ECONOMIC HISTORY
OF EUROPE

ECONOMIC HISTORY OF EUROPE

by

HERBERT HEATON

Professor of Economic History
University of Minnesota

HARPER & BROTHERS, *Publishers*
NEW YORK AND LONDON

ECONOMIC HISTORY OF EUROPE

Copyright, 1936, by Harper & Brothers
Printed in the United States of America

B-W

330.94
H44
Cop.2

To My Wife

CONTENTS

CONTENTS

MAPS AND CHARTS

EDITOR'S FOREWORD

IF ONE sought to characterize world history in the last three or four centuries in a single inclusive phrase, it might well be: the Europeanization of the rest of the world through the multiple influences and varied institutions that have gone out from the smallest continent. When the total of European influences and institutions—political, social, racial and economic—is summed up in justification of this generalization, the outstanding visible export item in the inventory falls under the rubric economic. No part of the world, no matter how distant or undeveloped, has been able to seal its ports and minds and ways of life against the products, the inventions, the techniques, the capital of Europe. And with these have gone significant, invisible exports in systems of thought, social and political inventions, ideas of liberty and state from Luther, Calvin and John Locke to Adam Smith, Marx, Mussolini and Lenin. The world has acted and reacted at every port of call and in every hinterland to the ceaseless outward thrust of Europe as a merchant adventurer.

But the Europe of the eighteenth and nineteenth centuries which we think about primarily in America when we think of capitalism, colonies, commerce and invention, is a debtor to its own sixteenth and seventeenth centuries and beyond that to the beginnings of what is most modern and the retention of much that is old from the lands around the Mediterranean. The economic history of Europe cannot leave these origins out, and Professor Heaton has given due weight in this volume to the oft forgotten background. Modern history, not even modern economic history, does not begin in this volume on January 5, 1769, when Watt filed an application for a patent on an improved steam engine. This is distinctly a genetic history. The student is not misled into any idea that history is a process of hopping from one epochal event to another. All the factors, human and geographical, within the whole area called Europe are here presented by a skillful selection of what is representative and significant for the understanding of the basic features in our present economic order. I have thought as I read it that aside from the author's gift in presenting his material crisply and interestingly the development of the whole account has profited by his intensive studies of such a basic industry as the English woollen industry and his residence in two continents whose life and institutions have been shaped by Europe's economic expansion.

This volume on economic history proceeds from no central idea that the economic factors are the only ones to consider in explaining our modern world nor that within the sector here covered there is some overshadowing organizing principle from start to finish. He is content to forego such seductive simplifications and has rather sought to explain how work was organized and done and why changes did or did not take place. The result of such a realism and restraint is to give us not only a text but a skillful synthesis of the latest scholarship in a field of history whose significance is more than European and more than economic.

GUY STANTON FORD

PREFACE

In the following pages I have attempted to survey the economic life and development of Europe from the emergence of the ancient civilizations in the eastern Mediterranean to the dislocation and perplexities of the nineteen-thirties. Nearly half the space has been allotted to the years since 1700, and as the book has been in preparation since 1930 it could not escape from excessive preoccupation with post-War problems. But I have tried to avoid writing a mere preface to this morning's news, and have given the ancient, medieval and early modern periods space which they merit because their story is interesting and their contribution is important. No understanding of current conditions can be obtained by beginning the study of economic history at 1760, or 1700 or even at 1492.

The book is intended for students, especially American students, who have done no previous work in the subject, apart perhaps from a brief excursion to a medieval manor or the Industrial Revolution in a general course of European history. Hence I have omitted discussion of those controversial topics which belong to the higher altitudes of economic historiography, and have been content to describe and explain conditions and significant developments. Sir William Ashley, one of the pioneers in economic history during the eighteen-eighties and nineties, was wont to chuckle when, in later years, some energetic young researcher proved that the things he had written twenty or thirty years before were incorrect. "The wonder is not that I was wrong," he would remark, "but that I was ever right." Today the researchers are amplifying our knowledge and revising our interpretations at an appallingly rapid rate. I have tried to embody some of the results of their labors in this book, but an article in the next issue of the *Economic History Review* or some kindred publication may shatter a whole paragraph or even an entire chapter. I would therefore urge teachers to watch the periodicals referred to in the bibliographies, peruse the articles and reviews of new books and note how new questions are being asked or how old ones are being given new answers.

My thanks are due to Dean Guy Stanton Ford, editor of this series, for his valuable suggestions and criticism of the manuscript; to my colleagues, Professors E. S. Osgood and D. H. Willson, who read some of the chapters and saved me from many pitfalls; and to those willing galley-slaves, Mr. Rodney Loehr and my wife, who read much of the manuscript and all the proof.

Acknowledgment for the use of maps and charts which are not original has in many cases been made in footnotes. I wish to thank the authors of the following books for their courtesy in allowing me to use additional maps: Carl Stephenson, *Medieval History*; James F. Bogardus, *Europe: A Geographical Survey*; Sellery and Krey, *Medieval Foundations of Western Civilization*, and N. S. B. Gras, *An Introduction to Economic History*. The map of the Parish of Weston Subedge is from C. R. Ashbee (ed.), *The Last Records of a Cotswold Community* (1904).

HERBERT HEATON

University of Minnesota,
November, 1935.

ECONOMIC HISTORY
OF EUROPE

CHAPTER I

INTRODUCTION—THE CONTENT OF EUROPEAN ECONOMIC HISTORY

Economic history can be most simply defined as the story of the way in which man through the centuries has obtained a living and satisfied his material wants. It is concerned primarily with the age-long sequence of *wants—effort—satisfaction*. The wants range from the fundamental need for food and shelter up to the desire for a great variety of necessaries, comforts, and luxuries. Beyond these may be the desire to accumulate wealth for its own sake, for the income it will bring when invested, for the sense of security it affords, or for the economic or political power and prestige it may confer. There may even be a want for something to do, an inability to be idle or to enjoy leisure.

The want for food still stands out foremost, and expenditure on food absorbs today at least half the earnings of most European wage earners. The other wants have grown in number through the centuries, and while at first new ones might be satisfied only by the rich and the ruler, cheaper methods of production or transportation gradually brought prices down to a level that created an effective demand from the middle class and the poor. The history of dining, of clothing, or even of personal cleanliness illustrates the way in which wants accumulate. Primitive man's dinner consisted of raw flesh, fish, roots, and so forth; he sat on the ground or a rock; he dismembered the food and conveyed it to his mouth with his hands. His descendant needs many kinds of food cooked in varied ways, served in a special room, with a lavish array of crockery, linen, and cutlery; he may even approach the ceremony garbed in a special suit.

To satisfy these wants effort is necessary to all living things, except those who can get others to work on their behalf. The nature of the effort depends in part on the environment in which men live—on the character of the soil and subsoil, the proximity to river and sea, the nature of the flora and fauna, and the climate. It also depends on the extent to which man has accumulated tools, implements, machines, and knowledge. Animals and birds work to obtain a living, but their only aids are parts of their bodies, and they take what they can find or catch. Their equipment and methods have probably not changed much in thousands of years. If their environment fails to yield sustenance they move on or die off. Once man resembled them in his methods of finding food, and must have fared badly if the race went to the swift or the strong. But he differed from them in developing the use of his eyes, brain, and hands to get tools, weapons, implements, machines, and knowledge, to make work easier and more fruitful, to harness other forms of power than his own muscles, to discover new processes, new uses, and new commodities.

For thousands of years the accumulation of knowledge and equipment was slow; the conviction that there must be a better way of doing things and the determination to find that way are comparatively modern human characteristics. If we are to get the "feel" of Europe's economic development from its beginnings until recent times, we must try to forget that such things as the automobile engine, mass production, the use of electricity, the assembly line, and high-pressure salesmanship have descended on us within about four decades. During the greater part of the story conservatism is more important than change. There might be very little alteration in ways of working for a hundred or a thousand years, and Russian peasants might be found tilling the soil in 1900 with equipment which was like that used in the days of Abraham. Efforts to clear land, to drain swamps, to dam back hostile waters, to erect adequate buildings, and to acquire flocks and herds might be nullified by flood, famine, fire, pestilence, war, or oppressive government. But much that was slowly done and discovered remained as a permanent heritage, to be used and augmented by later generations. The men who first learned how to domesticate animals, smelt ore, and extract metals, like the women who fashioned the first piece of woven fabric or discovered that seeds put in the ground would grow, made discoveries that were of lasting value. The labor that went into building a medieval market hall, bridge, water wheel or windmill, into clearing a road or draining a marsh, helped those who lived long after the laborers were dead. During the last two hundred years man has rapidly accumulated knowledge, equipment, and power to produce; but this has been possible only because of the inheritance he received from his near and remote ancestors.

The environment in which men worked limited the range of possible occupations and the character or quantity of the yield; but that environment might be capable of being changed or put to new uses. Men could not alter the climate or the rainfall, or get coal where there was none. But they could defy the cold by building shelters and by storing up food for the winter months. They could irrigate parched land, and make water-logged wastes cultivable by means of ditches and dikes. They could seek grains that would grow in areas of low rainfall or short frost-free seasons. They could give or restore strength to weak or exhausted soils by the use of fertilizers, find methods for profitably extracting metals from low-grade ores, and compensate for a lack of coal by harnessing falling water. This ability to defy nature and change environment becomes marked only as we draw nearer to the days of the modern scientist and engineer, but the ancient world was far from helpless.

Man does not live by bread alone, nor does he live alone. Even in the earliest stone ages he is a member of some group, and in historic times is always a social animal. We can grasp some of the economic consequences of this fact if we try to imagine the life of an isolated family which has no contact with the outside world, which is free to do as it wishes, which owns all that it uses, produces by its own labor all the commodities it consumes—and has to do without the goods it cannot produce. Even in a group most of the members may do the same kind of work, such as farming, hunting, or herding, and may make most of the articles they need, such as cloth, tools, bread, or beer. They may have virtually no contact with the rest of mankind, and do without the materials they cannot obtain on the spot. But even in such a community certain practices may develop for the more economical performance of work, such as cooperative ploughing or the appointment of a shepherd to look after the flocks of many farmers; certain rules may come into force to protect property rights or regulate the individual's enjoyment of property that is common to all; and a ruling or priestly class may claim a share of the wealth that is produced. The individual is thus helped by being in a community, he is regulated, and a portion of the product of his labor is claimed by a superior.

From this beginning has developed a network of social and economic relationships. The growth of division of labor is perhaps the largest single factor in weaving that network, for with the increasing concentration of individuals on special tasks and of regions on special products, the exchange of goods or services becomes widespread, a trading class arises to link producer and consumer, transportation and marketing facilities become necessary, and problems of money and price emerge. In a small Canadian town near which this book was written one can buy British shoes and socks, New Zealand apples, Australian canned fruit, South African oranges, Indian tea, and Brazilian coffee. The town contains, among its industrialists, a manufacturer of shovels, a maker of automobile springs, and a producer of corset steel. To link the consumer with producers in five other continents, and to link these small industrial specialists with their market, an elaborate organization has had to be evolved. The development of that organization is part of economic history.

Organization involves the joint application of capital, labor, and enterprise to natural resources. If the resources, capital, labor, and enterprise were owned or supplied by the same person the size of the business would be small, as in the case of the peasant proprietor or small craftsman, but all the income would belong to the same man. Economic effort cannot advance beyond a certain point on such a basis; consequently the different factors of production must be provided by different owners, and gathered together by some person who is usually called an entrepreneur. The word could be translated as "enterpriser," but the better translation, "undertaker," can be brought back to its original meaning since those who conduct funerals are now discarding it. The undertaker may have land, but need capital and labor; he may have land and capital but lack labor; he may have labor but little else; or he may have nothing but courage and a belief that he can run something successfully. The manner in which he obtains what he lacks determines the character of the organization he uses. The man with land and capital may buy slaves to work his estate or mine. Free labor may be hired, capital may be borrowed, land may be rented. The employer may provide only material, on which his men can work with their own equipment in their own homes; or he may provide buildings, equipment, and material, and gather his employees under his own roof. The landlord may supply just bare unimproved land to his tenants; or he may spend much capital on improving and equipping it, and even supply seed, livestock, and implements, leaving the cultivator to provide only his labor. It is possible to find undertakers who have worked with borrowed capital in rented premises and with hired laborers on materials that belonged to other people.

This division of ownership of the factors of production created the problem of distribution of the wealth created by joint effort. In essence it was a question of the price to be paid by the entrepreneur, whether the price was called rent, wages, or interest; and it is safe to assume that the purchaser would try to keep the price as low as possible and the seller to make it as high as he could. For centuries custom played a large part in keeping these prices stable, but by the end of the Middle Ages some of them became more mobile, and in the modern world they may move far and rapidly. Behind the shares that go to the different factors in production are the people who receive them, and even whole classes of people. Conflict of interest between these classes was possible even in slave or feudal systems, and slave or peasant revolts were not unknown; but with the emergence of a free laboring class and of entrepreneurs who controlled the work of many producers, conflict over the distribution of wealth became more likely. The relations in society between owner and slave, lord and serf, master and servant, employer and employee, landlord and tenant, or debtor and creditor, were not naturally harmonious; and since one economic class usually held political power as well as economic control, the "underdog" must growl quietly or be ready to bite hard.

The political authority, whether local, regional, or national, has played an important part in economic history. It has nearly always been engaged in some economic enterprises: ancient and medieval rulers had large estates, mines, and workshops, which were operated to supply the needs of the court in days when taxation was little developed. In our own day a government may own railways, ships, electric or gas plants, a postal service, factories, shipyards, banks, etc. In addition, the state has aided and regulated the enterprise of the subject. Its laws have determined his rights and obligations by defining such things as property and contract; it has helped him by protecting him against civil and criminal wrongs, and by providing roads, lighthouses, policemen, convoys, and currency. By 1800 there were few governments that would not do whatever was said to be "good for business," and the power of the state was readily put behind its citizens wherever a tariff, bounty, subsidy, or even a war promised to injure the trade of the foreigner and benefit that of the native. There was nothing new in this readiness; the ancient Greek and the medieval Italian cities had been just as eager to use political power for exclusive economic gain. Nor was there anything new in the state regulation of economic life; all through the story the town, the church, or the state has tried to control the individual's dealings with his fellows, in the interest of dependents, consumers, rivals, or the state. Finally, there was nothing new in the demand that the state made for a share in the wealth produced by its people. The state might well be included in any list of the factors of production; it certainly must be admitted to a list of the claimants when distribution takes place. The church might also seek admission to the first list, and would rank high in the second in most countries in most ages.

A fuller definition of economic history is now possible. It is the story of the way man has worked to satisfy his material wants, in an environment provided by nature but capable of improvement, in an organization made up of his relations with his fellows, and in a political unit whose head enjoys far-reaching power to aid, control, and appropriate. The study of that story has seemed worth while only within the last sixty or seventy years. Political, religious, constitutional, and military history were studied and taught much earlier, and some Germans had been looking at early urban and rural life since 1850. But only after 1875 did classes in economic history creep into university curricula. Wisconsin offered a course in the history of agriculture in 1876, Cunningham began teaching economic history at Cambridge (England) in 1878, Toynbee gave a course at Oxford in 1881, and Dunbar began to give one at Harvard in 1883. In 1892 the first professorship in economic history in any university was established at Harvard and occupied by W. J. Ashley. Since those days the amount of teaching and research has grown steadily; the first generation of economic historians has only recently passed away, and the second is pouring out a broad stream of monographs that has washed away many of the views and interpretations of the first. There are many questions that can be answered only tentatively, many answers given today will almost certainly be modified tomorrow, and some questions will probably never be satisfactorily answered.

The economic history of Europe is worthy of attention for at least three reasons. In the first place, it is concerned with the life of virtually the whole population. Whatever might be happening on the political, military, intellectual, or religious front, the mass of mankind carried on its daily round of production and consumption. Only the very great or long wars cut deep into the life of a large percentage of the population; most of the conflicts were small in the number of men engaged or in their direct effect on the life of the masses. Intellectual movements interested only the educated classes; constitutional battles were usually quarrels between the middle classes, landowners, and crown; and even the disputes of the Reformation might ruffle little more than the surface of the countryside. A history of "the people" must tell how they spent most of their time getting on with the important business of filling the larder and keeping a roof over their heads.

In the second place, economic conditions and developments had a powerful influence on political, constitutional, diplomatic, intellectual, and even military history. Historians have asked, "Why did some event happen, why were conditions as they were, and why did they change?" The answer often used to be found in some powerful personality, in legal, political, or religious ideas, court intrigues, victory or defeat, accident or chance, some act of God or gods, the sickness of some man or the influence of some woman. Such explanations Karl Marx (1818-1883) brushed aside and replaced with his *economic interpretation of history*. If, said he, you wish to understand any epoch or chain of events, the only key that will unlock the door is the economic. Men strive to get a living by working in society. The nature of the work and the relationships between individuals are the warp and weft out of which society, religion, politics, and ideas are woven. They create social classes, color ideas, shape forms of government, laws, and codes of conduct. The government represents the wishes and interests of the most powerful economic class, and laws are expressions of the will of that class. All struggles are class struggles, all wars are trade wars. Further, all change is due to change in methods of production or in economic organization.

This thesis had the defects of all attempts to explain varied results by one simple all-sufficing cause; but it did attract attention to factors that had been ignored, and the influence of economic forces on other sides of life is now universally admitted. A great English economist—Alfred Marshall—once said that religion and economics were the "great forming agencies" in history, and the declining power of religious considerations after the Reformation gave economic factors greater scope. International relations have been largely determined by rivalry for trade or colonies. The landed class used its political power to gain its own ends till it was challenged by the rising power of industry and commerce and, later, of labor. The Great War owed much to Anglo-German commercial conflict, and the peace settlement read like the distribution of the assets of a dead business man. The changes that came in the train of the Industrial Revolution have kept politicians in industrialized countries busy debating the rights and obligations of capital and labor, while every American student knows how the political life and thought of his country have been influenced by the clash between economic groups, classes, and regions.

In the third place, Europe's economic history is important because of the influence Europeans have exerted on the rest of the world. Europe was the birthplace of most of the modern developments in technique and organization—power, machinery, capitalism, etc.—that have given the economic life of today its chief characteristics. It was the source of the stream of population and capital that flowed out to settle and develop the New World. Its influence was ubiquitous, and few parts of the other continents could resist some degree of Europeanization. The continent's preeminence has been weakened during the twentieth century by growing strength without and by tragic divisions within. But Europe is still overwhelmingly the largest farmer, manufacturer, trader, banker, and shipper. Its resources—physical and human—are still great; "from the standpoint of business [it] is the most important of the continents" (Huntington), and "Europe, more than any other continent, holds in its hands the destiny of mankind" (Bogardus).

The European Environment.—A study of the European story is best prefaced by a bird's-eye view of the geographical factors that influenced the continent's development. The first is the existence of three main topographical and climatic zones: (1) the warm Mediterranean lands; (2) the mountain mass that

stretches from Spain to Asia Minor and passes on to the Himalayas and Thibet; (3) the cool to cold northern plain that reaches
from the Bay of Biscay to the Urals and beyond them across
Siberia. The soil, subsoil, and climate of these areas are sufficiently good to make labor productive, and sufficiently diverse to
make interchange of goods inevitable from the earliest days. This
leads to the second important characteristic—the comparative accessibility of most parts of the continent and the relative ease with
which communication and transportation could be carried on. The
mountain barrier was not impassable, and there was a well-
arranged river system by which passage from the Baltic to the
Black Sea, or from the Baltic, North Sea, or Bay of Biscay to the
Mediterranean was easy. The alternation of promontory and bay
brought a large part of the continent near to the sea.

Europe was favored by nature for production and for trade. It
had "sunshine without drought, rainfall that was not a deluge,
heat and cold that were never unbearable: mountains, but not too
high: plains, but not too wide or flat: rivers that were navigable,
seas split up into bays and sprinkled with islands: countries where
the shepherd could find grass for his flocks, the labourer soil
to till and plant, and the hunter forests full of game: countries
large enough for those who wished to wander, and small enough
for those who wished to settle down" (Thompson).

The third vital geographical factor is Europe's position as the
neighbor of Africa and the tail of Asia. The great barrier of the
Sahara prevented close contact with the tropics until a seaway was
found down the west coast after 1400. The products from the
tropics were largely luxury goods—gold, ostrich feathers, and
ivory—but America made the slave trade important; and in the
nineteenth century some other wares, such as rubber, copra, and
cocoa, came into demand. The North African coast was a market
and source of supply for certain commodities, the Straits of
Gibraltar were easily jumped by Moslem invaders, and the civilization of Egypt influenced ancient Europe greatly.

Asia was vastly more important. From northern Asia (i.e., the
plain north of the mountain belt) migrations of people came westward for peaceful or warlike purposes. There was little to stop
them, until powerful rulers arose, as they passed over the borders
of what is now Russia and moved to the Baltic, the Black Sea,
Asia Minor, and the great plain of the Danube. From prehistoric

times down to the end of the Middle Ages, people flowed westward out of the great human reservoir that was central Asia. From southern Asia the exports were goods rather than people, since the natural and manufactured products of Arabia, India, Malaya, and China were such as Europe could not produce for climatic reasons or was slow in learning to make. Thus Europe was exposed to the influence of Asiatic peoples, goods, and culture. It drew its racial stock and language; its taste for silk, sugar, cotton, and crockery; its compass, gunpowder, spices, and religion from the continent of which it was a peninsula. In course of time the tail grew strong enough to wag the dog, as Europeans went out by land and sea to the political or commercial conquest of Asia. After three centuries of that experience, the dog now shows a desire and determination to wag itself.

A GENERAL NOTE ON BIBLIOGRAPHY

At the end of most chapters a list of books and articles will be found. Most of them are works in English, for extensive citation of French and German titles would be affectation in a textbook. Some of the more important continental studies have, however, been included, and the student who can read Sée, Hauser, Pirenne, Kulischer, or Sombart will find his time has been well spent.

New contributions and revisions of old viewpoints appear in the periodicals, or are reviewed there, and the present state of knowledge or opinion is summarized in the articles in the *Encyclopædia of the Social Sciences*. The main articles in this *Encyclopædia* and in the periodicals devoted to economic history have been listed, but I would suggest that teachers prepare a card index catalogue of the articles contained in such periodicals as are available in their libraries. The catalogue can be as large as one wishes, but the following periodicals should serve as its base:

Economic History Review, cited hereafter as *Ec. H. R.*
Journal of Economic and Business History, cited as *J. E. B. H.*
Economic History, a supplement to *The Economic Journal,* cited as *Ec. Hist.*

These can be supplemented by two French periodicals:

Annales d'historie économique et sociale.
Revue d'historie économique et sociale.

Two valuable German publications are:

Vierteljahrschrift für Sozial- und Wirtschaftsgeschichte, cited as *V. S. W.*
Schmoller's *Jahrbuch.*

Articles on economic history occasionally appear in the following periodicals: *Economic Journal, Economica, English Historical Review, American Historical Review, American Economic Review, Journal of Political Economy, Quarterly Journal of Economics, History,* and in the kindred French and

German publications. *Social Science Abstracts* (1929-1932) contains digests of the articles published during those years, and its Index gives references to material bearing on every topic dealt with in the following pages. *A London Bibliography of the Social Sciences* (1931—   ) is a valuable aid. The *Economic History Review* has articles on recent French and German works in vol. i, and publishes lists of English, French, and German books and articles each year. It is also publishing a valuable series of bibliographical articles.

BIBLIOGRAPHY

"Economic History" and "Economics: the Historical School" (*Soc. Sc. Encycl.*, vol. v).

ASHLEY, W. J., *Surveys, Historic and Economic* (1900), pp. 1-30.

CLAPHAM, J. H., *The Study of Economic History* (1929).

CLARK, G. N., "The Study of Economic History," in *History*, vol. xvii (1932).

GRAS, N. S. B., "The Rise and Development of Economic History," in *Ec. H. R.*, vol. i (1927), pp. 12-34.

GRAS, N. S. B., "Stages in Economic History," in *J. E. B. H.*, vol. ii (1930), pp. 395-418.

HECKSCHER, E., "A Plea for Theory in Economic History," in *Econ. Hist.* vol. i (1929).

NUSSBAUM, F. L., *A History of the Economic Institutions of Modern Europe* (1930), Introduction.

SÉE, H., *The Economic Interpretation of History* (Eng. trans., 1929).

SOMBART, W., "Economic Theory and Economic History," in *Ec. H. R.*, vol. ii (1929), pp. 1-19.

TAWNEY, R. H., "The Study of Economic History," in *Economica*, February, 1933.

TAWNEY, R. H. (ed.), *Studies in Economic History: the Collected Papers of George Unwin* (1927), Part I.

USHER, A. P., *History of Mechanical Inventions* (1929), chap. i.

BLANCHARD, W. O., and VISHER, S. S., *Economic Geography of Europe* (1931).

BOGARDUS, J. F., *Europe: A Geographical Survey* (1934), chaps. 1-3.

FLEURE, H. J., *Human Geography of Western Europe* (1919).

HUNTINGTON, E., WILLIAMS, F. E., and VAN VALKENBURG, S., *Economic and Social Geography* (1933).

THOMPSON, J. M., *Historical Geography of Europe, 800-1789* (1929).

CHAPTER II

THE ECONOMIC CONTRIBUTION OF PREHISTORY AND OF THE ANCIENT EAST

EUROPEAN economic history might be labeled Chapter III of the story of man. Chapter I covers the long period of prehistory, a quarter of a million years or some such incomprehensible figure, during which man slowly discovered various ways of working, tools with which to work, and products that satisfied his needs. Chapter II begins when men were able, in favored areas of Egypt, Mesopotamia, and India, to use the accumulated heritage of knowledge, skill, and tools in building elaborate economic, social, and political communities. The events of these two chapters, and especially of the second, took place on non-European soil, and Chapter III is therefore first concerned with the way discoveries and developments passed westward into the European peninsula.

THE THREE SOURCES OF FOOD SUPPLY

Even man himself seems to have been an immigrant into Europe, though the site on which his cradle rocked has not yet been definitely decided. Wherever he did originate, his primary task was to obtain food, and there were three main ways by which he could get it—by collecting wild plants and edible animals, by domesticating animals, and by domesticating plants. In the beginning he was as much a part of nature as the animals, living by catching and collecting and by avoiding being caught or collected. Some foods were easily gathered, for they could not run away. Others might be taken unawares or in repose; but if the strong or the fleet of foot or wing were to be caught man must make up for his defective speed or strength by devising traps or weapons. To these he added tools for dismembering the carcass. If this equipment was of wood it perished, but if it was of stone or bone it might survive its maker and give us our first contact with man at work.

If all centuries were given an equal amount of space, the greater part of this book would be devoted to the story of catching and collecting. If the calendars compiled by the prehistorians are even roughly accurate, European man lived in this way for at least 250,000 years, a period eight hundred times as long as that which has elapsed since the landing of the Pilgrim Fathers. Food-gatherers still survive in some continents, and the fisherman, trapper, miner, and lumberjack still carry on the task of taking what nature has put or planted. Catching and collecting did not necessarily end when men found those two other occupations, herding and cultivation. Some animals were worth killing for their meat or hides, and others must be destroyed since they molested domesticated animals. Hunting appealed to those men who found the tending of tame animals and the tilling of soil unworthy occupations. If Isaac was content to sow (and reap a hundredfold), Esau preferred to go hunting for venison. In some areas pastoral and agricultural pursuits could not be practiced because of the character of soil or climate. Over Europe at large hunting declined in importance as food production and settlement expanded, for where the settler went the game and fur-bearing animals slowly disappeared; yet large areas remained under forest all through historic times, sheltering animals that gave food or fur, sport for kings and nobles, and villains for fairy tales.

How man and certain animals came to live together in amity is unknown. The dog seems to have been the first to be domesticated; perhaps it domesticated itself by following camps or hanging round human habitations, living on refuse. As it could be trained to help in hunting, in rounding up other animals, and in keeping guard, it was worth its food, and was getting it by 6000 B.C. Most of the other animals had been domesticated by 5000 B.C. Cows, goats, sheep, and swine were useful for their flesh and hides, and the first three for their milk. The ox became a draft animal with the coming of the wheel and plough, while donkeys and camels became beasts of burden.

The horse appears late as a servant. It provided a mount, it was a good pack animal, and mare's milk was the staple drink of some nomads. When warfare became more elaborate or raids were to be undertaken, its speed added to the terror of attack. It could carry officials, soldiers, or news quickly for long distances, and thus facilitate the policing of great states or empires. But for arid areas it was less useful than the camel and as a draft animal on field or road it was inefficient until at least the Middle Ages, because of incorrect harnessing. The harness was attached to a collar placed high up on the horse's neck instead of resting on its shoulders, and a heavy strain must have almost choked it. The horse was less sure-footed than the ox in slippery places and on slopes. It needed shoes on all four feet, while the ox was shod only on the forefeet. It was more liable to sickness than the ox, it ate more, and in the words of a medieval writer the ox was "mannes meat when dead, while the horse is carrion"—though not all Europeans were fussy concerning horseflesh. Hence the ox was the more valued and versatile servant; it shared with house, wife, and ass the honor of special mention in the Tenth Commandment, and in some religions was given sacred status.

The pastoralist was a mixture of parasite and protector. Until agriculture and hay made possible the provision and storage of fodder, animals had to forage for their own food, and their keeper did little more than lead or follow them to the pastures and protect them from attack. The search for food meant movement, and pastoral peoples spent little time at home. They might move with the seasons. In the Alps they snuggled in the valley villages during winter, but when summer came they drove their charges up the mountains. In Spain great flocks of sheep passed every spring from the south to the north and returned in the fall. In the lands south of the Baltic, wanderers returned to shelter when the cold winter approached; and in arid areas of western Asia, southern Russia, and North Africa an oasis or well served as a point of departure for an annual trek to the fringe of the desert when winter rains or melting snow had carpeted the bare land with grass. In the north the pastoralist was guided by the temperature, in the south by the rain clouds.

The arch enemy of the pastoralist was drought. Most parts of Europe were adequately watered, as was evident from the expanses of forest that covered the lower slopes of the mountains and a large part of the great plain. As the eastern frontier was reached rainfall became scanty, while from the Caspian and Arabia to Turkestan and Mongolia stretched an expanse with scanty or uncertain rainfall, at best fit only for pasturage and at worst a land to be left as quickly as possible. If drought came, the inhabitants deserted the area over which they had enjoyed a general proprietary claim, and invaded the areas of other tribes. If they were strong enough they might push the invaded population out, and thus start a movement which did not stop till it reached the sea or invaded some land of farms and towns where life was pleasant and goods were abundant. To go south and pierce the mountains that hemmed in southern Asia was not easy. The line of least resistance ran westward. From the foot of the Pamirs to Bucharest, going north of the Caspian and the Black Sea, there was not a single obstacle, apart from rivers. From southern Russia or Asia Minor migrants could pass to the Balkans, the Danube Valley, the Baltic, or the Rhine, and through the Alpine passes to Italy. Hence Europe was frequently influenced by waves from the east, or by the wanderings of its own peoples. Migrations were not all due solely to the weather. Pressure of population, the ambition of nomad rulers, the desire to enjoy the riches of some more advanced region, or the fervor of a new religion might start a movement; but climate east of Suez and Caspian has influenced the racial composition of the west.

Herding came when wild animals that had once been hunted were domesticated; agriculture came when wild grasses, grains, roots, and fruits that had once been collected began to be cultivated. The origin of agriculture is still a matter of inference from scanty data, and the question, "How, when, and where did it begin?" provokes a fascinating guessing competition. The best-informed answer is that barley and emmer (a kind of wheat) were first cultivated before 5000 B.C. in western Asia, probably in Syria, and that the practice spread northward to the Black Sea lands and the Danube, southward to Egypt, and eastward to Mesopotamia. The bread wheat, which was a hybrid of einhorn and emmer, came from Armenia or the area south of the Caucasus, while oats and rye were domesticated later north of the Alps and in southern Russia. Wherever tillage and planting may have begun, they spread far and wide; other areas either imported seeds or collected them from their own wild grasses, while traders or migrants played a part in spreading knowledge of the new farming. We know that by 2000 B.C. grain was being sown as far west as France, Spain, and Britain. Thus cultivation added a third source of food supply.

The patron deity of the cultivator has always been a goddess, from Isis in Egypt to Ceres in Rome. This is fitting, for woman was the first agriculturist. The cares of maternity, the tending of the young, and the accumulation of domestic duties made women stay behind while the men went out hunting, herding, or fighting.

They gathered roots, grasses, and fruits; looked after the tamer domesticated animals; worked on skins and fibers; cooked, wove, spun, and sewed. In food-collecting man brought home the meat, woman the vegetables and cereals; and somewhere, somehow, she stumbled on the discovery that seeds would grow if planted. A pointed stick, a piece of deer antler, or a stone hoe served to prepare the ground, until man became interested in agriculture and saved his dorsal muscles from fatigue by inventing the plow. Fish, marl, or chalk might be used as fertilizer, especially in areas where the supply of cleared land was limited. In the first great agricultural civilizations of Egypt and Mesopotamia irrigation served a double purpose, for the water contained silt which served as a fertilizer. The harvest was plucked by hand until the jawbone of an animal suggested a flint reaping hook and the coming of metals permitted a sharp-edged tool to be used. The ears of grain were threshed by being rubbed between the hands, and later by being trampled by cattle or beaten with flails. Stone querns allowed the grain to be ground, pots allowed porridge to be made, while bread or flat cakes could be baked on a hot stone.

Agriculture has been described as the discovery that put man's feet on the first rung of the ladder of civilization. We might change the metaphor and regard it as the first ball and chain fastened to his ankles, the first inducement to the establishment of a settled home. There may have been permanence of habitat in the cave, the pastoral nomad might return to the same well or winter shelter, while on the other hand the early cultivator might "mine" the fertility out of the soil and then move on, as did the farmer in the American north and the planter in the American south. But agriculture was a powerful inducement to "stay put," especially where a river offered opportunities for irrigation, or where stream, lake, or coastal strip was fringed with forests out of which the fisherman had to carve a clearing if he was to have room for crops. The larger the part that cultivation played in filling the larder, the more certain was it that roving habits would decline; and when vines or fruit trees began to be cultivated, mankind found a permanent anchorage.

The Coming of Industries

While the three methods of obtaining food were being developed, man was slowly improving his weapons and tools and discovering the basic industries. His earliest equipment was fashioned from wood, stone, bone, horn, fibers, or hides. During the long dawn of the paleolithic age, flints were chipped into various shapes and sizes to give an edge or point for piercing, cutting, cleaning, hammering, or scraping. A handle might be added to increase the force of a blow. The inedible parts of animals were put to use; bone and horn provided awls, needles, points for spears or harpoons, while fur or hide could be used for clothing. Methods of making fire were found, but until containers were available food could only be baked on a hot stone or grilled.

To these humble but important implements and occupations the neolithic age, which began about 6000 B.C. in favored parts of Asia, added many more. Stone implements were improved in shape and edge by being ground and polished. Handles came into more common use, flakes of flint were fitted into cleft sticks to make spears or arrows, and the bow gave greater skill in shooting at birds or distant objects. Pottery appeared, possibly to serve as a better container than the eggshells, gourds, wood bowls, or rush baskets smeared with clay that had preceded it, and food could now be stewed or boiled. Cloth came to supplement or supplant skins as clothing. Weaving probably originated in basket-making, or may have been preceded by felting, i.e., rolling, beating, or pressing wool or fur into a fabric that resisted wind or water. Spinning, weaving, and dyeing were very important additions to human work, for with simple equipment fine or coarse products could be made from wool, cotton, or flax fibers. Tanning also added to the variety of labor and commodities. Leather was useful for clothing, harness, ropes, bags, and armor, and a high level of workmanship was attained with the aid of a handful of simple tools.

The age that developed pottery, cloth-making, and leather work was also the age that domesticated animals and plants. It had thus nearly all the basic occupations and commodities. It had also learned to exploit the subsoil, for the best flints were often obtained only by mining. It had developed some exchange, since the flints, furs, or other commodities found in certain areas were wanted by people in other regions; and it had in some places "produced a Stone Age culture in which artistic taste was high" (Casson). It still lacked some important aids, of which the wheel and metals were perhaps the chief. These came in the course of time: the wheeled vehicle was well known in advanced communities by 3000 B.C., and some metals had been found a millennium earlier. But the most easily procured metals, obtained by washing alluvial deposits in the search for gold, or by digging into outcrops for copper, lead, or silver, were scarce and soft. Their scarcity made them valuable for ornaments, but their softness limited their use as tools or weapons. Copper, known in Mesopotamia and Egypt by 4000 B.C., made "a fairly efficient dagger, a rather mediocre ax, and a poor knife" (Kroeber); but when bronze was made (somewhere before 3000 B.C.) by putting a pinch of tin into molten copper, a good tool metal was available. Bronze was, however, too scarce and costly to be quickly or generally adopted, and for long it supplemented, rather than supplanted, stone and horn tools.

Iron came into industrial use much later, for good bronze was better than poor iron, and good iron or steel is hard to produce. Iron was found in meteorites as early as 4000 B.C., and was known as "the metal from heaven"; but there is little sign of widespread use until about 1500, and the main source of supply seems to have been the Hittite area of Asia Minor or Armenia. From that time its use as tool or weapon spread slowly; by 1000 B.C. the iron age was well begun, but smelting methods involved great effort for little output, and the Romans drew some of their steel from India. For the mass of mankind metal was a scarce commodity until at least the end of the Middle Ages and even until the eighteenth century.

Economic Life of the River Valley Civilizations

By 3000 B.C. the valleys of the Nile, Tigris, Euphrates, and Indus housed peoples who displayed great skill in agriculture and manufactures, were trading at home and abroad, were ruled by elaborate governments, and had evolved a system of writing, a knowledge of numbers, and a calendar. At that time most Europeans were living on shellfish, game, and other collectible or catchable foods. For two or even three thousand years more, many of those who dwelt north of the Alps passed little beyond the stage of being parasites to flocks and herds, but those who lived south of the mountains were increasingly influenced by contact with the civilizations of the East, and gradually developed more advanced societies.

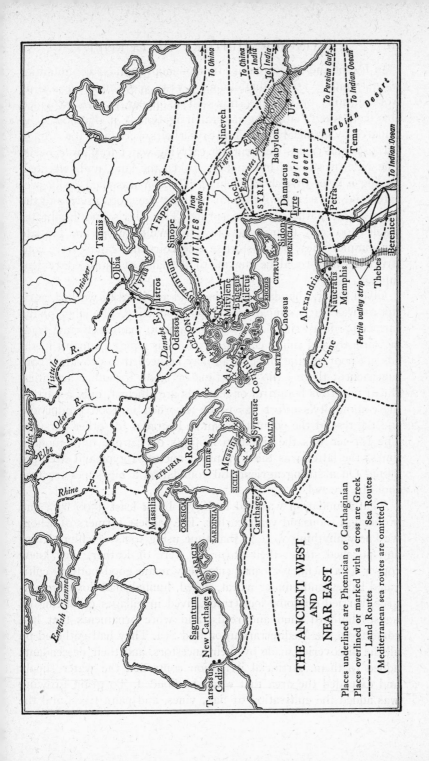

THE ANCIENT WEST
AND
NEAR EAST

Places underlined are Phœnician or Carthaginian
Places overlined or marked with a cross are Greek
— Land Routes — — Sea Routes
(Mediterranean sea routes are omitted)

In Egypt and Mesopotamia fundamentally similar communities were found. A river that annually rose very high because of tropical rains or melting snows in its upper reaches provided abundant water, either by natural irrigation if it overflowed its banks or by artificial irrigation if reservoirs were built for storage purposes and canals were cut for carrying water to plowed fields. The Nile overflowed in summer, soaked the land, and retreated, leaving a layer of rich silt behind. The soil was then easily prepared and sown; during the warm winter the crops grew, and the harvest was gathered in the spring. The Tigris and Euphrates flooded too early (April and May) for winter crops and too late for summer ones; but if storage reservoirs and canals were constructed water could be run on to the land at more convenient times.

Given water, abundant sunshine, and a soil easily worked, agriculture was fairly simple and highly productive. The labor of the farmer produced sufficient food to maintain manufacturing, trading, priestly and ruling classes. If nature is stingy or man's methods are poor, all the labor of all may be needed to provide a bare subsistence; there is no spare time or labor for other activities. But if nature is bountiful or methods are efficient, only a part of the community's effort has to be absorbed in food production, and the rest of the population can be liberated for other pursuits. The former was the situation in parts of Europe until modern times; the latter was the fortune of ancient Egypt and Mesopotamia. On a strong agricultural foundation a big superstructure could be erected.

That foundation was laid in Egypt by at least 3500 B.C., and probably a thousand years earlier. The earliest farmers of whom we know anything were at that time using tools of chipped flint and polished stone; their garments were of leather, they knew copper as a metal for ornaments, they made good pottery, cultivated barley and emmer wheat, fished, hunted, had domestic animals, carried on some local trade, lived in villages consisting of houses built of mud and reeds, and wore ornaments that had come from the Mediterranean or Red Sea. They had gathered up all the discoveries made by their ancestors, and their descendants added to them. Artificial irrigation controlled the water supply and extended the area that could be flooded. To grain growing was added the cultivation of flax, vines, and palm trees, and the more serious care of livestock. When the children of Israel were wandering in the desert they sighed for the flesh, fish, cucumbers, melons, leeks, onions, garlic, figs, and pomegranates they had enjoyed in the land of bondage. In the gardens of palaces and temples was a great variety of flowers, herbs, and vegetables, while flowers played a part in decorating the chambers of the living and of the dead. Of Mesopotamia a similar picture can be painted. It is still far from clear whether Egypt or Mesopotamia developed the first civilization, but by 2000 B.C. the land around any one of the cities dotted along the Tigris and Euphrates was covered with meadows, grain fields, orchards, and date groves. The people lived on barley bread, barley beer, wine, fruits, pork, fish, game, and vegetables—of which the chief seems to have been the leek.

On this agricultural foundation was built an industrial, commercial, religious and political edifice. There were farmers before there were kings, and possibly before there were priests. Where these two classes came from cannot be discussed here, but their influence on production and distribution must. One of their main contributions was the development of water control and conservation. Individual enterprise has rarely been able to undertake the construction of the large earthworks, canals, sluice gates, etc., needed for irrigation. The work must be done on a large scale, by someone who can command supplies of material or labor. In Babylonia the temples seem to have been the first organizers of water control; and as some priests became kings of the city-states and then welded these states into kingdoms the water problem could be more effectively handled by the use of slaves, by demands for forced labor from the farmers, and by laws punishing cultivators who neglected to keep their dikes in good condition.

The second contribution was protection against attack from the nomads who might sweep down on the fertile river strips or from neighboring river states. The valleys were not political units, except when some ruler from outside imposed unity as part of conquest or when the king of one part of the stream subdued his neighbors. Hence protection was necessary; but those who offered it were not always able to provide or preserve it, yet the price they asked was high. That price was the maintenance of a court, an official class, a priesthood, a nobility, and an army. The ancient civilizations, like their successors, had an economic machine that was obliged to grind out a large quantity of products for the maintenance of an upper class.

These products might be obtained in two main ways, one direct, the other indirect. On the one hand, monarchy, priesthood, or nobility might live on the produce of its own farms, vineyards, mines, and workshops, or on the yield of its own financial and trading enterprises. It used slaves or employed laborers, who worked under overseers, and gathered the produce into its larder, cellar, or wardrobe. On the other hand, the ruling class might live on the rents, fees, and taxes it collected by virtue of its position, in return for the use of part of its property, or as the price paid for permission to do something that could not be done without official sanction. The two methods joined hands when producers were bound to deliver part of their produce and also work on the landlord's farm in return for the use of the piece of land which they had from him. His needs were then met by the produce of his own "domain" and by the stream that flowed in from the separate farms of his tenants.

The ancient world, like the medieval, was full of instances of these arrangements. The royal estates of Egypt were so fruitful of produce and rent that they tempted every invader, and were rich prizes to be won by insubordinate nobles and priests in days when the Pharaoh was weak. The king had workshops to supply pottery, clothing, and luxuries for his household. He sold the surplus produce of his own fields or shops, along with that received as rent or taxes paid in kind and that which he claimed the right to buy at fixed prices. The domestic sale of certain goods and the whole foreign trade were a king's monopoly, and some goods could be made and sold only by the crown. The actual transactions might be conducted by the king's servants or agents, or by men who bought a concession conferring sole rights. The early Babylonian rulers monopolized foreign trade, Solomon traded with neighboring rulers, and the Achæan princes, Agamemnon and Menelaus, gained income from the sale of wine. The ancient kings would not have been scared by being called socialists or restrained by being labeled monopolists.

As with the crown, so also with the priesthood and nobility. In the twelfth century B.C., "fifteen per cent of the arable land of the Nile Valley belonged to the temples; two per cent of the population were their slaves; over 150 towns paid their dues direct to the priests; the temples owned nearly half a million cattle, over 500 gardens and orchards, over 50 workshops, and 88 ships, not to mention huge amounts of gold dust, silver, copper, and wine" (Olmstead). In Babylonia the temples were the early landowners; they directed the waterworks, assigned to each person a portion of land, gave him rations out of their storehouses, and at harvest time claimed most or the whole of his produce. Some of these goods they exchanged by external trade for the commodities needed by the temple and the community. Even when a merchant class arose, the temples still conducted production and trade, their workshops made much cloth and bronzeware, markets were under their control, banking was a priestly function, and the warehouse in which the peasant stored his grain and other products was temple or royal property. Nobles and temples made loans to farmers; and when bad luck, bad farming, or bad weather wrecked the debtor's ability to meet his obligations the creditor claimed the debtor as well as his property.

The luxurious needs of state, temple, and nobility lifted industrial production above the level of peasant handicraft. Palaces, temples, tombs, giant statues, and the need for defensive walls and towers took the art of building far beyond the mud or brick hovels of the farmers. The pyramids, the Sphinx, the remains of temples or kings' houses, and the great effigies—all tell the same tale of a "grandeur complex," of a religion that had strong hopes and fears for the hereafter, of a ruling class that commanded great supplies of material and labor, of sculptors skilled in use of bronze chisel and mallet, and of architects who knew most of the elements of stone architecture except the spire and a sense of proportion in relating width and height.

If the gods demanded that the dead be well housed they also insisted that the house be well furnished; and from this decree we get specimens which reveal the high level of ancient arts and crafts. The Egyptian tombs have yielded rare pieces of fine spun elaborately patterned textiles, and of pottery that shows the effect of the invention of the potter's wheel, of better ovens, and of improved methods of glazing. Glass beads, vases, cups, and bottles appear, and glass eyes for mummies. Like most people the Egyptians loved jewelry, and the goldsmith's and jeweler's arts were highly developed. King Tutankhamen's coffin was of gold, beautifully worked; gold statues were not uncommon, while combinations of precious metals and stones, or of stones and enamels, were sometimes most elaborate. Artificial pearls, amethysts, and emeralds were made of colored pastes. Cabinetmakers decorated furniture with inlays of gold, silver, ebony and ivory. Painters learned to mix and apply colors that are still vivid after five thousand years. The tombs of Mesopotamia tell a similar tale of skilled luxury production. From burial chambers of the fourth millennium B.C. have come jewelry of gold, lapis lazuli, and cornelian; harps decked with mosaics of gold and silver; gaming boards and dice; ostrich shells incrusted with mother-of-pearl and lapis lazuli; beautifully figured daggers, copper vessels, and silver lamps. The men who could make such articles in 3500 B.C. had behind them a long period of apprenticeship.

We must not assume that all industrial products were as good as those which have survived; we have the cream of craftsmanship, below which there were all grades of goods down to the homemade spare-time products of the peasant family. In the higher reaches there was a great degree of skill and specialization. In Babylonia craftsmen were organized in guilds to protect themselves and their trade, and guild or state demanded that young men be adequately trained by serving a period of apprenticeship. Some artisans worked in their own shops, but others were employed in the workshops of the great, producing goods for their eminent employer or for sale by his agents.

Many of the materials needed by these industries could not be obtained at home. Egypt had no forests, a little copper and gold but no silver or iron, and none of the tin that must be mixed with copper to turn it into bronze. Ivory, ebony, ostrich feathers, myrrh, and incense came from the south; the Levant and Europe could supply lumber and metals; spices, precious stones, and perfumes came from Arabia or India, and there were some manufactures in which other countries excelled. Babylonia was similarly devoid of all these things. To secure the desired commodities Egypt must go and take them by force, or develop foreign trade, exporting such goods as she had to offer in return. She did both at various times. As trader she sent grain, and eventually, in Roman times, became the most famous granary of the Mediterranean. Linen, glass, wine, wool, vegetable oils, and gold were exported, and also a commodity of which Egypt enjoyed a monopoly—papyrus. Parts of the river and delta were lined with big rushes—the bulrushes in which princesses hid babies. These were split, dried, and then gummed together to make a sheet. This papyrus was Egypt's writing paper, and was in great demand abroad. The literature of Greece and Rome was written on papyrus, and the government exploited its monopoly to keep the price high.

Some of Egypt's wants could be satisfied by Europe, and the routes along which she obtained goods from Asia were destined to be vital arteries of trade long after the Pharaohs were forgotten and the cities of Mesopotamia had been buried. They focused on the mouth of the Nile and the Levant. The discovery of the Cape of Good Hope route diminished their importance greatly, but when the Suez Canal was cut in 1869 and when the airplane was developed after 1900 the eastern Mediterranean once more became the hub of the eastern hemisphere.

The map (p. 19) shows the main intercontinental routes. The most southerly went overland from the Nile to the Red Sea, and then down that hot humid waterway. At one time a canal was cut to link the Nile delta with the Gulf of Suez, but the channel easily fell into disrepair, while the upper waters of the Red Sea were treacherous for navigation. How far Egyptians went beyond the mouth of the Sea is unknown; the way to Mesopotamia and India was along the coast, and thus exposed to Arab interference. In the first century B.C. navigators discovered that the monsoons would blow them safely across the Indian Ocean to India at one season of the year and blow them back to the Red Sea at another. When that fact was known the first really important transoceanic route could be drawn on the map.

The other eastward routes were chiefly land ways. Some of them crossed the Arabian Desert, from one oasis to another, till they reached a town on the Euphrates or a port (such as Gerrha) on the Persian Gulf. But the "Great Road" from Egypt crossed the Suez isthmus, and went up through Palestine to Syria. There it forked; one arm led to Asia Minor, to the land of the Hittites, to Ephesus or Troy; the other skirted the semicircular top end of the Syrian Desert, round the "fertile crescent" to the Euphrates. From this point one could descend the river or cross over and go down the Tigris to the irrigated lands and the cities—Babylon, Erech, Larsa, Lagash, Ur—to the Persian Gulf and thence to India. Or one could pass beyond the two great rivers to the Caspian, to the Himalayas, through spots which later were to have romantic names like Kashgar, Bokhara, or Samarkand, to India or China.

The growth of trade stimulated the development of a trading class, of a sense of exchange values, and of a medium of exchange. This was especially true in Mesopotamia, for the open valley was ringed round by lands that could supply invaders or traders, and it lay on the road between India and Egypt. Like Belgium in later days it was a cockpit of war and a hub, or highway, of trade. Of its traders we know something, thanks to the discovery of the baked clay tablets on which they made their business records; and we see them, as well as other kinds of workers, through the clauses of the Code of Hammurabi, compiled about 2100 B.C. From these private and public records a picture emerges of a people whose economic organization and methods were highly developed, with division of labor, clear ideas about property and contracts, landlords and tenants, employers and wage earners, apprenticeship, mortgages, leases, promissory notes, seed loans, partnerships, agents, doctors who operated unsuccessfully, tenants who neglected dikes, prices that seemed exorbitant, jerry-builders, and other features well known four thousand years later. The use of capital and credit was well established, and the use of metals for exchange fell just short of producing a currency.

This use of metals has been traced back to 5000 B.C., and was common by 3500 B.C. At first the metal was used as a common measure. The value of a cow, a rent, or a tax might be expressed in terms of a certain weight of copper and later of silver; but there was not enough metal available to permit its general use as a medium of exchange, and small payments were made in commodities, especially grain, to which a metal value was attached. Not till about 2000 B.C. were workmen paid wages in metal rather than in kind, and many other transactions were conducted by transfer of goods till much later.

After 3000 B.C. silver supplemented and then supplanted copper as a measure. The standard was a unit of weight, the metal was handled in bars, and a pair of scales was needed to discover the weight and therefore the value of the bar. Even then the fineness of the bar was not easily ascertained. In about 2000 B.C. the Babylonian temples began to issue bars or round pieces of guaranteed fineness, and as proof of quality stamped on them the head or figure of a god. Quality was now known, but scales were still needed. From standard fineness to the standard weight, shape, and imprint of a proper coin would seem to be a natural, easy step, but it was apparently not taken, and we have to wait thirteen hundred years until in about 650 B.C. Lydia in Asia Minor began to issue rude oval pieces of electrum, a mixture of gold and silver, stamped on one side.

We can now sum up the achievements of these Near Eastern civilizations. By exploiting an annual plethora of water a highly productive agriculture was possible; this gave subsistence to a large population and served as a basis for developed industries, extensive trade, much traffic on river, road, and sea, and a high degree of division of labor. Beyond the peasant class was a rich intellectual and artistic life, big cities, a religion that made great demands on material things, a wealthy nobility, and a resplendent monarchy. The development of writing, the framing of a calendar, and the study of mathematics and astronomy laid important foundations, while medical knowledge and practice were advanced at certain points. How these Near Eastern civilizations influenced Europe will be seen in the next chapter.

BIBLIOGRAPHY

Prehistoric and General

Breasted, J. H., *The Conquest of Civilization* (1926).

Burkitt, M. C., *The Old Stone Age* (1933).

Cambridge Ancient History (7 vols., 1923-1928). Contains many chapters on economic conditions, and has good bibliographies.

Childe, V. G., *New Light on the Most Ancient East* (1924).

Childe, V. G., *The Dawn of European Civilization* (1925).

Childe, V. G., *The Bronze Age* (1931).

Cleland, H. F., *"Trade Routes in Prehistoric Europe,"* in *Economic Geography*, 1927, pp. 232-238.

Cunningham, W., *Western Civilization in its Economic Aspects*, vol. i.

Gras, N. S. B., *Introduction to Economic History* (1922), chaps. 1, 2.

Hoyt, E. E., *Primitive Trade: Its Psychology and Economics* (1926).

Huxley, J., *"Climate and Human History,"* in *Atlantic Monthly*, April, 1930.

Knight, M. M., and others, *Economic History of Europe* (1926), chap. 1.

Kroeber, A. L., *Anthropology* (1923), chaps. 6, 14.

Marvin, J. L., *The Living Past* (1913), chaps. 1-4.

Myres, J. L., *The Dawn of History*, chaps. 1-8.

Neuberger, A., *Technical Arts and Sciences of the Ancients* (Eng. trans., 1930).

Olmstead, A. T., *"Materials for an Economic History of the Ancient Near East,"* in *J. E. B. H.*, vol. ii, 1930.

Olmstead, A. T., *"Land Tenure in the Ancient Orient,"* in *Am. Hist. Rev.*, vol. xxxii, 1926.

PEAKE, H., *The Origins of Agriculture* (1928).
PEAKE, H., and FLEURE, H. J., *The Corridors of Time* (1927-1933). Eight small volumes covering prehistory and early history.
PERRY, W. J., *The Growth of Civilization* (1923), chaps. 1-9.
ROSTOVTZEFF, M., *A History of the Ancient World*, vol. i,: *The Orient and Greece* (1925), chaps. 5, 10.
ROSTOVTZEFF, M., *Caravan Cities* (1933).
SEMPLE, E. C., "Ancient Mediterranean Agriculture," in *Agricultural History*, 1928.
SHEPHERD, W. R., *Historical Atlas* (7th ed., 1929).
WALLIS, W. D., *Introduction to Anthropology* (1926), part iii.
WESTERMANN, W. L., "Inland Transportation and Communication in Antiquity," in *Pol. Sc. Quart.*, vol. xliii, 1928.

EGYPT

BREASTED, J. H., *History of Egypt* (1912).
ELLIOT SMITH, G., *The Ancient Egyptians* (1923).
ELLIOT SMITH, G., *Human History* (1930).
PETRIE, W. M. FLINDERS, *Arts and Crafts of Ancient Egypt* (1923).
PETRIE, W. M. FLINDERS, *Social Life in Ancient Egypt* (1923).

WESTERN ASIA

CLAY, A. T., *Business Documents of Murashu, Sons of Nippur* (1898-1912).
HARPER, R. F., *The Code of Hammurabi* (1904).
JASTROW, M., *Civilization of Babylonia and Assyria* (1911).
LUTZ, H. F., "Price Fluctuations in Ancient Babylonia," in *J. E. B. H.*, vol. iv, 1932.
LUTZ, H. F., "Babylonian Partnerships," in *J. E. B. H.*, vol. iv, 1932.
WOOLLEY, C. L., *The Sumerians* (1929).

The Old Testament, especially Genesis to Judges, gives a good picture of a pastoral nomadic people.
Encyclopædia of the Social Sciences: articles on Anthropology, Archæology, Famines, Grains, Hunting, Migrations, Nomads, Prehistory, Slavery.

CHAPTER III

THE EMERGENCE OF SOUTHEASTERN EUROPE

THE rise of mature communities in Egypt and Mesopotamia could not fail to influence the backward regions that lay to the west. During the last three millennia of the pre-Christian era southeastern Europe emerged as a region of developed agriculture, industry, trade, politics, and culture, and at the end of that era could more than hold its own in most fields of economic, political, or intellectual effort.

The contacts between Europe and her neighbors were those of migration and of trade. They might be violent, for migration was often invasion, and trade was frequently piracy or plunder. Movement was along two main thoroughfares—a land bridge and a sea with many stepping-stones. The land bridge was Asia Minor, that promontory of plateau, high mountains, and western valleys that faced three seas and came within sight of Europe at the Dardanelles and Bosporus. Across those narrow straits was the European mainland, accessible either up the valleys of the Vardar-Morava Rivers which cut through the Balkans to the Danube Valley, or along the coastal strip to the mouth of that river. Along these routes neolithic Asiatics passed soon after 3000 B.C., seeking land and settling down to cultivate the banks of the Danube. Along them later came the Greeks, pressing down from the Danube into Asia Minor and the Peloponnesus. There was constant coming and going of people and goods across the straits, while the north shore of the Black Sea also offered an easy thoroughfare from central Asia.

The seaway was the Mediterranean, with its chain of islands from Cyprus to the Balearics, its great offshoots in the Ægean and Adriatic, and its big extension, the Black Sea. It was narrow and easily navigated; great peninsulas gave it a long coast line; it was landlocked, had little tide, and in summer its surface was fairly smooth. From some of its islands or from the northern mainland such important raw materials as metals or such desirable decorative articles as amber and furs could be obtained. The dawn of the metal ages made Europe a valuable neighbor, for she was well endowed with the ores that the river valleys lacked. The mountain mass from the Carpathians and Balkans to Spain was spotted with minerals, as were Scandinavia, Belgium, and the British Isles. Copper and gold were found in the Carpathians; silver, gold, and copper in Spain; tin in Bohemia, Brittany, and Britain; silver, copper, and gold in the Balkans. The Near East drew on these deposits to supplement supplies obtained from Asia Minor, the Caucasus, Nubia, and the rim of the Tigris-Euphrates plain. In return Europe obtained the products of eastern workshops and farms.

Land and sea contacts had been established long before 2000 B.C. The second city of Troy was built in 2400 B.C.; from it people and goods crossed the Dardanelles, and past it ships sailed to fetch amber and furs from the Black Sea terminals of river routes that came down from the north. In the second millennium (2000-1000 B.C.) the trade routes became longer, and important migrations took place. The people of the eastern Mediterranean learned the opportunities for settlement and trade offered by the west, and procured ships in which they journeyed to that area. In the last millennium B.C. the Greeks roamed far afield as colonists and traders. Carthage developed the western half of the sea as its trade area, the Greeks gave the eastern half a measure of economic unity, and the ancient world reached its climax when Rome welded the two halves and some lands that lay beyond into a great free-trade area.

If migration and trade were largely instrumental in pulling Mediterranean Europe out of its stone age, who were the migrants and traders? The Egyptians had learned how to build and navigate ships, and their vessels went out over at least the eastern half of the Mediterranean. The Anatolians of Asia Minor did some trading, for they lived on the bridge and had mineral deposits. But the traders of whom we have the earliest clear picture were the Cretans. Crete had many assets. Its climate was temperate all the year round, its soil was fairly fertile and well watered; there was little level land suitable for grain-growing, but fruit, olives, and grapes flourished. Its forests gave lumber for Egypt and for shipbuilding, while its position between Europe and the Near East put it within easy access of many sources of supply and markets.

For at least a thousand years (2500-1500 B.C.) Cretans went to all points of the compass. They moved among the islands and harbors of the Ægean, trading, freebooting, or fighting the city-states. They went to Cyprus and Eubœa to get copper, to the ports of the Levant, and to Egypt. In the west they visited Sicily, Sardinia, Elba, and the Lipari Islands (from which came the stone for vases), while beyond the Straits of Gibraltar was Tarsessus (near the later Cadiz) where Spanish silver and tin from Britain or Brittany were collected. In addition to metals, they traded in wine, oil, grain, lumber, and manufactured goods, produced at home or picked up in foreign ports. The discoveries made by modern excavators suggest that Cretan enterprise was richly rewarded. They also show that eventually it ended. The causes are obscure, but it seems that Crete lost her political and economic hegemony over the Ægean, saw markets and trade routes cut off or annexed by others, and finally was attacked and wrecked about 1400 B.C., probably by invaders from Greece.

Phœnician Traders.—If the Greeks wrecked Cretan trade they were slow in putting anything in its place, and until they were ready to send out their own ships and salesmen Mediterranean trade fell largely into the hands of Crete's rivals and successors, the Phœnicians. Phœnicia—a narrow belt in the middle of the Levant coast, with Tyre and Sidon as the central points—combined natural resources and good location. Its hillsides were covered with cedar, cypress, and oak trees; there was some metal underground, and at the foot of those hills passed the great road from Egypt to Asia Minor or Mesopotamia. Such a land tempted every Near Eastern power, and was captured by one after another. But whether it was in an empire or independent, its timber and metals were wanted, and its inhabitants were active middlemen, seamen, colonizers and pirates. They took their own products to the two valleys, and carried those of Babylonia to Egypt, or vice versa. They handled the copper of Cyprus and the metals of Asia Minor and Armenia. Stepping into Crete's shoes, they gathered the Ægean into their arms, and established colonies, or rather trading posts, in Malta, Sicily, Carthage, and at Gades (the later Cadiz).

Of the Phœnician outposts Carthage, established by 800 B.C., was destined to become the most famous. It commanded the narrow neck of water separating Africa from Sicily, and could therefore make trouble for the Greeks when they came west to colonize, or for the Romans when they developed a desire to expand. It tried to make the western Mediterranean a Carthaginian lake by placing posts at all strategic commercial points, by seeking alliances with native chiefs, and by using some of its profits to build fleets and hire mercenaries. These profits came from both sides of the sea. Sicily, Spain, and the Atlantic coast furnished raw materials; Spain, Elba, and Sardinia supplied metals. From the south came gold, ivory, ebony, feathers, precious stones, and slaves, brought by caravan across the Sahara or fetched by ships which went along the west African coast.

Tyre and Sidon added industry to commerce. They copied Babylonian and Egyptian products and patterns, and possibly sold their wares as "genuine" Egyptian or Babylonian. They became skillful in finishing and dyeing cloth. Insects collected from oak trees were ground into scarlet dye, while the famous Tyrian purple was made from tiny shellfish. Few dyers knew how to do the work, and an enormous number of fish produced only a small quantity of dye. Purple was therefore the color for rulers. Its use died out with the decline of the Roman imperial grandeur, the secret of making the dye was lost until at least the eighteenth century, and a purple chemical dye was not produced till 1906.

Phœnicia lost some of her commercial prestige and power when the Greeks became economically mature. Carthage gradually became an end in itself instead of a feeder of the parent cities, and to it many Phœnician merchants migrated as danger from western Asiatic empires drew nearer to the home land. But there was still abundant work and profit; the empires needed western goods, the contact between the Mediterranean peoples and the Orient became closer, and spices, silks, cottons, and other eastern goods came west in larger volume. Phœnicians handled much of the carrying trade in the Red Sea, they manned the Egyptian ships that were sent to circumnavigate Africa about 600 B.C., and Egypt long continued to be a profitable field for their shipping and trade. But domination of the Mediterranean sea routes gradually passed into European hands.

Greece.—Excavation is slowly pulling aside the curtain that separates the Greece of the literary records from that of the preceding two millennia. The picture (or series of pictures) shows people at work in a land of valleys, coastal slopes, and islands,

mining, cultivating, tending livestock, or living in towns which
are political centers, ports, and nests of pirates. Some town seeks
supremacy over the rest, and in the conflict destroys some of its
rivals or is destroyed by them. Then a strange people comes in
from the north or east, with better weapons (of bronze, or later
of iron) and a different culture. In the tumult life becomes more
primitive; but when the invaders have wiped out or subjected the
invaded, or have become assimilated with them, production re-
vives, trade recovers, and new towns are built on the débris of the
old ones. Then the wheel turns another cycle of migration, disturbance, and redevelopment; at each turn a different people is at
the handle, as northerners and easterners come (or are pushed)
toward the western peninsula of Asia and the eastern promontory
of Europe.

Disturbances occurred about 3000 B.C. and again about 2000
B.C., but the movement that made the deepest mark on the Ægean
area occupied the period from about 1250 to 1000 B.C. It came
from the north; it was one of pastoral and possibly farming
people, accustomed to the use of iron weapons and to fighting
under tribal leaders, used to the idea of private family tenure of
land, but with little experience in producing goods for a market.
These people pushed down the Greek mainland to the very tip,
entered Asia Minor, and crossed to the islands. That they destroyed the whole native population is improbable; they gradually
became merged with the conquered, to produce the Greek population of the Classical Age.

The Mediterranean Environment.—These people came to
a strange land, and had to adapt themselves to a new topography
and climate. The topography was, like that of the whole north
coast of the Mediterranean, one of hill, mountain, and valley.
Rarely does a Mediterranean valley or coastal plain cover a large
area; parts of Macedonia, the heel of Italy, the Po Valley, the
south coast of France, and bits of the Spanish littoral are the
only large level areas. In Greece ranges cut the country into a
jumble of valleys and thrust promontories out into the sea, thus
making the coast an alternation of forbidding cliffs and deep
indentations, and scattering the water with islands where the
ranges have been broken off from the mainland.

Over the valleys and slopes of Europe's southern fringe the
Mediterranean climate prevails. That climate, which is found be-

tween 30° and 45° latitude in such other parts of the world as California, Chile, southern Australia, and South Africa, has two main divisions. The winter is rainy and cool, but rarely reaches freezing point and has many sunny days. The mountain barrier keeps out the cold winds from the north. The summer is a season of drought broken by a rare thunderstorm, of burning southerly winds, blinding sunshine, shimmering heat, dust storms, parched brown grass, bare fields, and, if you are a wise southerner instead of a stubborn Anglo-Saxon, of afternoon siestas. The annual rainfall varies considerably from year to year and from district to district; it declines as one travels southward, descends the hills, or passes from the western to the eastern slope of a range. It may be 60 inches a year at the head of the Adriatic, 20 inches in Crete, and 10 inches on the north African coast.

These two factors—climate and topography—have controlled and shaped Mediterranean life all through the centuries; and the invaders, like the invaded, had to adapt their mode of work to them. There was room for livestock that were sufficiently nimble-footed and strong-legged to roam far on the slopes in search for food; but summer fodder was scarce, and water became scarcer as summer advanced. Hay cultivation and irrigation might mitigate this scarcity, but since the cost of feeding draft animals was large in comparison with the service rendered, man power, including slave labor, was in great demand, and animal products played a small part in the dietary. The area capable of easy cultivation was small, and the period of what one might call simple farming—plowing, sowing, and reaping—was limited to the winter. Even on the plains the uncertain or scanty rainfall called for the development of "dry-farming" methods. Fields were sown only in alternate years; they were thoroughly and frequently plowed to keep the soil loose so that the rain could penetrate rather than run away.

Even perfect farming on the plains could not meet the needs of a large population, and the area under cultivation must be extended, as in Japan and the Rhine Valley, by breaking up the hillsides. There the enemy was erosion. To combat it, the slopes were terraced. There was much breaking of stone and carriage of earth, and the newly made ground was then planted with figs, vines, or olives, which were able to live through the hot dry summer bceause their roots went deep down to tap the subsoil moisture. The olive was one of the foundation stones of Mediterranean life. Its oil was the butter and lard, the lamp oil, and the cold cream applied to protect the skin against intense heat and scorching winds. Wine held the place occupied farther north by water, tea, coffee, and beer. Grapes and figs, eaten fresh or dry, were the chief fruits; the fig tree generously gave two or three crops each year, while even foxes, according to Solomon and Æsop, liked grapes.

Orcharding involved intensive cultivation, close care, skill in pruning and trellising, and laborious work with hoe or plow. Wheat fed on winter rains; orchards could resist the normal summer drought; but summer hay, vegetables, and small fruits called for irrigation, while in drier areas or abnormal summers even vines and olives must be helped to quench their thirst. The city joined the countryside in making provision for the storage of water; the growth of large cities was impossible until waterworks had been erected, and great systems were planned and completed in Athens and Carthage long before the Romans built their famous aqueducts. Only by careful water conservation was it possible to maintain the beautiful gardens that surrounded the temples, the sacred groves, and the homes of the rich. One-eighth of imperial Rome was garden.

Greek Agriculture.—The development of Mediterranean agricultural methods occupied centuries. The farmer was "weak in theory, but strong in practice"; he learned by trial and error, picked up ideas from others, and slowly evolved "a precocious form of intensive tillage" (Semple). He worked hard and constantly, for his land quickly deteriorated if he neglected it. He probably began with grain-growing allied to cattle raising, and the picture we get in Homer is that of a land of grain fields and flocks, with orcharding still an infant industry, and with scarcely any trade in farm produce. But the yield of grain in many parts was not large and was quite insufficient to cope with any big growth in population. Further, its cost of production on any but the best lands was so high that when commerce brought competition from more favored and fertile areas in Egypt, Sicily, or the Black Sea, only the best Greek or Italian areas and producers could retain their market. Olive oil and wine could be produced more profitably, and beyond the domestic market could find a foreign one in areas which did not yet, or which never could, produce these goods. Profit and necessity therefore stimulated the production and export of wine and oil and the reliance upon imported grain.

This reliance was greatest in the big cities, especially Corinth and Athens. Corinth looked to the west for her grain and Athens depended on eastern or northern supplies. By the fifth century B.C. the food supply was a major issue in Athenian diplomacy and domestic politics, for any interruption of imports faced the city with starvation. Friendly relations were fostered with the Scythians, who grew grain on the north shore of the Black Sea or caught the tunny and other fish off that shore, for fish ranked second to bread as a solid article of diet. Control of the Dardanelles was sought by making treaties with those who ruled the land alongside it or by maintaining a big navy there. The route to Egypt must be kept open. Distribution of grain on arrival must be controlled by a board of commissioners, and forestallers or speculators must be checked.

Greek Land Problems.—The commercial production of oil and wine made its mark on rural society. The Homeric countryside had been the scene of a largely self-sufficing economy; the business of production was to meet the direct demands of the producers, the aristocratic class, and the king. There were large and small estates; the former were cut up into small farms worked by tenants who resemble the serfs of later days, or were tilled as larger units by slaves; the latter were cultivated by their owners, subject to payment of tribute to the ruling class. So long as the land's chief task was to feed its inhabitants, problems of ownership were not important, but when the task became the provision of goods for market and for profit difficulties developed. Vines and olive trees required more labor, so more slaves were needed; they called for capital to prepare the ground and plant the trees. Land was now more valuable to its owner, a big estate carried profit as well as social prestige, and the rich or powerful therefore sought to extend their boundaries. Where land was worked by tenants, the rent was either a fixed sum or a fraction of the produce, and might be raised if the number of land-seekers was great or the supply of land was small. Finally, the farmer resorted more frequently to the money-lender. He borrowed in order to expand his acreage or output, to tide over lean years and poor crops, to buy animals, seed, and equipment. Inability to meet payment on these debts resulted in the loss of the land or in enslavement of the debtor and his family, or in both; and the creditor was able to build up a large estate.

These developments eventually produced such an outcry from the small farmers as was to be heard in nearly every continent in later centuries when the cultivator who was working on rented land or with borrowed money was unable to meet his obligations. The Greek villain of the piece was the large landowner who operated big vineyards and olive groves, sold the surplus produce, and plowed back his profits into his estates, lent them to merchants, small landowners, and tenants, or bid for government contracts. With him was grouped the city merchant or manufacturer, who often lent money to farmers and exercised a creditor's rights when the debtor defaulted. The bourgeois might fight the aristocrat for economic and political control of the state, but both were the common target of the small rural producers, the common enemy in the class struggle. In that struggle political victory generally rested with the poor; they threw their rebellious weight behind some leader or found salvation in some lawgiver or tyrant who appeared above the battle. But the fruits of victory soon went bad, for the play of economic forces nullified the political reforms, old debts were canceled but new ones were incurred, and escape from one misfortune did not insure the farmer perpetual freedom from worry.

The Athenian story is the best known. Solon the Lawgiver (594 B.C.) softened the law of debtor and creditor, canceled many land debts, restored foreclosed land, liberated those persons who had become enslaved through debt, forbade such enslavement, and limited the area of land any person might own. Pisistratus the Tyrant (546-528 B.C.) went further, and therefore pleased the small men more; he exiled many landlords, distributed their land among the poor, and provided cheap loans. Yet within two centuries the land around Athens was back into large estates farmed on highly developed profit-making lines, and the free peasant had gone down again to defeat under the impact of interest charges, superior methods of cultivation at home, and competition from abroad.

Greek Industries.—While agriculture moved toward production for market, manufacturing did the same. In Homer's picture the household makes the things it needs, like a pioneer home on the New England frontier. Even the great men take a hand in manual work in the intervals of hunting and fighting: Paris helps to build a house; Odysseus is skilled in reaping, mowing, ship-building, and making furniture; a queen spends her days weaving, while a princess does laundry work for her brothers. In later centuries home industry continued to play a large part in supplying family needs; the small farmer's household made goods because it had little surplus produce available with which to buy them, while on the large estate and in the temples freemen, slaves, and women worked, often in special workshops, to supply the needs of the little community. But in the cities production for the domestic or external market expanded. Textiles, pottery, and bronze were the three chief industries, and each town developed a reputation for the quality and style of its wares. Production was carried on in the homes or workshops of the craftsmen or by groups of free, alien, or slave workers gathered together under the owner's or employer's roof. Some of these groups were comparatively large: we know of an Athenian shield-maker who had 120 men at work, and of capitalists with thirty or forty slaves working together, but usually only a handful of men were engaged.

Greek industry, like every other activity, relied partly on slave labor. Slavery was "a constant factor in the social and economic life of the Near East and Europe throughout the entire period of ancient history" (Westermann). The supply was fed in many ways; prisoners of war, victims of piracy and slave raids, defaulting debtors and their families, and children of slave parents provided most of the supply. The traffic in slaves was one of the oldest forms of commerce. The Phœnicians were especially vigorous traders, who combined audacity and lack of conscience in securing their supplies. Some towns, e.g., Delos, were important slave markets, auction sales supplemented private dealings, and governments collected a sales tax on every transaction.

Since slaves were drawn from various sources, their race and qualities were diverse. The slave might be white or colored, he might come from any of the lands or hinterlands around the Mediterranean, he might be a native-born Greek, he might spring from almost any section of society, and might have a simple rural training or possess great technical or professional skill. His work was as varied as his origins. On the land he tilled a small farm or toiled in great fields or orchards under the eye of an overseer.

At the oar of a galley, in the mine or quarry, or on some big building project he did arduous work, and there the exploitation of unskilled labor was often heartless. But as domestic servant, craftsman, or clerk in a shop, he might exercise much skill, receive wages, work alongside freemen or freedmen, and be put in positions of trust and even of authority. He could marry and own some property, sometimes his master set him up in a business and gave him a fixed percentage of the net receipts, while occasionally he won liberation as a reward for faithful service. His slavery was a legal rather than an economic or social handicap; "free and slave labor customarily worked side by side with little actual differentiation in respect to wages or treatment" (Westermann); and there was force in the complaint, made by one Athenian lover of the good old times, that one could not now distinguish in the streets between slaves, aliens, and citizens, since all dressed and behaved alike.

Currency and Banking.—Coins appeared in the eastern Mediterranean in the eighth century; Lydia in the seventh century made them from electrum, a natural mixture of gold and silver, but the value of such coins varied according to the proportion of gold to silver in them, and eventually coins of definite silver or gold content were minted by King Crœsus about 550 B.C. By that date coins were in wide use, though much exchange was still barter, with money acting only as a measure of value. For developing its currency Athens was well endowed. Mt. Laurium, at the tip of the Attic peninsula, was rich in galena, a silver lead ore. The lead was widely used for roofs, pipes, small statues, sling-bullets, and domestic utensils, and lead poisoning was prevalent. The silver was more valuable, and in the fifth and fourth centuries the Laurium deposits were vigorously exploited. Minerals were state property, but private enterprise extracted them, paying a rental or royalty, employing tens of thousands of slaves, and exhibiting great skill in sinking shafts, cutting tunnels, and devising equipment for crushing, milling, screening, and smelting. The public revenue and private profit drawn from Laurium added much to the fighting strength, economic energy, and cultural wealth of Athens; but the mines wrote one of the blackest pages in the history of slavery.

The coming of a money supply had many effects. In the first place, the circulation of coins of small value helped the small producer, for he could now take money instead of goods for the few wares he had to sell. Bars of precious metal had generally been large, and only the big producer sold sufficient goods to get payment in bars. In the second place, coins, even more than bars, helped to change the character of wealth. Real property, grain, slaves, and livestock were no longer regarded as its sole measure, and the new form of wealth could be more easily accumulated, consumed, or allowed to grow by being lent or invested. In the third place, money called for money-changers. In ancient Greece and medieval Europe the sovereign right of each city-state and the feudal right of noble, bishop, or petty prince gave power to mint coins. Since there were consequently scores of different coins, with different weights, names, and standards of fineness, and since cities occasionally reminted their money, adding or detracting from its precious metal content, a human ready reckoner was needed to tell the relative values of these coins and to change foreign ones for native currency.

The money-changer sometimes became a money-lender and by the fifth or fourth centuries was a fledgling banker. He began to receive deposits from those who wished to thwart thieves or put their money out to work earning interest. He made loans on the security of valuables deposited with him, or of farm or workshop products. He thus supplemented or competed with the temples, which were in Greece, as in Babylonia, safe depositaries, warehouses, and lenders. He transferred money from one person's account to another or from his bank to another on receiving an order in person to do so. He was rarely just a money merchant, but handled goods, conducted manufactures, or owned ships. Often he was an alien, used but hated by the natives, and since foreigners were forbidden to own land his energy and wealth went into building a fortune instead of building a country estate.

Greek foreign trade was sea trade; the land divides, the sea unites. Sea trade needed capital for ships and cargoes; but although something like joint-stock corporations were set up to farm taxes or work mines, maritime trade seemed too full of risks and was left to individual enterprise or to partnerships. In many trading ventures two parties were involved; one did the work, the other supplied the funds. The trader who went out with goods faced the risk of losing his life, while the stay-at-home financier lent him the money for goods and ship and risked the loss of his funds. The loan for the goods became known later as *respondentia*, that on the ship as *bottomry*. If the venture failed from loss of ship and goods, the debt was extinguished; if it succeeded the loan was repaid. A loan bearing such heavy risk naturally carried a high interest rate; the financier hoped to earn a good reward, while the merchant was insured against a legacy of debt if disaster came his way. This mixture of loan and insurance sometimes merged into a partnership, in which the capitalist got his money back if all went well, plus a share of the profits rather than a fixed rate of interest. The partnership had been well known in Babylonia, where kings, landlords, and temples had joined forces with traders. Like the sea loans just described, it was a common form of enterprise till at least the end of the Middle Ages.

Colonization.—Colonization played an important part in the history of many states, and between the eighth and sixth centuries B.C. groups of colonists swarmed out from Miletus, Corinth, Megara, and other parent cities. They went to the shores of the Black Sea, the Dardanelles, and the northern edge of the Ægean, to Sicily, southern Italy, Sardinia, Corsica, Marseilles, and the coast of Spain, to Cyrene, the delta of the Nile, and Cyprus. In some places they had to subdue or win the good will of the natives, while in others they met the hostility of rival colonizing and trading peoples. The Carthaginians checked them at many points in the western Mediterranean, the Etruscans kept them out of central and northern Italy, and the Phœnicians disliked them in the Levant. But there were many valuable sites left, and as some colonies in turn sent out further settlers, hundreds of colonies were founded. The Greeks finally squatted round the Black Sea and eastern Mediterranean like frogs round a pond.

Why did they go? The economic urge behind colonization in all ages has been one or more of four desires: (1) to find room for the excess population of the home country and land for the landless; (2) to secure supplies of food, raw materials, or precious metals, or to control the routes to them; (3) to develop markets for the produce of the colonizing country, or to control strategic points on the way to market; (4) to find fields for the investment of capital. To these economic forces, political or religious motives have often been added—the desire to spread the right religion among the heathen, or the belief that a country's strength and dignity are proportionate to the area over which its flag floats.

All four economic factors stimulated Greek colonization. A growth of population soon taxed the supply of cultivable land, and while intensive cultivation and attacks on hill-slopes made room for more people, four-fifths of the Greek peninsula and much of the islands and of the Asia Minor littoral were fit only for livestock—or not even that. Land hunger, whether of men who lost their holdings or of men who never had one, could be satisfied, the fear of revolution could be dispelled, and new opportunities for advancement could be offered by planting colonies. In Sicily or on the Black Sea the settlers could produce grain, tend livestock, catch fish, and ship food to the parent city. If the city wanted minerals, the colony might be planted where the ore was or at the sea terminus of a road or river that led to the mines. If the city was a growing commercial center its colonies were markets, gathering spots for raw materials, distributing points for manufactures, oil, and wine, or way stations on trade routes. It seems impossible to decide whether the need for trade or the need for land and food came first. Miletus and Corinth were the greatest colonizers, the first in the northeast, the second in the Mediterranean middle west. Both had limited land areas, and both faced the task of relieving a landless class; but both were early in the field as manufacturers and traders, needing raw materials and markets. If the land problem first led to colonization, the desire for trade outlets followed close on its heels.

Economic Rivalry.—Economically and politically Greek life was that of the city-state. The limits of coast and mountain range prevented any center from radiating its control over a large area. A single island might be subdivided, and there were six city-states on Lesbos, which was only about forty miles long and thirty wide. It is in the nature of trading cities to be rivals, and if they are sovereign states their commercial strife overflows into armed conflict or tariff wars. The towns of Babylonia and Greece in the ancient world, the Italian city-states of the Middle Ages, Melbourne and Sydney, Montreal and Toronto, Boston, Philadelphia, and New York, San Francisco, Los Angeles and Seattle —all have held limited views concerning the brotherhood or economic interdependence of man. East of the Ægean, Samos, Miletus, and Rhodes were the chief rivals; on the west Chalcis and Eretria wrestled for the profits to be made from the copper mines of Eubœa, while Corinth resented any attempt to break into its preserve, Sicily and south Italy. At times each of these rivals tried to strengthen itself by making loosely knit alliances with other towns, but these trade leagues were never strong or long of life. Sometimes the big rivals came to terms, but agreements were fleeting. Environment, history, and economic interests prevented the Greeks from thinking of strength through union.

The one force that for a time promised unity was the danger of attack from without. Yet when the Persian Empire absorbed Egypt, the Levant and Asia Minor after 500 B.C., and decided to add the Greek islands and peninsula to its dominion, joint resistance was not forthcoming and Athens was left to bear the brunt of the attack. She drove the invaders back, built up an anti-Persian confederation, and then turned it into an Athenian Empire of allied and dependent states. This political power brought great economic gain, but roused the anger of the outsiders. Sparta saw her military strength endangered, while Corinth and Megara felt the effect of Athenian commercial expansion, especially in western markets. The Peloponnesian War (431-404) was therefore in part a trade war, and the defeat of Athens wrecked the most ambitious attempt to unite Greece under the leadership of one of its states. Sparta could do no better, nor could Thebes; the task had to be left to two barbarians, Philip of Macedon and his son, Alexander the Great. The former absorbed all Greece west of the Ægean (except Sparta) into a realm that stretched to the Danube and Bosporus. The latter marched into Asia Minor, to Egypt and to India, overthrew the Persian Empire and linked the shores of Greece with the delta of the Nile, the Persian Gulf, and the banks of the Indus.

Alexander's empire was a military creation, and broke into three large pieces and a dozen smaller ones after his death (323 B.C.). The rulers of these pieces, like Alexander himself, were strongly imbued with Greek ideas and culture, and their armies were full of Greeks or of barbarians who had at least a Greek veneer. Hence it was natural that they should look to Greeks for help in organizing their conquests, in developing their resources, and in satisfying their wants. Greek traders already dominated the eastern Mediterranean, Greek goods set the fashions, Greek cities had become great markets for the food and raw material of the Mediterranean lands and for the wares which came from the Orient. This predominance was now so accentuated that historians have christened the region and the period *Hellenistic*, which may be translated as Greekish.

Greek became the common language of trade and cities. Greek traders and settlers were welcomed. On the land they were given holdings and stimulated to improve methods of cultivation and stock-raising; we know of one Greek who went to Egypt to manage a farm of 7000 acres. In Egyptian centers like Alexandria and Ptolemais they controlled the trade at the mouth of the Nile and upstream. In Antioch (at the western end of the road from the Euphrates) and Seleucia on the Tigris they dominated the trade with the Persian Gulf and the manufacture of most kinds of goods. If old centers such as Athens lost their commercial prestige, other ports and markets rose to prominence, such as Delos and Rhodes at points where sea routes converged. Greeks were the chief servants of the new kingdoms; in the army, in public administration, in tax-collecting, and in organizing or running the Egyptian royal monopolies they were active, and did not go unrewarded.

This Hellenized world can be painted in bright colors, full of life and vigor. Agriculture improves its methods, industry pours out more goods, trade and finance are stimulated by the enlarged area of the market, while the release of a great hoard of gold taken from the Persian emperor aids the development of money and credit. Postal roads are available, highway maps are drawn. Boats are bigger, harbors are better, and Egypt or Rhodes sweeps the pirates off the sea for a time. Alexandria, the hub of many trade routes, shows the range of commerce. In its harbor are goods that have arrived by the Red Sea and Nile from Arabia, Central Africa, India, and China; they are cargoes in transit, and their destination is Europe, including that growing market in central Italy, Rome. To these goods are added the grain, linen, vegetable oil, glass, and papyrus of Egypt, and the ointments, perfumes, rugs, mattresses, furniture, medicines, etc., made in local workshops. To Alexandria by sea come the goods Egypt needs—horses from Carthage and Sicily; tin, copper, iron, lumber, tar, pitch, and silver from Spain; sulphur from Sicily; tin from Britain; wine and oil. Some of these go upstream and cross to the Red Sea, for Arabia and Africa want wine, oil, grain, tools, and weapons from the north. Amber from the Baltic and coral from the Mediterranean are strange decorative products desired by the Indian, while gold coins will always pay for Oriental goods if no western wares can be exchanged for them. Such a center of long-distance trade needs a well-protected harbor, a great lighthouse, and a fleet to protect it from blockade or piratical raids. It offers opportunities to merchants from Greece, Italy, and Carthage; and in its cosmopolitan atmosphere scientists, mathematicians, inventors, and philosophers can work and teach.

Not all the colors of this Hellenistic picture are bright. Its civilization is urban and monarchical. Nearly all civilizations have been city products, "a flare-up on a few square miles of bricks and mortar." If the city grows out of the soil as servant of the rural producers, it may remain servant; but if it gains great industrial, financial, and commercial power it may become master of them. The city is nearly always the natural home of individualism, of opportunities for fortune-making unhampered by thought of social welfare, and of propertyless men who must sell their labor for what it will fetch. The Hellenistic world knew all this, and the dislike of traders expressed by Plato and Aristotle was in part a reaction against the effects of the "new commercialism" of their day. Prosperity built up a powerful bourgeois class, controlling agriculture, industry, and trade, and owning large estates or workshops. Land hunger and labor discontent sent some men to join the armies and some to emigrate in search of better conditions; others it drove to a class struggle which at times flared into social revolutions that rarely improved matters.

Monarchy was little kinder than city capitalism. Its ideas were absolutist, and since its power rested on military strength it must be able to do or take whatever maintained that strength or met its luxurious tastes. The Pharaohs had exercised wide economic control over the production and distribution of wealth, and the Persian Empire had state industrial and trade monopolies, vast estates worked by serfs, and huge treasure chests. When the Macedonians took charge they carried on the accepted tradition. In Asia Minor and in the new cities set up by Greek settlers a large measure of self-government, private enterprise, and private property was allowed, but in Syria the power of the state was expanded and the land and its people were exploited with the aid of Greek efficiency experts. The Ptolemies (the Egyptian rulers) went furthest in the combination of state control and state enterprise. They claimed labor, produce, sole right of sale, and added a banking monopoly to a trade monopoly. An army of officials and tax-collectors swarmed over land, workshop, and market. New agricultural methods and knowledge caused a great expansion of productivity, the population was driven to greater exertion, but an ever-greater proportion of the product was taken by the state.

The commercial and cultural unity of the Hellenistic world was stronger than its political unity. Its wealth and its weakness therefore tempted a far stronger power than Macedon. When Rome came east to conquer, the eastern Mediterranean had to pay the price in plunder, but from its fusion in a large empire it did not fail to find wider opportunities for profit.

BIBLIOGRAPHY

AUTRAN, C., *Les Phéniciens* (1920).
BOTSFORD, G. W., *Hellenistic History* (1923).
BURY, J. B., *History of Greece* (1922).
CALHOUN, G. M., *Business Life of Ancient Athens* (1926).
CALHOUN, G. M., "Ancient Athenian Mining," in *J. E. B. H.*, vol. iii, 1931.
CALHOUN, G. M., "Risk in Sea Loans in Ancient Athens," in *J. E. B. H.*, vol. ii, 1930.
GARDNER, P., *History of Ancient Coinage, 700-300 B.C.* (1918).
GLOTZ, G., *Ancient Greece at Work* (Engl. trans., 1926).
GLOTZ, G., *La civilisation Égéenne* (1923).
GLOVER, T. R., *The Ancient World* (1935), chaps. 1-3, 6, 7, 10, 11.
HALLIDAY, W. R., *Growth of the City State* (1923).
HASEBROEK, J., *Trade and Politics in Ancient Greece* (Eng. trans., 1934).
ORMEROD, H. A., *Piracy in the Ancient World* (1924).
ROSTOVTZEFF, M., *A Large Estate in Egypt in the 3rd Century B.C.* (1922).
ROSTOVTZEFF, M., *History of the Ancient World* (1925), vol. i, chaps. 12, 13, 16, 20, 23, 25.
TOUTAIN, J., *The Economic Life of the Ancient World* (Eng. trans., 1930), Parts I, II.
URE, P. N., *The Origin of Tyranny* (1922).
USHER, A. P., *History of Mechanical Inventions* (1929), chaps. 2, 3.
SCHOFF, W. H., *The Periplus of Hanno* (1913).
WESTERMANN, W. L., "Warehousing and Trapezite Banking in Antiquity," in *J. E. B. H.*, vol. iii, 1930.
WESTERMANN, W. L., "Greek Culture and Thought," in *Encycl. of the Soc. Sc.*, vol. i, pp. 8-41.
WESTERMANN, W. L., and HASENOSHOL, E. S. (eds.), *Business Papers of the Third Century B.C., Dealing with Egypt and Palestine* (1934).
ZIMMERN, A. E., *The Greek Commonwealth* (4th ed., 1924).
Encyclopædia of the Social Sciences: articles on Agriculture (Parts I and II), Archæology, Barter, Colonies, Commerce, Commercial Routes, Irrigation, Land Tenure (Introduction, Primitive Societies, Ancient World), Slavery.

CHAPTER IV

THE ROMAN WORLD

THE Romans appear first as a group of fighting farmers in a peninsula that had benefited much from immigration. Before 1000 B.C., waves of wanderers had come in through the passes from Switzerland and Danubia, and had settled in favored places from the lakes and Po Valley of the north to the heel and toe of the south. Then newcomers arrived by sea: the Etruscans came, possibly from Asia Minor about 900 B.C., and took root north of the Tiber, while after 800 B.C. Greeks sprinkled colonies on the south coast and Sicily. The Etruscans tended livestock on large ranches, tilled olive groves and vineyards, and drained the swamps that fringed the coast. They dug copper from the hillsides of Etruria and brought iron from the mines of Elba. They made hardware and textiles of good quality and design, which their traders took far afield to the western lands. Throughout Italy north of the Tiber, exploration of forgotten cities has revealed evidence of splendid cultures, of remarkable architectural and engineering skill, of a rich landed and military aristocracy, of skilled workers and wide-ranging merchants. In the south the Greek colonies reproduced the life and labor of the parent city-states, while from across the narrow sea Carthage exerted its influence and set up its outposts.

South of the Tiber lay Latium, a mixture of marsh and wooded hill slopes, occupied by the Latins and governed by a tribal aristocracy and a king. The patricians owned comparatively large estates, which were tilled by tenants who paid rent in kind, cultivated the patron's home farm, and followed him to war. The plebeians had less political power than the patricians, and were chiefly smaller landholders, traders, and artisans. Flocks and herds were driven from hills to valley each year, there was food for many pigs in the forests on the hillside, and a few acres of land on each farm were intensively cultivated by the farmer, his family, and a few slaves. Danger of attack called for defensive villages and towns, and Rome grew in importance because its site was good for defense and trade. Ravines and the river made the famous group of hills easy to protect, the site was sufficiently far inland to escape sea raids, and the river could be navigated as far as Rome. There an island in midstream made the crossing of the Tiber by ford or bridge easy. There was no other suitable spot on the lower river, and no other navigable stream on the whole coast. All roads between north and south led to this point, and during the period when Latium was under Etruscan control (700-500 B.C.) Rome became a thriving little town, with merchants and craftsmen.

About 500 B.C. Rome and its rustics shook off Etruscan over-lordship, became a republic, and during the next 250 years gained control over adjacent Latin tribes, over Etruscans and Gauls in the north, and over Samnites and Greeks in the south. That achievement, giving Rome hegemony over 50,000 square miles of territory, had important economic consequences. It facilitated trade, for the citizen of one place was given trading rights and protection in Rome and other cities. It fostered certain indus-tries, especially the making of weapons, and developed a class of rich army contractors. It also influenced the land problem. Dur-ing the early centuries of the republic that problem had been the subject of political discussion and even of class struggle. Debt or scarcity of land worried many cultivators. When Rome's enemies submitted they were compelled to hand over part of their territory, and this new public domain was leased or given to small farmers and colonies of settlers.

The Rome that dominated the peninsula was still the capital of an agricultural people. It had few craftsmen, little commerce, and no fleet for war or piratical trade. Industry and commerce were more highly developed among the subject or allied city-states than in Rome, and the patrician regarded agriculture, politics, and war as the only occupations fit for a gentleman. Hence com-mercial Carthage had looked with friendly eyes on the fighting farmers. They offered a good market for her produce, and were a thorn in the flesh of her Etruscan and Greek trade rivals. In 500 B.C. she had made a commercial treaty with Rome, and when the fight between Romans and Greeks was drawing to its critical stage she became Rome's ally (279 B.C.).

The ally of today is frequently the enemy of tomorrow, and Rome was soon at war with Carthage. The stake was the control of Sicily, rich in grain, oil, and sulphur. Carthage had the western end of the island; if she came to the eastern end she would control the Straits of Messina and might jump over to Italian soil. The First Punic War (264-241 B.C.) won Sicily for Rome. The second war (218-202 B.C.) broke Carthage's hold on the metals of Spain, and cooped her up in North Africa. She had to pay a huge indemnity and her commercial power was broken; but she set out vigorously to exploit her agricultural resources, and to plow such capital as was left into vineyards, olive groves, ranches, and wheat fields. This roused the enmity of the big landowners in Italy, for they now regarded the western wine and oil markets as their preserve. In 149 B.C. the landed and financial interests demanded that Carthage be destroyed, and destroyed she was in 146 B.C. The city was leveled with the ground, the population was enslaved, and a horde of greedy Romans shared the spoils.

By this time the Roman state was well on the way to becoming a big empire. What part economic motives played in taking the legions further afield one cannot say, for the motives were mixed. The boundaries moved relentlessly outward; at their widest expanse they stretched from the north of Britain to the fringe of the Sahara, the upper reaches of the Nile and the Red Sea, and from the Atlantic coasts of France and Spain to the Persian Gulf. The Rhine and Danube fixed the European land frontier, but for a time the camps were beyond that line, and though only one-third of Europe was inside the Roman fence economic contact with some parts of the barbarian remainder was close.

Economic Consequences of War and Conquest in Italy.— What were the economic consequences of war and conquest? Let us look at Italy first. The First and Second Punic Wars lasted twenty-three and sixteen years, respectively. The loss of life and property was enormous. At Cannæ (216 B.C.) half the Roman army of 50,000 men was slain. Fields were laid waste, the Italian soil deteriorated rapidly when neglected, villages were destroyed, and towns decayed. The burden of war costs was increased by rising prices and by the fact that there was now a fleet as well as an army to maintain. Loans carried some of the burden, but the rest had to be shouldered by the taxpayer. Hence post-war economic society could not be rebuilt on its old basis. Many farmers did not come back, and their land was sold or it

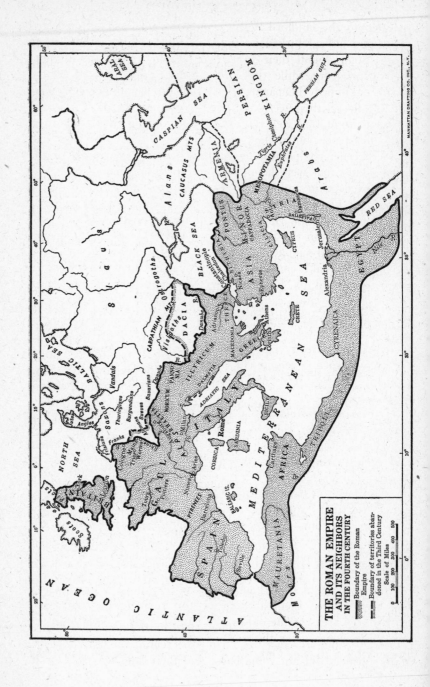

THE ROMAN EMPIRE
AND ITS NEIGHBORS
IN THE FOURTH CENTURY

▬▬ Boundary of the Roman Empire

┅┅┅ Boundary of territories abandoned in the Third Century

Scale of Miles
0 100 200 300 400 500

reverted to the landlord. Others came to a ruined or neglected farm, and either shirked or failed at the task of building it up again. Some found their farm had been mortgaged to support their dependents while they were away. Some drifted to the towns or joined the parties that went to found new colonies. Those who set their teeth and tried to resume the old life in the old spot might fare well if they were producing chiefly for their own subsistence; but if they were working for a market they had to face keener competition from the grain fields of Sicily or the large estates that were being built up on the mainland.

Imported grain and the large estate overshadow much of the subsequent history of Italy. After the First Punic War Sicily paid tithes to its new ruler instead of its old one and as this tribute came in grain the Roman cities became increasingly dependent on imported supplies, but the grain-grower in Latium found it harder to make ends meet. As Roman power was extended, grain from Sardinia, Egypt, Spain, North Africa, and even from the Black Sea lands came in trade or tribute. When Carthage was destroyed, Roman citizens took up much of the land and made North Africa into a great granary. The conquest of Egypt increased the already large flow of grain from Alexandria. In the face of such developments, field crops ceased to be profitable in many parts of Italy, and the land must be deserted or put to other uses.

If the small farmer found great difficulties in war and postwar reconstruction, the rich found great opportunities. The rich consisted of the senatorial class, already fairly large landowners and wealthy through money-lending, trade, and war contracts. When a law of 220 B.C. forbade senators to engage in trade, public contracts, or banking, they probably looked to land as an outlet for their capital. In addition, a rising class of business men made fortunes by feeding, equipping, and transporting the army, building ships, making roads, constructing public buildings, farming taxes, lending money, and by ordinary trade. They put some of their wealth into land for profit and prestige, foreclosed mortgages, bought land, kept pieces of the public domain which had been handed them as security for loans to the state, and leased large areas of the old or new public lands, especially in the devastated south after the Second Punic War and around Carthage after 146 B.C. Only by a big outlay of capital could the south be effectively reoccupied, and North Africa was such a fruitful field for large-scale operation that by Nero's time six men owned half the arable land there.

A big estate built up out of small holdings might still carry what was left of its old population, and be worked by tenants and slaves. But a big holding carved out of the waste lands and the domain was often colonized and exploited as one big unit, a *latifundium*. These latifundia might be simply huge ranches, for the character of the land or the scarcity of labor prevented any other use. But the wars which killed off Roman freemen brought in a swarm of slaves, who might be sold cheaply if the market was glutted. Cultivation could now supplement herding and take the direction decreed by the needs of its occupants, the character of the soil, or the potential net profit. A few tenant farmers might till small holdings, but on the main part of the estate gangs of slaves did the work under the supervision of their owner or of a bailiff and overseers (who were often slaves). The treatment varied, but sometimes was so brutal and heartless that it led to slave risings.

A latifundium was probably never less than a thousand acres in area, and often was much larger. When one owner died in 8 B.C., he left over 4000 slaves, 3600 yoke of oxen, 257,000 other animals, and much money. How efficient the slave plantation was one cannot say. Columella, a writer on agriculture about 50 A.D., reported that on large grain farms the slaves treated the oxen badly, and stole whenever and whatever they could. He believed, however, that if the land was fertile, the region healthy, and the bailiff capable and honest, slave labor might be more profitable than tenant farms. But the use of slaves was probably economical only so long as the supply was abundant and the price low. When the wars gave place to the *pax Romana* of the first two centuries A.D., the stream dried up, the price rose, and slave cultivation of plantations receded in favor of tenant farming.

Effects on the Provinces.—Conquest outside Italy opened the door to great wealth. When Rome subdued her Italian neighbors she left them a large measure of domestic self-government and imposed no levy of tribute. But the cost of the First Punic War loaded Rome with such heavy debts that this financial abstinence was abandoned. Sicily was ordered to pay tribute; when Spain was taken the same demand was made, and the practice spread to other conquered areas. Some provinces paid a fixed annual amount but others surrendered a tithe of their produce. At first these taxes were collected by the provincial governor and sent by him to Rome. He was a member of the senatorial class, his power was almost unlimited, and his opportunities for extortion were almost infinite. His aristocratic plunder preserve was invaded when the Gracchi began to farm out the collection of provincial taxes to groups of Roman capitalists who belonged socially and politically to the middle class (122 B.C.). These groups bid for the right to collect taxes in a province for a period of five years. The contract was let to the highest bidder, and the *publicani* (tax-gatherers) then set out to collect as much as they could. They gathered the taxes in kind, employed ships to carry them to market, and often bought the aid of the governor in making the venture fully profitable. The end of the republic was a boon to the provinces, for with it ended the farming of taxes and planting of unscrupulous politicians and military commanders in positions of power.

The second source of private profit in the provinces was the public domain—the public lands and also the forests, mines, quarries, and fisheries. These became the property of the Roman state, and their exploitation was leased to individuals or groups who bid high or stood high in official favor. In addition there were profits to be made when provincial roads, aqueducts, public buildings, etc., were constructed. If capitalists were criticized for making hay while the sun shone, they could at least retort that the proletariat was not forgotten. The Roman treasury was so full that after 167 B.C. direct taxes were not levied on Italian citizens, and in 122 B.C. Gaius Gracchus began the monthly distribution of grain to the Roman poor at half the market price, taking the other half of the cost from the public coffers. After 57 B.C. the grain was given free, and by the days of Cæsar 300,000 people were getting free bread and circuses.

The Economic Condition of the Empire.—The establishment of the Empire ended the period of chaos, restricted provincial plundering, and ushered in two centuries of comparative peace and prosperity. For the first time in their history about 1,300,000 square miles of land became a political unit, and apart from occasional trouble on the land frontiers their occupants need not fear attack. Piracy, whether as a profession or a form of guerilla warfare between a town and its trade rivals, was wiped out by Pompey in 67 B.C., and a strong navy made the Mediterranean much safer for ships, passengers, and cargo. Land travel and transportation were aided by the network of roads and by the patrols that checked highway robbery. Uniform coinage, weights, and measures, and the spread of Roman law made trade easier.

In comparison with earlier conditions the Mediterranean became a free-trade area. True, there were many internal and municipal levies on goods, and Italian wine and oil were heavily protected in the home market. In A.D. 92 Greece was forbidden to continue the cultivation of vines, since Italian growers complained of Greek competition, while Gaul was forbidden to plant vines till about A.D. 280, lest its wine steal markets from Italian producers or render the province independent of imported supplies. But, in general, duties were for revenue rather than for protection, and goods which could bear the costs of transportation had therefore a wider market at their command.

Roman occupation stimulated the economic development of the northern and western frontier regions. Its garrisons and administrative centers provided markets, its capital helped to develop natural resources, and while as a people the Romans made few agricultural innovations they took with them knowledge of methods and practices used elsewhere. In Britain they turned to the lead, iron, and tin deposits, introduced flax, fostered grain-growing in the southeast and the Thames Valley, and sent wheat to the Roman garrisons on the Rhine. Gaul was a much richer field, fairly well cultivated when the Romans entered it. It had rich grain and pasture lands, salt pans on the west coast, iron deposits in the north, and good river communications. Its blacksmiths made excellent arms and armor, its wool was good for coarse cloth, its potters made vessels which drove Italian wares out of the market, while flax, introduced from Egypt, was cultivated and made into linen by the Gauls. The ruins of aqueducts and other structures testify to the attention Rome gave to this treasure-house.

Spain was Rome's chief metal mine. Gold, silver, lead, copper, and iron were found there, and it has been estimated that during the three centuries of Roman occupation Spain yielded an average of over 300,000 ounces of gold yearly. The silver mines near New Carthage (the present Cartagena) employed 40,000 workers, and the rich iron deposits near Bilbao were vigorously exploited. Grain, wine, oil, and fruits were plentiful along the coast; sheep grazed on the central plateau, providing the highly prized merino wool; and hogs found plenty of food in the oak forests. The province took a long time to conquer, but was well worth the trouble; roads, settlements of soldier colonists, and large investments of capital all helped to Romanize it in customs and language.

The Rhine and Danube frontiers were fixed by strategic considerations, but they enclosed areas capable of great yields from soil and subsoil. Beyond them was a barbarian population which might buy and sell, and the two big rivers had long been used for the carriage of goods across the continent. The early camps at Cologne, Mainz, Strasbourg, Vienna, Basel, and elsewhere had to make for themselves or import the things they needed; but gradually the Germans inside and outside the frontier developed new industrial skills, acquired new tastes as consumers, adopted new cultivations and made new kinds of wares. When that day came, goods from Italy and the Rhine cities went across the river to be bartered for the produce of barbarian lands. Amber, furs, slaves, hides, cattle, goosedown, and red or yellow hair for ladies' wigs came in, to be exchanged for wine, pottery, glass, or coins.

In the eastern Mediterranean the provinces continued to produce and trade as they had done during the Hellenistic period, and much of what they paid in tribute they must have saved by the disappearance of piracy and war. The cities on the Greek peninsula had been hammered hard in the period of their conquest and never regained their old commercial power, but Asia Minor flourished, thanks to its natural resources, its industrial skill, and the wider opportunities for trade in the west. Egypt drew some benefits from Roman occupation, but paid heavily for them. The Ptolemies had exploited the country mercilessly, and when they lost it much land lay waste. In every addition to the territory of the Empire a portion of the land was earmarked for the emperor's use and income, and known as the *fisc*; but in Egypt the whole country went to him. Augustus did much (till he died in A.D. 14) to restore it to full productivity and make it yield more revenue, especially in the form of grain. He repaired the dikes and irrigation canals, and deprived the priesthood of its wealth and power; but he increased greatly his demands for forced labor and for taxes in kind. If his demands were within the peasant's capacity to work and pay, those of his successors often were beyond; and when individuals, unable to pay, were imprisoned or ran away, the scheme was devised of making some group—at first the family, but later a wider group or even the whole village—responsible for the dues of each individual. From this collective responsibility it was a natural step to forbid any peasant to leave his holding, a type of restraint that was to go out of Egypt and invade Europe. It was part of that inoculation of Roman economic policy with the despotic power of regulation common in eastern empires. "Rome's scourge of Egypt came back to plague the whole Empire" (Rostovtzeff).

The wealth of Rome and of the provincial towns created a demand for Oriental produce, spices, aromatics, ointments, drugs, cottons, furs, Indian metalware and textiles, precious stones, opium, Chinese silk, dyes, horses, and wild beasts for the circus. Opium—the "joy plant," as the Babylonians had called it—was popular in Rome, and was sold openly in shops or by quack doctors. Silk was highly esteemed, but its production was confined to China, and China regarded silk as the gift of a goddess, which should not be squandered on the heathen. The methods of production and preparation were kept a close secret, and attempts to export silkworm eggs were severely punished. Monopoly prices and transport costs were so heavy that a pound of silk is said to have cost a pound of gold in Rome.

Access to Oriental wares was made easier by the discovery (in the last century B.C.) of the behavior of the monsoons. A direct trip from the mouth of the Red Sea to India became possible, in place of the dreary dangerous journey along the coast. The voyage took at least forty days—the modern liner does it in about a week—but a boat could go from Suez to India and Ceylon, pick up cargo, meet the Chinese junks, and be back within a year of the date of departure. The other Asiatic trade routes, via the Euphrates or overland through Persia to India and China, were also used, but they were at the mercy of any strong power that controlled any part of them, and as the Parthian Empire grew in strength on Rome's eastern fringe the cost of transport and of tolls grew heavier. Failing to bring Parthia to terms, Rome tried to develop a new route through the Black Sea, across the Caspian, and round the top of the Parthian area.

How important this imperial and foreign trade was in the life of the Empire we cannot estimate. The towns scattered all over the Empire provided groups of consumers, not merely of local farm produce but also of luxury goods. The grain trade was large, and great grain ships plied between Alexandria or North Africa and Rome. But certain factors limited the volume and the range of traffic. The carriage of wine and oil was impeded by the difficulty of securing cheap earthenware or skin containers. Transport costs, especially on land, were heavy, and shipping in the rainy, stormy winter diminished or vanished. The efficiency of vessels was impaired by weak cordage, imperfect construction, and feeble masts. Oriental trade was restrained by transport costs and by the fact that Europe produced few goods which the Orient needed. Amber, coral, some metals, cloth, and wine—the list was short. Gold and silver were welcome in India then as now, and thousands of Roman coins, found in the Indian coastal ports, indicate one way in which the west paid the east; but there were limits to that kind of payment. Hence long-distance trade was confined to goods the rich could afford to buy, and the overwhelming majority of transactions were local in scope.

In order to get our trade picture into perspective, we must also remember that much production, both agricultural and industrial, was for direct consumption by the producer or his master. The modern home has so largely surrendered its domestic industries to brewery, bakery, laundry, cannery and clothing or shoe factory that the twentieth-century student finds it difficult to grasp the extent to which domestic production for family consumption dominated earlier centuries. In republican times the Roman large household, like that of Greece and like the courts and temples farther east, had its masons, smiths, carpenters, cloth and clothes makers, potters, and other kinds of workers. The growth of agricultural production for market gave the landowner some spending power, and the contacts with the Near East after 200 B.C. introduced him to the finer wares of that region. Domestic self-sufficiency was impaired and the purchase of imported luxuries increased as we draw nearer imperial days. Yet household production never disappeared from the homes of the rich, or even seriously declined; it supplied virtually all the needs of the poorer classes, and as the economic structure of the Empire disintegrated the big estate drew back into its shell and became self-contained again.

Roman Industrial Life.—Rome made very few contributions to industrial processes or products. Her construction industry was highly developed, for the task of supplying water to a big city during the long summer drought called for reservoirs, aqueducts, and pipes. One of the longest of the nine pipes serving Rome brought water a distance of sixty miles. The building of temples, forums, triumphal arches, amphitheaters, circuses, baths (with central heating), libraries, and market halls required a high degree of skill in architecture and surveying, the use of new materials (especially cement and long iron beams), and the employment of great hordes of laborers. But even the construction industry suffered at times from defective methods or from fraudulent contractors. When Pliny went to Bithynia as governor-general, he discovered that contractors had been robbing the treasury, that Nicodemia had spent a vast sum on an aqueduct which proved to be worthless, that the walls of a theater at Nicæa cracked before the building was completed, and that the walls of a gymnasium were too weak even though they were twenty-two feet thick.

In other industries Rome's contribution was insignificant. This may have been due in part to the standards of value which ruled the Roman mind. Its leaders regarded war, politics, money-lending, and agriculture as the only tasks to which they might put their hands. Gentlemen might grab the public domain, pile up booty and plunder provincials, shower bribes right and left to win elections, and lend money at high interest; but they must not touch industry or trade. One may hesitate to attach too much importance to this attitude, but it is true that industrial advance has been most marked in those countries or periods where the fashionable view was friendly to it, e.g., eighteenth-century England, seventeenth-century Holland, or medieval Venice.

The Roman list of ungentlemanly occupations was not solely industrial or commercial. It included doctors and schoolmasters, whom Juvenal associated with painters, attendants at the public baths, fortune tellers, and tight-rope dancers; it also included actors, charioteers, and gladiators, and even perhaps architects. Industry and much trade were thus left to the slave, the freedman, the alien, or the plebeian. The freedman was often a skilled

worker who might have been liberated by his master and set up
in a small business. He and his children played a large part in
carrying on many of the occupations listed above, as well as the
ordinary industries. He sometimes rose to wealth, became a local
civic officer, and presented a building, a statue, or a public spec-
tacle to his city. By the third century probably a quarter of the
members of the municipal councils of the Empire were freedmen.

Italian manufactures were usually carried on in the home or
small workshop by workers who might be independent masters,
slaves, or hired men. There were some large units. In Rome a
publisher employing slave copyists could produce 500 or 1000
copies of a popular work in a very short time at a low price. In
a few places in Etruria and Campania some special deposit of
raw material, some large local market, or the enterprise of some
employer gave rise to large plants for the production of bricks,
metalware, glass, or pottery.

Roman Guilds.—In Rome, as in most of the eastern cities,
many industries and trades had their guilds. In all ages men, especially in towns, have tended to band together for the defense or
promotion of their common ideas, faith, economic interest, or
amusement. Men producing the same commodity, using the same
wharf or market, living in the street devoted to one kind of industry or trade, traveling to the same fair or buying the same
raw material may be rivals, yet they have certain common interests to protect or promote. These need not be strictly economic,
and the ancient guilds seem to have been chiefly concerned with
the religious and social welfare of their members—a mixture
of friendly society, burial brotherhood, and luncheon club. In
Rome there is evidence of the existence of guilds (*collegia*) after
200 B.C. Some of them became embroiled in the wrangles of the
late republic and were abolished by the early emperors. Later
they were allowed to be formed again under official license, and
eventually there were eighty of them in Rome alone. In their
humblest form they were groups of poor free or freed workers,
whose business was to tend a member when he was sick and give
him a decent burial when he died, but there is no evidence that
they dealt with apprenticeship, wages, or hours. The groups of
builders, bargemen, barbers, smiths, pork merchants, wine dealers,
oil men, etc., were more wealthy or powerful, and some of them

sought to promote economic gain as well as social welfare and good fellowship.

The collegia probably began as voluntary groups, but were not long allowed to remain free from regulation from above. Whenever any association grows strong or becomes noisy enough to attract attention the state begins to suppress, regulate, or use it; and the later Roman emperors found the guilds very useful. By the third century the cost of government was growing heavy. Free bread was now being provided, and cheap oil and wine had been added. The cost of transporting and distributing these doles was becoming burdensome, as was also the general cost of government in a century torn by plague, civil war, and attacks on the frontier. Guilds were therefore formed for trades and industries that did not have them; they were given a monopoly over their occupation, and their members were exempted from military service. In return, they were commanded to give certain services to the government gratis, and the group was made a unit for tax levies or held collectively responsible for the taxes of each individual. The shipping guild must carry grain free from Egypt or Africa, the bakers must bake it free, the cloth or munition makers must provide the government with goods at cost price, some guilds must maintain the imperial post or transport officials, and some must operate the fire brigade.

As the needs of the state grew heavier, so also did these *munera*, these taxes in kind or labor. When they threatened to crush the urban middle class and the victims tried to escape from the guild, trade, or town, a decree forbade them to move and made membership in the guild hereditary. The government of the group passed under the supervision of some city official, and the guild became a part of the state machinery, directing the production and distribution of the wealth produced by its members. If the state had taken these steps in the interests of production, all might have been well; but it was solely interested in the golden eggs, and in its urgent need it killed the goose. There is a limit beyond which the state cannot appropriate the income of private enterprise without killing that enterprise. Craftsmen did escape from the towns or the trade, urban industries were weakened, and in the general damage to the middle and artisan classes Rome provided one cause of her "decline and fall."

The Disintegration of the Empire.—The story of the guilds has led us out of the centuries of peace and prosperity to those of decline and disintegration. No simple explanation of what happened is possible. Political, economic, social, intellectual and spiritual factors all played a part, reacting on and intensifying one another. Perhaps the least debatable simple economic explanation might be that the volume of income produced was reduced by certain factors on the one hand, while the state demanded a growing share of it on the other. The cost of government became too great, the instruments of government became restrictive and often destructive (e.g., when rival armies waged civil war), and two of the main functions of government (the protection of the frontiers and the maintenance of peace and order) were no longer discharged. A society with an agricultural foundation and some industrial and commercial superstructure was impoverished to support a state and army which could not render the services necessary for the maintenance of that society.

The cost of the army needed to defend the long land frontier was increased when barbarians pressed harder on the northern boundary and powers rose in the Near East. The efficiency of the army was impaired by the increasingly mercenary character of its personnel. The legions became less and less Roman. They were filled with provincials and barbarians, and the chief stimuli to loyalty were pay and booty. If these were not forthcoming the army melted away or revolted. At the head of the Empire puppet emperors came and went, chosen by the rattle of swords and deposed by violence. Between 217 and 285 there were twenty-nine emperors, of whom only one died in bed. This military anarchy encouraged the Germans and Persians to attack the neglected frontiers, and at the same time led to chaos and destruction along the mercenaries' line of march.

From the tumult of the third century Diocletian (285-305) tried to drag the Empire by drastic reforms. He recognized that the Empire was too big to be ruled and defended by one man, and therefore took steps which led to its division into two parts. Constantinople, built by Constantine as capital of the eastern half in 324-330, was well situated for defense and trade. Its territory included the richer and more developed areas of the Mediterranean, and for a thousand years its political and commercial history was a motley of color and squalor. The imperial ideas, laws, and methods of Rome, even the bread and circuses, were transplanted there, and emperors tried with varying success to extend or defend the old imperial boundaries in face of barbarian, Persian, Arab, and Turk.

In the west there was no power capable of preventing control from passing into barbarian hands, for the army was largely composed of barbarian mercenaries. Whole tribes were inside the frontiers of Rhine or Danube long before 400, and there was no force strong enough to bar their path as they moved into France, Italy, Spain, and North Africa. Rome's impotence is well illustrated when in 476 Odoacer, chief of the mercenaries in Italy, demands land for his men, slays the general who says "No," deposes the emperor, takes the title of king for himself and grants land to his followers.

To the cost of maintaining an inefficient army was added that of supporting the emperor and the civil government. Imperial luxury was lavish; when Nero erected a statue of himself 120 feet high, decked it with gold and jewels, sprinkled his dinner guests with roses and perfumes from a specially constructed ceiling, or used grain ships to bring cargoes of sand for the floor of the Coliseum, he merely showed a capacity for consuming wealth which his successors were able to exceed. The luxury of the court was reflected in that of the aristocracy and plutocracy. Huge public works, great buildings, the feeding or amusing of the city populace, the payment of a growing army of officials—all added to the demands on the public revenue and ate up a large part of the Empire's income. "No empire ever supported so many economically unproductive classes as Rome" (Clausing).

To meet these demands there was the yield from the state mines, the public domain, Egypt and other pieces of the *fisc*; there was the yield from monopolies set up after the Oriental pattern for certain trades and industries; there was booty, now less the yield from defeated foreigners and more the property of victims of imperial wrath or of civil war; there was debasement of the currency practiced in days of unbalanced budgets from Nero's time onward; and there was taxation. The taxes consisted of (1) tribute levied on the provinces, consisting of a poll tax, and a land and property tax (which might be a fixed sum or a fixed share of the produce), (2) customs duties, taxes on emancipated slaves, and sales and inheritance taxes.

The collection of many of these taxes was a duty of the municipalities. When tax time came the municipality was ordered to provide a certain sum, and the city fathers were responsible for the collection of that amount in the town and adjacent country. If they failed to collect enough they must pay the deficit out of their own pockets. Consequently the disturbances of the third century shook the municipalities. Trade was almost mortally wounded by civil war, invasion, pillage, and plague. Taxation had to be increased, *munera* became heavier, depreciation of the currency increased the cost of government and played havoc with prices, while some towns had been notoriously extravagant and corrupt in the handling of their finances during the palmy days. The added financial burden could not all be passed on to the surrounding country, but stuck on the back of the town. When the local magistrates tried to evade their financial responsibility by escaping from the magisterial class, membership of the class was made compulsory and hereditary for all who possessed a certain amount of property. Some of the wealthiest were able to escape into the higher clergy or the senatorial class, where there was exemption and immunity. Some ran away to the countryside or to the barbarians. The rest had to stay, pay, and extort as much as they could from their fellow townsmen or from the country-dwellers. But there were limits to this, and the middle class was crushed as its capital and income were sucked into state coffers. Starvation or suicide was the end of many a bourgeois.

The decay of industry and commerce, the monetary and military chaos, and the ruin of the towns threw Rome back on to the land as the one abiding source of income. If all else vanished, the land would yield something. We left the land at the stage where great estates had grown up or had been carved out of the public domain. The social and economic attractions of such estates had diminished little under the Empire, and after Christianity was officially tolerated (A.D. 313) gifts of land by the emperor and the laity set the church on a road which made it the greatest landowner of the Middle Ages. When peace reduced the supply and raised the price of slaves the cultivation of latifundia became unprofitable and landlords must therefore find some other way of using their estates. They reserved part of the land for a domain; the rest they rented in full-size holdings to free tenants (*coloni*) or in smaller cottage lots to slaves (*servi*). The cultivator paid his rent by handing over a fixed share of the produce or a fixed quantity of money or produce, and by doing a certain amount of work on the domain. Thus the landlord got his domain worked and drew income from the rest of his estate; the cultivator got the use of land on which to work and from which to live.

As late as A.D. 244, the colonus was free to leave his landlord if he wished, but in 332 we find a decree forbidding him to do so, and threatening to load him with chains "in the manner of slaves" if he tried to run away. He was bound to the estate as the townsmen were bound to their trades and the city fathers to their offices, and the bondage was (or soon became) hereditary. The colonus was legally free while the slave was not; he could own property, marry, appear in court, and sell his own produce. He paid a fixed rent, paid a poll tax, and must do some unpaid work on roads, bridges, etc., for the state. He could not be liberated from the estate on which he was born, and if the estate changed hands he went with it.

The reason for this imposition of bondage is not known, and many explanations, none of them generally accepted, have been advanced. The decrees of the fourth century probably tried to make general throughout the Empire conditions which had developed in some parts of it already. They were an attempt to guarantee that estates would not lose their producers or the state lose revenue. In the fifty years of anarchy which preceded Diocletian's reforms agriculture had become demoralized and the land tax receipts had fallen heavily. Farmers burdened with debt or taxes had apparently run away. To prevent a repetition of this and guarantee a stream of food and taxes, the cultivator must stay where he was. He was secure in possession of a holding, for if he was bound to the land the land was bound to him. His rent was fixed, and took a stipulated portion of his produce and his time. Only under stress of oppressive taxation by the state or of arbitrary exactions by his lord might he resent his bondage or want to leave the estate. Unless great opportunities of better land and income were available elsewhere, there was no desire to move. As a method of satisfying wants the colonate met the needs of cultivator, landlord, and state.

In the west the state slipped out of the picture, and the control of local life passed into the hands of the large landowner. In troubled times free peasants, runaway slaves, and harassed townsmen found protection under his wing. As a member of the senatorial class, he was immune from responsibility to the local municipality and later to the provincial governor. He gave up paying land tax, and neither city nor governor could force the money from him. He became local ruler as well as owner, policing his area and trying cases in his court. His *villa* became in effect a new economic and administrative unit. On it he had a market, church, mill, and often a prison. He had industrial as well as farm workers; and if the threads that bound his estate to the outside business world became frayed or snapped, so also did those which bound him to an imperial lord. Rome began with a group of patricians, small farmers, and slaves. The Roman Empire in the west ended with a group of large landowners who exercised far-reaching power over coloni and slaves, with a few stagnant or decaying towns, and with a commerce that had shriveled into insignificance. The great estates were carried over by their owners or taken over by conquering newcomers to form the basis of medieval society.

BIBLIOGRAPHY

See books cited in earlier lists by Cunningham, Marvin, Neuberger, Schoff, Semple, and Usher. Also:

BAILEY, C. (ed.), *The Legacy of Rome* (1923), chaps. 4, 13.
BARROW, R. H., *Slavery in the Roman Empire* (1928).
BOAK, A. E. R., *A History of Rome to 565 A.D.* (1925).
CHAPOT, V., *Le monde romain* (1927).
CHARLESWORTH, M. P., *Trade Routes and Commerce of the Roman Empire* (1925).
CLAUSING, R., *The Roman Colonate* (1925).
DUFF, A. M., *Freedmen in the Early Roman Empire* (1928).
FOWLER, W. W., *Rome* (Home University Library).
FOWLER, W. W., *Social Life at Rome in the Age of Cicero* (1909).
FRANK, T., "Recent Work on the Economic History of Rome," in *J. E. B. H.*, vol. i, November, 1928.
FRANK, T., *An Economic History of Rome* (2nd ed., 1927).
GRAS, N. S. B., *History of Agriculture* (1925), chaps. 2, 3.
GREENE, W. C., *The Achievement of Rome* (1934).
HEITLAND, W. E., *Agricola* (1921).
HUNTINGTON, ELLSWORTH, "Climatic Change and Agricultural Exhaustion as Elements in the Fall of Rome," in *Q. J. E.*, February, 1917.
KNIGHT, M. M., and others, *Economic History of Europe* (1928), chap. 2.
LOT, F., *The End of the Ancient World* (Eng. trans., 1931), part i, chaps. 4, 6, 7.
NILSSON, M. P., *Imperial Rome* (Eng. trans., 1926), especially vol. ii.
RANDALL-MACIVER, D., *Italy before the Romans* (1928).
ROSE, J. HOLLAND, *The Mediterranean in the Ancient World* (1933).

ROSTOVTZEFF, M. I., *Social and Economic History of the Roman Empire* (1926).

ROSTOVTZEFF, M. I., *A History of the Ancient World:* vol. ii: *Rome* (1927), especially chap. 20.

ROSTOVTZEFF, M. I., "The Decay of the Ancient World and Its Economic Explanation, in *Ec. H. R.*, vol. ii, 1930.

ROSTOVTZEFF, M. I., "Roman Exploitation of Egypt," in *J. E. B. H.*, vol. i, May, 1929.

THOMPSON, J. W., *Economic and Social History of the Middle Ages (300-1300)* (1928), chaps. 1, 2, bibliography.

TOUTAIN, J., *The Economic Life of the Ancient World* (1930), parts iii, iv.

USHER, A. P., "Soil Fertility, Soil Exhaustion, and Their Historical Significance," in *Q. J. E.*, vol. xxxvii, May, 1923.

VARRO on Farming (Eng. trans., 1912).

WARMINGTON, E. H., *Commerce between the Roman Empire and India* (1928).

WESTERMANN, W. L., "The Economic Basis of the Decline of Ancient Culture" (*Am. Hist. Rev.*, July, 1915).

Encyclopædia of the Social Sciences: articles on the Roman World (vol. i), Agrarian Movements (Rome), Colonate, Guilds (late Roman and Byzantine), Land Tenure (Ancient World), Latifundia, Manor, Slavery (Ancient).

CHAPTER V

THE MAKERS OF MEDIEVAL ECONOMIC SOCIETY

OF ECONOMIC life during the thousand years called the Middle Ages we know little until we approach the halfway mark, and even when A.D. 1000 is passed it is easier to ask questions than to answer them. As a student of French agricultural history recently lamented, "Nos ignorances sont grandes" (Bloch). Almost every topic has been the subject of controversy, and while the fire has died down in some spots for lack of new fuel, it still blazes fiercely in others. But on one point there is general agreement. There was no violent break between the ancient and the medieval world. The old civilization did not die a sudden death at the hands of barbarians, and even in its disintegrated form it contributed substantially to the economic making of the Middle Ages.

The makers of medieval economic society were seven: (1) the rural society that had taken shape in the later days of the Roman Empire; (2) the Eastern Empire; (3) the Italian cities which survived or rose to develop sea traffic with the Near East and land trade with northern and central Europe; (4) the church; (5) the Moslems, who advanced along the North African coast, crossed to Spain, and thus forged a new chain linking the two ends of the Mediterranean; (6) the Germans, who spread over the Low Countries, France, England, Spain, and parts of Italy; (7) the Norsemen, who gave northern Europe its first vigorous native seamen and traders. The first four carried on the economic or political legacy of the ancient world, but the last two emerged from an area that has hitherto figured little in the story.

Their appearance is a fitting reminder that not all Europe is Mediterranean. Behind the northern coasts of that sea is a great divide of hills and mountains. It has had its own economic life in the forests, on the pasture-covered slopes and plateaus, in the orchards or vineyards planted in the valleys, on the grain fields and pastures of the Danubian plain, in the spots where minerals are found, and in the towns that have grown up on the roads and rivers. The highlands have not been impassable to armies, migrants, or traders. The Morava and Vardar (or Maritza) Valleys provide a passage from Danubia to the Ægean; passes lead from northern Italy into Austria, Switzerland and France; the lowlands north of the Pyrenees and the valley of the Rhone give a western track to the Bay of Biscay or the north, while in the east the Russian rivers run round the end of the barrier.

The North European Environment.—The northern slopes of these highlands lead down to the great plain. It starts at the foot of the Pyrenees and swings northeastward to Belgium, Holland, eastern and central England, Denmark, and southern Sweden, and is bounded by the sea or by the belt of highlands in Wales, Scotland and Norway. It stretches over the northern half of Germany, and then broadens out to cover virtually all Russia. One can go by train from Bordeaux to the Urals without passing through a single tunnel. In places it is below sea level, e.g., in Holland; in others it is so flat, or the natural drainage is so slight, that rivers used to flood easily and seasonal or permanent swamps were extensive, e.g., in England between the Thames and the Wash, in Flanders, in Germany along the coast, and in the Pripet marshes of western Russia. Its soil is varied in quality, for while glacial action and rivers gave good soil to southeastern England, southern Sweden, central Belgium, Holland, and the Rhine Valley, the glaciers deposited clay, sand, gravel, and other coarse materials on many areas, especially round the Baltic. These areas of swamp and poor soil were of little use until they had been drained and their soil properties improved, and much of this could not be done without modern engineering and knowledge of soil chemistry.

The climate of northern Europe changes as one passes eastward. On the western fringe Atlantic cyclones and the Gulf Stream give a temperate climate to areas which are in the same latitude as the southern half of Hudson Bay. Snow, frost, and heat are equally rare, the Englishman can rarely use his skates, outdoor work is possible all year round, and in Ireland, southern England, and France cattle can be left in the fields all winter. The same oceanic influences bring plenty of rain throughout the year, fog and clouds, long springs and leisurely falls, with occasional raw winds that stir only poets to enthusiasm. The Atlantic loses its influence once the Rhine is crossed, and the climate gradually becomes continental, with smaller rainfall, long harsh winters, and in central and eastern Europe short hot summers. In the far north arctic conditions prevail, and the bleak tundras, covered with moss, lichens, and stunted shrubs, offer little sustenance. In the far southeast the rainfall fades away as we approach the steppes of western Asia.

Variations in soil and climate gave diversity to the natural environment, to the capacity of a region to carry population, and to the occupations of the inhabitants in all centuries. The far north was too stern for much human activity, but when that zone was left behind a broad belt of forest was entered. In places there was too much water for trees, and moorlands, peat bogs, or swamps prevailed, the bogs yielding a poor fuel, the fens swarming with wild fowl. But elsewhere, from the mountains of Wales across to the Urals, northern Europe had vast forest areas which provided a livelihood to various kinds of inhabitants but which must be cleared as the need for farm land grew. This forest gave place to treeless pastures up the mountain sides, and to prairie in south Russia and Hungary. In its better parts the prairie was rich soil—the "black belt" of Russia—destined to be one of the great grain areas of the world, but hard to "break," fickle in rainfall, and long shut off from markets. Beyond it lay desert around the Caspian.

Through the hills and plains of northern Europe ran many rivers, some of them navigable. Their estuaries provided safe harbors and permitted seafaring ships to go far inland. In some places the sources of rivers which flowed in different directions were so close together that a traveler could enter a country on one side, go up one stream to the head of navigation, make a short portage to another river, descend it and emerge at the opposite side of the country or continent. In France all the rivers except the Garonne radiate from one central area; in England the Trent, Mersey, Severn, Avon, and Thames approach each other; in Poland and Russia rivers which flow into the Baltic, Black, and Caspian Seas rise in the Valdai Hills, and southwest Germany is near the Rhone, Rhine, and Danube.

Northern Europe had rich assets in its mineral deposits and its seas. While there was never any great find of gold, most of the other metals were available, and by the end of the Middle Ages coal was being used. The seas were shallow, and therefore good fishing areas. They were not very wide, their coasts were dotted with good harbors, and they were rough enough to breed a race of hardy seamen.

If we add up the units of this environment, the total explains much of the workaday history of northern and western Europe during the last two thousand years. The climate was not enervating and it favored the production of a wide variety of crops or the tending of domestic animals. The soil was good in parts, but had to be worked and refreshed persistently. The area of naturally clear fertile land was small; extension of settlement called for pioneer work, draining swamps, felling trees, and fighting wild animals or natives on the frontier; and some regions required knowledge, methods, or materials which were not available till after 1800. Northwestern Europe was not hostile to her inhabitants, but she was not lavish in her hospitality to them. They must work hard for simple bed, board, and a little pocket money.

The Germans.—When the Romans came into contact with the north, they found three main groups of people. In the west, occupying France and the British Isles, were the Celts. In the center, from Scandinavia and the Rhine to the Vistula, and spreading later down to the Black Sea, were the Germans. In the east, in and around the Pripet marshes and the forests between the Vistula and the Dnieper, were the Slavs. How these peoples lived depended largely on the nature of the country they occupied. The Slavs of the marshes were almost amphibious; the waters gave them fish and fowl, swarms of bees gave honey and wax, rye and vegetables were grown for food, flax or hemp for clothing fibers, but there was not much ground dry enough for feeding livestock. Those who lived in forest areas hunted fur-bearing animals, produced tar and cultivated small clearings.

. Where the soil made tillage possible, the Germans were passing and the Celts had almost passed from a hunting and pastoral life to one in which cultivation was important. The Germans herded cattle and horses in open country and swine in the forests. They fished, hunted, kept bees—honey was used for making mead— cleared and cultivated some soil, and in places extracted and worked metals. For some tribes war was an attractive occupation, a way of life and a way of filling the larder, more exciting and satisfying than following cattle, and rich in promise of reward. Where herding and hunting were the main occupations the Germans attached greatest value to meadows and pasture lands. When the supply of grass was exhausted in one place they would desert that spot and the small cultivated patches they had broken. They rarely stopped more than a year or two in one place, and movement was thus a normal feature of primitive German life. It might take place inside some area recognized as belonging to the tribe; it might take the migrants farther afield; and, if stimulated by growth of population, by the desire for the fat lands and wealth of the south, or by attack from the rear, it might bring a Baltic people to the Black Sea or Mediterranean.

Even before the Romans were in contact with them, some Germans of the plain had ceased to roam, were practicing systematic agriculture and living in permanent village homes. In Gaul the Romans found many compact groups of Celtic farmers under the rule of big landowners, and in England villages and hamlets, perched on the ridges of the southern chalk hills, were centers of tillage and herding. In Gaul the Romans accepted the big estate and set up more like it. In England they expanded agriculture, settled Roman colonists, and established villas. Near the Rhine frontier Germans were settled as coloni. Tribute, the use of money, and the needs of towns stimulated production for market and gave agriculture some commercial flavor, especially in Gaul.

When the Germans began to move into the Empire in great numbers, their policy toward the land they entered depended on the conditions they found in existence. In southern France, Spain, and northern Italy they settled on deserted or empty lands and took over the public domain. They might also seize the big estates and transfer them to some tribal leader, but often they were satisfied with a fraction of the land or of the produce. As they became Christian they carried on the practice of granting land to church or monastery. In the southern lands the structure of rural society therefore remained much as it had become in later Roman days, with large landowners and coloni.

In the north the Germans were gradually pushed west of the Elbe by the Slavs, but continued to occupy the land between the Elbe and the Rhine, Denmark, and southern Sweden. Some of them went to northern France, the Low Countries, and England. Here they were less influenced by Roman survivals, were able to brush aside or overcome the natives, and settled down where they wished. In this area, from middle England to the Elbe, we see in its least diluted form the character of Germanic economic and social life. The political unit was the tribe, bound together by ties of blood and claiming the sole right to enjoy the area in which it dwelt. The economic unit was the village, consisting of a big family group or of a number of families. At its center were clustered the farmhouses, each with its barn, stable, and vegetable garden. Around this core might be the meadows, from which was obtained the hay needed for feeding the livestock during the cold winter. Since the cattle were private property, the hay crop was shared out among the villagers, or the meadows were cut into private patches and distributed by drawing lots.

Beyond the meadows lay the arable fields. So long as cultivation had to be carried on with little or no supply of fertilizer, exhausted soil might be abandoned and new fields prepared. But the available new supply might be limited and the labor of preparation very heavy. The alternative was to till land for a year or two and then let it rest for a season. In places a two-field or three-field rotation was worked out; each field was allowed to recuperate every second or third year, and only half or two-thirds of the arable land was under crop in any one season. This three-field system was widespread by the seventh or eighth century, and archæologists suggest that it goes back to at least 1000 B.C.

The distribution of the arable land among the villagers presented two curious features. In the first place, a man's acres were not in one compact block, but in a number of scattered pieces, possibly as many as forty. In the second place, these pieces were usually long and narrow; they might be about 220 yards long and 22 yards wide (an acre in area), but some were smaller. They were separated from each other by a strip (or balk) of unplowed land.

Many attempts have been made to explain these striped fields. Here are some:

1. When the village brought a piece of pasture or woodland under the plow, each family obtained a piece of it. In the course of time new fields would be added to the arable area, and each farmer would get a part of each field.

2. Plowing was often done cooperatively, for few farmers owned plows or sufficient oxen to make a team. If one field was plowed, and each farmer had a strip in it, he could get on with his seeding while the next field was being prepared.

3. Different parts of the arable land had different degrees of

desirability. They were good, fair, or poor, near or distant, swampy or well drained, stony or clear. In dry seasons lowlands might fare better than hillsides; in wet years the position would be reversed. Distribution of small areas over a wide expanse satisfied the demands of fair play and provided insurance against vagaries of the weather.

4. Periodical redistribution played its part. In places arable and meadow land seems to have been shared out, at first yearly, but later less frequently and only when the number of claimants had changed substantially. Such change would usually be due to an increase in the number of claims, and this might lead to the allotment of a smaller piece in each field to each claimant.

None of these explanations accounts for the long narrow strip. The reason for that shape seems to be found in the plow which the Germans used. The early Mediterranean plow, pulled by human beings or one or two oxen, was little more than a pointed stick, which scratched a shallow groove in the light southern soil and turned no furrow. When the ground had been plowed from east to west, it had to be scratched again from north to south to break the soil more effectively. Hence a small square field, perhaps 40 yards by 40 yards, was the normal unit for Greek and Roman farmers. The soil of northern Europe was heavier and wetter, and the southern equipment would make little impression on it. About the beginning of the Christian era a heavy plow, mounted on wheels and equipped with a broad plowshare which cut and turned a furrow, came into use. It disturbed the earth so thoroughly that cross-plowing was unnecessary, and a team of eight oxen could pull it a long way without pausing for a rest. Hence a plowed field consisted of a collection of long furrows, and when we finally reach a settled unit of area the acre is a furrow long (a furlong) and four rods, poles, or perches wide. The pole may have been the long stick with which the oxen were prodded to keep them moving.

Garden, meadow, and fields had been cut out of the tribal land, and their ownership or enjoyment had become private. What was left was the common property of the village or of the larger group to which the villagers belonged. Each householder had the right to turn his livestock on the common pastures and his hogs into the forest to seek nuts or acorns. He could collect turf or wood, hunt, fish, or take away any other natural product. These common lands faded away into the empty expanse that separated village from village. Bit by bit that land ceased to be empty as settlers came in. Sometimes they were individuals who left the old centers and carved out of plain or forest a lonely farm or ranch; often they were a group of the younger generation, which left the overcrowded hive to set up a new community; at times they were a band of monks.

When we turn from landscape to population we are confronted by one of the most vexed problems in medieval economic and social history. By the tenth century, at the latest, Germanic society was divided into two main classes—lords and servile tenants— and the former exercised lordship and landlordship over the latter. Lordship gave the right to govern, judge, and tax one's subjects. Landlordship gave the power to claim payments in labor, money, or produce. But while the lord and landlord exercised his authority over his subordinates, he in turn might have obligations to fulfill to some superior from whom he had received the land. His superior in turn might have to bow the knee and serve some overlord, until at the top of the scale we find a king who is lord and landlord in chief, king not only of the Franks or the West Saxons but of France or Wessex.

The historical problem raised by this social structure springs from the belief, held by many nineteenth-century scholars, that the migratory Germans were bands of free and equal warrior-peasants, tilling (individually or cooperatively) their own soil, and subject only to the lordship of the tribal chiefs. If this was so, the following centuries brought a degradation of political and economic status. Other scholars contended that the Germans were not all free and equal, that there was a large unfree and economically dependent element in the population, and that whole villages were composed of the servile tenants of some lord. When the wanderers entered the Western Empire they found in the Roman villa a social system that was familiar to them, and in regions remote from Rome they established the same kind of community of lord and serfs as they had known in their own lands.

The controversy between these two views has died down for lack of fuel, but it seems that both sides were right, since each picture portrayed part of the scene rather than the whole. The influence of the Roman estate was important, some German tribes had long been acquainted with social inequality and landlordship, and after they settled down "they merely continued further along the way of social differentiation which led to the great estate and servile labor" (Power). Some migratory tribes, however, such as the Anglo-Saxons, were apparently free peasant peoples. The society they transferred to England was one of free cultivators, but during later centuries it was gradually transformed.

Political, economic, military, and religious factors contributed to the building of that combination of lordship and landlordship which was to characterize rural society for quite a thousand years. War chiefs became territorial monarchs, gained sway over areas of land, and claimed the right to give or take away. Gratitude for past favors or expectation of favors to come made them grant estates to their lieutenants, favorites, or officials. Piety and the desire to retain the friendship of the church led to similar grants to bishop or abbot. These grants might be supplemented by seizures when weak kings were on the throne, when civil war broke out, or when invasion broke in.

A land grant was more than a reward; it might be a method of providing for local administration, public finance, and defense. Its recipient must give a certain amount of military aid, and at times some money. He must dispense justice, keep order, and enforce the king's decrees on his estates. To sustain him while he discharged these duties he had the income from his territory and its occupants. In an age when money was scarce and rulers had no large tax income from which to pay soldiers and public employees, the king financed the army and the administration by providing his servants with land from which they could draw sustenance. The provision might be only for life, but possession tended to become hereditary. The recipient of a royal grant might in turn make grants to his own lieutenants under similar conditions of military service, payment, and aid in administration. Each of them in turn might do the same, until we reach a fief which was too small for further subdivision.

Some of the land transferred by these grants or taken by force was empty, and its owner set to work to find settlers. Some of it was already occupied by free peasants. On these men was now imposed the intimate rule of a lord instead of the remote control of a king, and the alliance of lordship and landlordship probably grew closer and stronger. In the Frankish period (500-750) the seigneuries did not cover France, and there were still many small farmers who owed no dues or labor to anyone but the king. But the violence of internal wars or invasions, the need for protection from attack, the abuse of power by those who wielded it, and the weakness of kings combined to bring many free farmers into political and economic subjection.

If we look at the growth of lordship from above we see strong men gaining power, property, and privileges. If we look at it from below we see weak men sinking into dependence or reaching up for a protector. Some sank under the familiar burden of debt or taxes. Some abandoned freedom in order to escape military service, and others to secure protection in troubled times. Ties of kinship which had bound the clan or tribe together and sheltered its members had become weak. If a strong state, able to defend its subjects from attack and keep the peace, was not available, other sanctuary must be sought, and many found it under the wing of some lord. To "commend" one's life and land to him, to accept liability for certain obligations, and in return to get protection and the secure use of some land was a wise, even if a hard, bargain. It had the elements of a contract, though not one between equals.

To some areas the power of the landlord did not reach. Inhabitants of forests, marshes, or mountains might escape the general trend and remain a law to themselves. Those who lived around the Italian towns gained strength from the ability of those towns to maintain a measure of political or economic independence. But elsewhere in the lands west of the Rhine and lower Elbe society gradually took a pattern which, though varied in details, conformed to one general design in the relations between the landowning and the land-tilling classes. That design was feudalism in its broad aspects, and the manorial system in so far as the manor (the rough equivalent of the Roman villa) was its local unit. It has been described as "a form of government, a structure of society, an economic régime based on land proprietorship" (Thompson) ; as a land system wherein "every lord judged, taxed, and commanded the class below him" (Stubbs) ; and as a plan which "solved for a time two of man's perpetual problems —his social organization and his land system" (Jarrett).

With feudalism as a form of government we are not concerned, except to note that the political power which went with landownership carried many income-yielding perquisites. As a social structure it divided the population into a landed monarchy, aristocracy, and church on the one hand, and a mass of tenants on the other. As an economic régime it was a scheme for meeting the wants of all sections of society, for producing and distributing goods, and for defraying the costs of government and religion in an age that was predominantly agricultural, that had little currency and less commerce. The feudal division of labor was well expressed in the declaration that "The House of God is tripartite. Some work, some fight, some pray." It was even better expressed on the signboard of those later English inns which even today are called "The Five Alls." On this board are the pictures of five men, and beneath is the inscription: "I rule all. I judge all. I fight for all. I pray for all. I work for all." If the ruler, judge, warrior, and priest were to do their work, they must be supported by the labor of peasants and craftsmen.

The Northmen.—From the beginning of history Sweden had been the starting point of southward migrations. Burgundians had crossed to the south shore of the Baltic by 200 B.C., while Goths and Vandals were Scandinavian before they were German. But the great age of viking expansion began about A.D. 700, and lasted over three centuries. The forces which sent men out from the north were economic and political. Scandinavia had scanty resources. Denmark was a low sandy peninsula, with a poor climate and covered with grass and beech forest. In southern Sweden there was room for pasturage and tillage, but the soil was patchy, thin, and stony. Norway had little to offer cultivator or herdsman. The forest and the sea must be scoured to supplement the scanty returns from the soil, and if the Swede was a farmer who owned a boat, the Norwegian was a fisherman who had a little farm. Collecting and catching played a large part, hunting and trapping brought food and furs. On the fringe of the Baltic there was amber; around the coast were herrings or cod, and out west or north were whales, seals, and walrus.

Some northern wares had for centuries found markets in central and Mediterranean Europe, and were carried at least part of the way to the consumer by Scandinavian merchants. These men also gathered up produce from Russia and either exchanged it in such markets as Copenhagen or Wisby (on the island of Gothland), or went up the streams that flowed into the Baltic or North

Sea. The sea was a place for piracy as well as for fishing, while in lands beyond it were goods that could be obtained as booty or by barter. The boundary line between trading and piracy was as faint in the North Sea as in the Mediterranean, and a raid on town or ship was an approved method of replenishing a merchant's stock.

In their roving the Norsemen developed good ships and seamanship. When speed was important they built long narrow craft, seaworthy in the rough waters of northwestern Europe, propelled by oars and big woolen sails, and yet so shallow in draft

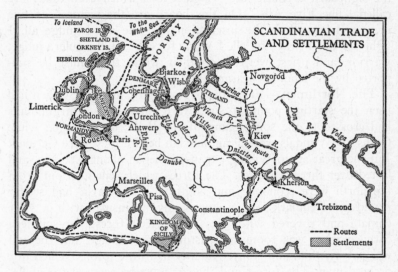

that they could be sailed far upstream when the Seine or the Ouse was reached. When the fighter gave place to the trader, broader slower vessels were built, and in these ships, of about sixteen tons capacity, sheep and cattle were transported to Iceland at an average speed of about three miles an hour. There were no decks to offer shelter for man or cargo, but huge woolen sheets might be stretched over the boat at night to keep its contents warm or dry. Navigation was limited to the summer, when darkness scarcely descended on the northern latitudes. The stars and the sun served as guides, but when these were not visible the direction of the wind or the color of the water gave clues. Armed with such scant aids the Norsemen groped their way to the British

Isles, Iceland, Greenland, and even to Cape Cod and Wineland the Good.

During the ninth and tenth centuries Scandinavia's reputation was foul and far-flung, and in French churches congregations cried, "From the fury of the Northmen, good Lord deliver us." The country was becoming overcrowded, tribal chieftains were wrangling with one another, and kings were asserting their power. The king of Norway, for instance, triumphed over his opponents and confiscated their lands, made the fur trade a royal monopoly, and took control of the traffic in walrus products. Landlords and tenants were dispossessed, especially of grazing areas and commons, while traders found their occupation injured. They therefore sought compensation and opportunity elsewhere.

For many decades the long ships descended on the coasts of the British Isles, the Low Countries, and France with sickening frequency. The towns and abbeys near the coast were sacked, the estuaries gave access to settlements farther inland, and Antwerp, Paris, and similar river cities were despoiled. Ireland and Scotland were easy plunder. Raiders went to the Bay of Biscay, to the Strait of Gibraltar, even to Marseilles and Pisa. While Dane and Norwegian scoured the western seas and coasts, the Swedes went eastward, to the White Sea in the arctic, to the Gulfs of Finland and Riga, up the rivers that led into Russia and then down the rivers that led to the Caspian or the Black Sea. Pisa was attacked from the west in 860 and Constantinople from the north in the same year. The Norsemen seemed ubiquitous.

The economic effects of these raids gradually changed in character. At first they were little more than a destruction or a redistribution of wealth. A sacked city was economic loss; booty, or a tax like the Danegeld levied by the English kings in order to bribe the vikings, was redistribution. But the Norseman was more than a mere brigand, and his raids gradually led to settlement. Iceland he colonized (874) and made a fishing center and sheep ranch. The Orkneys, Shetlands, and Hebrides became fishermen's farms. The east coast of Ireland attracted settlers, and Dublin, Limerick, and other towns became important Scandinavian outposts. If Alfred the Great had been less able, vikings might have taken possession of all England instead of only the northeastern half. By settling on the north coast of France the Norseman could quench his thirst with wine the whole year round. The English

Channel was a good fishing ground, and the French coast provided abundant salt. Wine, fish, and salt alone made it worth while to take Normandy, and Normandy in turn sent out conquerors to England and Sicily.

When the lust for raiding subsided the Norsemen turned to trade. With a foot in so many countries they exchanged the staple commodities of the North Sea and Atlantic region from Ireland and Iceland to Norway and Normandy. The North Sea nearly became a Scandinavian lake, and the Baltic became one entirely. There the Swedes and Danes penetrated the land of the Slavs to get furs, wax, hides, and slaves, and to traverse the ancient routes to the Black Sea and the Caspian. In the ninth century they took the area south of the White Sea, from which valuable gray furs came. At the same time they built fortified trading posts on the rivers that led to other parts of the country. Of these the chief was at Novgorod. From that point they crossed to the upper waters of the Volga and went downstream to the Caspian to meet traders who came over the Asiatic trade routes. The discovery of tens of thousands of Arabic coins and seals in Gothland shows that there must have been much commercial contact between the Baltic and western Asia.

In addition they traded with Constantinople. The way to the center of the Eastern Empire lay up the Dwina or through Novgorod, then to the upper waters of the Dnieper. On that stream stood Kiev, the center to which the Slavs brought their produce from marsh, plain, and forest in canoes made from tree trunks. Each June the canoe flotilla started downstream; when it reached the Black Sea at Kherson, the goods were sold to Greek merchants or carried to Constantinople, and there the furs of ermine, sable, or black fox, the honey, wax, amber, and slaves were exchanged for silks, spices, wine, fruit and metalware. The Norsemen had long been interested in this trade through the heart of Russia, but in the ninth century they swarmed into Kiev as merchants and mercenaries, quickly dominated and developed the river traffic, and controlled the political life of the Dnieper basin. When the Saracens disturbed the sea routes of the western Mediterranean this Varangian route was a convenient back lane between east and west.

Thus the Norsemen's trade spread like a fan, with one tip in Iceland, the other in the Caspian, and the handle in Wisby. Scandinavians were the middlemen of northern Europe until, in the twelfth and thirteenth centuries, they were elbowed out by the Germans of the Hanseatic towns. By that time their trade with the Black Sea had been injured by Tartar invasions of south Russia from the east and by the competition of Italians from Genoa or Venice.

The Eastern Empire.—The Eastern Empire shed liabilities without losing many assets by parting company with the poorer west, and Constantinople was a better imperial commercial metropolis than Rome. The new city stood at a vital spot on busy trade routes and was nearer the centers of wealth production in the eastern Mediterranean. For a time the Empire held its rich territories intact; Justinian took back Italy and the coasts of Spain and North Africa, and while much of his work was undone by Saracens and Lombards valuable parts of the Italian coast were retained. Slav and Scandinavian produce came to Constantinople from the north, and metals from central Europe; wine, cloths, and metalwares came from the industrial cities of Asia Minor or the Levant, grain flowed from Egypt, and oriental goods were brought over one of the long trade routes. When the Persian Empire rose astride the Syria-Euphrates route, Constantinople tried to open a new road to China round the top end of Persia. This route was slow, costly, and insecure, but had its uses. Along it some silkworm eggs were smuggled from China by two monks in 552, and silk production in the Levant soon became important.

As the political and economic hub of the Empire, Constantinople grew to great size. The church, court, bureaucracy, army, and navy provided a large market, while tribute flowed in as it had done into Rome. Like every great emporium, the capital developed a variety of manufacturing and processing industries. Craftsmen and traders were organized in guilds and subjected to elaborate regulation and taxation by the state; but the compulsory hereditary membership of Roman days had gone, and when Justinian abolished the free distribution of foodstuffs the more burdensome *munera* vanished. A fairly efficient bureaucracy carried on the government even in the days of incompetent emperors or in the face of hard blows on the frontiers. It maintained a navy to fight pirates, a police system to keep the peace in the towns and on the roads, a corps of inspectors to watch both native and foreigner, a code of law which fitted commercial needs, and a stable currency.

The merchants of the Empire did not forget the west. "Syrians"—who might be Jews, Greeks, Armenians, Persians, Alexandrians, or any other kind of easterner—traveled round the towns as far as Bordeaux or Paris, displayed their wares in fair, court, or abbey, supplied metalware and fabrics to cathedrals, and sold cottons, spices, perfumes, precious stones, and crucifixes. In exchange they took metals, furs, slaves, and other commodities from this commercial colonial frontier. As traders, financiers, musicians, and travelers the Syrians were known in every city; they had their special quarters, and their costumes, usages, and legends influenced their hosts. Eventually men of Amalfi, Venice, and Genoa took over the business of linking east and west; but for three or more centuries the Syrian was the middleman, bringing not merely goods, but also those instruments of commerce —the bill of exchange, the letter of credit, and various forms of partnership, insurance, and contract—which were to be useful in the life of medieval Italy.

Islam.—Mohammed began to preach just at a time when a long drought was making existence in the western Asiatic dry lands difficult. The movement begun by this merchant monotheist welded the Arab tribes into unity and sent them out on a career of conquest. They overthrew the Persian Empire by 642, chipped big pieces off the southeast end of the Byzantine Empire, pushed eastward to the frontiers of China and the mouth of the Indus, and swept westward to North Africa and Spain. They turned sailor and took Cyprus and Rhodes about 650, Corsica and Sardinia in 810, and Sicily (827-887). They ravaged and held part of the south coast of France, and set foot in northern and southern Italy.

The Saracens, like the Norsemen, turned easily from raiding to trading, and while there was frequent fighting and piracy on the fringe of their empire they soon settled down to exploit and enjoy the rich resources which had fallen into their hands. Ties of rule, religion, and language facilitated long-distance trade, and a large measure of tolerance allowed such conquered peoples as Egyptians, Syrians, and Jews to carry on their skilled production and far-ranging traffic. A people sprung from desert stock took intense delight in seeing what could be done with

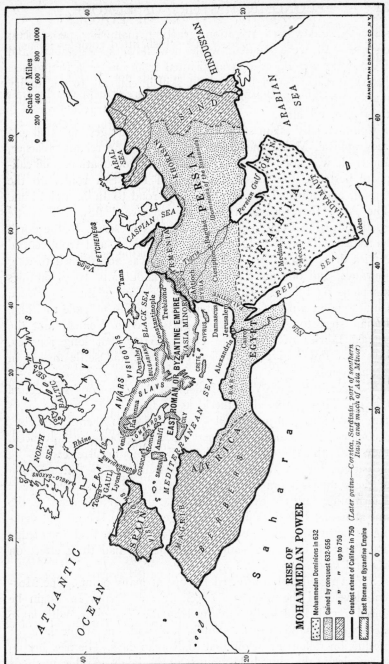

THE MOSLEM WORLD

RISE OF
MOHAMMEDAN POWER

Mohammedan Dominions in 632
Gained by conquest 632-656
"   "   "   up to 750
Greatest extent of Califate in 750 (*Later gains—Corsica, Sardinia, part of southern Italy, and much of Asia Minor*)
East Roman or Byzantine Empire

Scale of Miles
0 200 400 600 800 1000

MANHATTAN DRAFTING CO. N.Y.

soil, sun, and water. Irrigation, grafting, manuring, pests, plant diseases—all were studied, while new flowers, vegetables, and fruits were introduced or transplanted from one area to another. Industry reached a high degree of skill in catering to the luxury market provided by the court, the ruling and fighting classes, and the rich merchants.

Commercially Islam started with two advantages, spiritual and geographical. Mohammedanism began with a merchant preacher, and trade was not regarded as an unworthy occupation. The caliphate bestrode the Mesopotamian and Red Sea routes to the Orient, and touched the northern land road to India and China. The Arab therefore controlled the westward flow of Asiatic goods until the Portuguese broke into his preserve. In the north he traded with Constantinople and Scandinavia, and from central Africa drew gold, ivory and slaves. He was accustomed to long journeys, and one merchant, speaking about A.D. 1000, outlines his plans as follows: He will carry Persian sulphur to China, Chinese porcelain to Greece, Greek or Venetian brocade to India, Indian steel to Aleppo, Aleppo glassware to Yemen, and the striped fabrics of Yemen to Persia. After that long journey, says he, "I will give up foreign commerce and settle myself in a warehouse."

To economic energy the Moslems added vigorous intellectual activity. They gathered in the ideas of their Greek, Syrian, Persian and other subject peoples, and added to them. Medicine, chemistry, mathematics, astronomy, and geography advanced. How far this knowledge influenced economic life cannot be measured; but the experiments in agriculture, the introduction of the compass from China, the invention of the astrolabe (for determining latitude by measuring the angle of elevation of the sun at noon), the technical knowledge that lay behind the making of paper, fine glass, or good steel, and the medical knowledge that revealed cures for some complaints all had their effect on life and labor.

Saracen civilization affected Europe at many points. The Moslem developed the resources of Sicily and Spain. In Spain he found a rich land badly governed by the Visigoths, with large areas in the hands of the church, and with the whole level of production fallen far below that of Roman days. The new broom swept clean; the church lost much of its lands, Arabic methods of cultivation were introduced, irrigation was developed, and the watered areas were cut up into small holdings. To grapes and grain were added products brought in from the east—rice, sugar-canes, mulberry trees for the silkworm, palm trees, oranges, pomegranates, apricots, peaches, lemons, strawberries, roses, asparagus, and spinach. Industries were introduced: paper, carpets, shawls, and fine leather were made at Cordova, fine sword blades and armor at Toledo. Mineral deposits were tapped and silver mines were reopened. The central plateau became a great stock ranch. Intellectual life drew inspiration from the eastern Moslem centers, and a mixed population of natives, Visigoths, Jews, and Moors lived together under a tolerant and fairly efficient ruler. Cordova in the tenth century was the most civilized city in Europe, and probably the cleanest, with seventy libraries and nine hundred public baths.

The relations between the Moslem world and Christian western Europe are not clear. According to some historians, the Saracens broke the threads of trade between the two halves of the Mediterranean. They held Sardinia, Corsica, and Sicily, and occupied the coast of southern France. This strangle hold would permit them to stop, or at least render very hazardous, trade between west and east, and when Moslem rulers were well disposed toward Christian ships private pirates might inflict great damage. The Christian rulers and the Pope made no secret of their dislike of the infidel. The only thing to do with him was to evict him as soon as possible, and meanwhile the church forbade its people to trade with him. Pirenne and others therefore conclude that from about A.D. 800 the western Mediterranean was closed, that eastern wares disappeared from the west, that grass grew in the streets of many ports, and that western Europe was reduced to a self-sufficing economy, with no foreign and little domestic trade.

This picture is drawn in such strong lines that one may doubt its accuracy. It does not fit any estimate of the intelligence and tolerance of the Moslem. Pirates could not prey on commerce if there was none. Genoa, Pisa, Amalfi and other ports on the west Italian coast may have been hit hard when raided, but they recovered again, and there must have been some trade to make that recovery possible. Amalfi and Salerno came to terms with the Moslems and traded with North Africa, Egypt, and Syria. Pilgrims went from western Europe to the Holy Land. There was contact between Spain and her northern neighbors, Moslems took French wives, bishops of Liège in the tenth century were enthusiastic students of Moorish astronomical works, and young Christian scholars were sent to Spain to study mathematics. Further, if the seaways west of Sicily were blocked, eastern goods could come west along the Russian route, up the Danube, or up the Adriatic, since the Saracens did not control the Ionian and Adriatic Seas. It is hard to believe that the appearance of the Moslems in the western Mediterranean brought economic paralysis to the west.

Gradually the Moslem power was whittled away by internal weakness and external attacks. Italian cities fought the pirates or grew strong enough to negotiate trade treaties with their rulers. The Normans captured Sicily and south Italy (1016-1079). In Spain the Moorish frontier was gradually pushed southward by Castile and Aragon, and by 1250 it included only the southern belt, Granada. Long before that day came, the west had gone east crusading and trading. If Mohammed had once come to the western mountains, those mountains now tried to descend on him, with results which will be analyzed later.

The Italian Trading Cities.—The decline of imperial power in the west and the events of the next four or five centuries brought decay or ruin to many Italian towns. But even in the darkest times of migration or invasion, industrial, commercial or financial enterprise never quite ceased, and we can glimpse the gradual rise of those cities which were to loom so large in the economic life of the later Middle Ages. Some of them grew as centers of consumption, when some bishop or duke made his home there and goods flowed in from the neighboring country to feed the inhabitants of palace or fort. Some were market centers for an agricultural or pastoral area, and some rose to importance because they commanded the approach to Alpine passes or formed the terminus of some road from the interior of Italy and the European land mass. Most of the leading ports still belonged to the Eastern Empire and had access to its markets, while on some occasions Constantinople would seek the naval aid of an Italian city against Saracen or Norman, offering in return freedom from port and customs duties in imperial harbors.

For a long time Amalfi, on the ankle of Italy, was the leading Italian port. It was almost an outpost of Constantinople, but it made terms with the Saracens and thus had access to their ports as well. The products of its mint and the clauses of its maritime code were acceptable everywhere. Other southern ports, such as Bari, Naples, Salerno, and Tarento, crept back into the records. But rivals were growing up farther north, at Genoa, Pisa, Lucca, and Venice; and as the markets beyond the Alps expanded and the people of western Europe became more interested in Mediterranean products these ports overshadowed their southern forerunners.

Pisa and Genoa belonged to classical times. They suffered severely during the seventh century, and later were buffeted by Norsemen or Moslems, but they always came back. In the first half of the eleventh century they were strong enough to drive the Moslems out of Sardinia, Corsica, and the Balearic Islands, just when the Normans were overthrowing them in Sicily. They thus obtained a free run of the western Mediterranean, but did not go much into eastern waters until the crusades made the Levant the great terminus of all westerners.

Venice had no classical history. She was a medieval product, born of the migrations, taught by the Byzantine Empire, nourished by the trade between east and west, bloated by the crusades and deflated by the economic and political events of the sixteenth century. When Attila and his Huns swooped down on Italy (about 452), fugitives from several towns around the top of the Adriatic are said to have taken refuge on the mud flats and sand banks off the mouths of the Adige and Brenta. A dozen island villages gradually grew up. Their inhabitants caught fish and collected the salt left behind when the sea water in the lagoons evaporated during the hot dry summer. They found markets for these wares, refugees from later invasions swelled their numbers, and their island home was made virtually impregnable. By the early eighth century their traders were working up the valleys of north Italy, and going through the Alpine passes into France and central Europe.

Even before that century they had built ships, sailed down the sides of the Adriatic, and established trade relations with Constantinople and the Levant. With the Saracens they reached some working arrangement, and Egypt became a good customer for the iron, lumber, and slaves that Venice gathered in from the Balkans and the Slav country to the north. Some records of

Venetian galleys which carried these commodities to Egypt and returned laden with an Oriental cargo show profits which look like 1000 to 1200 per cent. To Constantinople Venice turned quite as eagerly. By A.D. 1000 she rivaled Amalfi there, and a great opportunity came when the emperor sought her aid against the Normans and repaid her with the Golden Bull of 1082. This document gave her for a hundred years the right to trade, free of duties or taxes, in any part of the empire. Venetians were thus probably on a better footing than were the native merchants of the empire. Even before the crusades poured wealth and power into her lap, Venice was a great city, gathering in the raw materials and slaves of Europe's northwest frontier, supplying in return Oriental wares, and in addition selling fish, salt, glass and various manufactured articles of her own production.

The Church.—As the Roman Empire declined in the west, the spiritual and material power of the church grew. The erection of buildings, the maintenance of a priestly class, and the discharge of such duties as education and charity called for large transfers of property and income from the hands of royalty, nobility, and commonalty. The Visigoths made the church the biggest landowner in Spain, and the Merovingian kings were so lavish that by A.D. 700 probably one-third of France was in church hands. As monastic orders were founded still more grants were made; and since church and abbey never voluntarily let any property leave their hands, the breadth of their acres and the weight of their purses increased steadily. The Pope at one time held nearly two thousand square miles of Italian wheat, forest, olive, or iron lands; some French bishops in the ninth century held over 100,000 acres, while in Saxony a nunnery held 11,000 farms and a monastery had 15,000.

Over these vast areas pope, bishop, or abbot ruled as feudal lord and from them drew a large income, either by cultivating the land or by letting it to free or unfree tenants. That income was chiefly in produce until money became more plentiful, and while some of it was consumed on the spot, surpluses were sent to market. Wool, lumber, minerals, salt, wine, grain, and oil from religious estates entered the stream of commerce. Feudal rights also included lordship over local market or fair, a monopoly of milling, possibly power to operate a mint, control of justice, and other revenue-producing privileges. The church also received income from its spiritual services, and a great variety of payments had to be made by the laity, or by the lower clergy to the higher. The tithe, a tax levied to maintain the church, took one-tenth of a person's produce. Then there were fees of all kinds, for marriage, for saying masses, and for trials in the ecclesiastical courts. Finally, the Pope collected taxes and levies from his subordinates. A bishop appointed to a diocese had to pay his whole first year's income to Rome, kings and princes might have payments to make, and the number of claims increased as the papacy grew stronger, after about A.D. 1000.

By that date the church was well on its way to being "a governor, a landed proprietor, a rent collector, an imposer of taxes, a material producer, an employer of labor on an enormous scale, a merchantman, a tradesman, a banker and mortgage broker, a custodian of morals, a maker of sumptuary laws, a schoolmaster, a compeller of conscience—all in one" (Thompson).

BIBLIOGRAPHY

GENERAL

Cambridge Medieval History (7 volumes) is a valuable reference work.

KULISCHER, J., *Allgemeine Wirtschaftsgeschichte des Mittelalters und der Neuzeit* (1928-1929), vol. i, chaps. 1-7.

MUNRO, D. C., *The Middle Ages, 395-1272* (1921). Chaps. 1-20 give the general history of the period.

NUSSBAUM, F. L., *A History of the Economic Institutions of Modern Europe: an introduction to "Der Moderne Kapitalismus" of Werner Sombart* (1933), chap. 1.

STEPHENSON, CARL, *Medieval History* (1935), chaps. 1, 2, 3, 6, 8, 9, 11.

THOMPSON, J. W., *Economic and Social History of the Middle Ages, 300-1300* (1928), chaps. 1-15. Very useful bibliographies and maps.

WEBER, MAX, *General Economic History* (trans. by F. H. Knight), chaps. 1-3, 14.

SPECIAL SUBJECTS

ARNOLD, T., and GUILLAME, A. (eds.), *The Legacy of Islam* (1931), chaps. 1, 2, 3.

ASHLEY, W. J., *Surveys, Historical and Economic* (1900), Part II.

BLOCH, M., *Les caractères originaux de l'histoire rurale française* (1931), chap. 1.

BOISSONNADE, P., *Life and Work in Medieval Europe* (Eng. trans., 1927).

CALMETTE, J., *Le régime féodal* (1924).

HEYD, W., *Histoire du Commerce du Levant* (French trans., 1895).

HUBERT, H., *The Rise of the Celts* (1933).

HUBERT, H., *The Greatness and Decline of the Celts* (1934).

KENDRICK, T. D., *History of the Vikings* (1930). Good maps.

KOVALEVSKY, M., *Die ökonomische Entwicklung Europas* (1901-1914).

LAPSLEY, G., "The Origin of Property in Land," in *Am. Hist. Rev.*, vol. viii, (1903).

LIPSON, E., *Introduction to the Economic History of England* (1915), vol. i, chap. 1.

PIRENNE, H., *Medieval Cities* (Eng. trans., 1925).

SEEBOHM, F., *The English Village Community* (1884).

VINOGRADOFF, P., *The Growth of the Manor* (1911), chaps. 1 and 2.

VINOGRADOFF, P., "Foundations of Society" (*Cambridge Med. Hist.*, vol. ii, chap. 20, pp. 631-655) ; and "Feudalism" (*Cambridge Med. Hist.*, vol. iii, chap. 18, pp. 458-484).

Encyclopædia of the Social Sciences: articles on Charlemagne, Commerce, Commercial Routes, Feudalism, Land Tenure, Manorial System, Migrations (Ancient and Medieval), Village Community.

Read a few stories in *The Arabian Nights*, noting the references to economic conditions, commodities, travel, and economic ideas. Cæsar's *Commentaries* and Tacitus' *Germania* might be read cautiously for the pictures they paint of the barbarians.

CHAPTER VI

THE MEDIEVAL COUNTRYSIDE

AN OCCUPATION census of Europe in the eleventh century would probably have shown that 90 per cent of the people were country-dwellers, drawing their livelihood from farming, fishing, or the forest. Here and there were towns, but few of them could boast of 10,000 inhabitants. Russia or India today is probably more urbanized than was any European country in 1000. An air photograph taken at that time would reveal a sprinkling of villages, linked by rivers or straggling trails and separated by expanses of unoccupied land, forest, moor, or swamp. A second picture, taken three centuries later, would show that the villages had grown larger and more numerous, and that medieval Europe had been pushing its frontier back, clearing, draining, and settling new areas. It would also show more people on the roads, rivers, and sea, carrying food and raw materials to the towns which had grown in number and importance during the preceding three centuries.

Any attempt to describe the European countryside during those centuries is made difficult by the refusal of its inhabitants to fit into a simple standard pattern or to stand still. Variety and change give point to two remarks made by the late Professor Levett, a student of medieval rural England: "In the history of land problems there is no sin like the sin of generalization," and "There is no heresy about the Middle Ages quite so pernicious as the theory that they were unchanging." No description fits all the people all the time or even some of the time; it can at best depict some of them some of the time. This is especially true of any account of the "typical manor," that community in which unfree villagers (villeins) cultivated the lord's domain as the price of their serfdom and of their use of a holding. A recent investigation of part of the English midlands shows that in 1279 only 60 per cent of the territory examined consisted of domains with villein holdings attached. The remainder was non-manorial; it had no unfree tenants, it had no domain, or it consisted of estates which were all (or nearly all) domain. In northern and western England, and also in Wales, the manor was not predominant, partly because the land was much more fit for pasturage than for tillage. Similarly, in France and other countries of the west, history or geography excluded large areas from the manorial economy. The manor was an important type of estate management, but it was not the only type, and the non-manorial regions cannot be dismissed as exceptional.

Further, while most Europeans probably lived in villages, there were regions where the land was so broken, hilly, or limited in supply of good soil that a village could not be sustained, and the farmer, forester, or herdsman lived alone or in a tiny hamlet. Some areas had better access to markets than had others, and their owners and cultivators were stimulated to turn from subsistence farming to an "exchange economy," producing goods for sale. Finally, conditions varied with the size of the estate and the nature of the owner. A great landlord, whether lay or ecclesiastic, might employ competent managers and plan production more rationally than a smaller owner; the large monasteries especially were progressive farmers and responded readily to the rise of markets for land produce. The great landlords were also more accustomed than the smaller men to keeping records; at different times they caused detailed surveys, "extents," or inventories to be made of their property, their stewards kept accounts, and on the rolls of the manor courts civil and criminal proceedings were reported. Many of these documents have survived, and from them we draw most of our knowledge of medieval rural society. It is largely knowledge that illustrates the life of the villager who lived under manorial conditions; of the others we do not know very much. It is also knowledge that comes from the twelfth or later centuries. By that time the development of towns, trade, and money is breaking down the "natural economy" of the self-sufficing countryside or has broken it down completely.

The Problem of Sustenance.—The business of the villager was to sustain himself and discharge his obligations. He cultivated land that he did not own, and his time or produce, or both, was divided into two parts: (1) that which was used to meet his own needs, (2) that which went to meet the claims of landlord, church, and possibly the state. In the joint satisfaction of these needs and claims we have the essence of most medieval country life. Until towns and trade developed, everybody had to live on the land. There was little taxation that a ruler could spend to stock his larder, little work for wages to buy bread, cheese, and ale, and little money that could be put into the collection box to keep the priest. The peasant household must make the goods it needed with the labor of the family; the *château* must make them with the labor of serfs or slaves. The peasant must feed himself by working his own land; the lord's household must be fed with the produce wrung from the domain by the labors of the peasants and with that paid as rent or as some other kind of due.

Household production, reservation of a domain, and the collection of payments and services from those who used the remainder of an estate ran through the various layers of feudal society. The kings kept certain estates, and on each of them might reserve a part for their own enjoyment or sustenance. Charlemagne is said to have kept over sixteen hundred, scattered over France, the Rhineland, Belgium, and Italy. Some of them might contain fifty farming villages, some were covered with forests famed for their hunting, some were rich in stone or metals, some had towns on them. When William the Conqueror shared out England, he kept about one-fifth of the country. In most villages was a royal farm worked by the villagers; and the produce, plus that collected in rents or other dues, was consumed by the local royal officials, by fighting forces, or by the king and his entourage when they visited the area. Neither Charles nor William had a fixed capital, but each traveled round from one important estate to another, eating what had been produced there and such foodstuffs as could be transported from neighboring estates.

From Charlemagne's famous instructions to his estate stewards we see how these men were expected to keep the villas well equipped, productive, ornamented, furnished, and staffed with farm workers and craftsmen. Two-thirds of some food products were to be sent to the places where the king sojourned on his tour, and the steward was to see that he had in his district good "blacksmiths, goldsmiths, silversmiths, shoemakers, turners, carpenters, sword-makers, fishermen, foilers, soapmakers, men who know how to make beer, cider, berry, and all other kinds of beverages, bakers to make pastry for our table, net-makers who know how to make nets for hunting, fishing, and fowling, and the others who are too numerous to be designated."

As with the king, so with the subordinate landholders. The church estates, whether held by bishop or abbot, were often handled in the same way. In the early days the Benedictine monks did much labor on their own land, but later they became too tired, rich, or feudal. Endowments sometimes came in the form of whole villages; in days of civil war or invasion peasants flocked to an abbey, and craftsmen gathered round or even in' the abbey. Hence the monks were able to live on the labor or produce of others. The Cistercian order, founded in 1092, preached the gospel of manual work with fine fervor. Its rule forbade it to receive gifts of villages, serfs, or mills, lest these tempt it to live on the labor of others. Its members must do their own work, whether it be farming, herding, manufacturing, building, or domestic service. But gradually these tasks were delegated to lay brothers, who did the work, supervised that of hired laborers, or served as stewards managing estates tilled by serfs or free tenants. One monastic manor in Essex had two-fifths of its land in the domain and the rest in the hands of tenants. Since monasteries could not go round eating up the produce of their estates, the outlying villages had to send it to the abbey to feed the monks and their guests.

This sustenance economy became diluted when markets became available, for then the cultivator might sell part of his produce, the landlord might sell part of the yield from the domain and from the rents paid in produce, and money offered a means by which labor or produce could be bought.

Village Classes.—When William the Conqueror's commissioners surveyed England in the Doomsday inquiry of 1085-1086, they squeezed all the cultivators into four categories—*freemen,* who comprised 12 per cent of the population, *villeins* (38 per cent), *cottars* and *bordars* (32 per cent), and *slaves* (9 per cent). Each of these labels covered a great diversity of grades and shades of tenure and status, but the classification is helpful. The number of slaves employed in domestic service, in working on the lord's farm, or in cultivating small holdings declined steadily in the west after about A.D. 1000. Slavery was gone from England by 1200, but survived in Mediterranean lands much longer. Emancipation helped to eliminate it in France and England, and when wars of conquest by the Norsemen and Germans ended, the supply of captives was reduced. Hence most villagers belonged to one of the other three Doomsday classes.

Economically the freemen and villeins were farmers who held enough land to keep them occupied and to provide a family income. The cottar was an industrial worker or agricultural laborer whose holding was so small that it did not occupy all his time or yield sufficient to keep him alive, and who therefore depended much on what he earned by working for others. The bordar was in the same economic condition. The English rural population was thus divided into two great classes that can be called farmers and laborers. The size of the laboring class—32 per cent—was not much less than that of the villeins and freemen combined—50 per cent. For other parts of Europe no comparable figures exist, but we know that there were large classes of men who lived by the sale of their labor rather than by the produce of their own holdings.

The village classes differed from each other in the size of their holdings and the terms of their tenure, but the freeman differed from the others in his *personal status* as well. The freeman must bear arms, the villein did not; a freeman had access to the king's courts, a villein could go only to his lord's court; a freeman could give his daughter in marriage, let his son enter the priesthood, or sell an ox or horse, but a villein could do none of these things without getting his lord's permission and paying a fee. More important economically, the freeman might hold his land on payment only of an annual quitrent in money or produce, or both. In some places the payment was purely nominal—a pound of pepper or even a rose each year as a token of obligation, but usually it was more substantial than that. If payment was made partly in labor the freeman did not have to spend three, four, or five days a week on the domain as the villein did. He worked for the lord only at special busy times, such as harvest. He was not tied to the land, but could terminate his tenure if he wished, or bequeath his farm to his son. The villein was bound to the soil, as were his children after him; yet at his death the landlord had the right to take possession of his holding, and if the villein's family was allowed to keep possession the landlord claimed the best beast as *heriot* and imposed a money fine as *relief* when the son stepped into his father's shoes.

These distinctions were found wherever feudalism developed. France had its *vilain libre* or *vilain franc* who resembled the English freeman, while its *vilain serf* was the counterpart of the English villein. The border line between the classes was sometimes ill-marked, but the chief economic difference was that the lord had a double claim on the labor, produce, or income of the serf—one on him as a person of servile status and one on him as a tenant. On the freeman he had only one claim, that on a tenant.

When lawyers began, probably in the twelfth century, to puzzle about the legal basis of serfdom they decided that the serf had only those rights which the landlord granted him. The "will of the lord" (*voluntas domini*) ruled, and could impose heavier burdens or take away what had been given or been taken for granted. The freeman could appeal to the royal courts if the landlord tried to get more out of him, but the unfree had no protection except an appeal to "the custom of the manor" (*consuetudo manerii*). Any arrangement, privilege, or obligation that had been accepted "since time whereof memory runs not to the contrary" had thereby gained in tenant eyes the right to continue unchanged. Its basis was not a document, but human memory and the testimony of the graybeards that the custom was at least as old as they were. Any attempt of landlord or bailiff to curtail it or to impose new obligations might be met by protest or even by revolt.

That *consuetudo* and *voluntas* might clash is obvious. That they must do so is not so obvious. What mattered to the landlord was the yield he obtained from his estate; and while he might try to squeeze every possible bit of labor and payment from his tenants, a discontented peasantry might be unproductive or might run away to the towns or frontier. We twist or color our picture if we assume that every landlord was a selfish monster and every peasant a sweet-souled innocent. The older view has been to regard manorial custom as a strong defense; but a recent Russian scholar (Professor Kosminsky) finds evidence in the thirteenth century of a complex class war, in which the lord exploited to the full the wide undefined limits of his *voluntas*, and in which the peasants found *consuetudo* an insufficient safeguard against increased claims on them.

The Tenant's Dues.—The tenant paid his dues in one or more of three ways—labor, produce, and money. If the estate had a domain and many villeins the labor dues (*corvée*) were important, and when we find them set forth in the manor records they are most elaborately and precisely detailed. The "normal" villein, holding a virgate of about twenty-five to thirty-five acres of arable land, must work three, four, or even five days a week on the lord's domain. Sometimes he had to bring another man with him for this *week-work*, and possibly oxen and equipment. If he had no family to do some of his work for him, his own land and stock might suffer, but if the virgate supported the father and some grown-up sons, along with their wives and children, the family labor supply would be large enough to meet the demand. Some tenants held only half a virgate, and they would have spare time available for sale, while the cottars and other very small tenants provided a labor reserve.

In the busy seasons of the farming calendar the amount of work demanded of the tenant increased. He had to work more days, bring more assistants, or perform a prescribed quantity of plowing, harvesting, shearing, or carrying. The need for this extra labor (*boon-work*) was as urgent as it is on a prairie farm, but since it had to be given just when the tenants were anxious to work on their own land, it was probably as vexatious to them as it was valuable to the lord. The landlord salved the sore by providing meat or drink, or both, and the custom of the manor decided when the boon-worker should get beer but no bread, when bread but no beer, when he should get black bread, when brown, when meat, broth, or cheese, and so forth.

A glance at the terms of two tenancies illustrates the elaborate details of these labor dues. The first tenant holds thirty-six acres on an estate owned by a Gloucestershire abbey. He works four days a week with one man from Michaelmas to Lammas (i.e., from September 29th round to August 1st, or ten months in all). During the other two months he and his mate must give five days each week. His boon-tasks are as follows: Plow half an acre in winter, and again in Lent, and harrow it at seedtime; carry loads by cart to Gloucester twice a year; wash and shear sheep for two days; cart hay for four days; carry brushwood one day; do ten days' reaping at the lord's bidding, with two men; carry the lord's corn twice a week for four weeks; carry corn to the lord's grange one day and carry millstones for the lord's mill.

The second tenant is a virgater on the estate of the Earl of Warwick. From the 24th of June to August 1st he must work for his landlord every other day, Saturdays and feast days excepted. He must mow while there is mowing to be done, and he can have as much grass as he can lift with his scythe. When the mowing is ended he and his fellows are to have the best sheep save one of the lord's fold, or sixteenpence, and the best cheese save one, or sixpence, "and they shall have the vessel full of salt in which the cheese was made." For the rest of the year two days a week will suffice, but the tenant and all his family except his wife must come when they are bidden and reap a fixed area. He must carry two and a half carts of hay and cart twenty-one loads of stone, he must gather nuts for three days, plow a certain amount of land, and carry goods as far as twenty leagues.

The total amount of labor due from the tenants might be quite large, but Kosminsky finds that in the thirteenth century it was insufficient, even where payment in labor was most highly developed. As it came from so many hands, and as it often had to be given on days when the peasant wished to get on with his own work, the bailiff who managed the estate would need to be an ingenious, keen-eyed, and sharp-tongued organizer and disciplinarian, while the reeve, who was chosen by the villagers as their foreman and spokesman, must have held an unenviable position. Sometimes *corvée* was unprofitable to the landlord, for the meals which had to be provided for the boon-worker might cost more than the work was worth. Battle Abbey in 1307 discovered that it was giving meals worth fivepence or sevenpence, yet getting work worth only fourpence from some villeins. The total boon-work done on one estate was worth 60^d, but the voracious villeins literally ate up two-thirds of this amount.

Payment in money was difficult until the development of trade and the growing circulation of currency in the eleventh to thirteenth centuries brought cash to the village. Payment in produce was easier. At quarter day or on some holy day the villagers delivered such money as they must pay and a stipulated amount of produce to the manor house. Eggs and poultry were part of most rents, especially at Christmas or Easter—hence the Easter egg. In Germany on *Pulltag* (cock-rent day), cocks were handed over to pay part of the rent. Christmas cake, a Yule log, a lamb, ram, pig, or ox, eels, wine, cloth, clothes, grain or malt, plow-shares, horsehoes, cheeses, and salt are mentioned in the rent rolls. One tenant gives a quarter of seed wheat at Michaelmas; a peck of wheat, four bushels of oats, and three hens at Martin-mas; a cock, two hens and 2^d of bread at Christmas. Another finds forage for three horses for three nights if his lord is at home for Christmas, in addition to 27^d, seven bushels of oats, and one fowl each year. The tenants of one manor pay £4/11/4 and "to the love feast of St. Peter" bring ten rams, 400 loaves, 40 platters, 34 hens, and 260 eggs, while the miller pays 60/- and 500 eels. Another group of tenants rendered £9/5/- and 3000 loaves for the dogs before 1066, but later paid £20, 20 cows, 20 hogs, and 16/- instead of the dog biscuits. A Swiss community of cattle farmers sent its landlord 300 cheeses.

These annual payments were more than mere rent. They had in them elements of feudal taxation, and were payments to a lord as well as a landlord. Thus the English villager might have to "give an aid according to the quantity of his land and beasts"; in one case "he, himself, and his fellows shall give aid 12 marks at Michaelmas." In France the lord levied the *taille* on the pro-duce of all grades of his subordinates, from the meanest serf to the freeman. From the latter he could demand only a fixed cus-tomary amount, but on the former he could levy as much and as often as he wished until, in the thirteenth century, his power was restrained. Often he collected the tithe, for he controlled the local church, and the village curé received a scanty portion of the tribute paid by the faithful.

Many occasional payments were also incidents of feudalism. *Merchet* was the fee paid by villeins on the marriage of their daughters, by widows when they remarried, and even by some villeins at marriage. It was the commonest badge of serfdom, but had economic justification where a person was marrying outside the manor and thus was reducing the local labor supply. If the villein's son was to be "tonsured" or "crowned," i.e., trained for entry into the clergy, the lord might well claim compensation for the loss of a worker. *Heriot,* the claim of the best beast, was a heavy death duty, while *relief,* which often amounted to one year's rent, was a heavy inheritance tax or entrance fee paid by the heirs. Fees on the sale of livestock, on the business of innkeepers and wine dealers, and on the beer brewed for sale by villeins were part of the landlord's market rights. Those on the transfer of land were the price paid for winning the owner's approval of a transaction which affected the use of his property. The lord's control of local justice had a real economic value; the various fines and fees paid in court went into his pocket and proved that *Justitia est magnum emolumentum*—justice is a great source of income.

One important source of income—the *banalités*—was partly a perquisite of feudal power and partly a price charged for the use of such medieval "public utilities" as flour mill, wine press, brewery, oven, dye vat, sawmill or fulling mill. The landlord tried to claim the sole right to provide these utilities, to force the villagers to use them, and to collect a service charge. This claim was sometimes stubbornly fought, and in parts of France and Germany successfully resisted; but in England the lords prevailed, while some monasteries built large mills—one had six pairs of stones—and pressed hard their attack on the villagers' querns and hand mills. The mill was one of the earliest instances of a substantial fixed-capital investment. In Germany the Teutonic Knights became great mill-builders; they approached landlords who owned water rights, provided one-third of the cost of erecting a mill and of damming up the stream, and in return claimed one-third of the profits. Often the lord leased his monopoly to some man, who thus became the official miller, dyer, baker, or fuller for the village. Some places did not free themselves from restraint until they bought out the landlord's claim in the nineteenth century.

The Tenant's Holding.—In return for these many payments the villager who was not a cottager received a house, appropriate farm buildings, a holding in the arable fields, a share of the meadow, the right to graze livestock on the common pastures, and permission to get peat, wood, and food for his hogs from the woodland or waste. The amount of cultivated land varied according to the quality, and might range from less than 25 to more than 36 acres. The cottars had much smaller plots, up to five acres and down to less than a quarter acre. The villager might increase or decrease his holding by renting more land or parting with some. Some men prospered and took up more land, while others failed and had to let some of theirs go. By the thirteenth

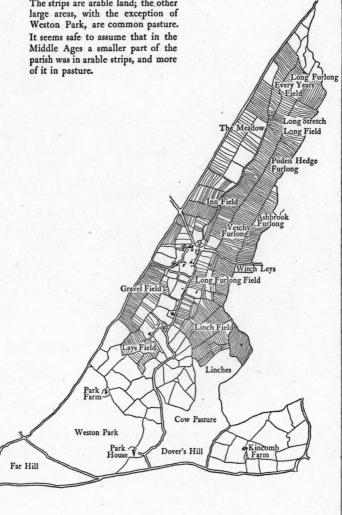

Map of the
PARISH OF WESTON SUBEDGE
(Gloucestershire) in 1840

The strips are arable land; the other
large areas, with the exception of
Weston Park, are common pasture.

It seems safe to assume that in the
Middle Ages a smaller part of the
parish was in arable strips, and more
of it in pasture.

Long Furlong
Every Years
Field

Long Stretch
Long Field

The Meadow

Poden Hedge
Furlong

Inn Field

Ashbrook
Furlong

Vetchy
Furlong

Witch Leys

Long Furlong Field

Gravel Field

Linch Field

Lays Field

Linches

Park
Farm

Cow Pasture

Weston Park

Kincomb
Farm

Park
House

Dover's Hill

Far Hill

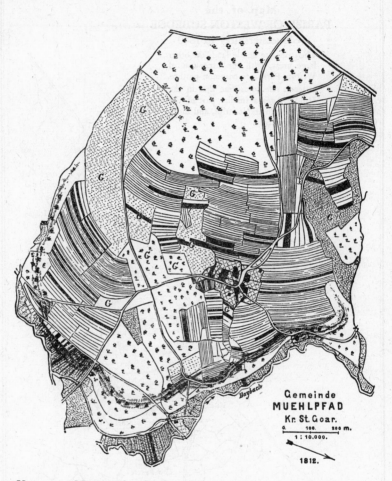

Gemeinde
MUEHLPFAD
Kr. St. Goar.

0   100.   200 m.

1 : 10.000.

1812.

VILLAGE OF MUEHLPFAD (ST. GOAR DISTRICT, MIDDLE RHINELAND) IN 1812
G = Gemeindeland (commons). The shaded strips represent one man's holdings. One man held 21 Morgen (acres) in 105 parcels.

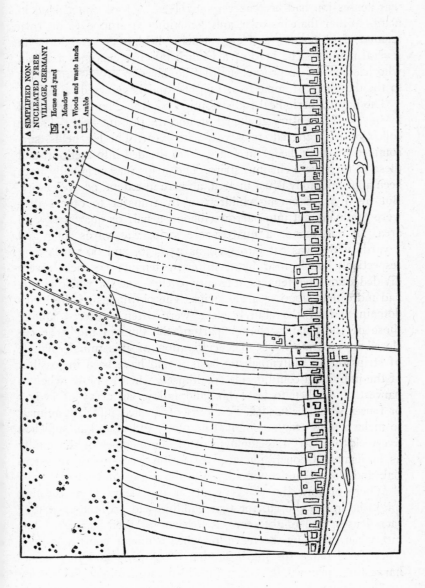

A SIMPLIFIED NON-NUCLEATED FREE VILLAGE, GERMANY

House and yard

Meadow

Woods and waste lands

Arable

century transfers of land in England had become so common that possession had become very involved. A lord rented land in manors other than his own, and sometimes from one of his own tenants; free tenants and even villeins held of several lords in several manors. The hero of a French tale is sometimes a villein who has become so prosperous that he dares to propose marriage to the daughter of some poor knight—and is accepted.

The day of periodical redistribution of arable lands had ended by the twelfth century at the latest, and the peasant held the same collection of scattered strips year after year. The big fields, surrounded by ditch, hedge or fence, were divided into sections, and these in turn were cut into strips. The strips may originally have been approximately equal in area, an acre in extent, or even more. But by division among children or by transfer to others they were gradually cut into narrow ribbons, a half or quarter acre in area. In one manor a quarter-acre strip, 240 yards long and 5 yards wide, was cut into sections 24, 156, and 60 yards long respectively, each held by a different tenant; six acres were divided among ten tenants in twenty patches, and the whole village had more than 2000 separate strips. The plowlands of the lord's domain and of the church glebe were often scattered among those of the tenants, though part of the domain might be enclosed in separate fields. The cultivation of this mingle-mangle of strips on an individualistic basis would have been impossible. If the individual could decide for himself when to plow, when to harvest, and when to leave his land fallow, an array of hedges or fences would be needed. Few peasants owned sufficient animals to make a plow team, some had no plow, and none had sufficient livestock to justify the employment of one member of the family as herdsman. Cooperation and regulation were therefore essential, and the village community was the organ of control.

Where or how the villagers met is not clear. Their meeting might be in the church, for that building had profane as well as sacred uses, and might serve as a barn for their harvest. They met when called by the reeve, or when a manor court was held. They fixed dates for the beginning of plowing and the end of harvesting, planned the order in which the different fields were to be cultivated, and controlled the cartage of grain, gleaning, and the picking of peas and beans. They decided when the grain fields and meadows should be thrown open—or become *vaine pâture*, as the French called it—so that livestock could come in to graze on the stubble or second growth of grass. They punished those who let cattle wander into the crops, summoned the village to haymaking, and gave the signal—by blowing a horn—to start or stop the picking of peas, thus preventing anyone from picking as he wished, presumably off the plants of other tenants. They defined and punished trespass; appointed shepherds, cowherds, vine-guards, and swineherds; controlled the use of the pastures; and took some care of drains, roads, and bridges. In this local control the village seems to have acted autonomously, though occasionally a veto came down from the big house. The manor court would lend its authority to enforce the rules, while at the same time retaining the power to issue its own decrees on matters touching the relation between lord and tenant.

One regulation—that of rotation of crops—was taken for granted even if there was no explicit rule. The three-field rotation was the high-water mark of medieval agriculture. Under it each field gave a crop of wheat or rye—the food crop; then a crop of oats, barley, peas, etc.,—the porridge, drink, and fodder crops; then it lay fallow for a year, and was plowed and harrowed two or three times to keep down the weeds and prepare it for the next two crops. The use of manure was limited by the available supply, but since the cattle spent the summer on the pastures, and in the fall were killed in large numbers for lack of winter food, the supply of manure was small and scattered. Here was a vicious circle: scarcity of manure meant small fodder crops, which prevented the building up of larger herds, which limited the supply of manure. The three-field system was the best plan that could be devised, and it is apparent that even this best was not universally attained. Professor Levett has called the three-field rotation described by some medieval writers a "vain imagination," "what they hope rather than what they expect to see." She points out that grain was sown on the same field seven or eight times in succession in some places, and that the land was then allowed to go back to pasture or waste for a few years; this practice has been called "convertible husbandry." In parts of France a two-field system prevailed in some areas, while in others land was tilled for three, four, or even eight years and then reverted to pasture.

Of the crops grown, rye was an important breadstuff. On the

continental plain from Belgium eastward it was, and still is, the chief bread grain; it will grow farther north than wheat and does better on poor soil. It was also widely used in England, and only in the eighteenth century did better farming allow the English consumer to go completely over from "black" bread to white. Barley would also grow well under northern skies; and while France and the upper Rhine could produce wine, Germany, Belgium, and England had to rely on water or ale. But good water was not everywhere available, and created no enthusiasm among consumers. It was regarded as a sign of British prosperity and economic superiority that Englishmen in the fifteenth century drank "no water unless at certain times, upon a religious score, and by way of doing penance." Oats were good for man and beast, would grow in cool latitudes, and in the form of porridge or cake were the staple food of many northerners.

While the plow ox remained the "central figure of the farm-yard economy," the horse slowly came into wider use for plowing and carting. Better methods of harnessing had been developed by A.D. 1000, and the collar had been padded and moved down the horse's neck to rest on its shoulders. Horse power at last could be really effectively used. The furrows turned by the heavy plow usually had to be broken by hand, harrows were tree branches or trunks, seed was scattered broadcast, and harvesting was a heavy drain on manual labor. In 1380 the harvest on one English manor farm of 250 acres occupied 275 people for two days, i.e., 2.2 man-days per acre.

Various figures are available from which we get a rough idea of the reward of this labor. From two bushels of seed wheat one rarely drew more than ten bushels of crop, and four bushels of oats or barley gave not more than fifteen bushels, though Walter of Henley, the thirteenth-century farm expert, talked about forty bushels as a possible yield. A recent study of the yield of eight English church manors from 1200-1450 shows that from 2.5 bushels of seed per acre a yield of 9.4 bushels, or nearly four-fold, was reaped. This yield is about one-third that of English wheat farming today, and suggests that "a threefold increase in productivity of seed seems to measure broadly the difference between medieval and modern farming" (Beveridge).

After the arable fields, the most important piece of land in the village was the meadow, since the peasants depended largely on its hay crop for their winter supply of fodder. Pending the development of corn, turnips, and other arable fodder, improvement in the quantity and quality of the hay crop would seem to be one of the most important tasks of the medieval village, but there is little evidence that the task was seriously faced. In France no village had enough meadow, and the cutting of a second growth of hay was usually impossible because the meadow became *vaine pâture* after the first crop was cut. The hay might be shared among the virgaters, the meadow might be divided into sections and distributed annually by lot, or each peasant might have permanent possession of one piece; but annual reallotment seems to have been most common.

The rest of the village lands consisted of the common pasture, marsh, moor, and woodland. Here sheep, swine, cattle, horses, and poultry sought their food. During two-thirds of the year they had to feed themselves; and if the medieval sheep and hog were leaner and longer of limb than their descendants, this was due in part to the distances they had to travel to find food. Here also the peasants sought their lumber, peat, rushes, and litter for the beds of themselves or their animals. The common lands were thus one of the three angles—arable, meadow, commons—of the rural triangle.

When the lawyers began to puzzle over common rights they evolved interesting definitions and distinctions. They defined the right of common as "a profit that a man hath in the land of another," and a common as "that soil or water whereof the use is common to this or that town or lordship." There was common of *pasture*, "the right of taking the produce of land by the mouth of cattle," common of *turbary* (cutting turf or peat for fuel), common of *piscary* (fishing rights), and common of *estovers*, which meant the right to take wood for making or repairing houses, plows, gates, fences, and farm equipment. The right of pasture was in theory proportionate to the size of the tenant's arable holding, and must provide food for as many animals as were necessary for plowing and manuring the arable fields. To prevent overstocking, villages might impose the rule that "None shall oppress or overcharge the commons or wastes by putting more goods thereon in summer than they can, out of the profits of their farms and tenements, keep in the winter." This "stint" was not always enforced, but the lack of adequate winter fodder acted as a brake, for in the fall the surplus animals were killed, salted, dried, or pickled in brine, and the village went on to a salt meat diet for the winter. The animals which were spared were left to forage for themselves or given scanty rations in barn or farmyard, and emerged in the spring looking like bags of bones. Eventually reliance on open pastures had to be diminished, and grazing areas were enclosed; but when this development came large areas remained open, overcrowded, breeding places of mongrels and murrain.

Sheep and swine have been called the sheet anchor of medieval farming, while the goat was the general utility animal along the Mediterranean fringe. Sheep gave milk (from which butter and cheese were made), meat, skins, and wool. They were gregarious, easily cared for by the shepherd who drove them out to grass in the morning and folded them—usually on part of the fallow field—at night. The hog was the medieval garbage pail, "the husband's best scavenger and the housewife's most wholesome sink." He could eat foods that were useless to other beasts, and his carcass salted well. Poultry contributed their quota to the larder, bees provided the only substitute for sugar, and the farmer who could afford a peacock had "a bird of understanding" which would "keep the farm premises clear of snakes, adders, newts, and toads."

Effort and Income.—Agriculture in northern Europe probably gave a smaller return for a greater effort than it did on the sunny slopes of the Mediterranean or the silt-covered banks of the Nile. Soil and climate were less generous, and until experiments in field or laboratory had laid the foundation of scientific high farming the cultivator must be satisfied with a meager return for hard work. Then, even more than now, his wife was a Jill-of-all-trades; and if she appears all too frequently in the manor court as a scold, virago, or even malefactor, we can lay that at the door of industrial-agricultural-domestic fatigue or count it as part of the streak of cruelty that ran through the period. Child labor was normal, and boys and girls carried a full share of miscellaneous tasks. The whole household worked, yet from its labor there emerged incomes which left little over when necessaries had been supplied. The fact that two or three generations were crowded into one small house suggests that the reserve of capital and labor for building houses was scanty, while the small supply of personal and domestic effects detailed in wills (when such documents appeared) shows that even comparatively well-to-do peasants were able to accumulate few worldly goods. It would take the cottage contents of a whole village to stock an antique shop.

The scanty margin of income and the slow accumulation of capital might be wiped out by three destructive forces—war, famine, or pestilence. War brought loss to the areas over which armies moved. To take what was movable and destroy what was not, provided sustenance to the taker but starved the enemy and the non-combatants as well. Such events as the investiture struggle in Germany (1075-1122), the civil war during Stephen's reign in England (1135-1154), the almost perennial Scottish raids on northern England, and the Hundred Years' War caused much destruction of life and property, with increased taxes and feudal levies, with kings exercising their right of purveyance to buy at their own price whatever food they needed for themselves and their followers, and with outbursts of robbery by powerful and poor alike.

Famine was more serious, for it affected even larger areas, and defective means of transportation prevented supplies from being brought from distant areas to counteract local scarcity. If the weather of medieval Europe resembled that of today, periods of good harvest never lasted more than two or three years, and were then followed by two or three years of poor or bad weather. At the same time there seem to be longer cycles marked by a few decades of predominantly good seasons and then by decades of inferior weather. The eleventh century had some black patches of widespread famine and the early fourteenth century fared even worse. The famine of 1315-1318 affected the continent from the Pyrenees to Russia, from Scotland to Italy. Between November, 1315, and June, 1316, grain prices in Antwerp rose over 300 per cent. As ever, starvation was followed by pestilence; underfed peasants and townsfolk were especially susceptible to epidemics, and the death rate was high all over the continent. Wars had to be suspended or converted into brigandage and robbery, plow teams were slaughtered for meat, and rats and mice were eagerly sought for food.

Pestilence followed in the wake of famine, but even when the ground had not been prepared for it the "plague" might still come. Of the two chief kinds, pneumonic plague was directly infectious, while bubonic plague was spread by rats, or rather by the fleas which got it from the rat and then passed it on to human beings. Rats and fleas are still part of the animal kingdom, as every war veteran knows; but whereas the modern brown rat is a shy animal which keeps to drains, sewers, and outside burrows, the medieval black rat did not shun human society. A medieval house of wood and mud, with a refuse heap before the door, and a floor of earth covered with filthy straw or rushes, was a fine home for the flea-infested rat. The disappearance of the plague from western Europe in the seventeenth and eighteenth centuries coincided with the disappearance of the black rat and the appearance of the brown one.

Of the plagues which did much damage, the best known is the Black Death, which arrived in the Crimea from Asia in 1346, spread over Europe during the next four years (1346-1350) and burst out again at various times between 1361 and 1391. The first attack was probably the worst in the severity and range of its devastation. It spread from the Black Sea to Iceland and Greenland. It struck very unevenly in different parts of the continent; in some regions a third to a half of the manorial tenants died, the death rate in monasteries ranged from ten per cent to fifty per cent, some districts lost forty per cent of their clergy, while in seaport towns like Bristol the mortality was so heavy that "the living were scarce able to bury the dead." Many more local records have to be studied before we can make a well-informed guess at the total size of the death toll, but it is clear that the outbreak was one of the most serious in Europe's history. The long-run effects of such events are hard to calculate, but the immediate result was economic and social chaos.

The picture painted in this chapter would probably not be accurate in all its details for any single village at any one time. No brief account can convey an idea of the great variety of conditions or organization prevailing in rural western Europe during the five centuries from 800 to 1300. Even in a small country like England the striped arable lands were rarely found outside the midlands and south. In the southeast men worked compact holdings; and in the west and north, where animals fared better than crops and population was thinner, scattered homesteads or hamlets dotted the pastoral areas. In France north of the Loire closely knit communities lived in the center of their big open fields and practiced a triennial rotation; in southern France the arable holdings were broad oblongs, homes were scattered, and the individual was more free from communal control; in Brittany the village was scarcely known, and in other areas the farmer tilled his own enclosed fields but shared the use of great pastures with his neighbors.

The relations between lord and tenant were as varied as was the landscape. In the English midlands and south villein holdings and domains preponderated, especially on the big abbey and church estates. But even in the midlands Kosminsky finds 30 per cent of the territory was held by free tenants and 34 per cent by villeins. The middle-sized and small estates had few or no villeins, but were worked by their owners with hired labor, or by free tenants. Some of them were all domain, some had none and some villeins did no *corvée*. The estate of the landlord is often not identical with the village. The land worked by the villagers may belong to several persons, a free tenant who holds from a lord may have tenants, villeins, and a court of his own—a sub-manor, and there are instances of sub-sub-sub-sub manors. "It is not only in the mingling of their strips in the open fields that manors were intermixed; they were intermixed in ownership, tenure, and economy as well" (Kosminsky). In France and western Germany the lands of one village were often owned by two or three lords; the peasant did little *corvée*, but was subject to heavier levies than in England. The French *seigneur* had greater judicial power than the English or German lord. Variety was the spice of medieval country life; but through it all ran the common thread of a peasantry that worked to maintain itself and worked or paid to sustain its economic and social superiors.

BIBLIOGRAPHY

See end of next chapter.

CHAPTER VII

RURAL CHANGE AND EXPANSION

IF A description of medieval rural life must be a composite photograph, it must also be a moving picture. The movement was slow, measured in decades or even centuries rather than in years. It was apparent in some countries earlier than in others, and in all lands many details are obscure. But the broad movements are clear enough: they involve changes in agricultural methods, in the purpose of production, and in the relation between lord and tenant. The chief driving force behind them is the development of trade and towns, the rise of local and distant markets for food and raw materials, the growth of a merchant class, and the increasing use of money. As opportunities grew for the sale of farm produce and the purchase of manufactured or other desirable wares, the sustenance economy of the countryside could be tempered by production for sale. The economic and social consequences of the emergence of an "exchange economy" were far reaching.

Agriculture by its very nature has always contained a substantial element of production for sustenance rather than for sale. Even American farmers, perhaps the most commercialized in the world, consumed in 1923 to 1928 about a fifth of their own produce, and the division of the farmer's output into subsistence crops and cash crops is almost universal today. At the same time the farm family may still convert raw farm produce into goods to be eaten, worn, or used in other ways. In every period of commercial chaos or when goods cannot be sold, procured, or afforded, production for use grows more important. This was apparently the case with the disintegration of the Roman Empire and during the disturbances caused by Saracens, vikings, and civil upheaval during the ninth century. But long before and long after that century, and long after towns and trade had developed, the greater part of the needs of the rich and nearly all those of the poor were met by the labor of the consumer or of his servants. Only within the last fifty or one hundred years have baking, brewing, laundry work, or the making of clothes, rugs, candles, soap, butter, cheese, bacon, jam, and pickles ceased to be domestic industries, especially in rural homes. To this list the Middle Ages added the making of cloth, leather, boots, furniture, wooden platters, spoons, forks, and farming utensils. The big house of king, bishop, or lord had its team of specialized workers, and the peasant household consumed what had been produced on its own land or made at home, "down to the last crumb or drop or stitch" (Coulton).

Self-sufficiency was probably rarely complete anywhere, and was tempered as quickly as possible when the roads were open. No village was so situated that it could produce everything it needed. Iron or steel for the blacksmith or armorer must be brought in from iron-producing regions. Salt was needed for curing or pickling meat, tar was the best-known treatment for sheep scab, spices were welcome if one could afford them, and certain areas, especially Paris, were famed for the quality of their millstones. Good knives could not be made locally, the scribe at the manor house needed parchment and ink, while hemp for ropes and flax for linen were not grown everywhere. The gentry up at the hall had some tastes that called for the purchase of cloth, saddles, spices, cosmetics, and perhaps soap, while the commonalty found much to desire when the peddler opened his pack full of strange things from afar.

If such goods came in as the village was physically unable to produce, goods also went out. At first they might be largely the transportable part of the rent paid in kind, or of the domain produce, sent to the abbey to which the manor belonged or to a *château* in which king or lord lived for part of the year. But when we pass A.D. 1000, and earlier in some areas, Europe witnessed a great growth of trade, of towns, and of currency supply. (See Chapters VIII-IX.) The movement came first and went furthest in the Low Countries and Italy, but in Germany old towns revived and new ones sprang up, while in France and England urban centers became more important. These towns were centers of consumption, and although their inhabitants might still till fields and tend livestock their demand for rural products grew. Some towns could satisfy their needs from nearby sources, but others had to draw supplies from a distance, as for instance the Italian or Belgian textile towns which came to depend largely on British and Spanish wool.

The farmer who was situated near such towns, or could produce a staple which they needed, might turn at least part of his efforts to commercial farming. If he was a free tenant there were few obstacles, except the distribution of his holding in the village fields, to prevent him from pursuing this policy. If he was a villein subject to labor dues, he might chafe at the time he had to spend on the domain farm, and seek for ways that would allow him to devote most or all of his days to his own land. He might wish to get his strips out of the mingle-mangle and fuse them in one compact piece on which he could do as he wished. At the same time the landlord might begin to regard his estate in a new light, as a place which could provide him with money instead of produce. That money could be increased in quantity by turning some of his waste lands into rent-producing tenancies, by increasing the labor dues or other claims on serfs, or by sweeping away the old order and those who were practicing it and reorganizing his estate as a big grain farm to feed cities, or a sheep farm to feed looms. If he did not see so far into the mysteries of economic life, others did, especially the merchant class that gradually grew strong and rich in the larger towns. To these men land had a triple attraction. It might pay handsome returns on the capital invested in its purchase, equipment, and improvement, give social prestige to its owner, and permit his fortune to lose the odor of leather or herrings.

These possible effects of the growth of towns and trade explain much of the agricultural and agrarian history of the last eight or nine hundred years. Sometimes the peasants got the chief benefit of the new possibilities, while the landlords gained little, e.g., in France. Sometimes the landlords were aggressive, rode roughshod over the peasantry, and merged the villagers' holdings in large grain farms, e.g., in Germany east of the Elbe in the sixteenth and seventeenth centuries. Sometimes the landlord and a few big farmers triumphed over the smaller men, as in Tudor and Georgian England.

Town and Country in Italy.—In northern Italy the estates around towns were held by lords, abbeys, and churches, whose tenants tilled their fields, vineyards, and olive groves on a crop-sharing system. The landlord provided the land planted with vines or olive trees, supplied seed and probably equipment, leaving the tenant to supply only labor. The yield was divided on some pre-arranged plan—a third, a half, or two-thirds to the lord, the remainder to the tenant. This type of tenure is known in English as share-farming, in French as *métayage*, and in Italian as *mezzadria*.

As the cities grew larger they needed more supplies. They also needed to bring the landlord to heel, for his castle controlled the road or river, and when he did not plunder the goods that passed by he imposed heavy tolls on them. Around Florence in 1100 there were 130 castles, on nine miles of the River Arno five fortresses commanded the route to the sea, and on every road and pass similar obstacles stood in the way. During the eleventh and twelfth centuries these dangers were removed. Florence sub-dued the lords, compelled them to live part of the year in the city, and put the administration of their estates into the hands of city officials. With the road between the peasant and the towns-man cleared, rural production supplied urban needs. Serfdom was wiped out, some towns abolishing it at a stroke. Money was spent on roads, canals, and ambitious drainage or irrigation projects. Irrigation overcame the summer drought, dikes and drains turned swamps into fertile fields, while canals linked up the rivers and made the carriage of goods easy and cheap. Some towns, such as Brescia, appointed officials to inclose land and abolish commons as a prelude to the extension of cultivation. Rich merchants acquired large estates, and let them on short leases or *métayage*. Often the terms were so heavy, when supple-mented by tithes and land tax, that the peasant could not live on what was left and had to work for wages part of his time. A rural proletariat emerged in place of the old hereditary servile tenants. The Italian cultivator was not the first, or the last, to learn that if the abolition of serfdom freed the peasant from the soil it also freed the soil from the peasant.

Rural Change in the Low Countries.—On the other side of Europe the relation between town growth and rural change was equally strong. The Low Countries were actually low, and much of the northern part was below sea level or was sandy heath. Without a great expenditure of effort such land could not be made safe for cultivation. In Belgium the land was higher, drier, and richer, except along the coast, but even there the water had to be watched. Yet the position of the area at the mouth of rivers which led far inland made it the meeting ground of the great lines of communication from the south and east.

In Roman days British tin, wool, and grain entered Europe along these rivers *en route* for the Rhine frontier or the Mediterranean. Local wool, hides, dairy produce, hams, and geese went as far as Rome. The ore deposits of eastern Belgium and the imports of tin made possible the rise of important metal-working towns. English and Frisian wool and local flax fields fed flourishing textile centers, and the coast dwellers caught herrings or plied their ships on the North Sea. The Germanic invasions disturbed production and trade, but both soon revived. The vikings wrought havoc for a time, but recovery gradually came, and Pirenne estimates that by the twelfth or thirteenth century half the Belgian population lived in towns. The need for food and raw materials was therefore great.

In Belgium and to some degree in Holland manorial estates had been owned by abbeys, bishops, and lay lords, but the obligations of the serfs became fixed at an early stage in terms of money. As the urban demand for farm products grew and the supply of money increased, prices rose steadily. The serf who produced for market prospered, but the landlord became poorer as the purchasing power of his income from customary payments fell. Two ways of increasing his income were available: (1) He could free the serfs, and then let them have their holdings back on short leases, at rents that could be raised when the lease expired. (2) He could increase the area of land under cultivation by attacking the commons, wastes, swamps, heaths, and woodlands.

The first way was easier than the second, and serfdom gradually disappeared. The second called for patient, persistent struggle, for great expenditure of money and labor, and for a refusal to be daunted when river or sea, scoffing at human effort, swallowed up more land. Time after time the North Sea broke through the sand dunes built by nature and the dikes piled up by man. In 1135 it flooded part of Flanders, and farther north took the first big bite toward making the Zuyder Zee. In the thirteenth century there were over thirty serious inundations. Faced with such disasters, many people emigrated to England or Germany. Those who stayed behind kept up the struggle, and if landlords could not afford to pay the costs, city merchants lent them the money or bought their estates. By 1200 most of the Netherlands was owned by rich townsmen, who poured capital into sea walls, dikes, drainage channels, and pumps worked by windmills. The land thus regained was intensively cultivated in small plots by tenant farmers. As there was no room to spare for fallow, rotations, stretching over five, seven or more years were worked out. Manures, cattle-breeding, root crops, better hay crops, and vegetables received attention, and by the expenditure of much labor on little land Dutch and Belgian agriculture became a model for the rest of Europe.

Rural Change in France and England.—France and England moved more slowly toward better use of the soil and new relations between landlord and cultivator. They were less dominated by town activities, their land supply was larger, they did not feel so soon the pressure of population on limited rural resources, and they were not worried by the lack or excess of water. But the rise of local markets, the development of merchant middlemen, the growth of export trade (especially in English wool and French wine), the financial interests or needs of landowners, and the desire of some cultivators for greater economic freedom exerted a slow but sure influence. We can study the results under five headings: (1) changes in the cultivators' obligations; (2) the spread of wage labor; (3) the rise of the *rentier*; (4) changes in the village map; (5) the organization of commercial farming.

1. *Changes in the Cultivators' Obligations.*—In general the status of the servile class improved, obligations became fixed, and payment in money became important. Peasants who were selling produce were willing and able to pay for emancipation from claims which irked them, and sometimes a landlord needed cash badly. In France this emancipation of serfs from arbitrary or unpopular demands was sometimes done *en masse*, for the French village was a vigorous communal group, and when twelfth-century towns were wresting charters from their lords some villages followed their example. As Bloch remarks, agrarian revolt was as characteristic of the seigneurial system as the strike is of modern capitalism. Violence rarely achieved much, but the steady pressure of the group and the self-interest or the need of the landlord produced results. The French peasant finally gained a virtually perpetual tenancy. So long as he and his descendants

fulfilled certain prescribed obligations they could not be moved. One might almost describe him as an owner who had to do certain things as the price of possession. As such he remained until the French Revolution relieved him of the price.

In England we know little of village action. There the large landowners—the greater barons and the church—were the chief controllers of villeins and possessors of domains. They readily responded to the call of markets, and seem to have sought to get more labor dues and money out of their unfree tenants and to deprive their free tenants of some rights. Against such efforts, the peasants struggled, and the Peasants' Revolt of 1381 was chiefly concerned with the grievances of men who lived on the great estates. Elsewhere the pressure was less severe, and over large parts of the country the peasant's obligations came to be fixed. Often they were inscribed on the court roll, and each tenant was given a copy of the terms of his tenure. He became known as a *copyholder*; so long as he observed the written obligations he was immovable, and the title might pass to his descendants.

While the villager's duties became fixed, the way in which he did them was gradually changed by the *commutation* of labor services for money or produce. This decline of *corvée* was apparent in France by the tenth century. In Charlemagne's day the tenant had owed dues and labor services, but chiefly the latter. By the twelfth century the position was reversed. Many more dues had appeared, but the *corvée* had almost vanished. As Bloch puts it, a tenure that had once been a source of man power was now a source of rent. The explanation was that the domain had been cut up and let to tenants.

On the English non-manorial estates, which comprised a large part of the country, labor dues were not common; villein and free tenant paid in kind (or money), and domains were insignificant or non-existent. On the manors with domains and villeins, some lords might have more labor dues available than they needed, and were ready to commute them; but on the big estates there might not be enough unfree labor, and the villein might find he was ordered to give more rather than less as production for market expanded. Hence while payment of rent in money grew and by "the thirteenth century had become the chief form of feudal rent" (Kosminsky), there was no universal willingness to let villeins change from labor dues to money rents. Commutation came slowly on the great feudal estates, and had made little progress by the Black Death. During the next hundred years it gathered pace, and by 1500 the cultivation of domains by unfree labor had become rare.

2. *The Spread of Wage Labor.*—Commutation stimulated the demand for hired farm workers to cultivate the domain. Such workers were already well known; they had been used to help on villein and free holdings, had worked alongside unfree tenants on the domain, and had been used by smaller landowners who had no villeins. They might be wanted to help the prosperous peasant who added bit by bit to his holding until eventually he possessed far more land than he could work unaided. The laborers might be cottars, men who had failed to make good on their holdings, or sons of peasants whose lands were not large enough to employ and sustain the whole family. In the summer season they were reinforced by the townsmen who came out to help gather in the hay and grain. By the fourteenth century at the latest, western European agriculture was leaning heavily on its hired labor class. The Black Death created a scarcity of workers —possibly only temporary—led to demands for higher wages, caused much anxiety to the rulers in London and Paris, and provoked attempts to keep wages down to the old level. A recent study of Essex in the late fourteenth century shows the influence of the growing textile industry in East Anglia and of the expanding commerce of London on the condition and outlook of farm laborers. These men were asking for money wages rather than for money and food, and getting rates far above those fixed by statute. They were demanding day wages rather than annual stipends, since they would then be more free to leave their jobs when they wished. They were leaving the land to take up woodcutting or carting, to work on ships, or to drag for oysters. The picture portrays landlords and farmers buying labor that knew how to demand its price and sell itself to the highest bidder.

3. *The Rise of the Rentier.*—As the landlord received more of his dues in money his dependence on the yield of the domain diminished. He might ask, Why face the risks of wind, rain, flood, drought, murrain, and incompetent bailiffs? Why spend on hired labor the sixpence received as money rent in the hope of getting sevenpenny worth of produce? Why not abandon the cultivation of the domain farm, and lease it whole or in pieces to

tenants? If the domain held a quarter to a half of the whole arable and meadow area, it could be cut into a number of holdings, or bits of it could be leased to tenants who needed a little more land. From at least the tenth century onward this was being done in France and Italy, then in England, and more slowly in Germany. Often the tenure was leasehold for, say, nine years; the rent might be payable in money or in produce—a fixed quantity in England, a fixed fraction in Italy and France, and sometimes the landlord provided the livestock and the first year's seed. Some Flemish monasteries as well as lay lords abandoned domain farming, but the English abbeys were more conservative (or enterprising), and some of them were still farming their lands when the dissolution of the monasteries came in 1536 and 1539. Where the domain passed away, the landlord became a passive income-receiver. His welfare depended on the amount of money he received and on its purchasing power. In France, much of it came from perpetual tenants whose dues had been fixed, and he received the same number of deniers or livres generation after generation; in England the income from copyholders was similarly stabilized.

Landlords who had to live largely on these fixed receipts were vitally interested in price movements. From about 1150 to 1400 prices rose, at times rapidly. Sir William Beveridge has shown that the price index number of produce sold by nine English manors rose from an average of 65 in the period 1200-1249 to 119 in the period 1350-1399. During the fifteenth century prices declined, but advanced rapidly and far during the sixteenth. Rising prices benefited the peasant but hurt the fixed-income receiver, and this impoverishment was probably accentuated by taxation, personal factors, and the demands of a higher standard of living. Some landlords lost their social standing and had to sell part or all of their estates to the bourgeoisie of Paris, Lyons, Bordeaux or other towns. These men got them cheap, and brought their capital and business outlook to bear on the task of making their property yield a greater income.

4. *Changes in the Village Map.*—With more time to spare and with a market available for surplus produce, energetic farmers wanted more land; they got it by leasing part of the domain, by renting holdings from their fellows, or by taking land out of the common pasture and waste. In England by the thirteenth century

"a busy land market was in operation, through the medium of the lord's court, for the sale, exchange, and lease of the villein holdings" (Levett); and the trend toward variety in the size of holdings continued as the prosperous man added to his acres while the victim of debt, incompetency, or restlessness let some or all of his go. With this movement went some consolidation of arable strips. If a farmer could lease strips adjacent to his own, or by exchange pull his scattered plowlands into two or three compact blocks, less time would be wasted, land lying idle and weedy in balks could be plowed up, and boundary disputes would end. Some landlords withdrew their domain arable strips from the open fields and welded them together. Even before 1300 some groups of tenants agreed to consolidate arable lands, and by similar pacts cut into the common or waste land to increase the supply of arable or meadow or to enclose pastures for sheep.

While the villagers cut pieces out of the commons and wastes in some places, they opposed any such action by the lord, especially when he added bits to the domain or carved out new farms and leased them. If the villagers were villeins, they got little support in their protest from lawyers, crown, or legislature. An English law, the Statute of Merton (1235), said the lord had power to occupy waste land provided he left sufficient for his *free* tenants. Encroachment on commons was one of the chief economic causes of the peasant revolts which sprinkle rural history from the fourteenth to the sixteenth century. There were other causes, but the economic ones can be summed up as resistance to the landlord's attempts to collect more money, goods, or services and to draw a bigger yield by better use of his estate. If the landlord was persistent enough he got much of his own way. In France he had least success, but he did finally get much of the commons in return for other concessions. In southern and western Germany, where serfdom had been slowly ebbing as it had in France and England, and where land was apparently becoming scarce because of the growth of population, the peasant revolts which spread at intervals from 1476 to 1525 all failed. In England the greatest tumult arose in the fifteenth and sixteenth centuries, when enclosure, chiefly for wool production, disturbed village life in some places. (See Chapter XIV.)

5. *The Organization of Commercial Farming.*—The rise of markets for rural products stimulated a measure of regional spe-

cialization. Production must still meet most local needs, but beyond that point a district could turn its attention to those commodities for which it was best fitted and which would give the greatest net return. The task of feeding a large town such as Bruges, Paris, or London determined the character of production in areas near these places, but international trade influenced some districts. Large areas in Gascony and Guienne served the English market, England had some grain and hides for export to the Low Countries, flax and rye were produced largely for export in some parts of Germany, and wool was the chief staple in the export trade of England and Spain.

The organization of production for market as well as for sustenance reached its highest level on some church and monastic estates. If an abbot or bishop controlled a group of manors scattered over a wide area yet not too far apart for easy communication, he might give each manor some special task and let it draw on the others for the goods it did not produce. A recent study of Crowland Abbey has shown that those in charge of its lands possessed well-developed ideas on farm management. The abbey itself stood on an island of fairly dry ground in the fens of East Anglia. Beyond the five waterways which surrounded it were several manors, some of them in grazing lowlands and some in the drier wheat areas which lay to the west. Each was part of a group and none tried to be self-sufficing; the grain villages grew a surplus to feed the graziers and the abbey, livestock went from place to place wherever the grass was best, and all the manors sent produce to feed the abbey and provide a surplus for sale. From 7000 to 10,000 bushels of wheat came to the central granary each year, along with 5000 to 6000 bushels of malt for the monks' ale, and much oats, beans, and peas to feed man, pig, or poultry. The abbey itself therefore could devote the whole of the island to rearing cattle and sheep. On its big central farm it had in 1160 over 2000 sheep; from this farm and the manors the abbot sold over 9000 fleeces in 1309-1310 to Italian, Flemish, and German merchants. In addition there were two or three cattle farms on the island, and much cheese was sent to market.

These conditions were not peculiar to Crowland. The Cistercians who penetrated the lands south of the Baltic sent produce to Lübeck, grain and wine to Norway, and wheat to Holland.

They had their own warehouses and stalls in every big market town, and while the monks themselves were not allowed to go far afield their agents did so. In England they were content to produce, for tne buyers came to their door, seeking to buy the wool clip, sometimes offering a ten years' contract, and if necessary paying in advance.

The changes in rural life described above were generally slow, and the areas affected did not embrace the whole continent or even a whole country. The landlords were not all burning with a desire to wring the last penny out of their estates, most peasants were conservative, and the commercialization of agriculture was a very slow process except in favored areas. Open fields, extensive commons, wide wastes, village control of production, two- or three-field systems, and fragments of manorial tenure were widespread even as late as the eighteenth and nineteenth centuries.

THE MEDIEVAL FRONTIER

For nearly a thousand years before western Europeans began to move overseas they had been pushing into new areas at home. Sometimes they had gone only as far as the fringe of the village; at times they had fought swamp and forest, sometimes wild beasts as well; and in the great movement eastward from the Elbe they had met and subdued or annihilated a native population—the Slavs—just as in later days they met the redskin, the Hottentot, or the Maori. In England and France the great empty spaces between or on the edge of the earlier settlements were gradually filled up, but for the German the call, "Go east, young man!" was the forerunner of the later American call to go west.

The motives that took men to the frontier were as mixed as the men. Lords went seeking estates, bishops sought new realms to conquer for Christianity, monks wanted land and solitude, and merchants searched for goods and customers. In the movement were dispossessed peasants, debtors, younger sons to whom the family holding offered no future, men who sought refuge from justice, invasion or civil war, adventurers and restless fellows. Some came from the Low Countries, crowded out by the growth of population or washed out by inundation. Some were transferred, willy-nilly, by their lord to help settle his new fief. Some were attracted by offers of cheap land and by pictures of a land of Canaan flowing with mead and honey. Some were knights who went crusading south of the Baltic instead of east of the Mediterranean.

The monasteries were the earliest big force working on the frontier. Not all the Benedictine abbeys were posted out in the wilds, but many of them were. In the seventh century they were dotted along the fringe of the Frankish kingdom from the Jura Mountains and Moselle Valley to Frisia. When Charlemagne devastated the Franco-Spanish marches in his campaign against the Saracens, he handed much of the captured land to abbeys. At each spot the monks might spend four to six hours every morning draining, felling, and tilling, while settlers came to live around the abbey, attracted by the security and the market it provided. "The founding of a monastery was usually an act of colonization" (Thompson), and even of town planting.

What the Benedictines began the Cistercians carried on, and they were far more intrepid frontiersmen than their predecessors. When they appeared, in the early twelfth century, the best areas had been taken up and land was beginning to possess a greater value to its holder. Hence the Cistercians settled mostly in naturally inferior places—the valleys of northern England or Scotland, the fringe of wild Wales, the dreary sandy stretches along the Bay of Biscay, or the racial frontier where German was steadily pushing back Slav. Most of the land was fit only for pasturage, and in England and Scotland the Cistercians became the chief flockmasters; but they cultivated the soil assiduously whenever possible. They drained, irrigated, studied the relation between the soil and the kind of trees that grew on it, and experimented in seed selection, grafting of vines, and horse breeding. They taught the tenants how to farm, and attracted settlers by offers of cheap land. They dug minerals, produced salt, built mills, fostered the production of linen or woolen cloth, and traded widely. They spent little on churches or education, took all they could get, grew avaricious and lazy, and eventually ceased to justify their existence. But they had done a fine piece of work from Wales to Poland.

In France the extension of settlement by monk and layman was vigorous from about 1000 to 1300. There had been much before that time, as Celt, Roman, and Frank had cut into the forests. Much of the earlier work had been a reclearing of areas over which the forest had spread its dominion when men deserted

them. In France, as in New England, the trees came back when
men went out, and reforestation was a process of nature, not an
act of man. With the end of the attacks from without and the
emergence of comparative domestic peace, reclamation and expansion could be undertaken with some degree of security.
Normandy, Flanders, and areas in the southeast were cleared,
land was won back from the sea, and the Marais de Dol, which
had been turned from fertile land into coastal swamp about
A.D. 700, was in the twelfth century reclaimed by building a
dike over twenty miles long. Lords saw the axe and spade cutting
paths to increased income, the church saw more tithes rolling
into its coffers, and the crown saw its frontiers strengthened
against the English. There was some transfer of serfs, but much
of the work was done by men who were offered "improvement
leases" to persuade them to come. By these leases they secured
hereditary possession subject to payment of a fixed quitrent; or
they were given half the land they had cleared; or they kept all
the land but handed over half its produce.

During the Hundred Years' War the French frontier stood
still or even receded. Villagers took to the towns or to the woods;
many once fertile areas no longer heard "chanter coq ni poule,"
and the forest reinvaded field and vineyard. The work of clearance began again in the sixteenth century, and Dutch engineers
and capital were brought to drain the marshes; but even in the
eighteenth century there was still much wild land waiting to be
tamed.

In England the breaking of new ground went on round the
fringe of the midland area. In the east there were swamps, in
the north the Scotch, in the west the Welsh. On the swamps no
serious attack was made till Tudor and Stuart times, but by
1300 the Welsh had been subdued, and pioneering on the Celtic
fringe was possible. Over half Cheshire was covered with forest,
moorland, marsh, or heath, and the rest could not be profitably
worked with the energy that was left over after holding back
the Welsh. When the Welsh danger passed, the enterprising abbot
of a local monastery set an example which the lay landlords and
peasants quickly followed. Forests were cleared, marshes were
drained, the inroad of high tides was checked, and pits were dug
to obtain marl for use as fertilizer. Thousands of pigs were
turned into the forests, then slaughtered, and with the aid of

Cheshire salt became ham or bacon. Grain and wool were produced, timber and minerals were exploited. A flourishing sea trade grew up in the export of salt, bacon, metals, and lumber, and the import of Irish grain and Gascon wine. Similar work was done in other parts. Monasteries were given marshy wastes on improvement leasehold. But England still had large unimproved areas until the eighteenth or nineteenth century.

The greatest pioneering movement was the mixture of missionary work, conquest, and colonization across the Elbe. Its starting point was a line from Venice to Hamburg. East of that line lay the territory rather sparsely occupied by the Slavs in the north and by the Magyars in the Danube Valley. The northern part was not easily cultivated, and the Slavs apparently did little tillage, except in a few favored spots. Into this area German merchants had ventured, seeking slaves, amber, honey, and furs. In their wake followed men who had been flooded out of their homes, adventurers, refugees, misfits, or men with a grievance. Behind them came the monks and the armies. Charlemagne pushed his conquests to the lower Elbe, the Saale (a tributary on the west bank of the Elbe), and the upper waters of the Danube. Here he established a chain of fortified posts and handed his new territory to nobles and churchmen, who set out to settle it with their own serfs or by inviting freemen from the Low Countries or other regions west of the Rhine. When Charlemagne died the push stopped; it was renewed in the tenth century but made little headway till the twelfth century, when it became almost irresistible.

At each step, whether to the Elbe, to the Oder, or to the Vistula, conquest was followed by the establishment of fortified centers whose name usually ended with *burg* (a fortress), e.g., Brandenburg, Mecklenburg. The country was cut up into marks or marches, each under the control of a margrave. Archbishoprics or bishoprics were set up, abbeys were founded, noblemen received big holdings, and the work of bringing settlers began. These settlers came chiefly from the Rhineland and the Low Countries. In the ninth century buffetings by the North Sea and the Northmen had driven Low Countrymen eastward, and in the twelfth century their skill in reclaiming land caused them to be eagerly sought for and welcomed on the frontier. An archbishop of Bremen brought them by the hundred to tackle the swamps around the lower Weser and a margrave of Brandenburg used them to develop similar land round his headquarters. Adolf, Count of Holstein, founder of Lübeck and one of the most energetic colonizers of the early twelfth century, sent messengers into Westphalia, Holland, and Flanders "to proclaim that all who were in want of land might come with their families and receive the best soil" in "a spacious country rich in crops, abounding in fish and flesh and exceedingly good pasturages." Henry the Lion, Duke of Saxony, who took Lübeck from Adolf in 1158, sought immigrants both for the city and for large areas he had captured from the Wends. The time was favorable, for in 1135 the North Sea had begun to create the Zuyder Zee, while war, feuds, and unrest caused by the early crusades made many people willing and eager to move. The response to Henry's invitation was embarrassingly large, and he passed some of the immigrants on to Hungary.

By the thirteenth century German control reached as far east as the lower Vistula. Cattle ranches and lumber camps had been supplemented by farms, vineyards, and thousands of villages. Land was usually granted to the pioneer on attractive terms. The landlord owned the land, but the settler who made a farm out of virgin country held it henceforth on payment of an annual quit-rent. He did no labor for his lord, and was personally free. While land was plentiful and labor scarce the lord had to be generous, but when the land had been thoroughly settled the tables were turned; labor became plentiful and land scarce. Further, a market arose for grain and wool in the Low Countries and elsewhere. The landlord therefore tightened his grasp on the descendants of the free settlers, absorbed much of their land in a great domain farm, compelled them to work it, and sent the produce to distant markets.

As plain and forest filled up, systematic settlement of villages was accompanied by systematic planting of towns. Often these towns were on the site of some old Slav center, and some kept their old names, e.g., Leipzig, Danzig, and Berlin. To attract merchants and artisans, liberal forms of municipal government were granted by the lordly town promoter, and usually the constitution and code of laws were copied, word for word, from those of some well-known town, such as Lübeck or Magdeburg. These towns gathered up from the interior far more goods than had ever come from the Slavs, helped Germans to oust Scandinavians from the Baltic trade, and served as stepping-stones to the great fair at Novgorod.

In the thirteenth century the frontier crossed the Vistula, and added lands east of the Baltic to the German sphere of settlement and trade. The conquest of Livonia, Prussia, Lithuania, and Estonia called for a special effort, made by two military orders—the Brethren of the Sword and the Teutonic Knights. During the siege of Acre (1191) some German crusaders turned their sails into awnings and their ships into floating hospitals. Thus the Teutonic Order was born, to function like that of the Templars and the Hospitallers; but it soon realized that not all the rewards for fighting infidels were in the Levant, and went to battle with Tartars on the Transylvanian frontier of Hungary. Its conduct and greed made it only a little less unpopular than the enemy, and it was expelled. At that moment the Prussians, who lived east of the Vistula, attacked Poland, and the Teutonic Knights were invited to protect Poland. They accepted the invitation on condition that they were allowed to keep what they captured.

Then began half a century of conflict; the struggle was fierce, but the military steam-roller moved eastward, and conquest was followed by colonization. A hundred knightly families obtained fiefs, about 1200 villages were founded between 1290 and 1350, and while such Prussians as were not killed or driven out were regarded as serfs, immigrants from the west were offered the usual liberal tenures. The familiar story of drainage, road-making, and forest clearance was repeated, and the land from which the Prussians had wrung so little was made much more productive as sheep, cattle, horses, swine, and new crops were brought in. The plains and reclaimed lands yielded far more grain than the settlers could consume, while the forests of southeastern Prussia produced a great surplus of lumber, potash, and furs. The country became a large exporter of timber and grain to Scandinavia, the Low Countries, or even the British Isles, and the Vistula basin became one of northern Europe's few granaries.

The Order was generous in its grant of civic rights, and gave eighty or ninety towns charters based on precedents of Lübeck or Magdeburg. It improved roads and rivers, and policed them. It had a keen eye for revenue, and while it gave much to townsman and villager it kept enough to insure a large income for itself. It collected much in land tax and rent; it retained rights over fishing, hunting, mining, and milling, and either exploited them itself or charged a substantial rent or royalty to concessionnaires. The mill rights alone were of great value in a country where much grain had to be ground or much lumber was being cut. The produce received in payment of these various dues had to be sold, and the Order therefore turned merchant and shipowner. It made its spare money work by lending it at interest, and gained a reputation as a rapacious creditor.

After 1350 the eastward movement drew to a close. The population of western Germany was now being absorbed by the growing cities, while the supply of land available was running low or was being taken up by native-born easterners. In 1410 the Order was crushed by Poland at the Battle of Tannenberg. It had few friends among the merchants, who regarded it as a serious trade rival, or among the peasants, who disliked the charges it imposed on them. By standing between Poland or Bohemia and the sea it provided an adequate excuse for Polish dislike. Out of its defeat it came with only East Prussia. There it carried on a little colonization among the great forests of the south, but the day of its greatness and of its service had ended.

German migrants did not stop at the political frontier, and foreign rulers eagerly welcomed them as farmers, lumberjacks, and miners. In Switzerland during the fourteenth and fifteenth centuries the Bishops of Basel and the Counts of Neufchâtel offered special privileges to German settlers who came up from the lower Rhine Valley. Bohemia was predominantly agricultural till the thirteenth century, but the immigration which then began helped to develop mining and industry as well as agriculture, and made the king of Bohemia the richest monarch of his day. German mining skill had become highly developed in working the gold, silver, and copper deposits of the Harz Mountains; and when important discoveries of precious metal were made between 1100 and 1300 in the Erzgebirge (on the boundary of Bohemia), in the Carpathians, and in Transylvania, German miners were sought for. In the sixteenth century their skill was enlisted to develop mineral resources in places as far apart as Russia, England, and South America. In the eighteenth century rulers and landlords invited German woodcutters to exploit the Carpathian forests, while Russian landlords attracted settlers to the Crimea and southern Russia. In the nineteenth century they made their mark in North America and the antipodes. If the German makes a good settler, it may be because he has had a long experience on the frontier.

BIBLIOGRAPHY

One scarcely knows where to begin in choosing a brief list of books or articles on medieval rural life. English and American writers have studied chiefly English conditions, and few continental works have been translated. The most ambitious effort to present the general story in brief compass is J. W. Thompson's *Economic and Social History of the Middle Ages,* chaps. 20, 24, 27, 29; other attempts to look at Europe as a whole are H. D. Irvine's *Making of Rural Europe,* chaps. 1-3; P. Boissonnade's *Life and Work in Medieval Europe,* book ii, chaps. 1, 2, 3-10; and Max Weber's *General Economic History,* chaps. 4, 5. See also Power, Eileen, "Peasant Life and Rural Conditions," in *Cambridge Medieval History,* vol. vii (1932), chap. 24. *Select Readings in Rural Sociology* by Sorokin, Zimmermann, and Galpin, vol. i, contains valuable extracts drawn from important works. In German, the most recent general surveys are Kulischer, J., *Allgemeine Wirtschaftsgeschichte des Mittelalters und der Neuzeit* (1928-1929), vol. i, chaps. 8-16; and Kötzschke, R., *Allgemeine Wirtschaftsgeschichte des Mittelalters* (1924) (see table of contents). In French, H. Pirenne, *Le Mouvement économique et social au moyen âge* (1933) is excellent. For the rest, regional studies must be used.

FRANCE

BLOCH, M., *Les caractères originaux de l'histoire rurale française* (1931), chaps. 1-3.

CALMETTE, J., *Le régime féodal* (1924).

COOPLAND, G. W., *The Abbey of St. Bertin and Its Neighbourhood* (1914).

LUCHAIRE, A., *Social France at the Time of Philip Augustus* (1912), chap. 13.

SÉE, H., *Esquisse d'une histoire économique et sociale de la France* (1929), part ii, chaps. 1-6; part iii, chap. 2.

SÉE, H., *Les classes rurales et le régime domanial en France au moyen âge* (1901).

GERMANY

MEITZEN, A., *Siedelung und Agrarwesen der Westgermanen und Ostgermanen, der Kelten, Römer, Finnen und Slawen* (1895), especially the *Atlas* to vol. iii.

THOMPSON, J. W., *Feudal Germany* (1928), part ii.

ENGLAND

ASHLEY, W. J., *The Bread of Our Forefathers* (1928).

ASHLEY, W. J., *Economic Organisation of England* (1914), chaps. 1, 3.

ASHLEY, W. J., *Introduction to English Economic History and Theory* (1888), vol. i, chap. 1.

BLAND, A. E., BROWN, P. A., and TAWNEY, R. H., *English Economic History: Select Documents* (1914), part i, sections 1, 3.

COULTON, G. G., *The Medieval Village* (1926).

GRAS, N. S. B., *A History of Agriculture* (1925), chaps. 4, 5.
GRAS, N. S. B., *Evolution of the English Corn Market* (1915).
GRAS, N. S. B., and ETHEL C., *Social and Economic History of an English Village* (1930).
GRAY, H. L., *English Field Systems* (1915).
HONE, N. J., *The Manor and Manorial Records* (1925).
LEVETT, A. E., *English Economic History* (1929).
LIPSON, E., *Introduction to the Economic History of England* (1915), vol. i, chaps. 1-4.
PAGE, F. M., *The Estates of Crowland Abbey* (1934).
PEAKE, H., *The English Village* (1922).
PROTHERO, R. E. (Lord Ernle), *English Farming, Past and Present* (1912), chaps. 1, 2.
SEEBOHM, M. E., *Evolution of the English Farm* (1927).
SEEBOHM, F., *The English Village Community* (1883).
STEPHENSON, CARL, *Medieval History* (1935), chaps. 11, 24.
WALTER OF HENLEY, *Book of Husbandry* (trans. by Miss Lamond, 1890).
Translations and Reprints from the Original Sources of European History (Univ. of Pennsylvania), vol. iii, No. 5. Students can get the feeling of manorial records from this collection, or from those found in Hone; in Bland, Brown and Tawney; or in Gras' *Social and Economic History of an English Village.*

Intensive work on medieval records frequently results in articles in the historical journals. Among recent ones the following are valuable:

AULT, W. O., "Some Early Village Byelaws" (*Eng. Hist. Rev.*, April, 1930).
BEVERIDGE, W. H., "The Yield and Price of Corn in the Middle Ages" (*Econ. Hist.*, 1927).
GRAY, H. L., "Commutation of Villein Services in England" (*Eng. Hist. Rev.*, October, 1914).
KENYON, N., "Labour Conditions in Essex in the Reign of Richard II" (*Ec. H. R.*, April, 1934).
KOSMINSKY, E. A., "The Hundred Rolls" (*Ec. H. R.*, 1931).
KOSMINSKY, E. A., "Services and Money Rents in the Thirteenth Century" (*Ec. H. R.*, 1935).
LEVETT, A. E., "Financial Organisation of the Manor" (*Ec. H. R.*, 1927).
LUCAS, H. S., "The Great European Famine 1315, 1316, 1317" (*Speculum*, October, 1930).
NEILSEN, N., "English Manorial Forms" (*Am. Hist. Rev.*, July, 1929).
PAGE, F. M., "Bidentes Hoylandiæ: A Medieval Sheep-Farm" (*Econ. Hist.*, January, 1929).
ROBBINS, H., "A Comparison of the Effects of the Black Death on the Economic Organisation of France and England" (*J. Pol. Econ.*, August, 1928).
ROBO, E., "The Black Death in the Hundred of Farnham" (*Eng. Hist. Rev.*, October, 1929).
WRETTS-SMITH, M., "Organization of Farming at Crowland Abbey" (*J. E. B. H.*, November, 1931).
Encyclopædia of the Social Sciences: Articles on Agriculture (Medieval), Agrarian Movements, Aids, *Corvée,* Entail, Feudalism, Land Tenure, Manorial System, Serfdom, Slavery, Village Community.

CHAPTER VIII

MEDIEVAL TOWNS AND INDUSTRIES

VARIOUS attempts have been made to estimate the size of central and western European towns in the fourteenth century. These estimates give only four towns—Palermo, Venice, Florence, and Paris—a population of about (or at least) 100,000 each. Milan, Genoa, Barcelona, Cologne, and London seem to have held about 50,000 folk each in 1340. Between the limits of 20,000 and 40,000 lie many towns which loom large in the medieval story, including Ghent and Bruges (the great Low Countries centers), Lübeck and Hamburg (the stalwarts of the Hanseatic League), Strasbourg and Nuremberg in southern Germany, Bologna and Padua in Italy. In the large class ranging from 6000 to 20,000 come such towns as York and Bristol, Ypres and Antwerp, and many central European trade hubs like Augsburg, Frankfort, Zurich, and Basel. The rest of the towns might run down from 6000 to 600, and some of them were as small and limited in their economic influence as many a "ville" or "City" scattered over the North American countryside.

In spite of their lack of stature, these towns exerted great influence on the character of European life. They whittled away some of the isolation and self-sufficiency of the countryside. They developed division of labor and manual skill such as would otherwise be impossible outside the workshops of great courts and abbeys, and offered employment to the free artisan as distinct from the slave or serf who occupied those workshops. They transmitted from the Saracen world some of the technical knowledge and ingenuity of the Levant, and added to it. They accumulated supplies of capital, and devised methods of marketing, transport, and finance. They forged bonds of far-reaching interdependence, as when English wool was made into Flemish cloth, sold in a French fair, dyed in Florence with colors from Bagdad and alum from Asia Minor, and sold to a consumer in Cairo. They brought into being a new social class—the bourgeoisie—to rival in wealth and challenge in political power the landed aristoc-

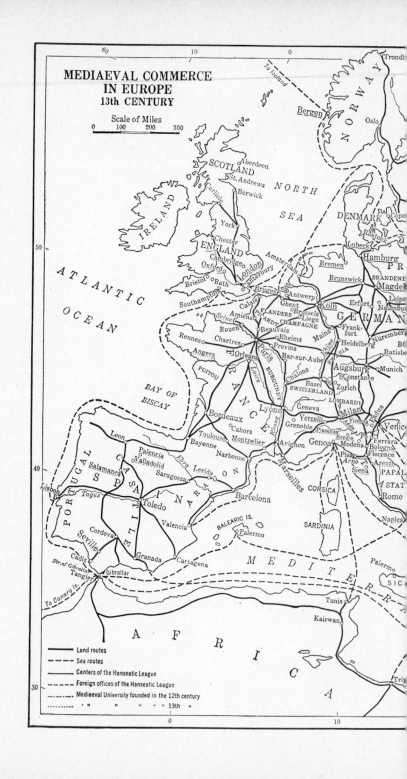

MEDIAEVAL COMMERCE
IN EUROPE
13th CENTURY

Scale of Miles
0   100   200   300

NORWAY

To Iceland

Bergen

Oslo

Trondh

SCOTLAND
Aberdeen
St. Andrews
Berwick
Carlisle

NORTH
SEA

DENMARK

Cope

IRELAND

York
Chester
Cambridge
Oxford
London
Canterbury
Bristol
Bath
Southampton
Calais
Amsterdam
Bremen
Brunswick
Rostock
Lübeck
Hamburg
BRANDEL
Magde

ATLANTIC
OCEAN

ENGLAND

Bruges
Antwerp
Ghent
Brussels
Liege
Köln
Erfurt
Leipz
Naumbur
GERMAN

Seine
Amiens
FLANDERS
PICARDY
CHAMPAGNE

Rouen
Beauvais
Rheims
Provins
Bar-sur-Aube

Frank-fort
Mainz
Heidelber
Nüremberg
BC
Ratisbe

Rennes
Chartres
Angers
Orleans
Paris
Loire
BURGUNDY

Châlons
Basel
SWITZERLAND
Augsburg
Constance
Zurich
Munich

POITOU

BAY OF
BISCAY

Bordeaux

Lyons

Geneva
LOMBARDY
Milan

FRANCE

Cahors
Toulouse
Bayonne
Montpelier
Narbonne

Vercelli
Grenoble
Avignon
Piacenza
Reggio
Modena
Ferrara
Bologna
Florence
Arezzo
Siena

Genoa

Venice

Leon
Palencia
Valladolid
Salamanca
Saragossa

Ebro
Lerida

Marseilles
CORSICA

Pisa
Arno
PAPAL
STAT
Rome

PORTUGAL
SPAIN
CASTILLE
ARAGON

Lisbon
Tagus
Toledo

Barcelona

Valencia

BALEARIC IS.

SARDINIA

Naples

Cordova
Seville
Cadiz
Str. of Gibraltar
Tangier
Gibraltar
Granada
Cartagena
Palermo

MEDITER
R

Palermo

SIC

To Canary Is.

Tunis

Kairwan

A F R I C A

Tri

—— Land routes
--- Sea routes
—— Centers of the Hanseatic League
--- Foreign offices of the Hanseatic League
···· Mediaeval University founded in the 12th century
···· " " " " " 13th "

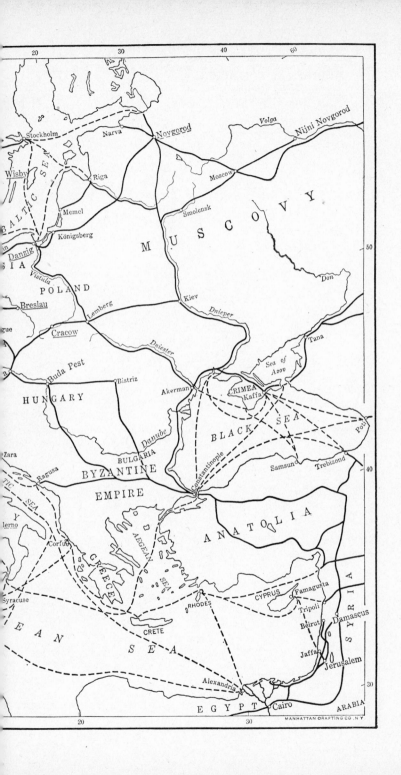

racy and church. They made distinctions of wealth and poverty rest less on real estate, and gave to the individual opportunities for personal advancement which were rare on the countryside. They provided new aspects of the class struggle in the clash of merchant with producer, of master with man. For the encouragement and regulation of economic effort they framed laws and ordinances, many of which are part of the statute law of today.

Town Origins.—The town had been the core of Greek and Roman life, as administrative center, fort, workshop, market, way station, port, or pleasure resort. With the recognition of Christianity it might become the seat of a bishop or archbishop. When the empire in the west collapsed, some towns were destroyed and others were deserted. The garrison towns decayed when the troops marched away; the administrative centers, baths, and pleasure resorts lost their occupation when the officials and patrons departed; the way stations had no guests when no one traveled the roads, and some places became scarcely habitable if the aqueducts fell into ruins. The Germanic invaders were primarily country folk, and their unit of government was a territorial area, such as the county, hundred, or duchy.

Not all the towns ceased to function. In the Eastern Empire they carried on; in Italy some survived, or if wrecked they soon recovered. In the west, especially on the Rhine, the bishop's city had been originally a Roman camp. When the soldiers left, the civilians, under his direction, protected themselves by erecting or repairing walls and forts, and during the invasions pulled down public buildings to get material for the walls. If the invaders did not at first respect the bishop, conversion soon changed their attitude, and from the sixth century to the ninth his buildings were the chief structures of the town. He provided peace and security, dispensed justice, established a market and perhaps a fair, and minted coins. He and his entourage provided a body of consumers of local farm produce or manufactured wares, and also of luxury goods brought from farther afield. The income that came to him from the episcopal estates or from the faithful gave him substantial spending power, and if his church possessed holy relics the pilgrims who came there would spend as well as worship.

Security and a market were also found around other centers— abbeys, castles, and lordly or royal courts—and some of these were in places where no Roman town had stood. If a bishop's palace and a noble's castle happened to be near together, the defense and the market were doubled, e.g., Durham; while if a king, a bishop, and an abbot lived near together, as at Tours, the situation was still more favorable. The protector was not slow to realize that his services had their reward in the revenue that flowed into his coffers from fairs, markets, rents, and courts, and the protector might therefore turn town promoter. When the eastward movement got into its stride the promotion of such towns as Munich and Berne in the south or Brunswick and Lübeck in the north became good defensive strategy and good business.

In the rise of medieval towns on the area between the lower Rhine and the lower Seine (i.e., Flanders, Brabant, and northeastern France) Pirenne finds a close connection between defense and trade. Trade recovery after the viking attacks came about largely through the efforts of wandering merchants who ranged far afield from castle to castle, district to district, fair to fair. There was not sufficient business in any one spot to give them a livelihood. For this hazardous calling they moved in armed bands, under a banner and a leader, crossing seas, traversing roads or rivers, and coming into fair or market like a circus. In their travels they needed halting places, and when winter came they must have quarters in which they could rest and store their goods, boats, and wagons.

The safest place was under the wing of an abbey or of one of the stronger fortresses (*castra, burgi*) which lords had built to protect themselves against the vikings or against each other. There the traders might erect a palisade or wall, and thus make a defended suburb, a *faubourg*. The occupant of the burg drew revenue in tolls and market dues from them, and therefore was willing to encourage and protect them. Victualers and tavern keepers settled there to supply them with food, artisans to make the wares they would sell, porters, boat builders, and longshoremen to handle the cargoes and containers, and a church dedicated to the merchants' patron saint might be built. As trade grew, the permanent population in such a *portus* increased, and in the fall the wanderers returned. The group of lodgers at the gate blossomed into a community which overshadowed and ringed round the defensive core and finally took over its name. The economic power of the trader and artisan grew stronger than that of the defender and chief local customer, and the castle, abbey, or cathedral became part of the larger community.

While religion, refuge, and a rich consumer played a large part in bringing towns into being, no town could grow much unless it possessed geographical or economic advantages. If it combined a strategic position for defense with a commanding position on trade routes and a rich agricultural or mineral hinterland, its growth was assured. Its economic importance was influenced by two factors. The first was its general *location* with respect to local developments, needs, and resources and to the general flow of trade. The second was its particular *site*, which determined why it blossomed into a town while a score of adjacent places remained farms or villages. In a mining area there must be some town which would bring in supplies, collect and send the ore, metal, or coal to the outside world, or make the metal into articles. A rich agricultural area needed a market center. On the edge of a sea rich in fish there must be spots where the catch could be packed and where salt, barrels, and other supplies could be obtained. In a textile area, dyers, finishers, wool sellers, and cloth merchants must be gathered in some central spot. The wider movements of trade called for towns along the main routes to serve as resting places, transshipment points, or warehouses.

These needs caused a town to grow up somewhere in a district, but did not determine the actual *site*. The deciding factor might be suitability for defense and command over roads or waterways. A town might grow where two trade routes crossed, bringing people from four points of the compass. It might grow at the highest navigable point of a stream, or the highest point that could be reached by seagoing vessels. Transshipment took place there; goods were brought to be loaded for the return journey, were stored till the boats or the land carriers came for them, and might be sold before they resumed their journey. A town might grow at the lowest point or the safest point at which a river could be forded or bridged, at some waterfall or rapid where portage was necessary, at the entrance to some mountain pass, or at the junction of two rivers. Some cities were blessed with good site and location, e.g., Constantinople, Cologne, and London. In others the location was so good that men put up with a poor site or strove to improve it by draining the land, dredging the harbor, fighting sand bars, or cutting into the cliff side to get more room for buildings.

The map of medieval Europe is full of illustrations of the above influences, working sometimes singly, sometimes in alliance with political, religious, or defensive factors. Cologne was the result of a happy combination. It was perhaps the most strategic point of the Rhine frontier, and became the center of a Roman colony and the seat of an archbishop. It was an outpost of the Frankish kingdom and the center of the Holy Roman Empire. To the west, by river or land, were the Low Countries, France and the British Isles; across the river stretched the expanding German world, while to the south lay the upper Rhine, the Danube, and the passes that led to Italy. With good location went a good site. The Rhine was comparatively quiet, shallow, and easily forded at the spot. Above Cologne the valley became narrower and the river could not easily be navigated, especially by the large boats that came from the North Sea. Hence landsmen crossed the stream there, and boats had to unload their cargo. Shipbuilding and repair work were done, there was a mint, eventually there were three fairs each year, and when the relics of the three kings who went to see the infant Jesus were brought from Milan in 1162 Cologne became a great pilgrim center. Some wares from the hinterland—cloth, swords and other metalware, leather, and wines—were marketed in Cologne, but the city's chief business was the handling of goods which came from a distance.

A list of towns that grew up at the junction of rivers would include such places as Lyons, Coblentz, Mainz, and Kiev. Milan commanded the roads to seven passes leading to the Rhone and France, to Geneva, and to the upper Rhine, while around it was the rich Lombard plain. Farther east the Brenner Pass, fairly low and wide enough to allow wagons to be used, helped to make Verona at the southern end and Innsbruck at the northern. Towns like Augsburg, Regensburg, Ulm, Salzburg, and Nuremberg owed their existence to the combination of passes and of upper reaches of rivers that flowed to the Baltic and Danube, and to the consequent crisscross of routes; but some of them also had such valuable local resources as flax or minerals, and were markets and workshops as well as crossroads. Paris began on an island in the middle of the Seine. The river was easily crossed by ferry or two short bridges, and roads converged there; the island was easily defended and became a fort and royal residence. On the banks *faubourgs* sprang up, occupied by traders, farmers, and artisans, while beyond them lay the fertile basin on the Seine. Politics also favored Paris, for in the disintegration of France after Charlemagne's death the Count of Paris became the King of France.

Many English towns tell the story of their origin in their names. Those whose names end in -burgh or -borough either grew round a fort or had one built there later. Cathedrals and abbeys played their part; Oxford, Hereford, Cambridge, and Uxbridge were at spots where rivers were easily crossed, York and Chester were at the end of navigation, the south coast was dotted with ports for the continental trade and forts to stop invaders, while such fishing villages as Yarmouth and Gloucester blossomed into towns. London began at the lowest point where the Thames could be forded or bridged. There was good anchorage, and above the bridge lay a fertile valley. It was a busy Roman city, with a wall, a mint, a bishop, and roads going in all directions. When the Romans left, London decayed, but a bishop and then a Saxon king revived it. The vikings hurt it, but Alfred and later William the Conqueror helped it. As the center of government slowly came to rest in Westminster, London benefited from the presence of a large customer, while across the narrow North Sea lay the Low Countries market. Location, site, religion, and politics combined to make London grow.

Though the rate at which a town grew and the size it eventually reached depended largely on its geographical and economic advantages, much hinged on the energy and ability with which the townsmen pressed and exploited these advantages. That energy and ability might be productive or predatory, or both. It might seek to expand industry and trade by efficient production or transportation, and by winning a reputation for good workmanship, excellent wares, cheap goods, and low freight costs. Or it might exploit every opportunity for monopoly, for exclusive enjoyment of some profitable field, and for driving or keeping a rival out of the market.

Both methods were usually employed in an age when almost every town's hand was against every other town. A town might seek freedom from tolls or harbor dues, or try to get its goods into port on payment of lower charges than were imposed on its rivals. It might demand that all goods passing through the town be unloaded and offered for sale for two or three days (*stapelrecht*), or that goods which did travel farther be sent only by its own merchants (*umschlagsrecht*). These claims were made by Dordrecht, Cologne, and the towns which bestrode the Alpine roads through the Tyrol. In the same spirit, but with sharper weapons, the Italian cities fought each other on land and sea. Almost every Italian town felt it had either to break a rival or be broken. Florence in A.D. 1000 was one of a number of small market centers for the farmers of Tuscany, no bigger or more full of promise than many of them, and a mere village when compared with Pisa. Its site on the Arno was good, and its location in a land of grain, grapes, olives, and sheep gave it a slight advantage over the others. But its subsequent fame and wealth came in part from the aggressive energy with which it subdued castles and rival towns, and mastered every center that might bar its path or compete with it.

The Town and the Feudal Order.—The rise of towns in a rural and feudal Europe created interesting problems, for the land on which the town grew up already belonged to some lord and landlord. That landlord was customer and defender, but he was also master. As such he might wish to claim all his rights and exercise the power that a feudal régime gave him. But a system framed for a sleepy village and a rural society might be a strait-jacket on the traders of a comparatively bustling town. These men needed at least as much freedom of action as was essential to the conduct of their trade and industry; they wanted to safeguard their property and income by fixing a limit to the lord's financial claims, and sought to get a measure of control over the making of laws which affected their business and the imposition of local taxes.

Landlords responded to these needs in every possible way, from ready grant to stubborn refusal. In general, lay lords and kings accepted the situation more readily than did the ecclesiastical and monastic rulers. They recognized that a growing town meant greater market or toll returns, higher ground rents for urban or adjacent land, and larger yield from taxes. Some of them therefore welcomed the traders round their doors, let them build wharves, warehouses, walls, and other public works, provided facilities for trade, and gave the townsmen a great measure of self-government. Sometimes necessity was stronger than long views. If a lord required a sum of cash for a pilgrimage, crusading trip, or some other abnormal need, he might sell his birthright for a lump sum, or a fixed annual payment, or both. Kings acted in the same way, but politics also influenced their attitude toward towns. If they were beggared by war or crusade, they would sell trade concessions and civic privileges. If they were engaged in a struggle with the church or the nobility, or if their title to the throne was weak, they might try to win the towns to their side by well-timed grants. But if they wished to keep or win the support of clergy or nobles, and disliked the growing power of the larger towns, they might try to check and even humiliate the rising bourgeoisie. Frederick I wrecked the walls of Mainz in 1163, after having almost destroyed Milan in the previous year. Such attempts at repression were doomed to failure in the long run. If force was the final arbiter, towns like Milan and Florence could muster an adequate supply of it, either singly or by banding together. Some towns took advantage of a period of anarchy; for nearly a quarter of a century after 1250 there was no emperor, and the cities on the imperial domain gave themselves a large measure of freedom, e.g., Ulm, Regensburg, Aachen, Frankfurt-on-the-Main, and Nuremberg.

The towns on church lands had greater difficulty in securing autonomy, yet many of them were extremely important places, e.g., Rheims, Strasbourg, Mainz, Cologne, Basel, Magdeburg, Cambrai, Milan, or Liège. Bishops and abbots clung to their control of the temporal as well as the spiritual life of their people. As big property owners they were conservative; as heads of a perpetual corporation they saw no excuse for alienating powers which they held in trust; as exponents of Christian ethics they had little respect for mercantile codes of conduct; and they were rarely in dire financial straits. Hence their attitude was often one of hostility to the townsmen's desires, and a firm assertion of feudal rights. There were disputes over minting rights, over the sale of goods without paying market tolls, and over the use of the lord's mill. But whatever the immediate cause, the clash of interests frequently struck sparks. There was a revolt against the Archbishop of Cologne in 1074, while similar uprisings occurred in Cambrai, St. Quentin, Amiens, Laon, and other places during the next forty years. Lay lords as well as ecclesiastics were attacked, villagers imitated the townsmen, blood was shed, at least one bishop was slain, and the rebels' ferocity was returned tenfold if the prelate got the upper hand.

In these uprisings rebels bound themselves by oath into an association or *commune*, and pledged themselves to stand together. They tried to seize control of the town and to replace seignioral law and jurisdiction by a government of their own, with officers who would look after the town's defense and foster its economic life. Some communes failed, but many succeeded, and their action was imitated elsewhere (e.g., in London in 1191). Where pressure was strong enough even bishops gave way, while some, either from fear or through good will, came to terms with the laity and sold what the townsmen were seeking to buy.

From these civic developments Europe got its third estate: to the clergy and nobility was added the citizenry. Its power varied greatly from country to country. In Italy it established independent city republics. In Germany some of the largest towns were virtually in the same position, with only a shadowy allegiance to the emperor. Over most of the rest of Europe civic freedom was limited and partial. The townsmen had their own officials and legislative body, their own courts, market, and police, levied taxes, maintained their own defenses and public buildings, and controlled the industrial and commercial life within their boundaries. But the lord, prince, or king retained some jurisdiction. In many French, Belgian, and German towns some officials represented the town while others represented the lord; in Flanders the same man might act for both town and count. The decrees of a national ruler or legislature supplemented or overrode those of the town in England and France. (See Chapter XI.) Minting remained a royal prerogative in England, in France the kings gradually regained control of coin-making after 1250, in Germany barons and bishops were loath to surrender their mints to the towns, and while some towns controlled currency others still used a feudal coin. Finally, the townsmen were collectively responsible to lord or king for an annual payment in place of the many varied individual dues of earlier days.

We see this collective responsibility most clearly in England. There most of the towns were on the royal domain. From them the king had received rent for the land, tolls from the market, fees and fines from the court, and the income from *banalités*.

When their merchants traveled throughout the kingdom they had to pay tolls at ports, bridges, markets and fairs. In place of these many payments the town agreed to pay a lump sum to the crown; it "farmed" the royal revenue, and paid the annual fee-farm or *firma burgi* (rent of the borough) out of the money it collected in court or market. In return it gained freedom from the royal officials: its citizens need not go to courts outside the city wall, need not settle disputes by ordeal of battle but by jury trial; and, in the words of one charter, "wherever they shall go in their journeys as merchants, through my whole land of England and Normandy, Aquitaine, and Anjou, by water and by strand, by wood and by land, they shall be free from toll and passage fees, and from all customs and exactions."

Urban Occupations.—Most medieval towns were of little more than local importance, and many of them retained a strong agricultural odor. Their citizens tilled fields outside the walls and kept livestock on the town commons. In Colchester half the people were farmers. There were a dozen barns in Cambridge (1279), and in one of the main streets of nineteenth-century Heidelberg there still stood a "large farm-house, with all its agricultural and pastoral appurtenances: horses and oxen in the stalls, and a dung-heap of gigantic size in the centre of the yard" (Coulton). Such towns had their petty tradesmen and craftsmen, serving the needs of the town and its environs. Once a week there was a certain liveliness while the market was being held, as farmers came in to sell what they had to spare and buy what they needed. Once a year there might be a fair in the town or on the outskirts, at which men from farther afield came with desirable outlandish wares, while others arrived to buy up the district's surplus of farm produce. The rest of the year was humdrum, except for the passage of peddlers, merchants, dignitaries, and soldiers, the holding of an election or the uncovering of some small-town scandal.

Some towns lifted themselves above the common level and won wide repute as centers of industry, commerce, finance, or all three. To the trade with their immediate hinterlands they added traffic with other regions, with one another, and with the smaller towns. Their importance might be chiefly commercial; they fetched, carried, and sold goods without changing their form or submitting them to any processes; but many of them built up industries and housed large bodies of craftsmen. From industry and commerce some townsmen accumulated large sums of capital which they used in banking and credit operations, and the range of their buying, selling, and lending might cover Europe. The development of industries must now be examined, but that of commerce is left till the next chapter.

The Rise of Medieval Industries.—Industrial production for market declined in western Europe as the Roman Empire disintegrated. The German migrants had the usual simple crafts; they made iron weapons, fashioned ornaments of gold, wove linen, made soap, tanned leather, and baked earthenware vessels. The women did most of these jobs, for with the exception of metal work the men spent their time chiefly in drinking, gambling, fighting, hunting, tilling, and tending their herds. In general, production was by the household, in the household, for the household. The big groups of consumers in abbeys, courts, and castles employed a supply of industrial workers on their estates, and this practice continued in part long after the towns had grown and trade become widespread. (See Chapter X.)

Self-sufficiency tended to be mitigated where an area was rich in some raw material, for on the least inducement such districts would produce a marketable surplus. Frisia and England, for instance, had much wool, and by the seventh or eighth century were making cloth for export. The makers apparently knew the tricks of their trade, for in 796 Charlemagne wrote to the king of Mercia complaining of a fraudulent reduction in the length of some woolen cloaks he had bought from England, and asking that the next consignment be "made of the same pattern as used to come to us in olden time." From such beginnings grew the great textile industries of the Low Countries, Italy, and, later, of England. As a merchant class arose the cloth was taken farther afield. In Tuscany sheep had roamed over the hills since at least Roman days, and the wool was spun and woven in the cottages, monasteries and nunneries. Surplus cloths were taken to market and those from the nunneries won high repute. Merchants came to buy, production for sale expanded, and Florence soon housed a growing number of wool workers. Similar developments took place in the metal trades. Areas which overlay metal deposits or were within easy reach of supplies did more than supply the local demand, and gradually became widely known for their weapons, armor, or other metalware, e.g., Dinant, Flug, and Liège. In the production of wine, leather, metals, or salt, many monasteries exploited their natural resources and sent goods to market.

Industrial advance owed much to the infiltration of patterns, methods, and tastes from more advanced areas. The Syrians showed western Europe what was being made in Levantine workshops. The church was a channel through which articles of fiber, wood, and metal were spread wide, bringing examples of artistic craftsmanship to the backward areas. The Saracens brought to Spain the technical knowledge of the east. Their skill in making and working leather goods was a revelation to Europeans. They also brought welcome knowledge of dyes and dyeing to a part of Europe that was poor in coloring matters and had to rely largely on woad or lichens. They revived the cultivation of madder in Spain, made rich carpets, and introduced silk culture and weaving to Spain and Sicily. From Sicily and Spain some of this knowledge and skill passed northward.

The knowledge the Moslem brought from the east was reinforced by that which the west fetched for itself. The growing trade of the Italian ports with Constantinople and the Moslem world helped much, the stream of pilgrims increased the number of Europeans who knew a higher material culture, and the crusades exerted a great influence. The crusaders came, saw, and were conquered by the dress, food, and houses of a people alongside whom they were rough backwoodsmen. In between the patches of siege and battle there were long periods of truce, in which enemies fraternized. Intermarriages were numerous, Moslem and Italian merchants traveled round the invading armies, while such industrial and trading centers as Damascus and Aleppo remained in Moslem hands, conducting business as usual.

The European was brought close to the luxury of the east; he saw it whole, not as fragments in a wandering Syrian's pack; and he liked what he saw. He bought pieces of silk, cotton, or woolen cloth and sent them home to his church or friends in Europe; he developed a taste for spices, sauces, condiments, and elaborate dishes; he ate the sugar and candies of Tyre and Bagdad; he learned to like rugs and tapestries on the floor and walls of his tent or around his bed, and the feel of underclothing next to his skin. He saw quantities of damask, brocade, cloth of gold, fine armor and swords such as few Christian workers could fashion; and if he used his ears he heard new ideas on warfare, religion, art, and science. Sometimes he stopped in the east, and even turned Moslem, but if he came home he brought new tastes with him. The ships which had taken him out returned full of Levantine and Asiatic goods; the number of towns, merchants, and ships engaged in trade with the Near East was increased; and the stream of goods flowing westward was widened.

Effects of the Crusades on Industry.—The crusades quickened the development of industry as well as of commerce. Europeans copied many of the eastern wares, improved their old industries, and set up new ones. In the twelfth century the Normans fostered the manufacture of silk fabrics in Sicily, and erected a big silk-weaving workshop in Palermo. During the next century the industry spread to the mainland, with Lucca and Naples as its centers, and from these towns emigrants took it to Florence, Genoa, and Venice. Florentine taffeta, damask, brocade, and cloth of gold eventually rivaled those imported from the east. The dye industry benefited, since rich Europeans wanted the colors of the east. Bagdad was the great dye market, especially for indigo from India and for certain Persian dyes. Venice became an importer and producer of dyes; the Venetian red of the painter or dyer is named after a color that Venice learned to extract from an insect. Florence learned from easterners how to get violet colors from a lichen, established a monopoly of the supply, and gradually added many other carefully guarded secrets to its dyeing lore.

The manufacture of glass and of metal was stimulated by new demands and new knowledge. Venice had begun to make glass by the eleventh century. New methods were discovered or transplanted, workers were brought from Constantinople when Venice captured that city in 1204, and the demand for vessels, mirrors, glass gems, and beads provided both luxury and popular markets. So important did the industry become that from the thirteenth century it was regulated by the state. The workers were segregated on an island just outside Venice, and the death penalty was inflicted on any artisan who tried to take the trade secrets elsewhere. As compensation the men were well paid, admission to the craft was carefully restricted, and a glass-maker became, by senatorial decree, a gentleman and burgess, entitled to marry a daughter of patrician blood. The industry did, however, spread to other parts of Italy, and even beyond, especially into Germany.

The making of armor and weapons had been carried on chiefly in feudal workshops, but the crusades stimulated the growth of several munitions centers, such as Brescia, Nuremberg, and Liège. A fourteenth-century Italian merchant bought his coats of mail from Milan or Nuremberg; his gold-handled swords from Florence or Lyons; his blades from Milan, Toledo, Nuremberg, or Solingen; his expensive spurs, leather cases, and trunks from Paris; and his arbalest cords from Hungary. Armament workers were highly specialized; in an Avignon shop one man made only visors, another iron gauntlets, another brassards, another spurs, and so forth.

Contact with the east stirred the west to improve its domestic furnishings. As the rich laity and the church developed a desire for decorated work in wood, metal, stone, fibers, and leather, Italy, the German towns, the Low Countries, and France developed the necessary labor force. Flanders produced not merely good cloth but also elaborate tapestries and carpets, for which Arras was especially famous. Lucca was a city of luxury trades; Florence exported religious pictures, church ornaments and costly cutlery, while Paris laid the foundation of her subsequent reputation as the luxury market of Europe. To her royal and aristocratic consumers she was adding a rich merchant class and gathering together a remarkably able body of craftsmen. Fine furniture was one of her specialties, and was in demand outside France. Ostrich feathers from Tunis were made into plumes for helmets, tapestry weavers rivaled those of Arras, and the work done with gold, ivory, and precious stones showed great skill, if not always good taste. The French crusaders wanted ornamented spurs, belts, bridles, and cases or trunks in which to carry their fighting apparel, and Paris made them. When the papacy was in Avignon, the demands of the papal court left their mark on French industry. Possibly no other country felt so strongly as did France the influence of the crusades in changing the standard of living, increasing the variety of foods, enriching the wardrobe and decorating the home.

The crusades also helped western industry by opening in the east a market for some of its wares. In the age-long exchange between the two ends of the Mediterranean the west had little

to offer except those primary products which Asia lacked. But
as the merchants followed in the wake of the crusaders, they
found a market for western woolen cloth, not merely among the
European armies but also among the natives. By the twelfth century cloths from the textile districts of northern Europe were
being gathered into Genoa, dyed and finished there, and shipped
to all parts of the Mediterranean. Cairo had a special market for
western cloths. Thanks to this growth of Mediterranean trade,
clothing-making expanded in both the Italian and North Sea
areas. Flanders had a double market: it supplied northern Europe,
and Ypres cloths were selling in Novgorod by 1100; in addition
it served the Mediterranean merchants, and such towns as Ypres,
Ghent, Verviers, Courtrai, and Malines grew large (for the
Middle Ages) and famous for special kinds of cloth. England
also served both markets; its cheap fabrics were exported to
northern buyers, but cloths of Beverley, Stamford, and Lincoln
fetched high prices in Italy.

The greatest woolen expansion seems to have been experienced
in Florence. That city had two textile groups, each with its own
guild. The *arte della Lana* consisted of those who made cloth in
or near Florence, the *arte di Calimala* contained the finishers of
imported pieces. According to Villani, these two groups employed
over 30,000 people in the early fourteenth century, the members
of the *arte della Lana* had two hundred or more workshops and
produced seventy or eighty thousand pieces of cloth yearly, while
over ten thousand cloths came to the warehouses of the importers.
By that time the Florentines were relying largely on imported
wool, and Italian merchants were going to the two great sheep
ranches of medieval Europe—Spain and the British Isles. In the
markets of Barcelona and Valencia they were the chief buyers,
but they also penetrated into the interior, bought from the monastic and other wool producers, and by 1400 had warehouses in all
the Spanish wool areas. In the British Isles they did much the
same, and in 1273 took 37 per cent of the wool exports. Some
Italians bought the whole yield of monastic flocks, and signed
contracts to take the clip over a period of thirteen years at prices
fixed in advance.

The Florentine industry owed much to imported skill. The
modern world, with its countless books on technical subjects, its
schools and colleges of applied science, may find difficulty in
realizing the obstacles that beset the spread of industrial arts. A

skilled occupation was fittingly called a "mistery"; knowledge passed orally and visually from one generation to the next, with apprenticeship as the channel. The passage from place to place depended on the migration of skilled workers, and from medieval times to the nineteenth century towns or countries which had skilled workers tried to prevent them from moving, lest backward places be enabled thereby to make for themselves goods they had formerly imported. Yet, with perfect consistency but imperfect sense of humor, even the most highly skilled centers welcomed newcomers who could add to their store of knowledge and set up new industries. Migration must move on a one-way road, inward but never outward. As the serf was bound to the estate, so also was the artisan to be bound to the town. Venice threatened death to runaway glass-makers, yet lured experts from Bologna to teach her people how to grow and harvest hemp, thus breaking the monopoly Bologna enjoyed of high-grade hemp needed for the Venetian rope factory. Knowledge and skill did nevertheless travel. When William of Normandy took England, many artisans followed in the wake of the army. Lords who were promoting new towns did their utmost to induce artisans to come and settle therein, and in every industrial center there were men who had traveled far from their birthplace and training ground.

Florence drew her textile lore from many quarters. Violet dyeing began when one of her townsmen brought from the Levant the secret process for extracting the color. Her whole textile industry was revolutionized with the coming of the Humiliati in 1239. These members of a religious order pledged to manual labor had concentrated their attention on making woolen cloth. They had developed a high degree of skill, a great division of labor, and something like mass production of fine fabrics. These skills they taught the Florentines; finishing processes were improved, the product was given a more attractive appearance, division of labor was made more minute, and workers were gathered together in large workshops, thus probably increasing output, insuring better work, and lowering production costs. At its height the Florentine textile industry was the best in Europe, selling its wares in the markets of North Africa, Spain, the Black Sea and western Asia.

BIBLIOGRAPHY

See bibliography at end of Chapter X.

CHAPTER IX

MEDIEVAL INTERREGIONAL COMMERCE

IF WE could examine European trade in 1300 statistically we should probably find that the local "neighborhood" exchange among villagers and between groups of villages and market towns was by far the most important, and some aspects of it will be examined in Chapters X and XI. But interregional long-distance exchange was not insignificant; there was enough of it to be worth fighting for, enough to interest monarchs in its control and taxation, and enough to produce wealthy men, powerful associations, and rich cities. It fell into three main fields: (1) northern, (2) southern, and (3) exchange between north and south.

The Northern Trade Area.—The exchange of wares between the different parts of northern Europe sprang from the monopoly (or the marked advantage) that certain areas enjoyed in the production of some commodities, both primary and manufactured. A few of these commodities were luxuries—e.g., wine, furs, and silver—but most of them were raw materials (copper, iron, tin, timber, hides, and wool) or necessary foodstuffs (fish, salt, beer, and grain). These products, heavy, bulky, and low in value, could not bear heavy freight charges, but since few producers or consumers were far from river or sea, water transportation could be used. Further, the Scandinavians and their German successors built roomy cargo boats. The *kogge* of the Hanseatic merchants was a vessel with a very capacious hold, well fitted for the carriage of large cargoes of fish, salt, lumber, grain, and even beer. Freight charges were consequently not prohibitive.

Of the luxuries, wine was the chief. The main vineyards were in the Rhine and Moselle Valleys, and in France south of the Loire (Guienne and Gascony). From Bordeaux wine went to England, the Low Countries, and Scandinavia; the chief customers were the great households of kings or nobles, the church, and the richer townsmen. In 1242 Henry III bought over 1400 casks (about 360,000 gallons) for the royal cellars. At that time about 10,000 casks (over 2,500,000 gallons) were coming to England annually, or more than a gallon per head of the population, and about three times as much per head as in 1913. The wholesale price of medium-quality French wine in England at the period was about 1/6 (36 cents) a gallon in modern money terms, and the retail price might be twice the wholesale. In terms of contemporary wages the price does not appear prohibitive. Wine was not too expensive to be bought by the growing upper middle class, and the vintner came into prominence in the larger ports and towns as purveyor to merchant and landlord.

Of the northern trades, that in fish touched most people. There were fasting days all through the year, and Lent came at an appropriate time, when the store of salted meats laid in during the preceding autumn had run low. Fish therefore supplemented local food production, and made fasting less unpleasant. Dried and salted fish was a staple ration for sailors and soldiers; every English schoolboy learns of the Battle of the Herrings (1429), fought to protect a convoy of fish destined for the troops. Some inhabitants of the sea—the seal, cod, and whale—provided northern Europe with oil that was used for lamps and as food.

The shallow waters of the northern region were rich fishing grounds. From the Bay of Biscay and Iceland to the Baltic and the arctic waters north of Norway, fish of many different kinds, from the sardine to the whale, were found. Some fishermen went as far as Iceland, and tradition says that Breton boats sailed to the Banks of Newfoundland. If they did they kept their own counsel for fear of drawing rivals after them to that fisherman's paradise. Until those Banks became known about 1500, the most famous fishing ground was the narrow Sound. Every year the herring shoals came to spawn in the shallow waters off the Scania peninsula in southwest Sweden. From August to October they were crowded so thickly together that, according to a contemporary fish story, "you could cut them with a sword." During these months thousands of boats hauled in easy catches, thousands of workers arrived to clean, salt, and pack the fish, while merchants came to buy supplies or to sell food, beer, salt, and barrel staves. A fourteenth-century observer declared that there were 45,000 boats at work, and estimated the total labor force at 300,000. These figures are almost certainly exaggerated, but they indi-

cate that this annual harvest of the sea must have rivaled in its
bustle the gathering of a North American prairie harvest before
the coming of the combine. Like the American grain, much of
the fish went far to its destination—even as far as Spain and the
Mediterranean. Its transportation called for a large fleet, and
the more profitable part of the business lay in distributing rather
than in catching. That profit went chiefly to the German merchants who, well endowed with capital, ships, and aggressive-
ness, pushed Norwegian, Danish, and all other traders out of a
lucrative enterprise.

The demand for fish carried with it one for salt, for the catch
was salted before it was packed. Salt was also needed for pre-
serving meat, and was one of the earliest goods to be carried far
by traders. It was obtained by evaporation of sea water and
from subterranean springs or rock-salt deposits. Every landlord
who had salt resources on his estate tried to develop them, and
from them many monasteries drew large incomes. The most important northern salt-producing areas were the Bay of Biscay
coast and the springs of Lüneburg, just south of Hamburg. "Bay
salt" supplied the English and other western markets, Lüneburg
salt was taken overland to Lübeck and thence to the Scania herring packers, but other shores contributed to the supply, and
springs (e.g., Salzburg) or rock-salt deposits (e.g., in the Carpathians) were exploited.

A seafaring people needed shipbuilding materials, the growth
of towns called for building lumber, and the trade in fish, wine,
salt, and beer created a demand for barrels. Where population was
thickest and the demand for lumber greatest the local supply was
soon exhausted, and the forests of Norway or the Baltic lands
became valuable. From them came furs for the nobility and bourgeoisie; tar, pitch, masts, spars, planks, beams, etc., for the shipyards; rafters, oak or deal boards for floors or for wainscoting
houses, and potash (extracted from wood ashes and used to make
lye or soap for washing or bleaching purposes). Sweden had
copper and iron ore deposits, as well as forests. The latter gave
her a supply of charcoal, which was the staple fuel in all metal
extraction until the eighteenth century. By 1300 Sweden was
winning that reputation as a producer of high-grade iron and
steel which she has held for centuries, while the copper mine of
Stora Kopparberg (the Great Copper Mountain) had already

begun to pour out a stream of metal that has not yet dried up. But the Scandinavian metal output was probably far less than that which German miners were digging out of the hills of central Europe.

How far there was regular interregional trade in the common farm products is not clear. A country like Norway was unable to grow much grain, and must have consumed little or imported supplies regularly. An English king of the twelfth century gave a Norwegian bishop the right to buy a shipload of grain annually, even in years of English scarcity. The new settlers south and east of the Baltic found markets for their rye in Norway, Flanders, and even England. England in good years might have a surplus of grain to spare, which went chiefly to Gascony in exchange for wine; but she "lived very near to the margin of [her] home-grown supplies" (Salzmann), and import was as likely as export. The Hansards carried butter and cheese from one country to another, but if we wish to think of farmers producing a staple for a distant market we must limit our picture to the English and Spanish woolgrowers, the Gascon vignerons, and the Baltic grain growers.

The Hanseatic League.—In the development of traffic over this northern area Scandinavian merchants played the first important part, but gradually the long-range trade passed into the hands of merchants who hailed from a hundred towns scattered between the Rhine and Reval and confederated in the Hanseatic League. The towns which were on or had access to the North Sea were the first to become important—Cologne, Bremen and Hamburg. Cologne's contacts were with all points of the compass—with the industrial and commercial Low Countries, with backward England, with the eastern frontier, and with the south. By A.D. 1000 the "men of the Emperor," who were chiefly Cologne merchants, were visiting London and enjoying royal protection. In 1157 the group (or *hanse*) had a hall there, and was selling German wine. It opened its purse when Richard I came back bankrupt from the third crusade, and in return was virtually exempted (1194) from customs levies and given the right to buy and sell in any fair. Groups from other German towns, especially Hamburg, Lübeck and Bremen, soon appeared in London, and by 1300 the traders from all these towns were working together, with common rights and a common residence.

For the next two hundred years they provided the strongest link between England and northern Europe. In the last quarter of the fourteenth century their ships carried three-fourths of the British wool exports and virtually all those of cloth. They lent money to kings, and as security might be given control of the collection of customs dues, of royal Cornish tin mines, or even of the crown jewels. Financial services won them preferential treatment even over native traders; in 1347, for instance, they paid only 12^d on each cloth exported, but Englishmen paid 14^d and others 33^d. Their walled headquarters included a wharf, a guild hall, armory, houses, and warehouses, giving accommodation for the men who came from some sixty towns to display their wares in the *staalhof* or sample yard. The term "steelyard" came to be applied to the whole settlement, and its occupants were known as the Merchants of the Steelyard.

Trade with England was only one string on the Hanseatic bow. Virtual monopoly of the goods drawn from the Baltic Sea, the Baltic lands, and Norway was the second. The eastward colonizing movement was welcomed by Rhineland and Westphalian traders, and when Lübeck was captured by Henry the Lion in 1158 it was soon filled with merchants from Westphalia. From that base traders advanced along the coast as well as inland, won trade privileges at Wisby and Novgorod, and became more effective rivals of the older Scandinavian traders.

In this trade expansion the German hanses and the towns from which they came were drawn together by common dangers and enemies. One of them was piracy on land or sea; another was the Dane, who owned the Scania peninsula, bestrode the Sound, and disliked the growth of traffic overland between Hamburg and Lübeck. Fear of a Danish attack and damage from pirates led to alliances between Lübeck and other towns; the earliest coalition of which we know was in 1227. Thus while the hanses of merchants in London, Bruges, Wisby, and Novgorod won a recognized, protected, and even favored position from their hosts, the home towns united to clear the traffic lanes, weaken rivals, and facilitate the commercial progress of their citizens.

This double development of merchant groups and of civic action reached high-water mark in the fourteenth century. All merchants trading outside Germany were organized into a kind of super-hanse, with headquarters on Gothland, and meanwhile the cities organized a league or confederation in about 1358. One of the League's first tasks was to crush Denmark. In the Treaty of Stralsund (1370) Denmark had to give her victors two-thirds of the Sound dues during the next fifteen years, hand over some castles defending the strait, give the League veto power in the selection of the next king, and grant or confirm various trading privileges.

With this victory the League reached the climax of its power. It consisted of about eighty towns on the coast and inland. Lübeck, the natural head, summoned and presided over the League diet, which met at least triennially to frame policy; decide questions of war, peace, protection, and privilege; consider problems of currency, shipping, and commercial law; and settle disputes. The League had no army or navy, and no regular sources of revenue, but had to rely on the ships, soldiers, and money of such towns as felt disposed to send them, or on emergency customs duties. Yet it wielded great power, for its field of operation lacked strong territorial monarchies, and its strength was enough to open doors for its own merchants and to close them against others.

German merchants now advanced with greater ease "on a broad front along the whole line of primitive northern Europe, seeking to exploit the wealth of its agriculture, forestry, mining, and fisheries, in exchange for whatever the Hanseatic towns themselves had to offer, either as producers or as middlemen of more abundant and less primitive goods, from wine and beer to the finished products of the textile and metal crafts" (Brinkmann). Apart from Bruges, their outposts were in primary producing lands which had few ships, no strong trading class, and little capital. Such countries were "passive" in commerce, they were "traded with." Economically they were *colonial*, and their commercial policy might be subjected to the control of the alien who served them.

The colonial front ran from Russia and Prussia in a great semicircle to Cornwall, the Bay of Biscay, and Lisbon. From Novgorod the Hansards controlled the westward movement of furs; through Danzig they handled the Prussian grain and lumber; the Baltic supplied them with amber and herrings. In Sweden they controlled forest products and minerals, and Stockholm was virtually a German city. Its mayor was often German, for a time half its administration had to be, and foreign participation in civic affairs was not finally swept away till 1611. Norway's trade passed into Hanseatic hands, and Bergen, center of traffic in cod, butter, and lumber, was even more German than was Stockholm. On the Icelandic fishing grounds English boats were elbowed out by Hansards, and German vessels penetrated as far as the Bay of Biscay and Lisbon, picking up salt and wine.

On all this front, diplomacy, aided occasionally by force, strengthened the Hanseatic grip. The Hansards suppressed piracy but were ready to be pirates themselves when foreign ships entered their preserves. They granted English merchants the same privileges as England gave them, but took care that the grant was more shadow than substance. The residence and activities of foreign merchants in Hanseatic towns were strictly regulated; the sale of ships, or even of fractional interests in them, to foreigners was forbidden; and native merchants were prevented from sending goods in foreign vessels.

The success of the Hansards was not, however, solely due to skill in waving a big stick, in exploiting backward peoples, in murdering rivals, or in aiding bankrupt monarchs. It was also a reward for the service they rendered in developing exchange over a large trade area, and for doing their job with a great measure of skill and efficiency. Their big boats of 1500 to 2000 tons reduced freight costs. Lighthouses were built, buoys were used to mark channels and reefs, and pilots were trained. A body of maritime law was developed or copied from elsewhere to govern relations between merchant, shipowner, captain, and crew; fix the responsibility for payment of damages; prevent overloading or undermanning; and settle problems of discipline afloat. Capital and management were supplied for the development of mineral deposits, and new trade channels were vigorously sought. If the Hansards were brutal to their employees and rivals, if they lacked scruples in their relations with foreigners who stood in their path, they were only true to the codes of their period and calling.

The Mediterranean Trade Area.—Mediterranean trade was partly a matter of selling Levantine and Oriental goods, but there was sufficient regional specialization around that sea to make certain areas stand out as suppliers of particular commodities. Spain had its wool, and while much of it went to Florence Saracen and Christian workers in Spain made and exported cloth. The Moors produced fine leather goods, dressed skins or furs of lamb, kid, hare, and rabbit, and gave superior appearance and names to the humblest pelts. Spain produced iron and steel, and its metal-ware was among the best in Europe. Rice, almonds, figs, oranges, onions, dates, and wine were exported; Seville oil was used for greasing wool before spinning and the reputation of Castile soap was already high. The Barbary coasts yielded one of Europe's few decorative materials, coral. Barbary, Sicily, the Levant, and southern Spain produced sugar, for the Moslem liked candy, and the confectioner was a storehouse of recipes and processes for producing colors and flavors. Behind the coral strands and the sugar canes of North Africa lay the desert; on its fringe sheep and goats were pastured, and across it came slaves, ebony, ivory, gold, and ostrich feathers from Central Africa. Lombardy and Spain were famous for their horses, much in demand as military mounts. Crete, Greece, and the Levant produced sweet wines, alum for the dyer was for a long time drawn from Asia Minor, and Egypt was still a granary. The Black Sea led to amber, furs, and grain; the western Mediterranean was a fishing ground for tunny; Sicily had the sulphur needed for spraying vineyards, and the Adriatic was the chief southern source of salt. Finally, the leading towns had their manufactured specialties.

Yet all this exchange of southern produce seemed of minor importance when compared with that in Asiatic goods, and every great city sought to gain a share of the trade between east and west. European workshops might learn to make some of these goods, but many could be drawn only from east of Suez, for Europe had no deposits of precious stones and was prevented by its climate from growing spices, drugs, and certain dyes. What the herring did for northern trade, spices did for the southern; and when seventeenth-century Holland held the herring trade in one hand and the spice trade in the other its pockets bulged.

The medieval poor probably could not afford spices, and had to rely largely on local herbs—mint, sage, etc.—to give flavor to the coarse meats supplied by elderly cattle, muscular pigs, and sinewy sheep. But the rich used spices lavishly on both salted and fresh viands, and poured sauces and condiments on dishes which were already elaborately compounded and flavored.

Medieval cookery books have no room for foods served *au naturel* or *au jus*. Stuffed pig or swan is eaten with yellow pepper sauce; eels are stuffed with a mixture of ginger, cinnamon, cloves, "grain of Paradise," and nutmegs. Ducklings and young rabbits are made into pasties and treated as follows: "Take plenty of good cinnamon, ginger, cloves, grain of Paradise, half a nutmeg, some mace, and galingale, and bray [mix and beat] them well; moisten with vinegar and verjuice [juice of unripe grapes]; when the pasty is almost cooked, pour the sauce therein and set in the oven to boil. In winter put in more ginger." The spice bill for Edward I's household in 1300 was about $100,000 in modern money.

Commercial Effects of the Crusades.—The Arabs brought Asiatic goods to the door of Europe, but left Europeans to carry them over the threshold. When the crusades began some Italian centers were already in close contact with the Levant, trading, carrying pilgrims, building ships, and accumulating capital and experience. To them the crusades came as a heaven-sent opportunity. There would be freight and passenger earnings for carrying the fighters, profits from supplying the army's needs, abundant space for return cargoes, and commercial privileges waiting to be claimed in conquered lands. The fighting men would need loans, and the lenders knew how to drive hard bargains. If the great warriors were to reap rewards by carving feudal fiefs out of the rich soil of Syria and Palestine, their bourgeois allies must have their share of the loot, and be granted their terms before they raised a sail or moved an oar. A city would transport the armies and their supplies, and its ships would help in capturing towns; but in return it was to receive a portion of the booty and a part of each city it helped to capture. In this ceded area it could have a church, market, mill, oven, and warehouses; it could unload its own ships and trade free of duties; its own court would settle disputes in which its citizens were concerned, and the tax-collector had no power over its property.

Genoa was the first city to take advantage of its opportunities. It helped besiege Antioch (1098), and in return got a church, a market, and thirty houses. In 1100 it was promised a third of every city it helped to capture, a slice of spoils and of port revenues, and thus got a big foothold in several important places. Pisa, Amalfi, Marseilles, Montpellier, and Barcelona obtained similar rewards for their services, but the largest beneficiary was Venice. Her strength was great and the rewards were commensurate. She was willing to hurl her fleet of 200 vessels against any port if she could have one-third of the prize. On such terms she took Sidon and Beirut almost single-handed, and helped capture Acre, of which she got a quarter. She won a quarter of Jerusalem, a third of Tyre and Ascalon, free trade throughout the kingdom of Jerusalem, lands and revenue in Acre, exemption from sales taxes in ports and markets, and courts of her own in each city frequented by her merchants.

For nearly a century the crusaders held most of the lands they had taken, and the western traders exploited their privileges. When the Saracens regained the Holy Land (1187), Venice was hit hard, but the fourth crusade gave her an opportunity to gain far more than she had lost. She agreed (1200) to transport the crusaders to Syria or Egypt and provision them for a season, but they must pay passage money and some other sums before sailing and give Venice half their conquests. When they proved slow in paying, Dandolo, the old, blind, but wily doge, offered to cancel the debt if the crusaders would oblige Venice by capturing Zara, an Adriatic port which had long been a thorn in her side. They did so, and the fleet moved on, only to be diverted to Constantinople, where Venetian merchants were feeling the heat of Genoese and Pisan competition and the coolness of the emperor. The city was captured and pillaged (1204), the emperor deposed, and the plunder divided. Venice got about three-eighths of the city, and the Genoese were evicted; she also gained a virtual monopoly of the trade of the Eastern Empire by controlling the Bosporus and taking the important islands, ports, market centers, and stepping-stones. Almost every strategic point came to her, and as she was already well established in Egypt and soon built up again her connections with the Levant, she was now the foremost trader in Europe.

The infidel who studied the new style in crusading might with justice comment on the way Christians loved one another. Yet such actions were in keeping with the general tone of relations between the Mediterranean trade rivals. Conflicts among Italian cities were real trade wars, fought with diplomacy, alliances, armies, navies, and privateers. Amalfi was sacked by Pisa in 1135, Pisa in turn was ruined by Genoa (by 1284), and Milan strove to damage Genoa by cutting the trade routes from the seaport to the upper Po and the Alps. Genoa and Venice fought almost without ceasing. Genoa in 1261 fomented a revolution in Constantinople which overthrew the emperor, broke the Venetian grip on the Black Sea, and established Genoa as the favored trader, even the monopolist, in the imperial lands. If Genoa attacked Crete, Venice attacked the Genoese quarter in Constantinople and destroyed valuable alum works. If the Genoese had the Venetians expelled from Tyre, the Venetians sacked the Genoese quarters in Acre. In the long process of give and take, Venice eventually emerged the less damaged of the two. By 1300, and certainly by 1400, she was much stronger than her rival; but meanwhile the conflict had helped to thwart the crusades and was partly responsible for leaving Europe's eastern frontier open to successful attack from Asia.

In addition to helping some cities to develop more rapidly than they might otherwise have done, the crusades had other economic effects. They ate up some of the wealth of western Europe, and redistributed some of the rest. The feudal class was in a measure impoverished, and some of its rights and property passed into the hands of peasant or bourgeois. Travel became part of the experience of more people, and facilities for movement multiplied. Some roads were built or improved, and the demand for ships led to a great increase in the size of vessels. One vessel built at Genoa for St. Louis' crusade (1270) was propelled by fifty-two oars, and could carry a hundred horses and a thousand passengers. The largest ships now needed a hundred sailors, had two or three decks and two or three masts. When the traffic in pilgrims and warriors declined these large galleys, propelled by sails and oars, were turned into merchantmen for the long journeys. Navigation slowly improved, for with more sails and better rudders the art of tacking in unfavorable winds was developed. The compass gradually came into use. The accumulation of wealth in Italian hands provided capital for industry and trade, the loans and advances made to the warriors improved the technique of credit, and in the later crusades the employment of mercenary troops helped to revive an old occupation—that of the professional soldier.

Mediterranean Shipping.—By 1200 the Mediterranean seaways were busy once more. Professor Byrne has given us a vivid picture of Genoese medieval shipping. Much of it was coastal, with ships crawling from point to point as far as Sicily or Barcelona. Danger of attack from the land and on the sea caused ships to carry crossbows, lances, headpieces, and fighting men, and to sail in fleets of three to ten vessels, convoyed by state galleys for part of the journey. Some ships went to the North African coast, calling at the Balearic Islands; but the important journeys were to the Levant, Egypt, or the Black Sea. Only one such round trip could be made each year, for much time was spent collecting cargo at each port, and since the Mediterranean can be rough in winter the big ships must hibernate. For these journeys great care had to be taken that the vessel was seaworthy, was not over-loaded or undermanned, and, if the merchant passengers were fastidious, that no mules, horses, falcons, or pilgrims were carried. The course of the voyage was determined by the merchants on board, who decided which ports should be visited or avoided and where the ship should call to pick up news about peace, war, and market conditions.

When the traders reached their destination they entered the Genoese *fondaco* where merchants and agents from Genoa lived and traded under the rule of their own consul. They collected spices, perfumes, fabrics, and slaves—Syrian female slaves were in great demand as domestic servants in the west. They sold the metals, furs, leather, lumber, wool, wine, cloth, soap, almonds, olive oil, etc., of Europe, or paid for their purchases in gold. In 1399 a fleet sailed from Venice for Syria, carrying 250,000 gold ducats.

In essentials this picture of Genoese shipping is true also of Venice, Pisa, Montpellier, Marseilles, and Barcelona. In the case of Venice the canvas would be bigger and would show a government regulating trade with great strictness and encouraging it with skill and energy. Venice had no agricultural class to complicate its political issues, and its policy could be shaped with a singleness of purpose vouchsafed to few governments in the world's history. That policy was a combination of state enterprise, aid and protection of private enterprise, regulation of shipping, and exclusive exploitation by Venetians of all sea trade leading to Venice. Every year from the twelfth to the eighteenth century the doge solemnly cast a wedding ring into the Adriatic, and every effort was made to keep the marriage monogamous by beating down or capturing rival ports, by restricting, taxing, or shutting out foreign ships, by imposing special tariffs or shipping dues, by forbidding merchants to use foreign vessels, by embargoes, and by seeking preferential or monopolistic favors from foreign rulers.

The building and equipping of ships were regulated to insure seaworthiness. A mark was made on the outside of each hull, and ships could not sail if they were so overloaded that this mark was more than a certain distance below the waterline. Ballasting, manning, provision of lifeboats, the supply of sails, discipline, the arrangement of cargo—all that bore on the safety of the trip and that might be neglected or scamped by shipowners eager for large profits—came under control and inspection. Since a ship's safety depended in part on the possession of good ropes and private enterprise apparently failed to produce them, the state in 1303 established a rope factory to protect "the security of our galleys and ships, and similarly of our sailors and capital." This factory was operated by the government till late in the eighteenth century.

Much of Venice's long-distance sea trade was conducted in state-owned ships. The cargo space was sold at public auction, but the actual work of transportation was kept in the hands of the government. The ships sailed in fleets, well armed, at fixed times on certain set routes; and by 1400 there were six regular liner services—to the Black Sea, Syria, Egypt, North Africa, Spain, and the North Sea. These ships were large for the Middle Ages, but their number was not great, for the traffic was chiefly in goods of small bulk. In 1388 the three fleets that sailed eastward contained only nine state galleys. The Flanders galleys never numbered more than five, and the Genoese in 1402 had only six galleys in the Levantine trade. But in addition there were swarms of smaller vessels, some engaged in local coastal traffic, some going far afield. In the fifteenth century the Venetian merchant fleet is said to have numbered over 3000 vessels employing about 36,000 sailors.

While Venice and Genoa dominated the Mediterranean picture, other centers farther west gradually crept into importance. Marseilles, Arles, Montpellier and Narbonne shared in the general trade expansion, looking southward to North Africa as well as eastward. Trade agreements with African rulers allowed

French merchants to set up their "factories" and obtain wheat, coal, wool, skins, and minerals in return for wines, spices, perfumes, and cloth. Marseilles was well established in Syria by 1250, and in later years Montpellier became an important spice market. In Spain the slow steady recovery of the country by Christian rulers led to the union of Aragon and Catalonia and to the emergence of a new commercial and political power in the Mediterranean. By the thirteenth century Barcelona had become a large manufacturing and trading city exploiting the wool and metals of the hinterland, and trading with North Africa and the east. It had consuls presiding over groups of its traders in the Levant, a strong grip on North Africa, much traffic outside the Strait of Gibraltar, well-developed banking institutions, and a code of sea law (framed about 1250-1260) which was remarkably complete. The capture of Sicily by Aragon in 1282 opened the trade of that island to Barcelona on favorable terms. Other conquests followed and put behind the trader the prestige of a powerful territorial state whose subjects must be respected.

Trade Between Northern and Southern Europe.—The third main division of medieval trade was that conducted between the Mediterranean lands and the north. It was partly an exchange of the wares of two different climatic areas, partly an exchange of manufactures of the advanced south for the food and raw material of the backward zones, but there was passage southward of some manufactured articles in which some northern centers excelled.

The early development of this trade was the work of the Syrians and the peddlers; but with the revival of the Mediterranean towns Italians and Provençals moved northward, while Scandinavians and Germans worked southward, and from the beginning of the crusades transcontinental traffic grew rapidly. Until about the beginning of the fourteenth century the traffic was almost entirely by land and river. The Alpine passes were bottle necks through which much of it passed. West of the Alps lay the corridor up the Rhone, the Saône, and thence to the headwaters of the Seine or Meuse. The Varangian route from the Caspian or Black Sea to the Baltic was damaged and even broken by the advancing Mongols, who by the middle of the thirteenth century had captured Kiev and cut Novgorod off from its old contact with the southern seas; but this only threw more traffic on to the roads farther west.

Some of the travelers on these roads went far afield. Italians pushed to the Rhine and Bohemia, crossed the northern seas, settled in towns like London or Prague, and in some centers had their *fondaci*. The northerners also came southward and either met them at some halfway point or descended into north Italy itself. Thus we find twelfth-century merchants gathering up cloth in northern textile towns ranging alphabetically from Abbeville to Ypres, carrying it to the Champagne fairs, and there selling it to men who transported it to Genoa to sell to cloth finishers and exporters. Every year six big caravans moved out of Genoa to buy and fetch these fabrics; they went with almost clock-like punctuality, despite the character of the country which lay between them and Champagne. In Venice land trade with the north was gradually allowed to pass into alien hands. The Venetians evidently found that sea traffic gave them a greater return, left the Germans to carry on the trade through the Brenner and other passes, welcomed them to Venice, and provided the famous *fondaco dei Tedeschi* (German factory). There only were they allowed to stay and conduct business, subject to strict regulations which sought to preserve order and prevent smuggling.

Land Transportation.—The modern road is the product of labor-saving equipment, technical knowledge, suitable materials, and governments with authority and money. Between the collapse of the Roman Empire and the eighteenth century few rulers had the essentials for good road-making on a large scale. Monasteries, churches, towns, or feudal lords might care for a ford, bridge or piece of highway; bequests might be made or guilds be formed for repair or maintenance, and a village community might be stirred into action by mud and flood. Crusades, pilgrimages, and trade led to some improvement and to an increased supply of inns. Strong kings or others who controlled a large piece of territory sometimes saw the value of good roads, and tried to compel landlords and tenants to repair the highways passing through their district. Hence while travel facilities seem primitive when measured by modern standards, they were not uniformly poor, they did permit movement, and they were improved slowly but substantially. Movement was slow, and even in the early nineteenth century travel at nine or ten miles an hour was regarded as extraordinary. Twenty miles a day might be a good journey; the Canterbury pilgrims took two or three days to cover sixty miles, and had time to tell many long tales. When news and mail had to be carried quickly couriers were employed. Some cities and big financiers had regular courier services; one went monthly from Bruges to Barcelona, a thousand miles, in about twenty-four days. On shorter journeys this pony express might cover a hundred miles in a day; but in the carriage of goods the barge, the pack horse, or the wagon, moving at a walking pace, was the normal method of transportation.

Safety was more important than speed, and the human enemies of trade were often more fierce than the physical. Europe still had its wild animals, but they were less to be feared than wild men of high and low degree. Not all highway robbers were as high-principled or romantic as Robin Hood, and the outlaw was more than a character in fiction. A pass or forest might be haunted by a gang which was supported by, or even composed of, prominent wealthy local inhabitants, and a feudal baron might regard a traveling bourgeois as fair plunder. Safety from such molestation varied with the strength of king or emperor. William the Conqueror suppressed brigandage so sternly that it was said "a man might go over his kingdom unhurt with his bosom full of gold," but during Stephen's reign anarchy prevailed and "every man robbed another if he could." When Henry IV restored peace to Germany in 1093 the chronicler said, "And now the boatman on the river glided in safety by the dungeons of the robber barons who had hitherto fattened upon his spoils; the roads were no longer infested by marauding bands; the forests gave no shelter to lurking brigands; the highways were open to the trader and the wayfarer to pass on their way in peace; and the professional depredators were themselves reduced to that beggary and penury that they had so long inflicted upon others." In France the kings tried to make nobles responsible for outrages committed on their estates. In England a statute of 1285 decreed that "highways leading from one market town to another shall be enlarged, where bushes, woods, and dykes be, so that there be neither dyke, tree, nor bush whereby a man may lurk to do hurt within 200 feet of either side of the way."

In Germany the cities formed leagues to protect their merchants against attack and toll abuses. Bishops and lords seized any opportunity to set up new toll stations, and in the thirteenth century the sum paid on goods passing from Bingen down the narrow castle-strewn gorge to Coblenz might amount to about two-thirds the actual value of the cargo. If new tolls had been the price paid for improved roads, rivers, or protection, discontent might have been allayed; but they were largely tribute exacted by titled racketeers. To protect themselves merchants traveled in bands, and the towns to which they belonged joined hands. In 1226 the middle and upper Rhine towns formed a league and in 1254 a larger League of the Rhine united seventy towns. It patrolled the roads, and operated a large fleet of armed boats on the main stream and its tributaries from Cologne to Basel. Having suppressed marauders, it then attacked oppressive toll-collectors, and many a castle or toll-station was destroyed. Eventually the League mixed in politics and was wrecked by faction and the superior strength of its opponents. A third league—the Swabian League—was formed in 1285, lived for a century, and then sank in the political morass. The Swiss towns opposed the levy of burdensome tolls on roads and passes, and in their case joint action led to permanent confederation and the birth of the Swiss nation.

Sea Transportation.—For exchange between the North Sea and the Mediterranean, water communication would seem more economical than land carriage; yet there was apparently little attempt to develop the sea route until the end of the thirteenth century, and even heavy raw materials like wool and metals went overland from England to the south. Perhaps the volume of trade did not justify the use of the sea; the journey would be long, the route lay through two bottle necks—the Strait of Gibraltar and the English Channel—where attack by pirates was easy, and the climatic conditions in the open Atlantic were uncongenial. In the last decades of the thirteenth century, however, there was a great outburst of maritime enterprise in Genoa. One venture would have been epoch-making if it had succeeded, for in 1284 a company was organized to circumnavigate Africa. Much money was raised, and in 1291 two ships sailed through the Strait of Gibraltar and turned south. Of their fate nothing is known, and Europe had to wait two more centuries for its sea route to the Orient. A second venture fared better, for it sought only to establish sea contact with northwestern Europe. The first Genoese galleys reached the English Channel about 1300, and the arrival of one of them in London in 1303 was regarded as "news" by a chronicler.

The Venetians quickly met this Genoese move by establishing a rival service. In 1314 their first galley reached Antwerp safely, and from that time onward a regular fleet of heavily armed vessels was sent annually. It crawled along the Italian coast, called at Spanish and North African ports, and put into Lisbon. In the English Channel it divided; some ships went to Southampton, Sandwich, and London, while the others sailed to Bruges or Antwerp to meet the Hansard and Low Countries merchants. The Flanders galleys took on a cargo of raw materials and manufactured goods, sailed to England to join their fellows who had been picking up wool, hides, tin, and unfinished cloth, and the fleet then returned to Venice.

The round trip might occupy a whole year, and it may be doubted therefore whether the actual cost and time of transportation were much smaller than those of the overland route. The assertion was made about 1500 that great quantities of English wool and tin were being carried overland to Venice, and at a lower freight cost than was charged by the galleys. By that time the Barbary pirates, who had never been suppressed, had become much more audacious, numerous, and dangerous. The chief advantages of the sea route were probably the ability to move more goods, freedom from interference due to land wars, the elimination of some middlemen, and the concentration of control and profits in the hands of a few entrepreneurs belonging to the city that sent out the ships.

Enough has been said to show how European trade quickened and extended its range during the later Middle Ages. Its volume was small when compared with that of a modern age equipped with facile transportation. Insecurity marked it at every turn because of the changeable moods and pressing financial needs of rulers, the seesaw of commercial rivalries, and the capricious opening and closing of markets. The eastern routes might be disturbed by movements of Asiatic peoples. The western highways might be blocked by some war, or by the anarchy which ensued when peace turned soldiers adrift or destitution drove villagers to desperation. A market might be starved of goods and prices might soar, only to have the former glutted and the latter smashed when a cargo unexpectedly came to port. Difficulties over exchange rates might make it hard or ruinous to settle debts incurred at a distance, documents went astray, ships were wrecked or plundered, couriers might be waylaid, and rumors were sometimes smoke without fire.

Yet despite what seem heartbreaking obstacles, merchants, fortunately ignorant of the facilities they lacked by being born five centuries too soon, adventured their money and wares. A man in Nuremberg would have his lines spread as far afield as Poland, the Black Sea, Bruges, and Barcelona. A lowly Italian dealer (Datini of Prato) gradually wove a net so far-flung that it covered Avignon, Florence, Pisa, Genoa, Milan, Barcelona, Valencia, Majorca, Bruges, Paris, London, North Africa, and the main ports of the Levant. He dealt in spices, arms and armor, cloth, religious pictures and ornaments, cotton veils, fruits, wool, handkerchiefs—anything that promised a reward. From his various outposts came 120,000 letters in fifty years (1360-1410). Some of their authors had written far into the night, laboriously penning their requests or reports in duplicate or triplicate, and had intrusted them to friends, pilgrims, priests, ship captains, or special couriers for delivery. The note of urgency with which they described events or sought information reveals the insecurity and sensitiveness of the markets in which they were working; but it also reveals the width of opportunity that lay open to the man who had courage, tenacity, energy, foresight, sagacity, and luck.

BIBLIOGRAPHY

See end of Chapter X.

CHAPTER X

MEDIEVAL INDUSTRIAL AND COMMERCIAL ORGANIZATION

MEDIEVAL industrial and commercial organization reveals as great variety as does rural society. The industrial unit ranged from the virtually self-supplying family to the large group of wage earners, each a specialist in one process, working together under an employer who sold the product in distant markets. Every kind of exchange was practiced, from direct barter to sale on long-term credit and to contracts which ran for more than a decade. The medium of exchange might be commodity money, coins, or the medieval equivalent of "commercial paper." Sales took place in fairs, markets, and shops, or in private transactions. The business unit ran from the one-man firm to the large group of men who pooled their money in a joint stock and in addition used sums lent or deposited by others. Income might be the product of humble production or petty trade, or, at the other extreme, it might be the reward of large-scale long-distance trade and operations in high finance.

The relative importance of these different types of structure or method depends on the time, the place, and the occupation. The further we come past A.D. 1000 the more complex and capitalistic is the organization of some branches of industry, trade, and agriculture; the further we get away from the influence of towns and trade the more simple and self-sufficing is the economic structure; but even in the largest cities the consumer produces some of the goods he needs or buys them direct from some petty craftsman.

INDUSTRIAL ORGANIZATION

We have seen the villagers at work in their homes and the craftsmen and women employed in the big households making goods for use in the home or on the farm. This type of production has been called *usufacture* and in the picture of world industrial history it covers by far the greater amount of the canvas.

167

But just as self-sufficiency had to be tempered by dependence on external supplies of materials that could not be obtained locally, so usufacture might be modified by drawing on the special or superior skill or equipment of others for certain processes or products. The special equipment might be the village mill, wine press, oven, or smithy; the skill was supplied by the miller, baker, and blacksmith, or by craftsmen who rambled from village to village carrying a kit of tools. Wandering weavers would come to a house which had prepared a quantity of yarn and possessed a hand-loom; they wove the yarn into cloth, and then passed on. Harness- or shoe-makers carried tools, thread, nails, cobbler's wax, etc., while woolcombers carried their combs and the charcoal stove in which to heat them. They worked on material belonging to their patrons, and wandered because there was not sufficient work to allow them to settle in any one spot. They might work in the manor house as well as in the farmhouse. Like the peddler, they ranged over a wide territory on a regular circuit, and when a rambling woolcomber confessed in a seventeenth-century folksong, "My failing is I drink strong beer," he was probably revealing a characteristic common to ramblers rather than to woolcombers.

With the rise of larger villages or towns the volume of business became big enough to allow some workers to confine their movements to a smaller area and even to set up permanent shops. Town workers in leather, cloth, and metals, dyers, fullers, finishers, and tailors labored on materials brought them by customers. Even the goldsmith often worked on gold, silver, and jewels supplied by his patrons, and a man who wished to have a piece of armor made might provide the metal. Itinerant workers have almost vanished; the knife sharpener and the seamstress who goes out sewing are pale-faced short-range descendants. The settled worker survives in the cobbler, the watch repairer, and the tailor who makes a suit from cloth supplied by his customer, while the dry cleaner, launderer, and repair garage are newcomers to the class.

The next step came when the craftsman, in addition to working on customers' goods, bought materials and made them into finished articles, either in response to orders or in the hope of finding a buyer. The front of his workshop became a store; he displayed his wares on a counter on the sidewalk or in a window, sold in market place or fair, or even peddled his products through the countryside. Professor Gras suggests that this organization be called *retail handicraft*; there was still direct contact between craftsman and consumer, but the former now sold the product of his equipment and skill, not the use of them. Retail handicraft remained an important part of economic organization until modern times, especially in industries which supplied a purely local demand for food, clothing, buildings and furniture. Tailors, shoemakers, butchers, bakers, and many others made goods and sold them to consumers. The unit of production was small; the craftsman used the labor of the members of his family, but might employ a journeyman or two and be training an apprentice. His equipment was not costly, and unless he worked in valuable raw materials or carried a large stock of finished articles, which was unlikely, his capital requirements were small.

Retail handicraft was unsuited to the production and distribution of wares which depended on distant sources of raw material, on scattered or distant markets, on customers who were slow in paying their debts, or on methods which called for a large outlay on equipment. If the craftsman could not go far afield to get his material or sell his wares, some middleman must do it for him. If the material was costly, the cost of production great, and the customer laggard in paying bills, the small craftsman must let someone else make the outlay and wait for the money. The rise of luxury trades, of industries which served large markets, and of long-distance carriage of raw materials therefore placed an increasing number of men between the producer of those materials and the craftsman or between the craftsman and the ultimate consumer. When the artisan produced chiefly for the middleman he had become a *wholesale handicraftsman*.

Middleman and craftsman might meet on terms of equality and independence. The latter might dispose of his goods in an open market, and be free to sell to any consumer or to any trader. But this condition gave way in some of the big export and luxury industries to a different relationship. The trader gave the craftsman orders for goods, or took his whole output at an agreed price; he might supply the raw material (especially if it was costly) and even the implements, or advance the money with which to buy material or pay wages. If he merely bought the goods, the craftsman was still economically independent, free to work for anyone; but the more the trader financed the producer the greater was the latter's dependence, and the nearer he drew to being a wage earner. Some craftsmen sank through debt into that condition; others may have relied on the trader for their equipment and raw material from the start; but others prospered, employed many journeymen, and rose to be traders, giving out orders and putting out material to their less fortunate fellows.

This development went furthest in the textile industries of Italy and the Low Countries. The Florentine cloth merchant (who was often a successful weaver) used his capital to buy English or Spanish wool in bulk, pay wages, and carry on till goods were sold and paid for. In his central warehouse he had the wool sorted, and then put it out to be spun by spinsters who worked at home. The yarn was brought back to the warehouse, wound on bobbins or made into warps, and put out to be made into cloth by domestic weavers. The piece was then sent out to be fulled, then to be dyed, finished, and packed; but these final processes might be done in shops owned by the merchant. If the last process of an industry consisted of the assembling of a number of parts, e.g., armor or harness, the material for each part was put out to be made up by different groups of workers, and the parts were then assembled in a central workshop.

In this system of production there was some congregation of workers under the employer's roof. In dyeing and finishing shops men had to work together under strict supervision to insure that the final processes were well done. In the silk-throwing shops of Bologna and Lucca large power-driven machines, attended by many women and children, were used by 1272 to twist and reel silk yarn, and the glass-makers of Venice were gathered together in a workshop on the island of Murano. But much work was done where it had always been done—at home or in a shop attached to the home, and in the Florentine woolen industry a corps of persons was employed putting out and fetching back the goods. Rural and urban workers alike were enlisted; and spinning, which had long been a part of domestic activity, now became a paid occupation, a minor source of income.

This type of industrial organization is called *Verlagssystem* in German, and the man who handed out material or orders was the *Verleger*. In English the only possible label seems to be *Putting-out System*, which is ugly but has the merit of explaining itself. The system was known in the ancient world, and was well rooted in Italy and the southern Netherlands by the twelfth or thirteenth century. It presented opportunities for an economical division of function between those who specialized on directing, financing, and selling on the one hand, and those who supplied skilled labor on the other. It also gave opportunities for the conflict of interests between capital and labor. In the early thirteenth century Sire Jehan Boinebroke, of Douai, organized the production of the cloths he exported by supplying material to small master craftsmen and wage earners. As a powerful member of the local ruling class, he was able to exploit his workers to the utmost and ruthlessly suppress any dissatisfaction they might express. He was accused of defrauding them, of paying in truck (goods) instead of in money, of threatening them if they murmured, and of evicting them from their homes. "Thanks to his overwhelming political influence the capitalist might permit himself anything he pleased where labour was concerned" (Pirenne), and the revolts of workers against their political and economic masters sprinkled the annals of Flemish and Italian cities with blood. In Germany, France, Holland, and England the putting-out system developed, possibly later, and was an important feature of industrial life till the eighteenth or nineteenth century.

Like manufacturing, mining showed great diversity of organization. Where minerals were found on or near the surface little capital was needed and the mining unit was small. German farmers dug iron ore and smelted it with charcoal, and there was some search for alluvial gold. Deeper deposits required large outlays for equipment and the sinking of shafts. A landlord might provide this capital, borrow it, or form a syndicate in which kings, nobles, clergy, and rich merchants would invest. Sometimes the right to mine would be leased, or granted as a concession in return for some loan. Mining therefore became a field for investment, and capital migrated from wealthy cities to the mountains and the backwoods. Shares, or fractions of them, were bought and sold—we know of a transaction concerning one-eighth of a share in the Störa Kopparberg. Most of the shares in that mine were owned by people who played no part in working it, including a bishop, a king, a royal official's wife, and the widow of a Lübeck merchant. Genoese financiers poured money into Polish salt mines, while Italian and German capital and German miners were to be found wherever there were minerals to be exploited. The miners were hired workers, with fixed hours and wages and subject to severe discipline. Mining was thus one of the first occupations to possess such capitalistic features as a wage-earning class, large-scale production, costly equipment, and constant need of more capital for development. In return it might give large fortunes to those who were willing to risk their funds and at the end of the Middle Ages some outstanding financiers, such as the Fuggers, the Welzers, and the Hochstetters, had both thumbs deep in the mining pie.

Building was an industry apart. Its products were not usually for sale, and the consumer took the initiative in bringing them into being. Most houses, even manor houses, were built of wood, clay, straw, reeds, and tiles; only gradually and for large edifices was stone introduced. Much work was done by amateur builders, who built or repaired their own dwellings, with some aid from carpenter or thatcher. Landlords' country homes might be the product of *corvée*, or of artisans attached to the house; but the big tasks were done for the crown, the great lords, the church, and the cities in answer to the call of defense, luxury, piety, civic pride, or rivalry. Only the lay and ecclesiastical great could command the money needed to buy and transport the material and pay the big wage bills. An army of 400 masons, 1000 laborers, and 230 other men was needed to build one Welsh castle. The workers were wage earners, who labored under the direction of some superintendent on plans prepared by an architect who was often the master mason. Some of them remained in one spot for years, but others wandered round seeking work, or were impressed and taken long distances when a king ordered his sheriffs to collect labor for some building project. Some tasks took a long time: one Welsh castle took thirty-eight years to complete, and the nave of Westminster Abbey took 150 years. Some pieces which demanded special skill—such as church interior decorations, images, and statues—might be bought from urban craftsmen who worked on orders and made stock in anticipation of demand. We get a hint of mass production of standard patterns when an English image-maker has trouble with an agent to whom he has delivered fifty-eight heads of John the Baptist.

COMMERCIAL ORGANIZATION

In much medieval commerce trader and traveler were synonymous. The humblest merchant was the peddler, carrying on his back, on a pack horse, or on a wagon, a stock of miscellaneous small goods. One thirteenth-century French peddler announced that he had girdles, gloves, cords for viols, needles, thimbles, purses, veils, arrow points of iron, shoebuckles, pins of brass and silver, kerchiefs of linen for young beaux and of hemp for clowns, rolling pins, brooches, cowbells, tablets and pens for clerks. For ladies' toilets he had razors, tweezers, mirrors, toothbrushes, toothpicks, combs, rouge and powder. He had dice large and small, including "two which when thrown fall on the aces." For children he had whipping tops, and for old women paternosters. Some of these men fared so well that they became big merchants. One twelfth-century English peddler made a fortune and became a saint, while an Icelandic peddler became a great landowner and founded a family so famous that one of the sagas recorded its history. But many peddlers had reputations far from saintly, and were sometimes accused of receiving stolen goods or of having killed a cat for its skin.

Higher in the scale came the merchants who handled the trade in raw materials, food, manufactures and eastern imports. These men accompanied their goods, and groups of them were to be found traversing the roads, chartering ships, attending fairs, or resting in a *fondaco* in a distant city. To some of them success brought the opportunity to stay at home, to conduct their operations from a city office and warehouse, and to work afield through partners, agents, or employees. The appearance of a class of *sedentary* merchants was a sign that medieval trade was growing up; but many traveling traders never grew rich enough to desert the road and sea.

MARKETS AND FAIRS

The formal exchange of commodities took place in market place and fairground. Much trade was conducted privately, but we know most about the transactions carried on in public. Market and fair were alike in some respects. Both were held at a set place and time, and sellers knew that if they took their wares to the appointed spot on the proper day they would find buyers gathered there. In an age of small trade volume and slow transportation, this knowledge centralized supply and demand and saved time. Both were controlled and protected by some sponsor; and while they had their strict rules and their tolls, stall fees, and other charges, they were free from some of the restrictions which towns imposed on retail trade in the interest of the local dealer.

The chief differences between market and fair were of degree rather than of kind. The typical market was a weekly gathering of people from a small area. The normal transaction might be between producer and consumer; but gradually the middleman crept in, buying goods for resale, especially those goods which a district or town produced in quantities beyond the needs of local customers. This was true of some industrial wares, e.g., cloth or metal goods, as well as of farm produce, and in some textile regions the weekly or semiweekly cloth market flourished until the nineteenth century. The area served by a market was limited; the producer could come, do his business, and get home, all in one day. Hence markets were sprinkled so thickly over the countryside that in parts of thirteenth-century England they competed with one another for custom, and attempts were made to prevent a new market from being set up within a certain distance of an existing one. Yet the fact that a lawyer could suggest 6⅔ miles as the minimum desirable distance between markets is an indication of the local character of the business transactions.

If a town grew large, foods must be brought in from a much wider area, a weekly market would be insufficient, and goods must be offered for sale two, three, or more times a week. The market place might be divided up, and each part reserved for the sale of one kind of commodity; or a number of specialized market places might be required; and the need for protecting goods from bad weather might lead to the erection of halls or sheds. Such developments gave the large town an almost continuous market, properly housed, and supplemented by shops.

The fair was a bigger market, held much less frequently, and attracting goods and traders from a far wider area. Sometimes it was little more than a special local market held for the sale of the district's wool clip, the harvest surplus, or the livestock that the farmer decided he would not try to carry through the winter. But often it had a national, a continental, or even a cosmopolitan flavor, and was frequented by middlemen who brought goods gathered in from a wide territory or who wished to replenish their supplies. Its trade was wholesale rather than retail, and the only consumers present were those who lived nearby. It gave merchants the right to deal with one another wholesale or to sell retail, a right which did not exist in ordinary town trade. It might last several days; yet even then the time might be too short. A second fair might therefore be established, or other fairs would spring up, within the same general district but so spaced in time as to provide an almost continuous fair for those who cared to move from place to place.

Periodical gatherings of buyer and seller were well known to the ancient world. They were held on frontiers, at neutral points, or alongside temples. The relation between gods and mammon was intimate, for the crowds gathered at a temple for a feast made a large body of customers, the gifts they gave the temple were sold, and the protection of the gods hovered over trade as well as worship. As Christianity spread, the church established fairs and markets, sponsored those already in existence, spread the peace of God over the trader and his wares, and profited by the sale of its own produce or the money collected in tolls and stall fees. The commercial value of relics in attracting pilgrims was realized by clergy and laity alike. Nidaros in Norway became a great pilgrim, healing, and trading center when St. Olaf was buried there; Venice got the bones of St. Mark and the hand of St. Bartholomew; and Cologne took the relics of the three kings from Milan as an additional magnet. Finally, the worshipers who gathered weekly in church exchanged goods before or after service. "The Sabbatical sanctity of Sunday was largely a growth of post-Reformation or Puritan times" (Salzmann), and despite occasional denunciation trade and worship were twin Sunday occupations.

If the church often led, lay lords were not slow to recognize the benefit of trade facilities both to the community and to their own pockets. In theory the right of a lord to hold a market or fair on his estate could be obtained only by a specific grant from the crown. The right was eagerly sought, and in times of weak monarchs might be taken without leave. In England a royal charter was needed to allow the lord to collect tolls and stallage and to protect him from the rise of nearby rural markets which might become "tortious nuisances." In the thirteenth century 3300 such charters were issued. On the continent the same expansion of market centers took place, and by 1300 every country was well equipped for exchange, large or small, wholesale or retail, local or long distance.

In the market the simple transactions between neighbors were fairly easily regulated by local officials. (See Chapter XI.) In the fair the task of control was more difficult and the need for speedy settlement of disputes much greater. Men of all nationalities were there; sales involving large quantities of goods were being made, usually on credit; many different currencies were brought together; and principals, agents, or partners were buying, selling, borrowing, lending, and making contracts. If this gathering was to function smoothly it must have protection from violence, and a court in which justice would be dispensed promptly. The Mediterranean traders had a long legacy of customs and usages for dealing with disputes concerning such matters as contracts, sales, debts, trespass, bankruptcy, and purchase or sale by agent or partner. The northern traders had worked out certain acceptable rules of the game, and in such great interregional meeting grounds as the Champagne fairs these rules met and fused in a merchant law which was one of the pioneer pieces of international law. In England the fair court was known as the Pie-powder Court (from *pieds poudrés*, i.e., dusty feet). Merchants came to it, with the dust of the road or fairground thick upon them, to state their case; rules of procedure were simple, red tape was rare, judgment was promptly delivered, and execution followed immediately. If the offender failed to meet the verdict he was banned from the fair. All important documents, contracts, acknowledgments of debt, or promises to pay were officially sealed by the clerk of the fair, and obligations might be enforced for as long as thirty years.

Of the hundreds of fairs scattered over medieval Europe, some won great fame. That of St. Denis in Paris went back to at least 629. In the eighth and ninth centuries the Scandinavian traders had many concentration points between Nidaros and Novgorod, and the latter place was already winning a reputation as fur mart. By 1100 a group of Flemish fairs was being visited by the merchants of Lombardy, and the Easter fair at Cologne was famous. In England the four great fairs—Northampton, St. Ives, Boston, and Winchester—were eventually eclipsed by Sturbridge Fair near Cambridge. There for three weeks each year were gathered English wool or cloth merchants, Venetians and Genoese with Oriental and Italian wares, Flemings with cloth, Spaniards and French with wine, Greeks with currants and raisins, and Hansards with Baltic and Russian fur, amber, timber, or tar.

The Champagne Fairs.—On the continent the most famous fairs were those of Champagne. Champagne was a fertile area east and southeast of Paris, on or near the upper reaches of the Saône, Loire, Seine, Marne, Meuse, and Moselle. It thus lay across one of the main land routes between south and north, with easy access to central France and western Germany. Its counts kept their territory fairly free from war, pursued an intelligent policy of internal improvements, and kept order. There was a fair at Troyes in the fifth century, one at Châlons and one at Lagny in the tenth. By the twelfth century, six annual fairs had become well organized and widely known, and as each one lasted some weeks or even months, there was a fair in full swing at some point during almost the whole year. The count nursed the traffic carefully, gave protection on the roads and rivers, provided a smoothly working court and erected halls and warehouses in each center. The trade in cloth, skins, and furs was most important; but there was traffic in almost every kind of commodity, including Oriental and Levantine goods, horses, cattle, wine, parchment, cutlery, pots and pans, peddler's wares, and even old clothes. On the fringe of the fair amusement or amazement was provided by jugglers, conjurers, minstrels, wild-beast shows, acrobats, and human or animal freaks.

The Champagne fairs played an important part in the development of credit. The practice of buying or borrowing at one fair and of promising to pay at a later one brought the fair letter (*lettre de foire*) into being, for this letter recorded the promise. Kings imitated their subjects in borrowing or buying in this way, as when the English king in 1240 agreed that goods bought for him at one fair should be paid for at the next. In some later fairs credits seemed more important than commodities. The papal agents or those who financed the kings of Spain and France went to the fairs of Lyons or Geneva after 1400, or to those of northwest Italy or Castile after 1500, to pay the kings' creditors or to borrow more from them. The interest on loans and the profits made in money-changing or other services made the fairs attractive to Italian financiers of all kinds, while the credit and clearing-house facilities permitted trade to be carried on more easily in an age which had little ready cash and few facilities for its speedy or safe movement.

The golden age of the Champagne fairs ran from about 1150 to 1280. Then the district passed by marriage to the French king, who imposed heavier taxes and charges and attacked his Jewish and Italian creditors. The fairs shrank in popularity, and belated efforts to restore life to them failed. Trade shifted to the sea lanes after 1300, as galleys began to ply from Italy to England, Antwerp, and Bruges. Bruges, the meeting point of northern and southern sea routes, granted foreign merchants the right to trade freely with one another and set up a special court to deal promptly with disputes. It thus provided many of the facilities of a fair, but the business could be transacted on several days a week or even daily all the year round. Overland trade found a new center in the fairs of Geneva, a city with a good location and a wide-awake duke. Then in 1420 a fair was established at Lyons, and the French king gave it valuable privileges. The Duke of Savoy retaliated by improving further the conditions at Geneva, but from this bidding and counterbidding Lyons emerged victor, and by the early sixteenth century was one of the leading commodity and financial centers of the west.

The fair gradually gave way to more direct or continuous trading contacts as the volume of business grew. Wool merchants went to farm or abbey to buy supplies. Cloth markets grew up in towns like Bruges. Hanseatic and Italian houses established branches in distant spots, employed agents, and thus got nearer to sources of supply or to customers. But markets and fairs showed great staying power, and in special cases or in backward areas continued to draw people together long after the end of the Middle Ages. Even today most European towns have their market days, when retailers purchase their supplies from farmers or merchants, and the vegetables, meats, and fruits sold in market places or halls to consumers compete with the goods offered all through the week by the stores. Wool, cattle, or horse fairs still take place; sale by auction is a popular method of selling some materials; while the Leipzig fair, once a great international annual market, is still an important shop window and shop to which sellers send goods or samples from all lands in order to show (and sell) their wares to customers who come from every continent.

THE BUSINESS UNIT

Medieval commerce, mining, and shipping could not in many cases be conducted with the labor and capital of one individual, and the business unit was often an alliance or fusion of interests. The sedentary merchant needed someone to take his goods to distant buyers and to gather in the wares he needed. He might send out an employee, or appoint an agent who went with the goods or received them at the end of the journey; the large Italian firms had branches or agencies in the chief trade centers of Europe and the Near East. He might intrust his wares to a merchant who was going abroad or to the captain of a ship; or he and his fellows might employ a *supercargo*, who would undertake the sale of goods for many merchants at various ports of call and spend the receipts on goods his patrons desired. Since many goods that were sent out had not been ordered beforehand, much depended on the ability and honesty of the person to whom they were intrusted.

Until the joint stock company appeared (see Chapter XV) the partnership was the usual device for uniting two or more persons in a common enterprise. Partnerships were of three chief types. (1) The capital partner might supply all the goods, defray all the expenses, and risk the loss of his funds; the trading partner provided no capital, but bore the burden and fatigue of travel and trade, faced storms and pirates, and took the risk of losing his life or of having no reward for his labor if the enterprise failed. If the venture was successful, the capitalist might receive three-fourths of the profits, and the trader one-fourth. This arrangement was well known in Babylonia, Greece, and Rome; the Arabs used it widely, and it was common in the Italian cities by 1100. It was known as *commenda*; the stay-at-home partner commended his goods to the care of a trader, whose interest and energy would be stimulated by the knowledge that his reward was proportionate to his success. The trader might carry goods supplied by many capitalists, and the capitalist might commend goods to many traders. The arrangement might last for only one trip or might become virtually a permanent partnership or *societas*.

(2) The trader contributed part of the capital. In 1073 a Venetian provided one-third of the funds for the goods he was to sell; for his labors he received one-quarter of the profits, for his capital he received one-third of what was left—i.e., a quarter—and his total reward was therefore half the yield of the venture. By the twelfth century this "fifty-fifty" practice was well known in Genoa and was probably general. The trader now had as big a stake in the enterprise as had the sedentary partner.

(3) All or most of the members of a group might contribute funds and labor to a real or complete partnership, a *vera societas*. They might be members of a family, or two or three friends; or a young inexperienced trader with some capital might be admitted to the firm—and sometimes by marriage to the family—of an older merchant. The partners worked together; some stayed at home, others traveled or managed the foreign branches. For their labors they received payment, and profits were divided in proportion to the capital each member had supplied. In 1300 the Bardi firm of Florence had fifteen partners, of whom ten were members of the family. All lived abroad, in England, Flanders, and France, where the main work was done.

These three types of partnership faded into one another and into many variations or extensions. Sometimes capital received only a fixed rate of interest, like preferred stock; sometimes a "real" partnership would supplement its own funds by accepting investments, loans, or deposits, at fixed rates of interest, from outsiders. Such Italian firms as the Medici, Strozzi, and Contarini secured large sums of working capital in this way, and were thus able to buy for ready cash or pay in advance, sell on credit, speculate in commodities, make big loans to rulers, or supply the capital needed for mining and similar ventures. Sometimes we can scarcely draw the line between a loan and an investment. For instance the *sea loan* was what its name implied, yet it had the element of risk of an investment; for while the lender got a fixed high rate of interest (20-25 per cent) if the venture was successful, he lost all if it failed. By the thirteenth century sea loans were such satisfactory investments that partnerships were formed to make them.

Loans or investments came from many quarters. Norwegian

kings put money into ventures bound for Iceland and the British Isles, and stay-at-home citizens in all walks of life provided sails, ropes, gear, oars, or bales of cargo to equip and stock a ship. A town merchant would furnish the wares in a peddler's pack, and a rich man would scatter his investments in the undertakings of many traders. In England the funds of orphans, widows, and wards, the purses of clerics, princes, and nobles, and even the dowries of brides went to supply capital. When a well-known Genoese privateer wished to sally forth against the enemies of church or state his fellow citizens rushed to invest their money in an enterprise which might, if history repeated itself, yield 25 to 100 per cent profit on the outlay.

At times the number of people interested in a venture was large. In 1248 over a hundred men of Marseilles put their money or goods into the hands of a group of merchants bound for Syria. In 1349 thirty-one English merchants united to guarantee a loan to Edward III. Mining might draw its funds from many purses. When a group decided to build a large Mediterranean ship, each member would solicit his friends to become owners of a fraction (*locum*) of the vessel, and sixty or seventy people might thus have a claim to a share of the ship's earnings. Each fraction might in turn be subdivided, and a man who wished to minimize his risks would own tiny fractions of a great number of ships rather than a large share in one or two. Title to these fractions was bought and sold freely by men and women in all grades of society, and a *locum* would be accepted as security for a loan.

Multiple ownership mobilized the capital of men who had only moderate means; but the giants did not need to consort with a legion of pigmies. Their resources were big enough to permit them to operate alone or in small groups. In Genoa by 1300 the "enormous concentration of wealth in the hands of individuals and of families with vast experience in foreign trade, in administration of commercial colonies abroad, and in shipping appears to have definitely subordinated the system of ownership of vessels by *loca* to one of ownership by smaller groups of capitalists and by financially powerful individuals engaged in large-scale operations" (Byrne). Professor Byrne tells of three brothers who operated alum works in Asia Minor, owned some galleys and sailing ships, leased other vessels, and ran shipping services to the Black Sea, Syria, Egypt, Tunis, the Balearics, and Spain.

MEDIEVAL CURRENCY

Europe's supply of metals suitable for coins was scanty until the sixteenth-century influx of American treasure. The yield from Spain, the central European mountains, Ireland, and elsewhere had to meet demands for decoration, currency, hoarding in high and low places, and shipment to the Levant. But trade and the payment of obligations did not depend vitally upon an abundant supply of precious metals, for other media of exchange played an important part.

Barter was still common, and while it might be direct, in that A got from B the goods A wanted in return for the goods B wanted, it might be more roundabout. Parts of Sweden lacked fish or salt, but had a surplus of butter and cheese. The dairy farmers wanted fish, but the only available nearby product was iron. They therefore took dairy produce to the mining region and exchanged it for iron which they carried to the coast and exchanged for fish. Further, much transfer of goods was one-sided, e.g., the payment of rent, taxes, or other dues. When the "men of the Emperor" gained the right to trade in England they had to pay annually "two pieces of grey and one of brown cloth, ten pounds of pepper, five pairs of men's gloves, and two barrels of vinegar."

In barter certain relationships of value soon became established. To the Swedes a barrel of herrings was worth so many units of rye or barley; salmon and iron could be equated, as could cloth, salt, butter, and malt. But the practice of using one or two metals or other commodities as media of exchange and measuring rods of value was so firmly established in the more developed parts of Europe that its spread among the northern peoples was inevitable, even if it did not grow up there of its own accord. In parts of Russia leather might serve as money, but the west used metals and other acceptable commodities. In Norway and Iceland silver and wadmal—a coarse, heavy woolen cloth—were used, and were made legal tender with a fixed statutory ratio; in the eleventh century seven and one-half ells of wadmal were equal to one öre of silver.

The Germanic peoples knew the precious metals both as medium and as yardstick. In the Anglo-Saxon codes the compensation to be given for various offenses was stated in terms of money; for striking off a nose the payment was sixty shillings, for a fore-finger fifteen shillings, for a forefinger nail four shillings. The Celts valued a cat "from the night it is kittened till it opens its eyes" at a penny; from then till the time it killed its first mouse it was worth twopence, but after that any one who killed it must pay fourpence. Such payments might be made in metal or "in any sound property." When metal changed hands, it might be in the form of coins; but coins mattered little, for the unit of currency was one of weight, whether it was called pound, öre, shilling, or mark. A money payment was made by handing over the required weight of metal. The Teutons seem to have carried much of their treasure in large bracelets or rings, the ends of which were not welded together. They paid a large debt or fine, or bought slaves and ships, by handing over a bracelet or two; but for a small payment they cut a piece off one end.

From these primitive methods the western fringe of Europe was slowly freed by the development of coinage in more advanced cities and areas. The silver penny (denarius) struck by the Frankish king Pepin in 755 became very popular and was widely copied. The Cologne penny, issued by the archbishop's mint and widely circulated from at least the tenth century, bore an official stamp which guaranteed the fineness of its alloy; but its weight fluctuated somewhat, and for large payments the pennies were weighed. For small retail payments the silver penny was too big, and sometimes it was cut into halves or quarters, but eventually coins representing these fractions were struck. For big wholesale trade it was too small; we know of a thirteenth-century debt payment in 6000 pennies and 12,000 halfpennies. Cologne therefore introduced the *mark*, which in 1100 had a value of 144 denarii. The imperial *bezant*, almost the only European gold coin of the early Middle Ages, was issued by Constantinople and circulated as far as England and Scandinavia. There was not enough gold to permit other countries to issue gold coins until the development of Crimean gold mines after the capture of Constantinople by Venice added to the supply. Florence in 1252 issued the gold florin; soon Venice had the ducat, Spain the pistole, England the noble, France the louis d'or, and Germany the gulden. The leading currencies then became bimetallic, and the relative value of the two metals was officially fixed.

The medieval coinage was defective in quality. In the first

place, minting methods were simple, and rogues could easily counterfeit or tamper with coins. Roman, Frankish, Visigothic and Anglo-Saxon law prescribed amputation of the hand as penalty for false coining, but the practice persisted. In the second place, there were many mints and kinds of coins. The situation was worst in Germany, where in the later Middle Ages six hundred cities, bishops, nobles, and princes issued coins. To mitigate confusion, a number of towns might agree to make their coins conform to a common standard and even carry a common imprint, but the babel of coins was still deafening. In Italy each city had its currency. Periods of feudal reaction in France usually saw an outcrop of new coins from lordly mints, but after 1250 the crown gradually asserted its monopoly of money-making. Between 1454 and 1474 a Castilian king granted possibly 150 mint franchises. England was comparatively free from this evil, and was the first country to centralize control; but she was an exception to the prevailing heterogeneity.

In the third place, there was little stability in the precious-metal content of the coin. Many currency controllers regarded the mint as a source of profit or an instrument of taxation. They charged a fee (*seigniorage*) for minting bullion or reminting old coins, and might even claim the right to remint annually. If the new coins contained less precious metal than the old ones, their value fell and prices rose. In days of war or empty treasuries the temptation to make a little silver go a long way was hard to resist, and the progressive debasement of the silver currencies became a normal part of public finance in an age that had no printing press. One French king, John the Good (1350-1364), altered his coins eighteen times in a single year to raise money to fight the English. Depreciation of the penny and elevation of prices eventually went so far that larger coins were needed, worth 12, 24, or more pence. These *grossi, gros, groats,* and *Dichpfennige* (thick pennies) were, however, debased by frequent reissue. People therefore turned more eagerly to gold coins, only to see them debased during the fifteenth century. Medieval money refused to discharge the first duty of a standard of value: it refused to stand still.

The final weakness of medieval currency lay in the lack of an internationally accepted ratio between the values of silver and gold. The ratio in the ancient world had varied between 10 to 1 and 12 to 1 and the same was true of the Middle Ages; but the rate differed from capital to capital, and could be changed by royal decree. At the end of the fifteenth century ten units of gold were equal to 98 units of silver in Spain, 105 in Italy, 110 in France, and 111.5 in England. If a man took 98 units of silver from England to Spain, he could exchange them for ten of gold, for which he could get 111.5 of silver when he returned to England. How much profit he would have left when transportation and other costs had been paid we cannot say; but if there was much of this kind of transaction, or much payment of foreign debts in bullion, it would disturb the money supply, as the metal that was undervalued was taken to countries where its value was greater.

Behind the whole monetary situation lay the comparative scarcity of precious metals. Countries which had no deposits of them strove to keep what they could get. At least seven times during the fifteenth century England forbade merchants to export gold or silver; exchange transactions were controlled by the Royal Exchanger, while foreign merchants were ordered to employ at least part of the money they received from the sale of their wares in the purchase of English goods. The increased output of central European mines made the metals more plentiful in the thirteenth and early fourteenth centuries, but between 1350 and 1450 some of the chief mines seem to have petered out. In the latter part of the fifteenth century new discoveries of ore and improved metallurgical methods swelled the European yield, and hard on the heels of this expansion came the influx of gold and silver from the New World. (See Chapter XII.)

"Paper" Money and Credit

Medieval trade fortunately did not depend solely on metallic money, or on prompt payment in cash. It had various methods for making payment even in a distant place or at some future date without much movement of coin. These methods were developed by money-changers, merchants, and bankers, and by 1500 were elaborate and comprehensive. Documents which contained an order to pay or a promise to pay bridged the gaps of time and space, served as media of exchange, and made possible the elaboration of credit and the expansion of banking.

Payment without transfer of coin or bullion was effected in

various ways. In the fairs merchants were buyers as well as sellers, and when they all came to settle up their crisscross of mutual debits and credits each might find that there was little due to or from him. Goods sold had paid for goods bought. In the towns banks of deposit appeared by about 1200. At first they were run by money-changers or merchants, but in 1401 the Bank of Barcelona was set up by the city. In them a man could make deposits, and have them formally placed to his credit. If he later wished to pay a debt he would go to the bank and authorize the payment of the money or its transfer to the creditor's account. Eventually he was allowed to write an order instructing the bank to pay or transfer the money, thus making out a check; but until the sixteenth century a signature on a check was rarely accepted unless the signer came to the bank and testified orally that it was genuine. The transfer of money from one account to another in this way economized the use of coin.

In the modern world a firm which exports goods frequently does not import any; but the medieval trader who took or sent out goods bought "returns," and therefore had no payment to collect or make in a far place. If he should owe money abroad he faced a transfer problem. He might buy the necessary foreign coins from a money-changer and ship them to his creditor; but the cost of freight and the risk of loss made that method unpopular and led to the development of bills of exchange and drafts. The bill of exchange seems to have begun as a promissory note, an acknowledgment of debt to a foreigner, and a promise to pay in the foreigner's currency before a certain date. It might read, "I, A. B. (a Genoese importer), have accepted from you, C. D. (an Alexandrian exporter), goods of the value of so many pounds of Genoese money, and I promise to pay to you in Alexandria, in bezants of Alexandria, so many bezants to the pound, before the arrival of a certain date." That note might be sold by C. D. in Alexandria to someone (E. F.) who owed G. H. pounds in Genoa. E. F. would pay bezants to C. D. across an Alexandrian counter, send the note to Genoa to G. H., who would present it to A. B. and collect his pounds. Thus two debts between Alexandria and Genoa would be settled with one document and two short-distance money transfers.

Settlement might be made in another way. The Genoese importer might pay his pounds to a local money-changer or merchant who had an agent, correspondent, or branch in Alexandria. In return he received a draft ordering that agent to pay the required sum in bezants, and sent the draft to his creditor. But whatever the actual procedure, payment over long distances and in foreign currency was made by the passage of documentary orders or promises rather than by the movement of coin or bullion. The scanty supply of coinage was not being badly reduced while metal disks idled away their time traveling to and fro.

The transfer problem was political and ecclesiastical as well as commercial in origin. St. Louis on his crusades bought supplies and obtained ready money in distant lands by issuing orders drawn on the treasury in Paris, and these documents might be handed from person to person in payment of debt until someone finally presented them in Paris. The biggest transfer problem was that of getting to the pope the immense revenue collected from every rank and section of society in every country, from Poland and Hungary to Scandinavia, England, and Spain. It was done by the merchant-bankers of Italy who had trading or financial interests in the lands from which the tribute was to be sent. These men received the money and used it to buy goods. In England they bought wool which they shipped to Florence or Genoa, and paid the pope what was due to him out of their Italian funds. The Knights Templars also served as transfer agents. Their religious order, founded to fight the infidel and care for the sick, the pilgrim, or the poor, accumulated properties in east and west alike, had treasuries in many capitals, and sailed fleets on the seas. They were therefore able to transfer bullion from place to place, or sell letters of credit or drafts by which money paid into the London Temple could be paid out in Paris or any other Templar center.

MEDIEVAL CREDIT

Medieval economic life was permeated with credit. Mr. Postan has shown that an unbroken series of credit sales stretched from the English woolgrower to the Polish purchaser of Flemish cloth, and that a cash sale of wool by dealers was a rare occurrence. Goods bought at one fair might be paid for at the next, and the exporter who consigned wares to a distant market must wait long for his money. Lending and borrowing were probably equally all-pervasive, and the debtor-creditor relationship was found in all classes, from peasant or petty craftsman up to king or pope. Some borrowers of high and low degree were perpetually in debt, others borrowed in order to lend, and some borrowed when they lacked funds but lent when they had money lying idle. There were short-term loans of a few months or a year or two, and there were long-term loans made on mortgages. The documents containing the acknowledgment of debt might become almost as negotiable as a modern government bond or piece of "commercial paper." The same was true of the "tallies"—pieces of wood in which government officials cut notches to indicate how much they had received from a lender.

. The needs of borrowers were met by various people or institutions. Some lenders were amateurs who intrusted their spare money to merchants, money-changers, banks, craftsmen, and peasants. The monasteries and some bishops lent their surplus income to peasants and even to big nobles; the abbots of Flanders and Lorraine were probably the largest lenders in those regions till the twelfth century. As security they took a mortgage on land, tithes, mills, and other income-bearing gages; the interest rate in twelfth-century Flanders was 12 to 24 per cent, and debtors' defaults added greatly to church property. In villages the priest sometimes lent money, and in the towns traders advanced money or goods under the putting-out system.

Of the professionals, some were petty pawnbrokers, others were money-changers who became Jacks-of-all-trades, while some were merchants whose resources and widespread branches permitted them to finance the great. The boundary lines between these classes were vague, and "In parts of Italy, the terms *money-changer* and *banker* were used indiscriminately, at least as late as the fourteenth century" (Usher). The money-changer often did more than change local coins for foreign ones, or trade in bullion. Sometimes he operated the local mint, and was the ruler's financial agent. His strong-room was used as a safe-deposit box by local merchants. He might tour the fairs, changing money and lending to traders who found they had bought more than they could pay for. He sold drafts. He took deposits in order to increase his stock of wares, allowed a depositor to transfer funds from his own account to that of another, and even let him overdraw. He lent money, taking valuables, plate, etc., as security. By 1200 he was doing some of these things in Italy, and gradually drew near to being a full-fledged banker. In Barcelona the city deposited its revenue with him, and through him collected its taxes and paid its bills until it established a municipal bank in 1401. It executed him if he went bankrupt.

The money-changer might become a great financial figure. The trader might develop a banking business as part of his work, receiving deposits, making loans, and facilitating transfers until he seemed more money merchant than dealer in goods. But no one could hope to scale the pinnacle of high finance unless he enjoyed the honor and profit of serving some important town, city-state, territorial ruler, or high ecclesiastic. Royal or papal finance could be handled only by those who had large resources, and towns occasionally needed large loans for defense, for rebuilding their walls as the population spread out, for public buildings, harbors, or war. Basel's public debt in 1400 was one-fifth of the total wealth of its inhabitants, Genoa's debt grew over fivefold in the fourteenth century, while towns in the Low Countries spent at least four-fifths of their income on defense and must borrow to meet emergency demands. Sometimes, as in Genoa and Venice, a syndicate was formed to make these large loans to the city. As security it was allowed to collect the taxes, and from them paid the interest to its members and other creditors. This syndicate of state creditors gradually expanded its operations, and eventually became manager of the public debt, a bank of deposit, discount, and transfer, and financer of public works. The Bank of St. George in Genoa was the most famous of these institutions, but like those in Milan and Venice it was often so strained by the city's demands that it had to suspend payment.

ROYAL AND PAPAL CREDIT

The work of the money merchant reached its zenith and had its greatest falls in the service of king and pope. Their revenue had to be transferred, safeguarded, and put to use until the time came for spending it. More important still, it often had to be spent before it was collected. Money must therefore be borrowed and repaid out of later tax or other receipts. In an emergency such as war the revenue of many years to come might be swallowed up. To meet short-term needs an exchequer might buy or borrow, giving some kind of bill which it promised to pay at a future date. In fourteenth-century England the "wardrobe bills" given the creditor were negotiable, were used as security for loans, passed from hand to hand, and were even forged. Often the crown "farmed" its sources of revenue or handed over some piece of property. It received a loan or was paid a regular sum by the farmer, and let the lender or farmer recoup himself by allowing him to manage and take the income from some piece of royal domain, to collect some tax, or operate some monopoly. Only a small part of the royal revenue, whether from levies or from crown properties, might actually pass directly through the exchequer's hands.

As financiers for the great the chivalric orders were prominent in the twelfth and thirteenth centuries, the Italian merchant-bankers supplanted them in the fourteenth, while men from the south German cities began to claim attention in the fifteenth. The Templars (founded 1118) drew large incomes from rich domains, city lands, mines, and markets in England, France, Italy, Spain, Germany and the Levant, and thus had a surplus available for loans. Their castles in various places and their headquarters in Paris and London offered safe deposit for treasure; the Temple in Paris was the chief cash box of the French king; that in London collected, guarded, and administered the royal revenue, and popes used the Templars to collect and transfer some of their income. Kings, princes, nobles, and ecclesiastics ran what were virtually current accounts and sometimes had overdrafts. To be a king's creditor was profitable but dangerous, and in 1307 the French king rid himself of his debts by trumping up a fantastic charge of vice and black magic against the Templars. The Order was destroyed and its treasure divided between the pope and the king.

By that time the Italians, and especially the Florentines, had swarmed into the places of financial power. From the wool trade and from small loans to clerics and landlords the Florentines passed on to finance the kings of France, England, and Naples. In Rome they displaced the Sienese bankers by backing the pope in his struggle with the emperor, and by 1300 had absorbed most of the work of collecting, transmitting, guarding, and investing the papal income. Firms rose and fell, won favor and lost it, but others took their place. In the fifteenth century the Medici stood highest, administering the papal funds, farming the customs, financing land reclamation, and helping to exploit the rich alum deposits found on papal territory about 1450. By 1500, however, favor had shifted toward an Augsburg firm, the Fuggers. In Naples, Florentines, having helped Charles of Anjou to capture the throne (1266), controlled tax collection, and ran the trade in grain and salt. In France they became the royal bankers when the Templars disappeared, collected the papal dues, made Paris a great financial center, and later did much to build up the Lyons fair.

In England Italians were transmitting Peter's Pence to Rome before 1200, and during the next two centuries they controlled royal finance and much of the wool trade. They supplied the sinews of war for the first two Edwards, and as they were bankers for Paris as well as Westminster the outbreak of the Hundred Years' War promised profit whichever side won. That promise proved illusory, and Florence learned that he who sups with royalty needs a long spoon; if rewards were great, so also were risks. By 1345 Edward III owed the Bardi and Peruzzi a sum worth £8,000,000 ($40,000,000) in modern values. The repudiation of this debt in 1345, coming on top of losses in France, Naples, and Flanders, caused panic and ruin in Florence. Something was saved from the storm, the debt was partly repaid between 1346 and 1391, and new firms were willing to venture on the treacherous sea.

The development of Florentine finance and of the medieval bourgeoisie reached its peak in the Medici family. By 1400 the combination of international lending, papal favor, and trade in wool, cloth, silk, leather, alum, furs, and spices was putting the firm ahead of its rivals. Those rivals had used their political power to exploit craftsmen and wage earners, but the Medici kept out of politics and won a reputation as "friends of the people." Eventually exploitation provoked revolt, from which Cosimo de' Medici emerged (1434) as "the people's choice." For three generations a Medici ran a business and a city. The third of the line, Lorenzo the Magnificent (died 1492), scrapped the constitution, became in effect a prince, lavished wealth on art, architecture, and letters, and played a prominent part in international politics. Two Medicis became popes, and the men who eventually became dukes of Florence and later grand dukes of Tuscany sprang from the Medici family. Meanwhile the firm continued its work, making loans to rulers, financing the papacy, farming taxes, and handling commodities. When governments repudiated debts (e.g., in England and Burgundy) and the pope turned to other houses, the firm was shaken, but Lorenzo escaped ruin by mingling the assets of the city with his own liabilities. In 1494 France invaded Italy, the Medici reign ended for a season, and the firm went to pieces. Its collapse added one more to the long line of Italian houses which had risen from small beginnings to great wealth and power, only to pass from the picture when the risks assumed in courting political power had exceeded the rewards, and when there was no stock exchange through which a financier and his depositors could unload their liabilities on the general public.

In range of action, scale of operations, and ingenuity of organization or technique the Italians led Europe; but big enterprises "were common enough and sufficiently important to prove that the capitalist spirit and organization on a scale truly Italian could also be produced outside Italy" (Postan). In Tidemann of Limberg Edward III found a big lender, who from 1340 to 1350 was one of his chief bankers, supplying him with cash, selling wool for him, and pawning his crown jewels. North German finance fed the capital and credit needs of the Baltic area, while south German merchant-financiers supplied funds to princes, exploited mines, and cut deep into Italian preserves during the fifteenth century. In Spain deposit banking developed in Barcelona as soon as in Italy.

In France the Manduel family looms large. Etienne de Manduel (about 1200-1250) scatters his loans or investments far and wide, enters into *commenda* partnerships with merchants bound for Spain, Italy, North Africa, or the Levant, and puts up a fraction of the capital in larger groups. By 1250 some of his ventures look like small joint-stock companies. But his name is overshadowed by that of Jacques Cœur (1395-1456). Son of a furrier, Cœur became a goldsmith and director of the mint at Bourges. He visited the Levant, determined to push French trade in that region, and soon had a fleet of ships plying between Montpellier and the Near East. For the collection and distribution of his wares he had over 300 factors in branch houses. He made some wares in his own plants—a silk mill in Florence, a paper mill at Bourges, a dyeworks at Montpellier; he operated silver, lead, and copper mines, and his passenger fleet carried pilgrims to the Holy Land. Energy, initiative, and unscrupulousness brought a fortune estimated at 27,000,000 francs. He lent heavily to the crown and nobility on the usual security, and for fifteen years was royal treasurer and master of the mint. His spending was as prodigal as his earning. He had a great house, abundant plate, and two score estates; he built an annex to Bourges cathedral, founded chapels and colleges in Paris, Montpellier, and Bourges, and patronized art and letters. Eventually royal disfavor and a multitude of enemies among the merchants and nobility led to his downfall. He was imprisoned, escaped to Rome, and died in 1456 in a naval attack on the Turks.

In other countries there were men similarly enterprising, similarly successful, and often similarly doomed to disaster. In Arras the Crespins and Loucharts put the money made in trade and land rents into loans to princes, lords, and cities of the Low Countries. In England the native merchant class rose after 1300 to a point where it could undertake substantial financial transactions. The de la Poles of Hull, "Dick" Whittington, and others in London or the provincial ports crept up steadily toward the powerful position held by Italians and Hansards. They were given, or bought, a place in the sun, persuaded the king to favor them rather than the alien, farmed taxes, and took increasing control of the country's export and import trade.

THE JEWS

In the ancient world the Jew did not stand out as financier or trader. "We are not a commercial people . . . and have no inclination to trade" said Josephus. Yet when the Jew came west during the early Middle Ages in the band labeled "Syrian," it was as trader in wine, oil, slaves, and peddlery wares. Christian Europe regarded him as an outsider who must not compete with natives in the occupations they pursued. He therefore took up the jobs which they, "through ignorance or by design, left vacant" (Postan). These might be agricultural or industrial, but usually he was excluded from all fields except trade and finance. His trade relations soon spread wide, and by the ninth century western Jewry was connected with Kiev and the routes into central Asia. Jewish communities grew up on the roads to Kiev—at Mainz, Regensburg, and other points; they sent merchants to buy goods in bulk at Kiev, and then distributed them by lot to the members of the groups.

Financial work began with money-changing and money-lending, and by the tenth or eleventh centuries the Jew was the chief lender in many countries. At the lowest he was a petty pawn-broker and old-clothes dealer; at the highest, a Christianized Jew was papal banker in the eleventh century and founder of a line that included a pope and the wife of a Sicilian king. In places he was welcomed, as for instance at Speyer, where he was offered special quarters by a bishop who was trying to make that city important. In Poland he was the moneyer during the twelfth and thirteenth centuries, and the coins carried inscriptions in Hebraic characters. But soon others trod on his heels. Men from the Italian towns, described generally as Lombards, and men who may have come from Cahors in Provence and were known as Caorsini, pushed outward on the trails that led to buyers and borrowers. Europeans learned to do the job, and found ways to circumvent opposition to payment of interest.

Hostility to Jews flared out of the dislike of infidels generated by the crusades, and was fed by the popular hatred of the creditor and his charges for accommodation. Philip Augustus expelled the Jews in 1180, but they were allowed to return, subject to heavy tax burdens. Philip IV evicted them again in 1306, after repudiating his debts and seizing their property; they returned in 1315, only to be ejected again within a generation. England expelled them in 1290, and the Low Countries in 1370. They were driven from the Dauphiné (southeast France) and many German towns during the Black Death, on such fantastic charges as that of having poisoned the wells; but they were soon welcomed back in Germany, for the towns needed the revenue collected from them, and traders, landlords, and governments needed access to their purses. Yet there, as elsewhere, their social status and economic power were gradually impaired by racial animosity and the rise of Gentile rivals. In Spain the tolerance granted by the Moor vanished with the Moor and persecution was followed by eviction.

BOOKKEEPING

Extensive and complicated trading or financial relations led to the keeping of records and the development of accountancy. Even feudal landlords had liked to know how they were faring and what their income and assets were. Charlemagne ordered his stewards to "make an annual statement of all our income," and prepare a detailed list of assets and stores, "in order that we may know what and how much of each thing we have." The preparation of the annual *compotus*, with its statement of income from rent, sales, fines, etc., and of expenditure on plows, buildings, wages, cartage, and miscellaneous petty services, was one of the most troublesome duties of the manorial bailiff. Treasuries kept rolls on which they recorded details of receipt and outlay; and merchants, investors, or lenders tried to keep track of their connections with agents, partnerships, and credit buyers or sellers. By the fourteenth century simple "single entry" bookkeeping was being supplemented by "double entry." Transactions were recorded in a journal and then "posted" in a ledger, with careful analysis of dealings with different people, partnership accounts, and profit and loss. The Genoese may have led in this improvement, but eventually the "style of Venice" became more popular, especially as young men went from all parts of Europe to study business methods there. Handbooks were written for traders containing advice on bookkeeping, and the ledgers of fourteenth-century merchants show that these men were conducting large complicated businesses with intelligence, foresight, and a detailed knowledge of their financial position.

With the invention of printing a book on double entry soon appeared, in 1494. Its author, Pacioli, was a Franciscan friar and a teacher of mathematics, and the "Particulars of Accounting and Recording" formed part of a textbook on general mathematics. The first chapter dealt with "those things that are necessary to the real merchant, and the method of keeping a Ledger with its Journal well in Venice and anywhere else." The necessary things were (1) cash or other "substance," (2) "a good accountant and sharp book-keeper," and (3) well-kept and orderly books "so that one may get, without loss of time, all particulars as to the debit and also the credit" of all one's business affairs. Pacioli outlined the essentials of bookkeeping "in a form which still prevails around the entire world. . . . Bookkeeping was spread throughout the world by a series of plagiarisms and imitations of Pacioli" (Hatfield). His book showed how far accountancy had developed in Italy; but when Schwarz, bookkeeper to the Fuggers, wrote a treatise in 1518 he said his aim was to teach his fellow countrymen a "wealth-producing art little loved by us Germans," and to wean them from the habit of carrying accounts in their heads, writing them on slips of paper or in scrapbooks, or chalking them on window ledges.

MEDIEVAL CAPITALISM

From the above description of medieval economic organization it will be apparent that many opportunities for capitalistic enterprise were being exploited by men who owned (or had access to) capital and whose actions in serving or supplying the community were motivated by the desire for profit. "By the end of the eleventh century the part played by capitalists in the exchange both of goods and money was considerable" (Pirenne). By the twelfth century the Flemish and Italian cloth industries were "based upon a wage system and an elaborate division of labour and . . . run by big entrepreneurs for an international market. . . . International trade and international finance, based upon an elaborate credit system, animated by the unbounded desire for gain and capitalistic to the tips of its fingers, was already in existence in thirteenth-century Italy" (Power). Mining and ship-building provided fields for investment, assumption of risks, and hope of profit.

It may be true, as Professor Brinkmann suggests, that the acquisitive instincts of medieval men were overlaid with religious and other non-economic interests, and that the creaking machinery of money and marketing retarded the spread of the capitalistic spirit. Yet the same author scolds Sombart and others who draw a thick line between the pre-capitalistic Middle Ages and the capitalistic modern world, and points to the danger of overrating "the qualitative differences between medieval and modern commerce or even of assigning too late a date to decisive cultural changes." The quality of medieval capitalism was mature enough to meet the needs of the period and to offer profitable opportunities to those who had the enterprise to seize them. The area of opportunity was small, but gradually widened during the later Middle Ages, and with the discovery of the New World it was to expand greatly. The spirit of gain was subjected to certain controls and restraints—religious, political and economic (see Chapter XI)—but these could be evaded by ingenious devices and were relaxed when the need was great or the pressure was strong.

The most powerful brake on the development of medieval capitalism may have been the slow rate at which one of its essential ingredients, capital, accumulated. The low productivity of medieval agriculture and of much industry left little surplus when simple consumption needs had been met. In Europe's main occupation, agriculture, the accumulation of farm capital was a slow process, undone all too often by famine, murrain, or war. The large landowners might do better, and have something to spare out of their rents, produce, tithes, etc. With many of them consumption needs pressed close on the heels of receipts; and the maintenance of a large body of retainers, the building of castle, abbey, or cathedral, or the costs of entertainment and war left little over. But the papacy, some abbeys, and the military orders were able to defer the consumption of part of their income and put it to work producing more.

In the towns, ground or house rents might yield enough to allow the landlord to use his spare income in making loans, in trading, or in partnerships, and Sombart maintains that rent was one of the main springs of capital. Other scholars see in the slow accumulation of trading profits the chief source of the medieval capital supply. In the present state of our knowledge rent appears as one contributor, e.g., in eleventh-century Genoa, but is less important than the capital accumulated by trade. In twelfth-century Genoa trade was breeding capital for more trade, large partnerships fused a lot of small investments into a large sum, and moneyed merchants were financing moneyless adventurers. In Nuremberg rent supplied a little capital, but trade did more. In Hamburg and Soest Sombart's theory was apparently reversed; money accumulated by traders was put into urban or rural real estate. This was a widespread practice, for land gave social prestige as well as a good return on capital. Finally, the growing practice of depositing money with money-changers, bankers, and merchants mobilized for active service much spare wealth that might otherwise have been consumed or hoarded by its owners.

If the medieval supply of capital seems meager to the modern world, the need was also much smaller. This was especially true of *fixed* capital, the sum sunk in buildings and equipment. Against the high productivity of modern production and transportation we have to place the heavy overhead charges for buildings, machinery, power plants, railroad tracks and rolling stock, power transmission lines, huge ships, and harbor facilities. If the Middle Ages did not have these devices, it did not have to earn interest on the capital expended on them. Productive equipment was simple, large industrial plants were rare, the outlay on roads was small, and it is possible that the capital cost of the means of transportation (horses, wagons, and ships) was a proportionately smaller item in the expense account than it is today. Capital was therefore largely a fund for operations, to be turned over, to be cast on the waters in expectation of a return. It was the basis of a commercial and financial capitalism.

BIBLIOGRAPHY

GENERAL

BOISSONADE, P., *Life and Labour in Medieval Europe* (Eng. trans., 1927).
BÜCHER, K., *Industrial Evolution* (Eng. trans., 1901), chaps. 3-5.
CLAPHAM, J. H., "Commerce and Industry in the Middle Ages," in *Cambridge Medieval History*, vol. vi, chap. 14.
CLARKE, M. V., *The Medieval City State* (1926), chaps. 1, 2.
DAY, C., *History of Commerce*, chaps. 6-13.
FAYLE, E. C., *Short History of the World's Shipping Industry* (1933), chaps. 2, 3.
GRAS, N. S. B., *Introduction to Economic History* (1922), chap. 4.
GRAS, N. S. B., *Industrial Evolution* (1930), chaps. 1-5.
KULISCHER, J., *Allgemeine Wirtschaftsgeschichte*, vol. i, chaps. 17-29.
NUSSBAUM, F. L., *History of the Economic Institutions of Modern Europe* (1933), part i, chap. 2.
PIRENNE, H., "Northern Towns and Their Commerce," in *Cambridge Medieval History*, vol. vi, chap. 15.
PIRENNE, H., *Medieval Cities* (Eng. trans., 1925).
PIRENNE, H., *Les villes du moyen âge* (1927).
PIRENNE, H., *Le mouvement économique et social au moyen âge* (1933).
PIRENNE, H., *Les périodes de l'histoire sociale du capitalisme* (1914).
POSTAN, M. M., "Medieval Capitalism," a valuable bibliography in *Ec. H. R.*, April, 1933.
SÉE, H., *Modern Capitalism* (Eng. trans., 1928), chaps. 1-3.
SOMBART, W., *Der moderne Kapitalismus* (1922), vol. i, pp. 31-309.
STEPHENSON, C., *Medieval History* (1935), chaps. 14, 15, 26.
THOMPSON, J. W., *Economic and Social History of the Middle Ages*, chaps. 17, 23, 28.
THOMPSON, J. W., *Economic and Social History of Europe in the Later Middle Ages, 1300-1530* (1931), chaps. 1, 4, 5, 7, 9-11, 17-19, 22.
Translations and Reprints from the Original Sources of European History (University of Pennsylvania), vol. ii, no. 1.
WEBER, MAX, *General Economic History*, chaps. 7-9, 10-21.

SPECIAL SUBJECTS OR COUNTRIES

ASHLEY, W. J., *Economic History and Theory* (1893), vol. i, book ii, chaps. 1-3, 6.

ASHLEY, W. J., *Economic Organisation of England* (1914), chaps. 2, 4.

BEARDWOOD, A., *Alien Merchants in England, 1350-1377* (1931).

BYRNE, E. H., *Genoese Shipping in the Twelfth and Thirteenth Centuries* (1930).

DAVIDSOHN, R., *Geschichte von Florenz* (1897-1925).

DOREN, A., *Italienische Wirtschaftsgeschichte*, vol. i (1934).

ESPINAS, G., *La draperie dans la Flandre française au moyen âge* (1923).

HEYD, W., *Histoire du commerce du Levant* (French trans., 1895).

LA MONTE, J. L., *Feudal Monarchy in the Latin Kingdom of Jerusalem* (1931), chap. 12 and Appendix.

LIPSON, E., *Economic History of England* (1915), vol. i, chaps. 5-10.

LODGE, E. C., "The Communal Movement, especially in France," in *Cambridge Medieval History*, vol. v, chap. 9.

PASSANT, E. J., "The Effects of the Crusades upon Western Europe," in *Cambridge Medieval History*, vol. v, chap. 9.

POWER, E. E. (ed. and tr.), *Le Ménagier de Paris* (*The Goodman of Paris*), written about 1393.

POWER, E. E., *Medieval People* (1924).

POWER, E. E., and POSTAN, M. M. (eds.), *Studies in English Trade in the Fifteenth Century* (1933).

PREVITÉ-ORTON, C. W., "The Italian Cities till c. 1200," in *Cambridge Medieval History*, vol. v, chap. 5.

SALZMANN, L. F., *English Industries in the Middle Ages* (1913).

SALZMANN, L. F., *English Trade in the Middle Ages* (1931).

SÉE, H., *Histoire économique et sociale de la France* (1929), part ii, chaps. 7, 8; part iii, chaps. 3-5.

ZIMMERN, H., *The Hansa Towns*.

RECENT ARTICLES

BEARDWOOD, A., "Alien Merchants and the English Crown in the Later 14th Century," in *Ec. H. R.*, January, 1930.

BRINKMANN, C., "The Hanseatic League," in *J. E. B. H.*, August, 1930.

BRUN, R., "A Fourteenth Century Merchant of Italy," in *J. E. B. H.*, May, 1930.

GRAS, N. S. B., "The Rise of Big Business," in *J. E. B. H.*, May, 1932.

HARTSOUGH, M., "Cologne, the Metropolis of Western Germany," in *J. E. B. H.*, August, 1931.

HARTSOUGH, M., "Treatise on Book-keeping under the Fuggers," in *J. E. B. H.*, May, 1932.

HECKSCHER, E., "Natural and Money Economy," in *J. E. B. H.*, November, 1930.

LANE, F. C., "The Rope Factory and Hemp Trade of Venice in the 15th and 16th Centuries," in *J. E. B. H.*, August, 1932.

LARSON, H. M., "A Medieval Swedish Mining Company," in *J. E. B. H.*, November, 1930.

PARSONS, TALCOTT, "Capitalism in Recent German Literature: Sombart and Weber," in *J. Pol. Econ.*, December, 1928, and February, 1929.

PIRENNE, H., "The Place of the Netherlands in the Economic History of Medieval Europe," in *Ec. H. R.*, January, 1929.

POSTAN, M. M., "Credit in Medieval Trade," in *Ec. H. R.*, January, 1928.

POSTAN, M. M., "Private Financial Instruments in Medieval England," in *Vierteljahrschrift für Social- und Wirtschaftsgeschichte*, 1930.

POWER, E. E., "On Medieval History as a Social Study," in *Economica*, February, 1934.

REYNOLDS, R. L., "Genoese Trade in the Late 12th Century," in *J. E. B. H.*, May, 1931.

SAYOUS, A. E., "Les transformations des méthodes commerciales dans l'Italie medievale," in *Ann. d'hist. éc. et soc.*, April, 1929. Sayous is a prolific writer of articles on Mediterranean trade. See the index of *Social Science Abstracts* and the bibliographical lists in the *Economic History Review* for the titles of other articles.

SIEVEKING, H., *"Der Kaufman in Mittelalter,"* in Schmoller's *Jahrbuch*, 1928.

STEPHENSON, C., "The Origin of Towns," in *History*, April, 1932.

STRIEDER, J., "Origin and Evolution of Early European Capitalism," in *J. E. B. H.*, November, 1929.

USHER, A. P., "Deposit Banking in Barcelona, 1300-1700," in *J. E. B. H.*, November, 1931.

USHER, A. P., "The Origins of Banking: the Primitive Bank of Deposit, 1200-1600," in *Ec. H. R.*, April, 1934.

Encyclopædia of the Social Sciences: See articles on Banking (Commercial, to the Close of the 18th Century), Bardi, Bills of Exchange, Capitalism, Jacques Cœur, Coinage, Communes, Crusades, Fraud, Ghetto, Hanseatic League, Industrial Arts, Interest, Judaism, Marine Insurance, Medici, Military Orders, Pole Family, Putting-out System.

CHAPTER XI

THE REGULATION OF MEDIEVAL INDUSTRY AND COMMERCE

THE medieval craftsman or trader was subject at almost every turn to regulation by his guild, his town, his church, and his territorial ruler. The motive varied with the regulator. The guild sought to protect its members, promote their welfare, and govern their actions in the interest of fair competition, good workmanship, and an adequate return for their effort. The town aided the guild, but imposed restraint on its members in the interest of other sections of society, especially of the consumers. The ruler might help town and guild by giving added force to their regulations or by issuing his own; but his policy might be shaped to foster the welfare of himself, of the country at large, or of some powerful interest in it. Finally, the church insisted that economic life was not an area removed from Christian standards or precepts. "Do unto others as ye would that they should do unto you" applied to all sides of life, and men's economic actions must be judged by "moral criteria, the ultimate sanction of which was the authority of the Christian Church" (Tawney).

THE CHURCH AND ECONOMIC LIFE

The church condemned covetousness, avarice, or "eagerness for gain," and urged the Christian not to "go beyond and defraud his brother in any matter." Its economic teaching concentrated on the relationships between lender and borrower and between buyer and seller. Its views on usury, i.e., the lending of money at interest, were not original, for Aristotle had condemned interest and Judaism exhorted the Jew to lend freely to his co-religionists. The church said that in general interest was bad, but gradually came to admit that in particular cases it might be permissible. The man who received more than he had lent committed a deadly sin; the devil would take his soul, the church brand him heretic, and the king get his worldly goods. The borrower was thought of as a person in need, and the lender as one who parted with that for which he had no immediate use. The loan should be an act of neighborliness; to exploit a fellow Christian's misfortune was "foul craft."

If this view of the debtor-creditor relationship had been complete its strength might have been unassailable. But it covered only part—a diminishing part—of the field. Money or its equivalent was sometimes borrowed for consumption, to stave off starvation and mitigate disaster; but sometimes it was borrowed for use as capital. Poor men in village and town borrowed grain, cattle, raw materials, clothes, furniture, or money, and bought goods on credit to tide over a bad season, an attack of murrain, or some other misfortune; but they also borrowed to bridge the gap between sowing and harvest, to secure a stock of raw material, or to set up farm or shop. The large borrowings of nobility, churchmen, towns, and rulers were often for unproductive purposes—to pay old debts, build, wage war, pay ransom, anticipate tax receipts, or buy luxuries. But beyond the little loans to the stricken or enterprising poor and the large ones to the necessitous rich lay the growing class of loans made to borrowers who hoped to make a profit from the use of another man's money in industry, trade, or finance.

In the face of such developments, what could church or state say? Each was a big lender, borrower, or both. Not even the pope could borrow unless he paid interest, and when he lent he usually claimed, in one form or another, a reward for his aid and a return on his money. The dignified line of action was therefore to hold fast to the doctrine that usury was wicked, but to admit certain exceptions. (1) Interest on a loan that must be repaid, no matter what happened, was usurious; but if the lender accepted the risk of losing his money interest was just. Risk made the loan worthy of its hire. (2) A good Christian would lend money free for a short term, but if repayment was not made when it was due interest was a just compensation for the loss or injury suffered through the delay and a fitting penalty for the breach of promise. (3) A lender surrendered the opportunity to use his own money in a venture that might have yielded him profit, and was entitled to compensation. In these and other cases the stress was on *loss* and *risk*; not till the fifteenth century do we find men like Archbishop Antonino of Florence admitting that loan capital had something to do with the productivity of an enterprise and was entitled to a reward.

These ideas influenced legislation in many lands. In Denmark a thirteenth-century code said interest on delayed repayments was legal. In 1390 the London city fathers ruled that the man who lent to receive gain thereby "for certain without risk" was a usurer. In 1485 the English parliament legalized interest charged as penalty if a loan was not repaid when due. For Jewish money-lenders interest rates were fixed by the crown, for the Gentile a similar practice gradually developed, and usury eventually came to mean the imposition of excessive rates. The loopholes in the doctrine and law were big enough to allow most commercial requirements to be met, and if there was no loophole evasion was not difficult. A trader might make a loan by selling £100 of goods on credit and buying them back immediately for £90 in cash. He thus lent £90, and charged £10 interest. There were still more ingenious ways, and one may doubt whether the church's attitude impeded seriously the satisfaction of any real need for credit.

The controversy on usury continued beyond the Reformation. Luther attacked the usurer with all the fervor of a monk or a peasant in debt. Calvin, on the other hand, talked like a "man of affairs, who assumed, as the starting point of his social theory, capital, credit, large-scale enterprise, and the other institutions" (Tawney) of the commercial society he knew in Geneva. To wring heavy interest from the needs of poor peasants, craftsmen, and wage earners was "evil and foul" to Calvin, but to take a moderate rate for a loan to a profitable producing or trading enterprise was as just as to take rent from land. Between these two viewpoints a bitter pulpit and pamphlet controversy raged throughout the sixteenth century; but governments gradually eliminated religious considerations, fixed maximum rates, developed special loan agencies (pawnshops) for the poor, and then let lenders and borrowers make their bargains.

The Church and Trade.—In selling, greed was equally anathema. One early Christian father said that the seller should point out defects in any article he was selling, while another contended that the man who bought a commodity "in order that he may gain by selling it again unchanged and as he bought it, that man is of the buyers and sellers who are cast forth from God's temple."

To Thomas Aquinas (about 1250) trade was an undesirable calling, a badge of man's fall from grace; but since it was a necessary (or inevitable) evil, it might be tolerated if the trader would rest content with a *just price*. Let him be satisfied with a price that repaid his outlay on material and paid him for his labor. Let him meet the needs of a modest livelihood and give any surplus that remained to the poor; then his activity would be lawful and Christian. Other writers were willing to let weight be given to (1) losses due to misfortune and miscalculation, (2) scarcity or abundance, (3) the labor involved in carrying goods from producer to consumer, and (4) the need for different rewards to labor according to the *conditio*, the social class to which the worker belonged. By the fifteenth century Antonino, Archbishop of Florence, was ready to admit that a just price should cover these items and also *industria*, by which he meant the zeal, enterprise, and business ability of the seller. But all writers agreed that justice was violated when any man monopolized the supply of a commodity and tried to extract exorbitant prices from the consumer.

THE TOWN AND TRADE

The church's views on price coincided with those of lay rulers, for the protection of the consumer was an important duty of state, city, and even guild. Dependence on local produce supplemented by foodstuffs brought from a distance exposed towns to danger of starvation or exploitation in an age which had no overseas producers and which could not easily transport a surplus of one area to break a famine in another. Few medieval towns could organize the grain trade as Athens and Rome had done, but they could build granaries, insist that no goods pass by until they had been offered for sale, and regulate trade to shelter consumers against avoidable scarcity and extortionate prices. They could impose rules on the victualing guilds, use the guild machinery to administer their decrees, and the state might supplement their action by passing legislation.

The cardinal trading sins were *forestalling*, i.e., buying goods privately outside market hours, outside the market, and possibly outside the town's walls; *regrating*, i.e., buying in bulk in order to sell retail; and *engrossing*, i.e., buying so much produce that one almost cornered the available supply. Since it might be hard to draw the line between legitimate trading and profiteering, price regulation was attempted. By 1202 the English crown was fixing the price of bread, and an act passed in 1266 laid down the principle which guided local authorities for five centuries. The price of the loaf remained constant, but the weight was reduced if wheat prices rose and increased if they fell. The price of ale varied with that of the grains from which it was made. In time of famine or distress the central government might fix other prices, even those of eggs, hens, pullets, and geese. But in normal times Westminster and Paris left the work of regulating prices, of safeguarding quality, and of checking forestallers or engrossers to the local authorities.

This regulation of the trade in foodstuffs goes back to Egypt, Greece, and Rome, where bakers were subject to strict supervision; and the price of bread is still fixed by French municipalities. It reached perhaps its highest point of development in the rules Constantinople copied from Rome and developed into a comprehensive code of market control. In that capital the Prefect of the City watched the guilds, approved or vetoed their ordinances, controlled exports and imports, supervised weights, measures, and coins, regulated prices, and generally protected consumers and the court. A tenth-century copy of his rules is detailed and drastic. Butchers must wait in Constantinople till the livestock arrived to be sold. Pork dealers caught meeting the pig drovers outside the city, or buying from them secretly inside the city, were to be flogged, shorn, and expelled from the trade. Fishmongers must not buy fish till the catch was landed. Cattle must be sold only in the market, cattle inspectors were to "detect and point out defects to would-be purchasers," and vendors must declare the shortcomings of their beasts.

Prices or rates of profit were fixed. Victualers found making more than 17 per cent were scourged, shorn, and expelled from the trade. The chief of the fishmongers' guild must go every morning to the Prefect, tell him the size of the previous night's catch, and the Prefect then fixed the price for the day. The weight of the loaf was determined by the supply and price of grain. Hoarding of goods was a serious offense. Perfume dealers must not store up supplies for times of shortage, those who slaughtered pigs must not keep back the pork, and those who sold fish must not pickle or sell them to foreigners for export unless there was a surplus. Any person found conducting his business to the public detriment was to be flogged and shorn, have his goods confiscated, and be expelled from his trade.

With the regulation of price went the protection of quality. Greece and Rome had tried to prevent the adulteration of flour and wine, and in the Middle Ages the attack on fraud was conducted by officials of manor, town, guild, or state. When a village grew large enough to have its own butcher, baker, and brewers, the manor court enforced the assize of bread and ale, and fined bakers who sold bad or short-weight loaves, butchers who sold "putrid and unwholesome flesh and likewise very dear," and brewers—or brewstresses, for usually they were women—who sold weak or bad beer or who "did not send for the ale-taster." In the towns civic laws, guild ordinances, and royal decrees dealt with the grosser offenses. In Gloucester butchers must not sell "rotyn shepe," and candlemakers must make "good light and sufficiently well brennying, not disseyving the kinges liege people." Paris forbade the adulteration of beer and the mixing or misrepresentation of wine, millers were forbidden to mix other cereals or legumes with wheat, and farmers or victualers must not artificially color butter or mix stale with fresh. In London the city punished those who made false bread—or loaves "of bad dough within and good dough without"—by fining them, standing them in the pillory, or dragging them through the streets tied to a hurdle, with the offending bread hung round their necks.

How far these efforts succeeded in eradicating tricks of the trade we cannot estimate. A study of an English town (Norwich) shows that however efficient the controllers were in detecting offenses, they did little to deter offenders from further misdeeds. By far the most fertile source of municipal income in Norwich was the offending brewer; but fishmongers, tanners, poulterers, cooks, and other victualers were fined year after year for breaking the law. If they had suddenly become honest the city might have faced bankruptcy. Price maxima were often exceeded. Only the cruder forms of adulteration could be detected in an age that had no microscope or knowledge of analytical chemistry; but the subtler forms of adulteration of a later day were impossible without the aid of the modern chemical laboratory.

The Guilds

Associations of men engaged in the same occupation were almost as widespread in the medieval world as in the modern. They were well known in the cities of the Hellenistic world and of the Roman Empire. Those of the Western Empire may have disappeared, but the *collegia* of Rome gave birth to similar guilds in Constantinople.

The Guilds of Constantinople.—From *The Book of the Prefect* (a tenth-century compilation of orders issued by the Prefect) we get a vivid picture of the manner in which individual enterprise was regulated. Some of the rules were probably made by the guild and approved by the Prefect, but others were imposed by him. The guild officials were responsible for their enforcement, the Prefect's staff helped and watched the officials, and the state punished offenders. Even if the guilds began as voluntary associations, they ended as part of an elaborate bureaucracy, as units for taxation, and as groups responsible for certain *munera.* The free distribution of bread, wine, and oil had ended, but there were still some tasks that the guild must perform.

The aim of the ordinances in *The Book of the Prefect* was to insure "that the human race may be governed fittingly and no person may injure his fellow." There was a high degree of division of labor, and each division must keep inside its own bounds. The weaver could not be a merchant, and the spinner must sell only yarn; leather-cutters must not soften hides, tanners must not cut or soften them. Victualers must not encroach on the preserves of the perfumer, soap-maker, linen merchant, tavern-keeper, or butcher "even in the slightest degree." The man who tried to increase his income by practising two occupations was usually flogged, shorn, deprived of his goods, led in mock triumph through the streets, and banished.

Applicants for admission to a guild must give proof of skill and good character. The banker had to be vouched for by respected and honest men who would guarantee that he would not pare down, cut, or put false inscriptions on coins. The notary must pass a very severe test "to ensure that he has a knowledge and understanding of the laws, that he excels in handwriting, and that he is not garrulous nor insolent, and does not lead a corrupt life, but . . . is serious in his habits, guileless in his thoughts, eloquent, intelligent, a polished reader, and accurate in his diction. . . . He shall also have received a general education so that he may not make mistakes in formulating his document and be guilty of errors in his reading," and must prepare a document in a meeting of the guild. Even then he could not be admitted if there were already twenty-four notaries at work in the city, but must await a vacancy.

The guildsman's actions were carefully ordered. The tavern-keeper must close his doors at seven P.M., in order to prevent the "habitual day-time patrons, if they have the opportunity of return-ing at night, from leaving intoxicated and shamelessly engaging in fights, deeds of violence, and brawls." The goldsmith must work in a shop on the main thoroughfare, so that he might have less opportunity for fraudulent workmanship. The metal worker who adulterated his raw material or the banker who tampered with coins was to have his hand cut off. The notary who failed in his job was to be whipped and have his long hair and beard—signs of dignity—shorn. The spinner who retailed raw silk or who gossiped, boasted, or stirred up trouble must be expelled from his guild with blows and insults. Joiners, plasterers, painters, and others who took contracts must finish one job before beginning another. Builders must take care that the foundations of walls, domes, or vaults be solid; and if a structure collapsed within ten years, except through an act of God, it must be rebuilt free.

When guildsmen depended on supplies of goods brought from afar each member must be able to get his share of the available goods. Imported merchandise must therefore be deposited at an inn, "so that all may meet together to divide it." The members of the guild made deposits and the material was then divided in proportion to each man's contribution. If a rich silk dealer had a big stock of material he must be ready to sell some of it to his poorer colleagues at a profit of not more than 8½ per cent.

Guilds in Western Europe.—We know little about guilds in the west till after A.D. 1000. There were some at Ravenna in the ninth century, the groups of traveling merchants in the northwest had rules and a leader, while many guilds were formed for re-ligious or social purposes, or for common protection in arms or at law. After 1000 evidence is more plentiful. The weavers' guild of Mainz is mentioned in 1099, the fish dealers' guild of Worms in 1106, the weavers' guild of Cologne in 1112. There is a mer-

chant guild at Burford in England by 1107, and weavers' guilds
in London and other towns by 1133. Paris had five guilds working
on leather by 1150. A century later the prefect of Paris compiled
a register of the laws and customs of 101 guilds, but that number
was exceeded later by Frankfurt (137) and Lübeck (129). London at one time had a hundred, while Florence, Venice, and the
Flemish towns were well supplied. A few towns or industries had
no guilds, or got them rather late in the day; but in most towns
of central and western Europe they were in existence by about
1300.

The Merchant Guild.—The earliest type of western guild was
the merchant guild (*gilda mercatoria*), hanse (*hansa*), or fra-
ternity (*fraternitas mercatorum*). It consisted of traders traveling about together, trading and residing in a town, or going from
one town to trade in another or in several others. Its aim was to
protect members and advance their interests in the home town,
in the places to which they went, and along the roads or rivers
they traversed. Such groups appear in the ninth century, but we
know little about them till the eleventh. By about 1050 the merchant guild of St. Omer was strong enough to have a guildhall.
In 1060, a group of Scandinavian traders had a guild in Utrecht.
In Flanders and France organizations were probably numerous
by 1100, a *fraternitas mercatorum* is mentioned in Cologne in the
twelfth century, and during that century scores of charters were
granted to merchant guilds in England. In Italy the merchant
guilds were probably older than those of the north.

In the local market the guildsman gained the exclusive right to
buy and sell, retail or wholesale, on market days and at other
times, without payment of tolls or customs duties. But this monopoly had loopholes. To shut out the "foreigner" from another
town or country might be neither possible nor desirable. He might
be allowed to trade "by license of the bailiffs of the burgesses,"
paying those tolls from which the guildsmen were exempt. But he
must not sell retail, open a shop, or deal with any but guildsmen.
Often he could not buy or take certain commodities out of the
town since the town needed them for its own use or the guildsmen
looked to them as the chief source of profit. The stranger passing
through a town might be compelled to offer his wares for sale,
and carry forward only those which were not sold.

The merchant guild sought freedom from tolls and other

charges in territory through which its members went and in towns they visited. Such concessions were probably most easily obtained in areas like England, where most of the towns were on the royal domain, for the king could grant freedom throughout all his land. Elsewhere there must be bargaining and mutual concessions, and reciprocal commercial agreements between towns were made both in England and on the continent. If lord or king granted the same freedom to a large number of guilds, or if two important towns made concessions to each other, the result was a growing freedom of interurban wholesale trade. Retail contact with the consumer was restricted to the local guildsman; yet even that restriction might be relaxed on market days, and certainly was at the fair.

Some English charters to merchant guilds allowed traders to have "their merchant guild and their hanses in England and Normandy," and York merchants were in 1275 protected in their right to have "their hanse and guild merchant in Boston fair." By this grant those who traveled to a distant town or fair could govern themselves and hold court to settle disputes in which they were involved. When merchants from a number of adjacent towns went to the same foreign markets the hanses of these towns joined in a bigger hanse. One such hanse smoothed the path for men who went from sixty towns in northern France and the Low Countries to the Champagne fairs; another, the Flemish Hanse of London, nursed, regulated, and monopolized the trade of seventeen (later nearly sixty) towns with England. The German town groups gained privileges in London, and in later days English merchants trading on the continent won permission to govern themselves in the ports which served as their headquarters.

On its own local market the guild, the town authority, or both, imposed controls of many kinds. Weights, measures, assizes of bread, beer, or ale were looked after, goods of unsatisfactory quality might be condemned, unfair competitive methods were stopped, and men who surreptitiously sold goods retail on behalf of non-members were punished. Any guildsman who bought merchandise must share it with another member if the latter had been present when the transaction occurred and wanted some of the goods. In this way the richer members were prevented from monopolizing supplies, and the poorer members could get quantities suitable to their needs. In places as far apart as Constantinople and Liverpool the guild or the town had the first claim on any cargo, bought the whole lot, and distributed it according to the needs of the various traders.

The merchant guild was a brotherhood. If a member was sick or fell upon hard times, it came to his aid. When he died it gave him a good funeral, and cared for his widow and children. Brawlers and scandalmongers were punished; when two members of the Leicester merchant guild fought at Boston fair, the guild fined them a barrel of beer, to be drunk by the other members. The members ate together on feast days in the guildhall, and worshiped together in a church which they might have built and dedicated to their patron, Saint Nicholas.

The Craft Guilds.—In small towns which had little external trade, the merchant guild consisted of men who bought to sell and those who bought, manufactured or processed goods and then sold them. It continued for centuries as a medley of miscellaneous tradesmen. But in larger centers with far-ranging traders and many developed occupations membership in the merchant guild might become restricted to the richer and important merchants. The number of men practicing the same industry or trade became big enough to justify the establishment of a separate guild to control each craft or the trade in each commodity. We do not know definitely how these craft guilds came into being, but two influences are evident. On the one hand, people came together to further some common end or resist some attack; on the other hand, the public authority exercised its right to control whatever seemed big enough or important enough to be controllable, and to sell privileges in return for cash.

Voluntary association was encouraged when people practicing the same occupation lived and worked in the same street or quarter. In Venice the fishmongers were all at the Rialto, near the landing place for fish. Bruges had many streets named after the occupation of the residents—needle-makers, furriers, rosary-makers, etc.; there was even a *Rue du Porc*. London had its Cordwainer Street, Bread Street, Ironmonger's Lane, and other thoroughfares with special trade names and odors. Men of the same craft lived, worked, and sold side by side, drank at the same inns, and worshiped at the same church.

The church might encourage the formation of groups. In Venice the early guilds met in the cloisters of an abbey, dined in the refectory, and kept their archives and funds in the sacristy.

They had their own altar in the abbey church, arranged for masses to be said for the souls of deceased brethren, and paid an annual fee to the monastery. So long as their purpose was not chiefly economic, membership was voluntary and was not confined to those who practiced one craft; but eventually regulation became part of their work, and an attempt was made to bring all craftsmen or traders into the appropriate guild. In London the smiths (sometime before 1299) quietly took an oath, with their hands on the Gospels, to defend one another in disputes with citizens, to work only for members of the group, and to cease work when curfew sounded. They made a casket, into which each master put a farthing a week to provide a wax taper in honor of the Blessed Mary and St. Landus and to build up a fund for the relief of smiths who fell into poverty. Anyone who violated his oath was taken before an ecclesiastical court. The spurriers made similar decisions, and one member who broke his oath was taken to the archdeacon's court, warned three times, and finally excommunicated.

While association and regulation came spontaneously from below, they also descended from above. In the first place, a ruler might confer power and privilege on some group, help the guild to enforce its decisions, make membership compulsory, punish offenders, but retain the right to veto its ordinances or to make them himself. In return the group might give him a lump sum of money and make an annual payment, thus becoming a tax-paying unit. In the second place, a ruler (especially a town government) might regulate an industry or trade by putting an official at its head, or by calling together those who practiced it and asking or commanding them to form a guild. Sometimes craftsmen said, "We will form a guild," and sometimes the lord or mayor said, "You must form a guild." This action was frequently taken when some trouble had occurred in an occupation. "Divers dissensions" among the London builders in 1356 led the mayor to summon delegates before him. They told him their trade customs, a code of rules was drawn up, and within a few years a full-fledged guild was in being.

Whatever their origin, the guilds moved toward the status of "publicly-regulated professional associations" (Pirenne), privileged groups, enjoying a monopoly over their occupations, but subject to civic or state control and possibly paying money or services to city or crown. The degree of public control varied. In the Low Countries, northern France, and the Rhineland the craft guilds claimed virtual autonomy, and demanded the right to share with the merchants in the government of the city, or to oust them from it completely. Elsewhere the civic or state power was greater. In Nuremberg the guilds could not hold a meeting without civic permission, and their correspondence with craftsmen in other cities must be submitted for perusal. In England the guild might have the mayor as its official head; its rules might be given it, or must be approved, by the town council and were enforced through the town courts. The town might receive part of the fees or fines, and demand *munera*; the Coventry clothworkers had to provide one-third the city's supply of armor, and in many cities guilds had to keep the watch from curfew to sunrise.

Aspects of Guild Control.—The guild ordinances touched every relationship of the guildsman—with non-members, fellow members, members of other guilds, future members, dependent workers, and consumers. The spirit that animated them was one of far-reaching protectionism: the group was protected against competition from outsiders, and the individual member was protected from the destructive, unfair, or fraudulent competition of his guild brethren. In an age of scanty return for much effort the guilds tried to prevent others from stealing their markets, and to guarantee each member an equal chance in the market. They distrusted human nature sufficiently to impose restrictions on the overenergetic, overenterprising, or unscrupulous. They learned by experience or were told by town or state that good workmanship, honest products, and a fair price might be the best policy.

Monopoly of the local industry was sought as an aid to higher income and a prerequisite of effective regulation. It was guarded against attack by workers who lived outside the town and by members of other guilds. Competition from without would be serious if the rivals paid lower rents, taxes, food prices, and wages, and were free from guild restraints. The Low Countrymen tried to suppress their rural rivals, and occasionally marched out to destroy their implements and handiwork. When country competition became intense in England during the fifteenth and sixteenth centuries, town and guild appealed to the state for aid; but the result was seldom satisfactory, even though the state might ban rural production and the guild be given power to search for illicit products and producers.

The guild tried to keep intact the boundary line between occupations. The line ran between processes or commodities, and where division of labor was pushed far the field was cut into very tiny plots. In Paris the tailor must not mend old clothes, the ragman could not make new ones. In London the state and the city endeavored for a time to maintain the principle of "one man one craft, one merchant one commodity, one craft one guild." The cobbler must not make new shoes, the bow-maker must not produce arrows, the brewer must refrain from making barrels, the innkeeper must not bake or brew. This policy was not easily enforced, and interguild strife over demarcation was fierce. The shoemaker wished to tan leather, the baker of white bread wished to bake black. The drapers trespassed on the preserves of mercers, tailors, merchants, weavers, fullers, dyers, and shearers. The grocer wished to handle metals, dyes, wax, drugs, spices, cloth, wool, wine, fish, and fruit, thus clashing with a dozen guilds. The outcome of these disputes might be amalgamation of kindred crafts or selling occupations; but peace and union often came too late, for the end of interguild conflict coincided with the end of guild restraint in the seventeenth, eighteenth, or even early nineteenth century.

Apprenticeship.—While every craftsman or trader had to be in his appropriate guild, entry was not free or easy. An adult newcomer to the town must prove he had the necessary skill and character, find sponsors, and pay entrance fees. A young man must complete a period of training which by the thirteenth century had become a formal apprenticeship, a contract between teacher and pupil, controlled by the guild, the town, and later the state. Apprenticeship provided a residential technical education. The youth promised to be good, industrious, honest, obedient, orderly, and loyal. His master's commands he would obey, his goods he would protect from theft, waste, and injury, his trade secrets he would keep. Taverns and gaming houses he would not frequent, matrimony he would not contract. He would not run away or be guilty of any form of "folly and jollity" that might injure his master. In return he was to be lodged, fed, clothed, taught, and chastised duly when he deserved it.

How the lad fared as learner and worker depended on his own

ability and temperament, and on the character of his master and mistress. The industrious apprentice is well known in literature; his runaway, idle, riotous, and ill-treated fellows were well known in law courts, charged with beating the watch, picking a quarrel with the servants of nobleman or ecclesiastic, indulging in sword-play, or setting heavy barrels rolling downhill. Some towns had a special prison for apprentices. The master might be a model foster father and teacher, or he might be dissolute, cruel, or incompetent; sometimes he neglected his task, supplied insufficient food, or acted like the Parisian goldsmith who hit his apprentice with a bunch of keys and "made a hole in his head."

Since the apprentices of today were the journeymen or masters of tomorrow, the guild was interested in the number of pupils, the length and character of their studies, and their career when education ended. The city also was interested, for apprenticeship was one way to gain the freedom of the city, a large body of youths living away from home created problems of public order, and there were fees to be collected. Hence guild and town regulated the age at which an apprentice could be taken, the length of his training, the number of pupils per teacher, and the fees to be paid. The training period varied greatly: in London it was from two to fifteen years, but gradually settled down at seven, and in 1563 that term was imposed by the state on the whole country. On the continent the youth worked two to six years in the master's household, and then spent three to five years as a journeyman in other towns obtaining further experience. The number of apprentices a master could take was limited in order to insure that each pupil received adequate attention, to keep down the number of skilled workers seeking admission to the craft, and to obviate such unfair competition and defective work as might result if one master was getting many goods made by immature unpaid learners. Many Parisian guilds had no restrictions, but others limited the number to one or two. In London some guildsmen had to obtain special permission to take pupils, but the rest might take one, two, or even more.

When the apprentice had "served his time" he might wish to become a master craftsman. If so, he must go through certain procedures and pay for initiation as burgess and guildsman. His skill was tested, his workshop was inspected, and he might have to prove he had sufficient funds to make good any damage done to his customers' goods. The test of skill might consist of the performance of a job in the presence of the guild officials, or the submission of an elaborate piece of work, a *chef d'œuvre* or masterpiece, the product of weeks or months of labor. If the candidate passed his test, had money for his fees, and possessed the equipment needed for his work, he gained the right to practice his craft. Not all ex-apprentices could take this step at once. A wife might be an indispensable economic asset not yet possessed, money might be lacking, and some time must therefore be spent in earning and saving. Some guilds, e.g., in Bruges, insisted on some years of work as journeyman and on some travel, and continental towns witnessed the constant migration of young men seeking postgraduate training. Some ex-apprentices never passed into the master class, but remained journeymen all their lives, and as the Middle Ages drew to a close the barriers separating dependence and independence rose higher in some occupations.

The Regulation of Enterprise.—The new master entered a world of regulated production and sale. We cannot decide how far the rules owed their origin to the guild's desire for good work and fair competition or sprang from the community's desire to protect the consumer; there was a mixture of motives. Work on Sundays and saints' days was banned to prevent the impious from making more money than the pious, and to promote true religion. Night work was forbidden, partly from consideration for the workers, partly because the light was too poor for accurate work, and in the case of the London smiths because of the unhealthiness of coal smoke, the risk of fire, and the noise. Bad workmanship was attacked by every guild and town. Punishments were provided for the weaver who put faulty material into his piece, the fuller who lost or damaged a customer's cloth, the tailor who pawned cloth intrusted to him, the butcher who mixed tallow with lard or sold dead dog or cat, or the brewer who strengthened the taste of beer by adding juniper or pimento. Alloys must contain the proper quantity of the right metals, and jewelers must not use colored glass. Work must not be done in chambers, cellars, or back rooms, but "only in halls and shops next the road in sight of the people" "so that the master and wardens can survey the defaults." Some guilds affixed a stamp, seal, or hall mark, or made the master put on his own mark. Punishment ranged from confiscation of the faulty wares, a fine or a scolding, to destruction of the worker's equipment, a period in the pillory, and eviction from the craft.

Many ordinances sought to secure fair play and equal competitive conditions between rivals. Masters must not try to steal one another's workmen or customers, or strive to gain an advantage in securing raw materials or soliciting purchases. Raw materials must not be forestalled, and members who lacked a supply might get it at cost from those who had some. Goods must not be hawked through the streets or from house to house, but be offered for sale in shop or market. The modern advertiser would shudder at the rules of St. Omer, where the seller was forbidden to greet a passer-by, blow his nose or sneeze when customers were around. The boatman bringing beer to Bruges must not display any notices singing the praises of his cargo. The professional ethics of medical and legal practitioners are a survival (or revival) of these rules against solicitation and advertisement.

Restrictions on the number of apprentices, journeymen, and implements, or on the quantity of goods produced might spring from the desire to let all masters share in a limited local market and to prevent anyone from winning more than his fair proportion of the trade. The same desire led guilds to frown on innovations or inventions which might help one master to increase production or reduce costs, to the injury of his rivals. In 1397 the tailors of Cologne forbade the use of a machine for making or attaching pinheads. But if an invention could be afforded by all masters its use might be permitted, as when the weavers of Speyer accepted the spinning wheel in 1297. How far guild opposition retarded technical advance we cannot say, but the attitude certainly tended to be cautious and suspicious. The ideal was "stability of conditions in a stable industrial organization" (Pirenne), "order rather than progress, stability rather than expansion" (Lipson).

The guild sought to fix minimum prices for the goods or services it sold, and to fix maximum wages for its journeymen; but in both efforts it was subject to civic supervision. In 1298 the London city fathers sent the coopers to jail for having decided to raise the price of barrel hoops, and later in the same year they denounced the carpenters for gathering together in a "parliament" and binding themselves "by corporal oath not to observe a certain ordinance made by the mayor and aldermen touching their craft and their daily wages." The regulation of wages by guild, city, and state probably became more important during and after the Black Death. The surviving wage earners seem to have taken advantage of their scarcity value to ask for higher pay. The English king in 1349 and parliament in 1351 tried to peg wages at the level prevailing before the plague, and half a dozen laws to check demands for "outrageous and excessive hire" were passed during the next 150 years. In France a royal ordinance of 1351 limited the increase in wages and prices to one-third. But in neither country was state, town, or guild effort successful, and some increase had to be allowed. The guild, with civic and then with state support, regulated the hours of labor. All the hours of daylight must be used. This meant a working day from 4 or 5 A.M. to 7 or 8 P.M. in summer, and from dawn to dusk in winter.

Social Activities.—In addition to wrestling with original sin and tricks of the trade, the craft guild had its social side; and religion, mutual aid, amusement, or politics at times seemed more important than economics. The brethren were exhorted to "be loving and gentle and friendly one to another," and to eschew quarrels. The York weavers in 1400 condemned the slanderer to expulsion, and the Bruges tanners in 1376 excluded a member from his trade for fourteen days for calling a fellow member a liar. If a member got into legal difficulties or fell sick, the guild must aid him; at his death the craft gave him a decent funeral, and gave some thought to the welfare of his widow and children. Often the guild had a livery, a common type of dress, to be worn by the members on such special occasions as processions, banquets, and masses; it was the badge of solidarity and of separatism. Nearly every guild had its patron saint, its chapel, altar, or at least a candle burning in some church. On the appropriate saint's day the liveried members celebrated solemn mass "for the brethren and sisters of the guild, living and dead," passed on to a business meeting, and then sat down to a banquet. In some English towns the guilds were responsible for the presentation of the Corpus Christi plays, a series of tableaux or scenes depicting human history from the Creation to the Day of Judgment, performed on Corpus Christi Day on movable platforms at different points in the town.

Thus the guild bound its members together in a little many-sided community, and guided them in matters as far apart as apprenticeship and amateur theatricals. Its warden presided over their meetings, its searchers came to their shops to see that the ordinances were being obeyed, while its power was used to protect them from interlopers without and unfair competition within. It tried to check dishonesty, fraud, or rapacity, and to promote the welfare of its members both at work and at play.

Guilds in the Later Middle Ages, and After.—In some occupations or countries the guilds retained and even strengthened their hold as the Middle Ages drew to a close. This was partly due to the grip they had on city government or to the support they received from the state. In France the crown saw in them an ally against the nobility and a useful instrument for industrial control; it therefore favored but regulated them. In Germany guilds often controlled a town and could suppress the rather feeble expansion of rural or capitalistic enterprise. In England the state occasionally helped the guilds in their efforts to resist the encroachment of new forms of organization.

Economic influences helped some guilds to retain their grasp. The craft guild was suited to the conditions of small retail handicraft. Many occupations remained of this type, and some had fewer wage earners than masters. The market was limited by the size and growth of the town; the work was such that a large unit had no advantage over a small one; the tools might be few, simple, and cheap, and the earnings were such that not even the most successful guildsman could hope to make a fortune. Hence the *organization* of these industries changed little during a long period, and the *association* of those who practiced them felt little strain on rules and customs.

Where economic or political conditions favored the continued existence of guilds, the innate tendency of privileged groups to become narrower and more exclusive asserted itself. Entry became less easy, apprenticeship fees and requirements were raised, the cost of admission to the rank of master became heavier, the masterpiece more difficult and expensive, and the livery more lavish. The number of masters was fixed, and the guild became a close clique, recruited from the sons of masters or from those who could pull the right strings—often the purse strings.

When an occupation served a large or rapidly growing population or an export market, the guild structure and policy must be capable of adaptation to changes in the organization of production and trade, or the guildsmen would find their power and even their occupations gone. The merchants and entrepreneurs of the great textile industries of Flanders and Florence did not fit snugly into a system of small independent guildsmen. They must either control the guild and shape it according to their needs or they must seek their supplies elsewhere than in guildsmen's workshops.

In Flanders many of them eventually did the latter. The conflict between producers' groups and traders was evident by 1200. The guilds fought hard and won a political victory. By 1400 they had ended the plutocratic control of municipal affairs, and were making their own rigid rules. But they gained little benefit therefrom, for while weavers fought demarcation battles with fullers and wage earners quarreled with masters, the merchants turned elsewhere for their supplies. Production in Ghent, Ypres, and Bruges declined, but flourished in Hondschoote and other small places which, coming late to textile work, escaped guild control. In these towns or villages there was no limit to the amount of labor or equipment men could use or the number of pieces they could make. There was no ban on immigration, taxation was light, living costs were low, as probably were wages. Hence the *drapier*, as the clothmaker was called, might have half a dozen looms gathered under one roof. The Counts of Flanders encouraged the industry and the traders of Bruges and Antwerp supplied it with capital and custom. By 1500 Hondschoote had 12,000 workers and was selling 100,000 pieces yearly.

In Florence the clothmakers' guild, the *Arte della Lana*, need not fight the big men, for it was made up of them. The members may originally have been weavers who had prospered and became great organizers and merchants. They naturally would impose no limits to their own scale of operations, but they did exercise the guild's power to regulate the wages and working conditions of their employees. They brought the small masters and the workers in suburb, country, and subject cities under control of the *Arte*. In the middle of the fourteenth century two hundred masters controlled twenty-five dependent occupations and thirty thousand small masters or journeymen. The *Arte* bought and imported raw materials and distributed them to its members, owned warehouses, workshops, dyeworks, and ships, sold goods for its members and had its own court and police force.

In London the successful guildsman gradually dominated his

less fortunate fellow members, and employed many of them. The guilds which were chiefly concerned with buying and selling elbowed the craftsman out of his right to sell his own products to the consumer, and drew more on rural supplies of goods. The distinction between rich and poor crafts or craftsmen, between sellers and makers, grew more marked. Where a guild became dominated by wealthy men, the entrance of poor men became difficult. The rich and the sellers intrenched themselves by securing charters of incorporation, thus getting for the guild a legal personality, the right to own property, and a chartered monopoly over the purchase or sale of certain goods. Eventually there were twelve of these "livery companies." Wealthy and politically powerful, they dominated the city's commercial life, and carried on beyond the Middle Ages something of the monopolistic and regulatory spirit of the guild.

In that respect they were not alone, for in such professions as medicine and law medieval principles were applied. No person could practice as a physician unless he had been trained and approved by the Royal College of Physicians (founded by Henry VIII) or by the Universities of Oxford or Cambridge. Pleading in court became the close preserve of men who belonged to one of the Inns of Court. In the field of foreign trade, guild principles were adopted, for as Englishmen developed the trade in English cloth in the areas around the North and Baltic Seas they formed companies which applied monopoly and regulation to their calling. (See Chapter XV, Part ii.)

Journeymen's Guilds.—With the growth of a gulf between master and man and the closing of the road to guild membership, a measure of class consciousness developed among wage earners, and associations were formed. These journeymen's guilds might cloak their purpose with the veil of religion, posing as a mutual aid society and a group of worshipers of some saint. So long as they were content with religious or social aims they might be tolerated, but when they tried to influence their employers they fell foul of the masters, the town, or the state. Encounters were violent and suppression was certain. In the thirteenth century Rouen strikers who tried to raise wages were imprisoned. At Ypres in 1280 opposition to increased hours of labor ended with the killing of the mayor and severe punishment of the strikers. Bruges in 1241 grouped under one law counterfeiters, thieves, and artisans. Florence had many turbulent periods in the fourteenth century, when the "blue nails" (textile workers) resisted or revolted. During the years 1379-1382 wage earners and small masters in many European cities were in revolt against their political and economic overlords, and demanded improvement of their lot; but in London, Paris, Cologne, Florence, and the Low Countries alike the power of the state, city, or employers was too great. The causes of association and unrest remained, and industrial friction was not unknown during the next two centuries.

BIBLIOGRAPHY

ASHLEY, W. J., *English Economic History and Theory* (1893), part ii, chap. 2.

DAY, C., *History of Commerce* (1907), chaps. 6, 8.

DOREN, A., *Studien aus der Florentiner Wirtschaftsgeschichte,* vol. ii (1908).

GRAS, N. S. B., *Industrial Evolution* (1930), chap. 5.

GROSS, C., *The Gild Merchant* (1890).

HAUSER, H., *Travailleurs et marchands dans l'ancienne France* (1920).

KEUTGEN, F., *Aemter und Zünfte* (1903).

KRAMER, S., *The English Craft Gilds: Studies in Their Progress and Decline* (1927).

LESPINASSE, R., *Les métiers et corporations de la ville de Paris* (1886-1897).

LEVASSEUR, E., *Histoire des classes ouvrières et de l'industrie en France avant 1789* (1901), vol. i.

LIPSON, E., *Economic History of England* (1926-1931), vol. i, chaps. 6-8; vol. iii, chap. 5.

PIRENNE, H., *Belgian Democracy* (1915), chaps. 4, 7, 9.

RENARD, G., *Guilds in the Middle Ages* (1919).

SAINT LÉON, M., *Histoire des corporations des métiers* (1923).

SALZMANN, L. F., *English Industries of the Middle Ages* (1913), chap. 11.

SALZMANN, L. F., *English Trade in the Middle Ages* (1931), chaps. 7-9.

SÉE, H., *Histoire économique de la France* (1929), part ii, chap. 8; part iii, chap. 4.

STALEY, E., *The Guilds of Florence* (1906).

THOMPSON, J. W., *Economic and Social History of the Middle Ages* (1928), chap. 28.

THOMPSON, J. W., *Economic and Social History of Europe in the Later Middle Ages* (1931), chap. 17.

UNWIN, G., *The Gilds and Companies of London* (1908).

UNWIN, G., *Industrial Organisation in the 16th and 17th Centuries* (1904).

UNWIN, G., *Studies in Economic History* (1927), part ii, essays 1, 2.

USHER, A. P., *Industrial History of England* (1920), chaps. 3, 6, 7.

WEBER, M., *General Economic History,* chaps. 9, 10, 11.

ARTICLES

BOAK, A. E. R., "The Book of the Prefect," in *J. E. B. H.,* August, 1929.

EVANS, A., "The Problem of Control in Medieval Industry," in *Pol. Sc. Q.,* vol. xxxvi (1921), pp. 603-616.

KNOOP, D., and JONES, G. P., "Masons and Apprenticeship in Medieval England," in *Ec. Hist. Rev.,* April, 1931.

MEYER, E. F., "English Craft Gilds and Borough Governments in the Later Middle Ages," *Colorado University Studies*, February, 1929, February, 1930.

PIRENNE, H., "The Place of the Netherlands in the Economic History of Medieval Europe," in *Ec. Hist. Rev.*, January, 1929.

Encyclopædia of the Social Sciences: Articles on Apprenticeship, Aquinas, Christianity, Fairs, Guilds, Journeymen's Societies, Just Price, Law Merchant, Usury.

CHAPTER XII

THE MAKING OF THE EARLY MODERN WORLD

THE economic history of the years which separate the Middle Ages from our own day can be roughly cut into two periods, with the eighteenth century as the dividing line. From the fifteenth century to the eighteenth the changes, developments, and expansions affected chiefly the volume, range, commodities, and organization of commerce. The center of interest lies in the way men distributed a greater variety of goods in greater volume over a larger area of the world's surface. Changes in equipment and methods of production were small when compared with those of later centuries; they were more important than has been generally realized, but we have to wait till after 1700 for the rapid advance in technical knowledge that gave producers an abundance of machinery, power, metals, and science. Hence if we like labels, but promise not to take them too literally, we can call the changes of the fifteenth to eighteenth centuries a "commercial revolution," and those after 1700 an "industrial revolution."

GENERAL FEATURES OF THE PERIOD 1400-1700

During these three centuries Europe witnessed the full flowering of the Renaissance, the Reformation, and the establishment of territorial states. Each of these developments was partly economic in cause and character, and each had far-reaching economic effects.

Economic Effects of the Renaissance.—The Renaissance, regarded narrowly as a cultural movement, gave active minds a new or greater interest in the physical world, and paved the way for the researches in physics which began to bear fruit in the seventeenth century. A bigger demand for books could be fed after printing became possible in the fifteenth century. As new tastes were created among the rich there was an increased call for buildings, furniture, apparel, and artistic objects. A "brilliant consumers' civilization" and a new elegance replaced simpler medieval standards in the life of the upper classes, and the inventories of sixteenth-century rich men's houses record great quantities of

Turkish carpets, feather beds, and other evidences of a new standard of material comfort. The Middle Ages built cathedrals, abbeys, and castles; the early modern world built palaces, town houses and country mansions, and made architecture a profession.

Economic Effects of the Reformation.—The Reformation did not touch all parts of Europe, but where it did its economic influence was many-sided. In the first place, it affected the distribution of property and income. In England the abbeys were dissolved (1536 and 1539). Their buildings and lands fell into the hands of the king and were distributed by him, chiefly to the new ex-bourgeois nobility. Much property belonging to the regular church was also taken by the king. Others were quick to follow his example, and a citizen of Hull wrote (about 1540) to a friend in another town, "We have taken all our church plate and jewels, and sold them and paved our town withal, and ye will do it too if ye are wise and mend your town, that is very foul withal." In north Germany the princes who broke away from the church despoiled it; in Scandinavia Gustavus Vasa in 1527 took most of the church lands. The breach with Rome ended the remittance of income to the pope.

In the second place, the Reformation accentuated religious intolerance and persecution of the unorthodox. Spain eventually drove out the Jews and Moors, and the former brought strength to the lands which gave them refuge. In France the Huguenot artisans and traders won civil, religious, and political rights in the Edict of Nantes (1598), but when they lost them (1685) great numbers of rich or skilled *emigrés* sought refuge and found welcome in Holland, Germany, England, Ireland, and the British colonies in America.

Finally, the Reformation carried still further the modification of those rules of conduct which the church had sought to impose on economic conduct. The church had tried to keep man's acquisitive spirit on a leash, but as that spirit grew stronger and the opportunities for acquisition increased the church had to be content to be pulled along or let go the leash. The later medieval writers on price and interest had let the needle's eye expand into an archway, and the Jesuits were to make several side entrances. Protestants might pass from an attack on Catholic doctrine and government to a criticism of its economic ethics; but they did so with varying degrees of caution and did not release business from all moral obligations. They frowned on usury if it involved robbing or exploiting the poor; Luther's condemnation was scorching, but Grotius contended that interest, if not oppressive, was not contrary to the law of nature, while Calvin saw it as a just reward for the service rendered by a loan.

Reformers attacked the worldliness of the church and went on to defend the laity against the contempt which the church had poured on its occupations. Luther denounced the idea that the monastic and priestly vocations were the only ones that found favor in God's sight, while Calvin maintained that the monastic ideals of hard work, prayer, and asceticism could be realized outside abbey walls. Every occupation, no matter how humble, could be a "calling," worthy of its full reward in this world and the next. The man who brought to his task the virtues of industry, thrift, sobriety, honesty, and abstinence promoted the glory of God and justified his own "election" to the eternal aristocracy of heaven. If his diligence and thrift led to the accumulation of wealth, if asceticism forbade him to waste his substance in riotous living and thus put much capital in his hands, he did no wrong. The really deadly sins were slothfulness, luxury, and self-indulgence; poverty might be the brand of the sinner, not of the saint. One sure road to sin was too many holidays; perhaps another was high wages, which let the unelect indulge in idleness and vice, dance round Maypoles, get drunk, and gamble. Satan had plenty of work for unoccupied hands in full pockets; hard work and little spending power were the best fences against the tempter.

This Calvinist view of life and work, and the puritanical view that was closely allied to it or sprang from it, were very stimulating (or consoling) to the bourgeoisie. Men who had been working hard in the service of mammon now found they had been serving God as well. Capitalism had gone far and grown strong in spirit, in organization, and in technique; but many of its aims and methods might not harmonize with the ethics of the medieval church. Now it had a restatement of rules of conduct in terms that would justify and sanction what it was already doing or wished to do. Calvin defended and justified it against those who judged it by the standards of a rural subsistence world; he removed its inferiority complex, and supplied it with sops in case its conscience should trouble it. Just as people had eaten spinach and liver long before dietitians gave their tastes scientific sanction, so the capitalistic spirit "found in certain aspects of later Puritanism a tonic which braced its energies and fortified its already vigorous temper" (Tawney).

Economic Effects of the Rise of National States.—The rise of national states and of rulers who exercised effective sway over large territorial units was perhaps the most important political development of the fifteenth to eighteenth centuries. A state might come into being with the eviction of a foreign ruler, as when Spain got rid of the Moorish power, Holland established its independence of Spain, or Gustavus Vasa pulled Sweden out of Danish hands. It might come from the persistent efforts of rulers to subject feudal, ecclesiastical and urban rights of jurisdiction to royal decrees, courts, and tax-collectors, as in France. Much of Europe thus passed under the control of strong centralized governments, each with a legislature or royal lawgiver, a corps of state officials, courts capable of overriding local dispensers of justice, an army of professional soldiers rather than of feudal bands, and a treasury with a large gaping mouth.

The economic effects of this rise of strong states were many. (1) The feudal or urban unit was merged in a wider trade area. Uniform laws, weights, measures, and currencies could now supplant those of city or fief, internal customs barriers could be reduced, roads could be planned or maintained as part of a national scheme, and the king's justice might have a longer arm in reaching for the enemy of trade or traveler. These elements of unity came only very slowly: local privileges and protection died hard; work on roads, rivers, and canals was given little attention unless it possessed military value, while internal customs boundaries survived in France and other countries, checking the free movement of grain till after 1750. England went furthest in achieving economic unity, and when she united with Scotland in 1707 Great Britain became the largest free-trade market in Europe. Yet even there better transportation facilities were needed before there could be much far-flung sale of goods produced in any one spot.

(2) A national state must have a national policy, in the light of which it regulated the economic life of its subjects. It must be strong, self-reliant, able to hold up its head and give harder blows than it received in the hurly-burly of diplomacy and war. To foster the strength of the state and of its ruler, industry, agriculture, shipping, and trade must contribute their quotas. Each must

be nourished here and restrained there; when the interests of different economic groups or areas clashed the state must decide which should be favored or sacrificed, and each interest must learn how to lobby. (See Chapter XVI.)

(3) War was almost a normal relationship among national states. From 1494 to 1559 there was fighting nearly every year in some part of Europe; the seventeenth century enjoyed only seven calendar years of complete peace, and England was at war during eighty-four of the 165 years between 1650 and 1815. Personal ambition of rulers, religious divisions, and desire for territorial expansion, glory, or revenge all played their part; but many wars were waged for economic ends, such as opening a market, driving a rival out of one, preventing one from being shut, or punishing a rival for passing a higher tariff or hitting one's shipping interest. The discovery of the New World threw new bones of contention into the ring. "Armed aggression was the heart of commerce" (Clark), trade was war fought with different weapons in the intervals between armed conflicts, and treaties of peace embodied more clauses of commercial significance.

(4) The prevalence of war imposed a heavy burden on national finances, and that burden was increased by new methods of fighting. Campaigns lasted longer, employed more men, and used more costly armaments. By the thirteenth century some kings were using hired troops instead of feudal levies or militias, while the townsmen of Italy and the Hanseatic area were too busy and valued their own lives too highly to fight their own battles. To meet the demand, leaders organized private bands of soldiers which might be hired by the highest bidder. Until 1700 or even later, European governments relied almost solely on these professional fighters, both for their wars at home and their colonial struggles overseas. The size of armies grew steadily, and by the middle of the eighteenth century the leading standing armies numbered from 180,000 to 300,000. Warfare required more elaborate equipment, defensive buildings, military highways, and other products of the military engineer. Maritime countries began to build navies; the Spanish Armada consisted of 200 vessels, and the British navy in 1780 had nearly 300, some of them armed with 100 guns.

To the heavy cost of war was added that of maintaining a class of public servants and of supporting courts which regarded luxury as an integral part of kingship. When Queen Elizabeth died, three thousand dresses and innumerable wigs were found in her wardrobes, yet she was a frugal monarch. The Stuart kings were extravagant in an age of rising prices, and the splendor of the French court under Louis XIV was dazzling.

To meet the growing obligations of a modern centralized state the governments of the sixteenth century had the revenue system of a feudal state. New sources of income must be found; indirect taxes were heaped on sales, exports, and imports; titles and monopolies were sold, crown properties were squeezed to increase their yield or were sold, the currency was depreciated, and taxes were farmed. Even then, monarchs often could not pay their way, and loans were raised either to supplement revenue or to anticipate its receipt. To the great loan markets of Florence, Genoa, Lyons, Geneva, Augsburg, Antwerp, Amsterdam, Lübeck and Kiel rulers sent their servants, cap in hand. Big financiers had offices there or in the capital cities, and native rich men contributed to the coffers of their own kings. The merchant-bankers of the south German towns forged ahead of the Medici and other Italian firms in this work; the Fuggers served the pope, the Hapsburg Charles V, and his son Phillip II. As reward or as security they collected customs and certain other taxes, and took land, mines, or any other accessible collateral.

These debts often grew so large that partial or complete default was inevitable. Interest or principal might not be forthcoming, the borrower might insist on a reduction of the rate or the principal, ask for a new loan with which to repay the old, or demand that a short-term loan be converted into a long-term one. Spain defaulted at least six times between 1554 and 1647, and wrecked the Fuggers. Henry VIII of England failed to repay a loan and thereby wrecked the Frescobaldi of Florence. Henry II of France evaded his obligations in the 1550's and converted his short-term debts into perpetual "rentes." The Thirty Years' War drove German princes of high and low degree to break their bonds and their bondholders. The popes, who were paying out half their income in interest after 1580, frequently forced their creditors to alter interest rates or principal sums. As old lenders were ruined, new ones emerged or were sought out. Creditors were offered annuities or the chance to win a big prize in a lottery; companies were offered trading privileges or the right to set up a bank. Compulsory loans were raised; Colbert took the deposits in the savings banks, Charles I of England took the treasure London goldsmiths had deposited in the Mint, and released it only when its owners agreed to lend him money. In 1671 his son Charles II defaulted on his debt to London bankers. The creditors had to be satisfied with a reduced interest rate and eventually with half the principal.

Only in the eighteenth century did conditions improve somewhat. Sovereigns became more willing to honor the debts of their predecessors, and better provisions were made for sinking funds. In England the growing power of parliament reduced the financial liberty of the crown; the tax system became less inefficient, revenue was earmarked for interest payment, and the debt was recognized as a national rather than a royal obligation. The security was thus greatly improved, money could be borrowed at a lower rate, long-term or even perpetual loans could be floated, and the national debt could mount higher with every war. In France and other parts of Europe borrowing, repudiating, and the depreciation of currencies continued to dot the history of war finance.

If kings were usually able to get more funds in spite of their bad record, the reason was that men forget or that the rewards were thought to be commensurate with the risks. Interest was high, collateral might be valuable, and the amount of money or goods actually supplied was often far below the face value of the loan. There was opportunity for great profit in army contracts. Some of those who supped with kings were able to wield a long spoon skillfully and leave the table well fed. But so long as the debtor was also the ruler the creditor was in a precarious position. The needs of governments diverted much capital from productive use, and the ability to obtain money allowed rulers to enter war more light-heartedly than they would have done had they been forced to pay as they went along.

(5) The states on the western fringe of Europe became empire builders. Apart from political or religious considerations, colonies offered opportunities for the investment of capital, the emigration of population, the securing of raw materials, the selling of European wares, and the consequent reaping of profits from trading and shipping. To stimulate these developments and concentrate the benefits in the parent land, the framing of colonial policy became an important part of western European statesmanship. It

might lead to war, for the New World, like the old, was regarded as a field of potential spoils, in which one country could benefit only at the expense of another. Whoever held a colony would strive to shut out the traders of all other states.

The Influence of the Maritime Discoveries.—The effect of the discoveries of new sea routes and continents was great, but must not be exaggerated. Economic activity remained overwhelmingly European in scope, interregional trade in the eighteenth century was still chiefly an exchange of European wares, and outside Great Britain it still is. If there had been no maritime discoveries, growth and change would have characterized the sixteenth and seventeenth centuries. Economically backward areas, such as England and Holland, would have become more active industrially and commercially, and the Hanseatic traders and towns would have been challenged by new rivals and strong states in the northwest. Florence, Venice, and Bruges would have faced the rise of other centers. The printing press, improvements in mining and metallurgical practices, and slow but sure innovations in industrial or agricultural equipment and methods would have come. The capitalistic class would have strengthened its grasp on industry, and the organization of banking, credit, and commerce would have become more elaborate. Fairs would have declined in importance as the machinery for transportation and distribution improved, while agriculture would have become more commercialized. In short, the movements which had all become more and more evident in the later Middle Ages would have continued. But the new routes and the New World opened up still more opportunities for those who were willing and able to seize them, made the whole world Europe's parish, and affected the pastor as much as his flock.

THE EXPANSION OF EUROPE

Causes of Exploration.—Until she found the new seaways, Europe was hemmed in on every hand. To the south lay the Moslem fringe of Africa, and beyond that the inhospitable Sahara, a thousand miles wide. Caravans traversed it, bringing ivory, gold, slaves, and ostrich feathers; but if the European wished to reach the source of these supplies he must circumvent the bad lands by going down the coast. To the west lay the apparently boundless Atlantic. In the northern part was a chain of stepping-stones— the Shetlands, Faroes, Iceland, Greenland, and Labrador. Leif the

Lucky had used them, and he may have had successors; but the seas around them were often rough, cold, fog-bound, and in the west were sprinkled with icebergs. To the east lay a land of invaders rather than a land to be invaded; a Europe torn by intercity or interfeudal rivalries could make little impression there, and when a strong power emerged in the east then not merely did Moslem Bagdad fall (1258) but so also did Christian Constantinople (1453).

Yet it was across or around these eastern expanses that the oriental produce needed by Europe had to come by one of the three famous and ancient routes: (1) overland from China and central Asia to the Baltic, Black Sea or Syria; (2) up the Persian Gulf, the Tigris-Euphrates Valley, and so to Syria; or (3) up the Red Sea, and then to Alexandria. If a strong power ruled the land areas trade might run fairly smoothly; but if tumult reigned, then the boat or caravan might not reach its journey's end. Even when there was peace, transportation costs and tolls added greatly to the f.o.b. (or f.o.c.) costs; there were many transshipments and handlings, much opportunity for damage and theft, and each link in the long chain of middlemen claimed its price for service and profit. Europeans were not welcomed on the trade routes as buyers or carriers; the Turks or Arabs kept the traffic in native hands till the wares reached the frontier of Asia. The Christian must make his profit by carrying on the trade from that point.

In the light of later events it is easy to point out the economies of the seaway opened up by the Portuguese; yet there is little evidence that the Italian yearned for a better way to the sources of supply. We know of one effort, made by the Genoese in 1291, to circumnavigate Africa; but the two great rival seaports preferred to try to oust each other from the old western termini, to defeat the Turks, or make the best possible trade treaties with them. There is no evidence to support the once popular thesis that Europe was driven to seek a way to India by the Turkish hostility to Christian traders, by the blocking of the trade routes, and especially by the capture of Constantinople in 1453.

This thesis fitted neatly into the nineteenth-century belief that the Turk was an "unspeakable" fanatic whose hobby was persecuting or massacring Christians. It pictured a Europe starved of spices, compelled to pay high prices, doomed to flavorless food, and therefore driven by desperation to find a new way. Professor Lybyer has, however, reminded us that Constantinople was not on an important spice route, and that the termini of the two important routes were not captured until 1516 and 1517; yet the Cape was rounded in 1487, America discovered in 1492, and India reached by sea in 1498. He has shown that oriental goods never ceased to be available in Europe during the fifteenth century. There was no increase in the price of spices, such as an interruption or excessive taxing of supplies would cause. The price of pepper actually declined during the period of "incubation of the great discoveries." The flow of oriental produce to Venice was normal up to 1502 or 1503, but in 1504 no spices arrived at Levantine ports; they had all gone round the Cape to Portugal. Finally, there is no hint in any of the explorer's narratives that the Turks were responsible for the maritime ventures.

The real explanation must be sought elsewhere. Many mixed motives—"gospel, glory, gold" (Shepherd)—inspired them, many improvements in maritime equipment and knowledge made them possible, and the personal enthusiasm of Henry the Navigator and his successor wedded the inspiration to the equipment. Henry (1394-1460) belonged to a land which had got rid of the Moors by 1250 and had gradually developed sea trade in wine, fruit, and oil with France, England, and Bruges. Its conflict with the Moor had made war on the infidel a normal permanent part of true religion, and two of Henry's main interests in life were to spread Christianity in Africa and make a flank or rear attack on Islam. To accomplish these tasks involved facing the almost unknown waters along the west coast of Africa. A few Genoese and French ships had been down there, but found little to stimulate enthusiasm for further exploits. The project called for systematic and serious effort, and Henry therefore withdrew from the camp to the study. On the promontory of Sagres (on the southwest tip of Portugal) he established what we should call a research institute. He built a shipyard, an observatory, and a school to study navigation and chart-making; he gathered in pilots, astronomers, cartographers, maps, books, and instruments from all parts, studied hulls and sails, and learned all he could about the west coast of Africa.

Fortunately for his plans, ship architecture and instruments had reached a point where navigation of the open ocean was now less hazardous. The *caravel* had been developed as a ship suited to Atlantic conditions. She carried two or three masts, with lateen (i.e., triangular) sails, easy to handle; her tall forecastle protected her from high seas; she was easily managed and faster than most other boats of her day. Henry improved her, added more masts, combined square-rigged and lateen sails, and produced a vessel capable of facing whatever the eastern Atlantic cared to do. For deep-sea navigation two of the three necessary instruments were now available. The compass had come from China by the twelfth century and was now widely used, while the astrolabe helped the navigator to determine his latitude. There was no instrument for finding longitude until about 1775, and mariners had to guess how far east or west they had moved. This handicap was serious, but not fatal; given a stouter ship, better sails, some instruments, charts, and a growing knowledge of winds, currents, and astronomy, one could desert the coasts and narrow seas of Europe, sail for weeks or months out of sight of land, and grope one's way to distant places.

The first Portuguese exploration went out in 1418, was blown out of its course and reached the Madeiras, which became the first Portuguese colony and a flourishing sugar plantation. Later trips went farther south, along the coast or to the islands that fringed it (e.g., the Cape Verde group), and went west to the Azores in mid-Atlantic. Henry died in 1460, but his work went on; in 1462 Sierra Leone was reached, and the coast was taking an encouragingly eastern direction. In 1471 the equator was crossed, but the coast had swung southward once more, thus destroying any hope that the Red Sea and Indian Ocean were just round the next headland. The length of that south-running coast was enough to break the heart of any explorer, and even when the corner had been turned (1487) the route to whatever lay beyond seemed too long to justify further effort. Not till 1498 was the final effort crowned with success, as Vasco da Gama reached Calicut.

In these gropings over unknown seas, politics, religion, and trade moved hand in hand. Colonies were planted, the Holy War went on, missionaries went out, the military Order of Christ took the African coast as its sphere of action, while trade in slaves, gold dust, and ivory developed. It is doubtful, however, if commercial interests alone would have been strong enough to push exploration to the end it actually reached. Diaz went as far as the Cape of Good Hope because he had been ordered to go on till he came to the kingdom of Abyssinia, the land of Prester John. If Portugal was to play its self-appointed rôle as savior of that Christian oasis and join hands with Abyssinia in an attack on the Moslems to the north, contact with the dusky crusaders must be by sea. The Cape was rounded, not in search of a new way to the produce of the Orient, but in search of colored Christians.

Portugal planned, spent, and worked hard for the material rewards that came from its discoveries. Spain's rewards fell into its lap accidentally, unexpectedly, and without much effort, for it found America in looking for something else, and at first was disappointed at the apparent failure of a venture into which it had been dragged by an incompetent braggadocio. Of Columbus at the end of the fifteenth century we know even less than of Shakespeare at the end of the sixteenth. He apparently mixed the gospel and gold motifs; he talked of reaching and tapping the fabulous wealth of Asia, winning converts, equipping an army out of the treasures of Ophir, and freeing Jerusalem from the Turk. His frantic fruitless search for treasure disappointed his sponsors, and others had to reveal the wealth waiting to be exploited in the New World. Moreover, it is not even certain that he was the first person from the Iberian peninsula to put foot on transatlantic soil, for evidence is slowly accumulating which suggests that the Portuguese had already crossed to Brazil from some such island outpost as the Cape Verde Islands.

Columbus' first voyage of 1492 was followed by three decades of vigorous exploration led by Spain and Portugal, but with Frenchmen and Englishmen playing a minor part around the mouth of the St. Lawrence. After the circumnavigation of the globe by Magellan's expedition (1519-1522) the rest of the story was largely a matter of filling in details. By 1600 the world map could be drawn with considerable accuracy except at one point— Australia. Many Europeans sighted or touched the big island during the seventeenth century, but always from the north and west. They therefore struck the worthless regions, and found nothing of commercial value, nothing but sandy waterless wastes, stunted trees, a strange beast with a big jump, and natives "the miserablest in the world." Not till 1770 did Captain Cook discover the more fertile east coast, and the whole rim of the continent was not charted till 1802-1803. Australasia does not enter the world's economy till the nineteenth century.

Effects of the Discoveries.—When Vasco da Gama reached India he is said to have announced, "We come in search of Christians and spices." The gate was now open for a great missionary movement and for securing oriental supplies in greater abundance with greater ease. The missionary work of the Jesuits was vigorous and successful in a parish that stretched from India to Japan. Sometimes the missionary turned trader, as the monk had done in medieval Europe. The Jesuits built up big trading enterprises in the Orient as well as in Mexico, the West Indies, and Brazil, and from these drew much income. The connection between religion and trade was close, and the first French company organized to penetrate Indo-China in the face of Dutch hostility tried to transport a party of priests whose business would be the encouragement of trade with France.

In course of time the trader with his aggressive individualism, his lack of scruples in dealing with colored peoples, his readiness with his weapons, and his active dislike of rivals who came from other parts of Europe, outlived his welcome in some parts of the east. So also did the missionary when he overstressed his by-occupation, when the feud between Protestant and Catholic was transferred to oriental soil, when the Buddhist priesthood found its influence threatened, and when rulers began to resent the power the Jesuits were wielding over politics. This anti-foreign attitude reached its height in Japan, where in 1638 Christianity was proscribed and all contact with Europeans was forbidden, save for a limited one with the Dutch, who managed to avoid the wide-swinging sword. From 1638 to the day when Perry's toe kicked the door open in 1854, Japan's only intercourse with the white world was through the little Dutch settlement on the island of Deshima. China also restricted the white man's movements, but in India, the spice lands, and most other regions he was able to get what he went to obtain.

The Influx of Oriental Produce.—The chief economic effect of the new sea route was to permit the carriage of oriental goods in great volume at lower transportation costs. The many sales, handlings, and transshipments gave place to one long continuous journey from the Asiatic port to Europe. Soon a dozen ships were leaving Lisbon each year; in 1503 they took on board 1300 tons of pepper alone, and in 1582 one ship reached Lisbon carrying 375 tons of pepper and cloves, "much cinnamon and other spices." It had spent only six months on the homeward journey. In return European goods which were not worth transporting along the old routes could now be sent more easily; and we find a European pepper merchant in India (1580) importing wine, oil, Dutch cheese, fish, and paper, but warning his friends at home that it was useless to send German merchandise, since tables split in the great heat while clockwork and iron goods deteriorated at sea. Copper, tin, pewter, lead, coral, cloth, mercury, and precious metals figured large in the eastward-bound cargoes. The same merchant also wrote, "The pepper business is profitable indeed; when the Lord God grants by his mercy that none of the ships take damage either in coming or going, then the merchants wax rich."

How far European consumers benefited through any substantial lowering of prices is not clear. The spice trade was in comparatively few hands; only big, heavily armed ships could visit the Orient; and the pepper trade was a royal monopoly which the king farmed out to a few large dealers. When the pepper reached Lisbon he claimed a fifth or a quarter of it, and sold it to big buyers or handed it to his creditors, who thus controlled its distribution. It seems safe to assume that the increased supply could be sold only by charging prices well below the medieval level; but prices fluctuated violently, for no one knew when a new cargo would arrive. In 1506, for example, the fleet left India in January. Some ships reached Lisbon in May, some in November, and some in January, 1507. Hence the market might alternate between famine and glut. When the Dutch gained control of the trade they tried to maintain high prices and avoid an overloading of the market by destroying plantations, crops, or cargoes. In the seventeenth and eighteenth centuries the taste for highly spiced foods slowly declined; less elaborate dishes became popular, and the taste of meats was not so thoroughly concealed. This probably weakened the demand for spices, and with the passing of the monopolistic controls of the Dutch and English East India Companies in the late eighteenth and early nineteenth centuries spices became more plentiful and cheap.

As Europe's contact with the Orient became closer, other eastern goods which had been little known found a wider market. Plain calicoes were imported, while chintzes, ginghams, and cretonnes, decorated with stripes or florid patterns, became popular. Defoe (about 1710) tells how they had "crept into our houses, our closets, and bed-chambers; curtains, cushions, chairs, and at last the beds themselves were nothing but calicoes and Indian stuffs," while cottons were used for underclothing and dresses. So strong was this invasion of the textile market that the silk and woolen workers clamored for a check on the importation of fabrics which they described as "tawdry, pie-spotted, flabby, ragged, low priced, made by a parcel of heathens and pagans that worship the Devil and work for ½d. a day." In Africa cotton goods were taken in payment for slaves, and in America they were worn by planters and slaves. These demands eventually stimulated the production of cotton goods in Europe in the eighteenth century.

Porcelain, indigo, tea, carpets, rugs, lacquered and brass-ware came in increasing quantities. Along the old trade routes porcelain would carry badly, and when Cecil looked round for a birthday present for Elizabeth, he could regard a China cup or plate as a dainty dish to set before a queen. But when the East Indiamen began to carry crates of porcelain with few breakages, fine pottery appeared on the tables of the rich, slowly displacing silver or plate, and stirring European potters to seek ways of making similar wares. Indigo, the product of a plant grown in India, was brought in greatly increased quantities, and the English East India Company fostered its cultivation. It met with bitter opposition from European woad producers and users, and in France and England the state attempted to protect these vested interests against the upstart, but with little success.

Tea was brought to Europe by the Dutch in 1606. By 1660 "that excellent and by all physicians approved China Drink called by the Chineans 'Tcha,' by other nations 'Tay' alias 'Tea' " was being advertised in London, buyers were being instructed how to make it "according to the directions of the most knowing merchants and travellers into those eastern countries," doctors were debating its effect on health, vendors of other beverages were attacking it, parliament was taxing it, and devotees were asserting that it made the body active and strong, cured headaches, giddiness, and heaviness, removed difficulties in breathing, vanquished bad dreams, strengthened the memory, the stomach, and the liver, and prevented tuberculosis. Gradually it became cheaper, and by 1800 the English consumption had risen to two pounds per head of the population; even the poor drank it. Architecture, gardening, and domestic decoration were affected by oriental influences. Wall paper was copied from China, and some German princes who had heard of the leisurely care-free life of the Chinese built palaces embodying Chinese architectural designs, hoping thereby to become leisurely and care-free.

African Produce.—Africa contained no surprises for European traders, but its staple wares could now be obtained at (or near) the source of supply. Gold was the most attractive; it was found around the headwaters of the Senegal and Niger, in Abyssinia and in Madagascar. Stories were told of a solid nugget weighing thirty pounds, and some company promoter declared that the natives had not yet "come to the main vein of any of their mines." Ivory was valuable for ornamental purposes; one enthusiast talked of the "prodigious number of elephants, which would not only facilitate the inland intercourse of commerce, but also afford a very beneficial branch of traffic in the teeth of these notable animals." Thus there was a Gold Coast and an Ivory Coast; but soon the Slave Coast transcended both in importance.

The Slave Trade.—Negro slaves had been known in ancient and medieval Europe, but the West Indies and the American mainland offered a bigger market than Europe had ever been. Native American labor might be forced into virtual slavery, but there was not enough of it, and workers must be imported for the mines and plantations. To buy and transport them, much capital and many ships were needed, and a regular triangular traffic developed. European ships went to the Gulf of Guinea, carrying trade goods—cloths of various fibers, qualities, and patterns; basins, bottles, beef, bells, beads, knives, swords, daggers, guns, sea shells, leather goods, and liquor. After much haggling with the slave dealers and generous use of the dram-bottle the price of a slave was decided; a woman slave might change hands for a gallon of brandy, six bars of iron, two small guns, one keg of powder, and two strings of beads; a man slave might cost eight guns, one wicker-covered bottle, two cases of spirits, and twenty-eight sheets. When at least three hundred slaves had been collected the ship sailed westward, lost from 10 to 25 per cent of its cargo from disease, and disposed of the remainder to the planters of the islands or mainland colonies. The ship then took on a cargo of sugar, hides, tobacco, indigo, or some other American product, and as much precious metal as it could secure, and made its way home to Liverpool, Bristol, Glasgow, Nantes, or Amsterdam.

For this trade in slaves or African produce the leading western European countries wrestled; even the Danes and Prussians tried to get a finger in the pie. Naval vessels protected their own nationals or destroyed the ships and forts of foreigners, and the Slave Coast bristled with guns. France, England, Portugal, and the Dutch owned colonies which needed slaves, and had staked out supply stations in Africa. Spain wanted many slaves but had no African possessions. She therefore made the delivery of slaves in the Spanish-American market a state monopoly, but farmed it out to Seville merchants and, when Portugal was annexed, to Portuguese traders. By the terms of the contract (*Asiento*) the crown was to receive a fixed fraction of the profit. But the Portuguese were not strong enough to keep their monopoly intact. Others smuggled slaves and merchandise into the market; the Dutch used Curaçao (taken from Spain in 1634) as their base; the English used Jamaica (taken from Spain in 1655) and Barbados for the same purpose, except when the Asiento traders were willing to buy the slaves.

In 1701 Louis XIV forced Spain to transfer the Asiento from Portuguese to French hands. England resented this, for if the French were strong enough to cut her out of the trade she would lose the supplies of precious metals and other desirable commodities she obtained from Greater Spain, and the Royal African Company which handled the slaves would be ruined. For this and other reasons she entered the War of the Spanish Succession (1702-1713), and emerged with the Asiento and full recognition of her claim to the Hudson Bay fur area. During the next thirty years she was to supply at least 144,000 slaves to the Spanish colonists; a quarter of the profits were to go to the Spanish king, and a quarter to the English crown. The concession helped English traders in their legal slave trade and gave a smoke screen to their illegal trade in commodities. Liverpool grew large in the eighteenth century on the triangular traffic, taking to Africa fabrics made in Lancashire, of cotton and linen, and bringing back from the West Indies sugar, cotton, and tobacco. Bristol did the same sort of trade; in 1760 her ships handled 30,000 slaves, and brought back the tobacco and sugar which were the two staple materials of her local industries. In France Nantes was the chief slaving port, and its ships were carrying 10,000 "pieces of black ivory" each year by 1750. A fifth of its shippers were in the traffic, and one of them christened his vessels *Voltaire, Rousseau,* and *The Social Contract.* Danes, Portuguese, Germans and New Englanders were also slavers, and big extensions in plantation production during the eighteenth century lifted the total traffic to 100,000 slaves a year.

The slave trade was thus an integral part of the economic life of both sides of the Atlantic. It was taken for granted as a respectable business, which differed from others only in being more risky and potentially more profitable. Captains of ships knew that their human cargo was too valuable to be treated with unnecessary harshness, and the death rate among it was often no higher than among the crew. It is estimated that in three centuries Africa contributed about 20,000,000 persons to the American labor supply—a migration which ranks second to that of Europeans themselves. For the purchase of slaves goods were produced and sent from America or Europe, and from their sale and labor vast supplies of plantation wares were obtained. In buying slaves the planters sank a great mass of capital; in transporting and selling them great risks were shouldered, large fleets employed, and some fortunes made.

American Produce.—Europe knew what Asia and Africa had to offer; but what would America yield to those whose path to the riches of Cathay it so rudely barred? Tradition and imagination always pave the streets of distant places with gold, and America, in spots, ran true to expectation. Away from the favored mineral zones the wealth was vegetable or animal, and had to be worked for. Fish from the Banks and the New England coast added substantially to Europe's food supply, and drew men to a region that had little else to offer. Furs were a rich natural asset; the beaver supplied raw material for the big heavy hats which bourgeois Europeans wore after 1650, and there were some furs of higher value. If fish brought Europeans to the coast, fur made them explore the interior, pushing their lines of exploration and trade ever farther afield from the Atlantic coast, the St. Lawrence, and Hudson Bay. Transportation costs kept American lumber out of the European market. England wanted lumber badly, for her forests were thinned woefully during the fifteenth to seventeenth centuries by the demand for ship material and for charcoal. Holland must import all the lumber for her shipyards. But the Baltic was the natural source of supply. When lumber was exported, it was chiefly in the form of ships built on the New England coast and sold in Europe. Farther south, Cuba, Jamaica, Honduras, and Brazil sent fustic, logwood, redwood, and other dyewoods, or mahogany and other timbers suitable for fine furniture.

America gave Europe five important indigenous products— tobacco, cocoa, cotton, corn, and the potato. Sugar was not indigenous; it was taken westward by Europeans, and took deep root in the West Indies. Cotton was a fiber found on both sides of the Atlantic, but the American mainland supply scarcely touched the European market until at least 1750. Corn crossed to Europe in the sixteenth century, but the area of its cultivation was climatically limited to the southern part of the continent. The potato came but did not conquer until the eighteenth century, when its cultivation spread rapidly over western Europe. The use of cocoa, the *chocolatl* of Mexico and the sacred drink of the Aztecs, passed quickly to Spain, became extremely popular, and after 1600 spread over the rest of central and western Europe. The Dutch fell in love with the beverage and established big plantations in Dutch Guiana; it was a Dutchman who first prepared the powdered cocoa of today.

Tobacco.—Tobacco's influence on personal habits, on the fate of some colonies, on the fortune of some European traders, and on British colonial policy was very great. Tobacco, consumed by the natives from the St. Lawrence to the Argentine, was quite new to the white man. Sailors brought some back to Spain, but the first Spaniard who smoked in his own land was imprisoned by the Inquisition. Tobacco seeds were soon introduced, and the plant and habit spread relentlessly from Spain. Jean Nicot sent seeds from Lisbon to France, and the plants which grew from them were called *Nicotiana*. By 1560 tobacco was being grown in France and Holland, and soon was known as far east as Turkey. Raleigh introduced the practice to the English court and polite society, and by 1600 men of fashion smoked at bear or bull-baitings, at the theater, and at home. Even Elizabeth is said to have "given it a trial."

Like all the new commodities, tobacco roused bitter controversy between its devotees and those who on moral, physiological, or economic grounds disliked it. The former claimed great medicinal virtues for it; applied externally, the leaves were a valuable antiseptic, disinfectant, and counterirritant in an age when soap, sanitation, and disinfectants were rare. Tobacco, said one advocate, "reduces filthy wounds and sores to a perfect health. It heals griefs of the head and cures colds in the head . . . [it] is useful also for evils of the joints, cold swellings, toothache, chilblains, [and] venomous wounds." Its smoke was "very good for loosening and carrying off the superfluous humours of the brain," and was both preventive and sedative.

To these eulogies of the new panacea, the opponents, headed by James I, replied with counterblasts, attacking the filthy, stinking habit which made bodies, rooms, dishes, and air evil-smelling, led men to ape the "barbarous and beastly manners of the wild, godless, and slavish Indians," and took money out of the country or sent it up in smoke. Governments tried to stop or restrain the use of tobacco. The pope threatened to excommunicate those who took snuff in church. France taxed tobacco heavily, and when this failed to restrain its use decreed that purchasers must have a physician's order and buy only at apothecaries' stores. The Greek Church forbade the use of tobacco and the czar ordered that first offenders be whipped, second offenders be executed, and snuff-takers have their noses cut off. Turkey decreed the death penalty.

All such prohibitions failed in varying degrees, and governments changed their policies when they saw that tobacco could be heavily taxed since it was not a necessary of life. Richelieu detested tobacco, but welcomed the revenue it yielded. Venice in 1659 set up a tobacco monopoly, and the practice of farming the right to produce or sell became popular. England, which shared with Spain the ownership of the chief American sources of supply, shaped much of her early colonial policy in terms of tobacco. James I and Charles I might order the struggling Virginia colonists to breed silkworms, produce pitch or tar, and regret that "this province is wholly built upon smoke"; but when an experimental cargo of leaf found a ready market in England in 1613 the settlers' worst troubles vanished. They now had a commodity with which they could buy what they wanted from Europe; they threw their whole energies into tobacco cultivation, and by 1700 were sending about 20,000,000 pounds to England.

Once hostility had been abandoned, a policy of fostering the industry and of regulating the trade was possible. Encouragement was offered by checking or eliminating competition from other producers. Spanish tobacco was loaded with increasingly heavy import duties, and at times forbidden entry into England; by 1700 Spain had lost the English market. But another rival was not so easily crushed. Tobacco could be grown in southern England, and in the early seventeenth century cultivation in Gloucestershire and the neighboring counties was spreading wide; one London capitalist spent £6,000 on the cultivation of a hundred acres. When Virginia tobacco entered the market the London importers and investors in the Virginia Company's stock decided that their trade and the colony's welfare would be helped if the English crop could be eliminated. They played on the prejudice of the king and offered to pay higher duties on imports in return for a ban on English cultivation. James accepted the offer, and farmers were ordered to destroy their crops and plant no more.

Eighty years passed before that order was effective. Prohibition produced the inevitable battle of wits and wills. The farmers continued to cultivate tobacco, and even extended their fields. The local justices, who owned the land on which their tenants were growing the tobacco, were ordered to enforce the decree, but folded their arms and did nothing, in spite of scoldings and threats from London. When sheriffs supported by regular troops tried to invade the fields, the farmers rose in a body, repulsed them, and killed one sheriff. The colonists and London merchants demanded firmer action; new laws were passed, but not till the end of the century did English tobacco disappear. Even then it did so because its Virginian rival was now being better cured and was selling at such a low price that the native produce could not profitably compete with it.

The tobacco trade was an excellent field for the cultivation of such commercial policies as were popular in the seventeenth century. It could be controlled to swell the national revenue, foster British shipping, keep foreign ships or merchants out of the trade, benefit British ports, gain access to foreign markets, and wring money out of foreigners who depended on Virginia for their supplies. How this was done we shall see later; it is enough to note here that by 1700 tobacco had become one of the main-stays of English commerce, played an important part in the colonial and foreign policy of the country, was the basis of colonial life in the warmer parts of North America, and had entered into the trading activities and consumers' habits of Europe.

American Treasure.—After a period of disappointment Spaniards discovered in America those precious metals and stones which Marco Polo and others had led them to expect if they got to Cathay or Cipangu (Japan). Adventurers and settlers des-cended on the "Pearl Coast" of Venezuela and Panama, pearls were found in the Gulf of California in 1533, and during the next two centuries the coast of Lower California was the scene of countless pearling and colonizing expeditions. The discovery of diamonds about 1725 made Brazil the chief world producer until Kimberley in South Africa revealed its treasures about 1870.

American gold and silver came to a Europe which was already getting a larger supply from its own deposits or from West Africa. The mines which produced most of the medieval supply had petered out, and the yield from the alluvial deposits of gold obtained in river valleys was small, in spite of the fame of Rhine-gold. Thus Europe in 1450 was probably facing a mild famine of precious metals. Relief came with the establishment of sea con-tact with West Africa, with the opening of new mines in Sweden and central Europe—gold near Salzburg and in Transylvania, silver in Bohemia, Saxony, and the Tyrol—with improved meth-ods of mining and metallurgy, and with the investment of much capital by south German financiers. Better pumps or chains of buckets made possible the drainage of deep mines; water wheels improved the vertical haulage of ore; trucks on rollers, run on wooden tracks, made horizontal movement easier, and an at-tempt was made to improve ventilation. Stamping mills were designed to crush the ore; smelting and refining methods became more efficient; but the discovery of a method of extracting silver by amalgamation with mercury did not come till about 1550—in time to be very useful in America.

In 1503 the first trickle of American treasure came from the

West Indies, in 1519 the first installment of Mexican spoils taken from the Aztecs arrived, and in 1534 was followed by similar booty from the Incas of Peru. This plunder made the *conquistadores* feel that their hazardous ventures were well repaid. In Peru they saw 1,300,000 ounces of gold all in one heap. They found four large figures of llamas of fine gold, and a dozen life-size golden statues of women. The king offered a room full of gold as ransom; his subjects had life-size trees, flowers, birds, and wild animals, all of gold, dotted about their gardens, households, and temples; utensils were of gold, and slabs of silver, twenty feet by two feet and two fingers thick, served as tables. Here was El Dorado.

The treasures already above ground were trifles when compared with those soon to be found underground. Natives, colonists, or German miners revealed rich deposits waiting to be exploited, and the amalgam method came into use. In 1545 the Potosi silver field in Peru began to be worked, and those at Zacatecas and Guanajuato in Mexico were soon attacked. The last was perhaps the richest silver vein ever worked, but Potosi was more easily pronounced and became a synonym for fabulous wealth. From mines and alluvial deposits a rapidly rising stream of silver and a small quantity of gold flowed to the assay offices, to the ports, and thence to Spain. The Spanish annual imports between 1580 and 1630 were about ten times those of the fifteen-thirties (the decade of Peruvian plunder). The high watermark was reached in the fifteen-nineties, when the imports were nearly thirteen times those of the 'thirties. After 1600 Potosi slowly became less productive, but the yield elsewhere remained high till about 1630; after that date output ebbed rapidly, but did not cease by any means, while just before 1700 Brazil began to produce large quantities of gold and continued to do so all through the eighteenth century.

Between 1521 and 1660 about 18,000 tons of silver and about two hundred tons of gold passed through official channels from America to Spain. At the 1934 value, the gold would be worth about $170,000,000, the silver about $200,000,000. These weights, given by Professor Hamilton, the latest authority on the subject, are at most only half the estimates made by earlier writers; the gold is about one-fifth of that held by the Bank of England, much less than the annual output of the South African gold mines, and one-fortieth of the gold held by the United States Treasury in 1934. But to sixteenth-century Europe it was a large and important addition to the continent's stock of metal. It was supplemented by supplies from central Europe, Russia, and Africa; in the Urals deposits of gold and silver were intensively exploited after 1574, and by 1584 German and English managers were directing the labors of 15,000 miners. Precious metal even came from the Far East, for the Dutch brought some gold dust from Japan along with the spices and other goods they had obtained for their hardware and cloth.

Spain made elaborate plans to insure that the crown received its full share of the new riches. Mining was done by private enterprise, but all bullion must be delivered to royal assay offices. There it was cast into bars or plates, and a *quint*—which was usually a fifth but might be as low as a tenth—was taken by the state as royalty. Then much of it was dispatched to Spain. The damage done to treasure ships by pirates led in 1565 to the organization of merchant fleets, which left Spain, one in April and one in August, convoyed by warships. These fleets gathered up and transferred the metal with apparently little loss; on only two occasions (1628 and 1656) did the English or Dutch divert any important part of it from its destination. All treasure went to Seville. There the House of Trade (*Casa de Contratación*) was stationed, to control and develop the traffic with America, and one of its tasks was to receive and distribute the bullion. Some of it belonged to the crown; some had been sent by emigrants to their relatives in the old land; but most of it went to pay merchants for the provisions and manufactured articles they had sent to the colonies.

Seville (or even Spain) was not, however, the terminus of the treasure. It was merely the bottle neck through which the metal flowed on its way to be scattered over western Europe. Some treasure never went near Spain, for smuggling, though fraught with very severe penalties, was continuous. If the producer (or the trader who bought it from him at the mine) could get his silver out of the country without passing it through the assay office he escaped the quint; and when French, Dutch, and English ships operated from Caribbean islands, buyers of unquinted metal were not far away. But much of the law-abiding treasure soon passed out of Spain. A large part of the king's share had to be handed over to his foreign creditors, and some went to pay the wages and other costs of Spanish armies fighting in France or the Low Countries. Of the privately owned bullion, some belonged to French and other foreign traders who had sent goods to America, while much of the rest seeped out to France, England, Holland, and Italy to pay for the manufactured wares which Spain bought for herself or for her colonies. Her own industries were incapable of supplying all these needs, her prices were higher than those of other countries, and she therefore imported much foreign produce. In these various ways the treasure of America was spread out among the traders and financiers of the rest of Europe.

Treasure and the Price Level.—Two chief results ensued. The first was a long and large rise in the general level of prices. The second was a general quickening of commercial activity in which the Spanish treasure acted both as lubricant and gasoline. The increase in prices was due to two causes—debasement of the currency and the larger supply of precious metal. Currency debasement, frequent in the fourteenth century, had been comparatively rare in the fifteenth, except in Spain. But the sixteenth, with its long, costly wars and spendthrift rulers, saw much devaluation, especially in France and England. In England Henry VIII and his successor led the penny down the slope, and the silver which had been in one penny in 1520 had been spread into six by 1551. Spain set its teeth and stuck to "sound money" all through the sixteenth century, but faltered and fell after 1600.

If debasement raised prices, the influx of new metal raised them still further, and Spain's honest coin did not prevent the country from feeling first and most fiercely the effect of the "price revolution" of the sixteenth century. An exhaustive international study of the history of prices is now in progress, and within a few years we may possess a satisfactory collection of graphs and index numbers for different countries and centuries. Professor Hamilton's study shows that Spanish prices around 1600 were over three times as high as those around 1500; for the years 1601-1610 they averaged about 3.4 times the average of the years 1501-1510. Once the metals began to flow eastward, the curves showing bullion imports and price movements run almost parallel throughout the sixteenth century.

For other countries less thorough studies are available, but those which we have all show a long, marked, upward trend. In France prices during the last quarter of the sixteenth century were 2.2 times as high as in the first quarter; in England the

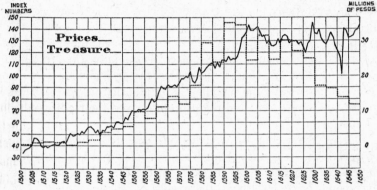

SPANISH IMPORTS OF TREASURE[1]

price ratio of the first and last decades was 1 to 2.6, but the highest point was not reached until the Civil War (1642-1648), when the price level was 3.5 times that of 1501-1510. In Alsace prices doubled during the century, in Italy they nearly doubled, and in Flanders the index for wheat prices rose from 100 in 1520 to 336 in 1599.

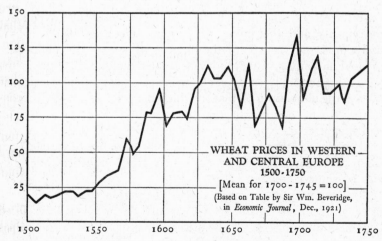

WHEAT PRICES IN WESTERN AND CENTRAL EUROPE
1500-1750
[Mean for 1700-1745 = 100]
(Based on Table by Sir Wm. Beveridge, in *Economic Journal*, Dec., 1921)

[1] From Earl J. Hamilton, *American Treasure and the Price Revolution in Spain, 1501-1650*, Harvard University Press, 1934.

This price movement was at times so large and rapid that it roused widespread discontent, especially among those whose incomes from wages, interest, or rent did not rise or rose less slowly than did the prices of the goods they had to buy. As in all such periods, everybody blamed everybody else, and all kinds of remedies were proposed. Farmers were accused of holding back wool, grain, oil, or wine, and they in turn blamed the greedy and covetous middlemen. The exporter (especially the foreigner) was accused of creating domestic scarcity by shipping too many commodities away; the merchant was pilloried as forestaller, regrater, and engrosser; and the usurer received the traditional condemnation.

Out of the welter of explanations emerged one or two wise observations. In France, Jean Bodin, scholar and lawyer, put two fingers on two vital spots in 1568. In the first place, he said that the rising price level was the result of currency depreciation. Depreciation ruined the state and the poor; only the hoarders, moneyed interests, financiers, and usurers gained when a higher value was given to a coin or some precious metal was taken from it. In this argument he echoed the view of an Englishman who had written Edward VI as follows: "Whether it hath made your Majesty rich or no I cannot tell, but I am sure the coinage since the first beginning (of the debasement) hath exacted upon your subjects already above eight shillings in the pound."

In the second place, Bodin stressed the connection between price movements and the influx of precious metals. The "principal and almost only cause" of the higher prices was the "abundance of gold and silver, which today is greater than at any time in the past four hundred years." "The principal cause of high prices is always the abundance of that in which the price of goods is measured." Bodin was not the first to say this; even Greek writers had hinted at it. Nor did he see the whole problem. But he did explain the relation between Potosi and prices more clearly than his predecessors, and his work, widely read, influenced the policies of some countries.

Almost every government took some action to cope with the price problem. In Spain the crown and the municipalities fixed legal maximum prices, yet the prices actually paid were sometimes two or three times those allowed by law. In France edicts of 1554, 1567, and 1577 fixed wages and prices, but with little effect. In

Flanders the seigneurs were allowed to raise their dues to compensate them for the fall in value of money units (1589). In England the middleman was subjected to more severe restrictions or even forbidden to buy some goods unless he held a license. Forestalling, regrating, and engrossing were more carefully defined by law (1552), and an attempt was made to keep the market free from extortionate dealers. At the same time, an effort was made to provide for the adjustment of wages. When prices nearly doubled between the fifteen-forties and 'sixties, parliament in 1563 admitted that the maximum rates fixed in various earlier statutes were "in divers places too small and not answerable to this time, respecting the advancement of prices of all things." It therefore abolished the old maxima, and ordered the justices of the peace in each county to review the wages question annually at Easter. They were to call before them "such grave and discreet persons as they shall think meet," confer "respecting the plenty or scarcity of the time, and other circumstances necessary to be considered," and then "rate and appoint" wages for the next year. In this way it was hoped a figure would be fixed which would "yield unto the hired laborer, both in the time of plenty and in the time of scarcity a convenient proportion of wages." Wages would presumably go up or down as prices rose or fell.

In practice this did not happen. The justices were usually landowners, their interest may have been with the wage payer rather than the receiver, and their natural inclination was to reissue the same figures year after year. In general, the statutory rates lagged far behind the price movement; if the rates fixed and those actually paid coincided, the result was a decline in the standard of living of the worker who depended solely or chiefly on his wages. The *real* wages of masons, for example, seem to have fallen by half between 1500 and 1600. There is evidence that sometimes the actual wage was higher than the justices' rate, but there were some prosecutions of masters or servants who gave or received more than they should. Many workers were not wage earners or were not solely dependent on their money wages, but many had little cause to bless Spanish treasure.

If the wage earner suffered, so also did the landlord who lived largely on rents fixed for many years (or generations ahead). His cost of living mounted, but his income did not. On the other hand, some classes of society were not injured, but even benefited from the price revolution. The independent craftsman or small master may have raised the price of his wares or services to meet the higher cost of the things he bought. The farmer would not be affected if he was self-sufficing, and would benefit from higher prices if he produced for market. The employer gained as the gap between the value of labor and the price of labor widened. The merchant profited by the greater volume of goods now entering the market, by the wider opportunities for trade, by the increased chances for successful speculation, as well as by the rising prices.

The expansion of the bullion supply had many other effects on European economic life, on commercial expansion, and on adolescent capitalism. More currency was available for operating a money economy, for building up a banking and credit structure, and for accumulating a supply of investing or spending power. Europe had a larger supply of bullion on which it could draw to pay Orientals for their wares, trade with the east could be expanded, and some of those who poured silver down the eastern sink—or, to adopt Hamilton's term, buried it in the oriental necropolis—won rich returns. The wealth that Spanish kings drew from El Dorado stimulated them to ambitious policies which had far-reaching political and economic effects, while the desire to conserve and increase the supply of precious metals influenced commercial policy at many points during the seventeenth and eighteenth centuries.

BIBLIOGRAPHY

ABBOTT, W. C., *The Expansion of Europe* (1925), vol. i.
ANDRÉ, M., *Columbus* (1928).
BEAZLEY, C. R., *Prince Henry the Navigator* (1904).
BOURNE, E. G., *Spain in America* (1904).
CLARK, G. N., *The Seventeenth Century* (1929), chaps. 1, 11, 12.
CORTI, COUNT, *A History of Smoking* (Eng. trans., 1931).
Day, C., *History of Commerce* (1907), chap. 15.
EHRENBERG, R., *Capital and Finance in the Age of the Renaissance* (Eng. trans., 1928), book i, Introduction.
FAYLE, C. E., *Short History of the World's Shipping Industry* (1933), chap. 4.
HAMILTON, E. J., *American Treasure and the Price Revolution in Spain, 1501-1650* (1934).
HANNAY, D., *The Sea Trader* (1912).
HARING, C. H., *Trade and Navigation between Spain and the Indies in the Time of the Hapsburgs* (1918).

HAUSER, H. (ed.), *La vie chère au xvie siècle: la réponse de Jean Bodin à M. de Malestroit, 1568* (1932).

HAUSER, H., *Les origines historiques des problèmes actuels* (1930).

HAUSER, H., and RENAUDET, A., *Les débuts de l'âge moderne* (1929), book i, chap. 2; book ii, chap. 6; book iii, chap. 1.

HELFFERICH, K., *Money* (Eng. trans., 1927), part i, chaps. 2, 3, 4.

KLARWILL, V. (ed.), *The Fugger News Letters* (Eng. trans., 1924).

KNIGHT, M. M., FLÜGEL, F., and BARNES, H. E., *Economic History of Europe* (1928), chaps. 7, 8.

KULISCHER, J., *Allgemeine Wirtschaftsgeschichte* (1929), vol. ii, chaps. 1, 2, 21.

LUCAS, H. S., *The Renaissance and the Reformation* (1934), chaps. 1, 8, 27.

MacINNES, C. M., *The Early English Tobacco Trade* (1926).

NUSSBAUM, F. L., *A History of the Economic Institutions of Modern Europe* (1933), part iii.

PRESTAGE, E., *The Portuguese Pioneers* (1934).

RENARD, G., and WEULERSSE, G., *Life and Work in Modern Europe, 15th to 18th Centuries* (Eng. trans., 1926), Introduction.

ROBERTSON, H. M., *Aspects of the Rise of Economic Individualism* (1933).

SALZMANN, L. F., *English Trade in the Middle Ages* (1931).

SÉE, H., *Modern Capitalism* (Eng. trans., 1928), chaps. 3, 4.

SOMBART, W., *Der moderne Kapitalismus*, vol. ii.

STRIEDER, J., *Zur Genesis des modernen Kapitalismus* (1904).

STRIEDER, J., *Jacob Fugger the Rich* (Eng. trans., 1932).

TAWNEY, R. H., *Religion and the Rise of Capitalism* (1926).

TAWNEY, R. H., Introduction to Wilson's *"Discourse upon Usury (1572)."*

WEBER, MAX, *General Economic History*, chaps. 22, 23, 30.

WEBER, MAX, *The Protestant Ethic and the Spirit of Capitalism* (Eng. trans., 1930).

ARTICLES

CLARK, G. N., "War Trade and Trade War, 1701-1713," in *Ec. H. R.*, vol. i (1928), pp. 262-280.

DONNAN, E., "The Early Days of the South Sea Company," in *J. E. B. H.*, vol. ii (March, 1930), pp. 419-450.

HAMILTON, E. J., "American Treasure and Andalusian Prices, 1503-1660," in *J. E. B. H.*, vol. i (November, 1928), pp. 1-35.

HAMILTON, E. J., "American Treasure and the Rise of Capitalism, 1500-1700," in *Economica*, November, 1929, pp. 338-357.

HAMILTON, E. J., "Imports of American Gold and Silver into Spain, 1503-1660," in *Quart. J. Econ.*, vol. xliii, pp. 436-472.

HAUSER, H., "The European Financial Crisis of 1559," in *J. E. B. H.*, vol. ii (February, 1930), pp. 241-255.

JANE, L. C., "The Columbus Controversy," in *Contemporary Review*, January, 1930.

LYBYER, A. H., "The Influence of the Rise of the Ottoman Turks upon the Routes of Oriental Trade," in *Am. Hist. Assoc. Report*, 1914, pp. 125-135. Similar article in *Eng. Hist. Rev.*, October, 1915.

MARTIN, G., "Commercial Relations between Nantes and the American Colonies," in *J. E. B. H.*, vol. iv (August, 1932), pp. 812-829.

NETTELS, C., "England and the Spanish-American Trade," in *J. Mod. Hist.*, vol. iii (March, 1931), pp. 1-32.

RICHARDS, R. D., "The Stop of the Exchequer," in *Econ. Hist.*, vol. ii (January, 1930), pp. 45-62.

Rive, A., "The Consumption of Tobacco since 1600," in *Econ. Hist.*, vol. i (1926), pp. 57-75.

Rive, A., "A Short History of Tobacco Smuggling," in *Econ. Hist.*, vol. i (1929), pp. 554-569.

Strieder, J., "Origin and Evolution of Early European Capitalism," in *J. E. B. H.*, vol. ii (November, 1929), pp. 1-19.

Encyclopædia of the Social Sciences: Articles on Asiento, Bodin, Jesuits, Mercenary Troops, Metals, Mining, Plantation, Plantation Wares, Slavery.

CHAPTER XIII

THE DEVELOPMENT OF THE CHIEF ECONOMIC POWERS

DURING the fifteenth to eighteenth centuries the center of interest is commercial expansion. In the light of that interest Europe falls into four areas: (1) Some countries felt little direct stimulus from the New World, saw no startling development in industry or trade, but jogged along down a country lane from one small town to another. Foreign traders might link them with the outside world, foreign financiers might come to tap their natural resources, and ambitious rulers might seek to westernize (which usually meant industrialize) them; but their essentially rural character persisted. Russia, Austria, the Balkans, Prussia, and Poland belonged to this class.

(2) Some regions slipped from the position of power they had enjoyed in the Middle Ages as the backward areas they had served rivaled and outstripped them, as the trade routes they had dominated lost their value, and as the supply of capital became more widely dispersed. Of this class the Hanseatic towns and the Italian cities were the chief instances.

(3) Spain and Portugal entered first into the riches of the New World, but lacked the domestic resources, population, political wisdom, or commercial class needed to consolidate their gains in the face of economic and political rivals.

(4) Holland, France, and England combined exploitation of the New World with aggressive development of domestic industries and participation in European trade. The foundation and much of the superstructure was local, European; it rested on the North Sea or Mediterranean, on supplying the goods needed by Russian, German, Spaniard, Turk, or Scandinavian as well as by the home market; but to this was added a superstructure of imperial distant trade or of breaking into other people's empires. The spotlights of economic history after 1600 shine chiefly on these three countries, but before seeing what they reveal the story of the other areas can be briefly told.

THE HANSEATIC TOWNS

The decline of the Hanseatic League was due to many developments, but few of them had much connection with the news explorers brought back. Inside Germany some towns progressed at the expense of others, and in foreign fields the Hansards faced keener competition from English, Scandinavian, and Dutch merchants. These rivals appealed to their governments for aid, whether by depriving the Hansard of his preferred position or by gaining easier access to some of his markets. Against such attacks the League was not able to put up a lasting defense, for a weakened confederation now faced strong territorial states in Poland, England, Brandenburg, Russia, and Scandinavia.

Only a few aspects of these developments need be noted. The eastern and southeastern Baltic coast towns, headed by Danzig, waxed prosperous on the trade in Prussian grain and spruce, shipped their goods through the Sound, and had therefore little interest in Lübeck or the isthmus route, while their sales of spruce may have injured Lübeck's trade in Norwegian lumber. In the south, Nuremberg and Augsburg took away some of the northern cities' exchange of western cloth for eastern furs, and Leipzig displaced Lübeck in the fur trade. Cologne occasionally broke away from the League and tried to gain privileges at the expense of its fellow members, while Hamburg in 1567 offered an open door to English merchants at a time when the League was being attacked in England. Thus harmony and unity of interest grew weak.

External rivalry or hostility came from many quarters. The herring shoal which for centuries had spawned in the shallow waters off Scania began to go elsewhere during the early sixteenth century. Bay salt displaced Lüneburg salt, and the shift of oriental traffic from Venice to Lisbon deprived the German towns of some overland transit and distributing business. The Dutch developed the North Sea herring fishery and crept through the Sound or up to Norway, and when Lübeck tried to restrict them the power of the Duke of Burgundy was behind them. English merchants gradually obtained a larger slice of the export trade in English cloth and metals, and in 1598 persuaded Elizabeth to close the Hansard headquarters in London. Gustavus Vasa loosened the German grip on Sweden and Denmark, the Czar evicted the

Hanse from Novgorod when he captured that town (1494), Poland's victory over the Teutonic Order in 1410 placed a strong territorial power on the League's flank, and the Hohenzollern Electors of Brandenburg compelled all their towns to sever connection with the League. In the new world of territorial states there was little room for an interurban association.

The League made a brave but futile fight against the rising tide of states and traders. Its last diet was held in 1669. By that time shrinking trade and the ravages caused by the Thirty Years' War had reduced many towns to positions of petty local importance, but the big ones lived on. Cologne felt the loss of Italian traffic, and as a bulwark of Catholicism she lost some Protestant artisans or traders, but she remained the chief city and market on the Rhine. Danzig throve on the export of grain and lumber. Hamburg found work to do serving the growing Berlin and Brandenburg markets. But there, as in Bremen and Cologne, the colonial produce that came to her wharves was largely brought in Dutch, French, or English ships. In spite of the grandiose plans of the Great Elector for colonies and a navy, few Germans traversed the lanes of long-distance trade until the eighteenth or nineteenth century.

THE ITALIAN CITIES

The Italian cities felt the influence of both European and external developments, and their preeminence as middlemen, manufacturers, and financiers gradually vanished. The Cape route to India deprived them of nearly all their trade in Far Eastern products, for Lisbon pressed home its advantage ruthlessly. In 1502 it sent da Gama east with a fleet of twenty-one vessels to break the Arab-Egyptian control of the Indian Ocean. Albuquerque took Socotra in 1506 and Ormuz in 1507, thus blocking the entrance to the Red Sea and Persian Gulf. Turk and Venetian discussed plans for revenge, and there was talk of a canal at Suez; but war in Europe distracted Venice's attention and funds.

Without the oriental wares Venice was no longer the middleman of Europe; the trade through the Brenner Pass declined, and the galleys made their last journey to Flanders in 1532. There was still much trade with the eastern Mediterranean and the lands beyond Syria, for some goods and people traversed western Asia and went overland as far as India and China; but the Italian cities failed to retain their old control even there. The Turks welcomed, or at least tolerated, English, French, and Dutch in their ports, and the newcomers made headway in competition with Italians. Frenchmen carried on the work of Jacques Cœur, and Englishmen, who apparently rarely ventured into the Mediterranean before 1400, were by 1600 well established in Constantinople, Smyrna, and Aleppo.

As Italian trade with the Levant and Egypt shrank in importance, the Italian towns depended more upon the manufactures and supplies of capital they had left. Their fine wares stood for a time supreme, and served the luxury market at home and abroad. The silk fabrics of Florence and Venice were famous; Venetian woolen cloth, velvet, cloth of gold, glass, lace, and leather were widely known; and the Aldine printing firm, founded in 1491, gave the world its first fine books. But gradually French, Dutch, and other craftsmen picked up Italy's industrial secrets. Lyons rivaled Venice and Florence in producing silks, French and Flemish lace competed with Venetian, Dutchmen became great printers and learned the art of finishing and dyeing cloths, while the rise of luxury-loving courts stimulated a dispersion of fine arts and crafts. New tools, processes, or sources of supply of raw materials freed the north and west from dependence on Italy, and state policies of protection closed the doors to her wares.

As international financiers the Italians maintained their position much longer, for the needs of new states and new traders called for more funds than the western fringe of Europe could supply. Genoa played a large part in financing crown and trader in Spain and Portugal, Italian firms had branches in Lyons and Antwerp, the Genoese fairs in the sixteenth century were the center of large transactions in foreign exchange or in the settlement and creation of debts, and Florentines were the leading figures in French high finance till about 1650. From Paris or Lyons, Italians or men of Italian stock born in France spread their agencies over northern Europe. One of them, Burlamachi, settled in London in 1605, became financial agent for the English government, and pawned the crown jewels in Amsterdam. These dealings with rulers frequently led to disaster; rivalry between Italian cities was still intense, and while the financiers in one city supported one side in an interdynastic conflict those in another backed the other side, thus providing fuel for fires which more than once scorched both lenders. Hence the great centers gradually ceased to be important dynamic forces in the economic life of Europe. Their economy became local or at most Mediterranean; they were living on their capital. In any tour of the continent a visit to Italy must be included, and by the seventeenth or eighteenth century the country was becoming a tourist center. But the western fringe of Europe had learned how to dispense with her services as it had with those of the Hansards.

PORTUGAL

Portugal's economic welfare depended on her ability to make the most of her embarrassment of riches in America, Africa, and the East. Her own natural resources were limited, for wool, cork, and port wine were her only staple exportable products. But her empire offered rare prizes, and to its expansion and exploitation

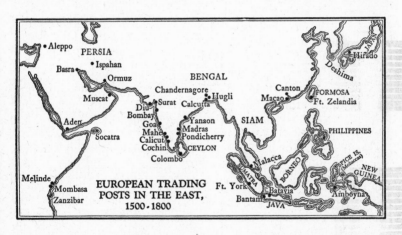

EUROPEAN TRADING POSTS IN THE EAST, 1500-1800

she brought at first intense energy and determination. Albuquerque, Governor-General of India (1509-1515), strove to drive Moslem traders off the Indian Ocean and secure control of the spice areas. He strung a chain of posts from the Red Sea to China; from the western ones he attacked the Arab ships, from the central and eastern ones—Goa, Calicut, Cochin, Malacca, Amboyna, Java, Sumatra, and Macao (in China)—he laid hands on the spice lands or ports. He cultivated the friendship of rulers in Siam, Java, and China, helped Hindus to throw off Moslem rule, put them in high posts in the Portuguese colonies, and encouraged his men to wed native women. A string of settlements on the east and west coasts of Africa and on the Atlantic islands provided stepping-stones between Portugal and the Orient and concentration points for local produce. Across the Atlantic Brazil was a valuable sugar colony long before gold and diamonds were discovered.

To get the full benefit of possessions in three continents called for greater strength than Portugal possessed. Effort was not lacking, and a German observer in Cochin reported in 1580 that "the Portuguese here are even more diligent than the people in Lisbon." But the country was too small to meet all the demands that conquest, colonization, and commerce made. Its population of at most two millions provided no great reserve labor supply for crews, emigration, and trade. The loss of life by wreck, disease, or war made the problem of man power serious; according to one estimate, the population fell from two millions to just over a million during the sixteenth century, but this decline cannot possibly have been all due to the exodus of men overseas. The drain was not beneficially counteracted by the importation of slaves.

Portugal also lacked the necessary capital and had to lean heavily on south German and Italian financiers for funds to equip her oriental ventures. The spice trade was a royal monopoly, but foreigners supplied much of the money needed by the crown, and played a large part in the trade in other goods. Portugal also lacked the central geographical position needed by a distributing center, for the hinterland of Lisbon offered no natural route to any great market except Spain. Goods must be carried by sea to some more central point, and as Bruges was now definitely supplanted by Antwerp it was to that port that the spices were forwarded. Contact between Lisbon and Antwerp was in large measure maintained by non-Portuguese ships and money; Low Country vessels often carried the cargo; and Dutch, German, or Italian merchants or financiers obtained possession of the goods before they left Lisbon. Thus a large slice of profit escaped from the hands of the Portuguese.

When foreigners went to Lisbon for supplies they felt an urge to go still farther and collect the wares in Africa and the Orient. When Spain annexed Portugal in 1580, and fought the English and Dutch, Lisbon became an enemy port, and the Portuguese monopoly of the Orient could be challenged in the interests of patriotism and profit. The Dutch tried in vain to drive the Portuguese from Macao, but did succeed in evicting them from the Malay Peninsula, Ceylon, and southern India, and in cutting large slices off their trade with Africa. Where the Dutch stopped, others carried on; an Indian ruler expelled the Portuguese from Hugli on the Ganges delta, and the Arabs evicted them from the Persian Gulf. When Portugal succeeded in regaining her independence (about 1665), her eastern possessions had shrunk to Goa, Macao, and one or two other points. Some outposts on the east and west coasts of Africa, along with the mid-Atlantic islands, were still hers, and she retained Brazil till 1822. Her African and Brazilian possessions were therefore still substantial, and Lisbon remained a great port, thronged with English, Dutch, and French ships, and with foreign merchants who wished to exchange the wares of northern Europe for the wool and wines of Portugal or the precious metals of Brazil.

SPAIN

While Portugal achieved greatness, Spain had greatness thrust upon her. By conquest, marriage, and discovery the empire that reached its height in the reign of Philip II (1555-1598) lacked nothing in size, quality or quantity of resources. When Ferdinand and Isabella wed (1469) they united the central pastoral kingdom of Castile with the eastern agricultural, industrial and commercial land of Aragon. Moorish Granada in the south was captured in 1492, thus uniting the whole peninsula except Portugal, and Portugal was absorbed in 1580. Outside Spain, Philip's realm included the territories of Milan, Naples, and Sicily, with their banking, industry, and agriculture. In the North Sea it embraced the Netherlands—the old industrial regions of Flanders and Brabant and the rapidly growing shipping, manufacturing, and trading towns of a later Holland. For a moment it included England. Beyond Europe, Philip ruled parts of North Africa, the Canary Islands, the possessions in America and those which fell into his hands with Portugal. He had a fine army, a big navy, great prestige until the English and Dutch shook it, and an intensity of religious fervor which made him regard himself as "the junior partner of Almighty God."

This political and economic power came almost simultaneously, just before and after 1500, to a country that had modest resources and some aptitude in their exploitation. Since the strength of an empire depends in large part on the strength of its home base, the best way to tell the Spanish story is to look at the strong and weak spots in that base, and then see how the acquisition of territories in other parts of Europe and in America reacted on Spain. As the empire was largely a political product, the policies of its rulers played a large part in determining its welfare, but economic factors were also important.

The greater part of Spain was mountain or plateau, with insufficient rainfall and long dry summers. Cultivation could be undertaken in the valleys or where irrigation was possible, but most of the land would not carry a large rural population and was fit only for cattle, goats, and sheep. On it grazed millions of merino sheep, whose fine wavy wool had won, even in Roman days, a high reputation. Spain had a monopoly of this kind of wool and forbade the export of merino stock till the latter part of the eighteenth century. Other animal products, especially hides and skins, were the basis of the Moorish leather industries. The pastoral areas were owned chiefly by large landlords, lay or spiritual, who had received much of the land reclaimed from the Moors, and who seem to have developed and managed their ranches fairly well.

To protect their flocks and pastures the ranchers formed an association about 1350. It was known as the *Mesta*, and during four centuries operated as a guild, with officials, council, court, and a large measure of political power and royal favor. One of its main tasks was to facilitate the migration from the southern to the northern pastures each spring, and the return in the fall. The broad path along which the sheep moved must be kept free from farmers, inclosures, and fences; agricultural encroachment must be resisted; and if the area open for grazing could be expanded, so much the better. Royal decrees were secured reserving a special wide strip of land; sheep could graze on any village commons *en route* and even on crop or orchard land after harvest. Within the track cultivation and inclosure were banned; outside that belt agriculturists were forbidden to turn pastures into arable. At various times decrees demanded that land taken from pasturage be allowed to revert to grass. Wool was king.

Eastern and southern Spain had soil, climate, and water supply suitable for the typical Mediterranean cultivations. There the Moors had developed and Christians continued the growth of grain and the production of wine, olives, fruits, rice, and silk. The Moor was forbidden by the Koran to consume alcohol, yet was a great wine producer—a good illustration of commercial farming. Here, as at some places in the interior, industry and trade created great towns. The skill of Moors and Jews built up important textile, hardware, and leather industries, while such ports as Barcelona and Valencia shared in the traffic along the Mediterranean, sending out raw materials, foods, and manufactured wares.

Spain in 1500 is thought to have housed about seven million people. To their ruler was now added sway over other parts of Europe and over the great transatlantic unknown. The first effect was to give a powerful stimulus to Spanish economic life; the second was to draw the country into costly diplomatic, religious, and dynastic disputes north of the Pyrenees, and dissipate a large part of the new-found national income in unproductive and unsuccessful enterprises. The heavy obligations in Europe eventually taxed, strained, and exhausted the new income from America and the old one from Spain; and when the flow of precious metal subsided after 1600 nothing else came that could adequately take its place. Spain lived at least up to her means, but her means declined after 1600; yet some of her obligations, especially the attempt to suppress the Dutch rebels, remained.

The story of Spanish agriculture, industry, and even commerce in the sixteenth century has been little studied, but certain developments seem fairly clear. The colonial demand for goods reacted on most forms of Spanish production. The colonists wanted the things they had consumed at home, and for a time were probably too busy seeking and getting treasure to produce them in America. The demand for wine, oil, hardware, textiles, furniture, etc., stimulated Spanish rural and urban activity, and industrial centers like Toledo and Segovia grew rapidly. To conduct the trade more ships had to be built (or bought) and more sailors employed; in the Middle Ages Genoese ships had conducted most of Spain's sea carriage, but by 1580 she probably had the largest merchant marine in Europe. Bullion offered an easy method of paying for colonial purchases, and therefore made the overseas buyer a better customer than he might have been if he had to find non-metallic exportable produce with which to pay his bills. The colonial church and government were erected on a large scale, and needed much equipment from home. The profits made by Spanish traders and the remittances to the crown or private persons increased purchasing power in the parent land. Finally, the rising price level stimulated industrial enterprise, for wages lagged behind prices till nearly 1600, and the entrepreneur's profits were therefore good.

This period of prosperity gradually came to an end during the latter part of the sixteenth century, and after 1600 agriculture, industry, and commerce stagnated or decayed. The merchant marine eventually dwindled to insignificance, the great industrial and trading cities shrank, the famous fairs of Castile lost their international importance, and the Mesta flocks diminished. The total population by 1700 seems to have fallen to 6,000,000. By the eighteenth century poverty had become so widespread that water was the national drink.

The causes of this decadence are not at all clear. The eviction of those Jews who were unwilling to become Christian cannot be a cause, for it happened too early, in 1492. The exodus of Moors when Granada was taken in 1492 is also too early, and the expulsion of Christian Moors (Moriscos) in 1609 apparently had little economic effect. Emigration to the colonies took away some young men, the cream and the scum of the country; but such figures as are available suggest that the drain was not serious. The fleets, army, and missionary organizations took men out of the country, while the church and the monasteries took them out of economic and matrimonial life. The sum total of these leakages may have been great, but no single one was large enough to have serious effects. Attacks on the growth of church lands and complaints concerning the excessive number of monks show that some onlookers felt that the price paid for spiritual services was too high, that the church was absorbing too much of the national dividend, and that men and money might be put to more productive uses. The church lands were often well and efficiently managed, but it is possible that the yield from them and from the contributions made by the laity took an excessive part of the total income of the country and the colonies.

The most severe strain on Spanish wealth was the cost of an ambitious foreign policy, of the splendid court in Madrid, of the protection of true religion, and of long wars. The furious attack on the Low Countries laid waste Antwerp and the manufacturing regions of the present Belgium, and drove the Dutch into successful revolt. American gold and silver were used to furnish the sinews of war and "were a factor in the shedding of the blood of Spain—sacrificed on altars of imperialism and religious fanaticism —on distant European battlefields" (Hamilton). The growing cost of royal consumption and conflict could not be met solely by quints and colonial contributions; domestic taxes must be increased, and large loans were raised. The fate that periodically befell the creditor has already been described. In 1639 the royal credit was so low that no one in Seville would advance money in anticipation of the arrival of the American treasure at less than 70 per cent discount. At other times the soldiers went unpaid, and recompensed themselves at the expense of the country in which they were stationed. Merchants at times refused to supply goods to the palace until some of the outstanding bills were paid, and courtiers went from house to house begging alms for the king. Of the taxes, the *alcabala*, a sales tax, was at times as high as 15 or 20 per cent; and while its payment was supposed to be shared equally by buyer and seller, the latter apparently had to bear most of it, and the tax fell heavily on the trading class.

Inability to make ends meet drove Spain's rulers to debasement of the currency after 1598. "Philip II opposed unsound money no less tenaciously than he fought the cults of Luther and Mohamed" (Hamilton), but his successor, Philip III (1598-1621), found the budget unbalanced and the revenue all earmarked for creditors. In 1599 he debased the vellon money, made of silver and copper, by extracting its silver, and in 1602 he doubled the face value of each coin. His successor's reign (Philip IV, 1621-1665) was full of strains and stresses, including a revival of the Dutch conflict, the Thirty Years' War, revolts in Spain, Italy and Portugal, and the drastic decline in the American export of bullion. It was therefore one of alternate periods of inflation and penitent deflation, of jumping and tumbling prices. In one period of seventeen months (1641-1642) wholesale prices in Seville jumped 93 per cent, but dropped 87 per cent in a few days when deflation took place. These fluctuations "upset calculations, stifled initiative, and impeded the vigorous conduct of business enterprise. Although in some respects a result of economic decadence, vellon inflation was one of the most powerful factors in the economic decline of Castile" (Hamilton).

The final cause of Spanish stagnation was the growth of foreign competition in the home and colonial market, and the decline in the colonial purchase of Spanish wares. The advance in Spanish prices was earlier, more rapid, and greater than that in France and other countries, and this probably handicapped Spanish export industries in competition with their rivals. Many of the goods that went to America were foreign, and were often sent by foreign merchants. A recent study suggests that nearly a third of the silver imported into Spain about 1600 found its way to France in payment for French goods sent to America. In addition, the colonies gradually developed the production of some goods formerly bought from Spain, and the decline in the imports of treasure into Spain, which was continuous after 1600, involved a falling demand for goods.

Of Spain, as of Portugal, it may be said that she politically overtaxed her economic strength. Her political unity was far from complete, and economically she was far from being united. She lacked easy land transportation; the passage across the Sierras from valley to valley was difficult, and the central plateau came so close to the sea in places that movement from the coast to the interior was hard. The rivers were in general too fast or shallow for navigation and the coasts were poorly supplied with harbors. Political divisions died hard and some of them never died; internal customs barriers and different systems of weights, measures, and currency survived, while strong sectional patriotisms and animosities made the country what it was officially called when Ferdinand married Isabella—*las Españas,* not *la España.*

Spain and America.—Spain was the first modern state with a colonial problem to face and a policy to frame. There was little precedent to guide her, except the general desire of all powers, civic or national, to keep all possible benefits for their own exclusive enjoyment, and the feudal assumption that whatever was found overseas belonged to the crown until it had been alienated into private hands. The control of commerce and the colonies was soon in the hands of three bodies. (1) The *Casa de Contratación* (House of Trade) was established at Seville in 1503 to act as the royal trading house; but since the traffic soon grew too big and complicated to be kept as a royal preserve the *Casa* became a regulator of private enterprise, issuing licenses to merchants, emigrants, and prospectors, supervising trade, dispatching ships, collecting customs, and receiving the treasure. It provided pilots, ran a school of navigation, appointed a professor of cosmography, and ran a court of law. (2) The *Council of the Indies* was set up in 1524 to frame and administer colonial policy and supervise the *Casa*. (3) The *Merchant Guild of Seville* was formed in 1543 to regulate and help traders, settle disputes, serve as a mouthpiece in dealings with the *Casa*, and raise money for convoys or government loans.

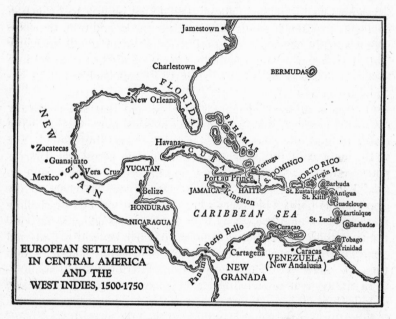

EUROPEAN SETTLEMENTS
IN CENTRAL AMERICA
AND THE
WEST INDIES, 1500-1750

These three bodies wielded great power. The first two at least were diligent and conscientious in their efforts to order colonial society and trade wisely, to promote material welfare, check acquisitiveness when it threatened to run amuck, protect the native, and prevent wealth from flowing into the wrong (non-Spanish) pockets. Their difficulties and failures sprang partly from the attempt to control even the petty details of colonial life from the eastern edge of the Atlantic in an age of slow communication. "Remote control" requires electricity. Even the best-informed and well-intentioned Council could not always grasp essentials, watch corruptly inclined officials, or understand the viewpoints of colonists living four or five thousand miles away. Settlers soon developed economic interests and attitudes that did not coincide with those of the home rulers. On the frontier in all continents they wished to seize all possible opportunities, demanded privileges from the parent land yet resented rules imposed by her, and lacked any sentimental ideas concerning natives. The local representative of the central government might try to enforce the imported laws, or be content to observe the letter and let the spirit evaporate. If he did not become indifferent or corrupt, he had to depend on an inadequate supply of underpaid minor officials who supplemented their incomes by closing one or both eyes. Thus colonial policies failed if they were too rigid, were framed by men who lived too far away, clashed with the colonists' interests, or needed a large, incorruptible administrative personnel.

The three main problems confronting the Spanish empire builder were those of land, labor, and trade. The first two belong to American history rather than European, and little need be said about them. Immigrants were attracted by the opportunities for booty or the hope of finding treasure, but when that appeal lost its early potency there remained the lure of a big estate and of a claim to the labor of those who lived on it. The natural tendency was to grant large holdings like feudal fiefs; hence the church and a small number of laymen held sway over a great area and a large (but not always adequate) native population. There was little room for the small cultivator, and peasant emigration was given scant attention. The New World did not offer a home to Spain's rural poor.

In the control of colonial trade there was for a brief period promise of a liberal policy. Charles V, a good European, was willing to open the American door to the non-Spanish trader and immigrant. This put the Spaniard at a disadvantage in competition with Italian and German rivals; and Philip II, a good Spaniard, bolted the door. All trade must flow through Seville, a river port fifty miles up the Guadalquivir, or through Cadiz near the mouth of that stream. Attacks on Spanish ships led to the concentration of traffic in two fleets each year, carrying goods to be distributed through the great fairs of Porto Bello, Vera Cruz, and Cartagena. From Spain only Spanish merchants who held a license from the *Casa*, and whose goods had paid the required heavy export duties, could trade with the colonies. The Merchant Guild watched its monopoly carefully. In the colonies those who trafficked with foreigners without express permission faced the risk of death as a penalty, any foreigner caught trying to enter a colonial market might expect execution or a life sentence in a mine, and smugglers of unregistered bullion might be sent to the galleys or to exile.

The temptation to take these risks was too strong to be resisted by Spaniard or foreigner. The former saved money if he could slip his goods out of Seville or Cadiz. Some licensed traders were simply shields for foreign merchants who supplied the capital and goods but used a Spanish partner (or commission agent) and trading name. In 1691, according to one estimate, between 94 and 98 per cent of the goods leaving Spain for the colonies belonged to foreign merchants, though the documents all carried the names of Spanish exporters. Colonists had many inducements to buy and sell without the law. They got their goods and slaves more cheaply if no duties had to be paid, and obtained a better net return on their bullion if they did not have to send it to the assay office and pay the quint.

Foreigners found patriotism and profit in climbing the ring fence. Like the French king, Francis I, they asked to be shown the clause in Adam's will which excluded them from a large part of the world. By 1514 Frenchmen and Moors were making sporadic raids into the Caribbean, and others soon joined them. Sometimes the foreigner went with a cargo for sale. John Hawkins in 1565 forced the Spanish officials to let him trade, to reduce the customs duty from 30 to 7½ ducats, and to buy his slaves at a good price—all by displays of bows, arrows, pikes, and arquebuses, or by the use of two small brass cannon. Sometimes the foreigner went to pillage ships or ports. Drake in 1572 raided several towns in the West Indies and ransacked 200 merchantmen; in 1577 he captured two treasure ships on the Pacific coast. Piracy became a normal occupation. The island of Tortuga was the center of the industry, and from it buccaneers of all countries roamed the sea lanes, from Boston to Brazil. A recently published diary shows how a bankrupt Frenchman set out "like an honest man" to pay his debts. From 1684-1688 he haunted the Pacific coast, plundering towns and ships, and returned to satisfy his creditors with gold, pearls, and jewels worth 30,000 "pieces of eight."

The seventeenth century saw growing foreign activity in Spanish American ports. Spain still maintained her trade restrictions, but grew less and less able to enforce them, for she could no longer maintain elaborate fortifications and big garrisons. Foreign ships sailed straight from Europe, or made such islands as Martinique, Jamaica, or Curaçao their bases. When the Spanish fleet arrived in western waters in 1662, it found the American fairs so fully stocked with smuggled goods that much of its cargo had to be taken back to Spain. The French were very active, and the traders of Nantes and St. Malo went out, even as far as the Philippines. English trade grew rapidly after the conquest of Jamaica in 1655. The Dutch were at least as active as their rivals, and the Spanish colonists had no cause to feel that an exclusive colonial policy really excluded.

The effective reply to this invasion of the colonial preserve would have been either a competent fleet—which Spain could not now afford—or a display of resourcefulness and energy on the part of the Spanish merchants themselves. But the merchants of Seville and Cadiz were either unable or unwilling to bestir themselves for a great effort. Moreover, Spain did not produce many of the goods the colonies needed. During the seventeenth century various proposals were made for the establishment of joint-stock companies which would do for Spanish trade what such companies were doing for Dutch and British. The government blessed the suggestions, but the Seville merchants successfully opposed them. Meanwhile others made the effort and reaped the reward. The trade with Spanish America helped to transfer commercial supremacy from southern to northern Europe, and the loss of the Spanish colonies in the early nineteenth century had scant effect on the economic welfare of a mother country that was doing little to serve its brood.

ANTWERP

Antwerp provides a good bridge from southern to northern Europe, and from medieval to early modern commerce. It displaced Bruges as the great trading and financial center of northwest Europe; on it was concentrated the energy generated by the enlarged oriental and new American trade, the capital resources of the German financiers, the vast credit operations of kings, and the activities of men who sought fortunes by adventuring bravely or speculating luckily. It was the home of the "new era of opportunity."

Bruges was hurt by many blows, such as the weakening of

Hanseatic trade, the growing use of Antwerp by the English for the export of wool or cloth, the silting up of the Zwyn (especially by a great storm in the winter 1404-1405), and wars in Flanders after 1482. The volume, speed, and character of trade were changing, but the little commercial oligarchy that ran Bruges was slow to realize this or to adapt the facilities and rules of the city to new needs. Antwerp had a better geographical position, and offered all comers a great measure of freedom and a minimum of control. The storm that damaged Bruges benefited Antwerp by sweeping away some of the shoals that blocked the Scheldt estuary. When Brabant (in which Antwerp stood) was annexed by Flanders (in which Bruges was located), the two ports became rivals inside the same political unit. When the dukes of Burgundy united the Netherlands (1419-1477), connected them with their inland possessions, established a uniform currency, fostered rural industry, encouraged the Dutch against the Hansards, and nursed Antwerp, the fortune of that city was virtually assured. To two old fairs Antwerp added two new ones, but it saw the value of providing facilities for continuous trade, and in 1485 the merchants erected a *bourse* which was open every day. It was so successful that by 1531 a bigger and better building was provided, and on its entrance were inscribed the words, "For the use of the merchants of all nations and tongues."

To Antwerp came the Hansards, the Merchant Adventurers of England, the Dutch, and the merchants and moneymen of south Germany and Italy. Portugal established a royal agency there to handle spices, and when Spain began to collect American cargoes Antwerp, the trade center of the Hapsburg Empire, became busier still. Goods from all parts of Europe and Greater Europe changed hands there. The concentration of trade in commodities produced a trade in bills and other means of payment, and developed a market in which public and private borrowers and lenders could meet. Loans were raised by kings, princes, and towns, and the bond or security they offered—a title to a quantity of silver or spices in a future shipment, or a claim on taxes as yet uncollected—was salable. Marine insurance developed, foreign exchange transactions were large, and speculation flourished, especially in pepper or other commodities which were subject to famine, glut, or attempted "corners."

To feed the needs of public and private credit, capital flowed in from all parts of western Europe and from all walks of life. Financiers took deposits from or sold bonds to all sorts of people, and men who had no skill or knowledge "had their flutter" in this sixteenth-century Wall Street. News of war, peace, and political prospects was eagerly sought, and its possible effect on trade and finance was weighed. Rumors, scares, "advice to investors," the bellowing of "bulls" and the growling of "bears," schemes to defraud simpletons, plans to make easy millions, all filled the air of what Professor Sée has called this "seat of unbridled capitalism." "Never since," says Ehrenberg, "has there been a market which concentrated to such a degree the trade of all the important commercial nations of the world"; never before had there been a market so free from restrictions and so full of opportunities for the manifestation of the acquisitive instinct.

The conflict between Philip II and the Netherlands wrought havoc on Antwerp. The attempt to extirpate heresy drove many Jewish and Protestant merchants, money-dealers, and artisans northward into the provinces of Holland, Zeeland, and Friesland. The sack of Antwerp (1576), the tumult in the industrial hinterland, and the growing aggression of Dutch privateers along the coast ended Antwerp's boom period. Its activities revived later, but other places—Genoa, Lyons, Frankfurt, Amsterdam, and London—had appropriated its financial work, the English took their cloths elsewhere, and the Dutch held the oriental trade. In 1598 Philip II shut its merchants out of direct trade with Spanish possessions (including Portuguese) in America or the Orient. When Dutch and Spanish made a truce in 1609 the former held all the islands of the delta and could close the approaches to Antwerp. For nearly two centuries they were kept closed, and Antwerp virtually vanished as a seaport. Only when the French in 1792 took the southern Netherlands from Austria and began to redevelop them did Antwerp regain freedom to exploit once more its geographical advantages.

The Dutch Republic

In the Middle Ages the region we now call the Netherlands was a mixture of water and sandy expanse, dotted with a few manufacturing, fishing, and shipping villages. Its inhabitants practiced intensive farming on the land they could keep dry, producing good cheese, fat cattle, and fairly good wool. Utrecht made fine cloth, while Amsterdam, with its sheltered harbor on the Zuyder Zee, had become a port of some importance by 1300 and a member of the Hanseatic League in 1358. These conditions contrasted strongly with those of the highly industrialized areas south of the Rhine delta. Yet by 1650 Holland had become the chief shipping, trading, manufacturing, and financial nation in Europe.

The steps to that position are fairly clear. The first was the extension of Dutch fishing in the North Sea. For the second time herrings were the foundation of commercial power. The Dutch were building up their herring industry long before the shoals of Scania ceased to be productive, but the decline of the Hansard fish trade made their position still stronger. Their success was due partly to the use of large boats (*busses*) manned by ten to fifteen men. In these they could go out to the larger and richer spawning banks off the British coast, instead of being compelled to wait till the fish came near the shore. They could use bigger nets, and could salt the catch on board instead of having to hurry it ashore for treatment. They also had a new improved method of preparing the fish for salting, and their government insisted on proper salting, packing, and grading in order to maintain the reputation of the product in foreign markets. Hence the industry advanced steadily from at least 1410 (when the busses were first used), and, by 1620, 2000 vessels were at work. The distribution of their catch employed a big fleet, and opened the way for the carriage of other goods and the picking up of return cargoes. In the words of a contemporary Dutch *bon mot*, "The herring keeps Dutch trade going, and Dutch trade sets the world afloat."

The second step was the extension of coastal trade up to Scandinavia and the Baltic, and the gradual displacement of German traders from some of their preserves. The herrings helped, the westward carriage of Prussian grain and lumber and the eastward traffic in cloth became important, Bergen was opened to Dutch trade in 1524, and the Dutch demand for lumber and naval stores for her shipyards made her a good customer in Scandinavia. Between 1559 and 1594 the Dutch share of the total imports of a remote area like Finland rose from 3 to 34 per cent.

The third step was the growth of traffic with Lisbon, Cadiz, and the Mediterranean. Fish, cheese, wax, manufactures, and other northern products went south, and in return wheat from Sicily, Levantine wares, wines, fruit, and oriental produce were brought north. Nearer home were the French and British ports, and during the first half of the seventeenth century much of the trade of Nantes and Bordeaux was in Dutch hands.

The fourth step came when the conflict with Spain, especially after 1580, shut Dutch ships out of Lisbon and Cadiz and embarked the seven rebel provinces on a colonial career. Like the English, they had been searching for a northeast or a northwest passage to the east, but now they determined to defy Spain by sailing on the orthodox routes. Between 1595 and 1601 at least fifteen fleets set out for the spice lands. Of eight ships that sailed in the spring of 1598 four were back by July, 1599; they had reached the Indies in seven months but returned in five and a half, and could boast that "never have the Portuguese accomplished such a journey." In 1599 thirty-six ships went east, and in 1602 the Dutch East India Company was set up, uniting various small groups which had nursed the infant trade. It was given a monopoly of oriental trade for nineteen years, and its charter was periodically renewed. It was vigorously supported by the government, and given sovereign power to make peace and war, found colonies, build forts, maintain an army and navy, and do whatever seemed necessary for the extension of its power and profit.

That extension was forcibly effected. In 1607 Jan Pieterszoon Coen entered the service of the Company, and from 1613 to his death in 1629 he was a second Albuquerque. His double aim was to oust the Portuguese, who had been in the east for a century, and the English, who had come about the same time as the Dutch. He founded Batavia on the ruins of a place taken from the English and the natives. From that stronghold he and his successors pushed out in all directions, driving the Portuguese from most places except Macao and Goa. With the English the fight must be under cover, for the two countries were allies; but Coen made the English traders' lot in the spice areas very unhappy, and in 1623 put a band of them to death at Amboyna, the center of nutmeg production. By 1680 the Dutch had made the spice-producing regions their own preserve, and the English and French had to be satisfied with posts on the Indian coast. Mauritius and Cape Town were valuable ports of call for East Indiamen, and became Dutch colonies. The spice trade was profitable; the Company regularly paid interest on a large bond issue and dividends of 15 to 25 per cent upon its stock. Its shares were sold on the Amsterdam Bourse from 1602 onward. In the spice areas crops were restricted, plantations or cargoes destroyed, and natives massacred in order to prevent prices from being lowered by a surplus of goods.

The western ventures were much less important. The search for the northern passages led to the exploitation of the whale, seal, and walrus regions, but the Greenland Company, organized in 1614, achieved little. As for America, there were treasure ships or coastal towns to be attacked, opportunities for smuggling, and furs in the north. By 1600 ships were parting company with the East Indiamen in the south Atlantic, slipping across to Brazil or the Spanish Main, attacking Brazilian ports and seizing cargoes of sugar. In 1609 Henry Hudson, in the employ of the East India Company and still searching for a way to the Pacific, entered the Hudson River and found an abundant supply of furs. This news failed to interest his employers, but in 1621 the West India Company was founded under the initiative of an Antwerp merchant, Usselinex, who had been forced to flee into Holland and had long sought revenge on Spain. The Company secured a monopoly for twenty-four years over settlement and trade on the "barbarous coasts" of Africa and America.

As fighter, trader, and smuggler the Company was successful; as settler, it was not. Profits from the fur trade looked meager in contrast with those made in other directions, and the trade did not call for a great population as did sugar production in the West Indies and Brazil or tobacco growing in Virginia. The settlements at Fort Orange (Albany) in 1624 and at New Amsterdam (New York) in 1626 were chiefly trading posts, separated by great but scantily developed estates. The government of the colony was either despotic or corrupt; the settlers resented the Company's restraint of their trading efforts, accused it of profiteering on imports, and were unconcerned, or even pleased, when its "neglect and forgetfulness" were ended by the British capture of New Netherlands in 1664.

Farther south the Company did better, for as the Spanish defense weakened the Dutch ability to raid and trade grew stronger. In 1634 Curaçao and two other islands—all a mere stone's throw from the coast of Venezuela—were captured, and served as splendid bases. Farther northeast was St. Eustatius, which in the eighteenth century offered free trade to the ships of all nations, and was used for smuggling goods into the British and Spanish colonies. In South America pieces of Guiana were secured. The development of sugar cultivation in the West Indies used much Dutch capital and shipping. Finally, the West India Company had the African coast in its parish, and from the posts dotted there it gathered gold, ivory, and slaves.

Trade with three distant continents, superimposed on the large traffic in European waters, made the Dutch the leading traders of the world. Geography helped, for a position on the North Sea and at the mouth of three important rivers—the Rhine, Meuse and Scheldt—put Scandinavia, the British Isles, western Germany, Belgium, and northern France within easy reach. But this factor, supplemented by successful displays of force overseas, was not enough in itself to insure preeminence; it had to be capitalized by fashioning an economic equipment better than that of any rival. That equipment consisted of a superior shipping fleet, a group of important industries, and the financial mechanism of Amsterdam.

Shipping.—The supremacy of Dutch shipping in the seventeenth century was admitted by French and English observers alike. The merchant fleet was more cheaply built, manned, and operated than that of other countries, and carried goods at the lowest freight rates in Europe. English and French ships still tended to be "reduced versions of men of war" (Barbour), for though both countries were building navies they were incapable of providing adequate convoys, and thought of the merchantman as a possible convert to war uses. For regions where trouble might be expected or ships had to face a long, grueling journey, the solidly built armed vessel was desirable, and on the routes to the Levant and Indies English and Dutch vessels—"rather tubs than ships"—were fairly evenly matched.

On the seaways of northern and western Europe the situation was quite different. There the journeys were short, the cargoes bulky and cheap. To carry them the Hansards had developed the *kogge*; the Dutch built the *fluitschip* (flyboat). She was a "light, slight, but practicable shell, employed to [carry] a ponderous and clumsy cargo. She had commonly one deck, but otherwise she was as nearly a closed hold and nothing more as a ship under sail could be" (Barbour). She was insignificant above the water line, round at stem and stern, long, broad and flat-bottomed, and carried three short masts with a simple set of sails. She was easily handled by a few sailors, offered little surface for wind resistance, and was so manageable and mobile that she could make one voyage per annum more than her Hansard forerunners. She might carry from 100 to 900 tons of cargo, was unarmed or carried only a few light guns, and was "about as warlike as a coal-scuttle" (Barbour); but in the North and Baltic Seas the power of the Dutch navy or the prestige of the government made the waterways fairly safe.

The flyboat cost little to build, for three reasons: (1) The material was bought in bulk, with prompt payment for low prices; Dutchmen paid less for Norwegian masts and planks landed in Holland than did builders in Norway. (2) In constructing the vessels, there was some standardization of design and therefore of parts. Labor-saving machines, such as wind-driven sawmills and cranes, were used. The lumber, masts, cables, sails, ropes, anchors, etc., were neatly arranged so that a ship could be put together and equipped by methods which foreshadow the modern assembly line. The shipwrights of Saardam on one occasion agreed to turn out ships at the rate of one a day, provided they were given two or three months' grace for assembling supplies and organizing construction. (3) The builder was able to borrow money at a much lower rate than his foreign rival, and since building and owning were profitable there was never any lack of loan or share capital; peasants, shoemakers, bakers, and brewers were part-owners of vessels.

These ships were easily and cheaply operated. Their crews were one-third or a half the size of those on English or French craft. While the English Navigation Laws of 1651 and 1660 demanded that ships have two English sailors out of three or three out of four, the Dutch used foreigners at lower wages in an age when the sailor had become the dregs of the labor world. Crews were harshly disciplined, taught the virtues of cleanliness, and fed on simple fare. The wide range of Dutch trade allowed food supplies to be purchased where they were cheapest, and when England forbade the importation of Irish cattle, the Dutch bought the banned beef and butter at lower prices.

All these advantages and economies allowed Dutch freight rates to be a third or a half less than those of other shippers. Rivals might try to destroy this advantage by shutting Dutch vessels out of certain routes or ports, especially in the colonies, as the English Navigation Acts sought to do. They might try to tempt Dutch carpenters to emigrate, as when Colbert sought some for the French royal shipyards; but merchants with goods to be carried sighed for Dutch vessels, and those who needed ships went to Holland to buy them. The Dutch built much of the fleet of the French East India Company; sold flyboats, fishing vessels, and colliers to England; provided big merchantmen for Spain's colonial traffic, and supplied Hamburg and Scandinavia with ships. Professor Barbour suggests that possibly a third or a quarter of England's merchant tonnage in the late seventeenth century had been built abroad, chiefly in Holland. At that time Petty estimated that nearly half of Europe's shipping tonnage belonged to the Dutch, and a quarter to the English. The fractions may not be reliable, but they give the contemporary view of Dutch supremacy. That view was shared by Peter the Great when he went to Amsterdam to learn shipbuilding, invited shipwrights and naval men to build and man the first Russian warships, and chose a Dutchman as his first admiral. In the nineteenth century Dutch naval officers and engineers instructed Japan's first naval cadets. In the twentieth century Holland has often ranked third (after England and Germany) as shipbuilder, and stood first when a vessel had to be salvaged or a dry-dock had to be towed from England to Singapore.

Industries.—Dutch industries were partly those of an *entrepôt* nation, a middleman who fetches goods in bulk from far places and distributes them in smaller parcels to consuming areas. Holland had few native raw materials, but she worked on raw or partly manufactured imports and exported what she did not consume at home. Her indigenous skill was substantially aided by immigration, for refugees came from all parts where strife or intolerance made life unsafe. From England Protestants migrated during Mary's reign, Catholics during Elizabeth's, and Puritans in Stuart times. From France Huguenots came before the Edict of Nantes (1598) and after its revocation (1685). The troubles in the Spanish Netherlands drove so many *emigrés* northward during the reign of Philip II that the country, once predominantly Catholic, became chiefly Protestant. The Thirty Years' War sent many Germans down the Rhine. Jews from Spain and Portugal were given extensive civil rights in 1593 and became prominent in industry and finance.

These migrants helped many industries. Belgian cloth workers strengthened the woolen industry in Leyden and the linen industry of Haarlem. French and Belgian experts brought silk dyeing and weaving to Amsterdam about 1580, and when in 1606 two large Portuguese ships were captured, laden with Chinese raw silk, the making of silk yarn was seriously begun. The East India Company took steps to secure raw material, city officials kept watch over the quality of the work, the industry became highly capitalized, and many foreigners sent their silk to Amsterdam to be "thrown" and dyed before selling or weaving it in other lands. Amsterdam became a world market for silk yarns and fabrics.

Sugar refining became a great industry in Rotterdam, drawing its supplies from the West Indies. English cloths were imported white and unfinished, and made ready for the tailor before they were passed on. Brewing, distilling, the preparation of lead, salt, tobacco, or cocoa, and many other "processing" industries flourished. Diamond-cutting, which had migrated from Venice to Antwerp, moved on to Amsterdam, and has remained there to this day. Skill found other outlets in the grinding of lenses, the making of microscopes, the perfection by Huygens of a clock with a pendulum, the construction of mathematical and shipping instruments, and the making of maps and charts.

Holland built up Europe's largest printing industry, serving not merely the local public but also publishing in foreign languages works that were too heretical to be printed in the author's own country. These books then had to be smuggled across the border in bales of cloth or cases of provisions. From the importation of Oriental china sprang the desire to produce better pottery in Europe, and delftware was one result. Physics, mathematics and chemistry were harnessed to industry, and various mechanical labor-saving devices were in use, e.g., a loom to weave several strands of ribbon, windmills to drive pumps, sawmills, flourmills and fulling mills, and a machine to print patterns on cotton fabrics. A country with such small natural resources at home, such great opportunities afield, and such a small population (about 2,500,000 people) had to make its labor count as much as possible in shipyard, printery, or workshop.

Agriculture.—In agriculture economy of land was more important than economy of labor. Today 40 per cent of the country lies below sea level, and in the seventeenth century some of this 40 per cent was under water. The three main tasks were to prevent further flooding, to reclaim some of the submerged regions, and to extract the greatest quantity of food from the *polders* (reclaimed lands). Dikes were built to hold back water, wind-driven pumps drained lakes into rivers and canals, and methods of tillage which were horticultural, rather than agricultural, were applied to the soil. There was no room for fallow and no profit in poor livestock. Improved breeds were sought; the hoe was kept busy; manure was applied; vegetables, root crops, and artificial grasses gave a bigger yield of food for man and beast; and cattle were virtually hand-fed instead of being turned adrift to hunt for food. Regions round towns were full of truck gardens, and to the cultivation of useful foods was added that of ornamental shrubs and flowers, of which the tulip was—and still is—the most valued. Dutch agriculture set the fashion and pointed the way to progressive landlords and farmers in other countries during the eighteenth century; and Dutch engineers were sought wherever a drainage problem had to be solved. Yet even at the end of the eighteenth century one-third of Holland was still sandy heather-covered waste, and some big reclamation tasks, especially the battle with the Zuyder Zee, remained.

Amsterdam.—The expansion of Dutch trade made Amsterdam the commercial and financial center of Europe. She never became the international money market that Antwerp had been, but inherited enough of the departed glory to make her rise from second to first class seem almost miraculous. Her Bourse expanded rapidly, offering a range of commodities as wide as Dutch commerce itself. It also became Europe's chief money and stock market, for trade in bills of exchange was a natural outcome of international trade in goods. The formation of the East India Company stimulated the sale of shares, for when the necessary capital had been obtained and the books were closed, those who wished to obtain shares had to buy from those who had them, and speculators joined with investors in the quest for sellers. The former were sometimes bullish; they sought shares for which they could not pay in the hope that a rising market would allow them to sell at a profit. Sometimes they were bearish, and sold shares which they did not have in the hope of being able to buy them at a lower price before the time came to deliver what they had sold. Amsterdam had little to learn from modern London or Wall Street, and in the sixteen-thirties passed through a speculative mania which foreshadowed in almost every detail the stock market booms and bursts of the nineteenth and twentieth centuries.

The center of that orgy was the tulip bulb. The tulip was introduced from Turkey after 1550, and its scarcity and rich color made it a popular but costly flower. Until about 1633 the trade in bulbs was confined to professional growers and experts, but the growing wealth of the bourgeoisie created that "optimistic atmosphere in which booms are said to grow. The country was increasingly prosperous" (Posthumus), and men turned to speculation in bulbs as a new road to easy wealth. Once the price level had begun to rise noticeably, outsiders entered the market, and soon all sorts of people—intellectuals, tradesmen, weavers, spinners, cobblers, bakers, and laborers—joined in the sport. They paid for their purchases with cows, fruit, cloth, silver dishes, land, houses, shops, pictures—anything that would pass in payment or serve as the basis of a loan. Rumors stimulated the price movement, and new ways of selling were devised to cater to small buyers. Prices soared: one kind of bulb rose in the ratio of 18 to 220, another from 50 to 1440, and in the widespread fever men made vast paper profits in a few days.

By 1636 speculation had gone mad. The non-professionals, uninformed and credulous, believed all the rumors and fantastic predictions that were whispered to them or that their own heated imaginations could invent. The crash came in February, 1637, when doubt arose concerning the future trend of prices. Almost overnight the prospects for profitable sale vanished, and the whole tower of prices collapsed, scattering ruin far and wide—not among the experts, the amateurs, or the big dealers, but among the middle class and poor who had so readily joined the mad dance. This was not the first Dutch boom and crash, nor was it the last, and history was to prove it was not a purely Dutch phenomenon.

As a loan and capital market Amsterdam served its own citizens and government and also those of other countries. For Dutch borrowers there was an abundant supply of cheap money available. The Dutch East India Company floated 12,600,000 florins of bonds at 3½ per cent, and merchants could usually borrow at that rate. Foreigners regarded this low rate as one of the main reasons for Holland's success, and when London or Paris failed to provide the capital needed for some venture a trip was made to Amsterdam. Government loans began when the Dutch rulers needed money for the struggle with Spain, and were made later for wars with England and France; but while the Fuggers and others had usually made short-term loans the Dutch borrowings were often for a long period. The lender took a bond which was negotiable; or he might prefer an annuity for his old age or a pension for his widow and children. The public debtor was thus rarely faced with the task of making a big repayment of principal. During the eighteenth century foreign loans became important; as Strieder says, the Amsterdam Bourse was a great gold reservoir which replenished the empty coffers of the princes of half Europe, and provided rich Dutchmen and foreign owners of large money capital with a field for profitable investment in colonial and European enterprise.

The Bank of Amsterdam was scarcely less important than the Bourse. Founded in 1609, it was the first institution of its kind north of the Alps. It was modeled fairly closely on the Rialto Bank set up in Venice in 1587, and was copied by Hamburg in 1619 and Nuremberg in 1621. The main purpose of these banks was to receive deposits and transfer money from one person's account to that of another. A merchant deposited such specie or bullion as came into his hands. The coins might be domestic or foreign, heavy or light, of various mintages with differing precious metal contents; the bullion might be in bars of different weights. The bank valued all this varied deposit in terms of the quantity of precious metal in it, and credited its owner with so many units of *bank money*; it said x grains of silver or y of gold equaled one guilder, florin, or whatever the unit might be called. The depositor could then draw to pay his debt to others, but as his creditors would almost certainly have accounts with the bank, payment involved merely a book transfer.

The Bank of Amsterdam also dealt in foreign exchange and handled bills. It was not supposed to issue bank notes or lend money, and hence could make no profit, but must charge a fee for its deposit, transfer, and exchange services. But it did not like to see great masses of coin and bullion lying idle in its vaults, and therefore frequently made loans to the city government or the East

India Company, and as a side line it operated a pawnshop. But its main service was to simplify the welter of currencies and make commercial payments easy for its two thousand clients.

From her far-reaching carrying trade, industries, and financial services, Holland drew a substantial income. Her industrial and business activities fostered town life, and probably more than half the population was urban. In its middle and upper levels society revealed the characteristics of solid comfort, energy, thrift, a tendency to measure private and public conduct in terms of material values, and some intellectual interests. The government pursued with some skill and, if necessary, with ruthless earnestness a policy dominated by commercial objectives. The business man was "in politics," and if he deliberately rejected an occasional opportunity to take Belgium, it was because he feared the competition that would come if Antwerp became Dutch. If he allowed the army and navy to decline, it was because he disliked heavy taxes. If he opposed reduction of the national debt it was because that debt offered a safe field for the investment of idle funds. He was sometimes interested in science and art, but the art of a Protestant bourgeois nation did not depict saints or Virgin. Instead, it took as its theme the secular life, and found fitting subjects in trim flat landscapes, streets, courtyards, kitchens, taprooms, workshops, docks, and ships, or in portraits of bankers, merchants, cloth-hall syndics, or women peeling apples. The subject might be as prosaic as a *fluitschip*, but the execution was as skilled and competent as was the operation of a tugboat or the cutting of a diamond.

The Passing of Dutch Supremacy.—In time the Dutch lost their economic preeminence, partly because they slipped back, but chiefly because others overtook them, copied their technique, challenged their monopoly, and dispensed with their services. The lack of raw materials and the dependence on foreign buyers became serious defects when the countries which supplied the materials or bought the wares became economically developed or politically hostile. A big export industry like silk-making had no advantages except of superior skill, abundant capital and trading connections; but when the French industry matured in the eighteenth century these advantages passed away, and when other countries tried behind high tariff walls to foster their own silk manufactures the Dutch maker was handicapped. For a time

Dutch finishing and selling of English woolen pieces was a great enterprise which the English failed to diminish seriously. The Civil War in England helped to weaken English traders and cause their displacement in northern cloth markets by the Dutch. But when that war ended England could take up the cloth trade again and improve her technique in cloth-finishing, and Dutch industry and commerce felt the effect. If France and England were at each other's throats or at those of anyone else except Holland, the Dutch benefited as neutrals or as allies of Protestant England. If France was trying to dominate Spain, Spain was glad of the aid of its rebel child. But if France or England turned on the Dutch, as they did during the third quarter of the seventeenth century, then Holland might be hard pressed, find greater difficulty in keeping her place in their markets, and even lose some of her colonies.

Fortunately for her, the main conflict between 1688 and 1815 was between England and France, and in that struggle it was to England's interest generally to have Holland neutral or friendly. But during the War of the Spanish Succession (1702-1713) it was apparent that Holland could henceforth play only a junior part in European affairs. Her burghers had let the navy decline in relative strength. The weakness of her central government left real power in the hands of the provinces and cities, and these units were dominated by lawyers, manufacturers, bankers, and merchants who counted their guilders carefully and frowned on any policy that did not offer a tangible commercial reward. In the drafting of the Treaty of Utrecht Holland's relegation to a secondary rôle was evident. She got little out of it, but England got much.

Throughout the eighteenth century her economic superiority passed away at one point after another; she ceased to be *the* fisherman, shipbuilder, distributor, finisher, and financier of Europe, and became *one* of them. British and Danish fishermen caught more herrings, and by 1736 only three hundred Dutch busses were at sea. English merchantmen swarmed into the Baltic, got a larger part of the Spanish American trade, and strengthened their position in the Orient and the Levant. English industries learned more of the secrets of Dutch organization and technical efficiency, made silk, printed cottons, finished cloth, developed little printing presses, and utilized the findings of physical science, while the Bank of England began to give London a more adequate financial service.

Holland still remained a great *entrepôt* and money market, a fountain of public and private investment and loans. At one time in the eighteenth century a third of the shares of the Bank of England and of the English East India Company and over 40 per cent of the English national debt bonds were in Dutch hands. When France gave financial aid to the American Revolution she did it through Dutch banks. 'The position of the creditor and middleman is, however, precarious. Many loans to foreign governments and private persons became valueless during the upheavals after 1789. During the American Revolution Holland declared war on England (1780), and many of her ships were captured by English privateers. When she was taken by Napoleon still more of her shipping and sea trade fell into English hands, as did Ceylon and South Africa. In those turbulent decades her two great pillars of commerce and finance—the East India Company and the Bank of Amsterdam—tottered and fell. The Company had been shaking for many years under the stress of war, mismanagement, and corruption. Its managers in the east had been building large fortunes, but its finances had gone awry. It ceased to pay dividends in 1783, and when the end came in 1794 its assets were worth only one-eighth of its obligations ($50,000,000). In its fall it pulled down the Bank, which had long since departed from its original function and had lent heavily to the Company.

Holland entered the post-Napoleonic world with some funds saved from the wreckage and with her East Indian empire almost intact. In that world, where coal and iron were more important than spices and herrings, her place was that of a small economic state; but her skill in industry and agriculture, her geographical position, her capacity for accumulating capital, her tradition in shipbuilding and seafaring, and the valuable remnants of her colonial empire gave her an opportunity to repair her damaged fortune.

FRANCE

In the French story from the eviction of the English (about 1450) to the French Revolution it is often hard to see the economics because of the politics. Much of the politics was economic, as one ruler or minister after another tried to extricate the country from the financial mess into which some war had plunged it, or strove to erect an ambitious industrial, commercial, financial, and imperial structure on a foundation that was persistently peasant and on a country that could be prosperous without departing much from economic self-sufficiency.

In periods of peace the progress of industry and commerce was marked, the state's efforts achieved a measure of success, and the country's resources were adequate for the support of a population which numbered possibly 15,000,000 in the seventeenth century and 20,000,000 in the eighteenth. But long periods of civil or foreign wars separated the peaceful patches, and usually caused heavy economic loss. Religious conflicts occupied many of the years 1562 to 1598. Then came thirteen years of peace under Henry IV (1598-1610); private enterprise made great strides, while the king and his chief minister, Sully, worked hard on economic problems. The national finances were reformed and the tax burdens lightened; agriculture was fostered; marshes were drained; silk production and weaving spread; various luxury industries were nursed; roads, rivers, and canals received attention; the merchant marine expanded; trading companies were set up, and a settlement was made on the St. Lawrence.

The half century following Henry's assassination in 1610 was marked by civil strife, the Thirty Years' War, and a fight with Spain. During those years the towns and the feudal nobility were beaten into fairly satisfactory subjection to the central power, and Richelieu and Mazarin achieved much of their twin aims of making the monarchy supreme in France and France supreme in Europe. But the price was heavy, and the next twenty-five years (1661-1685) were spent in valiant endeavors to straighten out national finances, develop industry and commerce, crush the Dutch, and sustain an extravagant court. This was the period of Colbert's herculean efforts to strengthen every side of French economic life. He achieved much, but some of his efforts failed because of the strength of the Dutch, and some because of the policies of his master, Louis XIV.

Then came thirty years of almost unbroken conflict with England, Holland, Scandinavia, Prussia, and the Holy Roman Empire. From them France emerged broken in prestige and bankrupt; Hudson Bay, Nova Scotia (Acadia) and the Asiento went to England, and most of the other allies nibbled something off the fringe of France or of her subordinate, Spain. Once more the task of reconstruction and economic expansion was taken up, and by 1740 great achievement could be recorded; but during the next twenty years France and England locked horns, and from the Seven Years' War France emerged defeated, losing Canada and her footing in India. Again peace came, and with it economic opportunities were seized; but participation in the American Revolution availed France little, and all efforts failed to make the state solvent. The France that went into the gloom of 1789 was, as Hauser puts it, "a state at the last resources of its poverty in the midst of a nation comparatively rich." The nation showed no lack of enterprise, powers of recuperation, or ability to produce a large income, but its head was more often bad master than good servant, and always an expensive one.

Agriculture.—Of the three sources of national income—agriculture, industry, and commerce—the first was by far the most important. Agricultural methods changed little during the period we are here considering, but when the tumult of the Hundred Years' War subsided the attacks on forests, swamps, and moors were resumed, and whenever peace ended civil strife the villagers came back to restore the fields that had been laid waste. Books describing better methods of land utilization appeared during the sixteenth century, and Henry IV and Colbert both strove to aid farmers to improve their ways or turn to new products. Many of these efforts failed or were abandoned when the enthusiast died or war came, while the state often took away with one hand —especially by taxation—what it had given with the other.

The extension of commercial production of France's two great staples—grain and wine—depended upon the markets available and on the ability to get goods to them. For wine there were good markets at home and abroad, but political events frequently interfered with exports, as when Anglo-French friction led London to exclude French wine or tax it heavily in favor of Portuguese vintages. For cereals, however, problems of transportation and of policy cramped the domestic and foreign markets. Rulers did something to improve transportation and remove the interprovincial tariffs and the obstacles to export; but their policy was checked by the rise in prices of the sixteenth century and by occasional severe famines in all centuries. The latter led provinces which had crops to prevent their export to famine-stricken regions, and induced the government to protect the nation's food supply by forbidding export. The farmer was thus limited in his market; he could not take advantage of scarcity in other areas, nor was he stimulated to produce that surplus for export in normal years which might have given the country an adequate supply in years of poor harvest. Further, in order to provide adequate supplies of raw material for home industry and prevent foreign manufacturers from waxing fat on imported supplies, the export of wool and hemp was forbidden, as was that of cattle. Those who demanded free movement of foodstuffs remained unsatisfied till the Revolution.

In France, as in most parts of western Europe, the "price revolution" reacted harmfully on those landlords who were chiefly dependent on fixed dues for their income. The steady depreciation in the purchasing power of this income had impoverished the landlord and benefited the tenant even before the sixteenth century. The landlord had to tighten his belt, sell his estate to some bourgeois, go to court in search of a post, or find some way by which he could wring more income from his estate. All these things happened; some landlords sold their lands, some starved on them, but others, especially the new ones, set out to get more from land and tenants. They restored the domain where they could. They changed the dues on any holdings that fell vacant from fixed money payments to fixed shares of the produce or to short leases. They increased the fine paid when a holding changed hands. They told their lawyers to search for lapsed rights that could be revived, lent money to tenants and foreclosed when the borrower defaulted, or supplied the cash when a village lacked money for its taxes and took in exchange part or all of the common land or rights. Over the common land and the grazing rights on cropped lands and hay fields (*vaine pâture*) there was long dispute. Lawyers tried to establish the doctrine that common property rights did not exist; the common lands belonged to the seigneur, who could do as he wished with them, and the community enjoyed them only at his pleasure.

These efforts on the part of the landlords had uneven results during the sixteenth and seventeenth centuries. To them were opposed the tenacity of the peasants and the general hostility of the crown. The landlords voiced their interests in the local *parle-*.

ments (courts), but the power of the state was wielded by the intendants, who watched the seigneurs, tried to check their encroachments, and protected the peasants against the more obvious attacks.

Industries.—France shared with England and Holland the desire to develop manufactures and commerce and to get a share of the expanding sea trade. Some raw materials could be produced on the spot; native skilled labor might be supplemented by offering foreigners adequate inducements to immigrate; a growing market for luxury goods existed in the needs of the court, nobility, and rich bourgeoisie; and some French *articles de luxe* had found foreign buyers even in the later Middle Ages. The establishment of industries and the consequent reduction of imports would check that drain of precious metal abroad which was the bogey of nearly all statesmen from 1500 onward, while elaborate regulation of production would win for French goods a reputation for high quality and good taste in foreign markets.

From at least the fifteenth century some such arguments had found favor. Louis XI and Charles VIII welcomed shipbuilders and silk workers from Italy, and miners, metal workers, and printers from Germany. They tried to turn Lyons into a silk textile town, and when the Lyons merchants persisted in preferring to import Italian pieces they transferred their efforts to Tours. Heavy duties were imposed on imported fabrics, the production of raw silk was fostered, immigrants came, and by 1550 Lyons, Tours and Nîmes were important producers of silks, cloth of gold, and other rich fabrics. Every king offered favors, privileges, freedom from taxation, and even contributions from the treasury to help found new industries. If men with money, whether merchants or nobles, were reluctant to invest in untried fields, Richelieu and Colbert brought pressure to bear on them or tempted them with generous concessions and monopolies. Dutch shipbuilders and cloth finishers, Swedish miners and foundry workers, Flemish tapestry-makers, English inventors seeking a refuge from angry workers and a reward for their ingenuity, all were induced to make France their home. Some goods were produced in state factories: in 1662 a royal workshop was set up at the Hôtel des Gobelins to make the tapestries needed by the court, while the Sèvres porcelain factory gradually won a high reputation for its wares.

If the new industries were to be helped and protected from foreign competitors, they and their elder brothers must also be controlled in order to insure that their products were of the highest possible quality, artistic, reliable, and durable. "Made in France" must be a trade-mark appreciated and accepted in foreign markets. Guild ordinances were supplemented by a network of state decrees defining the conditions of labor, the nature of the processes and materials to be used (or not to be used), the character, size, and even weight of the product. Colbert issued thirty-eight regulations and 150 edicts—nearly all for the textile industry—and under some of his successors regulation was pushed much further. Hats could not be made of wool and fur mixed, even though people liked them, for this would injure the Canadian fur trade. The stocking knitting machine must not be used since it was said to do bad work. Cloths must be of certain dimensions, and steel goods must be properly tempered even though they were not to be used for cutting purposes. An army of guild or state inspectors went around to enforce the decrees. Sometimes it did its work thoroughly in spirit and in letter, but sometimes it was willing to be bribed to put the telescope to its blind eye. The results were a good name for French goods, a comparative freedom from "tricks of the trade," and a traditionalism in practice and product which may have checked initiative and invention.

These state efforts to encourage industrial development produced some hothouse industries which relied solely on the court for custom, could not live without heavy subsidies, and made no impression on open markets. Other industries were helped to grow up, and catered to markets at home and in the Mediterranean, the luxury-buying classes of western Europe, and some purchasers overseas. To the one important medieval textile manufacture—linen—was added the making of high-grade woolen cloth in and around Rouen, Amiens, and Abbeville in the north, and in Languedoc (west of Marseilles) in the south. Southern fabrics held their own against those of England and Holland in the markets of the Levant, and French linen occupied the place held today by the products of Belfast. Tapestries, silks, lace, dyes, pottery, glass, paper, soap, sugar, books, furniture, and jewelry were being produced within the country by 1700, were supplying most of the home needs, and were finding external markets when not prevented by war or hostile tariffs.

Commerce and Transportation.—To develop French trade seemed as politically important as to develop French industry. Though medieval France had been more commercially active than England, her reliance on Italians or Hansards had been large. To foster French markets and merchants, to facilitate domestic trade and transportation, and to help French ships and traders win a larger share in intercontinental traffic were therefore aims to which the government frequently gave attention.

One important step was the extension of markets and fairs. Geographical location and the favor of Louis XI made the Lyons fairs important. Four times a year Spanish wool, French linen, Italian silks, lace, and gloves, Lyons books, Gascon wines, Languedoc cloth, and oriental produce were exchanged there. Trade in commodities led to elaborate exchange and credit transactions. Italian and German bankers established branches there, bills on Lyons were used for payment of external debts, and the French rulers found a reservoir of money that was all too easily tapped when they needed funds for their ambitious campaigns and policies. The inability of the crown to honor its huge debts in 1557-1559 gave France her first terrible financial crisis, for many of the creditors were French.

The second important step was the improvement of means of transportation and the reduction or elimination of provincial barriers and excessive tolls. Henry IV began the task of linking up the main streams and of removing weirs, mill dams, and toll barriers from them. Richelieu and Colbert carried on the work. In 1642 the Seine and the Loire were linked. Sully's dream of a waterway from the Mediterranean to the Bay of Biscay came true with the completion of the *Canal des Deux Mers*, from Toulouse on the Garonne to the Mediterranean coast. The canal was about 190 miles long, was a fine piece of engineering, and reduced transport charges by three-fourths. In the northeast the Picardy canal, finished in 1738, joined the Oise to the Somme, and when these rivers were in turn connected with the Meuse and the Scheldt a network of waterways covered northeastern France and the Low Countries.

Much roadmaking was done. In France, as in England, the medieval "king's highway" had been a right of way, but not necessarily a treated surface. In 1500 three-fourths of the French royal roads had virtually reverted to the state of nature or were dilapidated fragments of the old Roman roads; but during the sixteenth century interest in their preservation, repair, and maintenance was real, though spasmodic. Royal progresses through the realm, the movement of armies, the growth of trade and travel, all called for better highways. A road guidebook appeared in 1552, a postal system was set up in 1576, and by 1600 public diligences were running between the main towns. Sully was a vigorous road builder and repairer, but Richelieu and Colbert gave more thought to waterways, and heavy munitions or siege artillery were transported on barges as far as possible. In 1698 Burgundy bought a statue of Louis XIV; the article was carried by water to Auxerre, and then set out by road for Dijon, but the vehicle on which it rested sank in the mud, and the statue had to be stored in a shed for twenty-one years until a road was made strong enough to bear it.

During the peace which came after 1713 a big road program was planned, and the royal claim to *corvée* was extended and systematized. In 1737 all peasants over twelve years of age who lived within four leagues of a main road must work for thirty days a year for the state, or pay for the employment of a substitute. This demand was not always or everywhere enforced, and sometimes led to riots. Turgot abolished it in 1776, and imposed taxes with which to pay free laborers; but the taxpayers objected, and a modified *corvée* was therefore reintroduced. It was abolished in 1789, revived by Napoleon, and in one form or another survived till 1903. Yet, in spite of resistance, unwilling labor, and incompetent work, roads were made and improved. By the Revolution France had 25,000 miles of the best main highways in Europe.

Foreign Trade.—The encouragement of French foreign trade was part of every policy from the fifteenth century onward. It had two aspects: (1) the transfer from foreign to French hands and ships of the carrying trade to and from French ports; (2) French participation in trade with the Levant, the Baltic, Spanish America, and the Indies, and the carving out of colonial spheres of influence or monopoly. In the Mediterranean area Jacques Cœur had shown that his motto—"To valiant hearts nothing is impossible"—was no empty boast. Louis XI endeavored to squeeze Italians and their ships out of his ports, but his power was not equal to his plan; France could not dispense with foreign ships, capital, traders, or goods, Louis' own merchants turned a cold shoulder on him, and he had to retreat. The next century witnessed greatly increased trading and state activity. A treaty with the ruler of the Ottoman Empire (1536) recognized France as protector of all Catholics in that empire, and gave her merchants the right to have their own consuls. Italians, Dutch, and English competed with the French in the Near East, but Marseilles grew into a large port, and fine cloths of Languedoc, silver from America, and French luxury articles were exchanged for the wares of western Asia or North Africa.

A richer trade area was Spain. French luxury goods found a ready market among the wealthy Spaniards, French foodstuffs supplemented the products of Spanish farming, and in 1691, according to one estimate, a third of the wares taken from Cadiz to America were French. When ships returned from Spain they brought much silver, and a contemporary remarked that the Spaniards worked the mines of El Dorado to enrich the French. Much of this Spanish trade was, however, carried in Dutch ships, as were the French wares sent to the North Sea or Baltic countries. France, like England and Sweden, tried to upset the Dutch supremacy in near and distant waters. Colbert sought to do so by building ships like the Dutch vessels, by uniting with England in a war against Holland, by raising the tariff on Dutch goods, and by establishing a state-subsidized Company of the North (1669). These measures achieved little; the Dutch were not defeated either by war or by the competition of rival traders, and the Company was a failure. The only sure way of beating the Dutch was to do what they did better than they did it—a harder task than winning a war.

The French Empire.—From the villages and towns of the English Channel and the Bay of Biscay men had from time immemorial gone out to catch fish. In the Middle Ages Norman, Breton, and Basque had sought the fishing grounds where sardines, cod, and whales were found, and by the middle of the fifteenth century this quest may have drawn them to the western ocean and the banks off the shores of *Terre Neuve* (Newfoundland). Meanwhile tradition asserts that ships from Dieppe had been on the Guinea coast and even as far as India about 1350, and that journeys had been made from Honfleur to the Canary Islands and Brazil soon after 1400.

The Spanish and Portuguese discoveries stirred the French crown, merchants, and shippers to a desire for a share of the wealth Lisbon and Madrid had appropriated. In 1503 a Frenchman went to Brazil, and was followed by many others. In 1506 the St. Lawrence was entered, in 1523 the treasure ships of Cortez were raided, and in 1527 Frenchmen were in the East Indies. In 1534 Cartier passed through the fleet of French fishing boats on the Banks and wormed his way far up the St. Lawrence. In 1535 Rouen traders formed an association for trade with India, and in 1550 they organized a colonial exhibition to entertain and educate the king when he visited their town. On a great barge a Brazilian village was represented and fifty natives were imported to supply local color. Royal interest in Brazil and other possible fields was heightened, but the wars after 1560 ruined this promising development. The Portuguese were too strong in Brazil, Canada yielded no treasure, and when peace came (1598) France's only strong points were the fishing grounds of the northwest Atlantic, some smuggling or lawful trade with Spanish America, and some free-lance traffic in furs on the St. Lawrence.

When there was time and energy to spare, Henry IV, Richelieu, and Colbert tried to encourage colonial trade and settlement. In 1599 two Honfleur sea dogs were given a monopoly of the fur trade in New France on condition that they took out fifty colonists each year. This monopoly passed from hand to hand, but the settlement requirements were usually ignored. Sometimes it was canceled, and at all times interlopers went in to buy furs. In 1627 Richelieu handed the rule and trade of Canada to the Company of the Hundred Associates, of which he was patron and chief stockholder. The Company must transport colonists, but not Huguenots, and thus a valuable class was excluded. It collected much fur, and its men worked far into the heart of the continent; but it did virtually nothing for settlement, and in 1663 the colony had only about a hundred farms and 2500 white people. Its total population was less than the annual immigration into New England during some years.

After 1663 Canada was a royal colony, ruled by the king's officials. At first efforts were made to foster settlement; some intendants encouraged farming, fishing, shipbuilding, and trade with New England and the West Indies. Explorers, missionaries, and traders reached the prairies and the big river. Some seigneurs became lords of quasi-feudal villages on the banks of the St. Lawrence, while Quebec (founded 1608) and Montreal (founded 1642) were political, religious, and commercial centers. But the colony never became a great economic asset to the crown or to commerce. Its soil or climate unfitted it for easy development, the fur trade called for few men and was hostile to settlement, while the competition of New England and of the English stationed on Hudson Bay, combined with the hostility of some native tribes and with frequent overstocking of the European fur market, made profit precarious. Population grew slowly, and in 1763 there were only about 60,000 French Canadians. In the long fight with England, France regarded Canada chiefly as an outpost to be used in the conflict, and threw great burdens on it; but she did not adequately man or nourish it for that task. Officials were sometimes incompetent or corrupt, supplies were not forthcoming, colonial finances and currency fell into chaos, British ships barred the road, and nature added to the strain by closing the seaway to the motherland from November to May each year. France let Canada go without shedding tears, keeping only two little islands in the Gulf of St. Lawrence and the right to fish in adjacent waters. New France began and ended with fish.

France achieved her greatest imperial success in the Caribbean. At first she was chiefly interested in conquering something from Spain, securing military or naval bases at the mouth of the Gulf of Mexico, and setting foot on the mainland. In the last aim she had little success, but secured French Guiana in 1625. In the islands she got Martinique, Guadeloupe, Haiti, and two or three less important spots. To their economic possibilities she gave little thought at first, but in 1639 a Rouen emigrant laid out a sugar plantation in Martinique, and prospered. He was widely imitated, planters spread over the other islands, and the French colonies became Europe's largest sugar provider. For a time the Dutch were the chief buyers, shippers, and refiners; but Colbert and his successors tried to close the island ports to foreigners, to confine the trade to French ports, and to develop further the islands' tropical resources. The development went far, and tobacco, indigo, cotton, fruits, coffee, and chocolate were produced in great quantities. At the end of the seventeenth century it was estimated that over 400,000 persons in France were drawing their livelihood directly or indirectly from colonial commerce, and on the eve of the French Revolution goods worth 160,000,000 francs annually were imported from the islands. Nantes, Bordeaux, Havre, Dieppe, St. Malo, and Marseilles grew greatly during the eighteenth century, handling colonial wares, refining sugar, or taking slaves from Senegal to the islands.

The growth of a restrictive colonial policy had its good and bad effects. When the Dutch were excluded, the planters found themselves with a surplus of sugar on their hands, for France could not take all that the Dutch had bought. They tried to refine the sugar in the islands, but failed. They therefore smuggled as much as they could, and the Dutch and English were near at hand to aid and abet them. They concentrated on plantation products, relied on outsiders for their supplies of other commodities, and exchanged sugar and molasses for lumber, flour, and fish. New Englanders were glad to find a nearby market for these wares, and to obtain in return a commodity which, converted into rum, was valuable for barter in the fur and slave trades. In time of war mutual smuggling went on, and in time of peace such a law as the Molasses Act (1773), which sought to keep French colonial produce out of New England, was virtually inoperative.

For a time the French West Indies suffered from their owner's desire to use them as stepping-stones to the conquest of the Spanish mainland. Anti-Spanish plans called for big land grants to fighters, took men away from the plantations, and subjected the colonists to heavy strain on their resources and to arbitrary rule from offices four thousand miles away. After 1713 this policy was partly abandoned, and the islanders at times staged vigorous protests and little revolutions when they disliked the orders that came from Versailles. In the French colonies, as in the English, planters and traders wanted the right to export freely to any part of the world and still retain their monopoly of the motherland market. When in 1761-1762 England considered which French possessions she would keep, the British West Indies planters demanded that Guadeloupe be handed back. They feared their London market would be ruined if that great sugar plantation was brought inside the imperial circle. Their wishes prevailed; France lost Canada, but was allowed to keep her sugar bowl.

In Africa and the Indian Ocean France was an early arrival but never gained a strong foothold. Henry IV and Richelieu sponsored various companies, and Colbert became a veritable com-

pany promoter. He set up East India and West India Companies
in 1664, the Levant Company in 1670, and the Senegal Company
in 1673. Their achievements were slender. The Senegal Company
was broken in a fight with the Algerians in 1682, and the Levant
Company was unable to cope with its English and Dutch rivals.
Beyond the Cape of Good Hope the French occupied Madagascar
in 1642, and contacts by missionaries and traders were made in
India, the Malay peninsula, and the archipelago. But the Dutch
were too strongly intrenched, and the wars from 1690 to 1713
played havoc with the East India trade. After 1713 the French
began to make headway in the Orient. The East India Company
was reorganized and began to seek trade with energy and success.
Individual traders and groups which enjoyed no chartered privileges ventured into the Indian Ocean. Dupleix, who had gone to
India in 1720 and gathered a fortune and an intimate knowledge
of Indian politics, became commander of the French outposts in
1741. To curb or even oust the English East India Company was
his aim. In the struggle economics and politics became intermingled, but the older Company proved the stronger, and from
the conflict France emerged defeated at the end of the Seven
Years' War, retaining only a few trading posts.

France's imperial history was thus checkered, but the losses
were not serious blows to her economic welfare, for Canada and
India were minor contributors to her income. The rich sugar
colonies remained, but soon lost some of their value, first through
overproduction, later by the uncertainty of sea communications
during the Revolutionary War, and later still by the rise of the
beet sugar industry in Europe. Outside the empire, trade grew
greatly during the eighteenth century, especially with Italy, Germany, and the Levant. French total external trade increased by
500 per cent between 1718 and 1787; at the later date it was
apparently worth more than that of Great Britain. On the eve of
the Revolution the prospects for still further expansion were
bright for the policies which had restricted international traffic
were losing favor. An Anglo-French commercial treaty of 1786
opened the markets of each country to certain staple goods from
the other, a treaty with Russia was concluded in 1787, and the
independence of the United States offered a new expanding market. Foreign ships were being allowed to load at several French
colonial ports, and at home restrictions on exports of farm prod-

uce were being attacked with increasing vigor and frequency. Agriculture was being improved, industries were adopting new machines and methods, French ships were numerous, and the bourgeois class was growing in wealth and power. But the Revolution and the two decades of war which followed thwarted some of these movements, and the country once more witnessed the check of economic development by political catastrophe.

The Bourgeoisie and the State.—France gave the world the word *bourgeoisie*. The history and outlook of that class in France were greatly influenced by the needs, character, and policy of the state, and by the opportunities which it offered for getting an income. In the first place, the crown's need for loans and advances was increasingly met by Frenchmen after 1500. The merchant who had accumulated any money invested it, singly or as a member of a group (a *parti*), in a tax farm or direct loan. The vast expenditures of Louis XIV and the growth of taxation and borrowings offered a large field for the profitable employment of funds; according to the best available estimates tax farmers collected two dollars for every one they paid the state, and some of them became immensely rich. Such rewards made merchants and financiers prefer this way of using their capital to trade or joint-stock investment.

In the second place, the centralized state needed a large army of officials of high and low degree to administer justice, finance, industrial regulation, etc. Some of these government posts brought titles and noble rank to their holders, conferred privileges (including exemption from certain taxes), and gave an income in the form of a salary or from the receipt of fees. Hard-pressed rulers sold these positions for cash, and a post might become hereditary or salable to others. Such posts attracted the trading class; many a merchant's ambition was to buy an estate and purchase an official position for himself or his sons. Rich men acquired the important posts. Gournay, early exponent of *laissez faire*, was a merchant who inherited an estate and bought the office of intendant of commerce. Many of the men who loomed large in the politics and thought of prerevolutionary France had come up to land and titles by dipping into their moneybags. Even the petty bourgeois was inspired by the desire to get a clerkship or other minor official post.

In this bourgeois ideal Professor Hauser finds one cause of France's failure to go as far as she might in economic expansion. There was "a constant hæmorrhage of capital, which removed it from business as soon as it had been created; and the commercial class was decapitated by the transformation of its best representatives into professional men" or into that other home of fixed sure incomes, the church. In these two tendencies Hauser finds the "explanation of that narrowing down of the French commercial horizon, that diminution of the spirit of adventure and enterprise, that triumph of the love of fixed income which was to give to France, which had been noted of old for its travellers and conquerors of distant lands, the psychology of a nation of *rentiers*."

In the third place, the size and splendor of the French court tended to steer production toward the making of luxury articles. For these there was a good but limited market, and while the French craftsman catered for the upper classes he left the Dutch and English to cater for the masses. It may be that he lacked abundant raw materials, especially metals, or that the peasant population bought little; but the field of his choice was not capable of great expansion, and the goods he made did not lend themselves to machine production. Thus the supplying of necessaries was left to the English, who built, on the basis of cheap cloth and hardware, their workshop of the world.

Not every successful bourgeois could climb the social ladder. The Huguenots, tolerated by the Edict of Nantes, were in the forefront of most economic developments, and prominent in banking, industry, trade, and shipping. So long as they were not subjected to discriminatory treatment they were content with their political lot, loyal subjects of the state, and warm supporters of its economic policies. But they were not in favor in the eyes of their ruler, they were virtually shut out of the colonies, and after 1660 the civil service and the professions were closed to them. A series of attacks culminated in 1685 in the revocation of the Edict, the suppression of Protestantism, and the expulsion of its preachers. Those who would not abjure their faith might lose their property and be sent to prison or the galleys. Some accepted conversion, more or less sincere; occasionally some members of a family changed their church, while other members emigrated to Holland, England, or Germany, but retained trade connections with those left behind.

How much permanent harm the revocation did to France cannot be estimated. Some towns and districts were almost entirely depopulated, while others, such as Rennes and Normandy, lost heavily in population and wealth, and much time elapsed before the loss was made good. Louis' action certainly benefited the Protestant countries, for the exiles took with them some of their capital as well as their great skill in making silk goods, paper, pottery, glass, hats, jewelry, etc. Berlin, Amsterdam, and London gained new or vastly improved industries, and Professor Clark ventures the opinion that Holland thereby replaced France as the leading industrial nation of the world. But their departure was far from being a fatal blow to France, as was shown by the later expansion of industry and commerce whenever political and military preoccupations faded into the background. The pity was that they did not fade more often.

BIBLIOGRAPHY

GENERAL

BREBNER, J. B., *The Explorers of North America, 1492-1806* (1933).

CLARK, G. N., *The Seventeenth Century* (1929), chaps. 1-4, 11, 12.

DAY, C., *History of Commerce* (1922), chaps. 19-25.

FAYLE, C. E., *Short History of the World's Shipping Industry* (1933), chaps. 5-8.

JEUDWINE, J. W., *Studies in Empire and Trade* (1923), parts iii-v.

KELLER, *Colonization* (1908), chaps. 3-11.

KULISCHER, J., *Allgemeine Wirtschaftsgeschichte* (1929), vol. ii, chaps. 5, 6, 16, 20.

NEWTON, A. P., *European Nations in the West Indies, 1493-1688* (1933).

PACKARD, L. B., *The Commercial Revolution, 1400-1776* (1927).

RENARD, G., and WEULERSSE, G., *Life and Work in Modern Europe* (1926), chaps. 1-4.

SÉE, H., *Modern Capitalism* (1928), chaps. 4-7.

PORTUGAL AND SPAIN

CHANG T'IEN-TSE, *Sino-Portuguese Trade from 1514 to 1644* (1933).

CHAPMAN, C. E., *Colonial Hispanic America* (1933), chap. 9.

HAMILTON, E. J., *American Treasure and the Price Revolution in Spain, 1501-1650* (1934).

HARING, C. H., *Trade and Navigation between Spain and the Indies in the Time of the Hapsburgs* (1918).

KLEIN, J., *The Mesta, 1273-1836* (1920).

PRESTAGE, E., *The Portuguese Pioneers* (1933).

Encyclopædia of the Social Sciences: articles on Albuquerque, Alcabala, Casa de Contratación, Council of the Indies, Mendoza, Peonage.

HOLLAND

BAASCH, E., *Hollandische Wirtschaftsgeschichte* (1927).

BARBOUR, VIOLET, "Dutch and English Merchant Shipping in the Seventeenth Century," in *Ec. H. R.*, January, 1930, pp. 261-290.

BLOK, P. J., *History of the Peoples of the Netherlands* (Eng. trans., 1907), vol. iv, chaps. 4, 10, 19.

DAY, CLIVE, *The Dutch in Java* (1904).

POSTHUMUS, N. W., "The Tulip Mania in Holland in the Years 1636 and 1637," in *J. E. B. H.*, May, 1929, pp. 436-466.

TORCHIANA, H. A., *Tropical Holland* (1921), chaps. 5-7.

FRANCE

BLOCH, M., *Les caractères originaux de l'histoire rurale française* (1931).

HAUSER, H., *Travailleurs et marchands de l'ancienne France* (1920).

HAUSER, H., "The Characteristic Features of French Economic History from the Middle of the Sixteenth to the Middle of the Eighteenth Century," in *Ec. H. R.*, October, 1933, pp. 257-272.

MAY, L. P., "La France, puissance des Antilles" in *Rev. d'Hist. Ec. et Soc.*, 1930, pp. 452-481.

SÉE, H., *La France économique et sociale au xviiie siècle* (1925).

SÉE, H., *La vie économique et les classes sociales en France au xviiie siècle* (1924).

SÉE, H., *L'évolution commerciale et industrielle de la France sous l'ancien régime* (1925).

VIGNOLS, L., "Early French Colonial Policy," in *J. E. B. H.*, November, 1929, pp. 101-145.

See also French titles in Bibliography of Chapter XVI.

CHAPTER XIV

ENGLAND, 1500-1750

By the end of the fifteenth century England had an agriculture that was becoming increasingly commercial, some industries that were serving home and foreign markets, some reputation as a mineral producer, and a growing trading, shipping, and financial class. During the next two centuries subsistence farming, petty industry, and local trade continued to hold the greater part of the stage; but farming for market became more important, old industries expanded, new ones were established, while English ships and traders won a larger place in the growing European and intercontinental trade. Capital accumulated, important trading and banking institutions were established, and colonies were planted which became large markets as well as producers of certain colonial commodities.

By 1500 national unity was almost complete, the country had become politically as well as geographically insular by losing its French possessions, and the old feudal nobility had largely killed itself off in the Wars of the Roses. A new monarchy, sympathetic toward industry and trade, was on the bridge, and a new nobility, supplemented by or recruited from the wealthier bourgeoisie, manned the ship. The crown and its landed or mercantile subjects were not always of one mind, but when differences developed the crown rarely prevailed long or completely. The capacity for resisting the royal will grew steadily; it beheaded Charles in 1649, and exiled James II in 1688. From that time onward the landed and mercantile classes were virtual masters of the country. Even before that date policies reflected the wishes and fears of these classes, or of those groups and sections of them that had the strongest pull, the best-lined purse, or the loudest voice. Since London played a double rôle as economic and political metropolis, the connection between business and politics was closer than in any other country except Holland. The relations between land and commerce or finance were almost as close, through investment, intermarriage, the entry of sons of the lesser aristocracy into business, and the ascent of traders into the landed gentry. A stockholders' list for the great trading or banking companies after 1700 looked like an abbreviated political *Who's Who*, and from at least Elizabethan times titled men were developing their land or mineral deposits or investing in commercial or colonizing ventures.

Agriculture.—The rural changes described in Chapter VII became more marked as 1500 was approached and passed. Three markets helped to bring parts of the countryside closer to commercial farming. The first was London, which in 1550 may have housed at most 150,000 people, but by 1700 probably had 700,000, or at least a tenth of the population. No other town offered such a good market for foodstuffs, and "as the years pass by it is possible to watch the city's tentacles spreading over the provinces until by the middle of the seventeenth century they reached to Berwick, Cornwall, and Wales" (Fisher). The provincial ports and mining or manufacturing areas were also growing, and the combined result was a steady increase in the need for grain, dairy produce, fruit, vegetables, and meats.

The second market was the woolen industry. In the fifteenth century a great expansion took place in the European demand for woolen fabrics and at the same time there was a marked growth of English manufacture for export. To the old markets in the Baltic, central Europe, and the Levant new ones were added as the colonists in North America needed warm fabrics and as larger armies required more blankets and cloth for uniforms. Even the tropical markets of Asia, Africa, and America bought some woolen goods. The third market came later, when in the seventeenth century England became a minor grain exporter to the continent.

The growing food and wool demands influenced areas which were capable of meeting them, and were seized by energetic farmers and wide-awake landlords. The former strove to wring more produce and income from their holdings, and the latter sought the same end. Some landlords might be newcomers, possibly with some city experience in the art of money-making, who had bought an estate or secured some of the abbey lands; or their estates might be in the hands of customary tenants who paid fixed rents which were shrinking in purchasing power as prices mounted. The landlord pursued his objective in two ways. In the first place, he tried to extract more money from his tenants. The leaseholder's rent could be raised when a lease was renewed, but customary tenants or copyholders, whose tenure ran for a series of lives or in perpetuity, were not so easily squeezed. Yet the landlord found some ways: he increased greatly the fines they paid when a farm changed hands, "doubling, trebling, and now and then seven times" (Harrison). He seized the land when the tenant made some trifling default, or he might resort to force and fraud.

In the second place, he sought to change the use to which his land was being put, and the processes which had been redrawing the village map since at least the thirteenth century gathered strength and speed after about 1450. For this he was not alone responsible, for farmers might take the initiative, consolidate their arable strips, and inclose part of the commons or wastes to provide more meadow and better pastures. They might convert their holdings from grainfields to sheepwalks, but for this conversion the landlord got most of the blame. He evicted tenants when he had a chance, threw holdings together to make larger farms, took pieces of the commons, and turned much of his estate into sheep farms.

Where inclosure was a prelude to better arable farming or to the introduction of other forms of cultivation it caused little disturbance to the rural population; but where it led to conversion of arable into pasture its social effects were more serious, since few shepherds and shearers were needed in place of many plowmen and harvesters. On economic grounds both types of inclosure were inevitable and justifiable: wool production offered a greater net return, cattle fared better on inclosed pastures than on overstocked commons, and one Tudor estimate said inclosed arable land gave a third more crop than did open fields. But on social grounds the cult of the sheep seemed to some country dwellers and contemporary observers a first-class tragedy. Sir Thomas More declared that "the gentle sheep has become a more ravenous wild animal than the wild beasts of Africa," and another writer said, "the simple and gentle sheep, of all creatures the most harmless, are now become so ravenous that they begin to devour men, waste fields, depopulate houses and whole townships." Sermons, pamphlets, and even poems denounced "these cruel inclosers." Riots and revolts broke out at various times. A series of laws from 1489 onward for over a century forbade the pulling down of houses, the conversion of tilled land into pasture, the erection of hedges or fences, and the possession of more than two farms or 2000 sheep. But the effect was apparently slight. Administrative machinery was too weak, the weight of economic advantage was on the side of the innovators, and the laws, like those passed in most countries in most centuries to control the actions of landlords and farmers, were easily evaded.

Recent research has shown that the area and the number of people affected by this inclosure movement were much smaller than the uproar would suggest. It is estimated that only half a million acres were inclosed between 1400 and 1650. There was little illegal eviction of tenants, but much oppression within the law. Farmers or small owners were as active in inclosing and converting as were the big landlords. Not all inclosure was for pasture, for much land remained arable or became dairy farm, vegetable garden, or orchard, and might need more labor than before. The statistical evidence on which these measurements are based is, however, so defective that the minimization is probably as erroneous as was the old exaggeration; but it is clear that the "agrarian revolution" was not a wide torrent that swept everything before it.

During the seventeenth century inclosure continued in a quieter way, largely for the improvement of arable. Some of it was done by agreement among the parties affected, and these agreements might be confirmed in the Court of Chancery, or given legal force in a private act of parliament. Reclamation of wet land was undertaken on a large scale with a great outlay of capital. In 1630 a group of English and Dutch capitalists engaged Cornelius Vermuyden, a Dutch drainage expert, to reclaim 400,000 acres of fens between Cambridge and Lincoln. The costs were heavy, the opposition of the natives (who lived by fishing, keeping geese, and hunting wild fowl) was persistent, ditches and canals were damaged during the Civil War, winter floods were hard to cope with, and success was therefore only partial. By 1750 nearly 750,000 acres had been drained, but the task of drying up the eastern lowlands was not finished till a century later.

On a smaller scale, landlords brought waste lands under cultivation, and introduced from the continent crops, tools, and methods they had observed there. Expanses of sand hill and moor were converted into plowlands or improved pasture; various kinds of grass were planted to improve meadows and pastures, while the turnip, which in the eighteenth century was to provide a plentiful winter food for livestock, received some attention. The environs of London became intensively cultivated market gardens or dairy farms, and root crops alternated with grain in the open fields. Books on agriculture appeared, and in 1664 the Royal Society, a group of scientists, sent out a questionnaire asking persons "skilful in Husbandry" what practices they might "think good from their own knowledge and experience to communicate hereupon." The answers revealed a certain interest in experiment and improvement.

During the seventeenth century England became one of Europe's minor granaries. In earlier centuries there had been some exports, but only in years of abundant harvest were they either possible or permitted. Control of the grain trade was part of national and civic policy, for there was no easy access to external supplies, and if plenty reigned for a time it was always followed by scarcity, and sometimes by acute famine. Europe had especially bad harvests around 1530, 1586, and 1709, but in between these years wheat prices swung from low to high at least three times in every two decades. In 1584 the index number stood at 52, but in 1586 it was at 113; in 1706 it was at 69, in 1709 at 183. Since famine was never far away governments protected their supplies, and the English practice was to allow exports only when a very large surplus pushed prices below a fixed very low point. The price rarely descended so far, and hence export was unusual.

After 1600 cultivation expanded, and a class of big grain merchants arose to organize the domestic trade and the carriage of supplies overseas. After 1660, under the pressure of the landed and commercial interests, grain-growing was officially encouraged. In 1670 exports were allowed, no matter what the price of grain, but might be suspended in time of famine. In 1688 a bounty began to be paid the exporter if the price fell below a certain price. Meanwhile the old policy of allowing grain to enter duty-free was abandoned, and a sliding scale of duties was worked out, by which imported grain paid a high tariff if prices were low but only a nominal duty if they were high.

The aim of these Corn Laws—"corn" is English for wheat and other grains—was to encourage the grain-grower by letting his goods escape from a low-priced market, and yet to protect the consumer from a high price. The actual effect has been, and still is being, vigorously debated. Adam Smith contended that the bounty, by encouraging exports, kept the home market less well supplied and made food dearer to the home consumer than it might otherwise have been. It prevented a surplus from being stored up in the fat years for use in the lean, and thus raised prices at all times. A modern student, Professor Barnes, finds that the bounty was necessary if English farmers were to find and keep a market for their surplus grain, and thus helped to increase the production of grain. When scarcity threatened the country the suspension of the bounty, the ban on exports, and the welcome given to imports helped to break the famine, while the yield in poor years was more than it would have been if farmers had not planted in hope of being able to export. Mr. Lipson holds similar views; he points out that prices fell in the decades after 1689, tillage was stimulated, methods of production were improved, and while growers had a greater assurance of steady and uniform prices consumers had a better prospect of more regular supplies. To this Mr. Fay replies that the lower prices were due to a general fall in the price level and a long series of good seasons. The bounty "raised home prices and landlords' rents a little, cost the Treasury more than it could afford, kept the farmer in good heart, and provided subsequent generations with abundant food for erroneous reasoning in speech, tract, and treatise." The bounty was the farmer's share in the general distribution of benefits to the various powerful economic groups or sections. To give something to everybody at everybody else's expense was good politics and popular economics. Lord Ernle may be nearest to the mark when he suggests that the balance of influence in promoting or retarding agricultural progress was probably "inconsiderable."

Whatever the outcome of this argument may eventually be, certain facts are clear. Up to the seventeen-sixties, exports were large and imports negligible. After 1760 the exports rapidly dried up; a growing population, a series of poor harvests, and a rising price level made the task of supplying the home market more difficult and probably more profitable. In 1773 exports were forbidden if the price went above a certain point, and during most of the next twenty years that price was exceeded. Exports stopped and imports rose; henceforth England could not feed herself.

INDUSTRIES

Between 1500 and 1750 English industries grew greatly in stature and numbers. Woolen cloth became the country's staple export, while new mining and manufacturing enterprises appeared, supplied the home market, and found customers abroad. Professor Nef has shown that between 1540 and 1640 a great industrial development took place: old industries adopted processes already known on the continent; new industries were transferred from France, Germany, the Low Countries and Italy; and new processes were discovered and developed, largely in consequence of the transfer from wood fuel to coal. The rate of change was possibly as striking during the lifetime of Shakespeare as during that of Wordsworth or Byron.

Textile Industries.—In the Middle Ages some high-grade fabrics had been exported, while cheaper cloths had supplied the frontier demands of central and northern Europe. Wool was produced in most areas and manufacture for sale was carried on in nearly every county; but certain districts forged ahead of the rest, and by 1470 East Anglia, Yorkshire, and the region behind Bristol were outstanding producers. Commercial production spread to villages and small towns where living was cheap and guild ordinances did not apply, and wool was put out to be spun by women and girls residing in farms and country cottages. The organization of the wool supply, of production, and of sale gave openings for the energy and capital of large entrepreneurs (see Chapter XV). There was a great division of labor: each merchant, each weaver or dyer, and each district tended to specialize on one kind or class or product. Many cloths were exported undyed to Holland, where they were finished and sold by the Dutch. Critics who objected to this "sending of work out of the country" declared that 50,000 Dutch workers were thus employed; but an ambitious attempt in 1614-1617 to finish the cloths in England failed dismally—the art could not be learned overnight.

The woolen industry was recognized by the state as the country's staple manufacture. For its sake farmers were forbidden to export wool, and valiant attempts were made to prevent the "owler" from smuggling bales of wool to the continent. Heavy duties were imposed on foreign fabrics, the importation of cottons was checked, and corpses must be wrapped in woolen shrouds. The colonies must not make woolens for sale, and textile workers were forbidden to emigrate. In 1698 Ireland was forbidden to export wool and cloth to any country except England, and there a high tariff wall had to be jumped. Countless laws sought to stamp out "tricks of the trade," maintain quality, and make producers conform to the state's ideas of industrial morality; in this way foreign customers might be won or held, and charges of "cheap and nasty" be avoided. Diplomacy tried to open new markets or ward off higher tariffs. This state solicitude can be explained by the fact that cloth supplied about half the English exports in 1700, and that in 1760 one-third to two-fifths of that cloth went to the American colonies. The industry was in Defoe's opinion "the richest and most valuable manufacture in the world," worth more to England than the mines of Mexico and Peru were to the king of Spain.

By 1630 the woolen clothiers were looking with anxious or angry eyes on a rival fabric. In the late Middle Ages cotton had been brought from the eastern Mediterranean and made into cloth in Venice and southern Germany. As English merchants pushed into the Levant trade (after about 1580) they conveyed this raw material to Liverpool, secured linen yarn from Ireland, and employed Lancashire spinners and weavers to make a cloth with a linen warp and a cotton weft, which became known as fustian. This light, cheap fabric was useful for covering; it could be decorated by printing stripes, checks, or other patterns on its surface; and it won favor at home, in the slave markets, and on the plantations. Meanwhile the East India Company imported patterned cottons which became so popular that the woolen and silk industries demanded and secured a ban on the import of these colored pieces (1700) and on the use of even home-printed cotton fabrics (1721). But Lancashire fustians were exempt from these laws; they could be sold at home free from Indian competition, and in addition were sent to Africa and the plantations. Lancashire therefore steadily built up a big industry; Liverpool merchants financed it, supplied its raw material, sold its wares, and paved the way for the rapid advance that came with the invention of various machines after 1760.

Of other textile industries, knitting was stimulated by **William**

Lee's invention in 1589 of a complicated "frame." Work could be done much more quickly, hose could be knitted instead of being made from cloth, and a big industry grew up, first in London and later in the Midlands. The silk and linen industries drew much strength from Huguenot refugees. In 1718 Lombe introduced from Italy a machine for "throwing" silk; it was a complicated monster driven by water power, and was housed in a great mill, employing hundreds of workers, at Derby. It made a strong yarn and reduced the cost of production greatly. The government encouraged some Huguenot white paper makers and their English backers. The French ambassador did his best to check the enterprise and finally induced the workers to return to France, but not before Englishmen had learned the necessary secrets.

Mining and Metallurgy.—The Tudor period witnessed a great attack on mineral deposits. The growing European interest in precious and non-precious metals, the improving metallurgy, and the expanding demand for material for munitions, currency, and various metal goods, all stimulated the exploitation of mineral resources from at least 1450 or 1500 onward. England had iron deposits in many places, and zinc ore was found widely scattered, as was copper. Copper and tin made bronze, tin and lead made pewter, but copper and zinc made the brass that was now being used for articles as far apart as cannon and candlesticks. There were other minerals useful for making alum, copperas, and gunpowder, and plenty of clay and limestone for the bricks and mortar of an age that was deserting timber dwellings. Finally, there was coal.

Some of these deposits had been worked a long time; those near the surface had been exhausted, and deeper pits were necessary. Where precious metals were found, they were always mixed with others—copper, lead, or tin. This made the task of refining more complicated; it also made the deposits royal property, for under Germanic law all minerals, and especially the precious ones, belonged to the crown. Gradually this royal right was pared down; a judicial decision of 1568 recognized the landlord's ownership of base metals and coal in his subsoil, and an act of 1688 confined crown rights to gold and silver. Hence landlords became more interested in the exploitation of mineral wealth; they worked mines themselves with their own capital or with the aid of lenders or investors; or they leased the deposits and took rent or royalties.

For mining and refining by the new continental methods much capital, costly equipment, and special technical skill were needed, and German or Dutch capital and labor were therefore called in. The Hochstetters of Augsburg were prominent in British mining for over a century; when any mining company was formed some of the shares were usually sold in Germany or Holland; and in 1642 a colony of 4000 foreign workers was mining and smelting copper at Keswick. The copper and brass industries were developed by an alliance between English enterprise and German money and skill.

In the light of later developments, the growth of the iron and coal industries was the most significant feature of Tudor and Stuart mining history. Iron deposits in the Weald (i.e., the forest) of Sussex and at other points had been worked in pre-Roman and Roman times, but medieval production, using a primitive forge for smelting, was small. In Tudor times the blast furnace displaced the forge, while the growing demand for cast iron for cannon, etc., and the transfer of land from monasteries to lay owners stimulated production greatly. When one Cistercian estate on the Weald passed into the hands of the Sidneys, a forge and a furnace were erected in the abbey buildings, workmen were brought from France, Germany, and Wales, and a Dutch employee was sent home to fetch more workers and equipment for making steel. For over two centuries the Weald had a virtual monopoly of gun-casting, and its wares, ranging from little weapons weighing two pounds to cannon which weighed four tons, were in demand all over the continent. Streams turned water wheels which blew bellows and drove great hammers, ore was abundant, and at first vast forests supplied charcoal fuel. But the timber was cut more quickly than it was replenished, and when the fuel cost rose from 50 per cent of the total cost of production in 1550 to 80 per cent in 1750 the industry was ruined by its charcoal bill.

Sidney's activities were duplicated by landlords, farmers, and capitalists in many other places, and after 1600 there were said to be 800 ironworks in the British Isles. Ore and streams were plentiful, but the fuel supply always failed eventually, and at one place after another ironworks had to be abandoned after a few years' work. The government sought to encourage iron production in the colonies in order to free the country from dependence on

Swedish or Russian supplies of metal. Men talked of using coal, but the iron picked up new impurities from the coal while it was ridding itself of those contained in the ore. In 1620 a young squire, Dudley, apparently discovered a way of using coal, but various difficulties prevented the spread of the practice. Coke was not discovered till about 1650, and sixty years later Abraham Darby, a Shropshire ironmaster, succeeded in using coke as fuel for smelting. His son improved on his discovery, but even in 1750 the process was not generally known or was not satisfactory. Only after 1750 did the iron industry escape fully from bondage to charcoal.

When it did so, it added one more to the many demands that had long existed for coal. The Romans had burned coal, medieval England knew its virtues and vices, and in 1307 London lime-burners were forbidden to use it because the smoke and fumes were a public nuisance. Coal was washed up from submarine out-crops and picked up on the northeast coast—hence its name, "sea coal." It was dug from outcrops on hillsides and from shallow pits. As wood became scarcer, coal found wider use, and by the early seventeenth century it was used by brewers, distillers, makers of tiles, bricks, salt, sugar, soap, glass, nails, alum, lime, cutlery, and brass. Big vats, pans, kilns, furnaces, ovens, or other containers were built and coal fires were lit underneath them. The demand for coal grew rapidly: in 1550 the output was about 200,000 tons, but in 1700 it was nearly 3,000,000.

Sometimes coal was used on or near the mine; but if transport facilities were available, it might be sent long distances, and its production, carriage, and distribution involved a large outlay of capital. Newcastle was sending coal to London by 1200, and to the continent by 1400; by 1700 great dirty fleets were carrying 1,250,000 tons to London, the Low Countries, France, and some German ports. Large sums were invested, not always profitably, in mines, ships, or merchants' stocks, and 15,000 to 18,000 men were at work in and around the pits in 1640. Producers or distributors made agreements by which output was restricted and prices raised. Such technical problems as drainage of the mine and movement of the coal led eventually to the development of the railroad, the steam engine, and the English canal system.

On the basis of coal and of growing supplies of homemade or imported metals, the manufacture of articles of iron, steel, brass, copper, or pewter became important. London was the home of scores of specialized industries to supply the varied demands of city, court, and commerce. Sheffield specialized on cutlery, but Birmingham produced almost every kind of metal small ware— knives, nails, arms, locks, hinges, snuffboxes, and the countless small articles needed for apparel, home, army, or farm. Then came improved methods of gilding, plating, and lacquering, and by 1750 Birmingham was "the toy shop of Europe," supplying that continent and the American colonies with whatever hardware they needed for peace or war, for use or ornamentation.

In addition to the mining, metal, and textile industries there were others, such as printing, glass, and pottery. In nearly all of them there was an improvement in equipment and methods, and a search for ways by which problems could be solved, obstacles removed, costs reduced, or quality improved. If genius is a capacity for picking other peoples' brains, the English showed that trait. The alien skilled worker was welcomed by the government and large entrepreneurs, but not always by native craftsmen; Lombe was given a patent and then a large sum of money for bringing the silk machine to England; London paper-makers sought the reason for the superiority of Dutch, French, and Italian paper; the East India Company tried to discover how the Indians made the rich red dyes they used on calico; cotton printers copied the methods of their Hamburg rivals, and tin-plate makers built mills such as were in use in Sweden. At every point some-one was willing to sit at the feet of the foreigner and learn what was to be taught; but at the same time the inventive spirit was growing strong, "hunches" were followed up, new methods or equipment were being designed, and science was reaching the stage where it could answer some questions asked by industry. By 1700 England was ahead of other countries in parts of its industrial equipment, far ahead in its use of coal, and entitled to boast, "Our artisans [are] universally allow'd the best upon earth for Improvements."

DOMESTIC COMMERCE

Domestic commerce was stimulated by the growth of London and the industries. Its marketing facilities probably improved more rapidly than did its means of transportation, for serious attention was not given to the roads until after 1700. In 1555 each parish was ordered to appoint two surveyors, under whose direction every householder must work four (later six) days a year on the local roads. The plan rested on amateur supervision and forced labor and made no provision for material, and the "statute laborers" seem to have done no more than level the surface by filling holes with earth or such stone as was at hand. After 1660 tolls were imposed on some highways to provide a maintenance fund, but this plan did not become general till the eighteenth century. Travel by land was therefore slow; passenger vehicles rarely moved more than four miles an hour and could scarcely be used in winter, many travelers and great quantities of goods were carried on horseback, and freight charges were high. Yet the roads were used; cloth, grain, cattle, wool, etc., had to be moved, and used the road if there was no other way.

The other way was the river or the sea. England was a small country and no part was very far from some water. The Thames, Severn, Trent, Ouse, and other rivers went far inland, and had large estuaries. Their courses might be broken by natural or man-made obstacles, but they flowed through fertile country, and the goods which traversed them soon reached a port from which a ship could carry them along the coast or abroad. Coastal traffic was therefore large; even in the early nineteenth century travelers from Edinburgh to London went by sea, although there was then an excellent road and stagecoach service.

In France domestic trade was impeded by tolls, interprovincial duties, and actual bans on movement of goods. In England national unity created a free-trade commercial unit, and when Scotland and England united in 1707 Great Britain became the largest customs-free area in western Europe. Union opened the Scottish market to English producers and traders, and gave Scotsmen a field for their goods and enterprise in England and the colonies. To Glasgow the Virginia tobacco and West India sugar trades proved a well of wealth; to northern England there came freedom from the age-long menace of raids; and to Scotsmen in general, whether selling cattle or seeking a career, there was opened up "the noblest prospect which a Scotchman ever sees— the high road that leads him to England" (Dr. Johnson).

Distribution gradually grew in complexity as new kinds of middlemen and new opportunities for contact of buyer and seller appeared. The fairs survived as on the continent, and were still important for wholesale dealings in sheep, wool, cattle, horses, butter, cheese, or fish. The price at which staple commodities were sold at a fair might rule all subsequent transactions until the next fair. As the volume of trade grew, especially in commodities which were not seasonal but were made or produced all the year round, the market overshadowed the fair. In the textile districts of Yorkshire, for instance, the cloth-makers began in the seventeenth century to carry their pieces to the market held once or twice a week in the nearest town, and displayed them on the walls of a churchyard or on tables set up in the main street. Eventually the trade grew large enough to justify the building of cloth halls, where in the space of about an hour transactions amounting in value from £10,000 to £20,000 might be carried through. Other special markets supplied wholesale dealers, retailers, and consumers; in London there were separate markets, each with its own site or day, for cattle, horses, meat, fish, vegetables, fruit, hay, leather, coal, and cloth.

In large towns there were by the eighteenth century a considerable number of retail stores. The craftsman sold goods in the front room of his house or the front part of his workshop; imported goods like tea or tobacco were sold over the counter, market places became a jumble of inns and shops, and the "down-town" shopping area slowly spread into residential streets. In Johnson's time a pickle shop stood next door to the London home of the Duke of Northumberland. Street hawkers wandered round towns crying their wares, while peddlers traversed the countryside. Thus the equipment and personnel of distribution became more elaborate, varied, and specialized as the volume of trade grew. Contact between middleman and consumer grew more intimate, and an increasing percentage of the population earned its livelihood by buying, carrying, and selling.

External Commerce

The development of Indian, African, and American traffic looms large in English history, but Europe was more valuable as a consumer of English exports and of oriental and American goods for which London was an *entrepôt*. Even in the first half of the nineteenth century it bought one-third to two-fifths of the exports of British and Irish produce, and in 1913 took a third. Anglo-French trade suffered when the two countries became bitter rivals in the latter part of the seventeenth century. That rivalry led to the imposition of high tariffs or prohibitions, to the ban on export of English wool or import of French silks, and to preferential treatment of Portuguese wines. At the end of the war of 1702-1713 some English interests pleaded, but in vain, for freer trade with France; not till 1786 did the two countries substantially reduce their tariffs to each other, and that compact was soon broken by the revolutionary wars. Smuggling blunted the edge of exclusion, for both coasts of the English Channel housed a hardy population and provided quiet havens. In war time privateering did great damage to the trade of each land.

Spain and Portugal were important as markets, but much more as channels through which goods could pass to their colonies. In return wine, oil, soap, fruits, iron, tropical American products, and bullion were obtained. Portugal and Brazil bought much English cloth, and in 1660 there were sixty English firms in Lisbon. In the late seventeenth century England placed heavy duties on Portuguese wine and sugar; Portugal retaliated by forbidding the entry of most English cloths and tried to develop her own textile industry. This blow hurt, and in 1703 the English woolen interests secured the Methuen treaty, by which Portuguese wine was admitted at two-thirds the duty paid on French wines, in return for removal of the ban on English cloth. The result was apparently a large increase in trade between the two empires; English merchants swarmed to Lisbon or found partners and agents there, and much Brazilian gold went legally or furtively to London. The desire to capture the trade of Spanish America was one of the chief causes of the commercial rivalries of the seventeenth century. France had the advantage of nearness to Spain and sought political control; but the Dutch and English resisted this with a large measure of success, and after 1713 the trade relations of England and Spain were very close. France did not abandon her efforts, but gained little, and in 1784 British commerce with Spain was five times as large as was that of France.

English trade in the Mediterranean scarcely developed until the sixteenth century. Cloth, lead, tin, hides, and herrings were taken to the Barbary Coast, Turkey, and the Levant, there to be pitted against goods brought by the French, Dutch, and Italians. In London young men learned the handwriting and language of the Near East and the art of buying and packing cloths for the

Levant. Then they went out to Constantinople, Smyrna, or Aleppo to complete their training. After this they joined the firm of some agent who was handling English cloth, and wrestled with problems of supply and demand in a difficult market that stretched to Persia and the Red Sea—for the land routes were not deserted after 1498. They staved off Arab thieves, bartered with Jewish or Armenian brokers, made loans or gave bribes to Turkish officials, and lived inside the heavy iron gates of khans (factories).

North of Calais lay the great cloth markets of the North Sea and Baltic lands. In 1598 the Merchant Adventurers succeeded in persuading Elizabeth to drive the Hansards from the Steelyard in London, and the export of English cloth to the North Sea and Baltic area passed into the hands of English traders. Many cloths went to Holland to be finished and reexported; others went to Hamburg, the Merchant Adventurers' headquarters, and thence passed inland to supply the needs of Hanover and Prussia. The Merchant Adventurers had the Dutch as rivals, and also many English "interlopers" or "free traders." The latter grew stronger during the seventeenth century, evaded and attacked the Company's monopoly, and in 1689 persuaded parliament to annul it. In the Baltic the Eastland Company was the privileged group after 1579. Its trade centered on Elbing and later on Danzig. It took out cloths and brought back grain from the Vistula, flax, linen, wax, potash, and naval stores. It faced the fiercest Dutch competition, and could make little headway, while parliament whittled away its privileges after 1673. Hence English participation in Baltic trade was not important until the eighteenth century. When it did develop it owed little to privileged companies, but was the work of energetic individuals who learned to build or operate ships as well as did the Dutch or who used Dutch and Scandinavian ships to carry their goods.

IMPERIAL ECONOMIC EXPANSION

Englishmen played little or no part in the maritime explorations, but wished to share in the benefits which came from them by getting oriental goods and finding markets for their own wares. For a time they did not feel strong enough to risk their necks by poking into the preserves of Spain and Portugal, and sought other routes to the east. Two ways seemed open for unmolested search—the northeast and the northwest. The northeast was explored first. It would, said the enthusiasts, be the shortest and nearest, "for six months in the year navigable and without impediment or let, and for that time almost all daylight, the air temperate and wholesome." It would permit a round trip to Japan in six months, and on the way there would be "good traffic" with the Tartar, exchanging English cloth for "rich furs and other costly goods."

In 1553 a London group financed an expedition to the regions beyond the top of Norway, and one ship reached Archangel. Its commander went by land to Moscow and won from the czar the grant of free intercourse for English merchants. After that promising start, the Muscovy Company was formed in 1555. It never found a northeast passage, but a land route through Russia (down the Volga) to Persia and India was used a little for the carriage of silk and other Chinese goods. The trade with Russia remained, and as the czars expanded their territory British and Dutch traders sought markets for their cloth, tobacco, and arms in Archangel, on the east coast of the Baltic, and in the Black Sea.

The search for a northwest road to Asia also failed. In 1574 Drake planned to seek it, and in 1576 Frobisher set out. He "tasted most boisterous Boreal blasts, mixt with snowe and haile in the moneths of June and July," encountered a "sea unicorne which had in his nose a horne" two yards long, saw Eskimos eating ice "as pleasantlie as wee will eate sugar candie," but failed to find either a passage to the Pacific or a profit for his sponsors. In 1610 Henry Hudson went a little farther, but not far enough, and his successors did no better. But from these failures eventually came the exploitation of the "traffic of beavers" around Hudson Bay after 1670.

Since the arctic offered no thoroughfare, the Portuguese and Spanish routes and areas must be invaded. Even before the victory over the Armada (1588) this invasion had begun. Hawkins made three slave-trading journeys to Africa and Spanish America between 1562 and 1567. Drake in 1577 set out on what was ostensibly a journey of discovery and trade in the South Seas, but he pillaged two treasure ships on the Pacific coast, circumnavigated the globe, and returned in 1580 with a ship ballasted with bullion. At other times and places piracy or privateering was practiced in Spanish or Portuguese preserves, while Gilbert in Newfoundland (1578-1583) and Raleigh in Virginia (1580-1595) attempted to make settlements. It is significant that Gilbert's first venture was crippled when his supporters transferred their money to a privateering enterprise, and that the ships which should have taken supplies to Raleigh's settlement in 1586 went off raiding while the colonists were doing little but search for treasure. The lure of plunder or of a discovery of precious metals was disastrous; the raids brought fortunes to some, but provoked retaliation on English ships and trade, and were in part responsible for war. As for the bullion searchers, their efforts delayed real progress in settlement, and not till the next century did the hope of finding El Doradoes east of the Alleghenies grow faint. If California, with its gold, had been on the Atlantic coast, the story of North America would have been very different.

The East India Company.—The defeat of the Armada and the Spanish annexation of Portugal removed any reluctance Englishmen might feel in going east or west. The Dutch successes in the Indian Ocean roused London's envy, and in 1600 Elizabeth granted a charter to "the Governor and Company of Merchants of London trading into the East Indies." The Company was given for fifteen years a monopoly of English trade between the Cape of Good Hope and the Straits of Magellan; no individual merchant could traffic there unless he received a license from the Company. Armed with these powers and with a capital of £68,000 subscribed by over two hundred "adventurers," the Company set to work. By 1613 twelve voyages had been organized; only one had ended in loss, and some had repaid investors their capital, plus a profit of over 200 per cent. In 1609 a factory was established at Bantam (in Java), near the spice areas and at a point to which ships came from China bearing silks or from India laden with cottons. By 1615 the Company had nineteen well-placed outposts—in the cloth markets on the southeast coast of India, at Surat on the northwest coast (where indigo, Indian pepper, saltpeter, and cottons were obtainable and where ships came in from the Persian Gulf and Red Sea), on the islands and archipelago, and at Hirado in Japan, where the buyer was nearer the Chinese silk supply.

During the next forty years the Company strengthened its position in India but had to retreat from the archipelago. In 1622 the Persian Gulf was cleared of Portuguese posts, in 1628 the first "Persian Voyage" was organized, and in 1668 the Company obtained Bombay. There were stormy episodes with native princes or traders and with European (including English) rivals; but fortresses, diplomacy, presents, bribes, tribute, weak native rulers and strong Company officials saved the situation, and trade grew fitfully but surely. The Company had to fight most of its own battles and build up political and military strength to retain or strengthen its grasp on Indian commerce. Consequently a trading group became a political power, and when Clive captured Bengal in 1757 the Company became sovereign, landlord, and commercial monopolist of thirty million people.

Farther east the Dutch were too powerful, and eventually the Company had to retreat from the spice islands and from Japan. It did, however, get a foothold in Canton, where it gathered up silk, china, and tea. Apart from that outpost, the Company was thrown back on India. It took out precious metal, copper, lead, tin, coral, and cloth, and brought back cottons, indigo, saltpeter, and some spices. By 1700 the European demand for highly spiced food seems to have been waning, but that for cottons, indigo, and tea was growing larger. Hence India seemed a less meager asset in contrast with the Dutch preserves. In 1601 the Company sent out only four second-hand ships—the largest was of 600 tons; by 1801 it owned 122 vessels, the biggest of them solid ships of 1400 tons, built and armed like men-of-war.

The Company had difficulties to encounter at home as well as in Asia. Its charter rights were occasionally ignored by English rulers, and rival groups were given (or bought) power to trade. At times there were two companies in the field, in addition to interlopers. Only in 1709 did organized rivalry end, when a new company (founded in 1698) and the old one were merged in the United East India Company. The Company was flogged with many whips by its opponents, but the three chief criticisms were that it was a monopoly, that it exported bullion, and that it imported undesirable goods. The outcry against monopoly came from those London and provincial traders who were not stockholders and who wished to enter the Oriental trade without getting a license. But the Company held its ground; its stockholders were powerful, its cheap or free loans to the state were large and necessary, its foothold in India was firm, and its value in the struggle with France became greater. Not till 1813 was the British trade with India thrown open to all comers, and that with China remained closed till 1834.

The export of precious metal, especially from a country that had no domestic or colonial source of supply, was one of the cardinal sins of the early seventeenth century. By its first charter the Company was allowed to export a limited amount, provided it brought as much back. The limit was raised later, and in 1663 was removed. At the beginning of the eighteenth century the average annual exports were over £300,000 in bullion and less than £100,000 in goods; but before the end of the century they were £620,000 in bullion and £770,000 in goods. Such a trade obviously seemed bad. It "carried away the treasure of Europe to enrich the heathen," and was "a public nuisance, a burthen to trade, and a danger to the nation" (Defoe). The Company retorted that it brought back goods worth far more than the goods and bullion taken out, sold a large part of them on the continent, in Africa, or Spanish America, and thus brought more specie into England than it had taken out. It also tried to open new markets for English goods in the Orient, and had some success in selling cloth in Persia, India, and China. But until Lancashire turned the tables on India with its machines and American cotton, and began to send cheap fabrics to the east, most trading ventures to the Orient carried silver or gold as trade goods. The agents in India reported that "the natives will not trade their pepper for goods, for if they cannot have ready [money] for their pepper they care not to dispose of it," and the Company argued that if Englishmen did not take the treasure their "never-to-be-reconciled enimys, the Dutch" or the French would capture the trade.

The undesirable imports were the cottons and silks. The Company fostered this branch of its trade, and sent out artificers to teach the natives how to make fabrics for the European market. The opposition thus aroused led in 1700 to the ban on the use of Asiatic silks or of cottons which had been "painted, dyed, printed or stained there." The Company could still import these wares for reexport; it could import *plain* calicoes, and printing works therefore multiplied to print patterns on them. In 1721 Parliament forbade the use of *any* printed cotton fabrics (except in blue), no matter where they were printed. Thus the Indian pieces were shut out of the English market, but were still sold on the continent, in Africa, and in America.

North American Settlements.—While the first Company ships were on their way to the Orient, other vessels were returning from the east coast of North America with such rich cargoes of fur that plans for transatlantic trade and settlement revived. Fishermen had for decades been telling tall stories about the climate and resources of the lands bounding the transatlantic fishing grounds. Lemons, olives, vines, and mulberry trees would grow there, and gold must surely exist in a land inhabited by fauns and unicorns. North America would yield commodities which England lacked, while the natives and colonists would provide a good market for English goods, especially woolen cloth. There would be work and profit for English ships and merchants, and rich reward for English capital.

In 1606 two groups of merchants, one from London, one from Plymouth and other outports, obtained power to plant colonies in North America. The story of these ventures and of their successors is an oft-told part of American history, but certain English economic aspects are worthy of examination. The Londoners did not see clearly the nature or the cost of the task they were facing. They thought much of trade, but little of colonization. The first charter made virtually no provision for settling a white population overseas; it was assumed that settlers would go out of their own accord, that the capital of the Company would be used chiefly in supplying ships and trade goods, and that when the vessels returned their cargoes would pay good dividends to stockholders, as did the East Indian ships. The first expedition was organized in early 1607, to carry about a hundred colonists, seek a passage "to the other sea," search for minerals, and trade with the natives.

Experience quickly showed that no easy fortunes were to be made from "returns" from a land that lacked spices and precious metals. The ships brought back little but "ifs and ands, hopes and some few proofes." The investors lost their tempers, and told the settlers that if they did not do better "they were like to remain as banished men." But this fit of anger soon gave place to a clearer view of the problem. There could be little commerce until colonization had been fostered. Men must be induced to cross the ocean and settle, land policies must be framed, and equipment for defense and development must be provided. Trading and colonization were two sides of the same coin; they must be handled by one company, and much capital would be required. The second charter

(1609) to the Company of Adventurers and Planters of the City of London for the First Colony in Virginia shows a recognition of the double task ahead. The Company was granted a bigger area and given authority to alienate land.

Armed with these powers, it set out to get colonists and capital. To the former it offered land, to the latter it promised land and profits. Shares could be paid for in three annual installments, and prospective stockholders were assured that their dividends from trade would be as valuable as the land grants. The response was good, and in 1609 a big expedition set sail. But returns were still slow and small, the need for more capital was persistent, disappointed stockholders refused to pay their second or third installments, and the venture was almost always at death's door during its infancy. It was kept from passing through by the valiant efforts of Sir Thomas Smythe, the company's treasurer, who borrowed right and left, wrote begging letters to provincial towns and Dutch capitalists, and gained permission in the third charter (1612) to raise money by holding lotteries. Only when the experimental cargo of Virginia tobacco found favor in London in 1613 did the black years of fruitless effort end.

The Company's finances now began to be more healthy, but still more capital was required, and subsidiary companies were established to meet some of the special needs of the colony. One of them provided funds to develop the Bermudas; others were to finance fishing voyages, provide supplies of apparel and other necessaries, build a furnace to make glass for beads, send out shipwrights, equip the fur trade, or transport "a hundred maids to Virginia to be made wives." The last one was profitable, for the planter paid for his wife in tobacco, and the venture gave the shareholders "great contentment." Most of the others failed to make ends meet.

The Virginia Company was dissolved in 1625, victim of some bad fortune overseas and of internal dissension at home. It had made most of the mistakes of a pioneer, and discovered the many problems attached to colonization. It had poured much capital across the Atlantic, but made little profit for its stockholders. Its experience was repeated by the capitalists who financed the Pilgrim Fathers, for there was no New England tobacco or any other commodity that could be shipped to England in sufficient quantities to pay dividends, and the sponsors were glad to get out of the project with the loss of only two-thirds of their capital. The Massachusetts Bay Company (1629) fared better, for many of those who founded it went to the New World and received their reward on the spot. In the proprietary colonies material reward for capital and enterprise was also scanty. Penn made a colony, but ruined himself, was thrown into the debtor's prison, and tried to sell his venture to the crown. As ends in themselves all the colonies eventually succeeded; as means to a profit on capital expended on their foundation they were failures.

In the islands England soon gained a foothold. The settlement of the Bermudas in 1609 was an offshoot of the Virginia venture, the Bahamas were occupied in 1612, and during the sixteen-twenties St. Kitts, Barbados, Barbuda, Antigua, Trinidad and other islands were claimed. A group of London merchants sent a settlement to Barbados in 1627. That island was suitable for tobacco culture, and between 1627 and 1647 about 50,000 persons of high and low degree settled on it. During and after the Civil War many Cavaliers went there, sugar production began, and, in 1667, 750 plantations owned 80,000 slaves. Sugar production spread to other islands, providing a commodity for export to England or to the American mainland, and calling for great quantities of slaves, barrels, food, and clothing from the outside world, as well as ships in which to carry them. The sugar planters and the London merchants who served them became a powerful vested interest whose influence was often felt in British colonial and foreign policy. Meanwhile Jamaica, taken in 1655, became sugar planter, slave buyer, pirates' nest, focal point for the traffic in goods and slaves with Spanish America, and channel through which treasure flowed from the New World to London.

Economic Effects of American Colonization.—The story of the English colonies is relevant to this book only in so far as the transatlantic possessions affected their owner. Those effects were far-reaching. In the first place, the colonies were the first to receive any really large body of European migrants. Economic distress, desire for economic advancement, religious or political dissatisfaction, love of adventure, philanthropy, the indenture system, and exportation of convicts all played their part. During the seventeenth century 500,000 persons, according to the best available estimate, left the British Isles, but three times that number emigrated during the eighteenth century. At the peak of the seventeenth-century migration, 10,000 persons left Britain in a single year, and while the *Mayflower* carried only 102 people in all, at least 20,000 had joined them in New England by 1640, chiefly from southern and eastern England. By 1700 about 100,000 indentured servants had gone to Virginia.

In the eighteenth century the net was spread more widely. Religious, political, and economic discontent caused a great exodus from Ulster after 1715, and a severe famine in 1760 gave further impetus to this movement. The Union of 1707 opened colonial doors to the Scot, and agrarian changes which led to the eviction of Highlanders from their holdings set the Scottish outflow in motion; but the emigration from Catholic Ireland did not begin until nearly 1800. In 1619 the Privy Council began to send convicts reprieved from the death sentence, provided their crime had not been violence or witchcraft; paupers and some offenders were sent after about 1670, but "transportation" of convicted persons grew large only in the eighteenth century. Germany became a great exporter of people after 1700, when bad harvests in 1707-1709, war, and political or religious stress drove many from the Rhineland and Palatinate. Hence there were about 3,000,000 white people living in 1775 between Georgia and Maine—a number equal to roughly one-third the population of Great Britain.

In the second place, progress came first and was most marked in the "supply colonies," i.e., those which produced a commodity capable of sale overseas. The first successes were in the tobacco and sugar lands. "Even after the great migration of the Puritans, there were in 1640 more than twice as many English settlers in the West Indies and the tobacco area as in New England" (Nettels). By 1700 the region from Delaware northward housed 120,000 white people, against about 80,000 on the southern mainland; but the addition of the island white settlers to the southern figures made the sugar and tobacco colonies by far the more important group. In volume of trade the same was true: in 1700 English exports to the north were only one-third of those to the southern mainland area, and in 1767 were only two-thirds. English rulers consequently began their imperial thinking and traders planned their enterprises in terms of colonies that would concentrate on supplying commodities that Englishmen could not, or should not, produce.

In the third place, the development of the colonies expanded the English shipping and trading class, and stimulated such manufactures as hardware and cloth. The American market became a vital factor in the welfare of Birmingham, Yorkshire, and Lancashire, while the Atlantic traffic accounted for some of the growth of London and much of that of Bristol, Liverpool, and Glasgow. In the tobacco season of 1703-1704, 126 ships left Virginia and Maryland, each carrying over 100 tons of tobacco leaf; and in 1706, 300 ships came to pick up the crop. Between 1698 and 1774 colonial trade with England increased fivefold; at the former date it comprised 15 per cent of English overseas trade, at the latter it was 33 per cent. The slave trade employed many ships and needed goods with which to buy slaves in Africa. The emigrant and passenger traffic was by 1770 calling for better and bigger North Atlantic shipping services.

Much capital sunk in colonization never came to the surface again, but money put into trade and ships fared better. Some of those who trafficked in slaves, sugar, and tobacco made great fortunes, but the risks in the slave trade were large, while the advances made to the planters were heavy and were not always repaid. A debtless planter was almost unknown, and the financing of colonial production absorbed great quantities of English capital. When war or defenses called for food, munitions, shipping and building equipment, English and, later, colonial merchants profited by getting contracts to supply these needs. With the exception of the Hudson's Bay and African Companies, transatlantic trade was free and open, and offered rewards to those individuals who had the necessary capital, enterprise, and good luck.

The Colonial Trade.—Trade with the colonies might be simple and direct, but much of it was triangular, rectangular, or even more complicated. In its simplest form, a ship would sail from England, and after a six to eight weeks' journey reach the wharf of a Virginia or Maryland planter, to unload a miscellaneous cargo of ironmongery, cloth, guns, beads, shoes, hats, stockings, ink, glassware, books, furniture, cheese, toys, spices, buttons, farming implements, jews'-harps, and other articles ordered by the planter. A cargo of tobacco was then loaded and consigned to the planter's London commission agent, who sold it to English or continental buyers, pocketed his commission, and bought the items set out in the shopping list brought by the skipper. The London agent was the link between the planter and Europe. He received the planter's children and put them into school, gave his sons a business training, paid his debts, advanced him money when tobacco prices or crops were too low to pay all the bills, forwarded his letters, saw to the transportation of the professors who were going out to William and Mary College, and lobbied in the planters' interests among cabinet ministers or members of parliament.

This direct exchange of English goods for colonial produce did not, however, fill the whole picture, for England could not supply all that was needed or take all that was for sale, and hence various triangular or more roundabout transactions took place. Liverpool traders took English goods to Africa, picked up slaves for America, and brought tobacco, cotton, and sugar back to England. Fishing fleets went from England to the Banks, took their catch to Spain or Portugal, and carried wine to their home port. As the island plantations grew and concentrated on commercial cultivation, they needed not merely slaves, but food for planter and slaves, horses to work the sugar mills, and lumber for buildings and barrels. The triangle might therefore go as follows: fishing supplies from England to the Banks, fish to the islands, and sugar to England. But the needs of the islands stimulated the development of the middle and northern colonies. These areas could produce little that England needed, and direct traffic with the mother country was therefore limited. But wheat and butter could be produced, fish could be caught offshore or fetched from Newfoundland, lumber was abundant, horses could be reared, and ships could be built in which to take these products to markets that needed them.

The English trader and shipowner was therefore supplemented and even supplanted by his colonial cousin. From Boston or Philadelphia two trips could be made in a year to the West Indies, with fish, lumber, and farm produce. In exchange English goods might be bought there, or a cargo of sugar, rum, or molasses secured. To the Banks rum, barrels, food, tobacco, clothing, and fishing supplies might be taken and exchanged for fish, European goods, coin, or for bills of exchange which could be used to buy wares in Europe. If the New Englander was venturesome he might make longer journeys and invade the preserves of European vessels. He might take fish and lumber to Portugal and the Mediterranean, pick up wine for England, and exchange his cargo (or even his ship and cargo) for English goods, fishing tackle, or for bills on London which he could sell easily in Boston to those who had debts to pay abroad. Finally, he might enter the slave trade, and by 1675 little two-masted ketches were going to the Slave Coast and even to Madagascar. The New England slaver took rum as trade goods, brought slaves to the West Indies, and reached home with more sugar, molasses, rum, and European goods.

Imperial Commercial Policy.—Over this labyrinth of trade routes and transactions hung a colonial policy which, by a combination of encouragement and restraint, of protection and prohibition, sought to help vested interests, foster desirable new interests, keep profits inside the imperial family, hit enemies, and add to the economic welfare and political strength of parent and children. That policy contained little that was new; it embodied ideas which have colored commercial policies in most centuries, and which find expression today whenever men begin to discuss economics in terms of politics. It dealt with two sets of relationships: (1) those between the empire and the outside world; (2) those between the various parts of the empire. The outside world meant at first the Dutch, who swarmed into colonial harbors almost as soon as there were any or any goods to be picked up there. The goods were barrels of tobacco, and colonial policy began with the control of the trade in that commodity. By 1620 the Dutch were selling goods in Virginia and loading tobacco for continental European markets. When the Virginia Company protested against this threat to its profits, James I ordered in 1621 that all exports of tobacco "and other commodities whatsoever" must be brought to London, and in 1624 decreed that the goods must come in English ships. Native shipowners would thus get the freights, native merchants would get the reward for handling that part of the crop which was sold on the continent, London would become a tobacco *entrepôt*, and the crown would collect more customs revenue. Charles I frequently repeated the orders of 1621 and 1624, and forbade the colonists to buy goods from the Dutch, but the illicit traffic continued.

This policy broadened and matured during the third quarter of the century into an elaborate legislative code. Dutch activities had expanded on both sides of the Atlantic while England was fighting its Civil War; the lost ground must be regained if English trade was to recover, and the Dutch had set a precedent by rigorously excluding foreigners from trade with their plantations. The Navigation Law of 1651 sought to revive and encourage English shipping by demanding that goods from Africa, Asia, or America be imported into England and the colonies in England or colonial ships; the master and two-thirds of the crew must be English or colonial. European goods going to any part of the empire (including England) must be carried in imperial ships or in ships belonging to the country from which the goods came or to the port from which they were usually shipped. Finally, foreign ships could not carry commodities along the coast from one home or colonial port to another. The penalty for any offense was loss of ship and cargo.

The second Navigation Law (1660) clarified and stiffened the earlier act. Goods could enter or leave the colonies only in English-owned or colonially built and owned vessels, and three-fourths of the crew must be imperial. A list of colonial products was drawn up, including sugar, cotton, dyewoods, indigo and tobacco, and these "enumerated articles" must be sent only to England, Ireland, or another colony. (Ireland was eliminated in 1671.) By an act of 1663 all foreign goods destined for the colonies must pass through England, thus making the country the *entrepôt* for colonial imports as the enumerated-articles clause made it the bottle neck for many colonial exports.

These laws remained on the statute book till the nineteenth century, when they were whittled away as part of the free-trade movement between 1825 and 1850. They were part of a wider policy, other aspects of which will be noticed in a moment. They did not attempt to center all imperial oceanic trade on England. Fish was never on the enumerated list, and naval stores were not there till 1705. Rice was added in 1704, but after 1730 was allowed to go straight to southern Europe, and in 1739 the same liberty was extended to sugar exports. After 1763 the list was greatly lengthened, yet almost immediately shortened by liberal exceptions. But, in general, English ports benefited by the *entrepôt* trade—probably at the expense of the planter. Of the British sugar imports between 1703 and 1722 a quarter was reexported, and during most periods at least three-fifths of the tobacco imported into Britain went out again. English shippers and merchants gained the reward for handling this trade, and the sale of tobacco and sugar opened the way for the disposal of other goods:

the public revenue gained a little, but the refund of half or all the duty on reexported produce pared the receipts heavily.

Not all westbound traffic had to pass through England. Salt could be taken from southern Europe direct to the colonies, as could wine from the Portuguese islands and Oriental goods brought by the East India Company. In the case of other goods, many of them would have been bought from England, or have passed through, under a régime of free trade, for there was either no other or no better source of supply, and the shipping service was available. If purchase elsewhere was deemed more advantageous, and if a route that avoided English ports meant lower shipment charges, smuggling was not difficult. Almost the only enforceable part of the Navigation Laws was that relating to the nationality of ships in which goods left or arrived; and even that part might break down when customers officers were few and ill-paid, when long indented coast lines made quiet arrival or departure easy, and when colonists, like the coast dwellers and consumers in most countries, were on the side of the "free trader."

Smuggling was a normal lubricant (or, as Lipson calls it, "a venial sin") of the colonial system. Newfoundland and the non-British West Indies were gathering points for vessels and goods of many lands. Prominent Boston traders like Hancock got cargoes of European and East Indian goods direct from Amsterdam or through such Dutch islands as St. Eustatius, bought molasses in a French island but shipped it in English hogsheads, and sent instructions to their agents abroad detailing methods of safe illicit traffic. Enforcement was difficult even when only English ships and traders were available; it became doubly so when the colonies got their own ships and merchants. Those merchants might express their "great discontent at the Acts . . . that restrained 'em from an open trade to all parts of the world," but it is very doubtful whether any market or source of supply to which they desired access was really closed by the operation of the Acts of Trade and Navigation.

The Navigation Laws fostered colonial as well as British shipping. American boats could be built cheaply, were protected on the Atlantic sea lanes by the British fleet, could share in the carrying trade between continental Europe and England, and could be sold readily in English ports. The opportunities and profit thus made available meant much to the commercial development of New England.

The second part of colonial policy dealt with relations between the different parts of the empire. Its basis was a belief in the economy of regional specialization—let each area do that job for which it was best fitted by resources, climate, and history, and be content to exchange its surplus goods for those of other districts. At times the idea of imperial self-sufficiency emerged, and rulers asked whether some part of the empire could not produce goods now obtained from foreign sources. In 1650, for instance, Cromwell asked a commission to consider how the plantations might "be best managed and made most useful for this Commonwealth, and how the commodities thereof may be so multiplied and improved as (if it be possible) those plantations alone may supply the Commonwealth of England with whatsoever it necessarily wants."

This policy required a nice alternation of restraint and encouragement. Restraint must be applied when colonists or homelanders threatened to develop an industry that might injure some other group. The English tobacco grower was repressed for the sake of Virginia, and English fishermen were excluded from New England waters. But the chief restraints were imposed on the colonists for the benefit of English manufacturing interests, especially where a colonial supply of raw materials offered a basis for the rise of some industry that might jeopardize the sale of English goods. In 1699 the export of colonial woolens from one colony to another was forbidden, and in 1732 a similar ban was put on felt hats. Plans for making sailcloth in New York, making shoes in Pennsylvania, and opening coal mines in Cape Breton were frowned on, while the Maryland planters were patted on the head for not making goods "which ought to be imported from this Kingdom" and were urged not "to turn their Thoughts to anything but the Culture of Tobacco."

Encouragement was offered by admitting colonial produce to English ports duty-free or subject to low tariffs. The duties on competing foreign goods were so high that the colonists had virtually a monopoly of the English sugar, tobacco, and tar market. Bounties were offered on some goods which England bought from foreigners but which the colonies might produce if given financial aid. Indigo cultivation flourished on a bounty of sixpence a pound granted in 1748 and died when the Revolution ended the grant; but most other bounties—on silk, flax, hemp, potash, etc.—had little effect, as did the ambitious effort to foster the production of naval stores in the northern colonies in 1705. Iron provided a good illustration of combined restraint and encouragement. In 1750 colonial smelters were offered a free market for iron in England, in order to break the English metal and fuel famine and end the dependence on Swedish or Russian supplies; but colonial iron-mongers were forbidden to make iron goods, since that would reduce the demand for English hardware.

The net effect of the British colonial policy on the economic progress of parent and children cannot be accurately or simply estimated. Professor Andrews doubts whether the Acts of Trade and Navigation "ever were a serious menace to colonial development." The benefits were substantial, the limitations not insurmountable, and the alternative to fairly lax British control was not freedom, but French, Dutch, or Spanish control. Professor Kirkland suggests that the Acts controlling trade were "not extensively violated" for the simple reason that they "coincided with the natural conditions of trade. The colonists benefited by their inclusion within the world of British shipping; they were protected in the English market; and as for European goods, they would have had them from England anyway," while non-English goods would probably have been obtained from London, that great assembling place of wares from all parts of the world. The Acts did not conflict violently with the natural flow of trade between a growing manufacturing and trading country and one engaged chiefly in frontier pursuits. After the Revolution Britain's industrial and shipping preeminence probably gave her a larger share of the American import trade than she had held in colonial days, while the British market in some years during the first half of the nineteenth century absorbed at least as great a fraction of American exports as it had done in the preceding century.

The effect of the colonial system on England was to accelerate the development of its carrying trade, its merchant class, and its export manufactures. But under any circumstances the possession of the colonies would have caused these developments, and the influence of a policy of exclusive enjoyment was one of degree rather than of kind. No other policy was historically possible, and no policy was without its price. If some Londoners and provincials made fortunes, others paid part of the cost in the money taken from the taxpayer to provide bounties on some colonial imports and some English exports, in the higher prices at which colonial wares were sold in a protected market, and in the growing cost of a navy which protected colonial and British ships but was maintained by the British taxpayer.

BIBLIOGRAPHY

GENERAL

ASHLEY, W. J., *Economic Organization of England* (1912), chaps. 3-6.
LIPSON, E., *Economic History of England* (1931), vol. i, chaps. 4, 10; vol. ii, chaps. 2, 3; vol. iii, chap. 4.
USHER, A. P., *Industrial History of England* (1920), chaps. 8, 9, 11.

SPECIAL SUBJECTS

ANDREWS, C. M., "The Acts of Trade," in *Cambridge History of the British Empire*, vol. i, chap. 9.
ANDREWS, C. M., *The Colonial Period of American History* (1934), vol. i.
ANDREWS, C. M., *The Colonial Background of the American Revolution* (1924).
BARNES, D. G., *History of the English Corn Laws, 1660-1846* (1930).
BEER, G. L., *Origins of the British Colonial System, 1576-1660* (1922).
BEER, G. L., *British Colonial Policy, 1754-1765* (1922).
CURTLER, W. H., *The Enclosure and Redistribution of Our Land* (1920).
ERNLE, LORD, *English Farming, Past and Present* (1912), chaps. 3-6.
FOSTER, W., *England's Quest of Eastern Trade* (1933).
HAMILTON, C. J., *The Trade Relations between England and India, 1600-1896* (1919).
KHAN, S. A., *The East India Trade in the Seventeenth Century* (1923).
MORSE, H. B., *Chronicles of the East India Company Trading to China, 1635-1834* (1926).
NEF, J. U., *Rise of the British Coal Industry* (1932).
NETTELS, C., *The Money Supply of the American Colonies before 1720* (1934).
POWER, E., and POSTAN, M. M., *Studies in English Trade in the Fifteenth Century* (1933).
REES, J. H., "Mercantilism and the Colonies," in *Cambridge History of the British Empire*, vol. i, chap. 20.
SCHLESINGER, A. M., *The Colonial Merchants and the American Revolution, 1763-1776* (1918).
SCOTT, W. R., *The Constitution and Finance of English, Scottish, and Irish Joint-Stock Companies to 1720* (1910), vol. ii.
TAWNEY, R. H., *The Agrarian Problem in the Sixteenth Century* (1912).
TAWNEY, R. H., and POWER, E., *Tudor Economic Documents* (1925).
UNWIN, G., *Studies in Economic History* (1927), part ii, chaps. 5, 8, 9, 11.

ARTICLES

DONNAN, E., "Eighteenth-Century English Merchants," in *J. E. B. H.*, November, 1931, pp. 70-98.
FISHER, F. J., "The Development of the London Food Market," in *Ec. H. R.*, April, 1935, pp. 46-64.

GEORGE, R. H., "A Mercantilist Episode," in *J. E. B. H.*, February, 1931, pp. 264-271.

GIDDENS, P. H., "Trade and Industry in Colonial Maryland," in *J. E. B. H.*, May, 1932, pp. 512-538.

KINGSFORD, C. L., "Beginnings of English Maritime Enterprise," in *History*, July, 1928.

LENNARD, R., "English Agriculture under Charles II," in *Ec. H. R.*, October, 1932, pp. 23-45.

NEF, J. U., "The Progress of Technology and the Growth of Large-Scale Industry in Great Britain, 1540-1640," in *Ec. H. R.*, October, 1934, pp. 3-24.

RIVE, A., "A Short History of Tobacco Smuggling," in *Ec. Hist.*, January, 1929, pp. 554-569.

CHAPTER XV

INDUSTRIAL AND COMMERCIAL ORGANIZATION,
1500-1750

Part I—The Organization of Production

THE expansion in the volume of trade, the lengthening of the traffic lanes, and the improvements in equipment or processes influenced the organization of production and trade. Production for the maker's own use (usufacture) or by small retail craftsmen remained the great broad basis of economic life, the predominant kind of work; but it was increasingly supplemented, or even impaired, after 1500, and a growing amount of enterprise was conducted by pure traders or by men who gathered together large numbers of producers or large quantities of their products to supply markets.

The predominance of usufacture can be understood if we remember that Europe was overwhelmingly agricultural, and that large areas, not merely in the center and east but in parts of the west as well, were little touched by a commercial economy. Raw materials were at hand, equipment was simple, skill was handed down from one generation to the next, and there was spare time when night or winter put an end to outdoor work. In the great country houses the supply of craftsmen might be almost as complete as on one of Charlemagne's villas, and the diary of a French countess (about 1700) shows her supervising the work of carders, spinners, weavers, seamstresses, builders, wig-makers, and other workers. In humbler homes the family made what it needed, aided by village or wandering craftsman. In Lombardy (about 1800) the women spun and wove linen, the men made harness, baskets, farm tools, etc., and periodically "the tailor or shoemaker arrived, set up his shop for a lively two weeks, even a month, and clothed and shod the whole tribe." In Wales almost every farmer combed and spun wool from his own sheep and sent it to the weaver. Nearly every German rural family spun and wove linen, and as late as 1843 less than a third of the looms in Prussia belonged to professional weavers. An English observer accustomed to

London was surprised to find in 1797 that in the north "almost every article of dress worn by farmers, mechanics, and labourers is manufactured at home, shoes and hats excepted," and to learn that "there are many respectable persons at this day who never wore a bought pair of stockings, coat, or waistcoat in their lives." In all parts of Europe peasant arts and crafts were practiced long before (and long after) the commercialized products attracted the attention of townsmen, traders, or tourists.

Independent retail or wholesale handicraft production was almost as widespread. The craftsman might still work on his customer's material, and the scale of operation was small. Prussian statistics suggest that in 1816 there were only 56 journeymen and apprentices for every 100 masters. The family was the main source of labor supply, and goods were sold direct to the consumer or to merchants in shop, market place, or hall. Independent craftsmen were usually townsmen, but some rural industries were in their hands. One classic instance was the Yorkshire cloth industry, carried on by thousands of "clothiers" living in villages or farmhouses in the valleys and on the hillsides southwest of Leeds. The clothier bought raw material in small parcels at one of the three or four market towns. With the aid of his family and possibly an apprentice or journeyman he made one or two pieces of cloth each week, sold the product in the weekly or semi-weekly market, bought a fresh supply of wool, and went home to repeat the process. Sometimes he received orders and sold all his cloth to the same merchant, but he was usually a free agent, with a well-organized market in which he could sell to the man who offered the best price. A piece of land or some common rights provided opportunity for gardening, grazing, and some cultivation. His equipment cost little: a clothier's inventory, dated 1779, valued the total textile equipment at less than £10, which was equal to the combined value of the "spangled cow" in the barn, the clock in the hall, and "one large bibell" in the parlor.

Similar conditions were found in most countries. French families grew flax, made linen, and sold it in the market at Valenciennes. In Scotland the farmer spun wool shorn from his own sheep, wove the yarn or had it woven by the local weaver, and sold the cloth at the nearest fair or market to traveling merchants. In such cases the independent worker had, in Adam

Smith's words, "stock sufficient to purchase the materials of his work and to maintain himself till it be completed. He is both master and workman, and enjoys the whole produce of his labour." His "stock" and supply of tools need not be costly. A writer in 1747 estimated the "sums necessary to set up as master" in each of the hundreds of London occupations. He found that eight of them needed only £5, ten required £10, twenty-five could be begun with £20, ninety with £50, and seventy-five with £100. Raw material might be produced on adjacent land or obtained on credit by a reputable worker, and adequate market facilities made easy the disposal of the product to consumer or middleman.

During the Middle Ages some industries had become dependent on large entrepreneurs and merchants for their capital, direction, and markets, and by 1700 this condition was much more common. Its two chief features were (1) a widespread use of putting out (the *Verlagssystem* described in Chapter X), and (2) the gathering of comparatively large numbers of persons to work in one spot under the employer's supervision. These features were the result of four factors. The first was commercial, for the task of supplying some markets was too big for the small producing and selling craftsman. This was especially true of the markets that appeared or expanded greatly after 1500, and which called for knowledge, capital, enterprise, and possibly even a skill he did not possess. Some of them were far away; some were large and needed great quantities of goods of a certain type for the armies, cities, and slave plantations; some were luxury markets, needing goods that were made of expensive materials, took a long time to produce, and often were not paid for until a still longer time had elapsed. Some goods were new, or new to Europe, e.g., cottons, printed books, cocoa, and sugar in abundance; if these were to be supplied someone who had capital and was willing to take risks must organize production.

The second factor was technological; changes in the industrial arts caused changes in industrial organization. Such occupations as shipbuilding or mining could not be conducted by the craftsman in his little shop; and when these or others became dependent on large capital outlays for machines, containers, power, buildings, and lifting or hauling equipment, or involved big operating expenses for fuel, raw materials, and labor, production by a congregated wage-earning force was inevitable. Even where no improvement was made in plant or processes, division of labor allowed cheaper production than was possible where one man did many tasks; and that division could be best or most fully developed by a large entrepreneur who directed many workers.

The third factor was personal. In any industry or form of organization some men would advance while others stood still or fell down. Special skill, energy, thrift, honesty (or its opposite), a fortunate marriage, or some other asset helped a craftsman here and there to rise above his fellows, to give employment to many journeymen, put out much material, and sell goods in great quantities. His neighbors called him a self-made man and his tombstone might describe him as "merchant." In the same way some traders grew richer than their rivals, and while some of them used their spare capital to run private banks others turned to financing or organizing the production of the goods they sold. Alongside the merchant-banker was the merchant-manufacturer.

The final factor in the spread of large economic units was the establishment of industries in countries that had not hitherto had them or that had practiced them on a small primitive scale. When Englishmen in Tudor and Stuart times began making paper, cannon, gunpowder, glass, alum and brass they adopted the equipment, methods, and large units known on the continent. In the same way Japan and Germany began their serious industrialization after 1870 with the equipment and scale of production that England had evolved during the preceding century.

The Putting-out System.—Instances of the play and product of these four factors can be picked from most parts of central and western Europe after 1500. Let us look first at the industries in which producers continued to be chiefly domestic workers, did their job at home or in their small workshops, but were tied by loans, advances, orders, or supplies of raw material to some person who provided part or all of the capital and sold their product. Many usufactures and independent handicrafts might eventually come under mercantile control; country producers who had made goods for their own use were drawn into the trader's net, while in the towns craft guildsmen worked on orders and material of merchants. In Lyons in the seventeen-eighties 48 silk merchants gave out work to over 800 master craftsmen, and in Nantes 2000 masters were in the service of 226 merchants. In the woolen industry of northeast France the merchant spread his net over town and country alike. He bought wool, had it washed and dyed in his own warehouse, and gave it out to carders and spinners who came for it or to agents who distributed it far afield. When it came back as yarn his workmen prepared it for the loom, and he handed it out to weavers or to agents who would take it to them. When the cloth came in he had it fulled and finished in his own mill or in one that did such work for customers, and then he sold it. In sixteenth-century Holland, Leyden and Haarlem were the chief textile centers, but the demand for cloth and the high urban costs of living and labor sent the traders to the smaller towns and villages in search of workers during the next two centuries. In Belgium the good tapestries, carpets, and lace were made by town craftsmen, but the cheaper varieties came largely from country workers. The small-arms industry of Liège became important after 1500 with the introduction of the arquebus and pistol; merchants built up a great export trade, organized production, ordered the craftsmen to put no trade-marks on their wares, and sold the weapons in different lands as native manufactures.

In Germany the handicraftsmen grouped in their guilds remained strong in many urban occupations until the early nineteenth century, but industries which produced for a wide market became organized in some form of *Verlagssystem*. The Fuggers provided money and equipment to over a hundred small groups of silver miners, bought their product, and deducted the amount advanced, or charged interest on it. In Nuremberg the trade which made the city one of Europe's armorers was in the hands of merchants or local aristocratic families who supplied the makers with raw materials. Flax spinning was carried on as a full-time or part-time occupation over a wide area to feed the looms of Silesia, while various articles of wood, bone, metal, leather, or fiber were made by peasant families in their spare hours or in the winter months and then delivered by them to the *Verleger* or collected by him or his agents. This organization of peasant production continued long after the advent of machinery and the factory system; in 1914 many states and local authorities were operating schools for homeworkers in wood carving, basket weaving, lace-making, embroidery, the making of glass, pottery, cloth, or small hardware; and a stranger tramping through a rural area might be mistaken for a new *Verleger*.

In England the industries which rose to prominence after 1500 did so largely outside the medieval centers, free from guild control and even from national legislation. In some of them the merchant supplied capital, raw materials, and tools in order to foster the production of the goods he wished to sell. The traders of Hull imported Swedish or Russian iron, sold it on long credits to the small cutlery masters of Sheffield, then bought and exported the cutlery. Scottish cloth merchants imported Spanish wool and gave it out to be made into hose, Liverpool merchants imported flax and cotton to be made into fustian, and those of Glasgow developed putting-out in order to secure goods needed for the colonies. Some Yorkshire clothiers became middle-sized or even large employers, while in East Anglia and the west of England the typical figure was the large clothier who bought wool in bulk, put it out to an army of domestic workers, and sold cloth. His employees might number 500 to 1000 persons. In the eighteenth century one sailcloth maker had 5000 people at work, two cotton merchant-manufacturers gave out material to 600 looms and 3000 workers, and a Manchester maker of ribbons, tapes, and other small wares employed over a hundred domestic looms. In Birmingham hundreds of small domestic producers made different metal articles or did different processes. The key man was the *factor*, who supplied raw material and sometimes tools, made weekly advances of money, and gathered in and sold the products. Nails and chains were made by domestic workers until the early twentieth century.

The English hosiery industry supplies one of the most interesting instances of the transfer from an urban handicraft to a rural putting-out organization. When the knitting frame came into use after 1600 London became a great producer, consumer, and exporter of knitwear. The industry was controlled by the framework knitters' guild, which became a livery company in 1657, and which was in turn dominated by the traders who bought the wares made by small masters. After 1650 knitting was taken up in the midlands, especially in Nottinghamshire, Derbyshire, and Leicestershire. The Company sought to regulate the provincial industry, but judges refused to enforce its rules, and in 1753 parliament declared the craft "free and unrestricted." In the midlands there was plenty of good wool; living and labor costs were low; but the great market which set the fashions was over a hundred miles away, as was also the supply of capital and the merchant.

To link up producer and distributor a far-flung putting-out system was devised, with the hosier as its central figure. He received orders and patterns from London, and in some central town gave out material every Saturday to knitters who took it to their homes, sometimes ten or fifteen miles away. There the children wound the yarn on bobbins, the master and his apprentice worked at the frame, and the wife sewed up the seams at the back or feet of the stocking. On Saturday the week's work was taken to the hosier, payment was received and a new supply of material obtained. The hosier also gave materials and large orders to a bagman, who distributed them to scattered farms and remote villages where people knitted a little in the intervals of farming or tending livestock. In the towns and larger villages, where an abundant supply of workers was available, the hosier developed a third method of production, based on division of labor. One home worker made stocking legs and took them to the warehouse, where they were handed out to another worker who added tops and feet, while in the warehouse itself women seamed or embroidered. Some knitters owned their frames, but many rented them from the hosier or from men who put capital into frames, paying as much as one-sixth of their week's earnings.

The essential facts of the putting-out system can now be summarized. The entrepreneur puts capital into industry to get the goods he wants, instead of going to market in the hope of finding them there. The system is capable of adaptation to various conditions, and the capitalist may be involved in varying degrees. At the least he supplies material to men who have their own equipment and regard themselves as independent craftsmen; at the most he supplies everything, and those who work for him receive only wages. He draws on the full-time labor of town craftsmen and their dependents, and on the full- or spare-time work of the country folk. In theory his workers are "self-directing"; they are subject to no discipline except that of making a livelihood, and are free to work for anyone they wish unless they are tied by debt to one patron. Division of labor can be developed, and if equipment is inexpensive (or is provided by the worker) the size of an enterprise is limited only by the size of the market or by the amount of working capital the entrepreneur has at his disposal. Hence some men, whether they begin as producers or as traders, may eventually become large employers.

To the modern student the question naturally arises, Why did not these men gather the producers together in workshops? The answer is that some did, some did not, while some gathered part of their workers together but left many at home. Putting-out had many defects. Much time was wasted conveying materials to workers or finished products to headquarters. What was saved in low wages was partly lost in time or transportation costs, though if the time was the workers' the employer need not complain. One group of workers might be idle till supplies came from a group responsible for the previous process, as when the weaver waited for his yarn or the knitter of tops found the hosier had run out of leg pieces. Standards of workmanship were not easily maintained, and embezzlement or theft of material by workers or by those who distributed it was a widespread sin.

If work was done in a central workshop some of these defects would disappear. Employees could be prevented from loafing at will, embezzlement could be detected, standards could be guarded, division of labor could be developed, and capital spent on material would not eat its heart away in interest while goods were meandering along highways and byways. But such advantages would have to be dearly bought. The cost of a building to house many workers would be great, equipment must be provided, and unless there was an adequate local labor force cottages must be erected to attract workers from a distance. Few organizers of production had money to spare for such outlays. They needed their funds for working capital in an age when there was a long lapse of time between buying raw material and receiving the finished product, and when an even longer period might elapse before customers paid their bills. A diversion of capital to buildings and equipment would strain the resources needed for other purposes.

Further, if the equipment in a central workshop was the same as that used in the home, it would move no more rapidly than in the hands of a good domestic worker, and its output would be increased only in so far as the disciplined toil of a supervised employee displaced the irregular labor of a man working at home.

Finally, many domestic workers resented any attempt to draw them from home. There they were free to work or play as they pleased, and to enlist the aid of the whole family. To obey the summons of a factory bell was loathsome; a big workshop was too much like the workhouse, that grim building in which local authorities made paupers work for their sustenance. When factories did begin to sprinkle the countryside, many domestic workers refused to enter them or allow their children to take jobs in these new industrial bastilles.

The margin of advantage might therefore be too slight to tip the scales in favor of the congregation of workers in industries which had been originally domestic. Sometimes the building problem was solved, as when the dissolution of the monasteries in England rendered many large edifices vacant. One big clothier said he would employ 200 more people if he could have some of these buildings. In one abbey every available corner of the structure was filled with looms, and even the church was converted into a weaving shed. A sixteenth-century ballad tells how one Jack of Newbury gathered together 200 weavers, and had about 400 other workers practicing all the processes from wool sorting to cloth finishing. During the next two centuries other similar large units existed, employing many workers in one place as well as a far greater number in their own homes. In Orléans in 1789 a stocking firm assembled 800 knitters and had about 2000 workers outside; at Rheims over half the looms were in weaving sheds, and in Nantes great workshops were built to make wares for the West African trade. But if the same equipment and processes could be used at home as in the large shops, the domestic worker held his ground; and even when machines began to invade the textile and hardware industries outwork persisted long and disappeared slowly. (See Chapter XXIII.)

Centralized Production.—The great majority of industrial workers "laboured in their homes, in town cellars or garrets, or in village cottages. But that majority was by no means so overwhelming as has been supposed" (Nef), and recent research has revealed widespread instances of congregation of labor. If there was a putting-out system there was also a gathering-in system, and while much material went to the worker many workers came to the material. In some industries the nature of the demand, work, equipment, or processes made domestic production impossible or at least uneconomic, and necessitated the rise of large units with great sums of capital and large bodies of employees. The new mining and smelting methods which came into use after 1450 made metal extraction more capitalistic than ever, and if mining and refining were done by the same firm the amount of capital and labor needed was often very great. One silver mine in the Tyrol had nearly 7000 workers in the sixteenth century.

Coal mining stood second to metal extraction in the use of much capital and labor. While small pits were still worked by a handful of men as late as 1800, Professor Nef estimates that half the English coal miners in 1700 labored in pits that employed a hundred or more men. Some mines had 500 to 1000 workers, and produced 10,000 to 25,000 tons yearly. The opening up and equipping of a deep mine might cost £20,000 or more, while the outlay on wagons, horses, wharves, and ships might be more than on the mine itself. The total capital invested in coal mining and in the coal trade exceeded that in the East India, African, and Hudson's Bay Companies. It had been provided in part by wealthy landowners, but as they often ran short of funds they had to call on the purses of local or London merchants or on the traders who sold the coal. In many cases they eventually got deeply into debt, and when they defaulted the creditors took the mine. A group of London grocers and fishmongers secured a midlands pit in 1618, and most of the mines in the Tyne Valley were by 1650 owned by Newcastle merchants or by landlords whose fathers had seized the property of their debtors. In France coal mining developed later; the chief center was Anzin in the northeast, and there one company employed 1500 workers in 1756 and 4000 in 1789.

Where the conversion of metals into wares required little equipment and much skill the small producer prevailed, as in Birmingham and such German hardware regions as Solingen. But where a big job had to be done, such as casting cannon or other heavy pieces, where waterpower was used to drive machines, or where all processes from smelting to the making of metal goods were carried on, large units emerged. One of the most famous of these was built up by Polhem at Stiernsund in Sweden about 1700. Polhem was an enthusiastic advocate of machine production, the use of power, division of labor, and consequent reduction of costs. He believed that "nothing increases demand so much as low prices," and that the way to lower prices was through the use of "machines and appliances which will diminish the amount or intensity of heavy manual work." He therefore copied machines he had seen elsewhere or invented his own, and drove them by water power. He had shearing machines for cutting bars, slitting mills for cutting nail rods, and heavy rollers for pressing iron into sheets or bands. He had machines to cut cogwheels, hammer pans, shape tinware, and make all kinds of household appliances, tools, plowshares, and clock parts. Each of his hundred workmen was trained for a special process, and their almost automatic manual movements probably did much to suggest those that a machine could perform.

The nature of the product or improvements in equipment brought workers together in other industries. Shipyards grew in size to build bigger boats, and the large-scale organization of Venetian and Dutch yards was copied by English and French builders. Calico-printing required large workrooms, drying sheds, much dye, and many printing blocks, such as no small craftsman could hope to possess. In the silk industry the big "throwing" machine was a complicated monster; the first English example set up by Lombe was driven by a huge water wheel which (according to the guidebook) revolved three times a minute, turned 26,586 wheels, and caused 97,746 mechanical movements. In the mill that housed it about 200 people, chiefly women and children, were employed. Woolen cloth finishing was done in shops, some of them quite large, by specialized workers who used simple implements with great skill.

Sugar refining, distilling, and the production of soap, candles, salt, beer, paper, gunpowder, or glass needed fairly large sums of capital for vats, pans, raw materials, fuel, buildings, and working expenses, and were carried on by large groups of wage earners. Brewing remained chiefly a domestic or small-scale occupation, but in the seventeenth century large producers arose to supply big towns, to win popularity for certain brands, and to quench the thirst of Englishmen overseas. A visitor to the East India Company's quarters at Surat in 1689 found factors drinking European wines and English beer, which "though sold at high Rates [were] yet purchased and drunk with pleasure." Thrale, Dr. Johnson's friend and patron, was a large brewer, who paid his superintendent £500 a year. He became a member of parliament, and when he died the brewery, which Johnson described as "not a parcel of boilers and vats, but the potentiality of growing rich beyond the dreams of avarice," was sold for £135,000.

On the continent some large units were established directly or indirectly by the state to supply luxuries to the court, furnish army supplies, and liberate the country from dependence on foreign supplies. Outside Holland and England, capital for such industries was scarce, and those who had funds preferred surer or more profitable forms of investment. Hence stimulus must come from the state, by the grant of bounties, special privileges, freedom from guild rules, prohibitive tariffs, monopolies, exemption from taxation, loans or investments of royal money, and even by the establishment of state enterprises. Industries set up under such conditions were often large. The Van Robais brothers, whom Colbert induced to come from Holland, had a thousand workers in and around their Abbeville textile works. Tapestry, pottery, glass, iron, arms, and some other commodities were made on a lavish scale in French subsidized or state establishments with the most up-to-date equipment and great division of labor. Frederick the Great set up some state factories, while Peter the Great established state or quasi-state works and used much forced labor. Few of these examples of *la grande industrie* had great or lasting success. Many of them were ephemeral and artificial, they drained money from the state's pocket, and except perhaps in France had scant influence on the development of industrial organization.

The Status of Labor.—Much of the industrial organization described above rested on a basis of open or veiled wage labor. The craftsman who owned his equipment and worked on his own material for an open market or to fill orders was economically independent. If he owned only the tools he might be free to pick his patron, but his earnings would be in effect a piece-rate wage. The apprentice might hope to pass through a period of hired labor to a place among the masters of an urban guild industry, but this road was often steep and narrow because of the oligarchic control exercised by the guild or the amount of capital needed. Hence the urban journeyman tended to become a permanent wage earner, as did many others who worked at home or on the employer's premises, whether in town or country. Those who dwelt in rural areas might supplement their wages by drawing some produce from the soil, but those who lived in towns had to rely chiefly on the price they obtained for their labor. They were dependent not merely on the rate of payment but also on the regularity of employment.

The rate of payment might be fixed by custom, though custom was now rubbed threadbare. It might be fixed by the state, as under the English law of 1563, but by about 1650 that law had become almost inoperative. It might be determined by competition between rural and urban workers, by the relative scarcity or plenty of laborers, by the degree of skill required, or by the demand for commodities. From scattered comments on wages in the literature of the period we can draw almost any kind of wages theory. Some writers urged the economy of high wages, but more talked about the economic and moral value of low ones. If workers received high rates they would toil only till they had earned enough to satisfy their simple wants, and idle away the rest of the week, dissipating their substance in riotous living. Low wages would make goods cheaper for the export market, thus fostering the trade of the country and the morality of its laborers at the same time.

We know too little about actual wage rates to be able to make generalizations, even for any one country. Apparently spinning, which was a by-occupation for some but a livelihood for others, and was easily learned, was poorly paid; but some crafts which were highly skilled, in which women did not compete with men, into which entry was for any reason difficult, or in which workers easily banded together, received relatively high wages. When hosiers first put out goods in the midlands they paid the rates current in London, but gradually whittled them down. Where workmen worked or lived with their employers they often received bed or board, or both, and even outworkers sometimes received payment in goods, especially when no adequate currency was available in a district.

The regularity of employment was influenced by many factors. Contracts of employment in many parts of Europe must be made for a year, and in France, England, and Holland a worker must have a testimonial or clearance papers from his old employer before he could find a new one. Whether he worked at home or in a mine, smelter, or factory, he had his periods of enforced leisure. Bad weather held up supplies of material; goods which were to be dried or bleached remained damp or yellow when the sun failed to shine; the supply of yarn ran out, and some industries had virtually to close down in winter. More serious still were the fluctuations caused by expansions and contractions, often sudden, of the domestic or external market. Industries which served foreign consumers might be hit by war, peace, a new tariff, or a bankruptcy, and unemployment was as well known in the sixteenth and seventeenth centuries as in the twentieth. In 1622 an English royal commission was appointed to ascertain why "trade in general is so far out of frame that the merchants and clothiers are greatly discouraged, so that great numbers of people employed by them and depending on them want work." A hundred and fifty years later John Wesley, touring England at a time when the prelude to the American Revolution had shattered Anglo-American trade, wrote (1775), "Trade is exceedingly decayed and thousands of people are quite unemployed. Some I know of have perished for want of bread: others I have seen walking up and down like shadows." The end of a war hurt the metal, cloth, and leather trades; if a king died, a fashion changed, a bad season came, or if speculators gambled and lost, the result was disastrous to some or all industries.

Given a class of permanent wage earners and groups of men working together in one spot, labor organization and occasional clashes of interest between employer and wage earner were inevitable. The journeymen's societies or *compagnonnages* (*compagnon* = journeyman) on the continent made themselves look as innocuous as possible; they guarded high standards of workmanship, insisted on moral conduct, fostered fraternal spirit, and had their mystic rites and elaborate initiation ceremonies. In Germany and France the local groups were linked in a loose federation, and the journeyman passing from town to town was welcomed and cared for by his brethren. Sometimes masters and men joined hands against a common enemy—the merchant—who, by trying to cut the prices he paid the master would cause a commensurate reduction of wages. More frequently the men locked horns with the masters in really bitter fights concerning hours, wages, or the number of apprentices. In times of disturbed trade or prices strife was especially fierce, and street brawls, strikes, and violence were frequent.

In England evidence of the existence of combinations of wage earners accumulates after about 1660, though there had been journeymen's guilds in the fifteenth century. They were formed ostensibly to care for the sick, injured, or aged, but when necessary they sought increased wages, fought for shorter hours, or resisted reductions of pay. They were strongest in London and in the textile industry, especially in the highly capitalistic west of England branch. Even where there was no permanent organization, wage earners would gather together, fight a battle, and then disband. "Industrial strife was often as acute in the eighteenth as in the nineteenth century" (Lipson), and Dean Tucker wrote of the west of England in 1757 as follows: "As the master is placed so high above the condition of the journeyman, both their conditions approach much nearer to that of a planter and slave in our American colonies than might be expected in such a country as England." The master is "tempted by his situation to be proud and overbearing, to consider his people as the scum of the earth." The journeymen in reply attempt "to get as much wages and to do as little for it as they can," regarding their employer "as their common enemy, with whom no faith is to be kept."

In all countries the state tried to repress this incipient labor movement. Unions either were declared unlawful or were only lawful so long as they did nothing to improve or protect the wages contract. In Holland the ban simply drove them underground, and in 1692 men who attended illegal assemblies were threatened with capital punishment. In France a long series of decrees stretched from at least 1539 to the fiat of 1791 which declared combinations unlawful. In the Holy Roman Empire a shoemakers' strike at Augsburg in 1731 provoked an imperial decree of suppression. In England an Act of 1548 threatened those who made any agreement on prices and rates, and the common law frowned on combinations, conspiracies, or any other act in restraint of trade. The London authorities indicted the feltmakers in 1698 for having "conspired and combined together to enhance the prices for making of hats," and parliament at various times (in 1721, 1726, 1749, and 1773) passed laws to prevent unlawful combinations. At the same time it tried to safeguard the interests of workers by fixing hours and reviving the assessment of wages by the local justices. The action on wages achieved little, and the efforts to suppress unions achieved about as much. "In spite of common law and statute law, trade unionism persisted throughout the eighteenth century and bequeathed its traditions to the unions of the nineteenth century" (Lipson).

Conditions of Labor.—Production called on the whole available labor supply, from the child of four or five years to the aged. Child labor was normal and as old as labor itself. Children helped in the fields and played their part in the industrial pursuits of the home, while if there was some neighboring workshop or mine in which they could find employment they worked there. Defoe almost gloated over the fact that in the textile areas a child of four or five years could, if well brought up, "earn its own bread." In straw-plaiting regions they began to work at four years, and by their sixth birthday were (in 1801) earning 2/- to 3/- a week, climbing to a wage of 10/- to 12/- by the time they were eight or nine. Radcliffe, born about 1760 of a spinner-mother and a weaver-father, describes his childhood. While he was too young to weave, his mother taught him to earn his bread by carding and spinning cotton and winding linen or cotton weft for his father and elder brothers at the loom; but when he "became of sufficient age and strength" his father put him to work at a loom.

In mining districts boys and girls went with their parent (or parents, for sometimes the mother went also) to work at the pit mouth or down in the mine. They hauled trucks, and in primitive mines carried baskets of coal up ladders to the surface. In silk-throwing factories many children were employed; they worked around such other machines as were in use, and one of the virtues claimed in 1678 for a new spinning device was that with it "a child of three or four years may do as much as a child seven or eight years old." As attendants to chimney sweeps, boys crawled up the chimney and swept it with a brush and their bodies. Not till the nineteenth century did an awakened social conscience condemn these practices and stumble across the revolutionary doctrine that childhood should be a period of leisure and learning rather than of labor. But this doctrine was tenable only when the devising of machines and the harnessing of power allowed the world to dispense with the contribution made to production by children.

Women worked before and after marriage. They had their place in domestic industry, in workshops and mines, on the wharves where fish were cleaned, and in the farmyard and dairy as well as in the fields. When their work received payment the rate was usually low; in the words of a Lancashire spinner, "The pay is not much, but it helps to boil the pot." In addition to agricultural and industrial work they had their domestic and maternal duties, and must climb far up the social ladder before they were relieved of any great part of their load.

Hours of labor remained unchanged from medieval times. They stretched from dawn to dusk, and even longer if artificial light was available. In London in 1747 the usual hours were from 6 A.M. to 8 P.M., but the domestic worker who was master of his own time might be at his loom or bench by 5 A.M. and stay there till 8 or 9 P.M. if the piece of work had to be finished by a certain time. How often he interrupted his work, apart from meal times, we cannot say. Lack of material might stop him; gardening, agriculture, and harvest work broke the tedium; the complaints that he alternated between idleness and strenuous endeavor cannot all be dismissed as untrue, and in Catholic countries saints' days scattered holidays over the calendar.

Some industrial processes carried great hazards of accident and occupational disease. Mining had scarcely begun to solve the problems of ventilation or safety from explosion, and the effect of dust or fumes on health was serious. Glaziers suffered from "the Palsey," pewterers became paralyzed, and refiners must have strong lungs. Woolcombers worked in an atmosphere laden with charcoal fumes, while many domestic workers labored, slept, and ate in air full of industrial dust, fluff, and odors. Many tasks were physically strenuous, since all the power came from the worker's muscles and were monotonous repetitions of one or two movements. There was little glamour of craftsmanship in throwing a shuttle from side to side of a cheap piece of cloth, in working a spinning wheel ten hours a day, in converting rods of iron into nails or chain links, in sawing or planing by hand, or in hewing coal in a mine virtually innocent of drainage or ventilation.

Since much manual labor depended on the skill, knowledge,

and judgment of the worker, training was still necessary for some occupations. Formal apprenticeship survived, and was demanded by custom, by guild decrees, or even by the state. The English parliament in 1563 forbade any person to "set up, occupy, use, or exercise any craft, mistery, or occupation now used or occupied within the realm" unless he had been "brought up therein seven years at the least as apprentice." This law remained on the statute book till 1814, but by 1700 it was being ignored or whittled away by amendment or judicial rulings, and apprenticeship was therefore largely a matter of local practice or trade custom. Some trades could be learned only by long training, and in carpentry, printing, dyeing, and many distributing occupations a formal indenture was customary. A youth who wished to enter wholesale, foreign, and even retail trade would be formally initiated and trained in the office, shop, warehouse, and "field work," going round the markets and visiting London and foreign parts with his master. Apprenticeship was still the gateway to freedom of some cities and to a master's rank in guilds or companies, while some trade unions were by the eighteenth century strong enough to keep out the unindentured.

By that century, however, many occupations called for little or no special skill, others could be learned in a few months or years, and those which were not practiced in England in 1563 were excluded from the scope of the law by the phrase, "now used or occupied." Campbell in 1747 urged parents not to indenture their children unless they had enough money to set them up as masters later on, and reported that in several occupations apprentices were rarely or never taken. When machines began seriously to invade the manual occupations, handworkers appealed to the state for protection and asked that the apprenticeship law be enforced to keep back the untrained hordes that were flocking into the factories. Yet many of those who made this appeal had not been legally apprenticed.

Part II—The Unit of Enterprise

Medieval enterprise was in the hands of one-man or family firms, partnerships, and large groups of investors. These hands were capable of conducting most of the business of the early modern period, but the need for great sums of capital in certain fields brought the large group of investors to maturity in the joint-stock company, with permanent capital and transferable stock.

Medieval business units reached high-water mark in the great family firms. These rested on the basis of kinship and of the family purse, but used capital deposited by outsiders, and might even admit non-relatives to a share in management and profits. This type of unit spread from Italy, found a congenial home in southern Germany and elsewhere, and produced one of the most famous firms of all time in the Fuggers of Augsburg. The Fugger saga begins when Hans Fugger, master linen weaver, left his Swabian village for Augsburg in 1380. There he became interested in the production and sale of the new fustians; he imported cotton from the Levant, put out flax and cotton, and sold the cloth. He prospered, and left a fortune. His son, Jacob I, made yet more money, still out of cloth. The third generation, contrary to tradition and much business history, did better still, for its head, Jacob II, had served his apprenticeship in Venice, had learned the trading and accounting methods of that metropolis, and had imbibed some of its ambitious spirit. When urged to take life more easily and enjoy his vast fortune, he replied that he wished to go on making profit as long as he could.

That wish sought fulfillment in three main ways. In the first place, Jacob added silks and velvets, spices, metals and jewels to the linens and fustians which had been the staple commodities of earlier days. Establishments soon appeared in Venice, Rome, Antwerp, Lisbon, Lyons, Danzig, Nuremberg, and other important cities, thus creating an "empire of counting houses and merchandise depots," a set of fifteenth-century chain stores. In the second place, Fugger gained control of much metal mining and selling. Princes were in the habit of claiming the right to buy the whole mineral output of their territories at less than market price, and when in need would lease this right to the highest bidder. Jacob was often that bidder, and gained control of silver, copper, and iron in the Hapsburg lands in central Europe and of silver and mercury in Spain. From buying and selling these metals to mining and refining them was an easy step. Small mines were bought or financed; new equipment was installed; mines, foundries and smelters were brought under single ownership; and agreements were made with rivals, especially with the Welsers, in order to bring the supply of metals under monopoly control and prevent the market from being glutted. Jacob II almost succeeded in cornering the world supply of copper.

In the third place, the Fugger firm became the giant in public and private finance. Its widespread trading posts allowed it to deal in foreign exchange and lend to private and royal borrowers in almost every part of Europe. It collected and transmitted papal revenues, and by its bribes influenced the election of two popes. For the Hapsburgs it would do almost anything—at a price usually paid or secured by metal concessions. When Maximilian, the first imperial patron, died, the Fuggers had to make sure that he was followed by another of the same line, and their loan of half a million gold florins provided the bribes that secured the choice of Charles V. When Charles was slow in repaying this loan, Jacob wrote him, bluntly reminding him that "it is well known that Your Majesty without me might not have acquired the imperial crown."

When Jacob the Rich died (1525) the firm was the wealthiest in Europe. Its capital had grown from 50,000 gold gulden in 1494 to 2,000,000, which might equal $70,000,000 today. Twenty years later it stood at nearly 5,000,000 gulden, but the loans to the Hapsburgs were absorbing a dangerously large part of it, and the fourth generation—an Anton, not a Jacob—lacked the business strength of the third. When Spain and France defaulted on debts in 1557, the Fuggers, like all other creditors, were hard hit. In the following decades loan after loan turned bad—the paper promises of the Spanish king, of the Brussels court, of the Belgian and Dutch provinces, and of Antwerp, while private as well as public debts went unpaid. By 1607 the firm was bankrupt, its activities soon ceased, and only the great estates which Jacob II had bought or had taken as security for loans survived.

The structure of this amazing firm was that of a family group, ruled during the reign of Jacob II by a despot, but supplementing the family funds by accepting loans and deposits. Much that was lent to governments or put into mining belonged to others, though in seeking outside funds the Fuggers were possibly less active than some of their contemporaries. When Hochstetter tried to corner lumber, wheat, and wine, or fought a great battle with the Fuggers for control of copper and mercury, he drew in money at 5 per cent from all kinds of depositors, from princes to peasants. The Fugger funds came from fewer pockets; yet when the firm failed it ruined so many clients that Augsburg had to build a larger debtors' prison.

Partnerships.—The partnership in various forms was capable of meeting most of the business needs of the early modern world, and with the discovery of America it was used in a novel way— to finance the exploits of the *conquistadores*. Velasquez and Cortes formed a partnership for the conquest of Mexico; each provided half the capital, each was to fight, and each was to get half the loot. For the conquest of Peru a rich cleric furnished 20,000 pesos in gold bars to equip Pizarro and Diego de Almagro. These two had no funds, but held a license to explore Peru, and bound themselves "to make the conquest and discovery and also to take part in the war all the time." The plunder was to be shared equally among the partners after the king had received his quint. The three men signed a solemn contract in 1526, and took mass together, each receiving a third of the wafer. In 1533 the booty was divided.

Spanish trade with America was first developed by merchants who sent out agents to buy and sell on commission, but when this plan proved unsatisfactory *commenda* partnerships were made. The Seville merchant provided the capital; the active partner took goods out with the fleet, sold them, returned with bullion or other colonial produce and received a share of the profits. Sometimes he settled in the colonies and handled goods on behalf of many exporters in addition to those of his colleague, receiving a commission on sales. On such resident partners or commission merchants Europeans have had to depend greatly for the disposal of their wares outside their own country or continent.

Gradually the partnership grew less important as an alliance for one trip or venture, and was made for a certain length of time, say three to seven years. It might operate a mercantile, industrial, or banking enterprise, incur debts and grant credit, and any one of its members could commit the firm in borrowing or buying. If it failed to meet such obligations as its members piled on it, who was responsible for satisfying the creditors? Some partners might merely contribute capital and play no part in management, but others put in work as well as funds. The latter must accept unlimited liability, and hand over all they owned to pay the firm's debts; but should the sleeping partner be put in the same parlous positions or should his liability be limited to the loss of the capital he had invested, as had been the practice in the *commenda*? A French ordinance of 1673 made all the associates liable to the full extent of their assets, and English law said the same. Eventually, however, the French divided partnerships into two classes: if all members were active the firm was a *société en nom collectif*, and all shouldered unlimited liability; but if some were passive investors the firm was a *société en commandité* and the inactive members were liable only to the loss of their investment.

Companies.—The joint-stock company differed from the partnership in kind as well as in degree. (1) More people provided the capital, for a partnership rarely had more than two, three, or four members. A company could obtain the large sums needed for big enterprises. (2) The company had a legal personality, conferred on it by charter and, in the nineteenth century, by company law. If it succeeded it might live till its charter expired and was not renewed. The Hudson's Bay Company, founded in 1670, is still alive. A partnership expired at the end of a fixed period, but might be renewed; or it was broken when one of its members died, became bankrupt, or wished to resign. It was not a legal person, and each of its members must sue or be sued separately. (3) A company was managed by elected or appointed officers, who might have small sums invested but had reputations for business experience and ability. Capital could be drawn from people who had no such qualifications, and could be used in trust by salaried experts. (4) Ownership of stock was transferable, and shares could pass from hand to hand without disturbing the structure or operations of the company. Thus a new form of income-producing property and salable commodity came into being, and a market gradually grew up to facilitate transactions in it.

The joint-stock company may have come to western Europe from Italy, or from the central European mining areas where joint ownership of mines by investors and occasional trade in shares were well known by the early sixteenth century at latest. But joint-stock developments in England and Holland took such steps and went so far that the great companies had to solve their problems unaided by any precedents. They drew their inspiration from three main sources: (1) the association of men to monopolize, foster, and regulate some branch of foreign trade; (2) the association of capital for one trip or venture; (3) the rise of the "promoter," that eloquent and energetic individual whose keen eye spied out new ways of making money, old industries or trades waiting to be profitably "organized," unborn industries or markets ready to come into being, or savings yearning to be brought out of their hoard.

Regulated Companies.—The association of men to foster, protect, control, and gain exclusive enjoyment of some branch of foreign trade was best seen in the English "regulated company," of which the Merchant Adventurers' Company was the most important. It was an extension of guild ideas into the foreign field, and had much in common with the merchant guilds or hanses. The merchant adventurer with his packs of cloth "voyaged far afield, east, west, north or south, wherever he could find an opening," from Spain to Norway. His destination was usually a fair, and especially the quarterly fairs held in the Low Countries. Adventurers going from any such town as Newcastle, York, or London banded together to secure the ship or ships they needed, obtain trading privileges, choose a governor, and frame rules to control their conduct abroad. Gradually the London group became so strong that its governor in the Low Countries brought the provincial groups under his control, and in 1497 parliament confirmed his right to impose an entrance fee on all Englishmen trading in the Low Countries. Thus a unified Fellowship (or Company, as it was now beginning to be called) of the "Merchant Adventurers of England in the Low Countries" received official recognition.

The London fellowship began when those mercers, grocers, drapers, tailors, skinners, and fishmongers who were exporting cloth began to form little groups inside the livery companies of which they were members. Gradually these groups came together. There were joint meetings of the "adventerers of dyvers ffelishippes," joint charterings of boats, joint petitions or protests to the English king or to foreign towns and rulers. Joint action led to fusion, and in 1486 the city fathers formally recognized a united London fellowship. "Its ostensible purpose as a corporate body was to equip and despatch the fleets from London to the quarterly marts, and to levy the necessary money for their safe conveyance thither. . . . It possessed the most distinctive feature of the fully developed guild or livery company—the right to hold a court with power to make ordinances and to enforce them by fines and punishments" (Carus-Wilson). It chartered ships, fixed freights, and decided when and where the fleet should go. It lobbied at court and in parliament, negotiated with foreign rulers and towns in an area and period of insecure trade facilities, and was often able to get its requests granted.

In the sixteenth century the Company was the most influential English trading group. It used its influence to drive out the Hansards and to seek exclusive enjoyment of the export of cloth to lands between the mouth of the Somme and the tip of Denmark. In the seventeenth century it was the target of almost incessant attack by the "free traders." These interlopers were welcomed by the Dutch, since presumably their prices were lower than those asked by the Adventurers. During the Civil War the Dutch and the free lances gained ground at the Company's expense, and in 1689 the cloth trade in the Adventurers' area was thrown open by parliament to all traders.

The Company was an association of men, not of capital. It had "no banke nor common stocke, nor common factour to buy and sell for the whole companie, but every man tradeth apart and particularlie with his own stocke, and with his factour or servaunt." Each member used his own capital, or worked in partnership with other members. He made his own profit or loss, but the Company helped and regulated him. It helped by seeking sheltered markets, by providing ships, by protecting him and his goods from violence or loss on land or sea, by asking the state for convoys, and by calling on foreign rulers to punish those who molested him. It regulated him by imposing entrance conditions, of which apprenticeship was a part. It restricted the number of pupils he could train or the quantity of cloth or lead he could ship. It controlled his conduct when abroad, limited the length of credit he could ask or allow, supported his claims as creditor, enforced his obligations as debtor, punished him for fraudulent actions, made him responsible for the quality of the wares he sold, and watched over his morals and manners. Thus it safeguarded the mercantile etiquette and ethics of men enjoying a profitable preserve.

The regulated company operated in intracontinental rather than in intercontinental trade. The member, or his representative, could go out with goods, transact business, get back home and settle the whole round of transactions in a fairly short time. He might fare well, even if some of his fellows did badly. The link between ownership and use of capital was strong, and the owner might handle his own business better than did a hireling agent. Hence some companies which began as joint-stock ventures, with "one stock and purse for all" and one agent or official handling the whole business, eventually reverted to the regulated type and "every man ran his own adventures." The Russia Company got its charter in 1555 and was the first English joint-stock company; but its experience and profits were unsatisfactory and in the seventeenth century it was converted into a regulated company. The Levant Company, founded in 1581, began with joint stock, but its members were allowed to take or send some goods out on their own account. Its career was checkered, and after twenty years it became regulated, though it still occasionally sent a joint-stock cargo.

Joint-stock Companies.—Joint-stock enterprise in the west began with the pooling of funds for one venture in trading, raiding, or exploring. In 1553 one group of London capitalists provided £6000 in shares of £25 each for "the discovery of the northern parts of the world," while another group fitted out three ships for a trip to the Bight of Benin. Hawkins' slave raids, Frobisher's explorations, and Drake's plundering of Spanish treasure ships were financed by groups of aristocratic and mercantile investors. Even the queen occasionally provided some capital; she supplied ships and provisions for an African trip in 1561 and got a third of the profits, she invested in Frobisher's search for the northwest passage, and urged others who "might be willing to venter sumwhat in the voidage" to take up shares of £100 each. The return on such investments varied greatly. The Benin journey gave a profit of nearly 1000 per cent. Hawkins' first two voyages paid a handsome profit, but the third failed, as did Frobisher's expedition. Drake's voyage of 1577-1580 cost £5000, but his return cargo was worth £1,500,000. The queen received £250,000 of it, and the other stockholders drew 4600 per cent profit.

The Elizabethan colonizing expeditions were joint-stock enterprises. Gilbert had no capital and assigned the potential benefits of his venture to a "great number of persons" who promised—but failed to give—him financial support. Raleigh spent probably

£40,000 of his own money on Virginia and Guiana, but had to draw on the funds of about thirty merchants as well. At about the same time there was some joint-stock exploitation of English mineral deposits. In fact, late Elizabethan London seems to have been swarming with men who were trying to sell some alluring project, endeavoring to persuade gentry, nobility, and merchants to invest, and seeking to extract some grant of monopoly from the crown. There were also men who became almost professional company directors. One of them, Sir Thomas Smythe, was at various times governor of the Russia, Levant, East India, and Virginia Companies.

From 1600 onward the Dutch and English East India Companies dominate the story of joint stock. The Levant Company of 1581 had been capitalized partly with the profits of Drake's journey; but when in the 'nineties it shared out its available funds and became regulated, some of its stockholders used part of their refund to establish the East India Company. Nearly 220 "adventurers" were named in the charter. The government of the Company was almost exactly like that of a regulated company, but in spite of the scanty success of joint-stock trading in Russia and the Levant it was recognized that the Indian Ocean was too remote to be approached in any other way than "by a joint and united stock." Yet sixty years elapsed before this phrase took on its modern meaning of permanent investment. Until 1613 each of the twelve voyages was financed by a separate contribution of capital. When the ships came back and the books were made up, the providers of that capital received their money back, plus whatever profit was available. Sometimes the money due to stockholders from one trip was merged in the next one, and bookkeeping became very tangled. Between 1610 and 1613 seven separate voyages were organized, and the finances of one journey could not be wound up before the next one started.

In such circumstances there was no continuity of policy, no opportunity for building up reserves, and no effective resistance to the heavily capitalized and equipped Dutch rival. Yet permanent investment was only slowly recognized as necessary. In 1613 the First Joint Stock was subscribed to finance four voyages; in 1617 the Second Joint Stock was floated on subscriptions, profits, and loans, and there were two later similar funds. After 1640 the need for permanence grew steadily more urgent. Forts, equipment for trade, and ships called for the sinking of capital. At last in 1657 the Company got its fixed permanent stock. Henceforth members received dividends only. If times were profitable the Company increased its share capital by distributing bonus shares; but if it wanted additional funds it borrowed them, and its loan capital was often more than its share capital.

The Company conducted its business through factors who went with the fleet and settled in one of the factories. Not all the trade was company trade. Stockholders could send out goods on their own account in proportion to the amount of stock they held, non-members could buy a license to trade with India, ships' captains and crews traded openly or secretly, and the resident servants, from the president of a factory down to the meanest white employee, supplemented their salaries by local or port-to-port trade. The rewards of such trade were often far greater than the salary received, and in the eighteenth century a post in the Company's service might be sought as the gateway to a fortune made in trade or in less reputable ways. The "nabobs from India's plundered land" returned wealthy men, and secured seats in parliament to protect themselves against questions concerning the origin of their fortunes.

The Dutch East India Company was at first bigger and more strongly organized than its rival. It was founded in 1602 by the loose union of half a dozen companies which, by competing with one another, had been raising the price of spices in the Indies and lowering them in Holland. In the interests of profit the need for alliance was great, and a larger body could more effectively attack the national enemy, Spain, and its satellite, Portugal. Yet even after 1602 each of the six "chambers" had its own directors, ships, and factories, and the central body exercised only general control until union became real about 1650. A return of capital to stockholders at the end of each decade seems to have been anticipated at first, but at an early stage the Company was forced to sink large sums in forts and munitions, and there was never any disbursement of capital; the Company had a permanent joint stock from the beginning.

By 1660 joint-stock companies had attempted, with very varied results, to develop distant trade, to promote colonies, to collect furs, and to operate some mines or manufactures. Capital had been drawn from all kinds of people. The English East India

Company began with 218 investors, but the Second Joint Stock of 1617 attracted nearly a thousand, including peers, knights, merchants, doctors, clergymen, widows and old maids. The Virginia Company in 1609 obtained funds from 56 livery companies and 660 individuals, and Dutchmen were often stockholders in English companies. The practice of having a permanent capital fund had become established, and the transfer of stock ownership by sale was fully developed in Holland and well known in England. But the rewards to investors were very uneven, and an "investment counselor" in 1660 would not have been able to recommend many stocks to his clients.

In the shipping industry fractional ownership of vessels was a popular device for spreading risks. The cost of building or buying a ship might be divided into 8, 16, 32, 48, 56, 64, or some such number of equal shares. A person might own one or more fractions, and a capitalist would buy bits of a great number of vessels rather than several fractions in one ship. Professor Barbour mentions an Englishman who had shares in 38 boats. His smallest interest was 1/56, his largest 18/32; his fractions, if added together, gave him 3 1/56 vessels, worth £18,500. The fractions were divisible and could usually be sold without much difficulty.

After 1660 joint-stock activity was extended in the three leading commercial countries. In France Colbert worked hard, but with meager success, to found companies that would emulate the Dutch and English. In England the Royal African Company, heir to many failures on the West African coast, was founded in 1672. The Hudson's Bay Company was established in 1670; its nineteen shareholders subscribed £10,500, and its early profits were large. The 1676 voyage took out trade goods costing only £650, and brought back furs worth £19,000; but trouble with French rivals caused much loss later, and during the war of 1702-1713 the Company tried to improve its position by opening an insurance business in London. Scotland in 1695 raised £400,000 for a "Company of Scotland trading to Africa and the Indies," but English hostility helped to wreck its attempts to penetrate India and to plant a colony in Darien. Prussia founded African and East Indian Companies in the sixteen-eighties, but neither of them succeeded.

Toward the end of the seventeenth century and during the

first two decades of the eighteenth, company promotion gathered speed and rushed into the bubble and panic of 1720. Professor Scott has collected information about the various schemes, good and bad, honest and fraudulent, that were hatched in Great Britain. Between 1553 and 1680 there were 49, from 1681 to 1718 there were 56, but in the hectic years 1719 and 1720 there were 190. The successes in foreign trade, in urban water supply enterprises, in some industries, and, after the foundation of the Bank of England (1694), in banking, were sufficiently numerous to persuade investors that new companies might do as well as old ones. The promoter was now fully aware of the profits to be made by floating companies, and wide fluctuations in the prices of existing stocks gave the speculator a field for action. The wars between 1689 and 1713 created acute problems of raising and repaying large loans and led to high-sounding schemes for painless and profitable manipulation of the public debt by great companies. Finally, the war of 1702-1713 was expected to transfer the trade with Spanish America definitely from French to British hands, and on that transfer high hopes were based.

The years between 1713 and 1720 were therefore full of promotions of all kinds. If some were sound and sensible, others were fraudulent and fantastic, e.g., those which promised to earn great dividends by trading in human hair, making square cannon balls, getting butter from beech trees, marketing an air pump for the brain, perfecting a wheel for perpetual motion, searching for rich wrecks off the Irish coast, or importing jackasses from Spain. But these will-o'-the-wisps were insignificant in their effects when compared with the collapse of the booms that centered on John Law in Paris and the South Sea Company in London.

Law was a Scot who in 1716 established the *Banque Générale*. It did well, and in 1717 he organized the Company of the West, raised much capital, and secured title to Louisiana. He believed that paper money was better than metallic, that it could be increased as the need for it rose, and that it could be obtained safely by issuing bank notes based on land. He therefore poured out notes backed with Louisiana land. He obtained a monopoly of the tobacco trade, gained control of the mint, became controller-general of the national finances, collected the taxes, and offered to lend the government sufficient money to pay off the national debt. To do all these things he issued bank notes up to three billion livres and raised more capital for his Company. The grandeur of his "system" made his Company's stock attractive, and speculation in it pushed the price from 500 to 20,000 livres, while the vast inflation of the currency raised the price level by more than 100 per cent. Eventually the bubble burst in 1720. The excessive note issue wrecked the Bank and the price of the stock fell heavily. The Company was reorganized later by Law and carried on a thriving trade with America; but the blow to banking development was severe and the building of an adequate French banking and credit system was retarded.

In England the center of the stage was held by the South Sea Company, founded in 1711 for "trading to the South Seas and other parts of America and for encouraging the Fishing." It took over £10,000,000 of national debt—mostly short term—from the state's creditors, paying them in cash or in its own shares, and converting the debt into a long-term obligation. On this debt the government paid interest and in addition gave the Company the Asiento and a monopoly of British trade in the South Seas. The slaving and trading privileges were not as profitable as had been expected, and the efforts to encourage fishing by hunting whales failed dismally. The Company's chief interest was in public finance, and in 1719 it offered to take over the rest of the national debt in return for additional trade monopolies. Its offer was accepted, and the state's creditors were invited to exchange their certificates for the Company's stock at a price below the market level. That level was rising, and promised to go much higher; hence two-thirds of the debt was exchanged for stock. The promise was kept, and South Sea shares rose from 126 in late 1719 to 1050 in mid-1720. All other stocks, new and old, behaved in similar manner; many new companies were floated; and Change Alley, the stock market of the day, became "a roaring Hell-porch of insane or dishonest speculators," to which all classes swarmed, "some to undo and some to be undone."

In September, 1720, the bubble burst. From the wreckage the Company emerged alive, was reorganized, and lived till 1855, chiefly as owner of national-debt securities. But the stain made on joint-stock companies during these mad years did not wash off for a long time. If Law retarded the normal evolution of credit in France, the promoters and stockjobbers gave a severe setback to joint-stock enterprise in England. Parliament passed the "Bubble Act" (1720), which declared that only companies formed by charter or a private act of parliament were legal. To secure this official sanction was a slow, costly proceeding; further, the granting of that monopoly which had been a vital part of a company's charter was now becoming unpopular, and legalized joint-stock enterprise virtually stood still for a hundred years. When large sums of capital were needed for making a turnpike road or cutting a canal, parliament passed the necessary law establishing a turnpike trust that could borrow money or a canal company that could sell stock. Some companies operated without legal status, working mines and refineries; but outside the limited fields of insurance, metallurgy, distant trade, roads, canals, waterworks, and some banking, the one-man firm or partnership was the typical business unit. It was often starved of capital or credit, and insolvency lurked round the corner; but in general it satisfied the needs of an age that did not need to sink large sums in equipment or rapid transportation.

Economic organization in 1750 was thus predominantly personal rather than corporate, and its outstanding figures were often men who had started life in humble circumstances. Many big merchants, financiers, slave traders, colonial adventurers, tax farmers, munitions makers, and luxury providers were self-made men. Defoe, Johnson, and other observers comment on this social mobility. "Men are everywhere starting up from obscurity to wealth," said Johnson; and a Manchester cobbler in 1756 said that nearly all the rich men of that town had once been "of very inferior substance" and his customers. A Lancashire pin-maker became a Manchester cotton manufacturer and trader; his son, Samuel Touchett, was a big figure in cotton, slaving, insurance, bill broking, money-lending, and underwriting state loans, asked for a monopoly of trade with Labrador and Senegal, and fitted out a fleet of five ships to help capture Senegal from the French. Anthony Bacon, a Manxman, went to Maryland, ran a store, and then returned to England to operate on an imperial scale. He secured contracts to victual garrisons in Africa and the West Indies, sent Negroes to Jamaica, bought ships, acquired a mine and ironworks in Wales, owned a coal mine in Cape Breton, and occupied a seat in parliament.

Touchett and Bacon were only two of the many who climbed

into the rich pastures surrounding government offices. Those who could get contracts to underwrite loans, serve as paymaster to troops abroad, remit subsidies to allies, or supply ships, food, or munitions for a garrison or army had every chance of prosperity. "Fortunes were made and the greatness of families founded in army magazines and bread wagons" (Namier). Those who wished to secure such work found it convenient to be in parliament, since they were thus on the inside track to a cabinet minister's door, and at least thirty-seven of the fifty merchants who were in parliament in 1761 had extensive business dealings with the government. The less ambitious could move "from a seat in parliament . . . to the easy chair of some place or sinecure, snug and genteel," for there were scores of commissionerships or similar posts with heavy salaries and light duties. If one was merely a social climber the House of Commons was "a very agreeable coffee-house" (Gibbon), a pleasant club in which one met the lesser landed aristocracy, and a stepping-stone to the House of Lords. Not for another century did the industrial and commercial classes dominate parliament; but by 1750 the business man was "in politics" far enough to be able to bend legislation and administration to his will and interests.

Part III—Currency and Banking

The Coinage.—The growth of large territorial states and of national currencies reduced the number of coin-makers; but central Europe, divided into hundreds of states, still had its jumble of coins, while in the large states of the west rulers might debase their currencies in times of financial stress. The debasements of the sixteenth century have already been described. The lowest point in England was reached in 1555, but Elizabeth took heroic steps to restore the currency in 1561 by raising the silver content of coins. From that time onward there was little serious alteration in the shilling, and changes in the content of gold coins were largely due to variations in the relative market prices of gold and silver, since the country was on a bimetallic standard. In 1666 free minting was introduced; foreign coins or bullion could be taken to the Mint to be coined without charge, and the state thus abandoned its old right to make money by making money. On the continent monetary changes were frequent; Spain witnessed the vagaries of vellon, while during the wars of Louis XIV there were many alterations in the metal content or declared value of French coins.

Minting methods were primitive until near the end of the seventeenth century. The making of a coin might cost from 5 to 25 per cent of its value, yet new coins varied as much as 10 per cent in weight. They were easily counterfeited, they were clipped or filed, or holes were bored into them from the edge and the cavity was filled with base metal. In remote valleys and carefully guarded workshops men made "lead half-pennies coppered over," and skilled counterfeiters or clippers plied their risky but profitable craft. In 1695 the English Exchequer found that coins handed in weighed only about 110,000 ounces, whereas they should have weighed about 220,000. When the coinage was re-minted in 1696 better equipment was available, and the edge of the disk was milled; but even then a skillful scoundrel could copy the milled pattern after he had clipped the coin.

In spite of the increased supply of metal, the scarcity of coins, especially small ones, caused a frequent or chronic famine of currency. In remote parts of France coins were scarcely known even in the eighteenth century, and in important trading centers the lack of small change often hampered trade and the payment of wages or debts. Private traders therefore issued their own *token* coins, made of lead or some other cheap metal, and by 1610 about three thousand London vintners, tapsters, bakers, and other retailers had tokens in circulation. Token money did not disappear until after 1800, and some of the disks issued by merchants in the late eighteenth century were as attractive in appearance as real money.

The problem of the currency supply and of the bullion from which it was made provided one of the main topics of discussion during the sixteenth and seventeenth centuries. In its simplest form the problem was that of increasing, or at least of preventing a diminution in, the national supply of precious metal. Some writers talked of wealth and treasure as synonymous; the kingdom waxed rich as its supply of treasure increased but grew poor as the supply fell, and the ideal trade would be one in which only goods were exported and only bullion imported. Other writers, the more able ones, were content to regard gold and silver as two among many forms of wealth, but as the most obvious, tangible, and liquid forms. Precious metals would provide the sinews of war, and a royal treasure reserve would be a useful emergency fund, provided any ruler could keep his hands off it till a real emergency arose. Specie was a desirable commodity for a private store of wealth, for capital, and for an ample currency. Thrift was an impracticable virtue unless there was a hoardable material that moth and rust did not corrupt. Money capital was the easiest form of loan or investment, while an abundant supply of coin would stimulate trade.

Medieval rulers had not been blind to the above virtues of treasure, and had attempted to conserve and increase the supply inside their boundaries. (See Chapter X.) By the end of the sixteenth century these attempts had broken down or were becoming obsolete, and Europe's precious metals were flowing from country to country in great volume. On every hand traders were eager to export gold and silver if thereby they could make profit or pay a debt more cheaply than by purchasing a bill of exchange, and were resenting or evading any attempts to check them. Something must be done. But what?

The answering of that question provoked a battle of tracts and pamphlets. On the one hand were those who urged the reimposition of the old prohibitions and controls, with royal exchangers, sumptuary laws to check the import of luxuries, and insistence that at least part of the money received for imported goods be "employed" in the purchase of native wares. These "bullionists" said that the best way to control bullion movements was to control them. Against this simple but difficult policy were ranged the interests which wished to export treasure as part of their trading operations. Their spokesmen suggested that the best way to conserve precious metals was indirect rather than direct, by controlling foreign trade rather than bullion. If that trade was such that more goods were sold abroad than were bought, the imports would pay for only part of the exports, and the "overplus," "remayne," "overvallue" (or "balance" as it finally was called), must be paid by an import of treasure. Bacon in 1616 expressed a view that was not new, but that was to be repeated in every possible key, when he hoped that foreign trade would continue to grow and be "wisely managed," "care being taken that the exportation exceed in value the importation; for then the balance of trade must of necessity be returned in coin or bullion." In such trade it might be permissible to export bullion to India if the goods which came back and were sold in Europe, America, or Africa brought in more gold or silver than had originally been taken to the east.

Into the thickets of this controversy we need not penetrate far. The bullionists waged a losing battle, but there was still abundant room for argument about the balance of trade. (1) Was the *total* balance between all exports and all imports to be considered, or was the balance of transactions with each country to be weighed? (2) Was the verdict to be reached by contrasting only *commodity* exports and imports, or was weight to be given to *invisible* exports or imports? A country might have a large favorable export balance of goods, yet its surplus might all be swallowed up in paying shipping freights, insurance, or interest to foreigners, in defraying travelers' expenses, making remittances to Rome, or investing capital abroad. On the other hand, an unfavorable balance of commodity imports might represent payment in visible goods for invisible exports. (3) How could the balance be measured unless a statistical service was established? (4) How could a favorable balance be secured and accentuated? Obviously the answer was, "By restricting the consumption of foreign goods or the dependence on foreigners for services, by the large production and frugal use of goods which found a ready sale abroad, by promoting shipping and fishing, and by fostering the *entrepôt* trade."

The balance of trade theory was adopted, in part or whole, by most countries as a guide (or excuse) for a policy of trade restriction (see Chapter XVI). In 1650, for instance, Cromwell asked a commission to suggest "some way that a most exact account be kept of all commoditys imported and exported through the land, to the end that a perfect Ballance of Trade may be taken, whereby the Commonwealth may not be impoverished by receiving commoditys yearly from other parts of a greater value than what is sent out." Six years later an act of parliament declared, "it has been found by long experience that the prosperous state of all islands is very much (under God) maintained and supported by a quick and flourishing trade and in a just endeavour and care that the exportation of the native commodities over-balance the importation of foreign commodities." The Commissioners for Trade and Plantations were appointed originally to exercise a general supervision of trade and foster a favorable balance, and in 1696 an inspector-general of exports and imports was appointed "in order to make a balance of the Trade between this Kingdom and any other part of the world" and to compile detailed statistics.

The plea of Thomas Mun (1571-1641) and others that the balance be thought of in terms of *all* exports and imports was often ignored, and when the statistics of trade with particular countries began to appear those lands which sold more than they bought were regarded as bad customers. Sweden supplied shipbuilding materials and iron, but bought little English produce or Virginia tobacco; trade with her should therefore be discouraged and the goods she supplied should be obtained from the colonies. France was notoriously a bad neighbor, for she supplied luxuries but wanted little in return except wool, which England would not let her have. Russia might be a good customer because of "the inordinate amount of tobacco smoked by the Muscovites," while Spain and Portugal were worthy of cultivation since they had few industries, great colonies, and the bullion-producing lands. Yet in those countries voices were raised at various times urging that the bullion be kept at home and that the supply which had already gone northward be repatriated. In 1619 the Spaniard Moncada urged that the death penalty be inflicted on specie exporters, and that the aid of the Inquisition be sought to enforce a prohibition of manufactured imports. At the end of the seventeenth century Juán de Castro said treasure, the blood of Spain, must be retained by balancing trade with England, Holland, France, and Italy. How all nations could sell more than they bought was a problem as mathematically insoluble as it is today.

In the eighteenth century the balance of trade theory lost much of its cogency. Protectionist arguments supplemented or supplanted it by justifying the fostering of industries which would promote employment and national self-sufficiency. Critics expressed doubts concerning the value of official trade statistics, and groped toward the idea that the distribution of specie was controlled by a self-regulating mechanism. David Hume in 1752 contended that the attempt to accumulate bullion might be as ridiculous as an attempt to keep water above its natural level. If a country acquired too much specie through a favorable balance, its price level would rise, its goods would become too costly for foreigners to buy, and its exports would therefore fall; but its own people would buy goods abroad, since they were cheaper than at home, and imports would therefore rise. This would create an unfavorable balance of trade; specie would flow outward, raising the prices in foreign lands and lowering them at home, until once more the country became a cheap place in which foreigners could buy. A new favorable balance would emerge and the process would begin all over again. A perpetually favorable or unfavorable balance was impossible.

Hume was not the first to enunciate this view of the relation between the quantity of specie, the price level, trade, and bullion movements; nor was he the last, for Adam Smith turned his heavy guns on the beliefs of the balancers. But long before Hume or Smith wrote, the need for treasure as the sinews of war, as emergency reserve, as a store of private wealth, as capital, or as currency had become far less urgent. The machinery of public finance had been strengthened, the crown debt had become a national debt, credit and transfer facilities had been improved, and methods of taxation were reaching the point where they could yield substantial revenues. At the same time the use of "commercial paper" and the development of banking had reduced the dependence on possession of coin and bullion.

During all this controversy the precious metals had been moving openly or furtively from one country to another. The Dutch had frankly regarded them as commodities of commerce; they had never banned the export of coin, and from 1647 permitted the export of bullion. England in 1663 permitted the departure of bullion and *foreign* coins, but English coins could not legally be exported till 1819. Treasure went abroad to India as trade goods; it also emigrated when an importer found that the cost of a bill of exchange or draft needed to pay a foreign creditor was so high that it was cheaper to pack, ship, and insure metal instead. On the other hand, specie came to northern Europe from Spain, Portugal, Africa, and the Americas. In the sixteenth century it gravitated to Antwerp or Genoa, in the seventeenth to Amsterdam, but in the eighteenth century London climbed to importance as a destination, especially for Brazilian gold. By 1750 half the gold which left Lisbon found its way to England; a regular weekly service of packet ships brought it, or it might be sent on a man-of-war. Trade between the British colonies and Spanish America expanded greatly after 1700, and deposited great quantities of silver in English ports, where, along with the gold, it was bought by the Bank of England or by bullion merchants. Thence it passed to the Bank's reserve or the Mint, was forwarded to continental creditors, or formed part of the next East India shipment.

The expansion of the Brazilian gold fields played a large part in leading England from bimetallism to the gold standard. In the mid-eighteenth century silver was undervalued in terms of gold; it bought less gold in London than in other bullion markets and was therefore exported. Meanwhile gold was becoming more plentiful, and for many purposes the gold guinea of twenty-one shillings was a more suitable coin than the silver pieces. In 1774 silver was made legal tender only for payments under £25; in 1816 and 1819 this amount was reduced to £2 and the quantity of silver in the coin was reduced, so that a shilling contained less than a shilling's worth of silver; it was henceforth a token coin. The monometallic gold standard had come.

Commercial Paper.—For the transaction of business, whether local or long distance, the trading world made its own medium of exchange on pieces of paper. Most business was conducted on a credit basis, with paper orders or promises to pay at some future date. Credits of two, three, six or more months were normal, though there was a flavor of medieval usury doctrine in the practice of allowing credit for two months free but of charging interest on the subsequent months. Until the use of checks became widespread and bank or government notes formed a larger part of the currency, almost every wholesale transaction produced its own paper. Every seller was also a buyer, a debtor as well as a creditor. The seller of cloth (A) to a London merchant (B) drew a bill on B ordering him to pay by a certain date to himself or to C (from whom A had bought wool or dyestuffs). He sent this bill to B, who wrote "Accepted" and his signature on the back of it and returned it to A.

Then one of several things might happen. (1) A kept it till it matured if it was payable to himself, or sent it to C if it was drawn in C's favor. (2) A or C might wish to turn it into cash, and might sell it to another person at a discount, leaving him to collect it at maturity; if he gave £99 for it and received £100 from B when the bill matured, the difference was interest. (3) Some neighbor of A or C (let us call him D) might owe money in London; he might buy the bill from A or C and send it to his creditor, who would then collect his money from B, while A or C had got his money from D. (4) A or C might *indorse* the bill by putting his name on the back of it, and then use it to pay some creditor, who in turn might do the same; and the bill might pass from hand to hand, gathering many indorsements and paying as many debts before the time came for it to mature and be paid by B. If B failed to pay, then the indorsers were in turn liable, and a bill thus "backed" was a fairly safe negotiable instrument, possessing the fundamental asset of currency, i.e., acceptability.

The bill just described is that of the eighteenth century; it differed from its medieval ancestor in being easily negotiable and discountable. The bill which had come into general use in the fourteenth century was not negotiable, and payment must be made to the person designated in the document. In the sixteenth century bills and promissory notes made "payable to bearer" came into wide use in France and Holland, but the negotiability of bills indorsed by the person to whom the money was to be paid was not legal in Amsterdam till after 1650 and in England till about 1700.

Given the boon of negotiability, the use of bills in domestic and distant trade grew large. In centers like Amsterdam and London, and also in large provincial towns, goldsmiths, private bankers, and others with spare funds would discount good bills and then sell them or collect the cash on settlement day. Merchants who did a large business in distant lands became well known out there; hence a colonist who bought goods in England would ask one of them to "accept" and pay for him the bill drawn by the seller, and would recompense him out of the proceeds of sale of the colonist's produce. When an order for cloth went from Boston to Leeds or Manchester, it would usually be accompanied by the request, "Draw on Mr. So and So, my correspondent in London." Provincial merchants had their accepting agents in London; their creditors were told to draw on them, and their debtors were ordered to pay there what they owed. By 1700 the "bill on London" was the most common form of negotiable document in English trade, and during the eighteenth century London became the center on which bills were drawn even when the goods involved never went near Europe. Some merchants found that the commissions earned by this acceptance work were so large that they abandoned trade in commodities and specialized on trade in bills.

Banking in Southern Europe.—By the end of the fifteenth century there were public or private banks in most trade centers. All accepted deposits, which could be withdrawn by their owner or transferred to another person. The check was being used, and the depositor was ceasing to come to the bank to authorize withdrawals or transfers. The grant of loans was hampered to some extent by the lack of negotiable securities which could be used as collateral or be bought by the bank at a discount; but loans were nevertheless made. The public banks in Barcelona, Valencia, Genoa, etc., were restricted to public lending, and financed the cities or provinces in which they operated. The private banks made loans to traders, shipowners, landlords, and clergy, while the big merchant-banking houses financed princes, kings, and popes.

Since many private bankers were still more merchant than banker they invested much of the money deposited with them in their own trade or in partnerships. "These investments were the greatest single source of weakness to the banking houses of the early period" (Usher), for the disturbance of Italian trade by political events, by economic crises, and by the shifting of the trade routes after 1500 wrecked many big merchant houses, the banks they operated, and those whose money they were using. Venice was as worried over bank failures in the sixteenth century as was England in the 1820's or the United States in the early 1930's. It appointed commissioners to watch the banks, forbade the use of the check, made the amount of money that banks could put into trade proportionate to the amount they lent the city, and ordered them to deposit some of their reserve in the hands of the commissioners. But banks still made unfortunate loans or investments, and continued to fail.

In 1587, after debating for a time the abolition of all private banking, Venice decided to establish a really safe bank; the Bank of the Rialto was set up in 1587 and the Giro Bank in 1619. They received deposits, effected transfers, but did not make loans. Milan established a similar bank in 1593, and meanwhile Sicily and Catalonia established public banks of the type built up in Barcelona. Thus by 1600 the Mediterranean cities had (1) private banks, regulated by the state and supplying commercial credit, (2) public banks, which took deposits and financed public borrowers, and (3) public deposit and transfer banks for private customers. Outside Venice they were permitting a limited use of checks, the bill was creeping toward negotiability, and some banks in Naples were giving depositors a receipt which passed from hand to hand and served as currency.

Banking in Northwestern Europe.—In northwestern Europe banking developments resembled those of the Mediterranean area, but went further. The Banks of Amsterdam (1609), Hamburg (1619), and Nuremberg (1621) were copies of the deposit and transfer banks of Venice and Milan. They had a monopoly of money-changing, provided safe deposit, converted the welter of currencies to a standard "bank money," and accepted checks; but the ban on loans was evaded, quietly in Amsterdam, and by the establishment of a loan bank alongside the Hamburg bank. These loans brought the Bank of Amsterdam to grief when its advances to the East India Company proved worthless. The Hamburg transfer bank twice had to suspend payment when the advances made to its loan partner weakened its resistance to drains on its funds. Eventually the two sections were definitely separated, and the transfer bank carried on a precarious existence till 1875, when it was absorbed in the Reichsbank of the then recently established German Empire.

In addition to these large institutions, banking facilities grew up in a variety of places and ways to serve (1) the needs of those who wished to find a safe place (and if possible an interest-yielding home) for their spare money, and (2) the demand of private and public borrowers for credit. The desire for a safe deposit led to much hoarding. London shopkeepers for a long time intrusted their till money to the care of their apprentices at night, but later they began to put it in the safe or strong room of a goldsmith. London merchants deposited their spare cash in the Mint until Charles I seized it in 1640 and demanded a loan as the price of its release; after that, especially during the dangerous days of the Civil War, they hoarded or sent it to the goldsmiths.

If an owner cared to sacrifice a little safety in order to make his money income-bearing, there were people ready and willing to serve him. In France the tax farmer offered interest on deposits. In England, Burlamachi played a leading part in providing James I and Charles I with money in anticipation of tax yields. He obtained much of his funds by welcoming deposits, and his failure in 1633 caused a small financial crisis in western Europe. The big English merchant would pay interest on money which he could use in his own business, in trafficking in bills, or in loans to the government. The broker welcomed deposits to help him in pawnbroking, buying and selling exchange, or dealing in bullion; while the scrivener, who wrote bonds and contracts and was in touch with property and business, was often intrusted with money and asked to find a borrower. Thus men in various walks of life in Tudor and early Stuart England were acting as money middlemen, buying the use of other people's money, selling the use of it, or acting as broker to bring borrower and lender together.

None of them was a full-fledged banker, and London's need for better banking facilities gave rise to countless projects, "reasonable observations," "humble proposals," and "letters in all due humility." The plea might be for a bank "in imitation of that at Venice" or for such "as is at Amsterdam." It might urge the accumulation of a "Bancke or Treasure permanent" which would supply the needs of the crown and help "ye merchants to traffic, ye gentlemen, yeomen, and husbandmen to stock, store, and till their grounds, and ye artificers to worke and trade." If skeptics asked what would be the basis of the abundant credit these banks were to provide, the reply would often be land, such valuables or commodities as jewels, silks, sugar, wines, tobacco, or even iron; if specie was scarce other tangible forms of wealth would suffice. Late in the century a few of these schemes came to fruition, but their career was nearly always short and tragic.

While the planners drew their cloud-castle pictures, the goldsmiths had steadily been advancing to the stage where they gave London a supply of private banks. After 1660 they displaced the scriveners as the leading money middlemen, and their work as bullion dealers grew, as did the value of their strong rooms. They took care of money and other valuables free of charge, and then began to pay interest. They gave the client a note on which they wrote the amount deposited and the amounts later withdrawn—an early pass book. They allowed him to write out an order to pay part of his deposit to others, thus bringing the check to England. Sometimes they gave him a note when he made his deposits, promising to pay him or the bearer in coin on presentation of the note. This brought the bank note; and as such notes passed into circulation, but were rarely presented, the goldsmith's coin supply tended to mount with the increase in deposits, or at least to be replenished by new deposits as old deposits were withdrawn.

On the basis of this reserve the goldsmith began to make loans to traders or the government, and to discount domestic and foreign bills. These loans might be made in coin or in his own bank notes; they were usually made for a comparatively short term by discounting a bill of exchange which might mature in a few weeks, or by discounting an Exchequer "tally," which was a government promise to repay with interest in the near future a sum of money borrowed by the Exchequer in anticipation of receipt of taxes. The security of a bill or tally was normally good, and each was a readily negotiable instrument that could be turned into cash if depositors suddenly decided to want their money back. Hence the goldsmith could safely make loans far in excess of the quantity of cash he had in hand, and serve more liberally the credit needs of commerce and the crown.

If the credit had all been for commerce the goldsmith's record might have been almost spotless; but the crown in 1671 ran true to tradition. The leading goldsmiths had lent heavily to the king. The loan seemed attractive, for if the bankers were paying 6 per cent to their depositors, the king was paying them at least 10 per cent, and provision had been made for repayment of the debt. In 1671, however, the Exchequer "stopped" all payments for a year, and then for an indefinite time. The lenders were unable to meet the claims of their depositors, and some were ruined. After three years' default, interest at 6 per cent was paid, but ceased when Charles died. From 1685 to 1705 the creditors got nothing; then payment of interest at 3 per cent was resumed and half the principal was offered in full payment of the debt.

This episode shook the credit of goldsmiths and king alike; it led to eager discussion of credit problems, to condemnation of greedy bankers, and to the search for some means by which credit could be made available at those low rates—3 or 4 per cent—which seemed to be the secret of Dutch success. Discussion achieved little, but the pressure of war after 1689 accomplished the unexpected. The government, headed by a Dutch king whose tenure was far from firm, was financially at its wits' end. It was approached by William Paterson, a Scot who had been to America and was now a large London dealer in colonial produce. He suggested that a loan of £1,200,000 be raised, and that the subscribers be given 8 per cent interest and permitted to form a bank. The money was obtained, and the Bank of England was founded (1694), with power to issue notes, buy and sell bullion, discount bills, and make loans. Its capital was the loan to the state; its working funds were obtained by taking deposits and by issuing notes up to the amount of its loan to the crown. That loan was soon more than quadrupled, and the note issue grew accordingly.

The value of the Bank to the state was very great. It acted as financial agent, making loans and raising large sums from the public; it reduced the rate of interest paid by the state and by private borrowers; it managed many state lotteries and annuities, and its notes supplemented the national currency. Its service to commerce was also large, though indirect. It confined its business chiefly to such big firms as the East India and South Sea Companies, and did not try to compete with the private bankers for the custom of the general trading or depositing public. Before the end of the eighteenth century it was beginning to be a bankers' bank, in which the private bankers kept accounts and through which they adjusted their debts to one another. It had its rash moments, especially during the Bubble period, and drew perilously near to bankruptcy; but in general its conduct was cautious.

In the history of banking the importance of the Bank of England lies in the successful union of the varied functions of banking —deposit, transfer, issue, advance, and discount—and in the Bank's ability to serve the state and the business world without losing its head—literally or metaphorically. It was copied on the continent in whole or in part, but without much success. Excessive demands by the state and overissue of notes spoiled the career of Law's bank; a Danish bank of issue, exchange, and discount lasted only from 1736 to 1757, and other banks which began to use notes had to learn, at great cost, the danger of overissue.

As part of the reward for its service to the state, the Bank of

England gained the usual monopoly conferred on seventeenth-century companies. Various acts forbade the granting of a charter to any other bank or the operation of a bank by any partnership with more than six members. The bulk of British banking was therefore carried on after 1697, as before, by private bankers, the descendants of the goldsmiths and scriveners, or by merchants who developed banking as a sideline. In London and the provinces the growth of banking as part of the business of a merchant, shopkeeper, manufacturer, or even farmer was steady and widespread. Such men took deposits and paid interest; they discounted, sold, or accepted bills; they advanced money on the security of commercial paper, commodities, or even personal reputation, to traders, putters-out, farmers, etc., and they issued notes. Some of them, having prospered in the provinces, marched up to conquer London. A *Bankers' Who's Who* of 1800 would tell of banks founded by a grain merchant in Edinburgh, a Quaker worsted manufacturer in Norwich, an ironmaster in Birmingham, a bookseller in Bristol, a grocer in Leeds, a linen dealer in Barnsley, a tea merchant in Manchester, and so on. It would include Francis and John Baring, heads of the largest merchant-banking house in Europe, grandsons of a Lutheran pastor in Bremen and sons of a German emigrant who had built up a flourishing cloth business in the west of England. But under the name of Smith it would say, *"See Debrett's Peerage"*; for one Smith, a Nottingham mercer, had started a bank before 1700, and his descendant, after twenty-five years of profitable parliamentary and financial work, had in 1797 become Lord Carrington, to the disgust of George III (who disliked Smith's connection with counting houses), and to the equal disgust of Arthur Young (who disliked his abandonment of family prayers when he became a peer).

In other countries the private banker held most of the field. In Amsterdam the Hope firm of merchant-bankers, founded by a Scot in the seventeenth century, was known wherever white men bought and sold. In France Law's failure made people afraid of bank notes, and no serious effort was made until 1776 to start a bank of issue. The Huguenot merchant-bankers had suffered in 1685, but while some of them left France others stayed and maintained contact with their *emigré* friends or relatives in London, Amsterdam, or Hamburg. During the eighteenth century merchant-bankers of Nantes, St. Malo, and other places used money gathered from all parts of France to finance production or trade with Spain, Africa, and the Americas. But French banking organization was weak; the tax farmers absorbed money which might have been useful in commerce. When Frenchmen remitted money to most countries they had to use the banks of Amsterdam or Hamburg, and when France sent money to help the American revolutionaries she used the financial machinery of Amsterdam to get it across the Atlantic.

In central Europe the merchant-banker served trade, but the Jew became the court financier. Driven from Spain and Portugal, Jews found refuge and profitable enterprise in Holland, England, and Bordeaux. In central Europe the Reformation was a dark period for them; they were not permitted to compete with Christian merchants or craftsmen, to use open markets, or own land. They were driven from some cities (e.g., Frankfurt in 1613), or the number of Jewish families in a town was limited (e.g., Strasbourg). During the seventeenth and eighteenth centuries the need for their aid in financing wars could not be denied, and in Frankfurt and other places they were given special military protection. They lent to princes and subjects, and provided army supplies for England, France, and Germany. They supplemented their capital by obtaining credit from their co-religionists throughout Europe, and by the eighteenth century had spread a network of financial affiliations over the capitals of central and western Europe.

In Edinburgh the Bank of Scotland was founded in 1695 to issue notes; the Royal Bank of Scotland followed in 1727, and the country therefore had two note issues. In addition she had several unchartered local joint-stock banks which served her well and were held up by English enthusiasts as models to be copied. When in 1826 joint-stock banks were allowed outside the London area, there was a great importation of Scottish ideas and bank managers. Scotland's two great contributions to the world's army of workers have been sound bankers and competent marine engineers.

Sweden had one curious chapter in its banking history. From about 1620 to 1740 it had a copper currency; one coin measured about nine inches across, weighed eight pounds, and was an inconvenient medium of exchange. In 1656 a trader of Dutch descent established the Bank of Stockholm, and in 1661 began to give bank notes for these copper coins. The notes were probably the first fully developed bank notes in Europe; they were received gladly, but the temptation to overissue them in making loans was irresistible, and the bank came to grief. In 1668 it was taken over by the state as the Bank of Sweden; it overreached itself again in 1745, but government funds set it on its feet once more, and it is still running.

The banks described above rendered service to business units which, according to the standards of the period, were medium or large. By 1750 loans might be obtained in England and Holland at 3, 4, or 5 per cent, except in time of crisis or heavy government borrowing. This rate contrasted strongly with the 8 to 12 per cent charged on the Antwerp Bourse in the sixteenth century. The small borrower, whose exploitation by the usurer had roused the loudest condemnation during the Middle Ages, was now helped in some degree by civic, religious, or private pawnshops, by advances from the merchant for whom he worked or to whom he sold his product, or by loans from professional money-lenders. The sum-total of the non-profit-making credit institutions was not large, the price that had to be paid for accommodation by the small man was still high, and the debtors' prisons of Europe were usually full. The provision of adequate rural credit and the elimination of the usurer from the countryside were twin aspects of one of the great problems waiting for solution in the nineteenth century. (See Chapter XX.)

BIBLIOGRAPHY

The best recent bibliography is by R. H. Tawney on "Modern Capitalism," in the *Economic History Review*, October, 1933, pp. 336-356.

BAASCH, E., *Hollandisches Wirtschaftsgeschichte* (1927).
CLAPHAM, J. H., "Economic Change," in *Cambridge Modern History*, vol. x.
CORTI, COUNT, *Rise of the House of Rothschild* (Eng. trans., 1928), chap. 1.
DAY, C., *History of Commerce*, chaps. 16, 17.
EHRENBERG, R., *Capital and Finance in the Age of the Renaissance* (Eng. trans., 1928).
FEAVERYEAR, A. E., *The Pound Sterling: a History of English Money* (1931).
GRAS, N. S. B., *Introduction to Economic History* (1922), chap. 5.
HEATON, H., *Yorkshire Woollen and Worsted Industries* (1920), chaps. 3, 5, 9, 11.
KULISCHER, J. M., *Allgemeine Wirtschaftsgeschichte* (1929), vol. ii, chaps. 9-13, 18-25.
LIPSON, E., *Economic History of England* (1931), vol. ii, chaps. 1, 2.

Lipson, E., *English Woollen and Worsted Industries* (1921), chap. 2.

Nef, J. U., *Rise of the British Coal Industry* (1932), part iv.

Nussbaum, F. L., *History of the Economic Institutions of Modern Europe* (1933), part iii, chaps. 1-5.

Perkins, J. B., *France under the Regency* (1894), chaps. 13-15.

Pirenne, H., *Histoire de Belgique* (1901), vol. iii, book ii, chap. 2.

Renard, G., and Weulersse, G., *Life and Work in Modern Europe, Fifteenth to Eighteenth Centuries* (Eng. trans., 1926). See especially Conclusion.

Richards, R. D., *The Early History of Banking in England* (1929).

Scott, W. R., *Constitution and Finance of English, Scottish, and Irish Joint-Stock Companies to 1720* (1910-1912).

Sombart, W., *Der moderne Kapitalismus,* vol. ii.

Strieder, J., *Jacob Fugger the Rich* (Eng. trans., 1932).

Tawney, R. H., Preface to Thomas Wilson's *Discourse on Usury* (1924).

Unwin, G., *Studies in Economic History* (1927), part ii, chaps. 5, 7, 8, 11.

Van Dillen, J. G. (editor), *History of the Principal Public Banks* (1934).

Wadsworth, A. P., and Mann, J. de L., *The Cotton Trade and Industrial Lancashire* (1931).

Weber, M., *General Economic History* (Eng. trans., 1927), chaps. 11, 23, 24, 25, 27.

Westerfield, R. B., *Middlemen in English Business, 1660-1760* (1915).

Articles

Ambrose, G., "English Traders at Aleppo; 1658-1756," in *Ec. H. R.*, October, 1931, pp. 246-267.

Barbour, V., "Marine Risks and Insurance in the Seventeenth Century," in *J. E. B. H.*, August, 1929, pp. 561-596.

Carus-Wilson, E. M., "Origins and Early Development of the Merchant Adventurers' Organisation in London," in *Ec. H. R.*, April, 1933, pp. 147-176.

Donnan, E., "The Early Days of the South Sea Company," in *J. E. B. H.*, May, 1930, pp. 419-450.

Fisher, F. J., "Some Experiments in Company Organisation in the Early Seventeenth Century," in *Ec. H. R.*, April, 1932, pp. 177-194.

Furger, F., "Zum Verlagssystem . . . im Textilgewerbe," in *V. S. W.*, 1927.

Gilboy, E. W., "Wages in Eighteenth-Century England," in *J. E. B. H.*, August, 1930, pp. 603-629.

Gras, N. S. B., "The Rise of Big Business," in *J. E. B. H.*, May, 1932, pp. 381-408.

Hauser, H., "The European Financial Crisis of 1559," in *J. E. B. H.*, February, 1930, pp. 241-255.

Heckscher, E., "Natural and Money Economy," in *J. E. B. H.*, November, 1930, pp. 1-29.

Judges, A. V., "The Origins of English Banking," in *History*, July, 1931, pp. 138-145.

Kulischer, J. M., "La grande industrie au xviie et xviiie siècles," in *Annales d'histoire économique et sociale*, January, 1931, pp. 11-46.

Lipson, E., "England in the Age of Mercantilism," in *J. E. B. H.*, August, 1932, pp. 691-707.

Namier, L. B., "Anthony Bacon, M.P., an Eighteenth-Century Merchant," in *J. E. B. H.*, November, 1929, pp. 20-70.

Nef, J. U., "Dominance of the Trader in the English Coal Industry in the Seventeenth Century," in *J. E. B. H.*, May, 1929, pp. 423-433.

NELSON, E. G., "The English Framework-Knitting Industry," in *J. E. B. H.*, May, 1930, pp. 467-494.

RICHARDS, R. D., "The Pioneers of Banking in England," in *Ec. Hist.*, January, 1929, pp. 485-502.

ROBERTSON, H. M., "Sir Bevis Bulmer: A Large-Scale Speculator of Elizabethan and Jacobean Times," in *J. E. B. H.*, November, 1931, pp. 99-120.

SAYOUS, A. E., "Partnerships in the Trade between Spain and America," in *J. E. B. H.*, February, 1929, pp. 282-301.

SUTHERLAND, L. S., "The Accounts of an Eighteenth-Century Merchant," in *Ec. H. R.*, April, 1932, pp. 367-387.

USHER, A. P., "The Origins of Banking: the Primitive Bank of Deposit, 1200-1600," in *Ec. H. R.*, April, 1934, pp. 399-428.

USHER, A. P., "Deposit Banking in Barcelona, 1300-1700," in *J. E. B. H.*, November, 1931, pp. 121-155.

VAN DILLEN, J. G., "La Banque d'Amsterdam," in *Révue d'histoire moderne*, 1928.

VINER, J., "English Theories of Foreign Trade before Adam Smith," in *J. P. E.*, June and August, 1930, pp. 249-301 and 404-457.

WASSERMANN, M. J., and BEACH, F. H., "Monetary Theories of John Law," in *Am. Ec. R.*, December, 1934, pp. 646-657.

Encyclopædia of the Social Sciences: Articles on Balance of Trade, Banking, Bill of Exchange, Bubbles, Bullionists, Burlamachi, Capitalism, Companies, Fuggers, Gresham's Law, John Law, Journeymen's Societies, Thomas Mun, Negotiable Instruments, Partnerships, William Paterson, Pawnshops, Putting-out System.

CHAPTER XVI

THE STATE AND ECONOMIC LIFE

IT HAS been impossible to keep politics out of the four preceding chapters, but at the risk of some repetition a general survey of the relations between the state and the economic life of its subjects is necessary. To the policies of the sixteenth to eighteenth centuries the term *Mercantile System* or *Mercantilism* has become attached. The term was used by Adam Smith to describe a policy which sought "to enrich a great nation rather by trade and manufactures than by the improvement and cultivation of land, rather by the industry of the towns than by that of the country." Its antithesis would be an *Agricultural System*. The label has two defects as a comprehensive title for the economic policies of states. In the first place, the state did show interest in agricultural affairs as well as in industrial and mercantile. In the second place, the word "system" suggests a neat comprehensive body of doctrine accepted and steadily pursued by statesmen for the realization of some objective. If we look from the stratosphere at the mass of decrees spread over two or three centuries, certain general common features may be seen; but if we descend and examine each item in detail we often find that action came from some desperate financial strait, some desire to strike or return a blow, some struggle with a war or post-war problem, some concession to a lobby, some sale of a privilege, or some imitation of another country. The one common feature was the exercise of state power over every side of economic life. If we could translate *étatisme* into some less ugly word than *statism* a satisfactory label would have been found; but "Mercantilism" has become hallowed by long usage, it emphasizes the great interest in merchants and trade, and may be accepted if we keep its deficiencies in mind.

State control usually took the nation as its unit, and German scholars have stressed the efforts of territorial rulers to subordinate feudal and urban economic policies to the interest of a larger political body. In England unity came early and fully; laws passed in the thirteenth and fourteenth centuries to deal with wages, prices, highways, etc., had been nation-wide in scope, and the statute of 1563 imposed a seven years' apprenticeship on the industries of the whole country. On the continent attempts at national control faced great difficulties. Landlords, towns, and the church did not readily surrender their right to impose tolls, tariffs, or other restrictions. The French kings got political unity but had to recognize some special local claims, and while Colbert in 1664 was able to abolish border duties between five customs areas (covering less than half the country) he could do little in the rest of the kingdom. In central and eastern Europe there were limits to the extension of central authority. "The results of mercantilist activity in overcoming the disruption caused by medieval conditions were thus rather limited" (Heckscher).

The state had a wide range of powers—power to help, to protect, to initiate, to regulate, to prohibit, and to claim a slice of the income of its subjects. It used all these powers. What did it seek to gain thereby? Strength enough to cope with its own domestic problems, to hold its own in the quarrelsome family of nations, to take what it wished from other states, to recuperate from the last war and to prepare for the impending next one. That strength must be drawn from well-developed and many-sided economic enterprises, especially from industry, commerce, and shipping. Agriculture might take care of itself, but an industrial and commercial superstructure was not so easily built; yet without it there would be no ships for the navy, little money for the treasury, and a scanty supply of munitions. Since strength is relative, the country that lacked these essentials or had them in smaller measure than its rivals must strain every nerve to remedy its shortcomings, to fortify itself, and to weaken the stronger.

National strength, translated then and often since as national self-sufficiency, would not come of its own accord through the free enterprise of individuals seeking their own personal profit. The state must aid in some directions and restrain in others. Rulers, courtiers, and officials might regard artisans or traders as men whose menial business was to work, obey, and pay for a lavish court and expensive international prestige. Or they might see the trader as one who cared for naught but his own private gain, and was willing to weaken his country and hurt his fellows if he profited thereby. Contempt of the trader's unsocial outlook was well expressed by James I: "The merchants think the whole commonwealth ordained for making them up, and accounting it their lawful gain and trade to enrich themselves upon the loss of the rest of the people they transport from us things necessary, bringing back sometimes unnecessary things, and at other times nothing at all." They sell bad wares at high prices, corrupt the currency, and generally behave in an unpatriotic manner. A century later an ex-merchant confessed, "I am afraid there are but few men in any country who will prefer the public good to their private interest when they happen to be inconsistent with one another." The ruler had a national and social duty to perform in restraining such harmful enterprise.

The case for control of international trade was sometimes based on the assertion that the state made such trade possible by the treaties it negotiated with other rulers; what it had made it had the power to control and to unmake. In 1718 a British official put the case as follows: "That particular subjects should have an uncontrollable liberty of all manner of trading is not only against the policy of our nation but of all governments whatsoever. . . . Since trade depends principally upon such treaties and alliances as are entered into by the Crown with foreign princes, and since the power of entering into such treaties is vested absolutely in the Crown, it necessarily follows that the management and direction of trade, must in a great measure belong to the King. . . . Foreign trades carried on by particular subjects for their private advantage, which are really destructive unto, or else tending to the general disadvantage of the Kingdom, are under the power of the Crown, to be restrained or totally prohibited."

Finally, officials and some onlookers might regard individuals as too short-sighted to see the paths that led to their greatest benefit in the long run. The ruler who was capable of taking a wider, wiser view must hold the reins and whip and control the brake. In Germany a series of writers known as the Cameralists saw in the well-run state the agent of recovery and source of welfare for regions that had been torn by war. In France Colbert believed that his own love of order, honesty, and industry, embodied in regulation and aid, could move mountains of debt, inertia, and incompetence. In England bullionists and balancers had plenty of suggestions for state control, while an onlooker like Nehemiah Grew, scientist and physician, in 1707 examined the national anatomy and called on the state to operate and prescribe. A planned economy would wring more produce from the soil, develop new industries, encourage inventions, abolish idleness, destroy parasitic occupations, and make England a happy home for 55,000,000 people or even more. Enlightened leadership was the one thing needed: "No reason can be given why men should always lett alone in their folly, when they may easily be made wise for themselves and their country."

Mercantilism, however, had two parents. It was not merely the product of rulers who were wise and solicitous for the welfare of their people or were greedy for power, prestige, and pennies. If kings wished to make economic means serve political ends, individuals, groups, and classes were equally willing to use political means to secure desired economic ends. Of the items that went to make up mercantilism, some may have originated with rulers, ministers, or "bald-headed men in [government] offices, with strong class prejudices, an inclination to magnify their own authority, and a comprehensive ignorance of the lives of nine-tenths of those over whom it [was] exercized" (Tawney). But many, perhaps most of them, sprang from below, were urged on the state by some interested person, group, or class, and were then imposed from above. In Holland and England, where the power of the trading classes was greatest, policy tended to reflect more and more the wishes of these classes or of sections of them; but even in France, Spain, and elsewhere narrow or broad economic interests stimulated and steered state action.

These interests had two things in common: (1) a desire to protect and enhance income, usually at the expense of others, and (2) skill in demonstrating harmony between this protection or enhancement and the national (or royal) welfare. There the similarity ended, and gave place to a clash of interests inside the country or between citizens and foreigners. Old vested interests fought new ones: the craft guilds sought protection against the advance of commercial capitalism, tenants sought shelter from inclosing landlords, while the woolen industry lobbied against Indian cottons, English wool exporters, Irish rivals, and colonial upstarts. But usually the pleaders promised some great expansion in a new direction, some improvement in quality of production or trade, some transfer from foreign to native hands, and a substantial contribution to the public purse if they were given the privileges they sought and if the necessary restraint was imposed on those outside their group, class, or country.

The history of almost every mercantilist measure illustrates the mixed (and often muddy) motives that influenced policy. The ban on English tobacco-growing was sought by the Virginia Company to benefit its trade; it was granted in return for an offer to pay extra duties on imported leaf. Cockayne's famous project (1613-1617) for dyeing and finishing English cloths before export aimed at benefiting the Eastland merchants, at the expense of the Merchant Adventurers (who exported undyed cloths) and the Dutch (who dyed them). Cockayne argued that the plan would employ many more English cloth-dressers, improve the balance of trade, and swell the customs yield on dyestuffs; but to clinch these arguments James I was offered half the profits, courtiers were lavishly bribed, while the king and his son also received large gifts of gold. So long as kings wielded great power monetary inducements were often offered; but as parliament grew stronger, lobbying, bribery, and support of a political party became the popular methods of approach. "Commercial affairs became the football of party politics" (Viner), and economic groups or classes advanced or protected their interests in ways familiar to all western democracies today.

The mercantilist state was thus servant as much as master. While it might try to subordinate the profit-seekers' efforts to the national welfare, it was very susceptible to suggestion or pressure, especially where its own financial position might benefit. Professor Unwin suggests that nine-tenths of the inventive ingenuity of the seventeenth century was engaged, not in exploiting the powers of nature, but "in the endeavor to manipulate the power of the state and the wealth of the community for the benefit of individuals." Adam Smith was equally caustic, for from his examination of some aspects of British commercial policy he concluded that "the sneaking arts of underling tradesmen are thus erected into political maxims for the conduct of a great empire," and in the restrictive parts of colonial policy he saw a "project . . . extremely fit for a nation whose government is influenced by shopkeepers."

Agricultural Policy.—When the state considered its economic needs the list was heavily weighted on the side of industry, trade, ships, and money. Agriculture was not neglected, for its political influence was great and it supplied not merely food but also raw materials for the industries that were to be fostered, while after such periods of destruction as the Thirty Years' War or the Seven Years' War there were soldiers to be settled and wasted farms to be restored. Prussian rulers made valiant efforts to colonize and settle their domains, and to repair the ravaged countryside. France under Sully nearly accepted the doctrine that the real treasure the country needed could be won from its plowlands, vines, and pastures, rather than from Potosi. Colbert gave some attention to agriculture and forestry, and England had its Corn Laws.

Industrial Policy.—The encouragement of industries could be justified by the balance of trade theory or by protectionist arguments, and there were never lacking men to plead the cause of existing manufactures or depict the benefits that would accrue from the establishment of new ones and the reduction of imports. Industrial encouragement took many forms.

1. Tariffs or prohibitions were imposed on imports. Definitely protective tariffs began to take shape in the sixteenth century, and Colbert's tariff of 1667 imposed rates which virtually prohibited imports of manufactured goods. Holland retaliated and the war of 1672 was precipitated. From that conflict Holland emerged strong enough to demand the restoration of moderate duties. England, which had an unfavorable balance of trade with France, now saw the balance tipped further against her. In 1678 she forbade French imports for three years, and from that time onward for a century prohibition or very high rates prevailed against French goods. France was as relentless as England in its attack on cottons, while Frederick the Great in 1763 forbade the importation of silks or cottons, and ordered that those already in the country be exported. The vagaries of the Prussian, Austrian, Hanoverian, Spanish, and Portuguese tariffs on woolens were the despair of English and Dutch cloth merchants.

2. The importation or domestic production of necessary raw materials was encouraged, and the export of those materials to competing industrial areas abroad was forbidden. The outstanding instance was wool. France forbade its export in 1278, and on many later occasions. England began to limit export in the sixteenth century, and stopped it entirely in 1660.

3. The export of tools or implements and the emigration of skilled artisans were forbidden, but the arrival of foreign equipment or of skilled workers was welcomed. We have seen Colbert scouring western Europe for craftsmen. Dutchmen and French artisans were invited or welcomed by English kings, towns, entrepreneurs, and landowners. Peter the Great's efforts to develop shipyards, cloth works, and armament plants caused an influx of technicians which recalls the efforts of the Bolsheviks after 1920. On the revocation of the Edict of Nantes the Great Elector welcomed a colony of Huguenots in Berlin, and 20,000 Frenchmen gave Prussia a range and quality of production it had formerly lacked. In Ireland the Dundalk chamber of commerce in 1737 invited a merchant-manufacturer from St. Quentin to establish and direct the manufacture of cambric, as was being done by refugees in other Irish towns.

Immigration was good, but emigration must be prevented. The States General of Holland occasionally complained about the drain of skill to the country's chief rivals. England became increasingly worried when her industries and equipment grew good enough to make her craftsmen welcome elsewhere. In 1624 the Privy Council was disturbed by a French attempt "to seduce beyond the seas the workmen in His Majesty's furnaces for making of iron ordnance." In 1718 an act was passed to check the activities of "divers ill-disposed persons" who had "drawn away and transported artificers and manufacturers out of His Majesty's dominions into foreign countries by entering into contracts with them to give them greater wages than they have or can reasonably expect to have within this kingdom, and by making them large promises and using other arts to inveigle and draw them away." This ban on emigration became much more important after 1760, when artisans were building or working the new equipment. In those days Wedgwood, the master potter, proposed that letters addressed to workmen or to foreign manufacturers should be opened by the post office to see if they referred to plans for emigration.

As with men, so with equipment. In 1718 the English parliament gave Lombe a patent, and in 1731 it gave him £14,000 (instead of renewing the patent) for introducing the silk-throwing machine. Yet in 1696 the same legislature had forbidden the export of the knitting frame, invented over a hundred years before, and in 1749 the export of silk-throwing machines was forbidden. When the inventions came in in strength after 1750, laws were passed in rapid succession—five between 1773 and 1786 —to prevent the export of machines, or even of models, drawings, and specifications. Foreigners and their baggage were carefully watched, a German was caught with a model of a spinning machine, and a departing Dane was deprived of a large notebook full of drawings of pottery equipment. The laws were not easily enforced, and no customs officer could prevent Samuel Slater from carrying to America, in his head, the knowledge he had acquired by building and working spinning machines.

4. Positive aid and encouragement might be given by granting exemptions from taxation or guild restraints, by providing some of the capital, by giving bounties, or by granting a monopoly. Frederick the Great gave subsidies to infant industries and continued them as bounties. Colbert spared no money to nurture the manufactures he wished France to have. In Austria the nobility emerged from the Thirty Years' War with shattered fortunes and tattered estates, sought to replenish their purses by establishing industries on their domains, and obtained subsidies. Maria Theresa helped textile works in Bohemia and porcelain plants in Vienna. England gave bounties on whaling and fishing boats and their catches, on big ships, sailcloth, rope, silk, and linen. Bounties were even offered to stimulate the growth of population: in parts of Germany premiums were paid to fathers of large families, and the French nobleman with ten children received a pension of a thousand livres.

The grant of a monopoly appeared an excellent method of rewarding those who established and nursed a new industry or raised the quality and quantity of production of an old one. But many monopolies were not capable of such justification, for they were given to courtiers, favorites, and petitioners seeking prizes for themselves or for some company. The strain on the Elizabethan and early Stuart exchequer guaranteed a favorable reception to any proposal if the crown was to share in the profits of monopoly. Hence the promoter hunted for fields worth monopolizing, much as his descendant searched for firms that could be absorbed by holding companies in the nineteen-twenties. The various regulated and joint-stock trading companies were at least as interested in restricting trade to themselves as in expanding the sale of English goods. Monopoly of the import of tobacco, the retail trade in wine, and the manufacture of soap, vinegar, starch, playing cards, pins, and gold or silver thread was sought by offering the crown a part of the profit that would be made by ousting independent producers or dealers and exploiting the consumer. Similar conditions prevailed in other countries. Austria had money-raising monopolies for tobacco and snuff, for honey and wax, for dancing and music licenses, for carnival masks and oysters. In few cases, such as the production of glass, paper, soap, salt, and metals, was there any honest claim that a new process or equipment was to be introduced.

Opposition to these monopolies soon grew loud and strong. Independents objected to the rights given to any group from which they were excluded. Consumers complained that prices were up and quality was down, while constitutionalists saw in monopolies a means by which the crown could raise money without recourse to the legislature. Parliament was hot on the monopolist's trail whenever it met; it wrung from Elizabeth the concession that the common law courts should decide on the validity of monopolies, and passed the Statute of Monopolies of 1624.

The judges and the statute settled some points which were important to the subsequent history of the English-speaking world. They decided that a monopoly was valid if its owner had introduced a new invention and created a new industry, thus providing the basis on which patent law has since rested. They agreed that the crown could grant privileges in order that a trade might be properly organized and governed; this left such companies as the Merchant Adventurers and East India Company intact, and paved the way for such bodies as the Bank of England and the South Sea Company. Privileges of old standing, such as the exclusive trading rights enjoyed by the freemen of towns and guilds or livery companies, stood and remained standing till 1835. The government was allowed to impose restrictions in the interest of the state (e.g., in the printing of books, thus providing a basis for copyright), or for the defense of the realm. But apart from these exceptions, trade ought to be free, and any attempt to restrain it was illegal.

5. Manufactures were subjected to regulation in order to guarantee the quality of goods, especially of those made for an

export market. A few defective articles or sharp practices wrecked a country's reputation abroad, gave arguments to those who wished to shut markets against the importer, and strengthened the foreign buyer in his efforts to beat down prices. Complaints frequently came from foreign governments to London respecting "the great defectes and fraudes in the Englische clothes brought thether," "the badness of the English draperie," and "the abuses which are in the making of the English cloaths." To raise the level of production, parliament passed countless laws fixing the length, breadth, and weight of cloths, and forbidding the use of certain materials or implements. It appointed inspectors or searchers, insisted that cloths be sealed and bear the name of the maker, used the guilds to some extent to aid in the work and thought of extending their powers to cover rural industries. By 1792, 311 laws had been passed to regulate workers or dealers in wool and cloth, while leather, linen, silver and gold thread, bricks, tiles, clocks, and some other goods were also dealt with.

In France Colbert handled the same problem in a similar manner. Son of a woolen merchant, he knew much about commercial and industrial ethics, and thought that a flourishing export trade could be built up by gaining foreign confidence in the quality of French goods and the honesty of French merchants. His elaborate regulations covered the processes and the character of the product, especially of cloth. His army of inspectors worked with the guilds or with chambers of manufacturers and officers chosen by them. In 1673 he issued an Ordinance of Commerce which regulated the structure, forms, and practices of business units, in the hope of restoring faith in the word of French merchants. He required special inspection of goods that were to be exported.

6. Consumption of domestic products was stimulated in various more or less humorous ways. When the Reformation reduced the demand for fish, the herring industry complained. Fishing was regarded as a training ground for sea fighters, a hard school in which men learned to brave the perils of the deep, a source of food supplies and provider of an export commodity. For its sustenance Edward VI ordered that fish be eaten during Lent, on Fridays and Saturdays, and Elizabeth added Wednesdays. "Let the old course of fishing be maintained," said Cecil, "by the straitest observation of fish days for policy's sake: so the sea-coasts shall be strong with men and habitations, and the fleet

flourish more than ever." When cap-makers grumbled because fashions in headgear were changing, parliament in 1571 solemnly ordered all persons over six years of age, "except ladies and gentlemen," to wear wool caps on Sundays and holidays. When the woolen manufacturers made one of their periodical lamentations concerning the lack of markets and the growing popularity of other fabrics, parliament responded in 1666 by decreeing that no person "shall be buryed in any Shirt . . . or Sheete made of or mingled with Flax, Hemp, Silk, Haire, Golde, or Silver, or other than what shall be made of Wooll onely" under pain of a fine of five pounds.

Shipping Policy.—A thriving merchant marine provided the sinews of naval strength; it was the means whereby native traders could take their own goods abroad, "keeping in the country" the profit of the middleman and the income from freight and insurance; it was essential if an *entrepôt* trade in colonial wares was to be developed. Colbert did his utmost to build up France's merchant shipping, carrying on the work that Richelieu had tried to do before him. England had her Navigation Acts. They began in a law of 1381, which tried to make English merchants use English ships, but enough vessels were not available. In 1486 and 1489 the importation of Bordeaux wine and French woad was confined to British ships, and there were other laws. But the effect was negligible or definitely harmful, and all the restrictions were repealed in 1559 on the ground that "forreyne Prynces, fynding themselves agreaved withe the sayd severall Actes, . . . have made lyke penall Lawes. . . . By reason whereof ther hathe not onely growen great displeasure betwene the forreyn Prynces and the Kinges of this Realme, but also the Marchauntes have been sore greved and endomaged."

For nearly a century shipping was encouraged by charging higher duties on goods using foreign vessels, by giving bounties to ships built in England, and by trying to encourage the fishing fleet. Attempts to revive restrictions under the early Stuarts were resisted, for exporters objected to being deprived of the services of Dutch ships, of the low freights they charged, and of the market they provided for English produce; but the colonial trade became limited. The Navigation Act of 1651 reimposed restrictions on the Atlantic sea lanes and on shipping between England and Europe, but the Act was not popular, and was not really enforced. The Act of 1660 was stronger both in its colonial and its European clauses. It remained substantially unmodified till the last decades of the eighteenth century and did not finally disappear till the middle of the nineteenth.

The effect of the Navigation Laws on Anglo-colonial shipping has already been discussed. Apart from the loss of colonial traffic, it is very doubtful whether the Dutch felt any harmful effects; they continued to dominate the Baltic traffic and the trade between the northern seas and the Mediterranean, while smuggling gave them considerable traffic across the Atlantic. They caught herrings almost within sound of English coast guards, and English fishermen could scarcely make a living. The benefits that came to English shipowners and builders were mitigated by losses elsewhere. Traders lost the benefit of low Dutch freights; naval stores and shipbuilding materials had to pay higher rates when imported in English or Scandinavian ships, and the cost of building English ships was increased. The insistence that three-fourths of the crew be English prevented shipowners from using cheap foreign labor as the Dutch did. Thus the country's maritime apprenticeship was an expensive one to those who used ships. The Acts were frequently relaxed by the grant of special exemptions, especially when war made the use of neutral vessels desirable, and shipowners continued to buy Dutch boats for use under the English flag.

Other European countries pursued similar policies. Sweden got her Navigation Act in 1724, and imposed such heavy duties on goods arriving in foreign bottoms that English ships transferred their cargoes to Swedish vessels in some Baltic port and let them enter under the national flag. Frederick the Great pondered long over a French proposal for a quasi-state shipping service between French and Prussian ports in order to free his country from the grip of Dutch and Hanseatic carriers. Spain and Holland tried to keep foreign flags out of their colonies. Everywhere nationality was conferred on such inanimate things as goods and ships. In every port complicated laws, treaties, and lists of rates were administered by officials of varied ability and honesty, and everywhere daring or ingenious men tried to get goods through cheaply within or without the law.

Critique of Mercantilism.—Criticism of mercantilism from a purely economic standpoint is largely irrelevant, for economic activity always goes on inside a political framework, and political ends may seem more important than economic. Historically, the mercantilist pattern of frame has been, except for brief periods in a few places, the popular one. The state has always tended to favor policies that promised to add to its financial and fighting strength; most countries that lacked manufactures and merchant marines have sooner or later come to resent dependence on foreign industrialists and ships; and capitalists, farmers, and wage earners have wished the state to take steps that would benefit them as individuals, groups, classes, or natives. Men are entrepreneurs or laborers, but they are citizens and subjects as well; and in Europe language, tradition, and history made intercivic and international differences real. Given those differences, and given the desire to get political aid in securing economic ends, there was no alternative to mercantilism. A generation that has witnessed the accentuation of economic nationalism since 1919 and lived through the discussions on gold and silver since 1930 will view more charitably the aims and efforts of the mercantilists.

Mercantilism was "of greater interest for what it attempted than for what it achieved" (Heckscher). It believed that encouragement and restraint could build up an industrial and trading nation, that causes could be so shaped as to produce desired effects, and that private or sectional interests could be trimmed and fashioned by the state stonemason to fit neatly into the national edifice. The mason did not doubt his own power, wisdom, and skill; but the history of many efforts shows that he overestimated his talents, or, to change the metaphor, the arrow often missed its target, fell short, flew wide, and even turned into a boomerang. Mercantilism achieved some of its objects, but at a price. It created some problems while solving others, and took from some people what it gave to others. A boon here involved a blow there, and if aid was given to every section at the expense of all others the result might be a general canceling of benefits. It opened the gates to corruption, favoritism, and lobbying, whether under a despotic or parliamentary government. It encouraged men to take full advantage of decrees that favored them but to evade those they did not like. By thinking of trade in terms of war it encouraged the striking of blows and led to war.

The framing and administration of policy required great powers of statesmanship, ability to resist popular or sectional clamor, a competent civil service, and willingness to punish offenders severely. Colbert's modest successes were due largely to the energy and honesty he brought to his task, and to his willingness to modify plans that did not work. Yet his regimentation became harmful in less competent hands, his hatred of the Dutch led to costly retaliation against his tariff, and his eviction of the Dutch from the colonial trade hurt the colonies more than it did the evicted. Regulation required more knowledge of the ramifications of industry and trade than most rulers possessed, and proved too much for the army of French inspectors or Prussian officials, not to mention the handful of overworked English justices of the peace and of underpaid searchers or anti-smuggling officers. The French officials often were complaisant to the wishes of the industrialists, while England found it necessary to appoint inspectors to watch the cloth searchers, and supervisors to watch the inspectors.

Many attempts at stimulation were doomed to abuse or failure by the nature of the inducement or of the project. The British fish bounty of 1750 was so generous that ships went out to catch the bounty rather than to catch herrings. The bounty on vessels fitted for whale fishing was so large that whaleboats multiplied too rapidly; it was therefore reduced a quarter, whereupon the whalers almost disappeared. When the early English Corn Laws forbade export until grain fell below a certain price, merchants sold small lots below that figure and thus gained permission to export. Subsidized industries succeeded in a few instances, but often their costs of production were so high that they could hold only such highly protected markets as the court or army. When their capital or subsidy was exhausted, they expired.

The state that was willing to help favored persons, sections, or classes exposed itself to a multitude of conflicting pleas and pressures for aid; but scarcely any plea could be granted to one supplicant except at the expense of someone else, and the state thus became a partisan in the tug-of-war of economic interests. Even when the benefit was supposed to be granted at the expense of the foreigner, the price was often paid by many natives in the form of lower prices for their wares, loss of markets, loss of cheap supplies of raw materials or finished wares, or higher freights. The state helped Paul to rob Peter, though it had been told that Pierre, Patrick, or Pieter would be the sole sufferers. That Peter in turn should seek for similar assistance was inevitable, and if all who were strong enough to make themselves heard had their wishes granted the result might be a network of more or less contradictory and conflicting concessions. This conflict was well seen in the colonial field. "The English political method of 1763 was to grant a favor here and a favor there as need arose. . . . Each issue that arose was treated on its merits, under the pressure of special groups and interests. . . . And because such favors were granted to different groups whose interests conflicted, the resulting policy was inevitably contradictory in some respects" (Nettels). Failure to reconcile those contradictions added some fuel to the fires of the American Revolution, and struggles between economic groups for state support have provided much of the raw material of modern politics.

The Ebb of Mercantilism.—The mercantilist tide began to ebb in different countries, and even in different parts of the policy of each country, at different times. Economically backward nations, such as Prussia, Spain, Scandinavia, and Russia, were trying in the mid-eighteenth century to do what England and France had attempted in the mid-seventeenth. Colbertism was growing in official favor there just when it was being belabored in France. The balance of trade doctrine was current in the Prussia of Frederick the Great when it was losing its appeal farther west, and in Portugal Pombal (died 1782) spent the last decades of his life pursuing a full mercantilist policy.

Even in the western countries there were many false starts and backward steps. There might be movement toward freedom from industrial regulation, yet no action on tariff policy or navigation laws. But, in general, the eighteenth century witnessed the strengthening of interests whose advancement depended on securing a greater measure of freedom, saw the weakening of attempts at industrial control, and heard voices exposing the economic fallacies of the old order or expounding a gospel of *laissez faire*. When these interests grew strong enough and the voices became loud enough, a change in policy was inevitable. The change was patchy, for the loudest advocate of freedom for himself would demand the continuance of old restraints or even the imposition of new ones on the freedom of others. Wedgwood clamored for a trade treaty which would allow his pottery to get more easily into France, yet demanded that the state ruthlessly prevent any export of machines or emigration of artisans. The trade treaty came in 1786, but artisans were forbidden to emigrate till 1825, and free export of machines was not allowed till 1843.

Trends in Commercial Policy.—Mercantilist control can be divided into the measures which bore on external trade and those which were concerned with internal aid and regulation. The first underwent some liberalization during the eighteenth century. Some prohibitions disappeared. Reciprocal trade treaties became more numerous and began to embody "most-favored nation" terms; each party agreed that if it should later reduce its tariff to a third country, the lower rates would be granted to the other. Even England and France nearly buried the hatchet in 1713. Some business men wished it, the landlords wanted cheaper silk and claret, and some Tory politicians had reached the conclusion that freer trade with France was desirable. Some economic writers were propounding the idea of regional specialization and suggesting that "each country flourisheth in the manufacture of its own native commodities" and in the exchange of the goods it can best produce for those which others are best able to supply. But the Whigs, supported by the silk and woolen interests, killed the proposal.

From that time till 1786, France and England enjoyed little legal trade with each other, but the Channel was crowded with smugglers, and a Sussex landlord complained in 1771 that he could get no farm laborers, since "all the lively able young men" could earn a guinea a week "as riders and carriers without any risk; therefore it is not to be expected they will labor for 8/— a week." The manufacturers who urged Pitt to make the treaty of 1786 were eager to get the wares made by the new machines and processes into the French market. The opposition this time came from French manufacturers who feared the influx of these cheap English goods; but France did not have Whigs or a bourgeois parliament, and the treaty was signed.

Protection of woolens and silks against cottons vanished in France in 1759, and the English ban on the use of cotton goods formally disappeared in 1774. The export of French wool duty-free came in 1716, that of hemp in 1719. Restrictions on inter-provincial movement or export of grain were removed in France in 1763-1764, but when famine came and the price of bread rose they were restored in 1769 and remained till the Revolution. In

Tuscany they were abolished in 1767, and in Spain interprovincial customs dues were wiped out by 1754.

Colonial policy was liberalized at a few points in the last quarter of the eighteenth century. Ireland, which for a century had suffered the most rigorous subjection of its economic life to English interests, yet had been deprived of any benefits springing from its imperial connection, was after 1780 freed from most restrictions on its industry and trade. In 1778 Spain abolished the monopoly of colonial traffic enjoyed by Seville, Cadiz, and Santander; all Spanish ports were permitted to send out ships, and the colonies were allowed to trade openly with one another. Marseilles in 1759 lost the monopoly of French trade with the Levant. If the Revolutionary and Napoleonic Wars had not come, the liberation of colonial and international trade might have continued; but that conflict arrested the movement for thirty years.

Decline of Industrial Regulation.—Industrial regulation gradually broke down because it was not or could not be effectively enforced, or because it no longer fitted the conditions of industry. In England regulation of wages became inoperative after 1650, was abandoned by parliament for the woolen industry in 1757, revived for the silk industry in 1773, and definitely wiped from the statute book in 1813. The apprenticeship clause of the Act of 1563 was repealed in 1814, but long before that time it had ceased to be observed. Attempts were made as late as 1766 to find better methods of regulating woolen cloth production, but the results were unsatisfactory, and the last law was repealed in 1821. When informers, eager to collect their share of the fine, dug out a long-forgotten law of 1605 regulating the leather trade and tried to bring offenders to trial, parliament repealed the law and several kindred measures in 1808.

The English guilds and companies saw their privileges fade away, and by 1750 few of them could either enforce their rules or secure support in the law courts. They lost the power to enforce apprenticeship, and their own members took as many apprentices as they wished or employed men who had not served their time. They lost the power of search, and could not exclude non-members from practicing their trade. Here and there a municipal authority in a sleepy cathedral or market town would throw its weight behind them; but judges grew too fond of condemning any "restraint of trade," and many guilds, after consulting a lawyer, decided not to go to court. Some of them disbanded, sold their guildhalls, distributed their funds, and silently vanished. Some of them carried on, reduced their fees, admitted persons of other occupations, and used the receipts from their property in charitable work. Any lingering power guilds might possess over trade was definitely destroyed when an act of 1835 allowed anyone to keep a store "for the sale of all lawful wares and merchandises within any borough whatsoever." The arrival of the age of free enterprise was thus once more officially recognized by the state, as it had been by the repeal of regulatory acts in 1813, 1814, 1821, 1825, and at other dates. But in domestic industry and trade free enterprise had arrived at least half or three-quarters of a century earlier. Economic liberty was a fact long before it was a law or a theory.

In France regulation by the state or the guilds was gradually impaired by the attacks of big merchants who wanted to get supplies where they wished, by changes in methods of production and trade, by the grant of exemptions, and by the growing criticism of Colbertism. The guilds were "already at the point of death" (Hauser) when Turgot in 1776 gave men freedom to work at any profession or craft they chose, to practice more than one trade, to use whatever machinery they wished, and to employ as many men as they could. When Turgot fell, the guilds regained some of their rights; but their final disappearance was only postponed till the Revolution. In Italy guilds lost most of their powers —in Florence (1770), Milan (1771), and Sicily (1786). In Germany the French revolutionary conquests swept guilds away in the west, and Prussia destroyed their monopoly in the reforms which followed her defeat at Jena; but in the industrially stagnant states guilds survived till the middle of the nineteenth century, and free choice of occupation was not finally established by law until the North German Confederation was formed in 1869. In Sweden guilds were abolished in 1864.

The Trend of Theory.—By the third quarter of the eighteenth century the elaborate structure of control was cracking at many points, and freedom of enterprise was being demanded, obtained, or taken without leave. There was sufficient resistance from tradition or vested interests and sufficient clash of rival groups to provoke discussion. In that debate those who sought economic freedom had to frame arguments which looked disinterested to justify their claims. These arguments gradually grew into general views of society, of the working of the economic order, of the function of government, and of the rights of individual and state. In the religious and constitutional controversies of the seventeenth century, the state's claim to omnipotence had been opposed by the individual's right to worship as he wished and to depose or execute a ruler who flagrantly violated his subjects' rights. Debates on the balance of trade and on monopolies raised the question of the ruler's right to dispense favors to some and withhold them from others. The Civil War in England proved "a powerful dissolvent of traditional economic ideas; the reaction against authority in the constitutional sphere extended inevitably to the economic sphere, and encouraged a critical attitude towards state interference" (Lipson).

The critic might turn historian, and assert that regulation had been imposed by ancestors who held "mistaken principles in trade" and were "unskillful in the mysteries of and methods to improve trade" (Child). He might turn prehistorian, go back to the origin of the state, and even peer beyond into days before the state existed. In those days man lived in a "state of nature," and enjoyed certain *natural rights* (especially liberty and property) under laws of nature which, "being coeval with mankind and dictated by God," were "superior in obligation to any other" (Blackstone). Man formed the state to protect these natural rights and laws, not to take them away, and the state must recognize that the individual's right to use his capital and labor as he wished was an ancient inalienable right.

Sometimes the critic turned social psychologist and philosopher. If the seventeenth century said the state must subordinate man's selfish activities to the common weal, the eighteenth retorted that this was quite unnecessary, since private and public interests harmonized. Man had his vices—pride, self-interest, and the desire to further his own material well-being without thought of others. Yet these private vices turned out to be public virtues, for the things men found paid best were things that were good for society at large. He profited most who served best. Mandeville said this in his widely read *Fable of the Bees* (1705). Dean Tucker said it in 1757: "The self-love and self-interest of each individual will prompt him to seek such ways of gain, trades, and occupations of life as, by serving himself, will promote the public welfare at the same time."

Adam Smith said it even better, and more people heard him. Man was a creature dominated by sympathy for his fellows and by prudent, enlightened self-interest. These two qualities were complementary parts of his being, but in his business dealings the latter was uppermost. "Every individual is continually exerting himself to find out the most advantageous employment for whatever capital he may command. It is his own advantage, indeed, and not that of the society, which he has in view. But the study of his own advantage naturally, or rather necessarily, leads him to prefer that employment which is most advantageous to the society." In another place Smith speaks of the individual who, pursuing a certain line of action, "neither intends to promote the public interest, nor knows how much he is promoting it . . . he intends only his own security; and by directing that industry in such a manner as its produce may be of the greatest value, he intends only his own gain, and he is in this, as in many other cases, led by an invisible hand to promote an end which was no part of his intention."

If an "invisible hand" guided selfish action to public good, state control was "a most unnecessary attention." "The natural effort of every individual to better his own conditions, when suffered to exert itself with freedom and security, is so powerful a principle that it is alone, and without any assistance, not only capable of carrying on the society to wealth and prosperity, but of surmounting a hundred impertinent obstructions with which the folly of human laws too often encumbers its operations." Smith was no whole-hog believer in *laissez faire*, but he did see the statute book cluttered with laws that were unnecessary, short-sighted, or foolish. Bounties, the old colonial system, the repression of Irish industries, the Methuen treaty, the attitude toward France, compulsory apprenticeship—these and many other pieces of policy were weighed and found wanting in economic common sense. One country does not get rich at the expense of another, for trade is a matter of mutual advantage. The wealth of a nation does not depend on a surplus of exports or a plethora of bullion. The only balance that needs watching is that between production and consumption. If a country produces much, but consumes only part of it, putting the balance into further production, it is growing richer. Unless that is happening, all the king's horses and all the king's men can do nothing for its welfare.

As Mr. Fay puts it, "the note of liberty rumbles through" *The Wealth of Nations*. The note was neither new nor strange, for when Smith and his forerunners proclaimed the idea "that the greatest common good is to be reached by every man pursuing his own individual advantage, this was not so much a eulogy of egotism as an apology for an existing practice" (Namier). State control was going, in installments, under the pressure of facts or of interests; but Smith supplied a development with a doctrine. He was widely read, he made converts, business men or statesmen picked out phrases or ideas with which they agreed, and on the continent he found a welcome among writers and statesmen interested in liberation.

In France discussion of economic policy was for long unpopular. When Vauban (died 1707), the brilliant military engineer, turned economist and suggested that the tax burden on the peasant be reduced, his plea was suppressed by the king. When the aristocrat Boisguilbert made a similar proposal for tax equalization, his plea met a similar fate. But suppression could not go on for ever, and the discussion of economic ills eventually produced a famous catchword—*laissez faire*—and a school of thought—the Physiocrats. The catchword was known in Colbert's day, but the phrase and the doctrine came to have real meaning only after the ruin caused by Louis XIV's wars and the collapse of Law's schemes. They found a spokesman in Gournay (1712-1759), a merchant and landowner who bought office as intendant and thus knew *étatisme* from without and within. Gournay struggled with the bureaucracy of which he was now a part, fought to liberalize the industrial regulations, came to grips with the guilds, and was driven to despair by the restrictions on the grain trade. He translated a number of foreign economic tracts, and reiterated his slogan *Laissez faire, laissez passer*—give free scope to production and free scope to the movement and sale of goods inside the country and even beyond the frontiers.

His pleas were welcomed by many men of his own social class—officials, with possibly a professional or commercial background, who were buying estates and climbing the social ladder. These men found the profitable exploitation of their lands hampered by the grain restrictions, the sales taxes, and the heavy export or provincial duties. To them the remedies were obvious. (1) Free the grain trade internally and externally; this would allow wheat to go in search of high prices, raise prices in France, and thus benefit farmer and landlord. (2) Reform the crushing tax system which fell so heavily on the peasant. If one asked why the towns-man's cost of living and taxes should be raised for the farmer's benefit, the reply was that land was the only source of real wealth, and that the agricultural class was the only really productive one. What had all the costly attempts to foster industry and commerce achieved? France was still primarily agricultural, and the Seven Years' War cut her foreign trade in half, ruined her merchant marine, and wrecked her empire. The real France was the coun-tryside, solid and self-sufficient.

Even if this be true, why should freedom be bestowed on agri-culture? In answering that question the group earned its name— Physiocrat: it believed in the rule of nature. Just as natural laws of chemistry or physics governed such physical phenomena as expansion, contraction, combustion, gravitation, chemical reaction, etc., so did natural laws govern economic phenomena—production, distribution, prices, wages, and so forth. If these laws were al-lowed to operate unfettered by man-made laws, man and society would benefit, production would reach its highest possible point, and labor and property would both get their natural reward. So-ciety would function automatically, and its movements would be as harmonious and orderly as those of the stars or tides.

Thought along liberal lines was not confined to France and England. In Italy men were keenly criticizing the balance of trade theory, and in Spain and Portugal statesmen were reforming or urging the reform of domestic and commercial policy. Their plans included the reduction of customs duties in order to make smug-gling less profitable, the abolition of tax farming, internal free trade in food, the reduction or cancellation of the privileges of the Mesta, the abolition of guilds, and the limitation of the economic power of the church. At the other edge of Europe, Chydenius, a Finnish pastor, was spending the "silent midnight hours" writing a fifty-page pamphlet on *The National Gain* (1765). In it he ac-cepted the balance of trade theory, but said the way to a favorable balance lay through freedom rather than restraint. Develop inter-national division of labor and let each individual pursue his own interest. The government will then be relieved from thousands of worries, laws, and tasks of supervision; the "harmful selfishness which always tries to cloak itself beneath the statutes can then most surely be controlled by mutual competition," and "the pillow of laziness will be snatched from the arms of those who, thanks to their privileges, can now sleep away two-thirds of their time." He therefore pleaded for one more "single statute, i.e., the one to reduce the number of our statutes."

BIBLIOGRAPHY

ASHLEY, W. J., *Surveys, Historic and Economic* (1900), pp. 268-308.

COLE, C. W., *French Mercantilist Doctrines before Colbert* (1931).

CUNNINGHAM, W., *Growth of English Industry and Commerce* (1910), vol. ii.

FAY, C. R., *Great Britain from Adam Smith to the Present Day* (1910), Introduction, chap. 7.

FRIIS, A., *Alderman Cockayne's Project and the Cloth Trade* (1927), chaps. 1, 3, 4.

FURNISS, E. S., *The Position of the Laborer in a System of Nationalism* (1920).

HEATON, H., *Yorkshire Woollen and Worsted Industries* (1920), chaps. 4, 12.

HECKSCHER, E., *Mercantilism* (Eng. trans., 1935). See also Heckscher's article on "Mercantilism" in the *Encyclopædia of the Social Sciences*.

HORROCKS, J. W., *Short History of Mercantilism* (1925), chaps. 3-10.

KRAMER, S., *The English Craft Gilds* (1927), Study Three.

LIPSON, E., *Economic History of England* (1931), vol. iii, chaps. 4, 5.

MIMS, S. L., *Colbert's West India Policy* (1912).

NUSSBAUM, F. L., *History of the Economic Institutions of Modern Europe* (1933), part ii, chap. 1; part iii, chap. 5.

PACKARD, L. B., *The Commercial Revolution, 1400-1776* (1927), chaps. 2, 3.

SCHMOLLER, G., *The Mercantile System and Its Historic Significance* (Eng. trans., 1910).

UNWIN, G., *Studies in Economic History* (1927), part ii, chap. 9.

USHER, A. P., *History of the Grain Trade in France, 1400-1710* (1913).

WEULERSSE, G., *Le mouvement physiocratique en France* (1910).

CONTEMPORARY WRITINGS EASILY ACCESSIBLE

CANTILLON, R., *Essays on the Nature of Trade* (1755. Edited by H. Higgs, 1931).

MANDEVILLE, B., *The Fable of the Bees: or Private Vices Public Benefits* (1714. Reprinted, 1924).

MUN, T., *A Discourse of Trade* (1621. Reprinted, 1930).

MUN, T., *England's Treasure by Forraign Trade* (1664. Reprinted, 1928).

SMITH, ADAM, *Wealth of Nations* (1776). See especially book iv.

TUCKER, JOSIAH, *A Selection from his Economic and Political Writings* (Edited by Schuyler, 1931).

TURGOT, F., *Reflections on the Formation and Distribution of Riches* (1770. Reprinted, 1898).

ARTICLES

ABRAMS, M. A., "English Gold and Silver Thread Monopolies," in *J. E. B. H.*, May, 1931, pp. 382-406.

GEORGE, R. H., "A Mercantilist Episode," in *J. E. B. H.*, February, 1931, pp. 264-271.

HOLDSWORTH, W. S., "A Neglected Aspect of the Relations between Economic and Legal History," in *Ec. H. R.*, January, 1927, pp. 114-123.

JOHNSON, E. A. J., "Nehemiah Grew: A Forgotten Mercantilist," in *Am. Ec. R.*, September, 1931, pp. 463-480.

JOHNSON, E. A. J., "Malynes and the Theory of Foreign Exchanges," in *Am. Ec. R.*, September, 1933, pp. 441-455.

KULISCHER, J. M., "Les traités de commerce . . . du xvi° au xviii° siècles," in *Revue d'histoire moderne*, January, 1931, pp. 3-29.

TAYLOR, O. H., "Economics and the Idea of *Jus Naturale*," in *Q. J. E.*, February, 1930, pp. 205-241.

VINER, J., "English Theories of Foreign Trade before Adam Smith," in *J. P. E.*, June and August, 1930, pp. 249-301, 404-457.

WARE, N. J., "The Physiocrats," in *Am. Ec. R.*, December, 1931, pp. 607-619.

Encyclopædia of the Social Sciences: Articles on Balance of Trade, Bounties, Cameralism, Colbert, Export Duties, Economists (the Physiocrats), Free Ports, Free Trade, *Laissez Faire*, Mercantilism, Protection, Adam Smith.

CHAPTER XVII

ECONOMIC CHARACTERISTICS OF THE LAST TWO CENTURIES

THE remaining chapters of this book will describe those developments of the last two centuries which have fashioned the economic structure and given color to the economic life of Europe today. Even a partial catalogue of those developments makes a long list.

1. Population has grown at a rate unknown in any earlier period.

2. While much of that population has left Europe to people other continents, a larger part of it has sought a livelihood in industrial and commercial pursuits. Europe is still, however, predominantly agricultural if we measure area or count heads; against the "industrial Europe" that lies chiefly between eastern Germany and the Irish Sea must be placed the predominantly "agricultural Europe" that includes Ireland, Denmark, the Iberian peninsula, and the region lying east of a line drawn from Finland to Sicily.

3. Agriculture has spread over much waste land, abolished open fields and commons, and developed intensive commercial farming.

4. Industry has passed almost completely into factories equipped with power-driven machines, has access to abundant supplies of steel and other metals, and is using many new materials or making new commodities. Mining and metallurgy have become huge industries.

5. Transportation has developed the ability to carry cheap bulky raw materials, minerals, foodstuffs, and manufactured articles half-way round the world, and to move people at speeds that would have seemed astronomical rather than terrestrial two centuries ago.

6. Commerce has permeated the greater part of European life, greatly reduced usufacture and subsistence farming, and linked Europe with the rest of the world for the purchase and sale of common necessaries needed by the masses.

7. Invention, discovery, and science have assumed an increasingly important rôle in influencing the methods of production and the nature of the product.

8. The organization of industry has become more capitalistic, while the capital requirements of the new forms of transportation, especially of the railroad, have called for vast aggregations of funds in corporate or state hands.

At least some of these developments would not appear strange to a well-informed observer who had survived the death of Queen Anne or Louis XIV. They were the continuation of trends in technique or organization that were already clearly visible before 1750 or even 1700, and that have been described in previous chapters. These trends were powerfully reinforced by the development of equipment and knowledge which increased greatly man's power over his environment. His work in agriculture, industry, mining, fishing, transportation, and trade was influenced by four factors: (1) the designing of new or better machinery; (2) the generation of virtually new kinds of power; (3) the ability to extract and use metals in abundance; (4) the accumulation of a body of scientific data and principles capable of application to production. These four aids—machinery, power, metals, and science—changed the way in which much work was done, reduced the cost and increased the volume of output, released production from some of the limits imposed by the available supply of human strength and skill, brought new industries and occupations into being (e.g., mechanical engineering and the electrical industries), made possible the production of goods hitherto unknown (e.g., rayon), gave new uses to old materials (e.g., by getting sugar from beet or paper from wood), and allowed waste lands to be given fertility. Transportation benefited as barriers of space, cost, and time were reduced or removed, as remote places and the interiors of continents were enabled to get their goods to distant consumers, and as ability to communicate with far-away places by telegraph or radio knit the world together in something approaching a world market. Commerce expanded as production increased the quantity of goods to be sold, as improved transportation brought buyers within easier reach, and as population grew.

The advance in equipment and technical knowledge reacted on economic organization and on the structure of society. In the first place, much more capital was needed. In parts of agriculture the peasant continued to supply the chief ingredient—his manual labor—with little outlay on equipment; but even he might spend much on fixed improvements, machinery, fertilizers, etc., while in England and some other parts of Europe inclosure, reclamation, and the "high farming" technique of large landowners or big farmers required that much money be spent. In industry the machines, containers, and power generators might be costly, needed large buildings for their accommodation, and absorbed great sums for fuel, raw material, and human attention. In transportation the capital cost of roads, canals, railroad tracks, rolling stock, and ships was enormous, while the operating expenses and cost of maintenance were great. In merchandizing, the large warehouse and store were outward and visible signs of the sums of capital involved.

In the second place, the organization of the factors of production and the conduct of enterprise became larger, more difficult, and more important tasks. There was still plenty of room for such one-man firms or partnerships as could accumulate sufficient capital or obtain enough credit; but in certain fields the need for assembling capital into big permanent heaps gave greater scope to the joint-stock company and placed an expanding part of enterprise under its control. The practice of assembling workers into one spot now spread slowly but surely over those industries which had been strongholds of domestic production. We shall see later the tenacity with which small units survived in agriculture, in retail distribution, and in some industries; but over a large part of the field the standard type of economic unit became one in which captains of industry or colonels of commerce ran businesses financed with their own capital, with borrowed money, or with that of stockholders, used comparatively costly plants, consumed much fuel and materials, and employed on their premises large numbers of wage earners who owned no part of the enterprise and were dependent for their livelihood on the sale of their labor.

This dependence gave greatly added importance to labor problems. These had made their entry long before, but they now advanced toward the footlights, and as those lights were now gas jets or electric bulbs instead of feeble candles, the problems cast a stronger as well as a larger shadow. Wages; hours; working conditions; the employment of women and children; the loss of income through unemployment, accident, invalidity, or old age; the cost of living; the supply of houses, and the provision of healthier urban living conditions all demanded attention. The interests and welfare of the laboring class became matters for thought and action by the wage earners themselves, by sympathetic onlookers, and by the state or its political subdivisions. They gave rise to occasional class conflict, for which each side organized and armed itself; they led to vigorous campaigns for economic and social reform, to propaganda and popular pleading; and they steered the state into pastures new and strange.

If labor's problems grew in importance, so also did those of capital. There was need for an adequate banking, currency, and credit system. The legal structure of joint-stock units must be carefully built if capital was to be accumulated and if stockholders and creditors were to have faith in the men to whom they intrusted funds or goods. The work of organizing production, of increasing efficiency, of winning and keeping markets, and of ending the year's efforts with a profit led to the study of management, of advertising, of costs, and of plans for the more rational direction of an enterprise. While any entrepreneur wanted the utmost possible freedom of action, the boon of free competition might become a boomerang, especially when the business cycle turned inevitably and at least decennially downward or when stronger rivals entered the field. The desire for security against the worst features and effects of competition led rivals to form associations which would protect their profits from mutual destruction, or to ask the state for protection.

The relation between the state and economic life was no less intimate than in earlier centuries, though the points of contact might be different. The movement toward strong territorial states advanced further with the unification of Italy, the formation of the German Empire, and the spread of the Austro-Hungarian Empire. The industrial, financial, and commercial classes gained in political influence as they grew in economic strength. In Westminster, Brussels, and at the Hague they became supreme, though they might have to bow at times to the demands of land, of labor, or of an aroused social conscience. In Berlin, Paris, and other capitals the landed classes retained more of their power, and their wishes could not be ignored; but occasionally the interests of industry and of agriculture coincided, especially on such issues as the tariff. In many countries laborers eventually sought to challenge the landed and bourgeois control of politics by forming labor or socialist parties, and by forcing the state to take action in the interest of the wage earner. But whoever was in power, the state had to act; and as we draw nearer 1900 any devotion that might have existed to *laissez faire* had to be abandoned. There were problems that industry could not solve for itself, evils that could not be stamped out by voluntary effort, restraints that only society could impose, and interests that only political action could foster or protect. There were also services that only the state could provide, or that could best be supplied by it, such as, for instance, water supplies, postal facilities, railroads, and electricity. Thus the state discharged its old duties of defending the frontiers and of protecting life and property; but in addition it aided and regulated private enterprise, undertook certain enterprises itself, provided certain amenities which came to be regarded as desirable parts of a nation's life (e.g., education or public health), and became a social service state.

In the history of social systems the last two centuries saw capitalism rise to what Sombart and many other observers regard as its zenith. The opportunities for profitable enterprise were never before so vast and varied. The old fields of commerce and finance offered richer pastures than ever as the volume of domestic trade rose, as the value of the world's foreign trade expanded possibly twentyfold between 1815 and 1914, as the public or private need for capital in the Old and New World became insatiate, and as customers for coal, cotton, and candies could be reached at the uttermost ends of the earth. To these old fields were added the comparatively new ones of transportation and industry. The capital requirements of railroads and steamships were vast, and the rewards for organizing and operating services were attractive. Old industries offered chances by which men could rise from small beginnings to great wealth, while new ones offered affluence to those who could create a new demand, transfer some of the demand from an older product, or obtain a share in supplying the needs for machines, engines, steel, or other "durable goods." Banking lost some of its risks without losing much of its rewards, speculation in commodities or stocks was easier and no more dangerous than in preceding centuries, while the underwriting of loans, the floating of companies, and the mysterious processes of combination and recapitalization brought large fees to the architects of this high finance. In short, the old ways of making money were supplemented by the invention of many new ones.

In this age of opportunity the old restraints imposed by state, church, and town were fewer and weaker than ever before, and some time elapsed before new ones were imposed. Labor was slow in building effective organizations to defend itself against exploitation, and the consumer was equally slow in finding ways to protect himself or in getting the state to shield him. Hence the track was comparatively clear of obstacles; on it the capitalistic engine could go as far and fast as it wished, subject only to the limitations caused by its own structural defects or lack of fuel. It overheated itself, broke down, and came to a standstill in a depression at least once a decade. Its engineers sought eagerly to improve its structure, lubricating system, brakes, and fuel supply, and succeeded in getting it moving again each time; but the effect of its smoke on the countryside, the liability to derailment, and the frequency of accidents at grade crossings led its owners to seek safety devices, forced the state to frame traffic rules, and made some passengers suspect that they had the wrong driver, were using the wrong form of locomotion, and were on the wrong track.

In the history of material welfare these two centuries have seen a lifting of the standard of living over the greater part of the western world. The increased yield from agriculture and industry, the tapping of the resources of the New World, and the growth of cheap transportation have made this possible. Lower prices permitted luxuries to become comforts or even necessaries, and the money left over when food supplies had been obtained went to buy more clothing or furniture, better housing accommodation, or means of pleasure and recreation. Poverty still remained a big black mark on society, and production was probably insufficient to give every European the income needed for enjoying the standard of living of the better-paid artisan. But famine and famine prices virtually disappeared from Europe west of the Vistula, and if the rich grew richer the poor grew less poor. Improving public and private health facilities reduced the loss of income and man power caused by sickness and insanitary surroundings. The state's efforts to protect health were supplemented by its other social service activities in providing education, organizing insurance schemes, paying old age pensions, etc.; and its transfer of income through taxation, chiefly from the middle and richer classes, for such purposes was virtually a redistribution of income and a subsidy to the earnings of the poor. Finally, the increased volume of wealth was produced with a smaller expenditure of labor time. It became possible to reduce the hours of all industrial workers toward or below the eight-hour day, to free many married women from industrial or mining work, and to dispense with child labor. The exclusion of children from factory or mine was sought on humanitarian grounds, but it was possible only because the new mechanical equipment and the productivity of industry allowed producers to supply the markets' needs without the aid of tiny fingers. No earlier century was rich enough to be able to regard childhood as a period of play and education, free from the necessity of adding to the family income.

These gains in material welfare were not uniformly spread, did not come in a steady stream, and were not obtained free. Sometimes they had to be fought for. Sometimes one class paid heavily for the benefits obtained by others, as when the cheap food flowing in from the New World after 1870 was a boon to the wage earner but a bane to the European farmer; and it would have cheered the farmer little to know that if he could carry on till 1896 his prices would begin to rise and the purchasing power of the wage-earner's income would fall. The advance of the machine was over the body of manual workers, to whom there was scant consolation in the news that goods would become cheaper, demand would expand, and more workers would eventually in the long run be employed. Further, the standard of living was subject to the ebbs and flows of the business curve, and the wage earner who spent fifty years offering his labor for sale found a scarcity of buyers during at least five depressions in that half century.

If at the end of the period he could still make a sale, he was often more fortunate than his first employer, for the insecurity of labor was paralleled by insecurity for capital. The century of great opportunity was also the century of great risk. Depressions wiped out profits, dried up markets, stopped supplies of credit, and scattered bankruptcy. The mortality rate of enterprise was high, the average expectation of life was not long, and for many families and firms—or even whole industries—the business cycle was "three generations from shirt sleeves to shirt sleeves." Competition was not merely a rivalry between firms selling the same goods or services, but also one between rival commodities or services.

The railroad hit the canal and the improved highway, and in turn was hit by the automobile. The improved sailing vessel was slowly evicted by the steamship, oil and electricity shook the throne of King Coal, cheap steel displaced cheap pig iron, rayon hurt cotton and wool, while science, having taught farmers how to produce more wheat and potatoes, tells people to eat less of them. The age that developed speed has discovered that in its dynamic world nothing is stable, nothing safe from the hands of the innovator. Arthur Young declared, about 1780, that he had no fixed principle except "the principle of change"; but twenty years later he was driven to admit that some of the agricultural changes he had so enthusiastically advocated had been accomplished at the price of much suffering among some sections of the rural population. Since Young's day his principle has always charged its price, has made the old the victim of the new and the new the victim of the newer. It has destroyed the value of invested capital as well as of acquired skill, and caused a harassed world in the nineteen-thirties to wonder if security and stability may not be worth more than innovation and insecurity.

"The Industrial Revolution."—When the economic history of the last two centuries first began to be studied, certain changes seemed so rapid, deep, and drastic that the word "revolution" was applied to them. Men who lived in the days when spinning machines, coke-smelted iron, and Watt's steam engine were becoming known had felt they were in the presence of "great and extraordinary developments" and that "a revolution is making" which would "produce great changes in the appearance of the civilized world." Frenchmen after 1789 used the word "revolution" freely in describing the changes in equipment, organization, or commercial policy, and socialists made it part of their vocabulary. Finally Arnold Toynbee popularized a label when a volume of his essays, addresses, and the lecture notes of his Oxford students appeared posthumously in 1884 under the title, *The Industrial Revolution of the Eighteenth Century in England*. To Toynbee it was sometimes "an industrial revolution," sometimes "the Industrial Revolution," but limited to England and to three or four decades before and after 1800. To other writers it became *the* Industrial Revolution, the one great break in evolutionary development during the whole recorded past of industrial history, worthy of at least some attention in any survey of modern history and capable of being described in strong, dramatic or even melodramatic terms as one of the turning points in the story of mankind.

The story, as told by Toynbee and many of his successors, has three parts—quiet eve, stormy night, and murky dawn. On the eve, methods of tilling the soil and of making goods were those which had prevailed for centuries. Industry was conducted by small, independent master-manufacturers who lived in the country or in small towns, combined farming and industry, employed a journeyman or two, trained an apprentice, and worked in their home or in a small shed. The class of capitalist employers was in its infancy, with some putting-out and a few large workshops or factories. Production was chiefly for the local market; there were no great rewards and no marked class distinctions. This old system, this rural and virtually classless commonwealth, was "suddenly broken in pieces" in the last quarter of the eighteenth century "by the mighty blows of the steam engine and the power loom," some spinning machines, improved roads, expanding trade, and *The Wealth of Nations.* The "two men who did the most to bring [the revolution] about were Adam Smith and James Watt." *Laissez faire,* steam power, and machinery "destroyed the old world and built a new one." A period of "economic revolution and anarchy" followed; equipment and methods were transformed; population was "torn up by the roots" and dragged "from cottages in distant valleys into factories and cities," there to become a collection of landless wage earners, living tools, "of whom the employer knew less than he did of his steam engine." The factory system became the "all-prominent fact" in industry; overproduction and depressions—"a phenomenon quite unknown before"—became normal parts of economic life. Landlords and manufacturers waxed rich. The industrial capitalist climbed into the saddle, flogged his horse relentlessly, ignored all traffic laws or told the state to repeal them, knocked down everyone who got in his way, and provided the world with its most ruthlessly efficient example of the soulless pursuit of self-interest. But "the innumerable evils which prevailed in this age of confusion" made the wage-earners' sufferings acute and long. A new list of seven deadly sins was drawn up—factories, urban slums, long hours, child labor, the exploitation of women, periodical unemployment, and a propertyless proletariat dependent for its income on the sale of its labor at a price that was usually low.

Only gradually, after about 1825, did labor and the state begin to protect the worker against the wages of these sins, and make the new environment a more comfortable habitation.

Toynbee put the Industrial Revolution into the table of contents of every textbook on modern history, alongside the American and French Revolutions. Henceforth nineteenth-century Europe must be regarded as the child of English economic and French political history. The picture contained most of the features usually associated with a revolution: events come suddenly and cause a far-reaching change, a major break in the continuity of development. They move rapidly, are dramatic and catastrophic in their destruction of the past and their erection of a new order; and those whose interests were well cared for in the old régime suffer severely during the transition to the new.

Nearly all these neat, precise dates and identifying events have been blurred, if not rubbed out, by later research. The eve was not still, domestic, rural, non-capitalistic, or unchanging in technique, as the description of economic organization given in Chapter XV has shown. The Industrial Revolution had "been in preparation for two centuries" (Unwin) in 1760, and the technological changes after that date were "the completion of tendencies which had been significantly evident since Leonardo da Vinci" (Usher). "The developments which took place in the reign of George III must therefore be regarded as the quickening of an age-long evolutionary process, rather than a violent break with the past and a fresh beginning" (Redford).

In the second place, that quickening took place much more slowly than is often realized. In automobile language, economic change had a very poor "pick up." If two centuries were spent in low gear, there was a long run at gradually accelerating pace in "second" before top gear and the speed of the last forty or fifty years were possible. The Industrial Revolution has been described chiefly in terms of cotton-working machinery and the steam engine. But the cotton industry was peculiar in many ways, and its history between 1760 and 1820 "cannot properly be treated as typical of the changes then taking place in industry" (Redford). Its problems were fairly easily capable of mechanical or chemical solution, the supply of raw material could be expanded rapidly after Whitney's gin had simplified the cleaning of cotton, and a highly flexible market was available as the price of cotton goods fell. Yet thirty years elapsed between the invention of the spinning machines and the complete triumph of the spinning factory over the domestic handworker, while the power loom did not finally oust the handloom till 1840 or even later. Watt's steam engine was patented in 1769; yet in 1800 only 320 of them were in use in the British Isles. They were so huge in size yet small in power, so low in steam pressure yet hungry for fuel that water wheels were often preferred, and steam was used only as a second best. In 1830 the cotton industry was still drawing a quarter of its power from water wheels.

In that year "no single British industry had passed through a complete technical revolution" (Clapham). The old staple industry of woolen cloth-making had adopted the spinning machines, but some of them were so simple that they were being used in homes as late as 1840 and the power loom did not really displace the handloom till 1860 or even later. In other industries the same slow transformation took place. Mining had no great technical change, but a lot of little ones; building remained a manual industry till the coming of the steel frame and the concrete mixer, and even today houses are built in the same way, with the same tools, as a century or two ago. Pottery-makers got machines for some dirty laborious tasks, but many processes remained manual. Clothes-making, printing, glass-blowing, and the preparation of food slowly or tardily obtained mechanical equipment. Even in the great new industry, mechanical engineering, the development of machines capable of making parts for machines with a great degree of precision was a task that took at least half a century. Thus we have to come down to at least the middle of the nineteenth century before we find the transformation in technique or in factory production approaching a stage that can be described as complete, even in England. If we take such a date as 1850, cheap steel is not yet available, the supplies of cheap lubricants have not yet come, efficient cutting tools for lathes are scarce, wood is still being shaped by handsaw or plane, industrial chemistry is not yet adolescent, and electricity cannot yet be generated in great quantities. A revolution that was in preparation for two centuries and continued for more than another century may well seem to need a new label. It might almost be called a study in quickening slow motion.

BIBLIOGRAPHY

BEALES, H. L., "The Industrial Revolution: a Historical Revision," in *History*, July, 1929, pp. 125-129.

BEZANSON, A., "The Early Use of the Term 'Industrial Revolution,'" in *Q. J. E.*, 1921-1922, pp. 343-349.

BIRNIE, A., *Economic History of Europe, 1760-1930* (1930), Introduction.

CLAPHAM, J. H., "Economic Change," in *Cambridge Modern History*, vol. x, chap. 23.

HANSEN, A. H., "A Technological Interpretation of History," in *Q. J. E.*, November, 1921.

KNOWLES, L. C. A., *The Industrial and Commercial Revolutions in Great Britain during the Nineteenth Century* (1921), part i.

KNOWLES, L. C. A., *Economic Development in the Nineteenth Century* (1932), part i.

NUSSBAUM, F. L., *History of the Economic Institutions of Modern Europe*, part iv, chap. i.

REDFORD, A., *The Economic History of England, 1760-1860* (1931), chap. i.

SOMBART, W., *Der moderne Kapitalismus*, vol. iii, pp. 3-41. This volume covers the period since 1760, and describes what Sombart regards as the high point in capitalistic development—*Hochkapitalismus*. The volume is available in a French translation, but not in English.

TOYNBEE, A., *The Industrial Revolution of the Eighteenth Century in England* (1884).

Encyclopædia of the Social Sciences: Articles on Industrial Revolution, Industrialism, Capitalism, Progress, Individualism and Capitalism (vol. i), and the Rise of Liberalism (vol. i).

CHAPTER XVIII

BRITISH AGRICULTURE SINCE 1700

General Features of European Agricultural Development. —Europe's agricultural history during the last two centuries was characterized by the following features:

1. The spread and development of intensive cultivation of the soil and of systematic breeding and care of livestock. Waste lands were reclaimed, rotations were evolved which eliminated fallow, new crops were introduced, better tools and implements were designed, the use of fertilizer increased greatly, the production of fodder became important, and scientific research made discoveries valuable to cultivation and animal husbandry.

2. The decline of the village community as an agricultural organization. Common pastures, striped arable fields, and rules controlling rotation or grazing rights disappeared quickly or slowly, giving place to individual farms, each managed by its occupier according to his own plans and wishes.

3. The increasing commercialization of agriculture. Europe's population grew rapidly during these centuries, and in favored areas became intensely urban and industrial. To supply its food and raw materials the farmer bestirred himself, while improving transportation linked him with the consuming centers of his own country and with those that might be half a continent away.

4. The growing inability of Europe to feed itself, the increasing dependence on other continents for supplies, and a difficult period of competition and readjustment when these new supplies poured in from America and the Antipodes.

5. The reorganization of agrarian society. In England the trend was completed toward the large estate, cut into medium-sized farms worked by tenants with the aid of hired labor. On the continent the abolition of serfdom led in places to the English type of rural structure or to latifundia worked by hired men, but in many areas it allowed liberated peasants to become owners of small farms.

6. The development by the peasants of cooperative societies

which helped them to overcome the disadvantages of small-scale production, supplied them cheaply with credit, seed, implements, and other things they needed, and packed, processed, transported, and sold their produce.

The movement toward "high farming" first gathered speed in Great Britain, and was watched and copied, more or less slowly, by other countries. The British story must therefore be told first.

The British Countryside in 1700.—In Chapter XIV we noted the turbulent inclosure of some land in the sixteenth century, the quieter advance of the seventeenth, the growth of commercial farming, the expansion of grain exports, and the evidence of interest in experiment and improvement. Yet in 1696 Gregory King estimated that 10,000,000 acres of land, or a quarter of England and Wales, were heath, moor, mountain, or barren waste. Much of this territory lay west of a line drawn from Berwick due south to Dorset, a region where soil, altitude, or heavy rain made cultivation difficult, limited inhabitants to pastoral pursuits, or rendered the land virtually useless. Some of the wastes lay in the east, in districts covered with sand hills or swamps or exposed to risk of perennial floods. Between these two areas lay the broad central belt of better land, dotted with villages three or four miles apart, and devoted to a combination of grain-growing and animal husbandry. On this belt, running from Dorset and the Isle of Wight in the south to Norfolk and Yorkshire in the east or north, there was much under-utilized land, and much of the work of the incloser remained to be done in 1700. In the country at large half the parishes and half the cultivated lands were still in open fields.

In the middle belt the "typical" farmer held arable land in open fields, meadow rights in the hayfield, perhaps some inclosed pasture, and the various common rights. The passage of the centuries had brought some consolidation of arable strips, but "fragmentation" was still widespread. One farmer held eighty acres in 164 pieces, another had 166 acres in 217, a third had two acres in six lots, while a fourth had one acre in eight fragments. A village priest had 132 acres in 124 "lands" in 53 different places in seven fields. Cultivation was still on a two-field, three-field, or four-field rotation, one stage of which was fallow. The rotation was controlled by the farming group, and while a man could plant what he wished—grains, peas, or roots—he must have his crops harvested by a certain date, and let his plowlands be merged in the common grazing area till the next period of cultivation came round. His livestock fed on the straw from the plowlands, the hay from the meadow, and the grass in any inclosed pastures; but their main food supply had to be sought on stubbles, commons, and wastes. There they mingled with animals belonging to other farmers or to those cottagers who were the hired laborers of the village and who held the right (or had taken it without express permission) to pasture whatever livestock they owned.

To the eighteenth-century advocate of high farming this old system seemed utterly bad, and was condemned in such language as is commonly used on sin or gin. Some defects were inevitable results of the method of land distribution, but others were visible only in the light of knowledge of better ways of farming and were to be found on inclosed farms as well. The shortcomings of the strip system were many. There was waste of land in balks, headlands, roads and footpaths. There was waste of time and labor getting from strip to strip, or from home to the more distant fields. There were barriers to individual initiative and enterprise; drainage was impossible unless all farmers joined in the project, and the alert farmer could not experiment too freely on his acres unless his fellows were alert. To toe the line might be the line of least resistance.

On open and inclosed fields alike a crude tillage was practiced. Two men, one boy, six horses and a heavy plow might spend a day plowing one acre. Manure was inadequate, and sometimes had to be used for fuel. Undrained land lay water-logged in rainy weather. Seed was sown broadcast by hand, and the birds devoured much of it before it could be covered up. Far more seed was used than was necessary, and the yield was rarely more than sixfold. The fallow absorbed much labor in preparation for its next crop, yet produced nothing; and the village had to till more land than would have been needed with better methods. To the advocates of improvement "these very ugly things, common fields," seemed to be occupied by "Goths and Vandals," who reaped "bushels where they should reap quarters." Yet yields might be little better on inclosed lands.

The commons and wastes seemed equally obnoxious, "filthy blotches on the face of the country." They were often overstocked, and smothered with weeds, thistles, or bracken, but the tin can had not yet appeared. While Mother Hubbard's dog found the cupboard bare, her cow might find the common lacking in nourishment. Breeding could not be controlled when all the villagers' animals were jumbled together. The yield of meat and wool was small, and cattle diseases were a constant menace. Lack of winter fodder forced the farmer to kill or sell such animals as he could not carry through the winter. Consequently the number of livestock stood still or grew slowly, the supply of manure did not increase much, the land was insufficiently nourished, and the yield of fodder did not rise. The circle was still vicious.

The above picture is doubtless too rich in black paint. It does not reveal the great variety of methods and results that prevailed, and any agricultural expert today could type as damning an indictment of current farming as ever came off a quill pen. Yet the broad impression remains that the agriculture of open fields was not very productive, that village organization and tradition checked change, and that the treatment of inclosed lands was not much better. Open-field farming obviously satisfied the subsistence needs of a stationary or slowly growing population, or it would not have lasted so long; but if the strain of demand became great, if the prospect of larger income grew brighter and the knowledge of more productive methods spread, the old order must be shaken.

The Search for Improvement.—The eighteenth century supplied the strain, the prospect, and the knowledge. Let us look first at the knowledge. Between the introduction of printing and 1700, over a hundred British authors published books or pamphlets on rural problems or practices. Many of them described ways by which readers could get greater pleasure and profit from their lands. Their titles abounded with such phrases as "A Way to get Wealth," "Divers rare and profitable Inventions," or "The Profitable Intelligencer." The royal road to more profit was *improvement*, and the ways of improvement were legion. Bring heaths and moors under cultivation, drain swamps, use more manure, drill seeds instead of broadcasting them, plant turnips and clover in the fallows, and transfer the potato from the garden to the field. Establish schools of rural economics, and let each university have an agricultural college in which future landlords will learn principles and practice. Sweep away the open fields and inclose the commons. Then, when tenants have separate farms, encourage them to improve their holdings by giving them long leases and

promising to compensate them for any capital or labor they devote
to such work.

The seventeenth century, richer in plans and proposals than in
performance, was seedtime for the new husbandry; the eighteenth
was growing time, and the nineteenth was harvest. We pass from
the seventeenth to the eighteenth in the career of Jethro Tull
(1674-1741). Tull is important in many ways. (1) He was a
landowner, an early member of that unbroken line of propertied
experimenters that stretched to at least the middle of the nineteenth century. There were many "spirited farmers," but the pioneering work was done chiefly by the landlords. They had the
money to pay the bills for trial and error, their very livelihood was
not 'at stake, they could borrow money for permanent improvements, and their contacts with other areas and countries gave
them a width of interest that the ordinary farmer lacked. (2) Tull
gained his inspiration by seeing Frenchmen at work in their vineyards. Many other landlords picked up ideas in the same way.
One man learned much as an exile, another kept his eyes open
during a sojourn as an ambassador in Holland. A "grand tour" of
western Europe was undertaken by sons of wealthy families as a
postgraduate course, and during it the countryside might be looked
at as well as the towns. The British agricultural advance of the
eighteenth century owed much to foreign methods and seeds—
"Spanish clover, Burgundian and French grasses, the horse hoe
of Languedoc, and the French method of cultivating turnips in
fields" (Gras), and when the movement gathered momentum the
continent was scoured to find plants or animals that would flourish
under British skies. (3) Tull, like all other experimenters, had to
fight the conservatism of his laborers and tenants, and to realize
how great the *vis inertiæ* of a countryside can be.

Ill-health turned Tull from law to the land. Observation of
gardeners and of vignerons plying the hoe and plow around their
vines gave him his clue. The secret of success was to keep the irons
in the soil, to till incessantly, to fight weeds and prevent the soil
from becoming hard. His procedure was (1) to plow the land
very thoroughly; (2) to drill seed in rows some distance apart,
thus using about one-third of the quantity normally broadcast;
(3) to hoe between the rows as long as the plants permitted. In
1701 he invented a drill, and in 1714 a horse-hoe. He grew wheat
on the same piece of land for thirteen years, got heavier crops

than his broadcasting neighbors, yet used far less seed and no manure. Late in life (1731) he explained his theory and practice by publishing a book. This was his undoing, for though his facts could not be challenged his theories seemed ridiculous to well-informed readers, while his drill and hoe were unsatisfactory and cumbrous. The scoffers made merry at his expense; but here and there a landlord in England, an author in France, or an agricultural society in Scotland found inspiration in his pages.

The center of interest now shifts from a sickly squire to one who, in the words of Arthur Young, "quitted all the power and lustre of a Court for the amusements of agriculture." Viscount Charles Townshend (1674-1738) was born to rule. He served as ambassador to Holland, viceroy of Ireland, regent of England, and prime minister. Then he quarreled with Walpole, retired in 1730 to his estate in Norfolk, and spent the rest of his life wrestling with waste lands, rabbits, and stubborn tenants. Much of his land was a sorry expanse of swamp or sand on which a few sheep found starvation rations and "two rabbits struggled for every blade of grass." Townshend had seen such territory in Holland turned into fertile fields and set out to do likewise. He dressed the sandy stretches with marl (a mixture of clay and lime), and worked them strenuously and successfully. He also developed a four-course rotation of wheat, turnips, barley, and clover, thus producing human food and animal fodder in alternate years, and abolishing fallow. He drilled and hoed, planted trees, inclosed land, and welded small holdings into larger farms which he let on long leases.

Townshend pointed the way to more productive and profitable farming. Cultivation could be extended to poor lands, the yield per acre could be increased, the production of fodder became an integral part of arable work, and the cultivation of turnips not merely put the fallow to use but benefited the soil, since the hoe killed the weeds. Animals need no longer be killed in the fall or starved in the winter; the circle ceased to be vicious and became beneficial. What corn is to North American animals, the turnip, supplemented by other root crops, became to English livestock, and the man who first vigorously cultivated it comes down to us as "Turnip Townshend." He had his immediate reward in a larger income from his estate.

Tull and Townshend made possible the better feeding of more

animals, but did not face the task of breeding better animals. That task was not seriously attacked until the second half of the century. Here and there a landlord built up a good herd, but breeding on common pastures was the "haphazard union of nobody's son with everybody's daughter" (Ernle). Even where care was taken, the aim was not that of today. Sheep were valued chiefly for their wool and manure, were lean and long of limb, weighed 28 to 40 pounds, and gave two to four pounds of wool. Cattle were valued as milkers and draft animals rather than as butchers' victims, the quality and quantity of their flesh were not important, and the "roast beef of old England" was probably tough.

Between 1760 and 1790 Robert Bakewell, of Dishley in Leicestershire, changed the whole outlook. Improved roads were bringing the growing population and the grazier nearer together and opening a larger market for meat and milk, while fodder was now plentiful. Bakewell therefore set out to develop breeds in which bone and sinew were less important than prime cuts. He chose his animals carefully, inbred judiciously, made genealogical tables of his beasts, and produced greatly improved types of cattle and sheep. He kept his methods secret and charged such high prices that jesters said "his animals were too dear to buy and too fat to eat." But his work and that of other men revolutionized animal husbandry.

The "new husbandry" spread slowly at first. Even in Norfolk farmers were loath to spend time, labor, and money on drilling or hoeing. The chief converts were found among the landlords and gentlemen farmers, and a more or less serious interest in agricultural experiments had become fashionable by 1750. Walpole is said to have read the reports from his bailiff before he looked at the day's state papers, and Townshend's work became widely known. Royalty indorsed the fashion; George III turned part of his Windsor estate into a farm, trudged round it in heavy boots, and liked to be called the "Farmer King." The Marquis of Rockingham turned land covered with "rushes and other aquatic rubbish" into well-drained pastures, experimented with various manures, tried in vain to persuade his tenants to adopt the Norfolk methods, and finally brought in a farmer from that county "to convince their eyes." Coke of Holkham (1752-1842) transformed his sand hills, marshes, poor rye fields and rabbit warrens into a model estate by doing all the latest things; by spending much money; by encouraging his tenants with prizes, good buildings, and long leases; and by converting his annual sheepshearing into a mixture of big house party, short-course summer school, and agricultural show. The Duke of Bedford copied Coke, but had larger parties. In Scotland landlords planted forests, experimented with Polish oats and Siberian barley, and grew turnips—which at first they ate as dessert.

This interest in improvement gradually infected most sections of society. Burke discussed cabbages and pigs as earnestly as he did American colonies. A Yorkshire divine experimented with onions and carrots, and believed that the latter could be made into "a confection for the use of seamen." When Arthur Young rambled round the country (about 1770) he found enterprising farmers everywhere, including one who was famous for his drain-digging machine, his mechanical turnip slicer, his thresher, and his belief that electricity could be used to stimulate the growth of crops. Agricultural societies offered premiums, medals, and honorary awards for outstanding achievements or contributions, tested new implements, obtained land for experimental plots, published accounts of new methods or equipment, organized plowing matches or agricultural shows, and sent out questionnaires.

The zeal for agricultural improvement found its greatest publicity expert in Arthur Young (1741-1820). Young failed dismally on three farms, and then became one of the most powerful and voluminous agricultural writers of all time. He wrote of his own experiences, roamed round his neighbors' farms, and then conceived the idea of making a series of long observation tours. The idea was rendered more attractive by the fact that a nagging wife made home life unbearable. He toured England and Ireland, made three trips to France, rode 3800 miles on a mare that became blind after the first hundred miles, and in 1789 went as far as Italy. Each tour became the subject of one to four volumes in which he described and praised the work of the gentlemen pioneers and progressive farmers. He pilloried swamps, wastes, commons, open fields, fallows, small farms, short leases, broadcast crops, and unhoed fields. He urged that commons and open fields be replaced by big inclosed farms, well improved and equipped, and let on long leases to tenants who understood high farming.

Young's industry was amazing. In three years he produced sixteen volumes and some pamphlets. In the 'eighties he began to edit and write much of the *Annals of Agriculture*, which ran to forty-five volumes. In 1793 he became secretary of the Board of Agriculture, and thus gained more scope for travel, writing, and contacts with the high and mighty. His books were translated into foreign tongues; learned societies in Germany, France, Italy, and Russia bestowed honors on him; Bakewell, Bedford, Coke, Pitt, Burke, and Bentham sought his advice. Washington asked him about implements, Lafayette asked for a landscape gardener, Catherine the Great sent young men to sit at his feet, and Alexander invited him to make a series of Russian agricultural surveys. George III carried the latest copy of the *Annals* in his coach, and Napoleon in Elba read his *Travels in France.*

The Stimulus to Improvement.—The eighteenth century was thus marked, in a measure far exceeding its predecessor, by the spirit of change. In what still was this spirit made? What strains and stimuli stirred men to seek and apply new knowledge? Was agricultural advance just the product of curiosity, a new form of life and leisure, a fashion, a love of progress for progress' sake; or was it a result of economic pressure, a realization of profitable possibilities, a new manifestation of the capitalistic spirit? It was all these things. Imitation, curiosity, necessity, and the desire to make or seize opportunities for increasing income were the driving forces in agricultural and industrial advance alike. Imitation was evoked by observations made abroad and by the spread of knowledge at home, while curiosity was sharpened by the general quickening of what we may call the scientific mind. But both might be stirred by the pressure of necessity on prevailing methods of production or by the realization that higher yields, lower costs, and greater net income could be obtained.

Until about 1760 there was apparently no pressure of demand that could not be met in old ways. England was not merely able to feed itself but exported a surplus of grain, and wheat was cheaper than it had been during the seventeenth century. In such circumstances improvements which increased yields might "be grumbled against by landlords as the way to depress the price of victuals" (Petty, 1690). The urge to better farming or extension of acreage cannot be found in the lure of high prices or the stress of scarcity. It may have been due to the desire to reduce production costs or to make worthless or low rent lands give more produce and higher rents. The joy of achievement and a richer rent roll were the reward, and meanwhile possibilities were uncovered, ready for wider exploitation when the need arose.

That need arose after 1760. The population of England and Wales had grown about 1,250,000 (23 per cent) between 1700 and 1760, and rose over 2,000,000 (32 per cent) during the next forty years. It seems apparent that the birth rate from 1750 onward was very high for eighty years, but the death rate began to fall about 1730 and dropped rapidly after about 1780. Improving sanitation, the establishment of dispensaries and hospitals, better medical knowledge and practice, the decline in fever, scurvy, and smallpox, and obstetrical developments which reduced the number of deaths at childbirth, all played their part, while a decline in gin-drinking had some effect. The reduction of mortality rates was slow, and when Johnson consoled Boswell for the loss of a child he reminded him that "to keep three out of four is more than your share. Mrs. Thrale [the wife of a rich brewer] has but four out of eleven." But the reduction was sure, and it added especially to the population of the growing industrial and commercial towns. The need for bread, milk, meat, and wool rose accordingly.

While demand was thus stimulated, and while improving transport facilities were linking town and country more closely, a period of bad weather injured supply. Between 1765 and 1792 there were two really bountiful harvests and fourteen poor ones. The average price of wheat from 1716 to 1765 had been 35/- a quarter, but for the next three decades it was 51/-, 43/-, and 47/-, respectively. As much wheat was imported as was exported, and after 1792 imports grew but exports vanished. England had ceased to feed herself. The danger of this situation was made manifest when the war with France began (1793). For over twenty years imports of continental grain were uncertain, American farms were far away, and the home land must carry the load. Again nature was harsh, for between 1793 and 1814 there were fourteen poor seasons, of which seven were shockingly bad. Every available acre must be put to work, every belt must be tightened, and countless emergency measures were passed. Starch, hair powder, and spirits must not be made from grain or potatoes; bread must not be sold fresh, and there was even an attempt to use clay in place of pastry for the bottom of pies. The price of wheat averaged 93/- a quarter from 1805-1814, against 47/- in the pre-war decade; but in the worst year it rose to 126/6, which we can think of as $3.90 a bushel, provided we remember that few wage earners received $5 a week.

For more than two decades the stimulus of high prices encouraged an attack on waste lands and inefficient methods. High farming was now fortune-bearing as well as fashionable. Rents could be raised, land sold at high prices, and less fertile land tilled at a profit; and since there was no state control of prices a slight deficiency of crop caused a large increase in price. A country parson looking over his congregation one Sunday morning in 1796 noticed a farmer's wife wearing a black veil, and commented, "Times must be good for farmers when their wives can dress in such style." According to Cobbett, war prosperity converted the farmer into a totally different character, with a "fox-hunting horse, polished boots, a spanking trot to market, a 'Get out of the way or by God I'll ride over you' to every poor devil on the road, wine at his dinner, a servant (sometimes in livery) to wait at his table, a painted lady for a wife, sons aping the young squires and lords, and a house crammed up with sofas, pianos, and all sorts of fooleries."

Inclosures: The Last Phase.—If the growing pressure of demand after 1760 and the urgent needs of the war decades were to be met by taking advantage of the new methods of tillage and animal husbandry, the inclosure movement must accelerate its pace, put the commons or wastes to better use, and end the promiscuous breeding on the common pastures. Inclosure had gone on throughout the seventeenth century, but the rate quickened after 1700. Much of it was done by agreement among those whose claims and interests had to be respected, and agreement was most easily reached when the claim-holders were few.

If agreement could not be reached there were other ways of inclosing, but the most popular method was to obtain a private act of parliament. Parliament was a landlords' and merchants' club, full of enthusiasts for high farming. If a petition signed by the owners of a substantial majority of the value of "estates, rights, interests, and properties" of a district was submitted to parliament, an inclosure act was assured of passage. The act appointed commissioners who examined all claims, decided how much land was to be given the church in commutation of tithes, and then redistributed the land "in such quantities as the commissioners shall adjudge and deem to be a full compensation and satisfaction." The act might deal only with the arable lands, it might be concerned only with wastes, or it might make a clean sweep, abolish open fields, existing inclosures, commons, meadows, and wastes, and replace the diverse rights of each claimant with one piece of land.

The number of inclosure acts passed between 1700 and 1760 was about 240, i.e., about four a year. After 1760 resort to parliament became much more popular, and by 1792 about 1350 more acts had been passed, an average of over forty a year. During the war the legislators passed an average of eighty acts a year, but after 1815 inclosure slackened its pace, partly because of rural distress and partly because most of the land had been dealt with. By 1845 the movement was virtually completed; over 4000 acts had been passed, affecting at least 6,000,000 acres, or one-fifth of the country. The area inclosed by agreement cannot be estimated, but a study of one county (Nottingham) finds that the area voluntarily inclosed in the eighteenth century was 45 per cent of the county, while that affected by law was 25 per cent. After 1845 the fragments were dealt with, by 1910 an open field was a curiosity, and the 2,000,000 acres of common or waste land that remained were of little use for farming purposes.

The economic and social effects of this final chapter in the history of inclosure have been hotly debated, and the last word has not yet been said. It is apparent that inclosure was inevitable and beneficial, but that the rights and welfare of the small farmer and of the rural laborer might have been more tenderly handled. Given a landlord class determined to increase the yield of rent from its estates, a farming class eager to take advantage of high prices, a growing (and even urgent) demand for food and raw materials, and a conviction that high farming on larger holdings was most efficient, then social considerations were bound to give way to economic.

The cottager was the chief sufferer. If he rented a house, the share of the land that was allotted to his home in lieu of common rights went to the house owner, and his only compensation might be a reduction in rent. If he owned a house, he received a bit of land or was offered money instead. His fraction might be too small to supply what the commons and waste had yielded, and the cost of fencing it might be high. Thus he got less than he had obtained from the old order, his supplementary income was whittled or wiped out, and he became largely or entirely dependent on wages which rose far more slowly than did prices. Arthur Young, arch-apostle of inclosure, admitted that "by nineteen enclosure bills in twenty (the poor) are injured, in some grossly injured," and his admission is indorsed by most recent writers. "Without being sentimental about the poor man, there is ample contemporary evidence to show that whatever benefits may have accrued to the community at large from enclosure and the engrossment of farms, life for the lowest social grade in the rural community was deprived of many of its opportunities thereby" (Orwin).

The farmer fared well or ill according to the strength of his claim, the aim of his landlord, and his own ability to adapt himself to changed conditions. The copyholder and freeholder received farms, but the acts decreed that all leases were void and that their holders must be compensated. How strong copyhold and freehold were cannot be estimated. A recent study of six important agricultural counties finds that, in 1780, 90 per cent of the land was held on short leases or on "leases at will." On the other hand, a study by Lavrovsky of a number of actual inclosures reveals "the great vitality of manorial organization and the frequency of copyhold tenure" at the end of the eighteenth century. Tenants at will were at the mercy of the landlord; and if he was wedded to the belief that "poverty and ignorance are the ordinary inhabitants of the small farms," he might take advantage of inclosure to carve as much of the land as came into his hands into large units, especially in regions suitable for grain-growing. Where this happened, many small cultivators became landless.

Landlords, freeholders, copyholders, and favored leaseholders benefited from inclosure, but they had to pay the price, and the costs of inclosure might be heavy. There were fees and expenses to be paid to parliamentary officials, lawyers, commissioners, surveyors, and valuators. Roads, bridges, and fences had to be provided, and new farm houses and barns must be built. Those who owned their new farms must pay their own costs, while tenants must compensate the landlord for his outlay by paying higher rents. Hence the industry became more heavily capitalized, partly through inclosure and partly because of the increased equipment and operating costs of the new husbandry.

Rising prices after 1760 made the carriage of those added costs fairly easy, and during the war farming became geared to high prices and costs, much as it did between 1914 and 1918. Lease, purchase, and cultivation were extended to inferior soils, land was bought at high prices, long leases at high rents were cheerfully assumed, and the number of occupying owners increased as tenants bought their holdings. If farmers' wives could afford black veils, Coke of Holkham could take satisfaction from the knowledge that his investments and energy, supplemented by the war, had raised the annual rents of his estate from £2200 in 1776 to £20,000 in 1816. A Scotch estate, bought for £18,500 in 1779, and improved by the expenditure of £2000, sold for £57,000 in 1798.

The parallel between the two war periods continued into the post-war decade. Despite the protection of the Corn Law of 1815 (which forbade imports till domestic wheat reached 10/- [$2.50] a bushel), prices fell from 15/10 ($3.90) in 1812 to 8/2 ($1.96) in 1815 and averaged 8/9 ($2.10) for the first peace decade. Costs and taxes remained high; wages, rents, interest rates, national and local taxes, all had risen during the war and could not easily be lowered, and agriculture entered a typical post-war period of gloom. Farms were abandoned, mortgages were foreclosed, plowed land went back to grass and scrub. Farm relief came in reform of the poor relief and tithe systems, and in reduction or remission of rent. Those who had courage and were not excessively encumbered by debt weathered the storm; but many fell by the wayside, the number of occupying owners declined, and their land passed into other hands. When the clouds cleared about 1837 the English land system had become set in a mold different from that of any other European country.

The English Land System.—That mold contains three distinct sections—large landlord, tenant farmer, and landless laborer. In 1873 over half of England was owned by 2250 persons in estates which averaged 7300 acres each, i.e., the equivalent of 65 homestead quarter-sections. Political power, social prestige, and good rentals in prosperous years have made land a desirable investment since at least medieval times. "More than one city family of the fourteenth and fifteenth centuries ended . . . its connections with the city and entered the coveted circle of country gentry" (Postan) by buying a landed estate. Young rented a farm from a landlord who had been butler to a duke, a neighboring estate had recently been bought by a brandy merchant, and Young scoffed at the pagodas and temples erected as country houses by "some oilman who builds on the solid foundation of pickles and herring." The nineteenth-century merchant, banker, and manufacturer was as eager as his predecessors to acquire broad acres, and the landlord class was thus constantly receiving new blood and new capital.

Once an estate had been acquired, family pride decreed that it should be made larger whenever possible, but the sale of it was an unforgivable sin. To avert temptation, the practice of entail was available. Entail was a method of controlling inheritance which was found in most European countries at one time or another. On reaching manhood the heir to an estate was virtually compelled to settle his property on the next generation. When his father died he took possession, but only as life tenant. He enjoyed the income; but the property belonged to his son, who in turn was expected to convey it to his son. Entail and primogeniture passed estates down unimpaired from generation to generation.

The landlord did not work much of the land he owned. He might employ laborers to cultivate the home farm, but the rest was leased. Sometimes he was not a person, but an institution— the church, a college, or a charitable organization, and such bodies did not farm their estates. In 1910 seven-eighths of the farms and 90 per cent of the land in England were tilled by tenants. The landlord provided the permanent improvements, while the tenant supplied the working capital. If the tenant spent money on fixed improvements, it became the practice for the landlord to compensate him for such outlay when the tenant left his holding. In 1875 this "tenant right" to compensation began to be safeguarded by law, thus making the tenant more willing to spend money on his farm. In the inclosure days long leases (fourteen to twenty-one years) had often been granted, especially when a new farm was carved out of the commons or wastes; but when land had been broken in, the contract might be for a shorter period, even for a year. This policy allowed landlords to raise rents in prosperous times, and permitted tenants to seek reductions in bad years. Many families held their farms for decades, even for generations, on a year-to-year lease; the average occupation has been fifteen to sixteen years, which is longer than that of the North American farmer-owner.

The farmer's family might supply all the labor he needed, and in 1851 over 40 per cent of the farmers paid no wages. On the larger holdings hired help was required, and from 1851 to 1871 there were about 250,000 farmers and nearly a million employees, i.e., about 1 to 4. Since many small producers employed no laborers or only one to two, the largest farms must have had several. In such cases the farmer was a "clean-boot" rather than a "dirty-boot" farmer, concerned with direction, management, and marketing. He belonged to a rural upper middle class, his wife did only the pleasanter domestic and farm duties, and he was a valuable minor pillar of church and Conservative party.

The laborer was the third person of the rural trinity. The loss of the commons made him dependent on his wages, and some men had advocated inclosure in order "to have the laborers more dependent upon them." While he lost his supplementary land income, the passage of spinning into factories might deprive his wife of her money-earnings. His wages were low and rose slowly, except where proximity to manufacturing areas compelled the farmer to pay better rates in order to prevent laborers from going to the towns. His hours were long, and his house might be picturesque but poor. If he was ambitious he might migrate to town, or emigrate. At rare intervals unemployment, a threat of lower wages, the dislike of a new machine, or the voice of a trade union charmer might gather laborers together to smash threshers, burn haystacks, or join a union; but lack of energy, of education, or of class consciousness prevented farm hands from doing much to protect or advance their welfare. British agriculture in its palmy days "gave returns sufficient to reward adequately all the parties to production. It was the maldistribution of profits, rather than any lack of them, which led to the change for the worse in the lot of so many of the laboring class" (Orwin).

Agricultural Advance after 1815.—Inclosure and the new husbandry made possible the feeding of a population which rose from 14,000,000 in 1801 to 21,000,000 in 1821 (United Kingdom). Even twenty years later the country was growing 88 per cent of the wheat required for 27,000,000 consumers, and there was virtually no importation of other foodstuffs. Inclosure was not necessarily followed by better farming, but usually it was a prelude to improved methods, output, and rents. Light soils were given body, and drainage could be practiced effectively. Better breeding and feeding more than doubled the weight of animals coming to market, and most of the increase was in flesh rather than in bone. A Scotch mill manager found a new way of draining land, someone invented a machine which made drainpipes cheaply, and the reclamation of the fens was completed. Machinery received much attention, for iron was now cheaper and mechanical engineering was advancing. Better plows and harrows were designed, threshing machines were worked with animal or steam power, and some farmers used steam plows; but no satisfactory "harvester" was forthcoming till McCormick set up his factory in Chicago in 1845.

The most significant contribution made to agriculture during the second quarter of the nineteenth century was chemical, not mechanical. Even in the seventeenth century men had asked, "What is the food of plants?" and answered water, salt, air, earth, or all four. Tull said particles of earth, and Young had ideas about gases in the soil. The progressive farmer might have no answer, but he dressed his soil with any waste materials he could procure—rags, bakehouse refuse, city garbage, ashes, soot, bones, wood shavings, lime, and sweepings of London streets. Results varied; no one knew why, but by 1800 many people were believing that chemistry might solve the riddle. In 1802 Humphrey Davy, a young assistant professor of chemistry in London, gave a course of lectures on the connection between chemistry and vegetable physiology. His lectures were published and influenced the practice of many landlords and farmers. In 1840 Justus von Liebig, a German chemist, explained, largely from laboratory experiments, the relation between the food needs of plants and the chemical composition of the soil. Plants contained certain chemicals which they had taken from the soil. Soil was not just so much undifferentiated dirt, but a chemical complex. It might originally be devoid, or by cropping be deprived, of the essentials of plant nutrition; but by applying the right kind and quantity of fertilizer the defect could be repaired or the exhaustion prevented.

Liebig's findings opened a new volume in farming history. They were carried further in laboratories and on experimental farms.

One of Liebig's admirers, Lawes (a young English landlord), and one of his pupils, Gilbert, established a factory to make super-phosphates, and on the famous experimental farm at Rothamsted began investigations which have continued to our day. The use of superphosphates, Peruvian guano, potash, bone dust and, later, Chile nitrate spread rapidly. Arable and grass lands alike re-sponded to the treatment. More than ever before it was realized that farming could not be a mere extractive industry; he who put much into the soil would get more out, up to a point beyond which the law of diminishing returns began to operate.

Equipped with drains, machines, and fertilizers, English agri-culture began to enjoy a silver age, and then a golden age, after 1840. Good roads and canals were supplemented by railroads after 1830, the industrial areas were getting more crowded, and the import of foreign foodstuffs was still so small that farm prices varied with the size of the British harvest. In 1846 the Corn Laws were repealed and grain could be imported duty-free. The consumers of food defeated the producers, and the manufacturers and merchants, aided by a potato famine in Ireland, beat the landlords. The victims predicted speedy ruin when protection vanished, but foreign competition was not acute till after 1870 and British agriculture entered the best two decades in its whole history. The improvements came to a head, and British farming was regarded enviously by foreigners as a model of perfection. Wheat imports trebled between 1850 and 1875, and by the latter date half the people of the United Kingdom were fed on imported grain. But this did not worry the farmer, for wheat prices were good, wool had doubled its price in twenty-five years, and the urban demand for meat and dairy produce was excellent. Pros-perity was everywhere, except perhaps in the laborer's cottage, and even the hired men were stirred to seek a better share of the general well-being.

The Agricultural Depression.—Then came the deluge, and the period 1875-1896 was for European farmers in general, and English ones in particular, a time of deep gloom. The causes were partly monetary and partly agricultural. The upward swing of prices set in motion by the gold discoveries in California and Australia came to an end about 1873, and from that time till the next gold boom came (in the Klondike, South Africa, and western Australia after 1890) there was a relative scarcity of gold and a fall in the price level. Just as this dow ward movement began, English agriculture was struck hard by a number of bad seasons— a tragedy of rain and mud, of rotting harvests and dying animals. The yield of the blackest year, 1879, was about half that of the good year, 1874. Between 1874 and 1882 only two good crops were reaped, and the 'nineties were as drought-stricken as the 'seventies were sodden. Western Europeans were inured to climatic vagaries, and farmers could counterbalance short crops with high prices. But this time it was different, for Europe had been casting its bread on the water in the form of emigrants and capital, and now it came back on an ever-rising tide of foodstuffs from those cheap lands of the New World which had recently been reached by railroads and reapers. In 1850 three-fourths of the British wheat imports came from European farms, and only one-eighth (5,000,000 bushels) from North America. By 1870 the imports had almost doubled, but nearly half of them (34,000,-000 bushels) came from North America. By 1880 imports had nearly doubled again, but transatlantic supplies had nearly trebled (92,000,000 bushels) and accounted for 72 per cent of the imports.

These figures are in part an echo of the amazing expansion of settlement, production, and railroad facilities that followed the Civil War. Free homesteads, the steel plow, spring wheat, the binder, the new kind of flour mill, all facilitated the expansion of the prairie wheat fields. Elevators, bulk-handling, grading, and cutthroat competition between railroads and lake carriers reduced the cost of hauling grain from Chicago to New York from about 33 cents in 1870 to 14 cents in 1881. When the grain reached New York it found the old sailing ship and the new steamship fighting for freight. In 1874 the cost of sending a bushel of wheat across the Atlantic was 20 cents, but in 1904 it was 2 cents. Grain exchanges, the telegraph, and the ocean cable knit the world into one market; Chicago, Montreal, and Sydney knew the day's price in Liverpool; buying and selling became transoceanic, and a world price level took the place of a British or European level. That level seems to have been influenced chiefly by the state of the grain crops of Roumania and Russia, but developments there combined with those in the New World to depress it. Wheat sold in North American ports for $1.47 in 1871; by 1882 it was down to $1.18, and in 1885 to 86 cents.

Wheat was not the only villain of the piece. Lard, bacon, and pickled pork had been sent from America to Europe before 1860, the export of live cattle began about 1870, but that of goods from packing plants, canneries, and dairy factories was more important. Nor was the United States the only disturber of rural peace. Eastern Canada built up its food exports, and by 1883 the railroad was opening up Manitoba; but the flow of prairie grain across the Atlantic was not great until after 1900. Australia added wheat to wool exports after 1860; and when the refrigerated ship appeared in the early 'eighties, beef, mutton, butter, and even fruits could be shipped halfway round the world, carried across the equator, and arrive in edible condition in northwestern Europe. Nearer home, Russia began after 1860 to increase her outpouring of grain at a rapid rate, and while her rye went chiefly to continental markets, her wheat exports to Britain in some years rose to 40,000,000 bushels, placing her second only to the United States.

This revolution in food supplies pleased the consumer. As the general price level sank 40 per cent between 1873 and 1896, food became plentiful and cheap. Violent fluctuations of supply and price were now a thing of the past, for if Europe's harvest was bad that of America might be good. Food absorbed a smaller part of the wage-earner's income, money was released for other purchases, and the standard of living rose. The "hungry 'forties" and the old fear of famine were forgotten, and the British housewife put a girdle round the earth every time she prepared a shopping list. The manufacturer rejoiced, for cheap raw materials helped him to keep his prices low, cheap food kept his workers from seeking higher wages, and swollen imports created a demand for more manufactured exports. The investor was happy, for this influx of goods from the New World paid the interest or profit on the capital he had been pouring overseas since 1815 in an ever-widening stream.

To the farmer the influx was a tragedy, and from the Shannon to the Vistula he faced the prospect of ruin. If he had concentrated on grain he was hit first and hardest. An efficient British farmer could make ends meet if the price of wheat did not go below 6/- ($1.50) a bushel. In 1878 it sank below that figure, and after hovering for four years around 5/9 began a bumpy decline to a low point of 2/2 (53 cents) one day in 1894. Other products, such as meat and dairy produce, fell 20 to 30 per cent between 1876 and 1893, while the price of wool was cut in half. Every country in western Europe felt the effect of the invasion, and either sought tariff protection or readjusted its rural economy to meet the new conditions. The agricultural classes in some countries (especially Germany and France) were politically strong enough to secure protection, but in Great Britain wage earners and capitalists were too powerful to permit any return of taxes on food.

Certain concessions were given to farmers and landlords, local taxes were eased, and freight rates were lowered; but this farm relief had little effect in the face of the powerful economic forces which had created the crisis, and the rural community had to pass through the shadow and the valley. Farms were deserted and submarginal land reverted to grass, weeds, and thistles. Landlords had to absorb the financial shock by remitting or reducing rents, farm the land for lack of tenants, or use it for sport. The capital value of agricultural land dropped from £2,000,000,000 to about half that sum between 1875 and 1894. The total arable area fell a quarter and the wheat area a half, while the number of farm laborers declined from nearly 1,000,000 to just over 600,000 during a period in which the total population rose by 11,000,000.

Recovery and Readjustment.—Recovery came with the readjustment of production programs and a turn in the price curve after 1896. The general price level began to climb slowly again, and by 1914 had mounted 35 per cent. The devastating rush of American food spent itself after 1900, though this gave little relief to the grain grower, for Canada was now becoming England's granary, while Australia, India, and Russia were feeding the market freely. The farmer changed his direction, abandoned parts of the home market, and let the country rely on overseas producers for four out of every five bushels of wheat it consumed. In 1907 it was estimated that 20,000,000 acres of land abroad were growing wheat for British consumers, and that another 20,000,000 acres were supplying Britain with half its meats and much of its dairy produce. One-quarter of all the wheat, corn, barley, and oats that entered international trade went to Britain, as did virtually all the bacon, mutton, and lamb. Most of the exports of Australian, New Zealand and Canadian farm produce went there, along with 95 per cent of Denmark's butter and the larger part of the Argentine's beef and of Ireland's butter and bacon. The country produced about £170,000,000 worth of the foodstuffs it needed, and imported about £200,000,000 worth from the temperate zones.

Having surrendered some markets to overseas rivals, the British farmer set out to nurse those in which foreign competition was lighter, i.e., in perishable goods and high-quality produce. Cheaper bread left consumers with money for milk, meat, butter, fruit, eggs, and vegetables. The price of sugar fell more than half between 1880 and 1900, and the consumption of jam therefore multiplied, causing a demand for fruit and other ingredients. The stricken wheat lands of East Anglia were taken over by Scotsmen who were used to mixed farming, who had their race's genius for handling cattle, and who carefully improved their pastures to produce butter and milk for London or high-grade pedigree stock for export. Costs were pared by reducing the hired labor supply, the lessons of Lawes and Liebig were taken closer to heart, and the laws of heredity were now understood enough to influence the breeding of plants and animals.

On the eve of the Great War the clouds were passing from the rural sky. Everywhere there was a "quiet unexcited prosperity," some competition for land, and a recognition of the inevitability of vast food imports. On June 12, 1914, the London *Weekly Times* regarded the "alarming extent of our dependence on foreign imports" as "undoubtedly a disquieting state of affairs," but had to admit, "It is only in the production of butter, milk, eggs, poultry, and vegetables that we can hope to make the home supplies match our need. That is an undertaking well within our powers." Within less than sixty days war was declared and the country faced a far larger undertaking. The submarine gradually became more menacing, Russian food supplies were cut off, and Australia, Argentina, and India were so far away that few ships could be spared to fetch their produce. Greater reliance had to be placed on the nearer North American supplies, but America's harvest was poor in 1916, and ships were far from safe on the North Atlantic. Between 1913 and 1918 imports of wheat dropped a fifth, of beef and sugar a third, of mutton and butter a half, of eggs and apples three-quarters. Defeat by starvation was at times just round the corner.

To fight this menace farmers were urged to plow more land.

They were offered a guaranteed minimum price till 1922, but a maximum price was also fixed. Laborers were guaranteed a minimum wage, but landlords were restrained from raising rents at their pleasure. The labor shortage was fought by introducing tractors and better equipment, and by employing interned aliens, war prisoners, and women. The industrial population was urged to till allotments, of which there were over 1,400,000 in 1918. The acreage under wheat and oats expanded a third, that of potatoes a half, and over 2,000,000 acres of pasture were plowed up. The country grew enough wheat to supply its own flour for sixteen weeks a year instead of ten, and the increase in other products was equally good. This was a remarkable achievement, but it drove the wolf only as far away as the sidewalk.

Post-War Problems.—The end of the War reproduced many of the conditions that followed 1815, save that this time there was no powerful landed class to pass a Corn Law and the minimum price for grain was abolished in 1921. Prices fell more than half between 1920 and 1923, recovered a little, and then slid slowly toward the debacle of 1929-1933; but interest, taxes, wages, rent, and production or transport costs did not follow them, and could not be quickly adjusted. The only thing to do was to retreat again to those activities best suited to the country's climate and economic position. By 1925 the gain in arable area had been lost, the country was growing less than one-fifth of the grain it needed, and importing more than half its meat. Over two-thirds of the farm output consisted of livestock and animal products; the value of grains was less than that of potatoes and vegetables. A subsidy established in 1925 encouraged the farmer to begin growing sugar beet, while improvements in canning methods were inducing him to produce more fruit and vegetables for the canneries. In general, however, he had resumed his old place, filling only special shelves in the national larder.

In view of Britain's dependence on overseas producers for at least half its food, pleas for protection of the farmer fell on deaf ears until they were supplemented by cries for the protection of the manufacturer. When the depression of 1929 deepened into the crisis of 1931, free trade was abandoned and agriculture became again a ward of the state. Wheat-growing was stimulated by guaranteeing a minimum return of 45/- a quarter ($1.35 a bushel). The difference between the market price and this figure was met by a subsidy financed by a levy on flour. Fruit, vegetables, bacon, and dairy produce were taxed if they came from foreign countries, but entered duty-free from the dominions. Since foreign meat was too large an item in wage-earners' budgets to be taxed, a system of quotas was devised by which the quantity imported would be reduced or limited. Marketing schemes were devised to control the distribution of some domestic and imported produce, in order to bring the farmer a greater return.

This rediscovery of the farmer and the framing of a policy for his benefit has closed the one big open door through which foreign and dominion farmers have poured their produce without hindrance for three-quarters of a century. It has served notice on overseas producers that they cannot expect the British market to take all they care to offer. Depression revealed to Great Britain that she was buying more abroad than she was able to pay for out of the receipts from the sale of her goods, from her banking and shipping services, and from the interest or profit on her external investments. If she could not sell her wares, if her ships were idle and her investments unproductive, she could not pay for her imports. But the British farmer would not gain all that his distant rival lost, for Britain without a big export trade would be a poor overcrowded country, doomed to a lower standard of living, with a great army of unemployed, and less able to buy the produce of any farmer anywhere.

The War left its mark on land ownership. In the Napoleonic War there was no restriction on rents or prices, and landlord and farmer shared the benefits. A century later rents could not be greatly increased, and the limited additional returns were shared between laborer and farmer. The landlord got little; instead, he shouldered far greater tax burdens, was helpless in the face of rising prices and wages, and in many cases lost his heir in the War. It has been estimated that taxes and the cost of upkeep of his estate took 80 per cent of his rent receipts, and that his real income was diminished by half between 1914 and 1929. He became one of the "new poor" and might be forced to close his country house and even to sell his land.

Much land was bought by new-rich war profiteers. Much was bought by county councils for conversion into small holdings and allotments under a pre-war scheme which had sought to increase the number of small full-time or part-time cultivators and thus give the farm laborer an interest in a piece of land of his own. Tenants bought their farms to the extent of 3,000,000 acres by 1924. In 1921 there were 21,000 more landowners than in 1913, and over twice as much farm land was worked by its owners; but two acres out of three were still worked by tenants in 1927. Unfortunately many men paid boom-time prices for their land, and when the price of farm produce fell they had a millstone of interest or installments round their necks. Some succumbed, but some survived, and the country is today a little more the property of those who till it.

BIBLIOGRAPHY

See end of Chapter XX.

CHAPTER XIX

THE AGRICULTURAL DEVELOPMENT OF FRANCE AND GERMANY SINCE 1700

I—The Continental Countryside in the Eighteenth Century

Continental agriculture in 1700 was seen at its best in the advanced technique practised in Holland, Belgium, the hinterland of Paris, the Rhine Valley, Provence, and north Italy. These areas had long ago evolved, under the stimulus of urban demand, such features as water control and irrigation, elaborate rotations free from fallow, careful methods of tending livestock, lavish use of manure, and large expenditure of labor in tillage of vineyards or gardens. Foreign markets were served by some producers, such as the sheep ranchers of Spain, the vignerons of France, and the grain-growers of the southeast Baltic lands and Sicily. The feeding of armies necessitated the collection and transportation of much foodstuffs, and the Dutch moved grain, cattle, and dairy produce from country to country in the course of their shipping activities.

Outside these commercial farming regions production was chiefly for direct consumption and used methods and equipment that had changed little during the centuries. There had been attacks on forest and waste, consolidation and inclosure; but open fields, common pastures, and waste lands made up the landscape in places from northeastern France to Russia. In southern Sweden a score of farmers might occupy five to six thousand strips, some of them so narrow that one could not turn a vehicle on them without trespassing. In Spain a farmer might have 16 acres in 80 to 120 plots scattered within a radius of three miles, while some of a Russian peasant's strips might be from three to ten miles from his home. Two- or three-field rotation, village control of the farmer's calendar, lack of fertilizer and fodder, and *vaine pâture* were found wherever open fields prevailed. Young saw French farmers threshing their wheat by driving horses or mules over sheaves piled on the ground and by throw-

445

ing the trodden grain into the air to separate the wheat from the chaff. In the early twentieth century wood plows were in widespread use in Russia, while in Bosnia harrows were made of branches tied together, and weighted with stones or by sitting a child on them.

Of the peasant's status we may risk the generalization that it became more servile as one moved eastward or southeastward. In France possibly half the soil was tilled by *censiers*, customary hereditary tenants. They virtually owned their holdings, since they could bequeath or sell them, but must pay certain dues and discharge obligations to seigneur, church, and crown. They paid an annual *cens*, fixed long ago and now a mere mite in terms of purchasing power; they made other periodical or special payments, they must still use the *banalités*, the church claimed tithes, and the state claimed *taille* and *corvée*. The rest of France was in the hands of nobility, church, crown and bourgeoisie. They rarely cultivated it, but used some of it for hunting or pleasure parks, and leased the remainder to tenant farmers, *métayers,* or *censiers* who needed additional land. The tenant farmers often had large expanses; but the *métayer's* holding was usually small, the landlord often took half the produce, and the cultivator's share was scarcely enough for his sustenance. In this respect he resembled many other French country dwellers, for the great majority of them had not enough land, and many of them had none at all. When, in the eighteenth century, population began to grow rapidly land hunger became acute.

In the Low Countries servile tenures were dissolved early by the commercialization of agriculture and the demands of industry, commerce, and transportation for labor. In Denmark seventeenth-century landlords withdrew the domain arable strips from the open fields and consolidated them for more efficient production of grain and cattle for export; but when some of them tried also to absorb tenant holdings they were stopped by royal veto (in 1682, 1725, and 1769). In 1702 the liberation of the serf began, but so many peasants left the countryside that bondage had to be restored and was not swept away till enthusiasm for liberation became widespread in Europe in the seventeen-eighties. In Sweden feudalism never became intrenched. In southwestern Germany, the whole social structure was shaken during the

Thirty Years' War, for some areas lost over half their population. When peace came the nobility tried to regain their old power, and though they did not quite succeed, the peasants were more heavily laden with liabilities than in France. Many commuted labor for goods or money and their condition was similar to that of the *censier* or copyholder; but others had heavy obligations without security of tenure, *corvée* might still be onerous, while the tithe and other claims on produce caused much bitterness.

If the peasant in Bavaria or Württemburg was less free than his French counterpart, he was vastly better off than his fellow east of the Elbe. There the rising grain prices of the sixteenth century and the expansion of Baltic trade by the Dutch tempted landlords into wheat or rye production on a large scale. They increased the size of their domain farms by reclaiming more waste and by reducing the size or number of tenant holdings. They claimed more of the peasant's time, pushed him into hereditary subjection, and forbade him to leave the village. The eastern estates thus became latifundia fringed with sufficient servile holdings to provide labor and teams of draft animals. The work of the landholding serfs was supplemented by that of landless laborers, and by domestic workers bound to the landlord's house. The Thirty Years' War threw much peasant land into the domain, and the nobility of Poland, Pomerania, and Silesia exercised sufficient political power to enforce their wishes on their subjects; but in Prussia the royal power was used for financial and military reasons to protect the peasant, and to restrain the Junker (large landlord) from the exercise of omnipotence.

In the Hapsburg lands, Hungary, and the Balkans conditions varied. When Bohemia fell before the Hapsburg attack in 1620, much of the conquered land was distributed among the invading leaders, and the landlord was thus alien as well as feudal. In Austria some landlords pursued a liberal policy, while others kept their grip tight and demanded heavy "robot" (labor dues). In Hungary the nobility took the land freed from the Turks and used serfs to tend cattle or grow grain on vast ranches or farms. In Roumania every step in the eviction of the Turk was followed by an increase in the property of nobility and church.

The early modern movement toward serfdom went furthest in Russia. During "the time of trouble" (1580-1620) a series of decrees had bound the peasant to the soil, and subjected him to the supervision of some feudal lord. The lord in turn would serve the state by rendering military service, by dispensing justice, collecting taxes, and keeping the cultivators busy and orderly. The peasants must work on his fields, and in return received enough land for their own sustenance. As population grew, periodical redistribution of land insured that all had holdings. During the seventeenth and eighteenth centuries the landlord strengthened his hold on the peasants, but relieved himself (or was relieved) of his obligation to render military and other services to the state. Meanwhile some opportunities for commercial farming, for developing industries, and for tapping mineral deposits had presented themselves, and the large landowner sometimes became a capitalistic entrepreneur, calling on his bondsmen to provide the necessary labor for land, workshop, mine, or house.

European agrarian society thus showed almost every variety of structure, from the French and southwest German type, in which the landlord was a passive receiver of rents and other dues, to the eastern type, in which great demands for labor were made in order to cultivate a large domain for the sustenance of the lord or for market. Whatever the type, the structure was liable to be strained in any one of a number of ways: (1) If the peasant came to detest the obligations he had to render to lord, state, and church, or to resent attempts to increase them. (2) If the peasant became land-hungry and turned his eyes covetously on the great estates. (3) If landlords wished to enhance their income by increasing dues, by putting the commons and wastes to better use, by adopting new methods, by changing from *corvée* to wage labor, by redrawing the village map, or by getting land back into their hands in order to extend commercial farming on the basis of a latifundium or of large tenant farms. (4) If the state decided that agricultural improvement or agrarian reform was necessary. (5) If expanding markets, improved transportation, or large price movements set new forces to work on the old order. These strains, especially when combined, involved a possible conflict of interest between peasant and landlord. The outcome of that conflict might be decided by economics, but in almost every country politics, war, or revolution played a decisive part.

II—The Growth of Interest in Rural Improvement

After 1750 the continent developed an interest in agricultural and agrarian change. In Prussia Frederick the Great did his utmost to encourage and revive agriculture after the ravages of the Seven Years' War. He gave lands to ex-soldiers, drained swamps, dredged rivers, made roads, imported sheep, and welcomed rural immigrants. He even toyed with the idea of emancipating the serfs, and limited the claims that could be made on them. In Austria Joseph II freed the serfs on his own estates, leased land to them at low rents, and allowed *corvée* to be commuted. He limited the "robot" on private estates to two or three days a week, abolished personal serfdom (1781), and tried to shift taxation from the shoulders of the poor to those of the rich. In Russia Catherine and Alexander I showed little concern for agrarian reform but much for agricultural. Foreigners were invited as traders or farmers, land and money were offered them, and many Englishmen settled in the Crimea to grow grain, breed cattle, erect lumber mills, and develop mines. The Russian embassy in London was frequently asked to get answers to farming questions, and Young's son spent nine years in Russia making agricultural surveys.

This royal interest in rural affairs was shared by many great landlords. Some of it was native-born, but much of it was imported from England, and suffered from the sea passage. Some of it was dilettante, a glorification of the simple life, a new game of playing milkmaid; but in places it went deeper. French, Prussian, and Russian landlords formed societies to study English ideas and methods. Russia had a Free Economic Society which published translations of Young and Davy, while Smith's *Wealth of Nations* was translated by order of the minister of finance. In France Tull's book inspired Duhamel du Monceau to make experiments which he recorded in six volumes (1751-1760). Voltaire, the Physiocrats, and others quoted English examples and precedents. Agricultural societies and schools were founded, landlords experimented with crops and cattle, and scientists like Linnæus in Sweden or Parmentier in France tried to give reasoned answers to such questions as, "Is the potato a desirable food?" In Germany a doctor, Albrecht Thaer (1752-1828), published in 1791 the results of his experiments in a volume which showed the value of growing fodder crops, of feeding them to animals in stalls, and of using the animal manure to nourish the fields on which the fodder was grown. Thaer then began to expound the virtues of English agriculture, founded a school, taught in the University of Berlin, and poured out books which earned him a bronze statue in Berlin and a name as the Arthur Young of Germany.

In society meetings, salons, and books the virtues of rotations without fallow, of fodder cultivation, of inclosure and large farms seemed shiny and attractive. But how could they be transplanted to continental soil? The answer differed from country to country, and is perhaps best given by examining the agricultural development of the leading countries.

III—FRANCE

To the French wide-awake landlord two courses were open. (1) He might collect all dues to which he was entitled, raise those which were not fixed, and revive claims that had lapsed. (2) He might try to dissolve the village community, inclose, abolish the *servitudes collectives* (the common grazing rights), and build up a domain or carve out a number of large farms. He did both. He had been trying to do the latter in some places since the sixteenth century, and in Normandy and Provence had partly succeeded; but elsewhere the opposition of the peasants or of the local intendant had been too strong. After 1750 the state swung over from opposition to encouragement. High officials in the capital and intendants in the provinces had become converted to the new husbandry, to some of the pleas of the Physiocrats, and to an admission that the perennial fear of famine could be mitigated only by increased production and freer trade in foodstuffs. Between 1760 and 1780 decrees were issued authorizing the abolition of *vaine pâture*, allowing inclosures, permitting the partition of commons, and encouraging the attack on wastes by exempting improved land from taxation for a decade. In years of good harvest freedom was granted to export grain.

These attempts to increase income and efficiency succeeded chiefly in causing irritation and indignation among the peasants. The king had deserted his people and gone over to their enemies —the bigger farmers, the bourgeois landowners, and the aristocracy. He was taking more from them in taxes, and encouraging his new friends to take more from them in dues. The burdens of the seigneurial régime, "always troublesome and too often oppressive" (Sée), became more hated as they were increased. Apart from generating this bad temper, not much was accomplished. Lack of capital prevented some landlords from inclosing, the *censiers* were hard to move, while the small cultivators and laborers opposed bitterly any steps which reduced the pasturage available for their livestock. By 1789 the country had done little to improve its farm output, was still subject to famines (e.g., in 1785 and 1788), was facing overpopulation, and was housing a rural class that saw its lords as potential plunderers of peasant rights.

When the Revolution began, the peasants asked for three things: (1) a check on the landlord's encroachments, the "feudal reaction" of the last forty years, and the limitation or reduction of his claims; (2) more land, to be obtained from the crown and church estates; (3) a ban on inclosures, and the restoration of ancient pasturage rights. Attacks on *châteaux* and the burning of records containing details of peasant obligations moved the National Assembly in August, 1789, to grant the first demand, destroy the feudal régime, abolish personal serfdom, deprive the lord of his hunting and game privileges, and strip him of judicial power. Tithes were to be abolished (subject to compensation), while *cens* and other dues were to be redeemed by a payment from peasant to lord. In the dark days of invasion and internal strife of 1793 the peasant was excused from this unpopular payment in order to win his active loyalty. He thus emerged free of all the old obligations, a proprietor in fee simple.

The second demand was not so satisfactorily met. When, early in the Revolution, the church lands, along with those of the crown and the *émigrés,* passed into the hands of the state, the government put them up for auction in order to get income. The largest buyers were the men with plenty of money—the middle class, landlords who wished to add to their estates, speculators, large farmers, and prosperous peasants. The nobles and rich bourgeoisie who did not emigrate retained their property; many *émigrés* bought back their own estates by getting friends or agents to bid for them at the auction sale; and at least half the church lands were never sold. Petty proprietors did, however, get some land. Sometimes they pooled their money to make a purchase, or a larger buyer divided and resold land; but there was no spectacular transfer to the peasantry and no clean sweep of the large estates.

The third demand, for protection of common rights and restitution of *servitudes collectives*, was coolly received, for the Assemblies were bourgeois, believed in individual liberty, regarded the old order as barbarous, and said fallow was to agriculture what tyrants were to liberty. In 1791 they gave proprietors the right to vary the methods of exploiting their lands, authorized inclosure in all parts of the country, but imposed conditions to insure fair treatment of all claimants. They limited pasture rights by decreeing that meadows should not become *vaine pâture* until the second growth of hay had been cut. These powers were exercised very slowly. Conservatism, lack of capital, and the absence of any such autocrat as an English landlord or inclosure commissioner prevented the French inclosure movement from proceeding at more than a snail's pace until railroads and growing markets gave cultivators an incentive to change their methods and increase their output. That incentive was not felt till the second or even the third quarter of the nineteenth century. In 1889 the legislature voted to suppress *vaine pâture* on meadows, but was forced to reverse its decision a year later. Even today a peasant's holding may still consist of fragments scattered over the landscape, for the consolidation of land into compact blocks is far from completed.

The Revolution abolished entail and primogeniture, and made general the already widespread practice of dividing property equally among all the children. The *Code Napoléon* modified the rule a little: if there was only one child the father could bequeath half his property as he wished; if there were two children he could dispose of one-third, and if there were three or more the fraction was a quarter. The rest must be equally divided.

The outcome of the French upheaval was thus a modification rather than a fundamental transformation of rural society. The *censier* escaped from all his liabilities to lord and landlord, yet kept all his holding. Some land passed out of the hands of the crown, church, and nobility, but only part of it went to small cultivators or landless laborers. The inheritance laws strengthened the trend toward subdivision of holdings, but the freedom of the individual proprietor to use his property as he wished was not accompanied by any strong stimulus to use that freedom. During the next century ownership gained ground over tenancy, and in 1914 two-thirds of the soil, comprising four-fifths of the holdings, was tilled by its owners. Tenants and *métayers* held the remaining third, but *métayage* was declining. Some tenants held large farms comparable to those in England, but the preponderance of small holdings in 1908 is revealed by the following table. In that year France had about 5,500,000 farm units, about as many as had the United States.

Size of Holding	Number of Holdings	Percentage of Total Number	Percentage of Total Area
Less than 2.5 acres...........	2,088,000	38	} 25.6
2.5 to 25 acres...............	2,524,000	46	
25 to 100 acres..............	746,000	13.5	29.6
100 to 250 acres.............	118,000	2	} 44.8
Above 250 acres.............	30,000	.5	

The smallness of over four-fifths of the holdings was a result of the things grown, of the system of inheritance, and of a scarcity of hired laborers. An area of three or four acres was not small if it was used as vineyard or vegetable garden, while a holding that was statistically large might not be really large if used as pasture or grain field. Division of property among all heirs tended to subdivide holdings every generation; and if families were large the share of each heir would eventually become too small, even if supplemented by the *dot* of his wife, to provide a living. Birth control has checked this development since about 1870, and the French population has virtually stood still for six decades.

Agricultural Progress.—Professor Hauser enumerates the characteristics of the French peasant as slowness, love of routine, individualism, obstinacy, avidity for work, passion for acquiring land, and a spirit of economy and resistance. A fellow countryman (Bloch) says the French peasant's tenacious conservatism is the fruit of long resistance to new ideas and attacks. From such men, short of capital and eager to put their savings into a hoard or a new piece of land, no enthusiasm for new equipment or methods could be expected. Tools and methods changed little, and in 1852 a Frenchman could write, "a thirteenth-century peasant would visit many of our farms without much astonishment" (Delisle). Crops were uneven and famine was rarely out of sight.

After 1850 movement was more perceptible. The railroad came, and "five years of a railroad in France produced more tangible results than fifty years of emancipation" (Clapham). Rural and urban areas were brought into closer contact, rural credit facilities improved, and industrial towns expanded. Farm implements and steam engines were made or imported, 27,000,000 acres of waste land were reclaimed between 1840 and 1890, inclosures

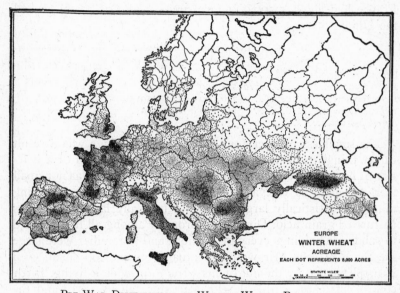

EUROPE
WINTER WHEAT
ACREAGE
EACH DOT REPRESENTS 5,000 ACRES

STATUTE MILES

PRE-WAR DISTRIBUTION OF WINTER WHEAT PRODUCTION

Europe grows about half the world's wheat. Russia produces much spring wheat in the region running from the Crimea up to the lower Volga. (U. S. Department of Agriculture.)

multiplied, and fallows disappeared. Chemical fertilizers freed the farmer from dependence on his dung heap and broke the old relationship between *blé et bête* (grain and beast). The wheat acreage rose 35 per cent, the yield per acre 14 per cent, and the output 47 per cent between the 'thirties and the 'seventies. Wheat became the staple food in place of rye and buckwheat, and the country was able to supply all its needs.

The wheat fields of the New World and the new low prices hit France as they hit England; but there were more votes in the French rural ballot boxes, industry did not tower above agriculture, and the industrialists were not free traders. The tariff was therefore raised on manufactured and farm products alike. From a nominal rate of 60 centimes a quintal on wheat (about 3 cents a bushel) it rose to 7 francs (36 cents). This substantial protection did not prevent French wheat prices from falling, but their descent was only about 28 per cent, against a British fall of 50 per cent. The French farmer let some land go to grass, but improved the cultivation of the better soils, and thus raised total production 20 per cent and the yield per acre 23 per cent in thirty years. His yield per acre (19.4 bushels) was nearly twice that of a century before, but only half that garnered by the high farmers of Belgium or Denmark. He lagged behind his neighbors, tilled far less intensively, used less fertilizer, and had little modern equipment. He got less out because he put less in. But in 1912 he grew over 300,000,000 bushels of wheat, or nearly half as much as did the United States; he ranked second to Russia as European grain-grower, and had once more made his country virtually self-sufficing.

France was a land of wine as well as of bread, and for every five acres growing wheat two were under vines in 1870. Of 86 *départements*, only nineteen had a few or no vines, and in 1910 1,500,000 vignerons supplied grapes for about 1,200,000,000 gallons of wine—30 gallons per head of the population. In the list of exports wine came second to textiles. Production was damaged by pests twice during the century. In the 'fifties a fungus called oïdium attacked large areas and reduced the vintage by two-thirds in five years. A sulphur spray brought salvation; but the phylloxera, a green fly which ravaged the vineyards in the 'sixties and 'seventies, was not so easily conquered. Between 1875 and 1879 two-thirds of the vines were partly or wholly ruined, and the output of wine fell from 84,000,000 to 26,000,000 hectoliters. Eventually roots which resisted phylloxera were imported from America, and French vines were grafted on them. By 1900 the pest was eradicated, and production rose toward its old volume. Unfortunately demand had adjusted itself to the shrunken supply, and when the wine began to flow in abundance once more it could not be sold except at ruinously low prices. The French had turned to other kinds of drink; Italy, Russia, and the United States had increased their tariffs; new areas were producing wine, and people who seemed (in French eyes) mad were crusading against alcohol. The only way to meet such a situation was to reduce production. This was done during the prewar years, with good results on prices; but after 1918 shrunken demand from prohibition America and poverty-stricken Europe damaged the market once more, and the task of readjustment has not yet been completed.

Among other French rural products, potatoes, sugar beets, silk, wool, meats, dairy produce, and vegetables are important. The

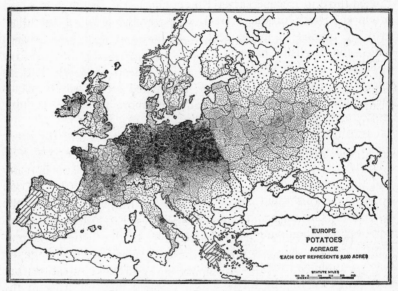

DISTRIBUTION OF POTATO PRODUCTION

Nine-tenths of the world's potato crop is grown in Europe, and half of it in Germany and Russia. (U. S. Department of Agriculture.)

potato passed from the garden into the field after about 1800. It had to struggle hard against popular dislike before it became accepted as human food, but once this was done it climbed to second place (next to the grains) as a food crop for northern Europe. The yield per acre eventually became four to six times that of wheat. Cultivation had to be continuous and intensive, and could be carried on by a peasantry accustomed to using much labor on little land. The potato was at home on the cool, sandy European plain, and was used as food for man, pigs, and cows, or for the production of alcohol. Hence a traveler entering the continent anywhere between Cherbourg and Hamburg and journeying to the Urals would find it hard to get away from the sight of a potato patch.

If the traveler failed to see potato tops he would probably be looking at beet tops, for the long plain became the home of the sugar beet during the nineteenth century. (See Part IV.) In silk production France never became more than a poor second to Italy, but her wool production benefited greatly by the introduction of merinos from Spain after 1760, and by 1900 she ranked third in Europe (after Russia and Great Britain) as wool producer. Dairy produce, fruit, eggs, and vegetables found a growing market in urban centers at home as well as in those across the English Channel.

Effects of the World War.—The World War hit French agriculture hard. About 7,000,000 acres were in the battle zone, and about one-third of them suffered severely. Of 8,500,000 land workers, about 5,000,000 went into the army; supplies of chemical fertilizer could not be obtained from Germany, and the area under cultivation fell heavily. Recovery was, however, very rapid. The devastated areas were reequipped and restored to fertility, and the physical volume of production was back by 1925 to its 1913 level. This rapid convalescence did not conceal disquieting tendencies. Out of war the country came stricken in manpower, for over a million rural workers had been killed or incapacitated; out of victory came a new impetus to industrialization; but there was no stimulus to a rising birth rate. Town and country therefore competed for the shrunken labor supply, and the town won. Between 1921 and 1926 nearly one-tenth of the agricultural workers left the farm, and the rural population declined from 22,100,000 in 1911 to 20,800,000 in 1926. The laborer's place was taken in part by Italians, Poles, Spaniards, or Belgians, and by 1929 one in every twenty of the "active rural population" was a foreigner. Scarcity of labor led to the conversion of some arable lands to pasture, to the subdivision and sale of large farms, and to further use of machinery. But on the smaller farms, especially those which consisted of scattered patches, the use of machinery was impossible and the cost too great. Meanwhile some peasant products were facing market difficulties; silk was meeting the competition of rayon, foreign wine drinkers had reduced their purchases, while sugar and wheat were headed for the price collapse at the end of the decade.

When that collapse came the state rushed to the aid of the farmer. Between 1924 and 1931 the tariff on wheat was raised six times, and in 1929 the quantity of imports was restricted. Most other farm products were similarly protected by higher tariffs or by fixing quota limits to imports. These steps sheltered the farmer against the full force of competition and ruinous prices. In July, 1931, wheat sold in free-trade England at 3/2 (76 cents) a bushel, but in France its price was 8/3 ($2.00). Behind this barrier farmers expanded production to take the place of imports, and eventually produced a surplus (1932-1934) which made them want to export grain into a glutted world market while depriving the native consumer of the benefits of cheap food. The French peasant has become a distorted Physiocrat; he wants free trade for exports, but he still has to be converted to some of the principles of high farming for which the Physiocrats stood.

IV—Germany

The End of Serfdom.—Some Germans gave heed to the ideas that were finding voice in England and France during the eighteenth century. They talked of *laissez faire*, said serfdom should be abolished, and repeated the slogans of high farming. Little happened, however, until a strong wind blew from the west, bringing the French occupation of western Germany and the later crushing defeat of the Prussians at Jena (1806). In the occupied areas the French abolished serfdom and introduced equal inheritance; but they did not blot out the landlord's claims, and when they left in 1814 the foundations of the old régime, with its manifold seigneurial money dues, was virtually intact. During the next thirty years peasants sought to end their obligations to their lords, and some governments helped them, but with little result until 1848.

The revolutions of that year were started by city workers and middle-class Liberals, but the peasants joined them, for the double collapse of credit and of the potato crop in the preceding years had made them desperate. Rulers quickly saw that if they granted what the rustics demanded the revolution would be fatally split, and hurriedly took steps to reform the land system. The peasant was to become completely free of his lord and keep his holding, paying in return a sum of money in installments. Unfortunately cholera, war, and ruined harvests made conditions bad between 1848 and 1853. Thousands of peasants, unable to pay their installments, surrendered or sold their holdings and joined the stream of German emigrants pouring across the Atlantic. Others survived, and when the painful transition ended, they emerged owners of their land, making southwestern Germany one of the peasant proprietor strongholds of Europe.

In Prussia defeat by Napoleon convinced many that a drastic reorganization of social and economic conditions was necessary, and led to the reforms of Stein and Hardenberg. Stein's library was rich in English authors, and he apparently read through Smith's *Wealth of Nations* at least two or three times. The plea made there for freedom was strengthened by the belief that France's invincible driving power came from a liberated peasantry. It gained further cogency from the declaration of Thaer and others that two free laborers did as much work as three unfree men. The Edict of Emancipation (1807) destroyed the peculiar caste system which forbade noble, burgher, or peasant to undertake tasks that belonged to the other two classes. Personal serfdom was to go: "From Martinmas, 1810, there shall be only free persons." Restrictions forbidding nobles to sell land to peasants or townsmen were abolished, and entail could be broken by a family resolution. When Stein was dismissed, Hardenberg carried on his work. By a decree of 1811 peasants with hereditary tenures—the Prussian equivalents of the *censier* or copyholder—were to surrender a third of their holding as the price for freedom and for receiving the other two-thirds. Those who held land on non-hereditary tenure were to surrender half.

These measures were far from popular among the Junkers, who had visions of losing the feudal services of their tenants and of seeing their domestic and landless ex-serfs drift away. By amendment, interpretation, and administration they succeeded in averting some developments unpleasant to themselves. The end of a complicated story was that only the larger hereditary peasants held much land after parting with a third, that medium and small holdings passed into the landlord's hands, and that domestics, landless laborers and small holders were little freer than before. If reform freed the serf from the soil it freed much soil from the serf, and the price paid in land and money for emancipation "left great masses of peasants either landless or with so little land as to leave them only the choice between labouring on the estates and more substantial peasant holdings or seeking the industrial labour market of the towns" (Brinkmann).

The transfer of freedom to the peasant and of land to the Junker was a doubtful boon to each party. The landlord had to find wage laborers and money with which to pay them; he had to reorganize and finance the larger holding now in his hands, and he was already loaded with debts incurred to provide capital. The collapse of prices after 1815, the glutting of grain markets, and the closing of the English market by the Corn Laws condemned him to a painful period of post-war difficulties, and during the 'twenties many of the old landed families had to part with much of their estates. By 1830 it is estimated that four-fifths of them had lost all or part. Thus a slice of Junkerdom went into the hands of a new race of owners, and "the mouldering race of the Prussian gentry" was in some degree replaced by "a new and more vigorous one."

These developments in east and west were not rapid. They were almost finished by 1871, but some Saxon peasants did not make the final redemption payments till 1907. Their chief result was to make Germany "a country of free landowning peasants and powerful cultivating squires" (Clapham). In 1907, 93 per cent of the farms, covering 82 per cent of the agricultural area, were owned by their cultivators. Of the two main types, the peasant predominated west of the Elbe, the Junker east of it, as the following table shows:

| | Area of Cultivated Land in Million Hectares | Percentage of Area in Holdings | | | |
		Up to 12½ ac.	12½–50 ac.	50–250 ac.	Over 250 ac.
East of Elbe.....	13.9	8.5	22.7	28.5	40.3
West of Elbe....	17.9	22	40	30	8
All Germany....	31.8	15.8	32.7	29.3	22.2

West of the Elbe 62 per cent of the area was in holdings of not more than 50 acres, and 40 per cent in those units of 12½ to 50 acres that could be regarded as big enough to yield a family income. Such units covered a third of the cultivated area of the whole country; they grew in number as the nineteenth century drew to its close, and in 1907 over a million of them occupied more than 25,000,000 acres.

The last column tells most vividly the contrast between east and west. Emancipation, the retention of judicial power, and the nature of soil or product played into the old or new Junker's hands. Between 1815 and 1850, 100,000 small holdings containing 1,-200,000 acres were swallowed up, and fractions were taken from the larger peasants. From this period of absorption the landlords emerged with the best lands, and a Prussian survey of 1925 showed that the large farms were on the better soil while the

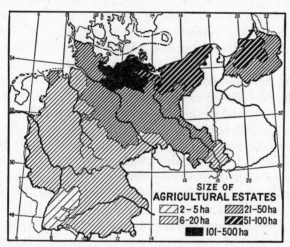

(From Bowman's *The New World*. Copyright, 1928, by World Book Company, Yonkers-on-Hudson, New York.)

peasants occupied the poorer patches. The enlarged estates were managed by their owners, with local hired (or rather bound) labor. After 1850 the bonds were weakened, and after 1870 the lure of the New World or of the new industrial German west pulled laborers away in such large numbers as to create a serious problem. To meet it the landlords encouraged the immigration of workers from Poland and Russia. Some came for the season, even just for the harvest, but some stayed. In 1912 over 500,000 foreigners were engaged on German soil.

Inclosure and the consolidation of scattered holdings moved as slowly in Germany as in France. After 1775 there was some division of commons in southwest Germany, Prussia provided in

1821 for the division of village lands into individual properties, and the Junkers consolidated their old or new lands. With the coming of the railroads and the expansion of the home market, progress was more rapid; and between 1870 and 1911 nearly 50,000,000 acres, owned by 2,500,000 persons, were consolidated in Prussia alone. Yet in 1908 nearly half the total area of farm and forest in Prussia was still unchanged. After the War the work was attacked energetically. An order of 1920 provided for the consolidation of parcels of land if they were dispersed or were uneconomic in size or shape. By 1929, 8,000,000 acres had been rearranged, but over 6,000,000 remained. The results suggested that production costs had been reduced by a quarter while output had increased by a third.

Agricultural Development.—During the first half of the nineteenth century the stimuli to agricultural expansion were external rather than domestic. The high prices of the Napoleonic War years had stirred eastern landowners to extend their fields, to reclaim and deforest, and to borrow money for improvements. After the painful period of deflation had ended, the British demand for wool and wheat expanded, the home market began to grow more rapidly after about 1840, and German agriculture became a bow with three strong strings—grain, wool, and sugar.

Of the three, wool and sugar were new. While America met the growing demand for cotton, the rising demand for wool was met by a great increase and improvement of flocks in Europe and then by a spread of sheep-grazing in the antipodes. Improvement was largely the result of the dispersion of Spanish merinos during the last third of the eighteenth century. Monarchs interested in agricultural advance obtained sheep, by gift or purchase, from the Spanish court. In Hungary the royal farm got 300 head in 1775; in Russia the emperor lent $75,000 for obtaining a supply (1802). In France the Rambouillet merino, bred on the farm of Louis XVI, revolutionized French flocks. In Germany the Elector of Saxony imported and popularized the breed, and soon Saxon wool was so much better than that of Spain that Spanish breeders imported Saxon rams. Pomerania, Hanover, Mecklenburg, and Silesia followed Saxony's lead; Junkers built up large flocks (e.g., one of 12,000); governments and banks financed and controlled production and sale, while wool fairs were held at Stettin, Breslau, Berlin, Prague, and elsewhere. After 1815 expansion was rapid. In Prussia the flocks grew from 8,000,000 in 1816 to 17,000,000 in 1837, and the number of merinos from 700,000 to 3,600,000. Buyers from all parts of Europe and North America attended the wool fairs or bought privately on the farms. Wool exports to Great Britain jumped from 5,000,000 pounds in 1820, to 32,000,000 in 1836. Germany ousted Spain from its position as the world's leading producer of fine wool, and held that place until dethroned by Australia after 1850.

In 1747 a German chemist discovered sugar in beets. In 1797 a Silesian, Achard, who had been wrestling with the double problem of increasing the sugar content and of extracting it more cheaply, set up a sugar factory and published a book. Little notice was taken of him, despite Napoleon's enthusiasm for a root that would allow France to do without the sugar it could not get from the West Indies. After 1815 production grew more rapidly. Junkers and smaller farmers assiduously cultivated the new crop, plowing, drilling, hoeing, using fertilizer freely, and including beet in a three- or four-years' rotation. In 1848, 250,000 tons of beet were grown, but in 1910 the yield was nearly 16,-000,000 tons, taken from 1,200,000 acres, or 13 tons to the acre. Meanwhile the sugar content was raised (from 7 per cent in 1800), and today it may be 24 per cent, while improved factory methods extracted a greater part of it from the root. Hence, whereas a ton of sugar was drawn from 20 tons of beet in 1848, it was obtained from only 6¼ tons in 1920. The pulp made an excellent food for livestock, as did the tops of the plant.

Germany led in beet production, and in 1914 grew a third of the world's crop. Russia and Austria-Hungary were rivals for second place, while the fourth area stretched from Paris to Holland. As the price of sugar fell the masses were able to develop a sweet tooth, and a luxury became a necessity. Since the same product could be obtained from the temperate zone and from the tropics, European producers competed with the West Indian cane growers, and each beet area fought the others. In that competition the beet farmers clamored for state aid, and the fingers of continental statesmen became sticky. Each country raised high tariffs against foreign supplies, but gave a bounty on its own exports, thus presenting non-producing countries like Great Britain and Italy with cheap sugar while its own people paid high prices. Eventually the folly of this international philanthropy led to the Brussels Sugar Convention of 1902, by which exporters abolished bounties and importers promised to ban imports from countries which refused to toe the line. Producers benefited, but consumers lost cheap imports, and in 1912 Rome and London decided to withdraw from the pact.

The War closed markets, reduced beet production, and stimulated a great expansion in sugar-cane planting, especially in Cuba

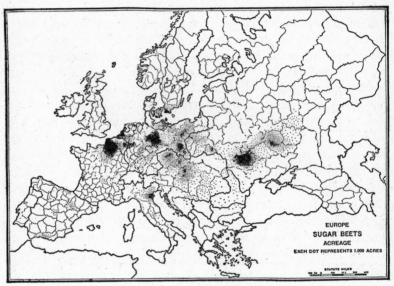

EUROPE
SUGAR BEETS
ACREAGE
EACH DOT REPRESENTS 1,000 ACRES

SUGAR BEET PRODUCTION
(U. S. Department of Agriculture.)

and Java. When the beet fields were restored, and when new production was encouraged by tariff in the United States or by bounty and tariff in Great Britain, overproduction ensued, stocks accumulated, and in the crash of 1929 sugar prices fell 30 per cent. In 1931 an international agreement was reached by the harassed producers, by which the output of sugar was to be limited or reduced, and the accumulated stocks were gradually to be fed into the market.

While feeding foreign consumers with grain, wool, and sugar, Germany had a home market which grew from 25,000,000 consumers in 1815 to 40,000,000 in 1870 (i.e., 64 per cent in fifty-five years). By 1870 the *Zollverein,* railroads, and improved waterways had knit the country together, reduced local self-sufficiency, and given farming a more commercial tinge. After 1870 industrial expansion and foreign agricultural competition became much more powerful influences on the German farm. The first offered growing markets as the towns expanded and as the

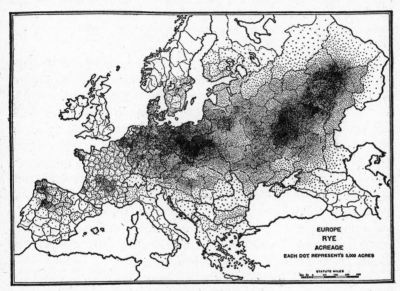

RYE PRODUCTION

Rye will grow on poor soil, and Europe produces 95 per cent of the world's crop. (U. S. Department of Agriculture.)

population grew even more rapidly than before 1870; but it drew labor from the countryside, raised rural wages, attracted peasants' children, and thus reduced the supply of unpaid labor on which family farming so largely depends.

Foreign Competition.—The second factor, foreign competition, struck chiefly from the east. Since two-thirds of the German population ate rye bread, the worst enemy was Russian rye, and the volume entering Germany jumped rapidly in the late 'seventies. It was followed by Russian, American, Hungarian, and Roumanian wheat. Junker and peasant alike saw their market invaded, the price of their produce falling, and the burden of their costs becoming heavier. They called for protection, and as the manufacturers were also seeking it for factory goods, it was granted. In 1879 a small duty of 10 marks a ton (6½ cents a bushel) was levied on wheat and rye. The rate was trebled in 1885, and by 1906 was 55 marks (36 cents a bushel). Agrarian policy sought to retain and strengthen the peasantry, protect the Junkers, and keep the country as near self-sufficiency in foodstuffs as possible. It did not prevent some fall in prices, for the Berlin price of wheat was higher than the London price only by the amount of the duty; but the fall was only 20 per cent on wheat and 12 per cent on rye.

The rural producer was spared the full impact of the agricultural invasion, and if urban consumers complained that they were paying the price in dearer food they were told that "it is a question of life and death for the whole country to help our agriculture against the impact of an international competition which is certain ultimately to pass away" (Schmoller, 1904). While prices were falling (up to 1896) and while industry needed its own protection, rural and urban interests might feel they were sharing in the benefits of national policy. When prices began to rise, and when it became increasingly evident that German agriculture could not supply all the nation's needs, town and country pulled apart. The town demanded free trade in foodstuffs, the country sought the removal of tariffs on manufactures.

On the eve of the War Germany was supplying about two-thirds of its wheat needs, all its rye, half its barley, and a third of its oats. It had not relaxed its grip on any form of rural production as Britain and some other countries had done. Behind the tariff wall a vigorous effort to attain efficiency had been made both on big and little farms. In 1870 the yield per acre was far below that of England. This was a measure of the poor quality of much German soil, of the uneconomic distribution of land, and of backward methods. During the next forty years the output per acre of rye and potatoes nearly doubled, and that of wheat, oats, and barley rose three-fourths, thus establishing records which bracketed Germany and Great Britain in fourth place after Belgium, Holland, and Denmark. Meanwhile the area under crop expanded steadily as drains and fertilizers brought sand, bogs, and heaths into cultivation. The growth of fodder crops (including the potato) received serious attention, and the number of cattle grew 28 per cent between 1873 and 1912, while that of pigs trebled. But in Germany, as elsewhere in Europe, the sheep lost favor. The number of sheep fell from 25,000,000 to less than 6,000,000, while the number of pigs rose from 7,000,000 to 22,000,000. The bleat of the sheep gave place to the grunt of the hog.

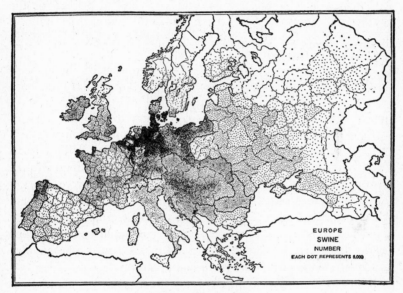

SWINE PRODUCTION
(U. S. Department of Agriculture.)

This great advance in productive efficiency was largely due to cooperation, science, and education. In certain forms of cooperation, especially cooperative credit, Germany pioneered (see Chapter XX). Formal agricultural education had little direct influence on the peasants, for the high schools and the institutes attached to universities were attended almost solely by sons of Junkers or by youths who wished to become teachers, technical experts, or managers of large estates. The peasant could not spare the time to go to school, and must learn his lessons informally from his cooperative society or from some neighboring larger farmer. But the beet taught him more than any school, for it demanded careful selection of seeds and systematic cultivation, and he could not escape the influence of at least one lesson in science.

Science was almost another name for chemical fertilizer, and for worship of the trinity of nitrogen, potassium, and phosphorus, the three great plant and animal foods. When the chemists had revealed that soils needed these ingredients, two questions arose: Where were they to be obtained in sufficient quantities, and how were they to be put into the soil? Answers were especially important to Germany because of the poor quality of much of its soil. Peru and Chile had rich deposits of guano, which contained all three chemicals, and these were raided by Europeans after 1840. Chile's deposits of nitrates (sodium nitrate), the only known supply in the world, were vigorously exploited after about 1880. In 1852 potassium salts were found in Stassfurt (at the eastern end of the Harz Mountains), and later in Alsace and other parts. Phosphoric deposits were found in various parts of the world and as an impurity in the iron ore of Lorraine. When, in 1878, a way was found by which these ores could be used for making steel, the German steel industry could advance rapidly and the phosphorus extracted from the ore could be turned into fertilizer. By that time ammonium sulphate (containing nitrogen) had become a by-product of the coke-oven and coal-gas plant. In the 'eighties agricultural researchers discovered that legumes (beans, peas, alfalfa, and clover) took nitrogen from the air, and that if they were plowed in as "green manure" the ground would be enriched.

From these varied sources German soil drew nourishment. Of potash deposits the country had virtually a world monopoly till she lost Alsace in 1919, and used over half of her output at home. She bought a third of Chile's nitrate exports in 1913, and supplemented it with the yield from her gas works. She tapped phosphate deposits on islands in the western Pacific to supplement the yield from her steel plants.

Effect of the World War.—War put the country to a severe test. The seas and Russian plains were cut off, and the supplies of food, raw materials, and fertilizer were thereby reduced. The withdrawal of man power and horse power hurt peasant cultivators. The soil could not be adequately dressed, and the manufacture of nitrates by taking nitrogen from the air had not developed enough to repair the damage. Productivity fell and livestock declined in number. By 1916 the pinch had become severe, rationing was instituted, substitute foods were invented, meatless days were decreed, and rations were reduced. Three decades of agrarian protection had kept the rural machine in a condition to deliver nearly, but not quite, enough goods.

Suffering did not end with the armistice. The loss of labor and of important food-producing areas, the demands for large deliveries of animals to restock French and Belgian farms, the conflict over reparations, the inflation and collapse of the currency—all conspired to send Germany through four or five years of misery. The Treaty of Versailles cut off nearly one-fifth of the rye lands, and from a sixth to a tenth of the wheat, barley, and oat fields. The potash and phosphoric fertilizers of Alsace-Lorraine were now in foreign territory, and could be imported only if there were exports with which to pay for them; but recovery of exports was hard. On the other hand, the collapse in the value of the mark wiped out a large part of the mortgage debts of landowners, there was no serious raid on the large estates to provide land for disbanded soldiers, and if Germany lost 12 to 15 per cent of her rural productive capacity she also lost about 12 per cent of her people. After 1923, therefore, as a measure of stability was restored, production began to revive.

In the general rebuilding of German economic life there was much talk about "rationalization," which meant, among other things, a careful reasoned planning of equipment and production. American books on "scientific management" were devoured (but not always digested) by a nation which had lost faith in itself and was looking outside for prescriptions for prosperity. For agriculture these prescriptions involved more use of machinery, implements, and power; more fertilizer, improved breeds and seeds; the study of marketing methods, and more careful keeping of farm accounts. The use of seeding or potato-planting machines, cultivators, steam plows, and tractors increased greatly; horse-driven threshers gave place to huge power-driven outfits, and electric motors were installed to drive apparatus on big and little farms alike.

Rationalization, like inclosure, cost money, and while inflation had blotted out old debts new ones must be incurred, though interest rates were at least twice those of pre-war years. By 1930 many farms, large and small, were mortgaged to the hilt or loaded with other forms of debt. When prices fell in 1929 this load became crushing, while the gap between the price of the goods the farmer bought and that of those he sold grew wider. Government efforts of every kind were made to check the fall in prices, to reduce foreign competition, and to relieve farmers of some of the debt load. Wheat and rye were protected by raising the tariff and then by fixing prices. Meat imports were limited, and the entry of margarine or its raw materials was impeded in order to encourage the consumption of butter. Debtors were helped by reducing mortgage rates from 8 to 6 per cent and then to 4½ per cent. In 1933 a new inheritance law said farm properties above a certain size could not be alienated or divided and could not be attached by creditors. This law protected the Junker, but not the small proprietor—an action with several precedents in German history.

BIBLIOGRAPHY

See end of Chapter XX.

CHAPTER XX

AGRICULTURAL DEVELOPMENTS IN THE REST OF EUROPE

General Characteristics.—Differences in soil, climate, markets, and historical setting make it difficult to tell in brief general terms the rural history of the rest of Europe. The student should consult some good geographical work if he wishes to know the present character of agriculture in the various European countries. Certain features are, however, sufficiently clear and general to be capable of description.

1. The growth of population was marked in agricultural as well as in industrial regions. Migration to towns and emigration to the New World absorbed some of the increase, but much remained on the land. It increased the density of the rural population, the labor supply, and the demand for foodstuffs, and thus emphasized those forms of production which used much labor and gave a large yield from a small area. Where the farmer could wring more from each acre by improving his methods or changing his product, a crowded countryside need not be a poor one; but if population outstripped productivity land hunger and bodily hunger might grow acute. Siberia offered some outlet to crowded Russian villages; fertilizers and drainage rendered some waste lands productive; but there were limits to this extension of the frontier, and intensive treatment was therefore essential.

2. The influence of the big urban markets was felt by native and foreign farmers alike. Industrial lands like Belgium and Holland (with 700 and 600 consumers, respectively, to the square mile) could not feed themselves. Denmark, Ireland, Spain, and the great triangle of "Agricultural Europe" that has its tips in Finland, Sicily, and the Caspian Sea found buyers in the industrial west, in spite of the protective measures of France and Germany. Russia and the Danubian lands joined the New World as granaries. Spain, Greece, and Italy exploited their climate to produce goods needed in cooler areas, and a rising standard of living in industrial Europe created a growing demand for such

things as fresh and dried fruits, oranges, lemons, nuts, silk, wine, and vegetables. In 1928 Spanish wool exports, once so important, were worth only half as much as the exports of onions. The northwestern lands, faced with the cheap grain supplies from the Black Sea and America, turned their attention increasingly to animal husbandry, to the cult of the cow, the hen, and the pig, and

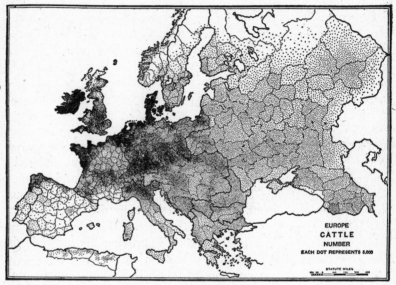

THE DISTRIBUTION OF CATTLE
(U. S. Department of Agriculture.)

found abundant markets at home or in neighboring countries, especially in Great Britain.

3. The peasant, cultivating his small farm with little or no hired labor, was the characteristic figure. If he emerged from serfdom he kept his holding as *métayer* or leaseholder, or became owner by compensating his landlord with money rather than by the surrender of part of his land. In Ireland he began as tenant and ended as owner. In Spain, southern Italy, Hungary, and Roumania the political power of the landlords, the character of the soil, and the production of grain and other staples kept or gathered the land into large holdings worked by armies of seasonal landless laborers; but the War led to an attack on these

large estates in many regions, and in Russia much of the land had passed into peasant ownership between 1861 and 1917. Outside Russia and one or two other regions peasant tenancy or ownership is today the rule, and the small cultivator has worked out with more or less success an economy suited to his needs and limitations, and adapted to a combination of subsistence and commercial farming. His attachment to the soil is just as strong as it was in days of bondage; his thrift is not always miserliness; his family solidarity provides an assured labor supply; his conservatism is partly the caution of a man who has little reserve to spare for experiment, yet it has not made him wholly deaf to new methods or ideas. At his best, in Denmark, Holland, and Germany, he has shown himself capable of adaptation to new conditions and of developing a highly efficient and profitable technique and organization.

Denmark.—Much of Denmark's soil is "poor sand-riddled stuff" (Haggard), and its climate is little better. Yet by 1900 Denmark had become "the demonstration plot of Europe." Its peasants did not lose their land when they gained their freedom, the landlord did not expand his domain, and the fusion of holdings was forbidden. By 1880 most of the country was held by men who owned an average of seventy acres apiece, but there were some larger estates—the relics of the domains—and many cottagers' small plots. In 1899 state lands began to be cut up for landless laborers, church lands and some estates have been parceled out since 1919, and the country today contains about 100,000 full farms (of which five-sixths are freehold), 100,000 part-time holdings, and a few of the old estates. Inclosure gathered speed after 1780, but in the process each farmer got his full share and the cottagers received four to six acres each.

The country exported grain and meat, but in the eighteen-sixties and 'seventies the price of butter rose while that of rye and wheat stood still and then began to fall. The large landlords therefore turned their estates into dairy farms, and when disaster hit the grain markets the peasants followed their example, with the British market as their chief objective. "Arable dairying" became the rule: the soil was cultivated assiduously to provide fodder roots and grains. These were supplemented by cultivated grass and imported fodder (especially corn and oilseeds), and fed to dairy cattle. The buttermilk was fed to hogs, thus permitting a large output of bacon; and since the Englishman who bought the bacon ate eggs with it 365 times a year hens were worth keeping, while beet gave food to man and beast.

At almost every stage cooperation helped the Danish farmer. The first cooperative dairy appeared in 1882, the first bacon factory in 1887. By 1890, 600 societies were at work, and, in 1909, 3600 societies served 450,000 members. The capital of these societies was subscribed by the members, and when it had received a fixed rate of interest any surplus that remained was distributed among the members in proportion to the amount of business each member had done with the society or the quantity of goods he had sent in to be processed or sold. To his society the farmer sent his milk and hogs to be processed cheaply, on a large scale, and according to standards that could not have been maintained on the farm. Cooperatives handled three-quarters of the milk output and over two-thirds of the hogs, an egg-exporting society had 550 collecting stations, while cattle-breeding societies helped to improve the quality of livestock. Societies bought rail or shipping space cheaply because they wanted much of it; they employed their own middlemen, bought fodder or fertilizer in bulk, and provided cheap credit for their members. They gave the producer the benefits of large-scale buying of the materials he needed, large-scale processing and sale of his produce, and provided loan capital at low rates. Cooperation became part of the Danish atmosphere.

If cooperation was the nitrogen, education was the oxygen. In the 'fifties and 'sixties Bishop Grundtvig and Kristen Kold, son of a shoemaker, began to organize "peoples' high schools." By 1885 over a hundred existed, with 10,000 students. To them young men went in the winter and young women in the summer. Their work was not vocational or technical, but cultural and civic. In them the young Dane could get an interest in life at large, a pride in his place in society, and an enthusiasm for his class and country. The spirit that gave leadership and loyalty to the cooperative movement was distilled in these schools.

As a food factory Denmark became very efficient. The average yield of butter fat per cow rose nearly fourfold in fifty years. The high uniform quality of the product and the ability to supply fresh goods all the year round made the country an ideal producer. Exports of butter, bacon, and eggs grew from 32,000,000 crowns in the early 'eighties to 300,000,000 on the eve of the War, and to 750,000,000 in 1928. In that year nearly 90 per cent of the butter and all the bacon were exported. The United Kingdom was the chief consumer, and in the post-War decade took almost all the bacon, two-thirds of the butter, and five-sixths of the eggs. Germany was a poor second customer. The measures taken by these two countries since 1929 to protect their dairy and hog farmers may therefore permanently injure Denmark's staple export industries. They may also lead the Danes to eat more of their own produce, for the townsmen eat margarine and the country has for many years past eaten twice as much imitation butter as real.

Holland.—The Dutch development of arable dairying, cooperation, careful breeding, and import of cattle foods ran along the same lines as in Denmark, and was in keeping with the country's long experience in intensive farming. Interest centered on milk products, but cheese and condensed milk were more important exports than butter. In 1928, 55 per cent of the butter and 70 per cent of the cheese were exported. Horticulture expanded, and the area under bulbs rose from 700 acres in 1850 to 12,000 in 1930. To produce bulbs cheaply, true to name and grade and free from disease, was a stern discipline, demanding an infinite capacity for taking pains. Variety gradually increased and prices declined; a good hyacinth bulb that was sold for $1.25 in 1860 can be bought now for ten or fifteen cents. In 1928 horticulture supplied one-fifth of the country's rural exports.

Holland's agriculture is that of a small, crowded countryside. Over half the country's 220,000 full-time holdings have areas ranging from 2½ to 12½ acres. The attack on waste and water was far from finished in 1800, for one-third of the land was still heath and much was submerged. Between 1840 and 1870 some of it was reclaimed, and when the agricultural depression ended after 1896 the task was resumed. Meanwhile the state took steps to rearrange holdings where the inheritance law requiring equal division of estates had caused excessive or uneconomic subdivision of land. In one case 795 morsels were redivided into twenty-six farms. In 1918 parliament decided to begin its greatest reclamation project, the Zuider Zee. The task of damming and draining that sheet of water may take thirty years and cost $300,000,000. Its completion will add a tenth to the cultivated area of the country and find land for 300,000 people. The dike across the mouth was finished in 1932.

Ireland.—Lack of minerals prevented Ireland from developing many factory industries. Abundant moisture made her "emerald," encouraged the growth of grass and the feeding of beef or dairy cattle, but rendered grain-growing and even potato cultivation somewhat hazardous. Conquest imposed an alien landlord class on the country. In Ulster tenants and owners were of English or Scottish origin, the relations between them were fairly harmonious, and the "Ulster tenant right" gave the cultivator secure tenure as well as compensation for improvements or freedom to sell them to his successor. Elsewhere the tenant was Irish, vanquished, and Catholic; the landlord English, victor, and Protestant. The latter was often an absentee, who left the management of the estate to a bailiff. He had introduced the English practice of short leases or leases at will, but was often unwilling (or unable) to spend money on improvements. He might let the bare land, leaving the tenant to provide everything else; yet if the demand for land was keen a peasant might find, after unremitting toil had brought his patch of bog or hill into fair cultivation, that his rent was to be raised or his tenancy terminated without compensation.

The demand for land became keen during the eighteenth century and intense during the first half of the nineteenth. Markets for grain, wool, butter and meat expanded, especially in Portugal and Britain. Meanwhile the spread of potato cultivation gave sustenance to a population that rose from possibly 2,000,000 in 1740 to nearly 6,000,000 in 1811, and to 8,200,000 in 1841. In that year Ireland carried 252 people to the square mile, against only 274 in much more highly industrialized England and Wales. Competition for land was almost cutthroat, rents were stretched on the rack, and holdings became smaller. In 1841 more than half the farms occupied five acres or less. Those who tended them often had virtually no capital, and Bernard Shaw does not paint an altogether fanciful picture when he speaks of two brothers who "made a farm out of a patch of stones on the hillside, cleared it and dug it with their own naked hands, and bought their first spade out of their first crop of potatoes." If the potato crop failed there would not only be no money for a spade; there would be no food.

Warnings of the effect of such failure went out in 1822 and 1831, but dire disaster came in 1845 and 1846. In 1845 blight destroyed half the potatoes, next year's crop was worse, and on top of starvation came typhus. The death roll was heavy, and every ship was crammed full as men scurried away from a stricken land. In 1846, 100,000 persons left for North America, and the tide 'ran high for decades. Not till the 'nineties did the exodus fall below 50,000 a year. By 1911 the island housed only 4,400,-000 people—a drop of 47 per cent in seventy years. There had been nothing like it before, certainly not in modern times. The Irish took their place second to the Jews as a dispersed people. As population fell the land famine lifted somewhat, holdings became larger, and prices of produce rose after 1851; but rents were still high, capital and security were lacking, and failure dogged many footsteps. The countryside was the scene of guerrilla warfare, bailiffs were shot, and the English language gained a new word when some evicted tenants persuaded their neighbors to ostracize their landlord, Captain Boycott.

By 1870 the British government was forced to recognize that it must "do something" with the Irish problem. The first step protected the tenant, as laws of 1870 and 1881 gave him the "three F's"—fair rent, fixity of tenure, and free sale. The fair rent was to be fixed by a land court if landlord and tenant failed to agree, and was to remain unchanged for fifteen years. Fixity of tenure was assured by forbidding the landlord to evict a tenant except for non-payment of rent. Free sale gave the tenant the right to sell the unexhausted value of his improvements to the landlord or incoming tenant. This "Magna Carta of the Irish peasant" had some beneficial results, but came a generation too late. Rents were first fixed in 1881 and were to run unchanged till 1896; but prices fell a third during that period, and the fair rent became a grievous burden.

The second step met the cultivator's desire to own land. In 1885 the British government began to advance money to tenants who wished to buy holdings. The loan was to be amortized in forty-nine years. Later acts made more loans, gave an outright subsidy of £10,000,000, helped to build houses, and set up boards to aid those who wished to move from congested districts to sparsely peopled areas. Circumstances favored this policy, for education, cooperation, and rising prices increased the farmer's desire to own and his ability to pay the price. By 1916, 375,000 tenants out of 500,000 had begun to buy land. The area transferred, 10,000,000 acres, was half the total extent of the country and two-thirds of the area fit for farming. A nation of tenants was thus transformed into one of owners.

Land reform alone did not make good farmers. A country lacking capital and knowledge of modern methods was still overcrowded, even with only 5,000,000 people (1891). Cultivation and animal husbandry were far inferior to those of England or the North Sea lands, and men were still wrestling with land so poor that "the bones of the earth were everywhere sticking through its skin" (George Russell). Into this land of little promise came Horace Plunkett, with his gospel of education and cooperation and his slogan, "Better farming, better business, better living." In 1894 he established the Irish Agricultural Organization Society to promote cooperative societies. Within a decade eight hundred societies had been formed, and by 1917 over 110,000 farmers were members. The government helped by establishing a Department of Agriculture and Technical Education (1899), which set up colleges and demonstration farms, sent out itinerant teachers, and offered prizes or subsidies.

Ireland suffered severely from revolution between 1916 and 1923. Farm property was destroyed, land went out of cultivation, herds were decimated, and the quality as well as the quantity of production suffered. When peace came the new government and the cooperatives strove to repair the damage and to raise standards. In serving his only big market—Great Britain—the Irish farmer still lags behind his Dutch, Danish, and dominion rivals in methods of production and marketing. He is still also the victim of politics, and when Dublin in 1932 decided not to remit to London the installments collected from farmers under the land-purchase scheme, London placed a heavy duty on Irish goods.

Spain.—Seventy per cent of Spain's workers are engaged in agriculture. In 1928 they fed a population that had grown to 22,000,000, and in addition provided three-quarters of the country's exports. Spain had its land reformers in the eighteenth century, Napoleon loosened the landlords' grip on their people, but the essentials of the old order remained. In the fertile or irrigated valleys of the north and of the Mediterranean provinces *métayers* tilled small scattered holdings, from which in the nineteen-twenties many were drawing incomes as low as twenty cents a day. The great mass of the peasantry must therefore supplement its income by remittances from relatives in America and by working on the larger estates. These estates usually specialized on one commodity —wheat, grapes, olives, or wool. They needed a few regular workers and a legion of seasonal laborers. They drew the latter from the small cultivators, and also from villages or towns composed largely of landless laborers. Such villages are found also in Sicily, southern Italy, and Hungary. The thousands of men who live in some of them are hired by the week or season, and when the work is over they return to their homes to exist as best they can till the next season. They may work only 90 to 150 days a year, are well organized in unions, and fight hard at times. To diminish this landless proletariat, schemes of "inner colonization" were urged in the late nineteenth century, and in 1907 state lands began to be settled. Progress was painfully slow, but was speeded up in 1927; and after the revolution of 1931 provision was made for expropriating uncultivated or under-utilized lands, especially those belonging to the aristocracy. Enthusiasts say 40,000,000 acres are capable of better use, but the outcome cannot yet be measured.

Italy.—Italy witnessed one of the earliest European steps in emancipation, for in 1762, 1771, and 1778 the king of Sardinia freed the peasants of Savoy from personal serfdom and ordered them to redeem their obligations to the seigniors. Bonaparte helped to abolish what was left of feudalism in the north, and some church lands were sold. Some of them passed into the hands of the bourgeoisie, who set to work to exploit them along English high farming lines. Cavour, for instance, after 1830 conducted commercial farming, introduced technical improvements, and spent much time tramping round his fields in an enormous straw hat. Some of the younger nobles came back from tours of England and France talking about parliaments, elementary education, scientific agriculture, roads and railroads; and in the 'forties northern Italian rulers developed similar interests.

Some of these enthusiasms could be brought to earth, as for instance on the moist or irrigated Lombard plain, where capitalistic farming could be practiced with the aid of hired laborers. Silk production expanded, and wheat, flax, hemp, or vines might be grown in between the mulberry trees. Italy became the largest

European silk producer and the second largest vigneron, had olive oil to spare for export, and until 1910 grew enough wheat to supply her own needs. In the north large farms and small *mezzadria* holdings were intermingled, while in Tuscany and Umbria the latter type of tenure was deeply rooted in history and soil conditions. "No country is greedier in the demand which it makes upon labor. Without the constant care of peasants responsible for a small area of land—tending the surface of the soil, strengthening the terraces, looking to the ditches, repairing assiduously the ravages of sun and rain—the hills of central Italy would sink into a stage of arid desolation. The land is in a sense greedy also of capital. The vines, most sensitive of economic plants, must every year be sprayed with sulphur dust or sulphate of lime; the soil, not naturally fertile, calls for a constant application of manures, while every system of *petite culture* demands a large outlay for dwelling houses and farm buildings" (Hancock). *Mezzadria* combined the capital of the landlord with the labor of the tenant, and made both interested in the size of the crop.

Some landlords tried to teach their tenants the secrets of the new husbandry, helped them to produce for market, and carried out drastic changes in methods without altering the terms of the pact. Many did nothing, while others sought to increase their share of the produce from half to two-thirds. This stirred up unrest. There were unions of *métayers* and unions of landlords, and collective bargaining did not always run smoothly. After 1918 the tenants won better terms, and the cultivator kept a larger fraction of the yield or paid a fixed rent. In the south latifundia were worked by armies of seasonal laborers, hired in gangs under some leader. Revolts against leaders and landlords were frequent; but after 1900, when unions were legalized, labor organizations negotiated with employers and took contracts to supply labor. Conditions were still far from ideal, a landless seasonally employed class was easily stirred to turbulence, and in the post-War confusion the cry, "The land for the peasants" often meant "Land for the laborers."

To meet that cry and at the same time provide food for a growing population, Italy gave some attention to reclamation, especially after 1900. The Campagna marshes were attacked as early as 1878, the effect of devastating floods in the south was reduced by elaborate drainage and terracing schemes, and elsewhere irrigation or reforestation was extended. The costs were high, and Italy was not a rich country. Under the Fascist régime more ambitious plans were undertaken, and an attempt was made to reduce the country's dependence on imported wheat. In 1922-1924 half the wheat consumed was imported, but between 1924 and 1931 the tariff on wheat was raised five times. The effect was a substantial but fluctuating increase in output; Italy, like France and Germany, penalized the consumer to subsidize the production of wheat at high costs.

Austria-Hungary and the Balkans.—The area stretching from the southern border of Germany to Constantinople contained two great plains (Hungary and Roumania), the Carpathians, and the Balkan highlands or valleys. The plains could become vast grain fields if markets were available, whether near or distant. The near market grew large during the nineteenth century, as Austria and Bohemia developed their manufactures and as other rural parts produced special commodities and bought grain. The central economic fact of the Austro-Hungarian Empire was regional specialization and interdependence, with a good river and railroad system, and a good center in Vienna. In that economy Hungary became the granary.

Foreign markets became accessible with the coming of railroads, the greater use of the Danube, and the opening of the Black Sea to navigation. In 1829 the Bosporus and Dardanelles became open to the merchantmen of all powers at peace with the Porte, and the Sea thus ceased to be a Turkish lake. In 1856 navigation of the Danube was made free to ships of all nations, and an international commission was set up to improve the stream, give it a satisfactory mouth, and regulate its traffic. Railroads were built from the river on to the plains, and the Hungarian method of milling grain by use of rollers instead of millstones revolutionized the production of flour. These factors turned much of Hungary and Roumania from ranches into grain farms. Budapest became a milling center, and Roumania began the nineteenth century with 90 per cent of its farm land under grass but ended it with 85 per cent under the plow. Maize flourished better than wheat, but the natives ate the former and exported the latter.

To the south of the grain fields lay the deep valleys and high hills of the Balkans, cut off from the Mediterranean by ranges or political frontiers, and devoid of good means of transport. The life of Serbia, Bosnia, and Albania was that of self-sufficing village communities of corn growers, graziers, or hog raisers, subject to a mildly feudal Turkish suzerainty. Gradually railroads came, Adriatic ports became accessible, the Turk was expelled, serfdom disappeared, and governments fostered agriculture. Bosnia passed into Austrian keeping in 1878, while railroads knit Serbia into the economy of the Dual Monarchy and gave its people a market for five-sixths of their exports.

The Great War tore Austria-Hungary to pieces, dismembering an economy that had embraced 250,000 square miles and 51,000,-000 people. Austria lost two-thirds of its territory, Vienna became a big head on a puny body, and Hungary shriveled to less than a third of its old area. Some of the richest farm, forest, or mineral land went to Czechoslovakia, Italy, Serbia, Roumania, or Poland. Tariff walls fenced off these lost lands, cutting across the old lines of trade, and separating producer and consumer. A big free-trade area vanished, and trade must find new directions, jump obstacles along the old ones, or die. Experience since then suggests that it might be wise to reerect in some form the economic unit that was so light-heartedly destroyed.

The agrarian history of the area reveals almost every degree, method, and result of emancipation. Liberation in Austria led fairly painlessly to peasant proprietorship; but in Hungary the lords kept most of the land and farmed it in big units with the spare-time labor of small holders or the seasonal labor of landless villagers. In 1910 Hungary (with over 4,000,000 farm laborers) ranked second only to Italy (with 4,500,000) as the stronghold of the rural proletariat. In most of the Balkans the nature of the soil prevented the building of large commercial farms, and the villagers combined individual cultivation with common use of pastures, paying tribute—usually a fraction of the produce—to some Turkish lord. When that lord was evicted the peasants took the land for themselves, though in some parts they did pay compensation to the landlord.

On the rich Roumanian plain the story was different. In 1595 the king had created a feudal order to provide an army; but while its heads (*boyars*) were landlords, two-thirds of the land was reserved for peasant use. This system was not disturbed by the Turks, and when they were driven out the boyars were still lords.

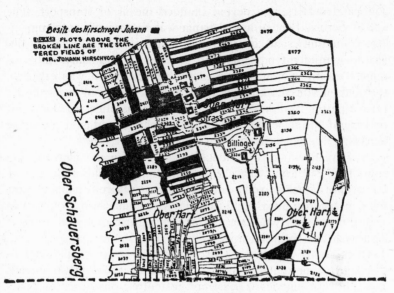

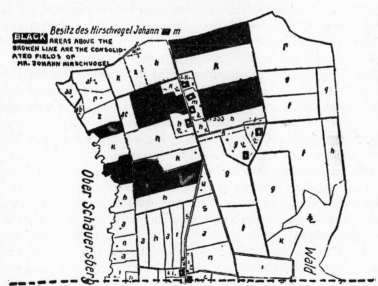

AN AUSTRIAN FARM, BEFORE AND AFTER CONSOLIDATION

In Austria, as in Germany, Switzerland, Holland and other countries the consolidation of scattered holdings has been undertaken, especially since 1900.

As grain fields and exports expanded they raided the peasants' labor and land in order to expand their domains and output. Revolts ensued, and in 1864 a liberal-minded prince abolished serfdom, gave the peasants land in proportion to the number of oxen they owned, but abolished the two-thirds rule and ordered the peasants to compensate the lords for the loss of dues. In the transition the landlords used their wits and political power to pull more land into their hands, and in 1905 three-eighths of the arable land was in estates of over 1250 acres. Few peasants had enough land for a livelihood, few could compete with the more heavily capitalized big grain farms, and many had no land at all. Unrest burst into flames in 1907 and won minor reforms, but the Roumanian landscape was studded with latifundia and covered with land-hungry poor when ten years later a great explosion occurred on the eastern frontier, in Russia.

Russia.—In 1914 over 80 per cent of Russia's people lived on the land, a percentage similar to that of most predominantly agricultural countries. They were not evenly spread, for nearly a quarter of the country was arctic or arid. Of the remainder, forests and pastures covered the area north of a line joining St. Petersburg and Moscow and running thence southeastward. For purposes of rural settlement Russia meant the country south of Moscow; yet in this area, and especially in the southeast, vagaries of rainfall, wind, hail, and late or early frost would make agriculture a gamble against famine, even for a people well supplied with machinery for quick seeding and harvesting, with knowledge of dry farming, and with equipment for water conservation.

In 1800 there were probably about 40,000,000 Russians, of whom a tenth belonged to the 14,000 noble families, the church, and the growing middle class. Most of the rest were serfs, dwelling on the estates of the state, royal family, nobility, and church. The royal lands housed 15,000,000 and the others had about as many. Perhaps a million worked in the homes of their masters, while the remainder divided their time between the domain and the village land. The landlord claimed sometimes as much as three days' labor weekly, and in places had been known to demand six.

Over the greater part of settled Russia the serf was not so much an individual as a member of a village community (*mir*). In Russian Poland, Lithuania and the Ukraine, the village and the landlord were less powerful, while some areas had free peasant proprietors. But elsewhere the landlord claimed services from the group in return for land. The village council shared out the arable fields in strips among the families, either according to "mouths" (in which case each child counted as one) or according to "souls" (of which a child had only a fraction). Redistribution might take place every few years (six to thirteen years) or even annually, in order to take account of changes in population.

Emancipation found advocates even before 1800, but little happened until the Crimean War, with its revelation of incompetence and corruption and its defeat of Russia, led to drastic reform. The Edict of Emancipation (1861) liberated the serf, but in spite of the desire of some landlords it did not liberate the land from him. He, or rather the *mir*, retained about half the cultivated land. The *mir* could rent the land or buy it; in the latter case the government paid the owner in bonds, and the *mir* became responsible for collecting money to repay the government in installments spread over forty-nine years. The administration of a decree affecting nearly 50,000,000 serfs and 350,000,000 acres was a difficult task. On the state and crown lands peasants were freed on fairly generous terms and obtained larger holdings at lower prices than did their fellows on private estates. Many nobles opposed the policy, officials could not always avoid injustice or blunders, and valuation was full of pitfalls. There was delay and friction, and, in 1880, 15 per cent of the peasants had not begun to buy. In 1881 purchase was made compulsory, but payments were reduced.

Emancipation did not solve the problem of an increasingly crowded countryside and of a diminishing share of it for each peasant. In 1861 peasant holdings averaged about eleven acres, 28 per cent of them were inadequate, and many were smaller after emancipation than before. Between 1860 and 1900 the population of the empire rose from 74,000,000 to 133,000,000; periodical redistribution reduced the share of each household, and by 1900 the average holding had fallen to seven acres. While quantity fell, quality suffered. Capital was lacking, and the annual installments hindered its accumulation. The strips grew smaller and more scattered, and continuous cropping without fertilizer mined fertility from the soil. Famines during the 'seventies and 'nineties had tragic results. Yet the installments had to be paid, and taxes fell chiefly on the peasantry. Finally, the price decline after 1875 hit the Russian as it did his western victims.

Russia entered the twentieth century with its rural problem still acute at many points. It had succeeded in building up its grain trade, and in 1909-1914 supplied a quarter of the world's wheat exports. It had many large farmers using efficient methods, and its rural governments were grappling with problems of health and education. A Peasants' Bank had been set up to buy and transfer more land, while migration to the towns or emigration to America and Siberia eased the pressure to some extent. Yet millions of peasants were food-hungry and land-hungry, were loaded with taxes, and were in arrears on their installments. Hence the revolution of 1905, though chiefly an urban affair, was supported by the peasants, and won them important concessions. The remainder of their installments were canceled, and large areas of state or crown land were thrown open for purchase. The chief reform went deeper; it aimed at liberating the peasant from the *mir*—a center of revolutionary discontent—and making him an individual proprietor. Stolypin, who became prime minister in 1906, was convinced that the dissolution of the *mir* as a land-dividing and controlling unit was essential to agricultural progress and political conservatism. He therefore decreed (1) that any peasant could withdraw his holding from the village lands into a separate farm; (2) that villages could dissolve completely by majority decision.

These reforms made complete emancipation possible. The peasant could become a peasant proprietor, free of lord and village, free to farm as he wished. Between 1907 and 1916, eleven per cent of the holdings under village control were withdrawn and consolidated, chiefly by dissolution of *mirs*. Some men sold their holdings once they were free to do so, and the buyers thus built up larger farms. The *Zemstvos* (district assemblies) fostered rural education, agricultural cooperation spread, and cooperative credit banks lent money at rates far below the 18 to 30 per cent charged by the usurers. The use of modern farm implements increased, prices rose after 1896, while the expansion of industrial centers and the construction of more railroads provided larger domestic markets. At the same time the eastward movement became strong, for the Trans-Siberian Railroad, begun in 1891, had opened a great field for colonization. Between

1906 and 1915 nearly half a million families received almost 50,000,000 acres in Siberia. Thus there were signs of improvement on every hand. But though four-fifths of the arable land of European Russia (500,000,000 acres) was now in the peasants' hands, the population was growing so fast that there was still land-hunger and fear of physical hunger. There were more landless laborers than before, and there were still large areas of state, crown, noble, or church land, on which rude hands would be laid if the chance came.

The chance came in the trail of war and revolution. When Russia was cut off from her allies and from German supplies of manufactured wares, her factories and foundries could not fill the gap, and her industrial plants and railroads steadily went to pieces. The withdrawal of men and horses had serious effects on an agriculture which relied much on manual labor. Collapse was inevitable by the end of 1916; the revolutionary government of March, 1917, soon found that the ship of state it had boarded was a wreck, and in November it was displaced by the Bolsheviks.

Bolshevik theory had been evolved in terms of industrial capitalism. It envisaged industry, finance, and transportation passing into the hands of a few giant units, lords of a mighty army of propertyless wage earners. Its aim was to displace these wealthy owners and managers, to strip the bourgeoisie of political power and property, and to run their enterprises by a classless society for the benefit of all workers. Industry provided plenty of evidence of the rise of big units, but agriculture did not. Apart from the latifundia of Hungary, Roumania, Italy, and Spain, the trend was toward small family farms, worked in many cases by their owners, and that trend was marked in Russia after 1905. Expropriation of the bourgeoisie had therefore limited scope. There were a few industries and the remnants of the big estates, but little else, unless one regarded any farmer who hired labor as a bourgeois.

When the Bolsheviks took control they found much expropriation had already been done. Laborers, peasants, and returning soldiers had seized the land of crown, nobles, church, and larger farmers (*kulaks*). All that the new rulers need do, therefore, at two o'clock one morning, was to declare these estates abolished without compensation and authorize their partition among the peasants. The peasant holdings grew in number from 15,000,000 to 25,000,000 and expanded 60,000,000 acres. The peasants now held 96 per cent of the land; but were they free owners? Communist theory abhorred private property, and the crying need for food in the towns and armies could be met only by requisitioning supplies from the peasant. The right of private property in land was therefore "abolished once and forever." Land was to be held in trust; it could not be bought, sold, leased, or bequeathed. Its possessor was a public servant, and must hold no more than he could work without hired labor. From his product he must take only "according to his needs" and hand the surplus to the state, receiving manufactured goods and necessary services in return.

This policy was not very stimulating to production, especially in a broken-down country. Either there was no surplus or the peasants concealed and sold it surreptitiously. The cultivated area fell, and famine was widespread. When the danger of counter-revolution ended, a milder régime was established by the New Economic Policy (NEP) in 1921. Requisition of surplusses was abandoned, the peasant paid a tax in kind, and was then free to sell what he had left. He could lease his land or rent some from others, employ hired men, and bequeath his holding to his son. He acquired the status of a perpetual tenant, and for six years was left more or less to do as he wished. True, he found that the state monopolized trade, bought his goods at prices below those ruling in world markets, and then sold them abroad at world prices in order to pay for machinery and other industrial equipment. But as the sky was growing less dark for him and his country, he felt a greater urge to produce. He got his cooperative society to work again, and if he was a good farmer he might once more become a *kulak*, while his less efficient neighbors groveled along the rim of starvation or slipped off it. His success and his bourgeois striving for property and profit made him hateful to the faithful, and his lease of liberty did not last long.

Meanwhile theory and need led to experiments in large-scale cooperative or state farming. Some royal estates were worked as units, and others were handed over to groups (*artels*) of landless men. They were not very successful, but they fitted the communist objective better than did the *kulaks* and NEP. The gulf between the methods and yield of the *kulaks* and those of the rest of the farming class was wide, the scramble for land in 1917 had accentuated fragmentation, and much agriculture was crude and unproductive. In 1928 the average peasant holding was 12 acres, three-fourths of the spring grain area was plowed with wood plows, and nearly half the crop was cut with scythes or sickles and threshed with flails. The solution seemed to lie in sweeping away the petty cultivation of the small men and the greedy energy of the *kulaks*, and in working the soil in large state or "collective" farms with modern machines and tractors. In 1927 the government decided to embark on this policy as part of its Five-Year Plan.

The policy had two parts. In the first place, more and bigger farms (up to 300,000 acres each) were to be operated by the state to yield produce and serve as models for the rest of the country. They would be run by managers, employ armies of laborers, and use tractors, giant plows, and combine harvesters. After 1930, 5000 of these farms were organized, but their record was far from happy. A farm refused to be a factory. In the second place, villagers were urged to merge their holdings, implements, draft animals, seed, and farm buildings in one great farm unit and operate it collectively. The government would supply credit, tractors, machinery, and expert advice; but in return for this aid and for manufactured goods the collectives would hand over their surplus produce.

The drive for collectivization was fiercely conducted; the *kulaks* were swept aside ruthlessly; great pressure was exerted on the smaller holders; and, by 1933, 200,000 collective farms, embracing 70,000,000 peasants, occupied three-quarters of the cultivated area. Peasant resistance was strong in places, the surrender of the surplus was as unpopular as before NEP, and in 1932 the state's claim was reduced to a grain tax, fixed before sowing each year. Thus the rest of the surplus remained in the hands of the producers, and was an incentive to greater effort, as it had been to the *kulaks*. The results of this policy cannot be foreseen. The younger generation has grown up in a collectivist atmosphere, the strips and fragments have been abolished, modern equipment and methods have been introduced, and some well-managed collectives have proved more productive than individual or state farms. But Russia still wrestles with the problems of an "economy of scarcity," and its agricultural future is in large measure dependent on the birth rate and the weather.

"The Green Revolution."—On the western fringe of the red revolution there occurred a contemporaneous "green revolution." From Finland to Greece the large estate was attacked by those who had no land or wanted more, and the results were almost everywhere the same. "Among the various social effects of the Great War the downfall of the class of large landowners has been the most outstanding on the continent . . . . Wealth in the form of land has become rare and may soon be unknown" (Mitrany).

The liberation movement of the nineteenth century left much land in eastern and central Europe in the hands of great proprietors, and sometimes increased the amount. Even in pre-War days men with too little land or none at all sometimes asked why a third of the arable land of Hungary should be in estates of more than 3000 acres, and why three of those estates should cover half a million acres in all. Why should 1730 men—mostly German-Austrians—possess nearly 30 per cent of Bohemia while a million peasants had less than five acres apiece? Why should 200 families in Estonia own 58 per cent of the land, why was 31 per cent of Russian Poland in the hands of less than one per cent of the population, and why was half of Latvia in 1300 estates? Bulgaria, Finland, Serbia, Roumania, and Lithuania all had big targets at which peasant or laborer could shoot.

The Great War made land redistribution a matter of practical politics for several reasons. (1) The peasant, as food producer or soldier, must be induced to fight, farm, and fast by promises of land as a reward. Defeat, demobilization, revolution, blockade, the collapse of currencies, and the misery of towns made the peasant's position stronger, for man must have food no matter what the color of his flag or the exchange value of his paper money. Sometimes the peasant formed his own political party, sometimes he was content to let other parties woo him, but he was never shy about naming his price. He wanted land, and the big estate must supply it. (2) The returning soldier must be cared for. (3) The new states had to frame plans for their political and social structure, and that structure was predominantly rural except in Czechoslovakia. (4) Many governments obtained lands which had been crown, state, church, or monastic property, or which had been taken by a foreign aristocracy when it conquered the country. Reconstruction in central and eastern Europe therefore meant land reform, just as farther west it meant the salvaging of industry, commerce, and currency.

The methods adopted ranged from a tender respect for property rights to a disregard that was little different from the Russian viewpoint. Estates belonging to church, crown, or alien nobles were taken over entirely. In many cases big landowners were allowed to keep a certain area, ranging from 250 acres in Latvia to 1250 in Roumania. Compensation might be promised, though Latvia took the land by one law and omitted to pass a second one providing the compensation. Valuation was low and payment rarely adequate. Bulgaria paid half the market price; Czechoslovakia paid the pre-War land value, but made no allowance for the depreciation in currency since 1913; and Estonia paid in bonds bearing 2 2/3 per cent interest. In Germany, Austria, and Hungary, where the program was reformist rather than revolutionary, owners received kinder treatment; but Hungary imposed a capital levy on large estates, payable in land, and got much property in that way. In redistributing the land, claims were received from men who had no holdings or whose farms were too small. The land was rarely a free gift. The peasant must pay the state, in installments, sufficient to cover the cost of compensation and redistribution.

These plans for rural reorganization were sometimes carried out with unwise haste or hate, sometimes with considerable care. The result has been a substantial transfer of territory, but the amount available has often proved much smaller than enthusiasts expected. In Czechoslovakia, the big estates held 10,000,000 acres. Of these, 7,000,000 were forests, 3,000,000 were cultivable, and of the latter one-quarter had to be left in the hands of the former owners. By 1929, 1,900,000 acres (one-tenth of the total agricultural land) had been transferred to 500,000 purchasing peasants and only 400,000 acres were left. Of the forest lands the owners kept about a quarter, and only a quarter of the remainder had passed to the village communes by 1929. The state lent small holders money for equipment, improved rural education, established peoples' high schools, sent traveling teachers round, and accomplished the transition more successfully than did any other country.

In Latvia nearly 100,000 holdings had been created or enlarged by 1928, and the peasants held 80 per cent of the land, in place of 40 per cent in 1914. Danish experts were engaged, cooperation took root, and this former grain field gained fame as a butter exporter. In Estonia 55,000 new tenancies were carved out, in Lithuania 27,000 new holdings were created and 25,000 enlarged, while in Finland 100,000 new holdings appeared. In Poland early plans failed for lack of capital, but in 1926 the state informed the landowners that if they would voluntarily sell or lease 500,000 acres yearly for ten years no compulsion would be used. They did so. Yugoslavia had little land to divide, Bulgaria's finances were strained in equipping refugees put on land, but Greece carved 145,000 holdings out of church, state, and private lands. Roumania did the largest job of all, for by 1927 nearly 1,400,000 claims had been met, 9,000,000 acres had been made into peasant holdings, 2,500,000 acres had been labeled grazing commons, and 1,200,000 acres had been proclaimed public forests. Only 10 per cent of the country was now in estates of more than 250 acres. In Germany some "internal colonization" took place, but in Austria reform was limited to land which had been turned from peasant farms to sporting reserves since 1870. In Hungary about a twentieth of the land was redistributed, but one-third of the country was still in large estates, and Hungary remains an "island of latifundia in a green sea of agrarian reform."

The whole movement, breaking up about 35,000 estates, was inspired by political and social rather than economic motives. Land was not given to those who could make the best use of it, but to those who had least. The size of holdings was fixed with a view, not to sound farming, but to the satisfaction of the largest possible number of claims. There was little thought of "the economics of the agricultural industry" (Mitrany), and certain general results were soon evident.

1. Land alone was of little use, and since most of its recipients had little or no capital, governments had to borrow money (from Sweden or America) to pay the landlords and provide the peasant with capital. The repayment of these advances and of the purchase price became difficult when farm prices sagged in 1929.

2. Many holdings were still too small, given existing methods, equipment, or lack of consolidation of scattered patches. Yet consolidation lagged, methods changed slowly, and governments had to check some peasants from further fragmentation of land.

3. The disappearance of the big estate ended the demand for

hired laborers, but not all the former hired men got land. They became jobless as well as landless.

4. When large farms were cut into small holdings land was often withdrawn from the production of some staple marketable crop, and devoted to mixed farming suitable to the resources and ability of the small cultivator. The peasant thought more about feeding himself and less about raising a crop with which to pay his rent. This reversion to production for family consumption probably raised the standard of living for millions; but subsistence farming without thought of markets was impossible, for there were interest and installment payments to meet, and things to be bought. The peasant must produce cash crops as well as supplies for the larder. Cash came from markets; but in "agricultural Europe" there were few industrial centers to serve as markets, and sale for export to "industrial Europe" was of vital importance. Yet just at that spot the new rural order received its severest test, for whether it tried to win back the old grain markets or sought to build up new ones for produce most suitable to peasant farming, it found rivals and obstacles.

In pre-War days "industrial Europe" bought nearly half its wheat imports from Russian and Danubian producers. Between 1909 and 1913 Russia supplied 25 per cent of the world's wheat exports and Danubia contributed 16 per cent, a total of 210,000,000 bushels annually. The remainder, 255,000,000 bushels, came from the New World and India. War, revolution, and land reform blotted out the Black Sea supplies, and the New World stepped in to take their place. From 1915 to 1924 no Roumanian grain entered a British port, and Russia had none to spare. Danubia gradually got back on to its feet, but Russia was prostrate much longer. Hence during the years 1924-1929 the New World supplied 94 per cent of the export wheat trade; in 1927 industrial Europe imported 600,000,000 bushels of wheat, but only 20,000,000 came from the eastern granary. That which did come was often of low grade, and the label "Of Danubian origin" was acquiring a "derogatory meaning in the international [grain] trade" (Mitrany).

The exporters' lot was hard even before prices crashed in 1929-1930. In that year Russia came back with a bound, for a bumper crop allowed her to put 100,000,000 bushels on a market that had learned to do without her and had its bins full of surplus stocks from earlier years. Of the chief importers, Italy, France and Germany immediately rushed to protect their grain growers and to foster still more production, and in 1931 Great Britain, the giant among importers, began to tax foreign wheat and encourage English farmers to plant more.

Faced with such conditions, eastern growers frantically gathered to seek salvation. But neither plans for restricting exports nor proposals that industrial Europe should give their produce preference had much hope of acceptance, and the grain exporter was left to scramble in a relentlessly shrinking market. If he turned to dairy or meat production others were there before him, beet sugar was in the general unhappy quagmire of excess production, and no commodity found a welcome in a foreign port. He was too deeply involved in a commercial and credit economy to retreat into the shell of subsistence farming, but must struggle on, the sport of economics and politics, the victim of low prices for the things he sold but of high prices for the wares he wanted to buy. No wonder he strengthened his reputation as the world's best grumbler.

Rural Credit.—The spread of peasant farming over a continent that was becoming increasingly commercial in its rural economy raised two acute problems. (1) How could the small producer get the benefits of large-scale buying, processing, transportation, and sale? Cooperation answered that question. (2) How could he meet his need for credit? He might want money for three purposes: (a) To buy land, erect the main buildings, or carry out the long and not immediately reproductive work of planting an orchard or vineyard. For such purposes he required *"long-term credit,"* usually in the form of a mortgage repayable in five, ten, or more years. (b) To buy implements, fencing material, livestock, or minor buildings. The cost would not be large, and the farmer could hope to repay a grant of *"intermediate credit"* in a year or two. (c) To buy seed, fertilizers, sacks, or other materials, and keep himself alive from the beginning of a season till his produce was sold and paid for. A debt incurred for such purposes might be repaid in a few months, and would be *"short-term credit."* Cooperation, with some government aid, strove to meet these needs.

In England the tenant farmer did not need long-term credit, for his landlord supplied land and fixed improvements; he could use his own capital for equipment and working expenses, or needed only intermediate or short-term loans. The peasant proprietor was not so happily placed. Often the country in which he lived had little loanable capital, the banking system gave scant attention to his needs, or there were no rural banking facilities. He had to rely on private or corporate money-lenders for his long-term loans and on storekeeper or produce merchant for his shorter credit. In both cases he frequently paid such high interest rates—ten, twenty, even fifty per cent—that it was difficult to keep abreast of interest payments alone. He was born in debt, lived in debt, and died in debt; and the savage attacks on Jewish and other money-lenders sprang from the bitter hatred felt by hopeless debtors toward inexorable creditors.

Germany was the first country to find a way out of the rural credit morass, and the methods there evolved were copied throughout Europe, the Orient, and the United States. The story begins with the efforts of Junkers to lift themselves out of distress after the Seven Years' War and with their later desire to buy more land for high farming. Lenders were unwilling to meet their needs except at high rates, for land was an uncertain security and mortgage deeds were not always salable, except at a loss, if their holders wished to turn them into cash. On the suggestion of a Berlin merchant, the Prussian government authorized an experiment. Let the borrowers form an association, which would raise money by selling bonds and lend it to its members. The first *Landschaft* (Land Mortgage Credit Association) was formed in 1770, and was soon imitated. Its bonds were backed with all the property of the members, i.e., the unlimited liability of all to honor its debts. The *Landschaft* then lent its members up to two-thirds the value of their property. It insisted that they repay the loan by instalments, disciplined them, and might even take over the administration of their estates. The government strictly supervised the group and appointed the higher officials. These precautions made the bonds almost gilt-edged securities, which sold at prices nearly equal to those of government bonds and never lacked buyers. The interest rate on them was low (3 to 4 per cent), and the borrower secured his credit at a little above that figure. Though primarily designed to help the Junkers, the *Landschaft* was later allowed to aid owners of smaller estates and eventually larger peasants. The system spread to neighboring countries, and in

Denmark was successfully adapted to the needs of the small dairy farmers. When in 1913 an American commission visited Europe to study rural credit, the land mortgage bond was hailed by one pilgrim as the greatest discovery since 1492.

Germany's attack on rural credit problems did not end there, for the *Landschaft* left most peasants unaided. In 1848 Frederick Raiffeisen, burgomaster of a group of Rhine villages, observed the difficulties under which peasants labored, the petty and costly scale of their buying and borrowing, and the tragedies enacted when a usurer gobbled up the stock and implements of his debtor. He therefore wrung capital from rich philanthropists and opened a loan society (1849). Success paved the way for expansion, but no big structure could rest on a philanthropic foundation. Cooperation was in the air, and in 1862 Raiffeisen induced the villagers of Anhausen to form a cooperative bank, in which the people of the district could deposit their savings and from which the local farmers could borrow. By 1905, 13,000 of these Raiffeisen banks were at work. Round their central task they gathered other such services as purchasing and processing, while a central bank took care of their surplus funds or lent them money if their deposits were inadequate.

Until 1889 a bank might have no share capital, but when the law demanded a capital basis each member contributed ten marks ($2.50). More important was the acceptance of unlimited liability by each member; he put his farm, cattle, implements, and other property behind the bank as a guarantee of its solvency. Each bank was small, with the village as its area of operation, and confidence in it could rest on a personal knowledge of those who ran it. Its operation was cheap and simple, for only the accountant, usually the schoolmaster or priest, was paid for his services. It received deposits and considered applications for long or short credit. Its decision depended on the applicant's personal character, on his project, and on his ability as a farmer. If he passed this triple test he obtained his loan at about 4 or 5 per cent. If the bank's funds were exhausted, it could draw on the central bank, and after 1895 a government central cooperative bank lent money at 3 per cent.

The Raiffeisen principles worked with remarkable success. Unlimited liability proved a sound foundation, the borrower's personal reputation and ability were good security, and operation on a non-profit basis, largely by honorary officials, permitted a low rate of interest. Raiffeisen's success in the Rhineland and south-west was duplicated when Dr. Haas started a similar movement in Hesse, Saxony, and Hanover. By 1910 the two movements embraced 17,000 credit banks, over 1,500,000 members, and an annual turnover of nearly $1,500,000,000. Yet so carefully were they managed that between 1896 and 1910 only nineteen of them went bankrupt. In 1913, however, a group of Haas banks failed. Money had been too easily obtained from the state, and too readily lent. The episode stressed the need of self-help, caution, and ability to say "No." But no amount of such virtues could bring the banks unscathed through the post-War currency inflation. As the mark sank, the value of their deposits and debts melted away, and when stabilization came the rebuilding of both had to be faced. The banks had to lean more heavily on the state for their funds, since farmers were borrowing heavily in order to "rationalize." In 1930 the Haas and Raiffeisen groups amalgamated, were joined by smaller federations, and thus linked over 36,000 societies with 4,000,000 members.

An indefatigable arithmetician has discovered that in 1930 Germany had one rural cooperative society for every 1594 inhabitants and for every 1760 acres of farm land. These figures indicate the extent to which cooperative credit, buying, processing, and selling have permeated the agricultural organization of the country. The German bank and the Danish creamery or bacon factory served as models for the rest of Europe's peasantry. In 1913 Russia had 13,000 societies with over 8,000,000 members, and in every other country the two pre-War decades witnessed a rapid spread of organization. War and post-War difficulties strengthened cooperation, and in the areas of land redistribution governments encouraged the new peasants to cooperate. In Latvia (1926) 300 dairies were handling two-thirds of the butter exports and one-eighth of the total exports. In Czechoslovakia a central marketing society imported half the fertilizer and took over the grain trade. In Italy 4000 societies had a million members; while in Greece 4500 societies were selling currants, curing tobacco, crushing olives, making wine, providing credit, or renting land. In Russia the revolution swept away the credit societies, but NEP accepted the other groups as necessary; and in 1928 there were 93,000 societies buying, processing, or selling for 11,000,000 members. Collectivization wiped out much of their work, and if it stays they may vanish.

Where cooperation has been strongest it has played a large part in reducing costs of production and distribution, and some part in increasing the efficiency of farming. It probably has had little effect on price levels, especially in international trade. These remain the sport of a supply that results from the uncoordinated efforts of millions of farmers scattered over parts of five continents; of a demand that may be injured by depression among city folks, or may change its direction under the influence of new consumer habits; of commercial policies that may close doors; of currency vagaries, or of weather. In such a changeable world the peasant often carries a large overhead load of interest that may have been fixed in days of happier prices. He cannot reduce his labor force as can the industrialist, for it is his family. He cannot quickly cut down the volume of production, once the seed is in or the cow has been bought. He cannot quickly change the direction of production, for soil and climate may forbid it, and if they do not he might merely be moving from one frying pan to another. He is thus helpless at many vital points, and in his latest period of distress has called on the state to help him as never before. Tariffs, quotas, subsidies, readjustment of debt, moratorium laws, compulsory cooperation, and marketing schemes comprise an unprecedented motley of farm relief. To estimate their efficacy would be prophecy, not history.

BIBLIOGRAPHY

GENERAL

BIRNIE, A., *Economic History of Europe, 1760-1930* (1930), chap. 2.

BOGARDUS, J. F., *Europe: A Geographical Survey* (1934), chap. 6, and agricultural sections in description of each country.

BOWMAN, I., *The New World: Problems in Political Geography* (1928).

FINCH, F. C., and BAKER, O. E., *Geography of the World's Agriculture* (1917).

IRVINE, H. D., *The Making of Rural Europe* (1923).

JONASSON, OLAF, "The Agricultural Regions of Europe," in *Econ. Geog.*, October, 1925, and January, 1926.

KNIGHT, M. M., FLÜGEL, F., and BARNES, H. E., *Economic History of Europe* (1928), chaps. 11-13, 19-21.

OGG, F. A., and SHARP, W. R., *Economic Development of Modern Europe* (1926), chaps. 2, 6, 8, 9, 15, 26 (good bibliographies).

SÉE, H., *Esquisse d'une histoire du régime agraire en Europe aux xviii°-xix° siècles* (1921).

SMITH, J. RUSSELL. *Industrial and Commercial Geography* (1925).

SOROKIN, P., ZIMMERMAN, C., and GALPIN, C. J., *A Systematic Source Book in Rural Sociology* (1930), vol. i. Contains excellent extracts.

Encyclopædia of the Social Sciences: See the list of titles under the headings, "Agriculture" and "Cooperation," in vol. xv, pp. 548 and 550.

The International Institute of Agriculture publishes a *Yearbook of Agricultural Statistics* and a monthly *International Review of Agriculture.*

ENGLAND

SURVEYS

ASHLEY, W. J., *Economic Organisation of England* (1915), chap. 6.

CLAPHAM, J. H., *Economic History of Modern Britain,* vol. i, chaps. 4, 11; vol. ii, chap. 7.

CURTLER, W. H. R., *Short History of English Agriculture* (1909), chaps. 17-21.

FAY, C. R., *Great Britain from Adam Smith to the Present Day* (1932), chap. 12.

GRAS, N. S. B., *History of Agriculture* (1925), chaps. 7, 8.

KNOWLES, L. C. A., *Industrial and Commercial Revolutions in Great Britain during the Nineteenth Century* (1921), part vii.

MANTOUX, P., *The Industrial Revolution in the Eighteenth Century* (Eng. trans., 1928), part i, chap. 3.

MARRIOTT, J. A. R., *The English Land System* (1914).

PROTHERO, R. E. (Lord Ernle), *English Farming, Past and Present* (1927), chaps. 14, 17-19.

SEEBOHM, M. E., *Evolution of the English Farm* (1925).

VENN, J. A., *Foundations of Agricultural Economics* (2nd ed., 1933).

SPECIAL TOPICS

BENNETT, M. K., "British Wheat Yields for Seven Centuries," in *Ec. Hist.,* February, 1935, pp. 12-29.

BLAND, BROWN, and TAWNEY, *English Economic History: Select Documents,* part iii, section 2.

BRODRICK, G. L., *English Land and English Landlords* (1881).

CURTLER, W. H. R., *The Enclosure and Redistribution of our Land* (1920).

DAMPIER-WHETHAM, W. C., *Politics and the Land* (1927).

DAVIES, E., "The Small Landowner, 1780-1832," in *Ec. H. R.,* vol. i (1927), pp. 87-113.

GONNER, E. C. K., *Common Land and Inclosure* (1912).

GRAS, N. S. B. and E. C., *Social and Economic History of an English Village* (1930). See especially the Enclosure Act of 1794.

GREEN, F. E., *History of the English Agricultural Labourer, 1870-1920* (1920).

HAMMOND, J. L. and B., *The Village Labourer, 1760-1832* (1911).

HASBACH, W., *History of the English Agricultural Labourer* (1909).

HEATON, H., *The British Way to Recovery* (1934), chap. 5.

LAVROVSKY, V., "Tithe Commutation as a Factor in the Gradual Decrease of Landownership by the English Peasantry," in *Ec. H. R.,* October, 1933, pp. 273-289.

LEVY, H., *Large and Small Holdings* (1911).

MARSHALL, T. H., "Jethro Tull and the 'New Husbandry,'" in *Ec. H. R.,* vol. ii (1929), pp. 41-60.

MIDDLETON, T. H., *Food Production in War* (1923).

ORWIN, C. S., Chapter on "Agriculture" in Turberville, A. S. (ed.), *Johnson's England* (1932), vol. i.

SLATER, G., *The English Peasantry and the Enclosure of the Common Fields* (1909).

STREET, A. G., *Farmer's Glory* (1931. A novel).

YOUNG, A., *Autobiography.* Also any of his Tours.

Articles on British agricultural problems will be found in such periodicals as the *Economic Journal, The Round Table, The Political Quarterly,* and *The Contemporary Review.*

FRANCE

AUGÉ-LARIBÉ, M., *L'évolution de la France agricole* (1912).

AUGÉ-LARIBÉ, M., *L'agriculture pendant la guerre* (1925).

BLOCH, M., *Les caractères originaux de l'histoire rurale française* (1931), chap. 6.

BLOCH, M., "La lutte pour l'individualisme agraire dans la France du xviii° siècle," in *Ann. d'hist. éc. et soc.,* vol. ii (1930), pp. 328-383, 510-556.

CLAPHAM, J. H., *Economic Development of France and Germany, 1815-1914* (1923), chaps. 1, 8.

DÉLÉAGE, A., "La vaine pâture en France," in *Rev. d'hist. mod.,* September-October, 1931.

KOVALEVSKY, M. M., *La France économique et sociale à la veille de la revolution* (1909), vol. i.

LEFEBVRE, G., *Les paysans du Nord pendant la révolution française* (1924).

LEFEBVRE, G., "Les récherches relatifs à la répartition de la propriété . . . à la fin de l'ancien régime," in *Rev. d'hist. mod.,* vol. iii (1928), pp. 103-125.

LEFEBVRE, G., "Les récherches relatifs à la vente des biens nationaux," in *Rev. d'hist. mod.,* vol. iii (1929), pp. 188-219.

LEFEBVRE, G., "La place de la révolution dans l'histoire agraire de France," in *Ann. d'hist. éc. et soc.,* vol. i (1929), pp. 506-519.

LOUTCHISKY, J., *L'état des classes agricoles en France à la veille de la révolution* (1911).

MARION, M., *La vente des biens nationaux* (1908).

MELINE, J., *The Return to the Land* (Eng. trans., 1906).

OGBURN, W. F., and JAFFÉ, W., *The Economic Development of Post-War France* (1929).

SÉE, H., *Economic and Social Conditions in France in the Eighteenth Century* (Eng. trans., 1927).

SÉE, H., *La vie économique de 1815 à 1848* (1926).

THÉRY, E., *Les progrés économiques de la France* (1908).

YOUNG, A., *Travels in France, 1787, 1788, 1789.*

GERMANY

BRINKMANN, C., "The Place of Germany in the Economic History of the Nineteenth Century," in *Ec. H. R.,* vol. iv, April, 1933, pp. 129-146.

BUCHENBERGER, A., *Agrarwesen und Agrarpolitik* (new. ed., 1914).

CLAPHAM, J. H., *Economic Development of France and Germany, 1815-1914* (1923), chaps. 2, 9.

DAWSON, W. H., *Evolution of Modern Germany* (1908), chaps. 12-15.

FORD, G. S., *Stein and the Era of Reform* (1922).

GERBER, H., *Geschichte des deutschen Bauernstandes* (3rd ed., 1928).

HANSEN, M. L., "The Revolutions of 1848 and German Migration," in *J. E. B. H.,* August, 1930, pp. 630-658.

KNAPP, G. F., *Die Bauernbefreiung und der Ursprung der Landarbeiter* (1887; 2nd ed., 1927). The classic work on agrarian reforms.

MIDDLETON, T. H., *Recent Development of German Agriculture* (1916).

PCGGI, E. M., "The German Sugar Beet Industry," in *Econ. Geog.*, vol. vi (1930), pp. 81-93.

SARTORIUS VON WALTERHAUSEN, A., *Deutsche Wirtschaftsgeschichte, 1815-1914.*

SERING, M., *Die Innere Kolonization* (1893).

SKALWEIT, A. K. F., *Agrarpolitik* (1924).

STEIN, R., *Die Umwandlung der Agrarverfassung Ostpreussens* (1918).

STOLZE, W., *Der deutsche Bauernkrieg* (1907).

VON DER GOLTZ, T., *Geschichte der deutschen Landwirtschaft* (1903), vol. ii.

WYNN, A., "A Note on German Agriculture," in *Ec. J.*, September, 1933, pp. 518-524.

OTHER COUNTRIES (IN ORDER OF TREATMENT)

JONES, H., *Modern Denmark* (1927).

WESTERGAARD, H., *Economic Developments in Denmark before and during the War* (1922).

SCHEFFLER, K., *Holland: the Land and the People* (1932).

ROWNTREE, B. S., *Land and Labour: Lessons from Belgium* (1910).

O'BRIEN, G., *Economic History of Ireland from the Union to the Famine* (1921).

PLUNKETT, H., *Ireland in the New Century* (1905).

POMFRET, J. E., *The Struggle for Land in Ireland, 1800-1923* (1930).

SMITH, G. L., and STAPLES, L. C., *Rural Reconstruction in Ireland* (1919).

NEWBIGIN, M. I., *Southern Europe* (1932).

HANCOCK, W. K., "Italian Métayage," in *Ec. Hist.*, January, 1928, pp. 368-384.

MICHAEL, L. G., *Agricultural Survey of the Danube Basin* (U. S. Dept. Agric., Bulletins 123 and 126, 1924 and 1929).

ANTSIFEROV, A. N., and others, *Russian Agriculture during the War* (1930).

DOBB, M., *Russian Economic Development since the Revolution* (1928).

MAVOR, J., *Economic History of Russia* (1914).

POKROVSKY, M. N., *Brief History of Russia* (Eng. trans., 1934), vol. ii.

ZAITSEFF, C., "The Agrarian Crisis in Russia," in *J. E. B. H.*, August, 1931, pp. 499-528.

POST-WAR DEVELOPMENTS

DELAISI, F., *Les deux Europes* (1929).

MITRANY, D., *The Land and the Peasant in Rumania* (1930).

TEXTOR, L. E., *Land Reform in Czechoslovakia* (1923).

World Agriculture (Royal Institute of International Affairs, London, 1933).

The Agricultural Crisis (League of Nations, Econ. and Fin. Section, 1931).

ENFIELD, R. R., "The World's Wheat Situation," in *Ec. J.*, December, 1931, pp. 550-565.

Social Science Abstracts (1929-1932): Consult complete index.

COOPERATION

AUGÉ-LARIBÉ, M., *Syndicats et cooperatives agricoles* (1926).

FABER, H., *Cooperation in Danish Agriculture* (1918).

FAY, C. R., *Cooperation at Home and Abroad* (1920).

CHAPTER XXI

EUROPEAN INDUSTRIES SINCE 1700

DURING the two centuries following the geographical discoveries the makers of economic history were the merchant, seaman, and financier. With some important exceptions, industry was the handmaid, or at best the butler, to commercial capitalism. The next two centuries turned the tables with a vengeance. Their central theme was production; their hero was the inventor, scientist, or manufacturer; and their story full of changes in the methods of making things, in the discovery of new things to be made, and in the equipment of transportation. The merchant and banker had to make room on the bench for the portly figures of industrialist and carrier, and if the bench was too short it was the merchant who must stand up.

The industrial innovations of the eighteenth century did not come suddenly out of a clear sky. The ancient and medieval worlds had faced and solved some production problems as they arose, with the knowledge, materials, and tools at their disposal. The German miners of the fifteenth and sixteenth centuries grappled sucessfully with metallurgical and mechanical difficulties, and Leonardo da Vinci (1452-1519) brought a powerful imagination and well-stocked scientific mind to bear on a wide range of problems. He was artist, sculptor, poet, musician, architect, canal cutter, and military engineer. He observed and designed improvements on the industrial appliances of his day, dreamed of a flying machine that would bring him fame or a needle-polishing machine that would bring him fortune, and filled notebooks with sketches of spinning machines, power looms, roller bearings, universal joints, gears, lathes, screw cutters, turbines, and a steam cannon. Whether he drew what he had seen or what he would like to see is not clear. Many of his devices never got off the paper on which they were drawn, but he did begin lines of thought that others were to carry on, in both pure and applied science.

Science grew in stature during the seventeenth century, and the value of its discoveries concerning the vacuum and atmospheric pressure was soon realized by men who were seeking better pumps for their mines. Newcomen, a mining engineer, appealed to a physicist for aid about 1700, just as Young submitted his soil problems to the chemist Priestley seventy years later. But it was only in Young's day and later that the work of Lavoisier, Leblanc, Priestley, Volta, Galvani, Franklin, Davy, Faraday, and others, on chemistry, heat, and electricity produced a body of knowledge that was useful to production. Discovery, invention, and improvement had therefore to come largely from industry itself until we approach or pass 1800. They came in quantities that were far from insignificant even in the sixteenth and seventeenth centuries. The making of glass, clocks, chemicals, and munitions advanced; metal refining, knitting, cloth-finishing, ribbon weaving, wood cutting, shipbuilding, and other occupations found new or improved equipment. The harnessing of animal, wind, or water power expanded, the use of coal grew, and steam was on the threshold. "New projections are every day set on foot," said an English writer in 1695.

These instances may seem to make a meager total when compared with those of almost any decade after 1750. The obstacles to advance were still powerful, and while some were technical, others were human. If lack of fuel checked the expansion of iron production, popular or state opposition damped the enthusiasm of inventors whose devices might reduce the demand for labor. In Tudor England a ban was placed on the use of some cloth-finishing machines, and in 1623 the Privy Council suppressed an engine for making needles. Danzig in 1586 forbade the use of a new loom which wove several strands of ribbon, and suffocated its inventor. The use of this loom was limited or forbidden in nearly every country during the seventeenth century. If any vested interest could show it was threatened and was strong enough to make its hostility felt, the inventor might deem it safe to retreat or the state might compel him to do so. How far state decrees were enforced we do not know; it is probable that they made the wheels turn more slowly, but did not stop them entirely, and advance was quickest where opposition was weakest, especially in industries that were comparatively new in a country.

As we pass into the eighteenth century the obstacles grow weaker, the movement gains strength, and the advance captures point after point along the four fronts—machinery, power, metals, and science. In that advance Great Britain and France led. The British success was chiefly in machinery and metallurgy, while that of France lay in chemical discoveries. Each learned from the other, for while some English inventors found refuge and reward in France, French dyeing and bleaching lore helped British manufacturers greatly. French mechanical ideas were improved by British hands, and a well-known proverb announced that "for a thing to be perfect it must be invented in France and worked out in England." Each country had governments and groups interested in technical progress and each had a large and growing market. France housed at least 20,000,000 people in 1789, and her external trade increased fivefold between 1715 and 1787. The British population was only one-third that of France, but it was growing rapidly, occupied a large free-trade unit, and was being knit together by roads and canals. Foreign and colonial trade, especially in cloth and hardware, doubled between 1720 and 1760, and doubled again by 1795. Ports like Liverpool and Glasgow rose to importance, and the profits made in the textile, hardware, tobacco, sugar, spice, slave, and other trades fed a rising reservoir of capital to finance banking, shipbuilding, and manufactures.

This expansion of domestic and external commerce was both cause and effect of manufacturing changes. On the one hand, a growing demand for a commodity might call for quicker or larger production and for an effort to design machines that would allow more work to be done per person. On the other hand, a producer might see a great slumbering demand waiting to be wakened if goods formerly sold to a few at high prices could be sold to the multitude at low ones. Demand creates supply, but supply creates demand if the price is low enough. If cheap cottons, cheap crockery, and cheap iron could be put on the market the demand for them would be enormous, just as was the demand for cheap automobiles, rubber, grapefruit, or radios in a later generation. There was no conscious actual demand for them till they appeared, and the mass of mankind got along without them. It is no mere accident that the makers of these three cheap commodities—cottons, crockery, and iron—were in the advance guard of modern technological change, for in creating virtually brand new markets and stirring up a vast consumer consciousness, they set a fashion that many other producers have followed.

Supply and demand do not explain the whole search for new

equipment and methods. The wave of curiosity and zest for experiment that swept agriculture washed over industry as well, and by the third quarter of the eighteenth century was becoming a flood. The motives were mixed. There were geniuses and quacks, inventors who sought a solution for the joy and fun of success, men who were eager to make money, and men who must find new ways if they were to avert the extinction of their business. The mine manager must cut haulage costs, fight the water that flooded deep seams, and rid the underground of poisonous or explosive gases. Unless he could do these things, his mine could never be more than a shallow pit with a short, damp, dangerous life, and vast mineral deposits must lie untapped. The ironmaster was faced with extinction unless he could find a substitute for charcoal. Necessity was the mother of invention, and invention turned the tide in what threatened to be a losing battle.

Many inventions sought to "abridge labor," dispense with skilled workers, counteract the lack of them, or permit the use of children. In 1770, for instance, a Scotch papermaker claimed that his new rag-cutting engine did more work than eight men had formerly done. In 1760 the London Society of Arts offered a prize for a spinning machine, on the ground that "manufacturers of woollen, linen, and cotton find it extremely difficult in the summer season, when the spinners are at harvest work, to procure a sufficient number of hands." Four years later it gave its prize "for a masterly improvement in the spinning wheel, by which a child can do double the business that even a grown person can with the common wheel." Campbell in 1747 reported that watchmakers had invented engines for cutting the teeth of cogwheels, thus reducing the "expense of workmanship and time to a trifle in comparison to what it was before and [bringing] the work to such an exactness that no hand can imitate it."

Some inventors were stimulated by the prospect of profits to be made from the operation of their engines or of large patent royalties. Leonardo da Vinci calculated that ten of his needle-polishing machines would bring him the income of a Medici, and Arkwright set out to make a fortune by erecting mills to use his waterframe. Kay, Arkwright, Watt, and others fought with varying success to protect and exploit their patents, and to punish pirates who stole their ideas. Manufacturers did not like the command to pay, and urged that reward should come in the form of a gift of money instead of patent rights. With this view the British and French governments occasionally concurred. State rewards were supplemented by those of numerous societies set up to foster technical progress. The Society for the Encouragement of Arts, Manufactures, and Commerce was even wider than its name. Founded in 1754, its aim was "to encourage ingenuity and industry by bestowing of premiums." It offered money, medals, and other rewards for specified achievements, it built up a museum of machines and models, and its publications circulated widely. In the British provinces and in such continental towns as Hamburg and Paris similar societies were at work.

The decades after 1750 were thus marked by a lively spirit of inquiry and innovation. The atmosphere was favorable to individual inspiration, and men grew more convinced of their ability to alter and adapt their environment and implements to new wants and plans. Magazines, encyclopædias, and dictionaries chronicled new machines and methods. The first balloon flight in 1783 created a temporary but enthusiastic "air-mindedness," men played with ideas of submarines and horseless carriages, and clock-makers designed elaborate mechanical figures, including a robot that played chess. All things seemed possible and credible. One man came forward with a "very ingenious piece of mechanism . . . for the easy capture of sea-fish. One person may operate 500 hooks." An English mechanic took out a patent "for a perpetual power that will give motion to all kinds of machinery, mills, engines, carriages" and boats. A genius informed the world that he had made a "composition for shaving without the use of razor, soap, or water."

Of the growing army of inventors and improvers some are known, but many who made important contributions are not. "At Birmingham, Wolverhampton, Sheffield, and other manufacturing places almost every master manufacturer hath a new invention of his own, and is daily improving on those of others" (Tucker, 1757). Many of them were small craftsmen, who by accident, inspiration, or the play of a fertile mind "hit upon" a new device or fundamentally improved an old one. Some were onlookers, who by chance strayed into the company of problems that practical men said were insoluble, and brought a fresh mind to the task. Edmund Cartwright, the first designer of a power loom, was a country parson who had never seen a loom, who had never turned his mind to any mechanical problem—beyond the writing of eighteenth-century poetry—but who heard some hard-headed Lancashire manufacturers say that a power loom could not be made. Eli Whitney, prospective school-teacher, heard cotton planters declare "that if a machine could be invented which would clean the cotton with expedition, it would be a great thing both to the country and to the inventor." But they were as empty of hope and ideas as the Lancashiremen had been, and it was left to Whitney to solve their problem.

The outsider grew greatly in importance during the nineteenth century, but he was usually a professional inventor or a pure scientist. The former explored unknown fields for the joy of the venture and for the monetary reward. The latter might be little concerned with the practical application of his discoveries, but the industrial world could not be indifferent to him. Sometimes it took up his findings, sometimes it took its problems to his door. When Scheele found chlorine in 1774, and Berthollet discovered that it bleached colored fibers (1785), one of the first important chemical contributions was made to industry, for the length of time taken to bleach cotton or linen was cut down from months to days or even hours. When a series of big explosions drove mine owners to Davy's laboratory for aid against the underground demon, a big industry recognized its dependence on the scientist. As the nineteenth century progressed, physics or chemistry gave birth to new industries, such as electricity, rayon, dyes, or fertilizers, and helped old industries to understand the nature of the materials they were using. Manufacturers began to employ their own research staffs, but the fundamental discoveries continued to come chiefly from inventors and scientists working outside industry, and the staffs improved the details. Within the last forty years moving pictures, dial telephones, television, radio telegraphy and telephony, triode valves, airplanes, synthetic resins, and safety razors have been brought into the world by pure scientists or free lances.

Changes in the Textile Industries.—The making of cloth has always been one of the world's most important industries, and changes in its equipment therefore had far-reaching results. Its raw material was present in most inhabited regions, and its products could range from humble homespun to fabrics of fine texture, rich color, and elaborate pattern. Its technology rested on three main divisions: turning the fiber into yarn, weaving the yarn into cloth, and giving the cloth its finished appearance; but the first and third were capable of great subdivision. At almost any point in the flow of material from plant or animal to finished article the traffic might be held up by a lack of spinners, weavers, or finishers, but the worst jam came where the yarn-makers and the weavers met. In the early eighteenth century one cotton loom used the product of four spinners, a woolen weaver kept nine or ten persons busy preparing yarn, while in the sailcloth industry Young found "20 spinners and 2 or 3 other hands to every weaver." Thus for every additional weaver employed, many more hands must be found. The spinners rarely lacked work, but the weavers were often idle for want of yarn, and as the demand for cloth (especially cotton or fustian) expanded during the eighteenth century putters-out had to send material farther afield to be spun.

Prior to the eighteenth century there was little change in textile equipment. The wheel displaced the distaff and made spinning less slow, while a Saxon wheel allowed two threads of yarn to be made at once. The silk-throwing machine spread from Italy after 1500, and reached England in 1719. It required a big building, much water power, and many workers, and was said to throw over 3,000,000 yards of yarn a day. When Lombe's patent expired in 1732, similar machines were erected in Lancashire and London, thus spreading factory production. Meanwhile the use of the ribbon loom had spread in spite of opposition, and on it one weaver could produce many pieces of ribbon or tape at once. But this list of alterations left the greater part of the industry untouched.

In 1733 John Kay, a Lancashireman who made loom parts and had a gift for invention, patented his fly shuttle. It was cigar-shaped, fitted with tiny wheels, and could be knocked from side to side of the loom, instead of being thrown from hand to hand. Weaving could now be done more quickly, and only one person (instead of two) was needed to weave a wide cloth. This invention was only slowly taken up. It roused jealousy and dislike among weavers, and while some workers used it without paying royalties, others did not. There may have been technical obstacles, but apart from these, quicker weaving was useless unless yarn was forthcoming in greater abundance.

That abundance came through a series of inventions which increased the quantity and improved the quality of yarn. In 1733

Paul (son of a French refugee) and Wyatt (an inventively minded carpenter) began to experiment with spinning by the use of rollers. In 1741 they set up a little mill, and used two donkeys to supply the power. Failure dogged the effort, and roller spinning had to wait till Arkwright, a Lancashire barber and wigmaker with little inventive ability but much business capacity, bought the idea, improved it, took out a patent in 1769, and established a factory driven by water power in 1771. At almost the same moment (1770) Hargreaves, a Lancashire weaver, patented his spinning jenny, which was virtually a multiple spinning wheel; it allowed one person to spin eight, then sixteen, and finally over a hundred threads of yarn at once. The jenny was an inexpensive simple device, was worked by hand, could be housed in a cottage, and thus increased the yield of yarn without requiring any great outlay in mills, machinery, or power. In 1779 Crompton, a Lancashire jenny spinner, combined features of Hargreaves' jenny and Arkwright's "water frame" in a hybrid appropriately called a mule. The mule was steadily improved, made automatic in action, and adapted to water power. By 1800 it might be spinning 400 threads of the finest yarn such as only the Orient had formerly produced. Lancashire and Glasgow could now compete with the best wares of the East India Company, and the textile workers of Asia soon felt the hard kick of a mule as British goods invaded their home market.

The yarn famine ended, only to give place to a famine of weavers. Jennies and mules were worked by hand in cottages, spinning factories of all sizes arose, and thousands of new weavers had to be found to consume the apparently endless supply of yarn. Irish emigrants flocked across the Irish Sea to join the army of hand-loom workers. Mechanics wrestled as Cartwright had done with plans for a power loom, but success came slowly. Yarns were so fragile that if a shuttle was hit hard the strain might break the thread or knock the shuttle out of the loom. We have to pass down a long line of improvements before we get a power loom that could beat a hand loom. The final triumph did not come till nearly 1850 in the cotton industry, but woolen yarn was for long too frail. As late as 1880 the clatter of the hand loom could be heard in many cottages in Yorkshire valleys, and the last generation of hand-loom weavers is only just passing away.

Other textile processes became mechanical between 1770 and 1860. The finishing of cotton goods was greatly helped when in 1784 a copper-plate printer patented a "new, peculiar, and improved art of printing one, two, three, four, five, or more colours all at one time." He used rollers, as in the modern printing press, and thus made the application of patterns easy, quick, and cheap. In New England during the next decade men applied the principle of the lawn mower to shear or crop the surface of woolen fabrics, but the hand shears were still being used twenty years later. In 1804 Jacquard brought to a head the efforts of many predecessors to perfect the mechanism for weaving patterned fabrics. His device was adapted for making lace, and an ancient manual occupation was turned into a machine industry by combining methods drawn from stocking frames, watchmaking, fishing-net machines, and the Jacquard loom. The scarcity of wool in the early nineteenth century led to the designing of machines which extracted the fibers from wool rags, cast-off clothing, old stockings, and tailors' clippings, and allowed them to be manufactured into "shoddy."

These developments caused a great increase in the output per worker and a reduction in costs of production. Between 1779 and 1812 the cost of producing a pound of cotton yarn fell from 100 to 7, and between 1779 and 1882 from 100 to 2. The mule's fine cheap yarn "brought to the masses of the people better goods than even the rich had been able to afford in the earlier period" (Usher). The British output of printed cottons rose from 21,-000,000 yards in 1796 to 347,000,000 in 1830. When the power loom became efficient women gradually displaced men, and one worker could look after two, three, or four looms. According to one estimate, a male adult hand weaver made two cotton cloths in a week, but a "steam weaver," aided by a twelve-year-old girl, could attend four looms and weave eighteen to twenty pieces a week in 1833. The weaver's task was to stop the loom when the shuttle was empty, put in a full one, start the loom again, and watch for broken threads. In 1894 Northrop produced an automatic loom which changed the shuttle mechanically without halting the work, but which stopped of its own accord if any threads broke. A weaver could supervise many more such looms, and the labor cost of weaving was reduced by half. The automatic loom was well fitted for weaving plain cheap fabrics, and found a home in the factories of the American south and in Japan. It was less satisfactory for finer grades of work, and was therefore much less popular in Europe.

In the woolen industry, machines had by 1800 reduced the number of workers needed to turn wool into yarn by four-fifths, and forty years later the savings were eight-ninths in time and two-thirds in cost. By that time the labor cost of making the best cloths had fallen by at least half, though weaving was still done by hand. In 1770 the labor cost of making some cloths was two, three, or even five times the cost of the raw material; but by 1830 labor, maintenance, and capital charges combined seem to have cost less than did the wool in the best mills. In the lace industry huge broad looms could make curtains or produce forty strips of lace. Lace trimmings became a feminine necessity, and curtains a standard domestic decoration.

Machinery in Other Industries.—Machines gradually invaded other industries. A Frenchman invented a sewing machine about 1820. Defective construction and the hostility of Parisian seamstresses delayed its adoption in France, but Elias Howe produced an improved machine in America in 1846 and Singer popularized it. It came into being just at a time when needleworkers were being gathered together or employed in their homes by manufacturers of ready-made clothing, and became the instrument through which the cheap cottons, woolens, and shoddy could be converted into garments for the masses. A stronger sewing machine came to the aid of the shoemaker during the 'fifties, and when supplemented by American machines for cutting, nailing, and finishing, it displaced the old shoemaker with his lasts, cobbler's wax, awls, and mouthful of nails. The group of keyboard machines was the product of European and American inventors. An Italian, Ravizza, patented a typewriter in 1855, American and British models soon appeared, and by 1874 serviceable machines were available. The printing industry got its first rotary press in 1847, and its first linotype in 1884. The first adding machine appeared in 1888, and the office slave to pen, ink, and mental arithmetic gradually gave place to the "error-proof machine operated by a vision in bobbed hair and bright-hued raiment, whose knowledge of Debit, Credit, and Balance is confined to the pressing of keys which bring about the desired result."

The rise of cities and factories called for large supplies of building material and stimulated the construction industry. After 1800 machines for making bricks were designed in England and America. Woodworking machines were American in origin, and in 1853 an English observer was surprised to find that many factories in New England were occupied solely in the manufacture of doors, window frames and stairs, with machines built specially for planing or making joints. In the furniture trades he found every process, "from sawing to sandpapering," done by machines. These methods were transferred to Europe, especially to the Baltic countries which produced lumber for the builders, and to the furniture factories which were thereby enabled to clutter up homes with cheap products. Into those homes after 1850 came an increasing supply of machine-processed foodstuffs. Large food factories were possible only when easy transportation and the spread of advertising opened up a wide market, and allowed the biscuits, candies, cocoa, jam, or flour of some large firm to spread over a whole countryside and even enter foreign fields.

The Rise of Mechanical Engineering.—While machinery conquered old industries it also created new ones. The bicycle, automobile, and electrical equipment industries were three of its numerous offspring; but of the newcomers the greatest was the production of machinery itself by a branch of industry that came to be known in Europe as "mechanical engineering." For constructing a water wheel or windmill, hand loom, jenny, or early mule, few metal parts were needed, and the builder was little more than a skilled carpenter. It soon became evident, however, that equipment driven at a rapid pace must have many parts of brass or iron, that cog wheels and bearings could not be left to grind themselves into a neat fit through much friction, and that steam engines could not be economical of steam or efficient in delivery of power unless pistons fitted cylinders snugly all through the stroke. Watt found that a cylinder made by the best workmen available in Glasgow varied by three-eighths of an inch in diameter, and Smeaton, a famous engineer, told him that "neither tools nor workmen existed that could manufacture so complex a machine with sufficient precision." Various workers in wood and metals had lathes or borers, but the production of large metal pieces was done by casting the metal in a mold and then giving it final shape or size by grinding or filing. The file was "the chief and ultimate instrument of precision in the heavy metal trades" (Usher).

The way to precision was to clamp both cutting tool and material firmly in a machine; then the tool could be adjusted and guided to do its work—grinding, boring, slotting, drilling, turning, or cutting. The development of such machine tools was the work of many men between 1770 and 1840. In 1774 John Wilkinson, who was so "iron mad" that he built an iron barge, an iron bridge, and an iron coffin (for himself), made an improved borer for cannon, and in 1776 used it to shape cylinders and condensers for Watt. At last cylinders could be cylindrical. In 1794 Joseph Bramah, a jack-of-all-trades as an inventor, and his ally, Henry Maudslay, designed an all-metal lathe with the cutting tool held in a slide rest. Maudslay made the lathe capable of adjustment to the thousandth part of an inch, and designed screw-cutting, planing, and other machines. James Nasmyth and others developed the steam hammer (1839) and various types of metal presses; engine-builders and textile machine-makers improved their equipment, and by 1850 mechanical engineering had a full kit of machine tools. Within a decade it was to begin to have an abundant supply of cheap steel and of lubricating oil.

The steel came with Bessemer's invention of the converter, the oil with the tapping of the Pennsylvania fields in 1859. Till that time all kinds of animal or vegetable oils had been sought and tried. Olive oil had been used for greasing delicate machinery; tallow, colza, neatsfoot, and whale oil served heavier machines; and the bearings of railroad axles had been lubricated with a mixture of palm oil, tallow, and lye. Hence the extraction of oil from petroleum was a great boon to all who built or used machines, by reducing friction and permitting movement at greater speeds. Oil and steel opened a virtually new chapter for the engineer.

While British engineers solved their problems, their American counterparts were advancing on a somewhat different line. The keynote of the American development was already quantity production of standardized articles made by the assembling of standardized parts. Each of these parts was made by a machine specially designed for that one task; it needed only to be fed, started, and stopped, and did not need a skilled worker for its operation. The designing of machines to make the necessary parts for guns, clocks, sewing machines, harvesters, or locks called forth great ingenuity, and English observers in the 'fifties contrasted the "fearless and masterly manner" in which "correct principles" were applied in New England with the "certain degree of timidity, resulting from traditional notions and attachment to old systems," in old England. Gradually the products and the machine tools crossed the Atlantic. Colt set up a pistol factory in England in 1851, the sewing machine and the harvester were made there by 1860, while the British Ordnance Department bought a complete set of machines for making rifles. In later decades European production of cars, shoes, and electrical appliances benefited from "Yankee ingenuity" in equipment and organization.

The Generation of Power.—From at least medieval times there had been slow but sure improvement in the generation, transmission, and use of power. The treadle and treadmill had their place, and many an apprentice obtained part of his training by turning a wheel. Animals were harnessed to work gins or windlasses geared to machines; Wyatt and Paul used two donkeys, Cartwright a cow, and the first two power looms in Scotland (1793) drew power from a Newfoundland dog. Windmills dotted many a landscape; but water was the main source of power, driving fulling stocks, millstones, saws, bellows, and ore crushers. When cities began to improve their water supplies in the sixteenth century water wheels worked the pumps to raise water from river or reservoir. The accounts of Lombe's silk mill show how elaborate had become the connection between the prime mover, the transmission, and the machinery. The textile inventions came in an area of hills, valleys, and streams, and the early mills were built on river banks. Every available water site was harnessed, and the early factory system was therefore dispersed, rather than concentrated in towns. If the supply of falling water was inadequate, steam engines were used to pump water to a height from which it could flow to the wheel.

Steam was known to the Hellenistic world, and had been used to open temple doors or perform miracles for the edification of the faithful and the confusion of doubters. Da Vinci thought about it, and the seventeenth-century scientists made two useful discoveries—that atmosphere had weight, and that if steam was condensed in a closed vessel a vacuum was formed. Pepys in

1663 found Charles II "laughing mightily" at the Fellows of the Royal Society for "spending their time only in weighing of ayre," but men who had to raise water for domestic or city use or fight floods in mines had cause to be grateful. One of the latter, Newcomen, discussed his problem with Hooke, the physicist, and in 1705-1706 made an engine model. His fundamental idea was to put a vertical piston and cylinder at the end of a pump handle. The cylinder was filled with steam; the steam pushed the piston up, and the pump plunger descended. The steam was then condensed by spraying cold water into the cylinder; as a partial vacuum was thus created, atmospheric pressure pushed the piston down, and the plunger was pulled up, bringing water in its train.

Newcomen's engine became popular, many were at work by 1720, and in 1769 Smeaton counted a hundred of them on the north of England coal fields alone. Some were big and powerful; one had a cylinder six feet in diameter, its piston stroke was over ten feet, it was rated at 76 H. P. and was said to "have the force to raise, at a stroke, above 307 cwt. of water." Even the smaller engines were more powerful than most water wheels, and were truly "the miner's friend." They moved slowly—about ten to fifteen strokes a minute, steam was only a device for getting the atmosphere to work, and the cooling of the cylinder meant a great waste of heat; but this was unimportant at a pithead where coal was cheap. Hence Newcomen engines were in use on the coal fields as late as 1830, three decades after Watt's patent had expired. Where, then, lies the importance and fame of Watt?

Watt was a Scot, and his engine was patented as "a new method of Lessening the Consumption of Steam and Fuel in Fire Engines." As maker of scientific equipment for Glasgow University, he was asked in 1763 to repair a model of a Newcomen engine. He realized the shocking waste of good heat involved in cooling the cylinder to condense the steam; if condensation could take place in a separate vessel (a condenser) the cylinder would not have to be alternately heated and cooled, and many sixpences could be cut off the fuel bill. Had Watt stopped there he would merely have improved the old engine; but he went further, and fed steam into each end of a closed cylinder to push the piston back and forth. The engine was thus changed from an atmospheric to a steam engine, which "worked" on each stroke, and when a crank and flywheel were added (1782) the engine provided rotary motion that would turn shafts and wheels to drive machines.

Watt took out his patent in 1769, and Roebuck, head of the Carron ironworks and cannon foundry, tried to give substance to Watt's plans in the face of crude tools and unskilled workers. Roebuck went bankrupt, and one of his creditors was Matthew Boulton, a Birmingham maker of metal small ware, whose energy as manufacturer and salesman had won wide fame for his Soho factory. He had spent £20,000 in building and equipping that factory, and employed 600 skilled workmen. He needed more power for his works and for Cornish mines in which he was a stockholder, and he saw that on Watt's patent a profitable business might be built up. He therefore let Roebuck pay his debt by handing over Watt, took the Scot to Soho (1774), and secured an extension of the patent to 1800.

When it expired 320 Watt engines were at work in Great Britain on mines, in metal plants, textile factories, and breweries. One or two were rated at 40 H. P., but the average strength was only 16 H. P. The steam pressure was still low, and mountainous engines produced mouselike power. After 1800 competition between Soho and other engine builders grew keener than ever, and great improvements were made. Higher pressures were developed, and methods of transmitting power from engine to machine were made less cumbersome. From mines, metal works, and mills the steam engine passed on to ships and railroads: a Watt engine propelled the *Clermont* up the Hudson in 1807. But water wheels continued to play an important part in the mechanized industries till at least 1850. Cotton, "the steam industry par excellence" (Clapham), drew a quarter of its power from water in 1830 and a seventh in 1850. In that year the other textile industries got nearly a third of their energy from water. Only where there was no water power, or when the available supply had been exhausted, was the engine's adoption rapid. With that adoption mankind tapped a source of power that was free from considerations of rainfall, climate, or the supply of muscle, and was bounded only by access to supplies of fuel.

Electric Power.—After seven years' labor Faraday in 1831 found the underlying principle of the dynamo, and showed how an electric current could be derived mechanically; but no dynamo capable of regular use was available until 1873. From that date electrical engineering began in earnest. For at least two decades the cost of power and appliances was too high to threaten the supremacy of steam, and electricity was used chiefly for illumination and street traction; but after 1900 generation became more efficient, transmission difficulties became smaller, and electrical equipment became more reliable and less costly. Parsons' steam turbine, invented in 1884, provided a better engine for driving dynamos. Countries which had coal used steam engines to turn dynamos, but those which lacked fuel turned eagerly to the harnessing of falling water. In the late eighteen-sixties Bergès, a Grenoble papermaker, had seen in the water that tumbled down from the towering Alps a new kind of fuel, which he called *"la houille blanche"* (white coal). He steered the water into big pipes, out of which it squirted with tremendous force on to the flanges of turbines that drove his paper machines and later turned dynamos.

Bergès' pioneer work attracted attention and started a movement. In France, Alpine falls and rapids were harnessed, and by 1911 were yielding nearly 500,000 H. P. for the aluminum, calcium carbide, and other electro-metallurgical or electro-chemical industries, as well as for the general light or power needs of the region. Italy, devoid of coal and apparently doomed to industrial insignificance, followed closely on her neighbor's heels. Italian engineers improved transmission methods, pioneered in the adoption of the now familiar steel towers, sent current under high voltage over distances as great as 130 miles without serious leakage, built steam plants to supply power during dry seasons, and linked their stations together in a network. Electricity invaded almost every place and industry north of Rome, fed power to chemical works, and turned the wheels of textile or automobile factories in Milan and Turin. The first electric street car in Europe ran through the street of Florence in 1890. From the south "hydro" spread to Switzerland, the hilly areas of central Europe, Norway, and Sweden. It compensated for lack of coal, but even where coal was available hydro-electricity was cheaper than thermo-electricity (made by steam-driven dynamos). Installation costs were higher but operating costs were lower, while the cleanliness and the decentralized production favored white coal at the expense of its black rival.

Since 1918 the electrification of Europe has been very rapid.

The harnessing of water has been carried on with greater vigor. Italy in 1929 was generating 2,300,000 H. P. (against 500,000 H. P. in 1909), and thus ranked third in the world, after the United States and Canada. Russia rejoiced that a Bolshevik government could get water into pipes, and its great plant at Dnieprostroi (on the Dnieper) was one of the foundation stones of communist industrialism. The Irish Free State regarded the harnessing of the Shannon as the first outward and visible sign of the constructive statesmanship of a self-governing people. At the same time the production of thermo-electricity was made much more efficient by building larger turbines and dynamos, and by discovering methods of using such cheap fuel as lignite. The amount of coal required to produce a given quantity of power fell from 6 lb. in 1900 to 1.8 lb. in 1930, but some large stations used only 1 lb. Thermo-electricity can now be made as cheaply as hydro. The range of transmission was extended to 200 miles or more, and "super-stations," serving large areas, supplanted the motley of smaller generators. Public and private interests joined hands to rationalize the industry: Germany divided its territory into four big zones, and Great Britain in 1926 established a Central Electricity Board to build a "grid" that would convey power from great stations to every nook and cranny in the country. In 1929 electricity supplied three-fourths of the power used in German industry and two-thirds of that used in British.

The Extraction of Metals.—The development of machines, tools, power generators, and high speeds was closely connected, both as cause and effect, with the production of great quantities of metals, especially iron and steel. Iron ore deposits were found in places under an area stretching from South Wales to south Russia and flanked by Spain and Sweden; but their exploitation was in every place eventually checked by the rising price and exhaustion of the charcoal supply. England felt that exhaustion by Stuart times, and Réaumur in 1721 warned France that the spread of cultivation and the growth of the iron industry were threatening the country with deforestation. In Sweden, government control was imposed as early as 1633 to preserve the forests, and during the eighteenth century the erection of new forges was forbidden, while the output of old ones was restricted. Swedish exports stagnated just as the demand for metal was expanding rapidly, and British users turned to Russia and the American colonies.

Salvation came with Abraham Darby's discovery (about 1709) that coke could be used for smelting. His son improved on his work, but the practice spread slowly. Newcomen and Watt engines were introduced to work bellows or air pumps which blew a draft into the furnace, thus aiding the combustion of the coke and making the smelting more effective. In 1828 Neilson, a Scot, heated the air before passing it into the furnace, and found he not merely could use some kinds of coal instead of coke but needed only half the former amount of fuel. Thanks to these and other innovations, the production of iron could now be increased greatly. Between 1740 and 1840 it expanded eightyfold, and iron became much cheaper. In France coke helped to build up the great iron works at Le Creusot, but small producers in France and Germany continued to use charcoal till at least the middle of the nineteenth century.

The metal that ran out of the blast furnace was cast iron. It might contain 5 per cent of carbon, silica, and other foreign materials. It would break rather than bend, and was too brittle for use where strains or blows must be endured. Wrought iron or steel was needed, but to make either of these more impurities must be extracted. In 1784 Onions and Cort independently patented methods of making wrought iron. While a flame played from above on the surface of molten iron, a long puddling rod stirred the metal; more carbon was thus burned out, and the iron was cleaner and tougher. Cort also designed rollers through which white-hot iron bars could be passed and turned into plates, rods, rails, or girders.

The puddling process helped to put British ironmasters well ahead of their continental fellows, and in 1825 they were producing the cheapest bar iron in Europe. The cost in Cardiff was £10 a ton, but in France was over £26. Nearly three-fourths of the British output of iron in 1830 was wrought iron, one-fifth of it was exported, and the exports quintupled between 1806 and 1832. Britain had joined the small army of iron exporters.

Given cheaper metal, the machine and railroad builders could go ahead. The iron age dawned, but soon gave place to the steel age. Steel can be defined for the lay reader as iron with less than one per cent of carbon, and the task of production was therefore that of extracting more carbon than could be eliminated by puddling. It was being done by intense prolonged heating, the output was small, and in the early nineteenth century the best steel cost £50 a ton, or five times as much as wrought iron. Great Britain in the 'fifties was producing 3,000,000 tons of pig iron, but only about 40,000 tons of steel. Cheap mass production was made possible by Henry Bessemer. Son of a French refugee, Bessemer flitted from one invention to another. He designed an embossed velvet, built a machine to make bronze powder, invented a sugar press, made plate glass, and spent his old age trying to devise a steamship room that would not rock—for he was a bad sailor. In the 'fifties he was experimenting with cannon, and saw that they would be more efficient and durable if made of steel. But how make enough steel? The answer came in 1856. Pour molten iron into a big container (a *converter*) which had a number of holes or jets in the bottom. Blow air through these jets into the liquid iron; the oxygen would combine with the carbon and silicon, the impurity would be burned out, and to the cleansed iron the required amount of carbon could then be added. This process might take only twenty minutes, yet tons of steel could be made cheaply.

Between 1856 and 1870 the price of British steel fell about half, and production rose sixfold. Some kinds of ore failed, however, to respond to Bessemer's process; they contained phosphorus, and .1 per cent of phosphorus sufficed to make iron inconvertible. Bessemer sought in vain to remove the offender, and the phosphoric ores remained useless to steel-makers. Meanwhile William Siemens, a German living in England, offered a rival method of making steel. His "open hearth," perfected in 1866, was in essence a big shallow pan. Into it he poured liquid iron, on which he blew a hot stream of air and a torch-like flame of gas. The carbon was burned out slowly, the conversion could be controlled, samples could be taken out at any time for analysis, the steel was more uniform in quality, and the hearth could hold more metal than one dared put in the largest converter. Yet the German was as baffled by phosphorus as was the Frenchman, and had to be helped out by a Cockney and a Welshman. In 1878 Thomas (a London police court clerk who studied chemistry in his spare time) and his cousin Gilchrist (a chemist in a Welsh iron works) solved the riddle. They gave the converter or hearth a basic lining which extracted the offending substance and left the iron free to become steel.

Few spare-time studies have exerted such far-reaching influence. British phosphoric ores could now be used, and Germany awoke to a full realization of the value of the territory taken from France in 1871. In that year Lorraine had only about forty little furnaces producing cast iron; but underground, and spreading into Luxembourg, Belgium, and France, was one of the richest beds of phosphoric ore in the world. The Ruhr Valley had a fine supply of coking coal, and the Thomas process therefore opened a new door to this region. By 1894, when the patent expired, Germany had already passed Britain in steel production, and she increased her output sevenfold, to nearly 19,000,000 tons, in 1913. France also benefited, for the ore under such places as Nancy and Longwy contained from 5 to 8 per cent of phosphorus, and even the pig iron made from it had been poor; but good fuel was lacking in France, and as it was easier to take the ore to the coke than the coke to the ore, much French ore went into German furnaces.

On the eve of the Great War the iron and steel center of Europe rested on this low-grade phosphoric ore bed and on Ruhr coke. An area smaller than Vermont, and including bits of Germany, France, Luxembourg and Belgium, contained two-thirds of the furnaces, converters, and hearths of Europe, and produced 24,000,000 tons of steel against 8,000,000 tons in Great Britain and 31,000,000 in the United States. Of the 28,000,000 tons of ore fed into German furnaces in 1913, three-fourths came from Lorraine. Steel as well as sentiment therefore demanded the transfer of Alsace-Lorraine to France in 1919. Germany lost the source of 75 per cent of her iron ore output to France, and 5 per cent to Poland. She also lost about a quarter of her iron and steel plants. France now had 95 per cent of the ore field; but Germany still had the coking coal, developed her remaining ore beds, imported ore from Sweden and elsewhere, and built new and better plants to take the place of those she had lost. Her steel production soon regained its pre-War level, and added to the already adequate productive capacity of the continent. When cutthroat competition drove producers to seek international agreement in 1926, Germany's claim to 40 per cent of the market was admitted, thus recognizing her supremacy. The fact that France's share was to be 32 per cent was, however, an indication of that country's advance in consequence of the redrawing of the map.

The steel age dawned rapidly after 1856. In 1860 steel began to be used for boilers, and thus allowed far higher steam pressures to be developed. In 1863 the first steel locomotive was built,

THE RUHR-LORRAINE-BELGIAN-FRENCH COAL, IRON ORE, AND LIGNITE AREA (From Blanshard and Visher, *Economic Geography of Europe*, McGraw-Hill Book Company, Inc., 1931.)

and Bessemer converted the railroads to the use of steel rails by showing them a steel rail that had outlived twenty iron rails. A steel ship was launched in 1863, cheap steel sheets and a new tinning process made possible the canning industries, while cheaper galvanized iron, wire, and wire netting were useful to farmers and ranchers. When Eiffel, the French engineer, completed his tower in 1889 he thought that he had symbolized the new age as

Notre-Dame did the Middle Ages. But that tower was only a sight-seer's elevator shaft, and the real temples to steel were built on the other side of the Atlantic. The Flatiron Building in New York was the first steel-framed chapel of the new faith, and the Wool-worth Building was its first cathedral.

Once steel could be made in abundance, the next task was to develop steel alloys, each possessing some special characteristic which fitted it for a particular duty. From research and from accidents observed by trained eyes, metallurgy advanced in the art of giving new or added properties to steel. In 1850 Mushet had produced tungsten steel, and from it tools were made that cut metal four or five times as quickly as did the ordinary steel tool. In 1888 Hadfield produced manganese steel, tough, strong, and non-magnetic, suitable for railroad crossings, curves, or other points where severe friction had to be borne. Armament-makers sought steel that would allow shells to penetrate armor plate, then sought for armor plate steel that would resist the penetrating shell, and so on *ad bellum*. Chromium made steel rustless, vana-dium gave it greater strength, and some alloys might be given a combination of virtues by being dosed with several stimulants.

Other Metals.—Industry did not live by steel alone. The nine-teenth century needed the already well-known metals—copper, lead, tin, and zinc—and found at least one new one—aluminum. The copper alloys, bronze and brass, had a long history, and in the early nineteenth century ranked next to iron in general use-fulness. Cannon, bells, sheathing for wooden warships, boilers, vats, piping, kitchen utensils, and many metal parts of the early machines were of brass or bronze. Cornwall had become the lead-ing European copper producer, Anglesea yielded rich supplies after 1768, and in 1830 over half the British yield was exported, especially to Asia, France, and the United States. The coming of electricity expanded the demand for copper, but the British mines petered out after 1850. The Rio Tinto mines in Spain be-came famous, and Bulgaria, Norway, and Germany increased their output; but these sources were insufficient, and Europe had to rely increasingly on North America, Chile, and later on the Belgian Congo. By 1925 Europe produced about a fourteenth of the world's output of copper, but consumed over a third. By that time it was also dependent on other continents for half its lead and zinc; the ancient glory had long since departed from the

Cornish tin mines and Malaya, Bolivia and Nigeria supplied most of that metal. Only in the case of aluminum could Europe satisfy its own appetite for an important non-ferrous metal.

Coal.—British coal production has been estimated at nearly 3,000,000 tons in 1700. In 1800 it was 10,000,000 tons, but this threefold increase was a mere prelude to the twentyfold expansion of the nineteenth century. Such growth was due to the play of commercial factors rather than to any remarkable or drastic changes in mining methods. The driving force was the growth of markets, of new uses for coal, and of improved transportation. The middle decades of the nineteenth century saw a "headlong, almost devastating expansion" (Ashton), for that was the period of rapid metallurgical and steam transport development. During this fierce attack on the coal seams Stanley Jevons created a sensation in 1865 by calculating that all Britain's coal would be gone in about 150 to 200 years; but a royal commission allayed the panic by ruling that the coal-less day might not dawn for another 1273 years. When the rate of expansion became slower in Britain, Germany began to gain speed. The following table tells the essentials of the story:

COAL PRODUCTION

(in million metric tons)

	1841	1871	1900	1913
United Kingdom	35	117	225	292
Germany and Luxembourg	3	29	109 black[a]	190
			40 lignite	87
France	3	13	33	41
Belgium	4	14	23	23

[a] Bituminous or anthracite.

Europe's coal production, according to Mulhall, rose sevenfold between 1820 and 1860, and over threefold between 1860 and 1894. The above table shows a more than threefold expansion between 1871 and 1913.

Behind this great growth lies a long story of varied improvements in mining methods, and a great increase in the number of mines and workers. Three questions had to be answered by the mine manager. How could mines be freed from the menace of death from gas, fire, and water? How could more coal be hewed per pair of hands? How could the coal be moved more easily underground, to the surface, and on the surface? The steam

engine helped to fight water and made possible the attack on
deeper seams; but as mines became deeper and galleries longer
the menace of choke damp (which suffocated), fire damp
(methane), and coal dust (which exploded) became more serious. Choke damp gave warning by putting out the miner's candle,
but fire damp gave no signal. Many "fiery" mines had to be deserted; in others, owners tried to get a safe light to the working

THE COALFIELDS OF EUROPE
(U. S. Department of Commerce.)

places by using phosphorus, putrescent fish, and even a mirror at
the shafthead!

To combat these unseen foes, improved ventilation was a necessary weapon. A second shaft was sunk, and a fire burning at
the bottom of it made an upward draft which pulled fresh air
down the first shaft. By 1840 powerful fans were available. Attempts to obtain safe illumination were spurred on by bad explosions after 1800, and the Davy lamp (1815) kept flame and
methane apart. Explosions continued, sometimes because miners
were careless with their lamps, sometimes because of the growing use of gunpowder, and sometimes because coal dust might

explode, especially when mixed with methane. The discovery of this dust hazard by Lyell and Faraday in 1845 gave an added understanding of the causes of danger, and led to better ventilation and the use of explosives which gave less flame. Today explosions are the least important contributors to the death roll in European mining accidents, but an occasional great disaster bears witness to the intense watchfulness that is needed in the struggle against the spirit of the nether world.

The second problem was that of increasing the output per worker and of leaving less coal underground in the pillars needed to support the roof. These pillars might contain 30 to 60 per cent of the coal in a seam. Gradually the practice spread of taking out all the coal, of filling up the space with soil, sand, or refuse, and of lining roadways with brick or wood. Cheaper bricks and lumber for props made this possible, but it involved constant struggle against sagging roofs, and falling earth is the heaviest life-destroyer underground today. Eighteenth-century inventors tried to put better equipment into the miner's hands. "Willie Brown's iron man" (1761), was a mechanical pick driven by levers, gear wheels, and a crank handle. A horse-driven pick was tried, as was a circular saw. From these crude beginnings there slowly evolved various implements driven by compressed air or electricity, but their adoption was far slower in Europe than in North America. The coal seams were often steeply inclined, full of faults, and shallow; labor was not friendly to the new tools, and employers were not enthusiastic, especially when their mines were hallowed by fifty or a hundred years' history. During or after the War the pressure of demand, the scarcity or high cost of labor, or the keenness of competition led to some change of attitude. In Britain the percentage of mechanically hewn coal rose from 8 in 1913 to 24 in 1928. The Ruhr coal field was reequipped, and the percentage rose in the same period from 5 to 85.

The third problem was that of transporting the coal from the working face to the head of the pit shaft. In the crudest mines boys, women, and girls carried it in baskets on their backs, and even climbed ladders to the surface. Elsewhere the baskets were put on sleds which were dragged to the shaft by men or boys, and later by ponies. The first advance came when parallel boards were laid down, on which the runners of sleds or the wheels of trucks could move more easily. When iron became cheaper, iron plates took the place of wood. John Curr (about 1770-1790) made a flange on the edge of these plates to prevent the wheels from leaving the track. He then put the flange on the wheel and turned the plate into a rail, thus producing the railroad. On these rails men or ponies moved trucks underground, and after 1800 mining engineers like Trevithick and Stephenson used engines on rails around the pit head.

A versifier who looked back on the bad old days burst into song:

> God bless the man wi' peace and plenty
> That first invented metal plates.
> Draw out his years to five times twenty,
> Then slide him through the heavenly gates.

To the more prosaic mine owner the saving in transportation costs was substantial, for in the early eighteenth century far more labor was needed to move the coal than to hew it. The more efficient the haulage methods the fewer were the men needed to serve the miner, or, turning the statement round, the larger was the percentage of workers actually hewing coal. In mechanical transportation, as in hewing, no European country went nearly so far as did the United States, though the movement was much more marked during the post-War rationalization decade, when every mine was trying to cut costs, raise the output per worker, and generally increase efficiency. Consequently the annual output per mining employee rose considerably. In the Ruhr coal field the number of workers fell 10 per cent between 1913 and 1928, but the output of each rose 26 per cent.

Improved methods and the tapping of new coal beds allowed the industry to meet the ever-expanding needs of industry and transportation. In Britain coal mining knit itself into the very fabric of economic life. In 1914 it employed more workers than any other industry except agriculture, and one-twelfth of the population was directly dependent on it. Iron and steel, shipbuilding and engineering lived on cheap coal. Coal provided one-tenth of the value and four-fifths of the volume of exports. The home market grew from 50,000,000 tons in 1850 to 190,000,000 in 1913; but the overseas market grew relatively more rapidly, from one-sixteenth of the total output in 1850 to one-third, or

90,000,000 tons, in 1913. Those exports went to supplement the domestic production of Germany, France, and Belgium; to supply lands devoid of coal, such as Italy and Scandinavia; to fuel the Argentine railroads, to replenish bins in coaling stations the world over, and to fill the bunkers of foreign ships leaving British ports. Coal paid for part of the country's imports of food and raw material, provided outward cargoes or ballast for ships going out to deliver manufactured wares and fetch foodstuffs, and by giving ships a paying cargo on both journeys made lower freights possible.

Other countries expanded production, especially after 1870. Germany nearly doubled her output (excluding lignite) between 1900 and 1913, and exported about a quarter of it to her neighbors, while importing some from England. Belgium exported and imported a little, but France had to supplement her own yield by buying from Germany and England. Acute observers in 1913 might detect danger signals beyond the record output and abounding prosperity of that year. Lignite, hydro-electricity, the internal combustion engine, and oil fuel were clouds bigger than a man's hand on the horizon, but few could see them through the coal dust. Coal was king. Its price rose between 1880 and 1900 when other prices fell, and after 1900 went still higher. Mine owners were prosperous, new pits were opened, and miners, well organized in unions, received wages which made them the rich men of the labor world.

The War took many miners away, and strained productive capacity in all countries. In Great Britain and Germany export markets had to be almost abandoned, in France some mines were destroyed, while Russia's production was decimated. Europe therefore emerged with a shrunken output and a deteriorated or damaged plant. Germany lost the fields which supplied a quarter of her fuel, and had to pay some reparations in coal. France had 200 mines to recondition, and Britain had lost 60 per cent of her export trade. The task of restoring production proved easy; by 1924 the European yield (excluding lignite) was almost equal to the average for 1909-1913; but this restoration of production did not encounter a corresponding restoration of demand, and the industry therefore suffered severely. King Coal was sick, and, instead of calling for pipe, bowl, and instrumentalists, was crying for subsidies, bounties, tax exemptions, reduced freight rates, tariffs, lower wages, and even for state purchase of coal at high prices.

The failure of demand to spring back to "normalcy" was due to many factors:

1. Depression, especially in the heavy or export industries, reduced coal consumption by iron and steel plants, factories, railroads, and steamships.

2. Former coal-importing countries which had coal beds were exploiting them more vigorously. Holland mined less than 2,000,-000 tons in 1913, but in 1929 produced nearly 13,000,000 tons; France, Spain, and Russia also exceeded their pre-war output. In other continents production expanded, and dependence on European coal weakened.

3. Substitutes for coal grew in popularity. Hydro-electrical developments in Sweden, Switzerland, and Italy checked the demand for coal. Oil fuel, used by only 1,500,000 tons of merchant shipping in 1913, was used by over 20,000,000 in 1925; the world's navies had installed oil burners, and the Diesel motor engine had won its spurs in ocean traffic. Lignite, "the Cinderella among the coals," found a fairy godmother, to the discomfiture of its two elder sisters (bituminous and anthracite). It was earthy and watery, and gave only about a fifth of the heat provided by the same weight of black coal; but it was easily mined in "open cuts," and before the War German engineers had found a way to dry, pulverize, and mold it in briquets. It could be burned in the improved furnaces of thermo-electric plants, and in 1922 a German chemist, Bergius, obtained liquid fuel from it. By 1929 Germany was mining 175,000,000 tons of lignite.

4. Marked economies were effected in the use of coal. Pre-War Europe burned its coal wastefully. Much heat and soot went up the chimney to warm and foul the atmosphere, the use of raw coal involved the loss of valuable by-products, and the generation of steam power in thousands of plants or of electricity and coal gas in hundreds involved losses from small-scale production. After the War greater care was taken. Gas displaced coal or coke in some boilers, machines were driven by electricity, boiler and furnace designs were improved, powdered or brown coal was used, central power stations were built, and even the production of coal gas began to be centralized, with pipe lines to carry the product long distances. Germany in 1927-1928 used only two-fifths of its

coal raw, and converted the remainder into coke, briquets, electric power, gas, and oil fuel.

The post-War coal industry was therefore characterized by increased productive capacity and sluggish demand. Competition for the few foreign markets became intense, with Germany, Britain, and Poland as the chief rivals; Poland entered the field when she obtained the Upper Silesian mines from Germany. In the contest, reparations coal loaded the dice against the British exporter for a time, the French occupation of the Ruhr in 1923 checked German exports and helped the British, but the long British coal strike of 1926 presented Germany and Poland with some British markets, especially in the Baltic. Lower wages, longer hours, rationalization, and price cutting were weapons in the struggle. Six years' discussion between owners, governments, and the League of Nations failed to produce any agreement to equalize wages or hours, limit production, or share out markets. In 1929 depression descended on a world glutted with coal as with wheat, loaded with mines capable of producing far more than was wanted, and flooded with an oversupply of coal's chief rival, oil.

The post-War troubles of the industry must not blind us to the fundamental importance of coal. In the leading European industrial countries water power is insignificant, and liquid fuel must be imported or manufactured. Germany in 1928 drew 98 per cent of its energy from black coal, and most of the remainder from lignite. To imagine, therefore, that the supremacy of coal is passing is to see only the fringe and ignore the shawl.

The Chemical Industries.—Coal has become more than a fuel, and for over a century has been known as a treasure house from which other things than heat can be drawn. In 1792 Murdock, one of the mechanical geniuses of Soho, illuminated his house and office with coal gas, and a plant installed by him (1805) in a Manchester mill reduced the lighting bill from £2000 spent on candles to £650. After 1817 companies were formed to supply some of the leading cities, and after the old candle or whale oil lights the new yellowish gas flame seemed a miraculous manufacturer of daylight. In the 'eighties Welsbach devised the asbestos mantle, which was heated by a Bunsen burner and set a standard of illumination that the electric bulb only slowly equaled.

While coal gave a valuable gas it also gave a liquid (coal tar)
which soon roused the curiosity of chemists. Faraday, Hofmann,
and others experimented with it, and Mansfield extracted aniline
from it. Perkin, one of Hofmann's assistants, tried to obtain
quinine from aniline, but instead he produced a mauve dye (1856)

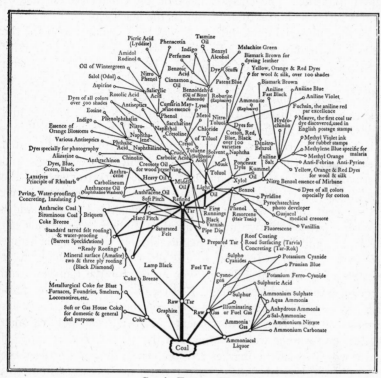

COAL'S FAMILY TREE

and then other colors ranging from purple to pink. Mankind had
scoured the animal, vegetable, and mineral kingdom in its search
for colors for its cloth. It had used beetles, crocus blooms, shellfish, wood, plants, mosses, walnut peel, and even bullock's blood.
Perkin and his successors spared it from further search, for once
they had discovered the composition and structure of a dye mole-
cule—often a hard task—they were able to create that structure
by working from some point in the branches of coal's family tree.
On the twigs of that tree nearly a thousand dyes are now to be

found; but to reach them we have to pass a motley of other tar products, including aspirin, wintergreen, saccharine, disinfectants, laxatives, perfumes, photographic chemicals, high explosives, and essence of orange blossom. Nearer the trunk or the roots are roofing or road materials, ammonia fertilizers, lubricating oils, and liquid fuel. The chemist has not yet exhausted the list of commodities he hopes to draw out of the black hat.

In the industrial exploitation of coal tar Germany soon led the world. Hofmann returned from London to Germany, university research became intensive, technical schools poured out a stream of trained men, and chemical firms established large research laboratories. Eighteen years' work (1880-1897) and $5,000,000 were needed to discover the structure of the indigo molecule and devise methods of commercial production. Ruhr coking coal supplied plenty of coal tar, the production of fertilizers had created a strong chemical industry and a class of chemical engineers, and Germany therefore soon dominated the dye market as she did the potash market. By 1913 six large companies were making about 88 per cent of the world's dyes, had ruined the French madder growers, put nearly two million acres of Indian indigo fields out of action, and supplied textile manufacturers with a wider range of better dyes at a fraction of the old cost. Their plants were capable of quick conversion to war needs, for the materials and processes that produced Congo Red could also be used for making high explosives and tear gas. During the War other countries established dye works, government aid was given, and German patents or formulæ were appropriated. By 1928 Germany supplied only two-fifths of the market (41 per cent), or just a little more than did the United States (24 per cent) and Great Britain (13 per cent) combined.

The dye industry is the most colorful example of the application of chemistry on a large scale. It found treasure trove in a waste product. Yet its achievement seems little more remarkable than that of taking nitrogen out of the air to make ammonia fertilizers, or that of turning wood pulp into artificial silk. Hooke in the seventeenth century wondered whether a shiny fiber like that of the silk-worm could be produced artificially, but two centuries elapsed before a Frenchman, the Count de Chardonnet, took out a patent in 1884 for a fiber which the French call "chardonnet." By that time the manufacture of paper from wood was well established, and the nature of cellulose, which forms the main body of all vegetable fiber, was fairly well understood. Almost every step in the conversion of cellulose into a shiny fiber was full of chemical problems, but in 1900 rayon was shown at the Paris Exhibition and a thousand tons were produced. In 1913 the output was 11,000 tons (about one-third that of real silk), and after the War progress was astonishingly rapid. New processes were devised, other raw materials were used, vast sums were invested in plant by existing chemical firms, and as the cost of production fell garments could be sold at prices which rivaled those of other fabrics, especially of cottons. By 1929 the output had risen to 180,000 tons, a fivefold jump since 1923. This advance was too rapid, and 1929 found the industry glutted with goods and productive capacity.

The growth of production by chemical processes expanded the demand for those acids and alkalies which had begun to be produced and used in the eighteenth century. When in the seventeen-forties Barth of Saxony found that a weak acid bleached linen fairly quickly, the manufacture of sulphuric acid began in earnest. At almost every step in the subsequent application of chemistry to industry, sulphuric acid played a part; most materials in general use today have depended directly or indirectly on the acid at some stage in their production. The consumption of sulphuric acid might make a good barometer of business activity. Meanwhile Leblanc's discovery of a cheap method of making soda in 1791 and Solvay's better process of 1863 made sodium compounds available to meet the demands of bleachers, soap-makers, glass-works, pulp mills, oil refineries, rayon plants, and many other producers. England was the first country to develop these heavy chemical industries, but France, Germany, Belgium, and the United States followed; and as Germany added potash, phosphates, and nitrates to sulphur and soda, a quarter of the world's chemical industry was carried on inside her borders in 1913. War lessons and transfers of territory have reduced the fraction to a sixth.

Pottery.—Medieval and early modern Europe had its peasant pottery industry, but few craftsmen capable of producing fine wares. The poor ate or drank from wood platters, leather mugs, horns, or crudely glazed earthen pots. The rich used pewter, copper, silver, some glass and later some silver plate. In the cargoes from Asia after 1500 a crate of porcelain (or china, as it might be called) occasionally found a place, and as the East India companies developed their traffic china became more widely known among the very rich. It stimulated Europeans to improve their own industry; to seek supplies of such white clay as gave the oriental article its white texture all through; to experiment with colors, glazes, and oven temperatures; to create a skilled force of artists and craftsmen; and to secure transport facilities that would make breakages less common.

Venice and Florence were making good pottery by 1600, Huguenots achieved some success, and the Dutch produced the famous delftware. The first real European porcelain, made of kaolin—the white clay used by the Chinese—was produced by Böttger at Meissen in 1707. He kept his factory locked and guarded like a prison, but some workmen escaped to Vienna. By 1760 porcelain factories had been set up in Berlin, St. Petersburg, and Sèvres to supply goods to the courts; in London, Bristol, Derby, and Liverpool potters were hard at work producing attractive wares. In all these places the product was too costly for any but the rich, and Dr. Johnson said he could buy vessels of silver as cheaply as those of Derby.

Josiah Wedgwood (1730-1795) did much to improve the methods of production and to extend the market. A realization that two markets were waiting to be served led him to divide his plant into "useful" and "ornamental" units, each with its own ovens and workshops. In the former he set out to produce table crockery of all grades from the most elaborate to the plain, while in the latter he made vases, cameos, and other articles for personal or domestic decoration. The discovery of a rich deposit of kaolin in Cornwall in 1755 gave him good raw material, but as the clay had to be carried two or more hundred miles to his works he became an enthusiast for better roads and canals. In his factory at Burslem (1759) and later at Etruria (1769) he experimented ceaselessly with clays, glazes, colors, and temperature control; built new ovens and then tore them down; employed artists to make molds and patterns; ransacked the treasures of the classical world for models and ideas; developed great division of labor; designed new equipment, and tried to turn "dilatory and drunken idle worthless workmen" into skilled operatives.

Wedgwood studied marketing as keenly as he did making. He

sent out printed and illustrated advertisements, established a London showroom which became a fashionable resort, and traded direct with almost every country. His vases, cameos and snuff-boxes were bought by the rich; a dinner service of 952 pieces, each carrying a different English scene, was ordered by Catherine the Great; and his plainer cream-colored plates, cups, and teapots became part of the equipment of humbler homes. "In his own person he combined three men of unusual capacity: a scientific potter, an enterprising business man, and a man of taste and artistic talent" (Hower). His tombstone did not flatter him when it said he had converted "a rude and inconsiderable manufacture into an elegant art and an important part of national commerce." Others followed closely on his heels or were alongside him, and found great home and foreign markets. By the early part of the next century a traveler could record that "from Paris to Petersburg, from Amsterdam to the farthest part of Sweden, and from Dunkirk to the extremity of the south of France, one is served at every inn upon English ware. Spain, Portugal, and Italy are supplied with it, and vessels are loaded with it for both the Indies and the continent of America." By 1830 over £500,000 of pottery was exported in a year; over half of it went to the United States, and much to Germany and Holland—lands that had been far ahead of England in pottery skill a century earlier—while far more went to the Orient than had ever come from there. Machinery did not seriously impair the dependence on skill till after 1850, but as it came and as other countries developed large-scale production the price of crockery fell still further. Eating and drinking became more delicate and hygienic, pewter and plate passed into the antique shop, wood platters were used as kindling wood, and washing dishes became a heavy domestic chore.

BIBLIOGRAPHY

General

Bogardus, J. F., *Europe: a Geographical Survey* (1934), chaps. 7 and 8, and sections describing chief industries of each country.

Bragg, W., *Creative Knowledge: Old Trades and New Science* (1927), chaps. 2-6.

Epstein, R. C., "Industrial Invention: Heroic or Systematic?" in *Q. J. E.*, February, 1926, pp. 232-272.

Gilboy, E. M., "Demand as a Factor in the Industrial Revolution," in *Facts and Factors in Economic History* (1932).

Gras, N. S. B., *Industrial Evolution* (1930), chaps. 8, 10-13.

HATFIELD, H. S., *The Inventor and His World* (1933).

MARSHALL, A., *Industry and Trade* (1919), book i.

NUSSBAUM, F. L., *A History of the Economic Institutions of Modern Europe*, part iv, chap. 3.

ROSSMAN, J., *The Psychology of the Inventor* (1931).

ROSSMAN, J., "The Motives of Inventors," in *Q. J. E.*, May, 1933, pp. 522-528.

SOMBART, W., *Der moderne Kapitalismus*, vol. iii, pp. 74-124.

USHER, A. P., *History of Mechanical Inventions* (1929), chaps. 7, 9, 11-13.

WEBER, M., *General Economic History*, chap. 27.

Encyclopædia of the Social Sciences: See the list of titles of articles under the heading "Industry," vol. xv, pp. 551-552.

Social Science Abstracts: The complete index gives references to articles dealing with most of the industries described above.

SPECIAL INDUSTRIES OR COUNTRIES

The literature is very large, and only the more accessible and important books are listed here. Useful annotated bibliographies for British industries have been prepared by Professor Eileen Power, "The Industrial Revolution, 1750-1850" 1927) ; by T. S. Ashton, "The Industrial Revolution," in *Ec. H. R.*, October, 1934, pp. 104-119; and by H. L. Beales, "The Basic Industries of England, 1850-1914," in *Ec. H. R.*, April, 1935, pp. 99-112. For continental countries no such bibliographies are available.

ASHTON, T. S., and SYKES, J., *The Coal Industry in the Eighteenth Century* (1929), chaps. 1-4.

ASHTON, T. S., *Iron and Steel in the Industrial Revolution* (1924).

BALLOT, C., *L'Introduction du machinisme dans l'industrie française* (1923).

BENAERTS, P., *Les origines de la grande industrie allemande* (1933).

BLADEN, V. W., "The Potteries in the Industrial Revolution," in *Ec. Hist.*, vol. i (1926), pp. 117-130.

BLANCHARD, W. O., "White Coal in Italian Industry," in *Geog. Rev.*, vol. xviii, (1928), pp. 261-273.

BOWDEN, WITT, *Industrial Society in England toward the End of the Eighteenth Century* (1925), chaps. 1, 2.

BOWDEN, WITT, *The Industrial Revolution* (1928). An excellent collection of extracts from contemporary accounts of developments.

BURN, D. L., "The Genesis of American Engineering Competition, 1850-1870," in *Ec. Hist.*, vol. ii (1931), pp. 292-311.

CLAPHAM, J. H., *The Economic Development of France and Germany, 1815-1914*, chaps. 3, 4, 10, 11.

CLAPHAM, J. H., *Economic History of Modern Britain* (1926, 1932), vol. i, chaps. 5, 10; vol. ii, chaps. 2, 3.

CLAPHAM, J. H., *The Woollen and Worsted Industries* (1907).

DANIELS, G. W., *The Early English Cotton Industry* (1920).

DAWSON, W. H., *The Evolution of Modern Germany* (1908), chap. 3.

DAY, C., *Economic Development in Modern Europe* (1933), chaps. 2, 9, 12.

DODD, A. H., *The Industrial Revolution in North Wales* (1933).

DUNHAM, A. L., "The Development of the Cotton Industry in France and the Anglo-French Treaty of 1860," in *Ec. H. R.*, vol. i (1928), pp. 281-307.

FAY, C. R., *Great Britain from Adam Smith to the Present Day* (1932), chaps. 13-16.

FLEMING, A. P., and BROCKLEHURST, H. T., *History of Engineering* (1925).

HAMILTON, H., *The Industrial Revolution in Scotland* (1932).

HAMMOND, J. L. and B., *The Rise of Modern Industry* (1926), chaps. 7-11.
HECKSCHER, E. F., "The Place of Sweden in Modern Economic History," in *Ec. H. R.*, vol. iv (1932), pp. 1-22.
JEANS, W. T., *The Creators of the Age of Steel* (1884).
KNOWLES, L. C. A., *The Industrial and Commercial Revolutions in ·Great Britain during the Nineteenth Century* (1922), part ii.
KNOWLES, L. C. A., *Economic Development in the Nineteenth Century* (1932), part iii.
LEVASSEUR, E., *Histoire des classes ouvrières et de l'industrie en France, 1789-1870.*
LORD, J., *Capital and Steam Power, 1750-1800* (1923).
MANTOUX, P., *The Industrial Revolution in the Eighteenth Century* (Eng. trans., 1928), part ii, chaps. 1-4.
MARSHALL, T. H., *James Watt* (1925).
MEAKIN, W., *The New Industrial Revolution* (1928), chaps. 1-3, 5-7.
MIALL, S., *History of the British Chemical Industry* (1931).
OGG, F. A., and SHARP, W. R., *Economic Development of Modern Europe* (1926), chaps. 7, 10.
REDFORD, A., *Economic History of England, 1760-1860* (1931), chaps. 1-3, 9.
ROE, J. W., *English and American Tool Builders* (1916).
SARTORIUS VON WALTERSHAUSEN, A., *Deutsche Wirtschaftsgeschichte, 1815-1914* (1920).
SCHULZE-GÄVERNITZ, G., *The Cotton Trade in England and on the Continent* (Eng. trans., 1895).
SÉE, H., *La vie économique de la France, 1815-1848* (1927).
SLOSSON, E. E., *Creative Chemistry* (1919).
USHER, A. P., *Industrial History of England* (1921), chaps. 10, 12, 13.
VEBLEN, T., *Imperial Germany and the Industrial Revolution* (1915), chap. 6.
WADSWORTH, A. P., and MANN, J., *The Cotton Trade and Industrial Lancashire, 1600-1780* (1931).

The League of Nations Economic and Financial Section prepared a series of reports for the International Economic Conference of 1927. These deal with Coal, Shipbuilding, Mechanical Engineering, Cotton, and the Chemical, Iron and Steel, Electrical, Natural Silk, and Artificial Silk industries.

Index (published periodically by the *Svenska Handelsbanken*, Stockholm) contains excellent surveys of the important industries, commodities, and economic developments.

Statistics of production and trade can be found in various annual publications. The *Commerce Year Book*, vol. ii, published by the U. S. Department of Commerce, is invaluable, as is the *Statesman's Year Book. The Statistical Abstract of the United Kingdom, Statistisches Jahrbuch für des deutsches Reich,* and *Annuaire Générale* are useful. The League of Nations publishes a *Statistical Yearbook*, a *Monthly Bulletin of Statistics*, an annual *World Economic Survey*, and an annual volume on *World Production and Prices* covering the years since 1925.

CHAPTER XXII

THE DEVELOPMENT OF MODERN TRANSPORTATION

THE connection between changes in production and improvements in transportation was close. While some of the improvements were impossible till cheap iron and the steam engine were available, expanding production depended on greater ability to bring in raw materials and send more goods to a wider market. The story can be divided into two chapters. The improved river, the canal, the good road and the larger sailing ship enable men to move greater quantities of cheap, bulky, heavy, or fragile commodities more quickly over long distances at lower cost. Then steam and the internal combustion engine increase further the size of the load, give certainty of movement, defy climatic obstacles, add greatly to speed and flexibility of movement, reduce costs still more, and give power to penetrate areas inaccessible by river or canal.

Improvements in inland transportation owed far more to the state than did the developments in industry. In Great Britain the canals and railroads were constructed by private enterprises which raised their own capital, made their own profit or absorbed their own losses. In most parts of the continent capital was much more scarce, the tradition of state enterprise was strong, the prospect of profit was not bright enough to tempt capitalists to risk their funds, and the military authorities needed facilities for quicker movement of troops and supplies. Hence the state not merely undertook the work on rivers, canals, and roads, but either built and ran the railroads or subsidized private enterprise.

ROADS AND WATERWAYS

The improvement of rivers, the cutting of canals, and the construction of good roads had gone far in lands west of the Rhine when the railroad came to supplement or supplant the older forms of transportation. In France the work on waterways begun by Sully, Richelieu, and Colbert was carried further, and by 1900 the country had about 7500 miles of improved rivers and canals.

French roads, already the best in Europe, were improved and extended before the Revolution, and military reasons made Napoleon an enthusiastic road builder in France and western Germany. After 1815 Lemoine invented the steam roller, which helped greatly in making durable surfaces.

England carried through the biggest revolution in inland transportation in pre-railroad days. Having improved many rivers by 1750 and discovered that freight rates fell by about three-quarters when goods left the land for the water, the country became "canal conscious" when, in 1761, the Duke of Bridgewater's canal was completed to convey coal from Worsley to Manchester, seven miles away. The price in Manchester fell by half, the Duke extended his canal to the Mersey, and offered freight rates one-sixth of those charged by land carriers. Between 1758 and 1807, 165 canal acts were passed, the main rivers were improved and joined together, and flights of locks carried canals over the central backbone of the north. By 1830 England south of York was covered with a network of nearly 4000 miles of improved river and canal.

The effects were far-reaching. Goods could be moved in tens of tons instead of in hundredweights, freight costs fell greatly, coal from inland mines became cheaper than sea-borne coal, and farmers could serve distant markets. Roads were relieved of heavy traffic, prices were equalized between districts, passengers could travel cheaply, and Wedgwood ceased to worry about broken crockery. Canal construction employed armies of "navvies" (i.e., workers on "navigations"), and offered a great field for investment. Porter estimates that at least £11,000,000 was spent on canals. Many investors were robbed, some canals failed, but those which served busy districts and had no costly engineering difficulties to surmount made large profits. In 1832 nearly thirty companies out of eighty paid 10 per cent or more, one paid 75 per cent, but forty distributed little or nothing.

This canal era was paralleled by a great period of road-building. All road construction faced two problems: How could the necessary supply of labor, money, and material be obtained? What was the best method of constructing a durable surface? Statute labor or *corvée* had proved unsatisfactory and was inadequate for the maintenance of much-traveled roads. On the continent central governments were assuming control, and were still using *corvée*, but were supplementing it from the exchequer. England in 1663 established its first turnpike trust to take charge of a piece of road, and in the eighteenth century set up so many trusts that, by 1830, 1100 of them were dealing with 20,000 miles of road. The trust consisted of local landlords, traders, clergy, and farmers. It had power to borrow money, employ a surveyor, improve the road with hired and statute labor, and collect tolls. The tolls, forerunners of the gasoline tax, were to defray the cost of maintenance, pay the interest on the bonds, and redeem them. By 1830 over £7,000,000 had been borrowed, and over £1,300,000 was collected annually. This was not enough; expenses often exceeded income, interest could not be paid, administration was in the hands of an unwieldy "promiscuous mob" of amateurs, and when canal or railroad rivalry grew intense the trusts went bankrupt. Eventually statute labor was abolished (1835), local taxes were imposed, the trusts were disbanded, and road maintenance was recognized as a public obligation. That obligation was lightened as the railroads relieved the highways of all but local traffic, and roads were more than adequate until the automobile came to tear up their surface.

By 1830 the second problem had been solved, for during the decades after 1750 Metcalfe, Telford, Macadam and other road engineers had evolved methods of producing hard-surfaced roads that would bear traffic all through the year. Competition and better surfaces had increased the speed of travel by coach from four miles an hour to six, eight, or even ten; but when the Liverpool-Manchester coach did one journey of about thirty miles at fourteen miles an hour there were loud calls for a judicial inquiry into this attempted manslaughter. Night travel became possible, and the journey from Edinburgh to London, which had once taken fourteen days, was reduced to forty-four hours. Speed was dangerous and costly in horseflesh, but it accelerated the movement of persons, packages, and mail; freight wagons and livestock could get more easily and quickly to their destination, and the carriage of goods or persons on horseback virtually ceased. The country became more tightly knit together, and McCulloch in 1835 declared that "Manners as well as prices are reduced nearly to the same standard. . . . Everything is, as it were, brought to a level."

After 1830 the railroad challenged both waterway and road.

It defeated the latter by providing greater speed and safety as well as lower freight, and by its ability to move goods in greater loads than could have been taken over the highways. It defeated the waterway by carrying even such cheap heavy commodities as coal at rates below those charged by canals. To make sure of this, some railroads bought or leased canals and let them stagnate or pass out of use. "The canals attracted no new capital and, with few exceptions, carried out no improvements" (Clapham). The new private enterprise played havoc with the old one, canal towpaths are today little more than unhedged lovers' lanes, and the canals were "an episode" (Fay), but an important one, in the passage from bad to better transportation.

Germany's "rich natural network" of rivers "enabled the country to put off the chief problems of artificial canal building to the twentieth century" (Brinkmann). The Congress of Vienna opened international rivers to the ships of all countries, and in 1831 an international commission was set up to regulate Rhine traffic. The tolls and restrictions which Cologne and Mainz had for centuries claimed were abandoned, and the steamship or steam tug made upstream haulage easier after 1840. For a time railroad construction diverted attention from waterway improvement, but after 1870 money began to be spent freely on river beds and canals. By 1903 the country had 9000 miles of navigable waterway, of which 4000 had been improved or made. The upper Rhine was made navigable as far as Strasbourg almost the whole year round, and in 1886 the Rhine-Ruhr area was joined by canal to the River Ems, thus gaining a German outlet to the sea. Plans for a *Mittelland* canal, along which vessels of 600 to 700 tons could steam through the heart of the country from the Rhine to the Vistula, found favor; much work was done before 1914, and the last link of the chain has been forged since 1930. In 1929 the waterways carried 110,000,000 tons of freight, or one-fifth the amount moved by rail. Coal and coke were the chief cargoes, while sand, iron ore, bricks, grain, fertilizers, lumber, and other heavy goods of low value were carried. Half the cargoes went to or came from abroad. Berlin was a veritable port, for a third of the goods it bought in 1929 came by water.

At its best the waterway is today a minor part of European transportation. Its freight rates are usually lower than rail rates for two reasons: (1) Where the government owns both forms

of transportation it fixes rail rates well above water rates in order
to insure the use of the waterway by some kinds of cargo; (2)
boats are charged very small tolls or none at all, and do not
contribute much toward meeting the interest on the cost of making the waterway. In some cases, such as the Rhine, this cost has

(From Bowman's *The New World*, copyright, 1928, by World Book Company, Yonkers-on-Hudson, New York.)

been comparatively slight, but where construction and subsequent
improvement have been expensive the burden is heavy. It is borne
not by the shipper, but by the railroads and the general taxpayer.
A water freight rate large enough to bear all costs of construction, maintenance, and carriage would rarely be lower than the
rail rate. Germany kept a wide gap between water and rail rates
for the carriage of the same freight, lost heavily on its water-

ways, but made up the deficit from the profits on the railroads. After the War, when the Rhine became part of the French frontier, French and Belgian railroads competed more keenly with the German lines and compelled them to lower their rates. This reduced the advantage that the Rhine had enjoyed, just at a time when the automobile and truck were stealing some of the river's passenger and parcel traffic. Meanwhile the division of the thousand miles of Danube, once within the Austro-Hungarian Empire, into five pieces and the erection of tariff obstacles in Danubia reduced the movement of goods on that stream. Water communication in central Europe may have seen its best days.

THE RAILROAD

The railroad came in two installments. First the plate or rail track, developed in the mines, was copied elsewhere, and "iron railways" were laid down near London, Sheffield, Munich, and other towns. On the Munich wagonway it was claimed (1819) that a woman or child could draw with ease a cart laden with three-quarters of a ton, and that one horse could do the work of twenty-two. When these roads were public, tolls were collected from those who used them.

The engine came next. In 1769 a Frenchman made a steam carriage to run on ordinary roads, and by 1830 steam buses were running on some British highways. Eventually they disappeared, but the steam truck is still a common sight. By 1801 Trevithick, a Cornish engineering genius, had an engine pulling a few trucks on rails around the mine at which he worked. In 1808 he built a steam railroad near London, but his lone engine ran off the track and he lacked money for its repair. He went to install engines for draining a mine in Peru, and thus let the pioneer's fame fall into the lap of another mining engineer, George Stephenson. Stephenson used an engine to pull coal trucks six miles from a mine to the River Tyne, and urged the promoters of a plate road between Stockton and Darlington to give steam and rails a trial. They agreed, and in 1825 an engine weighing seven tons hauled a train weighing ninety tons at four to eight miles an hour. At all speeds its chimney was red-hot; but it did the work of forty teams of horses, the price of coal in Stockton soon fell by half, and only a financial panic late in 1825 checked the first epidemic of railway promotion. Five years later much better results were obtained. A line was opened in 1830 from Liverpool to Manchester. On it Stephenson's *Rocket* pulled a train thirty-one miles at an average speed of fourteen miles an hour; and as Huskisson, one of the country's chief cabinet ministers, was knocked down and killed, the opening ceremony received abundant publicity.

These two lines proved there might be "something" in steam railroads. The Lancashire passenger trains were soon running at twenty miles an hour, a result which went "far to strike space and time out of the calculations of the traveller"; the amount of freight carried rose rapidly, and the line earned 8.4 per cent on its capital. Soon other lines were planned. They had to wrestle with technical problems, as boilers burst, engines broke down, and construction costs exceeded the estimates. Even before they turned the first sod they had to fight the vested interests of the old order or rival projectors of the new. Canal stockholders, turnpike trusts, innkeepers, coach owners, horse breeders, and fodder merchants saw that they would be injured by "this smoky substitute for canals," and tried to stop its progress, while two or more companies might fight each other to obtain the right to build a potentially profitable line. The main battle, especially between rivals, was on the floor of parliament, and its cost during the boom years 1845-1847 was estimated by a contemporary at over £10,000,000, or enough to build a first-class line from London to the top of Scotland. If to this are added the sums spent in buying or leasing nearly a thousand miles of canal between 1845 and 1847, the money used to lease rival lines or build branches to forestall a rival, and the high prices paid for land, then we get a glimpse of the cost of competitive private enterprise.

To the burden of these initial costs was added that of speculation, extravagance, and mismanagement. In four frenzied years, 1844-1847, 628 railroad acts were passed, authorizing the raising of £250,000,000. These figures represent much solid achievement and a top layer of froth. The profits that were being made by some lines and the powerful "sales talk" of promoters like Hudson, the Railway King, were bait enough to catch a shoal of eager credulous investors, and much capital never saw a dividend. The cost of mismanagement and fraud also seems to have been heavy. Herbert Spencer in 1855 charged directors with multiform dishonesties, declared that the morality of railroad construction engineers was not far above that of railroad lawyers (he had been an engineer), and quoted a current estimate that a quarter of the £280,000,000 already raised had been filched or squandered. Many investors lost heavily, and the railroads were loaded with a burden of interest which was far greater than it need have been.

The growth of the British railroad system is shown in the following table:

UNITED KINGDOM RAILROADS

Year	Miles	Paid-up Capital	Passengers	Freight (in tons)
1838........	500	....	....	....
1850........	6,600	£240,000,000	73,000,000	....
1870........	15,500	530,000,000	337,000,000	....
1890........	20,000	897,000,000	818,000,000	303,000,000
1910........	23,400	1,319,000,000	1,307,000,000	514,000,000

By 1850 the main routes had been built and the chief features fixed. Most companies had laid only short lines—ten to fifty miles —but competition, amalgamation, and leases gradually welded the fragments together. Two companies controlled about 450 miles apiece in 1849, and twelve operated nearly three-fifths of the total mileage, leaving at least a hundred in charge of the rest. By 1850 the engineers had solved most of their early problems. Cheaper iron and better machine tools aided them, and cheap steel was just over the horizon. The electric telegraph was introduced in the 'forties to transmit information about train movements. In the 'fifties hydraulic brakes were introduced, but Westinghouse's air brake (1868) gave much more satisfaction. Wood ties replaced stone blocks, rails became stouter, and engines larger. By 1850 speeds of 30, 40, or 50 miles were well known, 60 was "far from uncommon when in full motion," and 70 had been reached. Edinburgh was forty-four hours from London by coach but only twelve hours by express train.

Effects of the Railroad.—In 1850 two-thirds of the railroad revenue came from passengers. For their accommodation three classes of carriages and even of trains were offered. The first-class coach resembled three stagecoach bodies mounted on a chassis, and thus originated the "compartment" of today. The early second-class coach was cheerless, but had seats and a roof. Third-class passengers stood in open trucks on trains that started at inconvenient hours, dawdled along, and reached their destination at no fixed hour. In 1844, however, parliament insisted that they be given better service; and this decree, combined with competition among rival lines, led to such improvement of the cheapest travel that second class was eventually abandoned, while by 1900 first class was used only by rich men and honeymoon couples. Cheap excursion fares permitted Demos to visit the coast, the inland scenic areas, or the capital. Even by 1845 Wordsworth was becoming annoyed at the crowds arriving by excursion train to see the lakes and mountains of which he had sung; while in 1851 trippers could go 200 miles to see the Great Exhibition in London and be brought back, all for five shillings. The cheap weekly or season ticket dispersed urban workers, and opened a way of escape for "the sickly artisan, pent up in the densely populated city, or inhaling the pestilential atmosphere of the crowded manufactory."

After 1850 freight steadily grew more important than passengers, but even today British railroads draw a third of their revenue from the sale of tickets, as against a sixth in the United States. Coal and coke provided the greatest weight, and in 1913 supplied two-thirds of the tonnage; other minerals came next, and general merchandise ranked third in weight but first in yield of revenue. The carriage of mail was undertaken in the 'thirties, and when penny post came in 1840 the postal service became cheap as well as quick. The railroad ended long-distance driving of livestock along the highways; one of the earliest pictures we have of a freight train (1833) shows trucks of sheep, a wagon full of cattle, and two trucks in which green-coated Irishmen are trying to keep pigs in order. Milk and other farm produce could be sent quickly to market, and fresh fish could be distributed far inland.

For handling small consignments of produce and merchandise the railroads soon built up a rapid service. Regular freight train schedules were in operation by 1850; rates were the same for small shipments and carloads; and the farmer, storekeeper, or manufacturer could send or receive his can of milk, sack of potatoes, bale of cloth, or packet of clothes cheaply and quickly. The buyer need sink less capital in stock, and hand-to-mouth buying became a feature of trade. Even today the average consignment is only 500 pounds, the average load per car is about five tons, and the average car capacity less than eleven tons—a fact which makes the North American visitor think he has strayed into a toy shop when he first sees a British freight train.

The railroad reduced the time and cost of movement. Stage-coach fares from Liverpool to London in 1835 ranged from 45/– on the roof to 90/– inside the coach. In 1845 the same journey by train cost 16/– third class and 45/– first class, while the time had been shortened by nearly two-thirds. Road wagons charged 12d. to 15d. per ton-mile, and covered about twenty-four miles a day. Canal barges charged 6d. to 12d., and their speed was lower than that on the road. In 1849 railways carried coal at 1d. per ton-mile, and general merchandise for 2d. to 4d. They offered little time and opportunity for the pilferer or thief to do his work, whereas on road and canal "a system of plunder of the most extensive nature" had thrived.

The railroad provided new fields for the employment of labor. In 1847, 47,000 workers were operating British lines, 257,000 were building new ones, while many more were providing iron, rolling stock, building material, or the 700,000 tons of coal consumed by engines that year. One company had over 10,000 persons on its payroll. By 1907 British railroads employed 620,000 persons doing all kinds of work—manual, mechanical, clerical and administrative, skilled and unskilled, regular and casual, sedentary and strenuous. The railroad and the mechanical engineering trades were two large new employers.

The railroad was a great new sponge for capital, and according to one estimate it has absorbed about $100,000,000,000 in different parts of the world during the last hundred years. By 1853, £273,000,000 had been invested in British lines. During the next sixty years the total capitalization rose to nearly £1,300,000,000, of which bonds and guaranteed stock absorbed less than three-eighths (against three-fifths in the United States). "Home Rails" (as the stocks and bonds were called) were popular investments, and the better-paid wage earner regarded them as more desirable than a savings bank accumulation. It soon became evident, however, that the railroads would not make fabulous profits. An early company might pay 6 to 10 per cent, but the heavy capitalization of the later ones forbade any such rich return. Each mile of track bore a capital load of £34,600 in 1853 and of £64,000 in 1918, against about the same number of dollars in the United States.

The return during the second half of the nineteenth century never quite reached 5 per cent but never fell below 3 per cent.

In 1850 Porter wrote, "The *laissez-faire* system . . . has been pregnant with great loss and inconvenience to the country in carrying forward the railway system." Gifted with hindsight, we might say the country paid the penalty for not *planning* its railroad system. But a plan was not easily foreseen until men knew what the railroads could do, and parliament really did have a plan—the promotion of competition and the breaking of monopolies held by canals, roads, or by any one railroad in a district. In addition, the state fixed maximum fares and freights, protected the poor by demanding that a third-class train be run on each line each day at a penny a mile, and even coquetted with the idea of state ownership by decreeing in 1844 that the state might buy all the lines after twenty-one years. Considering the novelty of the car and the strangeness of the route, parliament could retort to Porter that it had been a fairly competent back-seat driver.

After 1850 the state had to change its plan of fostering regulated competition into one of regulating the railroads' monopoly of transportation. The granting of preferential rates to some traders or districts was forbidden (1854), a Railroad and Canal Commission was set up (1873) to settle disputes between customer and carrier, and maximum rates and fares were fixed (1888-1894). If American railroads had to bow to the phrase, "just and reasonable," their British counterparts had to submit to an interpretation of "general" or "public interest." The rates fixed gave none too generous a return on the capital sum, and remained unaltered until 1913; but meanwhile employees became organized and demanded higher wages, coal and materials rose in price, and the gap between receipts and operating expenses steadily narrowed, as the following table reveals:

OPERATING EXPENSES AS A PERCENTAGE OF RECEIPTS (*U.K.*)

1860	47	1913	63
1880	52	1920	97
1900	62	1927	81

The War found the railroads nearing a crisis caused by overcapitalization, rising costs, and state control. "Home Rails" were falling on the Stock Exchange, and the motor car had ceased to be a curiosity. During the War the twenty-six main companies and ninety-three subsidiaries were run as a unit, and when peace came the unscrambling of a hundred and nineteen eggs was neither desirable nor possible. Labor urged that the railroads be nationalized, but instead they were rationalized. Parliament in 1921 divided the railroad map into four main areas and handed the lines in each of them to one big company. Some water was squeezed out of the capital, a tribunal was set up to fix rates which would give the railroads the same net revenue as they enjoyed in 1913, while provision was made for cooperation between managers and employees in settling disputes and increasing efficiency. The railroads were to remain private property, but their public importance was such that their regulation, organization, and welfare were recognized as matters of national concern.

That concern grew great after 1921, for if King Coal was ill his iron horse was far from well. Depression in the export industries reduced the volume of freight, the wages bill in 1927 was twice that of 1913, and expenses ate up 81 per cent of revenue in 1927 against 63 per cent in 1913. The automobile grew to manhood, and in a land of short distances the bus, truck, or private car could skim railroad receipts of some of their cream. Fortunately for the railroad, the automobile in two of its three dresses (car and truck) is far less common in Europe than in America. Purchase price, running costs, and taxation are higher; road conditions prevent the automobile from approaching the best trains in economy of time; railroad fares (especially excursion rates) are low; and as the roads become congested the train becomes the safest, as well as the quickest and cheapest, distance between two points. Fast freight trains, supplemented by free collection and delivery, reduce the truck's advantage. The railroads began, rather tardily, to meet the new rival by accelerating and cheapening their services, by trimming costs, by securing tax relief, and by establishing bus services. But "overhead" is still a crushing load, and cannot be passed on to the taxpayer's shoulders as it can when railroads are publicly owned. The outcome of the struggle is not yet visible, but the day of railroad monopoly is ended after a reign of about sixty years. "Home Rails" will probably never again be what they were in 1900—nearly gilt-edged investments. The shades of the stagecoach driver and the canal boatman must be chuckling over the discomfiture of the enemy who drove them out of business.

Continental Railroads

The continent had its wagon ways, and the British success with steam traction led, during the years 1830-1860, to the building of railroads in most European countries. In this work British capital, equipment, and laborers played some part. In 1841 Thomas Brassey (1805-1870) took a small army of English and Irish

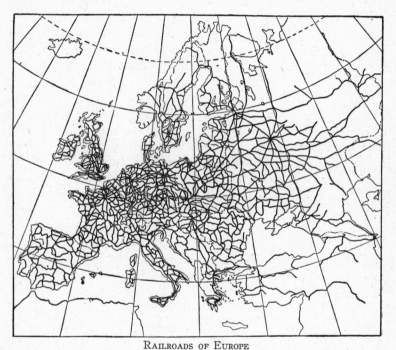

RAILROADS OF EUROPE

(From Blanshard and Visher, *Economic Geography of Europe*, McGraw-Hill Book Company, 1931.)

"navvies" to France to build a line from Paris to Rouen, and during the next two decades his engineers and men laid lines in Belgium, Denmark, Australia, Canada, Argentina, and India. Railroads became a staple British export, but the British system of private ownership did not export very readily.

Belgium.—Belgium was the first state to envisage a coordinated national system. She resolved to turn the cockpit of western Europe into the railroad hub, and by 1834 had launched a project "which should render this small Kingdom the great highway for a large share of the commerce and personal intercourse between some of the chief countries of Europe" (Lardner). Two trunk lines were built: one ran from Ostend eastward toward Germany, the other at right angles from Antwerp to the French border. This railroad cross tapped trade with Prussia, Holland, France and England. The lines were built with borrowed money and run by the state; and foreign railroad men praised the careful spending of the loans, the speed of construction, and the thorough study of engineering, fuel, and cost accountancy problems. Traffic was attracted by low fares and freights, and at first the lines did not earn enough to pay the interest bill. They did, however, aid greatly in building up the foreign trade of Antwerp, the sale of coal, the export of iron, and the general advance of factories and foundries in a country that had followed more closely than any other in Britain's industrial footsteps.

In later years Belgium planned two other innovations. (1) In 1872 she established a system of workmen's weekly tickets to induce urban wage earners to live in the rural areas. For twenty-four cents a week one could travel six miles to and from work, for twenty-nine cents a journey of twelve miles could be taken, and the stalwart who went to live sixty-two miles from his job could commute for sixty cents a week. In 1906 about one-sixth of the working-class population used this opportunity to live where rent was lower, fresh air less rare, and a plot of land offered a supplementary source of income. (2) In 1881 a commission was appointed to "study the best means of creating a system of secondary or local railways," and, by 1910, 3000 miles of light narrow-gauge line had been laid to bring steam traction nearer the farmer's gate. In 1927 at least 4,000,000 tons of beets, cereals, potatoes, fertilizers, coal, stone, and other requirements or produce were carried, along with 50,000,000 passengers. Pre-War Belgium had more transport facilities per hundred square miles than any other land; there were thirty miles of ordinary railroad, thirty of light railroad, and fourteen miles of navigable waterway.

France.—While Britain and Belgium were boldly plunging into unknown territory, France looked long before she crawled. Outside the north and east there were few large towns between center and circumference. From Paris to any place of importance involved a journey of 250 to 500 miles, and there would be little local traffic on the way. Inland transportation was controlled by the central government, and the bureaucrats were hard-hearted skeptics, quick to see problems and difficulties, but slow to reach solutions. Not till 1842 was a policy adopted, and meanwhile most of the few lines built by private companies came to grief.

The policy of the "Organic Law" of 1842 had two parts. (1) The railroad system was to consist of seven main lines radiating from Paris to the coasts and frontier, and two lines from Marseilles to the Rhone and to the Bay of Biscay. (2) The state and private enterprise were to join hands. The central and local governments would buy the land for the roadbed, and lease it for a long period to some company which laid the rails, provided equipment, and operated the line. When the lease expired, the whole property was to pass to the state, but the company would be compensated. At first the central government had to do more than its share, but by 1850 most of the main lines were at work under companies which held them on lease for thirty or forty years. During the next twenty years the length of track increased fivefold, and amalgamation reduced the number of companies from about thirty to six big units.

These six lines—the old system (*ancien réseau*)—were largely trunks without branches. To encourage the construction of spur lines, the state agreed in 1859 to guarantee interest on capital spent on such tracks, and extended the leases for a further ninety-nine years. In ten years the mileage doubled, but the building of this *second réseau* still left many areas without rail service. In 1883 the state agreed to guarantee interest and dividend on capital spent in filling up the gaps. The *troisième réseau* was added, and the mileage more than doubled between 1880 and 1914.

Money paid by the state under these guarantees was not a gift, but a loan. On it interest must be paid, and it had to be repaid; but the second batch of lines often failed to earn interest on its capital, and the third nearly always ran at a loss. Party politics and vote-catching were responsible for the laying of tracks which could never hope to earn much revenue, most of the companies sank deeper into debt, and in 1907 owed nearly 1,200,000,000 francs ($240,000,000). The *P.L.M.* (Paris-Lyons-Mediterranean), an important international highway, was profitable, and the *Nord*, serving industrial regions, never needed aid; but each of the four others went downhill, and in 1908 the bankrupt Western Company handed over its property. After the War the state established a Superior Railways Council to coordinate the lines, and encouraged electrification. The inflation of the currency and the reduction in the value of the franc by four-fifths lightened the interest burden; but taxes, wages, and costs of material rose, while the airplane and the automobile harassed the train. The day of track-laying has ended, and some lines may be abandoned. The state owns about a quarter of the 33,000 miles of railroad, but its lines are chiefly in the agricultural west and are unprofitable.

Germany.—Probably no area except Russia, Canada, or the American Middle West benefited so much from railways as did Germany. The railroad knit her together politically and economically and made the Empire a reality. It also knit her into the fabric of continental Europe, with strands that stretched westward to the North Sea and English Channel, eastward into Russia, and southward to Austria, Italy, and Constantinople.

The chief original business of the railroads was to supplement the waterways, improve the portage from one stream to another, and facilitate traffic between neighboring towns. Each state thought in terms of its own local needs, of tracks that would be suburban or interurban rather than interstate. The first line (1835), from Nuremberg to Furth, was three and one-half miles long, and in 1849 fifteen lines were twenty miles long or less. In most states the railroads were built by the government; but Prussia, having built one important military line from Berlin to the Russian border, encouraged capitalists in Cologne and the west to lay lines by taking up some bonds or stock, by guaranteeing interest, and by promising not to permit a second line to compete with the first one in any region.

By 1850 piecemeal building had given Germany 3600 miles of railroad and Austria about 1000 miles. Interstate junctions had been made, Cologne was linked with Belgian and French lines, Vienna was throwing out tracks in all directions, and only fifty miles were lacking in the route from Trieste to the Baltic. Engineers were following cheap American rather than costly British methods of construction; they put rails on the best surfaces they could find, took hills and valleys as they came, and laid only single tracks. Hence they built and equipped the railroads for about a third of the British cost. They offered very plain accommodation for passengers, ran no expresses or "limited" trains, put first to fourth classes behind the same engine, added freight cars, stopped at all stations, and completed journeys at speeds of 11 to 25 miles an hour. Yet in Germany as in France even this service had far-reaching effects in tying town and country together, in fostering interregional exchange of goods, and in stimulating industry and commercial farming.

Between 1850 and 1870 mileage trebled, gaps were filled in, equipment and service were improved. When the Empire was founded Bismarck tried to get all the lines transferred from state to imperial ownership, but had to rest content with coordination of the state systems through the Imperial Railway Office. In Prussia he bought the private lines, built more, and laid light railways to help the Junkers. By 1910 Prussia owned 21,000 miles of railroad—over half the whole system—and 6000 miles of light railway. Other states were equally energetic. The opening of the St. Gotthard tunnel in 1882 gave an outlet on the Mediterranean, and Genoa became almost a German port. As Russian lines came westward the eastward flow of German goods rose, and many Russian factories and markets were equipped or supplied with German machines or wares. But Russia ranked only sixth among Germany's customers, and it was toward Great Britain, Austria-Hungary, the United States, Holland, and France that the railroads conveyed most goods.

Public ownership allowed Germany to fit her railroads into her commercial as well as her military policy. A fairly consistent effort was made to give special encouragement to industries and districts which sought foreign markets, by lowering rates on export commodities. Lorraine ore went to Ruhr coke at freight costs which "largely cancelled the 150 miles of distance that lay between" (Bowman). The railroads were not, however, allowed to be milch kine, except for the waterways; they were run to yield a surplus, and in 1911 had $90,000,000 left over after meeting working expenses and interest charges.

In 1919 all the railroads were made national property, subject to payment of compensation to the states. They shared the general dislocation of the post-War years, but the inflation of the currency wiped out the debt incurred for their construction. By 1924 they were recovering their old efficiency, and were regarded as one of the sources from which reparations payments could be squeezed. Under the Dawes Plan of 1924 they were to earmark 550,000,000 gold marks (about $130,000,000) each year, and this sum, supplemented by the receipts from a transport tax, would provide $200,000,000 a year for reparations. From 1924-1929 Germany's rapid economic recovery reflected itself in railroad activity. Old plans for electrification were unearthed, and an attempt was made to coordinate railroad, river, and highway carriage; but the car, truck, and airplane could not be tamed, and the railroads estimated in 1929 that they lost traffic worth $100,000,000 to motor transporters on land or in the air.

Russia.—To Russia railroads brought easier and quicker transport inside the country and to the frontiers, an effective penetration of Siberia, and the junction of the waterways. The Crimean War was waged at the end of poor rivers and worse roads, but in the modernization that followed, the railroad mileage rose from 850 miles in 1855 to 15,000 in 1882. Companies were formed and aided by state guarantees of interest or investment in their securities. This plan was far from satisfactory, for competition led to rate-cutting, to heavy losses and to heavy claims on the guarantor. In 1881 the state decided to take over the railroads. Sergius Witte, who advanced from the rank of station master to be minister of communications (1888) and then minister of finance (1892-1903), reveled in buying up lines and making extensions. Loans were floated at home and abroad, the mileage rose to 47,000 in 1914, and a third of the national debt in that year had been incurred for railroads.

Witte's efforts brought far more farmers into contact with domestic and foreign markets, but his significant achievement was the Trans-Siberian line (1891-1905). Siberia was even less useful than the American prairies till railroads reached it, and few people went there of their own will. Though built mainly for military reasons, the line had great economic value. It ran through the Siberian black belt; to the north were large forests, and to the south lay grass lands fading into desert. Between 1893 and 1913 over 5,000,000 settlers crossed the Urals, and in the peak year (1908) 760,000 persons went east, a number equal to that entering the United States. Soon the westbound trains began to carry loads of Siberian grain and butter. Branch lines went north to the forests and south to Turkestan or other parts. Irrigation turned pieces of Turkestan into cotton fields, and the Bolsheviks fostered this development by completing the Turk-Sib line in 1930. They also finished the double-tracking of the main line, thus giving the world its longest double railroad (6350 miles from the Polish frontier to Vladivostok).

Russia's railroad achievement between 1856 and 1914 was remarkable, but it still was not enough. The network was unevenly spread, dense on the western front and the industrial areas of Poland and Moscow, but thin in the north, south, and southeast. Rolling stock and engines were insufficient, tracks were flimsily constructed, while repair shops and engines were often equipped with German tools and parts. When war came this semi-developed and lopsided system soon broke down, and its repair was one of the most urgent tasks confronting the Bolsheviks. Only with infinite labor were the lines restored; but more was needed, and the first Five-Year Plan (1928) called for construction which would give the country 59,000 miles of track, or 24,000 more miles than it had inside its present boundaries in 1913. During the last seven years Russia has been one of the very few countries in which new lines have been laid.

Of Europe's other railroads little need be said. Italian lines helped to give reality to political union, while the tunneling of the Alps removed the age-old barrier to rapid communication with the north and made the heel of Italy a point for jumping off to the Orient. From Vienna to Constantinople lay another transcontinental route, along which the first Oriental Express traveled from Paris via Vienna and Belgrade in 1888. What then? Constantinople, the end of Europe, was the beginning of Asia. Why not cross the Bosporus, and go on to Bagdad and the Persian Gulf?

French and English capitalists played with this idea, but the appeal came most strongly to Germany, for by the end of the nineteenth century that country was economically and politically in an expansive mood. Berlin-Byzantium-Bagdad was more than a good alliteration. There were minerals in Asia Minor, oil fields in Mesopotamia, and irrigable lands in the Near East. Basra on the Persian Gulf might become a mart where the wares of the Rhineland and the treasures of the Orient could change hands. Aleppo, near the north corner of the Syrian coast, might become the railroad hub of the eastern hemisphere, and its train announcer would have the romantic task of informing travelers that trains were due to leave for Berlin, Bagdad, Bordeaux, Bombay, Moscow, Mecca, Madrid, Calais, Calcutta, Cairo, or Cape Town. Of such stuff were dreams made in the last years of the nineteenth century. Canada had linked Halifax with Vancouver, Witte was busy with his Trans-Siberian, and Cecil Rhodes was talking of Cape to Cairo. The Bagdad Railway seemed quite as good business as any of these schemes, and it looked good foreign policy as well.

In 1902 Germans began in earnest to make the dream come true. In October, 1918, the first train ran from the Bosporus to Aleppo, and in the same month the Allies captured Aleppo! The railroads passed into British and French hands, and a new route was developed via Paris, Milan, Trieste, and Constantinople, to Aleppo. The shifts of power and frontiers have destroyed such unity as the old plan possessed, the bombing plane destroys the strategic value of the line, the automobile and airplane provide more elastic and rapid transit, and pipe lines take the oil to the sea. The Near East has not shrunk in economic or political importance since 1918, and oil has given a new taste to imperialism; but the glory has departed from "the Berlin to Bagdad."

The Automobile and the Airplane.—Although Germans and Frenchmen did most to make the automobile possible by 1900, the motor vehicle has influenced Europe less than it has America. Production has never exceeded one-tenth of North America's record annual output, and even in Great Britain there was only one motor-driven vehicle—two- or four-wheeled—to every twenty persons in 1933, against one to every four in the United States. The peasant is scarcely a potential owner; the wage earners go to work on train, street car, bus, cycle, or foot; and the middle class may not have a piece of income to spare for a vehicle that is costly to buy and operate. The popularity of cycling, the persistent enjoyment of walking, the lack of garage facilities in old residential areas, all combine to retard the spread of private car ownership. Nevertheless, the spread has been persistent, while the truck and bus have both taken some traffic from the railroad and added greatly to the sum total of movement. The automobile has created a large new field of investment and employment; made new demands for steel, alloys, and other materials; produced new types of salesmanship and service occupations, and revived the old industry, road-making. It has made more of the population suburban or rural, changed the character of leisure and holidays, brought new revenue and expenditures to the state, and given new work and worries to hospitals, insurance companies, and Scotland Yard.

Commercial aviation began when the War ended. Germany's central position, and the ban imposed by the peace treaty on military aviation, led to great development there. The country was soon covered with routes, and several companies were fused into the *Luft Hansa*. From the Tempelhof airport near Berlin planes left for nearly every European capital. Paris was almost as active, with Le Bourget as its hub; England, Holland, and other countries soon had their services. Each imperial power planned lines to its distant outposts: France sought quick contact with her North African empire, with Syria and Indo-China; Holland in 1930 began a service to the Dutch East Indies, while England began flights to India (1929), and later to Singapore, Australia, and the Cape.

Sixteen years have shown the potentialities and limitations of the new vehicle. Speed such as was impossible on land has come. Areas across which no railroad could be economically operated can be traversed. But the plane can lift only a comparatively small paying load, especially on long non-stop runs. The safe load in 1930 was twenty pounds per horse power, of which possibly seventeen pounds was dead weight. The plane's life is short and its fuel still costly. In 1927 the *Luft Hansa* found that of every 100 marks spent, 30 went to meet depreciation in engines and planes, 20 were absorbed in maintenance and repairs, and 14 in fuel. There has since been little change that would make operation much cheaper; hence the plane is limited to the carriage of small, valuable, or perishable loads that can afford to pay heavy freights, of passengers to whom time is more important than money, or of mail that governments are willing to deliver at a loss.

Communication.—By 1700 state postal services were becoming common, but the modern system is largely the product of steam transportation and of the practice of paying postage in advance. When Rowland Hill analyzed postal costs in 1837, charges varied with the number of sheets of paper, with the weight, and with the distance to be covered. Hill found that distance made virtually no difference to the cost of delivery. The heaviest expenses were incurred in weighing the letter, detecting inclosures, discovering the number of sheets, and collecting the money from the recipient. He therefore pleaded that all letters up to half an ounce in weight be carried throughout the country for a penny, and that postage be paid in advance by the purchase of stamped paper, envelopes, or labels. Penny post was inaugurated in 1840, the envelope appeared, and philately was born. Other postal facilities followed, other countries adopted similar plans, and in 1875 the Universal Postal Union was established to coordinate the passage of mail across frontiers.

Still quicker communication came with the electric telegraph, used first by the railroads but soon made available to the newspapers and the general public. The first British telegraph company was formed in 1846; in 1851 it accepted messages for the continent, as a submarine cable to Calais had linked the British telegraph with wires that stretched to Moscow and the Mediterranean. By 1865 the cables went as far as Calcutta, in 1866 they crossed the Atlantic, and in 1871 Australia was reached. These wires over land and under water knit the world together. Shipping movements, prices, supply and demand could be learned almost instantaneously. For stocks and for the great staple commodities that were capable of being graded, a world market came into being.

The telephone found favor slowly in Europe after Bell's first transmission of the human voice in 1876. Distances were short, postal delivery was rapid, and the telephone was for a long time slow and defective. Wireless telegraphy was, however, so revolutionary that it was quickly adopted after the first dots and dashes went through the air across the English Channel in 1899 and across the Atlantic in 1902. Merchant vessels and warships soon learned the value of the new ears and tongue, and the ability to communicate between shore and distant ship gave communication something of the same flexibility that had come to transportation with the automobile. Wireless telephony—radio—was of less economic significance to Europe than to North America, for the broadcasting services grew up (or became) government systems, were maintained by the license fees of listeners, and did not "sell" time for advertising purposes. The radio telephone, begun in 1927 between London and New York and since extended to cover most of the telephones of the world is still too costly to be of more than limited use.

The Development of Ocean Transportation

The revolution in sea traffic was marked by the triumph of the steamship over a greatly improved sailing vessel and of the steel hull over that built of wood. By 1900 the days of the sailing ship were numbered, but only after sixty years of struggle.

Europe's shipping supply in 1800 consisted of a few big East Indiamen of 500 to 1500 tons, and a swarm of smaller vessels ranging from 400 to 500 tons down to less than 100 tons. The largest were about 200 feet long and about 55 feet wide; the largest liner today is 1000 feet long. Speed depended on ship design, wind, and weather; so long as men relied on sails the date of journey's end was gloriously or grimly uncertain. A vessel might spend four to seven weeks crossing from Philadelphia to Liverpool, but hostile winds and currents spread the return journey over five to nine weeks, and one winter journey of seventeen weeks is known. A run from Liverpool to Marseilles might occupy thirty-seven days, and the Orient was four to seven months away.

The art of navigation improved slowly but surely after 1600. The telescope was perfected about 1610, map-making received more attention, ocean currents were marked on charts, lighthouses and buoys were provided. The sextant, invented in 1731, measured latitude more accurately than did the astrolabe, while in 1772 John Harrison won the £20,000 offered by the British government for a chronometer which kept perfect time and thus allowed ships' officers to ascertain their longitude. Some maritime risks did not disappear till after 1800. Privateering played a large part during the six Anglo-French wars waged between 1689 and 1815, as each nation authorized private merchantmen to attack and seize enemy ships. When the conflict between the two countries ended in 1815 the seas became safer, and in 1856 most nations agreed to the abolition of privateering. Meanwhile the nests of pirates in the Caribbean had been extirpated by British and American fleets in 1816, and the Barbary coast was rendered innocuous between 1816 and 1845. The quest for healthier conditions afloat was just beginning in 1800. Mortality rates on all vessels making long journeys had been appallingly high. Dirty unventilated quarters, lack of fruit, vegetables, or fresh water, and dependence on stale beer, salt beef, or ships' biscuits exposed crew and passengers to scurvy and fevers. At times the entire French navy was crippled by scurvy, and while only 1500 British seamen were killed in the battles of the Seven Years' War, 134,-000 died of disease or were posted "missing." Captain Cook revealed the beneficial effect of cleanliness and fresh food during his Pacific journeys of 1769-1770. After 1786 the French and British navies began to insist on cleanliness, health precautions, and the regular administration of lime juice as a preventive of scurvy. Hospitals and doctors became more efficient, and scurvy was defeated by Vitamin C.

In the story of nineteenth-century shipping two countries stand out: North America perfected the wooden sailing ship and Great Britain evolved the steel steamship. American shipping went ahead quickly after 1783. Trade with the Far East grew, the European wars of 1792-1815 stimulated a demand for American goods and ships, and when peace came transatlantic traffic in manufactured goods, cotton, and passengers (including immigrants) expanded rapidly. Among the ships of all sorts and sizes the *packet* ship stood out. Americans established lines which dispatched boats carrying mail, passengers, and high-grade cargo packages at regular intervals. The first line began work in 1816, and by 1840 packets of 1000 tons were crossing the Atlantic eastward in three weeks or even less, and often got back in less than five. Sailing days were advertised, but dates of arrival could not be.

In the 'forties the American shipbuilder excelled all his earlier efforts, and in the *clipper* produced the fastest and most beautiful craft ever launched. The secret of this vessel was its shape and sails. It might be five or six times as long as it was broad, its shape was "stream-lined," it cut the water instead of bumping it, and on the longer hull more masts and square-rigged sails could be used. The first clipper, the *Rainbow*, was built in New York in 1845, and was quickly copied. Vessels with such names as *Flying Cloud, Typhoon, Sea Witch,* and *Flying Fish* attained speeds which were as startling as fourteen miles an hour had been on the road from Liverpool to Manchester. British builders, who had been slumbering behind the protection of the Navigation Laws, awoke and took up the Yankee challenge. Soon the British public began to read of the achievements of its *Cutty Sark. Ther-*

mopylæ, or *Heather Belle,* and both sides of the Atlantic settled down to enjoy two decades of thrilling international contest.

Speed was sought, not for fun or glory, but because it paid, and the clippers ran on routes where time meant money. The lure of gold in California and Australia made men willing to pay high fares for a quick passage to El Dorado. The first cargo of each season's tea crop brought from China to London always fetched the best price. The Crimean War made France and England desire the speediest contact with the distant war zone. Even the North Atlantic gave a field for profitable record-breaking, since a faster boat could make more round trips in a year, and the clipper cut the passage down to fourteen days or less.

Against packets, clippers, schooners, and other types of craft the steamer began its advance after 1840 and eventually triumphed. Some factors weakened the advantage the sailing ship had enjoyed. The decline in the gold diggings and the completion of the American transcontinental railroads reduced the demand for fast ships. The Suez Canal, opened in 1869, could be navigated by steamers under their own power, but a windjammer would have to be towed through at prohibitive cost. The journey to China via Suez was 3000 miles less than round the Cape. But the more important fact was that gradually the steamer improved until it was more efficient than the sailing ship at every point and was free from some of the defects of its victim. Its power cost money; a lot of its hold was filled with machinery, fuel bins, and water tanks; and it needed a larger crew. But its speed was increased, its cost of operation pared, its dead space reduced, and its range of action extended as its engines were improved. It was more certain in its movements; doldrums had no terrors for it, it did not lie becalmed or stormbound, it need not go off its direct course to take advantage of favorable winds, and it could come into port under its own power. Its efficiency was eventually four times that of a sailing vessel of the same tonnage, and while the task of handling spars and sails limited the size of iron or steel sailing ships to 5000 tons, steamships could be increased far beyond that size. A ten-thousand-ton steamer "making eight round voyages a year in the North Atlantic trade will do in a year the work of at least a dozen sailing vessels of the largest type formerly employed in that trade" (Fayle). "The net effect of the substitution of steam for sail is that an enormously greater volume of trade can be carried on without any corresponding increase in the number of ships employed; that this trade can be brought forward in a steady regular stream, instead of in seasonal rushes, and that arrangements for its reception and disposal can be made in advance, with absolute confidence in the arrival of cargoes at the time expected" (Fayle).

These advantages were slowly realized, especially on long journeys to fetch Australian wool or wheat, Chilean nitrates, American cotton or lumber, and other cheap heavy goods. But by 1893 the world's steam tonnage exceeded that under sail; in 1914 only 8 per cent of its shipping was driven by wind, and today less than 2 per cent. One may travel all the oceans, yet never see a big ship flying along under a spread of canvas.

THE STEAMSHIP

The steamship had a long infancy, as men in France, Scotland, and America groped toward the use of an engine afloat. At least one of them committed suicide and another died in a London slum, but out of their failures success emerged on both sides of the Atlantic. In America, Fulton gathered up their ideas, bought a Watt engine, and in 1807 men saw "the Devil on the way to Albany in a saw-mill" as the *Clermont* traveled 150 miles up the Hudson in thirty-two hours. In Scotland, Bell built the *Comet* (1812), which for eight years ran between Glasgow and a port twenty-five miles away.

The *Comet* and the *Clermont* proved that a steamboat could navigate the sheltered waters of lake, river, canal, or inlet. The next ten years saw the construction of many boats for such waters, and the establishment of ferry services from Holyhead to Ireland (1816) and from Dover to Calais (1820). Experience with these early vessels showed the technical problems that must be solved. Engines were crude, boilers burst, and the weight of the machinery broke the back of the wood hull. There was little room for cargo, and not enough room for fuel for a long journey. The *Savannah*, a sailing ship with an auxiliary engine, used steam for only 80 hours out of 29½ days when she crossed the Atlantic in 1819, used up all the fuel in that time, and went back entirely under sail. Could any ship carry enough coal to cross the Atlantic? The experts said, "No." Lardner, the chief of them, "had no hesitation in saying" that a direct run from New York to Liverpool was "perfectly chimerical, and they might as well talk of making a voyage from New York to the moon."

The chimerical was soon accomplished. In 1833 the *Royal William*, built in Quebec, took on coal in Nova Scotia, and used steam and sails all the way to England. In 1838 the *Sirius* and *Great Western* steamed and sailed from Liverpool to New York in 16½ and 13½ days, respectively, or two weeks less than the usual packet time. On its return journey the *Sirius* overhauled a becalmed packet, took off the mail, and was soon out of sight. Samuel Cunard, a passenger on the packet, thereupon decided that mail ought to be carried by steamers, and in 1839 gained from the British government a contract to carry mails fortnightly between Liverpool, Halifax, and Boston, receiving a fixed annual sum which was virtually a subsidy. The first Cunarder left Liverpool on July 4, 1840, and reached Boston in seventeen days. If the boat had ended its journey, instead of beginning it, on July 4, Boston could scarcely have made a greater celebration. Flags flew, toasts were drunk, Cunard received a silver vase, and Daniel Webster made a speech. Rapidly the service improved, and Cunard began to publish dates of arrival as well as departure. He referred to himself as operator of an "ocean railway," who had replaced the "maddening irregularity inseparable from the days of sail" with an almost clock-like regularity and speed.

By 1850 the steamship had established itself as the best vehicle for carrying mail, passengers, and merchandise that was fairly small in bulk but sufficiently valuable to bear a high freight rate. Its field of action was limited to European waters and the North Atlantic, it could not carry enough fuel to take it farther afield, and coaling stations had not yet been established. The world had probably 10,000,000 net tons of sailing ships, but the steam tonnage was only 750,000, of which nearly 500,000 tons were on the rivers and lakes of North America. The next sixty years saw European steamship registration expand as follows:

Year	Europe, Net Tons	United Kingdom, Net Tons	Germany, Net Tons
1850	186,000	168,000	...
1870	1,483,000	1,113,000	82,000
1890	7,816,000	5,043,000	724,000
1910	19,045,000	10,443,000	2,257,000

This expansion was accompanied by important improvements in hulls, engines, fuel, and driving methods. The first began when Brunel in 1839 planned a big iron steamer, and fitted it with the "Archimedean screw" or propeller in place of the ungainly paddle wheel. An iron hull did not leak or become waterlogged, and its weight was little more than half that of a wood vessel of equal capacity. The wood ship could not safely exceed 300 feet in length, but the only limits to the size of an iron steamer were the strength of the engines, the amount of cargo available, and the ability of ports to accommodate the vessel. By 1855 even the cautious Cunard had deserted wood and paddle wheels. Steel was even better than iron, and in 1879 the first ocean-going steel ship was launched.

The second improvement came when compound engines, with four cylinders, became efficient about 1860. Steamers equipped with them cut their fuel bills in half, got more miles per ton of coal, had more spare space, and could compete with the sailing ship for the carriage of general cargo on long journeys across the equator. On shorter runs the speed and size of vessels could be increased, two or more propellers were used, and the race across the Atlantic entered a new phase when the *Alaska* made the passage in less than seven days in 1882. Turbines, Diesel engines, and oil fuel have since brought greater speeds or more economical operation. The turbine, introduced about 1900, required less steam and hence less fuel, weighed less, occupied less room, and developed more speed with less noise and vibration. Oil fuel began to be used by ocean vessels in 1904. A ton of oil gave nearly 50 per cent more steam than did a ton of coal, yet took up 12 per cent less space. It was easily pumped aboard and could be stored anywhere. It dispensed with an army of stokers, the labor cost of attending the fires was reduced by two-thirds, much space was released for passengers and cargo, while the dirt, discomfort, and laundry bills of coaling days were eliminated. By 1914, four per cent of the world's merchant tonnage was burning oil, but by 1929 the four had expanded to forty.

In 1903 a German, Dr. Diesel, made a motor engine which used crude oil and was suitable for marine work. It was much smaller and lighter than a steam unit of equal power, and in a German warship launched in 1931 it weighed only about one pound per horse power. No boiler was needed, no water tanks,

and no funnels. A ton of exploded oil gave the same power as
four tons of coal or 2 2/3 tons of oil burned in a furnace. The
savings in space and fuel were therefore great. In 1933, 15 per
cent of the world's tonnage was driven by Diesel engines, most
new ships were described as M.V. (motor vessel) instead of S.S.,
and the demand for bunker coal was less than three-fourths that
of 1913.

Types of Shipping.—The racing palaces of the North Atlantic,
now grown to 1000 feet, 70,000 tons, 100,000 horse power, and
29 knots an hour, do only a tiny part of the world's shipping
work. They carry little cargo, few harbors can give them berths,
and only the large volume of traffic on that route, the number of
round trips made in a year, the government subsidies or well-
paid mail contracts, and the ability of some passengers to pay
heavy fares make their operation possible. The bulk of sea carriage on the North Atlantic and the whole of it on other seaways
is done by vessels of much more modest dimensions and performance. In 1914 the world had only 291 steamers of more than
10,000 gross tons. The rest of the fleet was distributed as follows:

5,000–10,000 gross tons	1,747	vessels
2,000– 5,000 " "	5,882	"
100– 2,000 " "	16,523	"

Apart from the greyhounds, hustle was too costly to be a shipowner's ideal. The medium-sized boats on the Canadian, South
American, Oriental, and Australian runs steamed 350 to 450
miles a day, carrying at most 600 passengers and a large amount
of general cargo. An attempt to reduce the length of their journeys would involve a heavy increase in fuel bills. Below these
middle-sized vessels the motley array of passenger and cargo
steamers or of freighters moved at eight to fourteen knots an
hour. Regularity, certainty, cheap operation, and low charges
were more important than speed.

The modern merchant fleet can be divided roughly into the
liner, the tramp, and the boat built specially to carry such cargoes
as oil, coal, cattle, or meat. The liner, whether passenger or cargo,
belongs to a company which provides a regular service over a set
route, and sails at fixed times for a certain destination, whether
it is full or not. The "tramp" is the free lance of the seas. It will
go anywhere to take or fetch almost any kind of cargo. Nitrates,
wool, ore, cotton, lumber, steel, merchandise—the commodity

matters little more than does the route. In 1913, 60 per cent of the world's tonnage was tramp. The typical boat was about 2000 to 3000 gross tons, with large cargo capacity, a speed rarely exceeding eight to nine knots, and a low fuel consumption. A tramp might steam six miles on a ton of coal. Professor Kirkaldy gives an illustration of the roving life of one such vessel. In 1910 a tramp left England laden with rails and general cargo for West Australia. There she picked up lumber for Melbourne, where she loaded harvesters for the Argentine. In Buenos Aires she took grain aboard for Mauritius and Calcutta, and in the latter port was filled with jute for Boston and New York. In New York a cargo of American general merchandise was shipped for Australia, and when this had been delivered the hold was filled with lead ore, wool, and wheat for England. When the ship reached London it had traveled 72,000 miles in seventeen months, and put into port thirty-one times in six continents.

Of the special types of ship, the oil tanker and the refrigerated vessel are the chief. The growth of the demand for gasoline and oil fuel has been so great that by 1931 a ninth of the world's tonnage consisted of tank steamers. The carriage of refrigerated cargo became feasible when in 1880 a consignment of solidly frozen Australian meat reached London. New Zealand followed with a shipload in 1882, and the Argentine in 1883. The first sale of New Zealand meat in the Smithfield market was fittingly described by the *Times* as "a prodigious fact," for refrigeration afloat opened a new world of possibilities to the southern producer, the European consumer, the ocean traveler, and the shipowner. As the prejudice against "frozen mutton" faded, as engineers solved the problems surrounding chilling and freezing, and as southerners became able to send out steady streams of good well-graded produce, Europe became a ready customer. By 1894 the total cost of killing, freezing, and delivering New Zealand lamb in London was only four cents a pound. Liners turned part of their space into cool chambers, and special ships were built capable of carrying 150,000 carcasses. To the carriage of meat was gradually added that of dairy produce, apples, oranges, and such very perishable fruits as peaches, plums, and apricots; and while the southern hemisphere benefited chiefly by being placed in contact with the great food markets of Europe, refrigeration made it possible to gather goods into the British larder from

Nova Scotia, California, the West Indies, Spain, the Levant, and other lands north of the Equator as well.

Interoceanic Canals.—The Suez Canal was begun by de Lesseps in 1859 and finished in 1869. It might have been constructed much earlier if British statesmen had not feared it would strengthen French influence in the Near East and endanger British interests in India. Yet as soon as the canal was open to traffic the benefit to Anglo-Indian trade was seen to be great, and in 1875 Britain bought the shares held by the Khedive, following this with the establishment of a protectorate over Egypt in 1882. At first the canal was shallow, narrow, and unlit, and a boat spent three days passing through it; but after 1880 it was steadily improved, and vessels of 20,000 tons can traverse it today in about fifteen hours. It reduced the distance between London and Bombay from 10,700 miles to 6300. Hongkong came 3400 miles nearer to the Thames, and Yokohama 3000 miles. The Mediterranean awoke to a new day and soon became the second most important ocean route, while Port Said grew to be the world's most famous coaling station and sink of iniquity. In 1928 nearly 33,000,000 net tons of shipping, or 6000 ships, passed through the canal. Of them, two-thirds were British.

When Suez began to pay good dividends, de Lesseps and a group of French capitalists resolved to repeat their success by cutting Panama. In six years (1883-1889) the company spent $350,000,000 and then went bankrupt, victim of graft, a financial rake's progress, and the mosquito. Where France failed, the United States, aided by Sir Ronald Ross' discovery that mosquitoes spread malaria, succeeded, and the canal was opened in 1914. Its chief effect was to shorten journeys between the two coasts of the Americas, and to bring the west coast nearer to Europe. But the canal also brought that west coast, along with New Zealand, Japan, and the eastern half of Australia, nearer to New York than to London. Valparaiso was now 2500 miles nearer, Vancouver 2600 miles, Sydney 1600, Wellington 2600, and Yokohama 1000 miles.

These figures seemed ominous even before 1914, for they gave the American exporter an advantage over his British and German rivals in Pacific markets; but the next four years proved that the canal was most opportunely timed. American exports would have won many Pacific markets in any case, but the World War made the campaign easier. When peace came the ocean shipping map was redrawn. Boats which went from Europe via Suez to New Zealand and the Orient now returned home via Panama instead of through Suez or round Magellan. Nearly two-thirds of the 30,000,000 net tons of shipping that used the Panama Canal in 1928 was foreign—an indication of the extent to which trade routes had been affected.

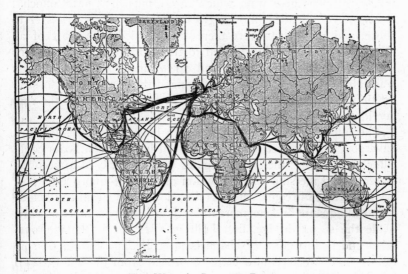

THE WORLD'S SHIPPING ROUTES

The thickness of the lines is proportionate to the tonnage. (From Bowman's *The New World,* copyright, 1928, by World Book Company, Yonkers-on-Hudson, New York.)

The Growth of Ports.—Since the end of every sea voyage is a harbor, the growth in the size of vessels and in the volume of traffic must be accompanied by the provision of better facilities at ports of call and termini. The depth of a channel or route was that of its shallowest point, and a boat with a draft of forty feet has nearly double the capacity of a ship drawing thirty feet. Most of Europe's great ports developed as far up rivers as could safely be reached by a seagoing vessel at high tide. Ships had to navigate carefully amid sand banks and shallows, watching tides and currents, and often requiring two or three tides to reach port. London had a "rather intricate navigation at the mouth of the river," the road to Amsterdam was treacherous, while Liverpool had sand banks and a tide that rose and fell thirty feet. Vessels drawing four feet of water needed a pilot for the seventy miles of river leading to Hamburg, and large vessels had to stop sixty miles down stream.

Few ports had quays in the eighteenth century, and anchorage was usually in midstream. At Hamburg in 1830 ships were tied to piles, and "in this position they are not exposed to any danger unless the piles give way, which rarely happens" (McCulloch). Goods were unloaded into barges or small boats for transfer to shore, and busy ports were therefore crowded with craft of all sizes. Repeated handlings added to transportation costs, customs were collected with difficulty, and cargo landed on bank or quay was fair game for thieves who thronged the ports, ready to steal anything from a bag of coffee to an anchor. Meanwhile the ship lay idle, earning nothing.

The improvement of ports has been long and costly. In 1715 Liverpool made a wet dock, an artificial basin which boats could enter at high tide; the entrance gates were then closed to keep the water in and the ship afloat. London did little to improve its port till 1802, when it constructed its first dock. The steam tug helped both sailing ships and steamers to berth or leave port more quickly, while the steam dredge, first built in 1824, made the improvement and maintenance of channels possible. The cutting of ship canals gave Amsterdam a better approach from the sea (1825), put Manchester on the coast (1894), and started Rotterdam in 1872 on its advance to second place among European ports. Public and private enterprise shared in the expensive task of providing terminal facilities, and when the muddles of competition and lack of coordination drove the British parliament in 1909 to establish a public trust—the Port of London Authority—that body took charge of thirty-six miles of quay and 3000 acres of land and water devoted to docks. While vessels were thus able to berth and unload more quickly, warehouses had to be provided in which goods could be stored till they were passed on to factory, merchant, or outbound ship. Big importers built processing or packing plants, manufacturers chose sites near by, while shipbuilding or repairing might be carried on near a great ocean terminal. Hence the chief ports ranked among the largest cities in Europe. Glasgow and Hamburg contain more than a million people each, Liverpool has over 800,000, and Marseilles over 600,000.

Shipping During and After the War.—In 1914 the world had about 42,500,000 gross tons of steamships engaged in coastal and sea traffic. Of these,

19,000,000 were British,	or 42	per cent of the total	
5,000,000 were German,	” 12	” ” ” ” ”
2,000,000 were American,	” 4.4	” ” ” ” ”
1,900,000 were Norwegian,	” 4.3	” ” ” ” ”
1,900,000 were French,	” 4.3	” ” ” ” ”
1,700,000 were Japanese,	” 3.8	” ” ” ” ”

Italy, Holland, and Austria-Hungary had each more than a million tons. The outstanding facts of this table are the overwhelming preponderance of British shipping and the large German tonnage.

The preeminence of British shipping was due to priority in steamship building, the large imports of food or raw materials, the great exports of coal and manufactured wares, the widespread imperial, banking, and commercial connections, and the readiness with which capital had been obtained for the merchant marine. The victory over the American sailing ship was complete, but soon another Richmond was in the field. In 1871 Germany had only 80,000 net tons of steamships and 900,000 tons of sailing vessels. When she swung into her stride as manufacturer and exporter, the expansion of the merchant marine became inevitable. The government gave some generous mail subsidies, foreign-built ships or shipbuilding materials were admitted duty free, and orders for battleships stimulated shipbuilding. The growing export trade, cheap iron and steel, low wages, and the rising tide of emigration from central and eastern Europe all helped. By 1914 the German steam fleet had grown to 2,650,000 net tons (or about 5,000,000 gross tons). German ships were everywhere; the giant *Vaterland* was the largest floating hotel crossing the Atlantic, while tramps were loading nitrates in Chile, phosphates in Oceania, and lumber or scrap tin in Tasmania.

During the War over 12,000,000 tons of merchant shipping were sunk, of which 7,700,000 were British. Frantic efforts were made to repair this damage by building new ships—some were even made of cement. Hence, when the War ended, the world's tonnage was 2,000,000 tons larger than in 1914, many unfinished vessels were on the stocks, and the productive capacity of the industry had been vastly expanded. In the peace settlement, Germany was deprived of virtually all her ocean-going ships. The story of the next ten years is one of unparalleled expansion. From 42,500,000 gross tons in 1914, the world's fleet had risen by 1923 to 58,000,000, and by 1929 to 68,000,000, or 60 per cent in fifteen years. The United States ocean fleet grew from two to ten million tons; the tonnage flying the flags of Norway, France, Japan, Italy, and Holland increased two- to threefold; and Germany worked vigorously to replace the fleet she had lost. Only Great Britain stood apart from this multiplication of ships, and was content to replace some of her older boats with better ones. Her old predominance was thus whittled from 42 per cent of the world's tonnage in 1914 to 30 per cent in 1929.

If this growth had been accompanied by a comparable expansion in the volume of trade, all might have been well. But in 1923 that volume was estimated at only 80 or 85 per cent of the 1914 figure, and in 1929 it was still far below that of the shipping space waiting to carry it. Tariff obstacles and economic nationalism frowned on imports, and the stream of emigration shriveled up under such influences as the quota restriction in the United States, the growing reluctance of other countries to take all comers, and the higher fares. Competition became fierce, government subsidies permitted some lines to operate at a loss, and freight rates fell to pre-War levels or below; but operating costs declined more slowly, and shipping became an unprofitable enterprise. When depression descended on the world in 1929, the volume of cargo seeking carriage fell probably a third. Nearly one-eighth of British tonnage was laid up at the end of 1930, the world's idle shipping quadrupled in that year, and the remaining ships ran with half-empty holds and short passenger lists. Unemployment stalked the waterfront, and shipyards were as silent as graveyards. Ships, coal, and railroads, the three musketeers of the nineteenth century, were all sick men.

BIBLIOGRAPHY

GENERAL

BOGARDUS, J. F., *Europe: A Geographical Survey* (1934), pp. 146-162.

CLAPHAM, J. H., *Economic History of Modern Britain* (1926, 1932), vol. i, chaps. 3, 9, 10, 12; vol. ii, chaps. 5, 6.

CLAPHAM, J. H., *The Economic Development of France and Germany, 1815-1914,* chaps. 5, 7, 10, 12.

FAY, C. R., *Great Britain from Adam Smith to the Present Day* (1932), chaps. 8-11.

HASSERT, K., *Allgemeine Verkehrsgeographie* (1931).
KIRKALDY, A. W., and EVANS, A. D., *History and Economics of Transport* (1924).
KNOWLES, L. C. A., *Economic Development in the Nineteenth Century* (1932), part iv.
KNOWLES, L. C. A., *Industrial and Commercial Revolutions in Great Britain during the Nineteenth Century* (1922), parts iv, v.
McPHERSON, L. G., *Transportation in Europe* (1910).
OGG, F. A., and SHARP, W. R., *Economic Development of Modern Europe* (1926), chaps. 11, 27.
PORTER, G. R. (ed. Hirst, 1912), *Progress of the Nation*, chaps. 14, 28, 29.
Encyclopædia of the Social Sciences: See list of articles on Transportation, vol. xv, p. 557.
Social Science Abstracts: See Index for articles on history and recent developments.

INLAND TRANSPORTATION

ACWORTH, W. M., *The Elements of Railway Economics* (1924).
DICKINSON, H. W., and TITLEY, A., *Richard Trevithick* (1934).
GRINLING, C. H., "British Railways as Business Enterprises," in Ashley, W. J., *British Industries* (1907).
HINES, W. D., *Report on Danube Navigation* (League of Nations, 1927).
JACKMAN, W. T., *Development of Transportation in Modern England* (1916).
JAGTIANI, H. M., *The Rôle of the State in the Provision of Railways* (1924).
LEWIN, H. G., *Early British Railways, 1801-1844* (1925).
SHELDON, G., *From Trackway to Turnpike* (1928).
SHERRINGTON, C. E. R., *A Hundred Years of Inland Transportation* (1934).
TURBERVILLE, A. S. (ed.), *Johnson's England* (1933), vol. i, chap. 6.
WEBB, S. and B., *The Story of the King's Highway* (1916).

OCEAN TRANSPORTATION

BERGLUND, A., *Ocean Transportation* (1933).
CHATTERTON, E. K., *The Mercantile Marine* (1923).
COLIN, A., *La navigation commerciale au xixe siècle* (1901).
FAYLE, C. E., *Short History of the World's Shipping Industry* (1933), chaps. 8-11.
FAYLE, C. E., and WRIGHT, C., *A History of Lloyd's* (1928).
FAYLE, C. E., *The War and the Shipping Industry* (1927).
HARDY, A. C., *Seaways and Sea Trade* (1934).
HOSKINS, H. L., *British Trade Routes to India* (1928).
JACKSON, G. G., *The Ship under Steam* (1928).
JOHNSON, E. R., and HUEBNER, G. G., *Principles of Ocean Transportation*, part i.
KIRKALDY, A. W., *British Shipping: Its History, Organisation, and Importance* (1914).
LUBBOCK, B., *The China Clippers* (1914).
SALTER, J. A., *Allied Shipping Control* (1921).

ARTICLES

BERGLUND, A., "The War and the World's Merchant Marine," in *Am. Ec. R.*, June, 1920.
LEFRANC, G., "The French Railroads, 1823-1842," in *J. E. B. H.*, February, 1930, pp. 299-331.

LEVAINVILLE, J., "The Economic Function of the Rhine," in *Geog. Rev.*, vol. xiv (1930), pp. 242-256.

MAGNES, J., "The Recovery of Germany's Merchant Marine after the War," in *Harv. Bus. Rev.*, October, 1930, pp. 57-68.

PETERSON, G. S., "Motor and Rail Carriers in Great Britain," in *Am. Ec. R.*, December, 1930, pp. 640-657.

CHAPTER XXIII

INDUSTRIAL AND COMMERCIAL ORGANIZATION

I.—The Spread of the Factory System

During the last hundred and fifty years many industries which had been in the hands of domestic workers have passed within factory gates, the putting-out system has almost disappeared or has changed its character, while the new industries that have come into being have depended on the assembling of much capital and labor almost from their birth. The practice of gathering workers together would probably have spread over much of the old industrial field if there had been no great changes in equipment, for the expansion of the market would have strained the putting-out and handicraft systems. An entrepreneur could save time by bringing in labor instead of putting out material, could develop better standards of workmanship, train men to do jobs the way he wished, take advantage of division of labor, impose discipline and regular hours, and get goods produced in a steadier stream. Boulton, Wedgwood, and many other builders of large plants in England and France were quite as much concerned with skill and quality as with machines and power. The putting-out system was not a good technical school. True, there were obstacles —the need for capital and the possible hostility of labor; but these might have been surmounted. At any rate, they were overcome when machinery, power, and science added their economies to those already enjoyed by the central workshop.

The factory system made its most notable advance when it annexed the making of yarn and the weaving of cloth. These processes had been strongholds of domestic industry in all countries, and the central workshop did not offer marked net advantages except under special conditions. They were, however, well suited to factory production, once their equipment was changed, and were transferred to the textile mill along at least four roads. (1) Lombe's silk mill at Derby (1718) was copied in London, Lancashire, and Cheshire, and served as a pattern.

When the cotton spinning machines came, some of these silk mills were converted to the production of cotton yarn.

(2) The early jennies and mules were erected in homes to feed the family loom or to spin for some putter-out; but an enterprising person might erect a number of them in a shed to produce on a larger scale. One Lancashire man (Fielden) in 1780 converted three cottages into such a shed, and set his nine children to work jennies.

(3) Some occupiers of grain or fulling mills installed the new machines, attached them to the water wheel, and treated their own material or that put out to them by neighboring cloth-makers.

(4) As power-driving became easier and larger machines were designed, the building of mills became more general. Such mills might specialize on the processes using power, but some of them gathered under one roof the processes that did not need power as well. In the same establishment some workers might be attending power-driven machines, others might be operating hand jennies or mules, scores of men were working hand looms, while many outworkers might come each week to deliver a piece of cloth and take away a new supply of yarn. The extension of power and machinery and the disappearance of putting-out was a matter of time.

Some of these developments came fairly quickly after Arkwright, in 1771, set up a factory at Cromford (Derbyshire), and used a wheel to drive his spinning frames. By 1800 hundreds of mills of all sizes were strewn along the river banks of Lancashire, Nottinghamshire, Derbyshire, Yorkshire, and the hinterland of Glasgow, and steam was already supplementing water power. The supply of barns, old flour mills, and other adaptable buildings had been exhausted, and some of the new mills were built on a large scale, with four, five, or six floors, great boxes of brick and glass. If the owner or occupier could not use the whole structure himself he leased part of it to others, supplying power as well as space.

Several factors made the establishment of a textile factory enterprise easy. In the first place, the early equipment was not expensive when new, could be bought cheaply at a sale of some bankrupt's stock, and could often be rented with the room in which it stood. In the second place, a small factory with a few machines was not at a great disadvantage in competition with a larger rival. A mill using (say) ten units of each kind of machine was not much less efficient than one using fifty or a hundred. In the third place, the division of labor was great. The product was one of infinite variety of patterns, weights, and qualities, calling for a similar variety of yarns, dyes, spinning and weaving standards, and finishing methods. A producer might concentrate on the manufacture of one or two qualities, patterns, or kinds of cloth. He might perform only one process, such as weaving, buy his yarn ready-made or put wool out to be spun, sell his cloth unfinished or put it out to be finished. The comber, scribbler, spinner, fuller, dyer, printer, or finisher might be working on his own goods or on those of customers. In this highly subdivided industry a man might need only enough equipment for one task, and earn his living selling his skill and the services of his plant. A giant here and there gathered all processes under his roof, or built up a huge plant for one of them. In 1816 three cotton spinners had 1500 to 1600 mill workers each; one Lancashire firm had 700 workers in its spinning factories, and "a whole countryside of hand-loom workers, nearly 7000 people all told" (Clapham); a Leeds woolen factory employed over 1100 persons in 1830. But against these leviathans must be placed mills in which fifty or fewer people were at work. In 1900 the average British woolen factory employed only 80 persons, the worsted factory 200 people, and the cotton factory about 170 workers.

By 1840 the factory system was supreme (or was becoming so) in the production of cloth, paper, glass, iron, engines, and machines. This still left large fields in the hands of the craftsman and outworker, especially in the clothing, leather-working, small metal ware, woodwork, building, and food industries. Leather goods, metal articles, furniture, clothing, and food gradually became factory products after 1850. The new industries born after 1850—steel, chemicals, electrical apparatus, rayon, and vehicles—often depended on patents as well as on the use of complicated and costly equipment, and were part of the factory system from birth. The mechanical engineering industry gradually expanded its small workshop into a great factory, while the little shops in which the vast variety of Birmingham small wares were made gave way after about 1890 before foreign competition, the growing supply of cheap steel in place of brass, the use of presses

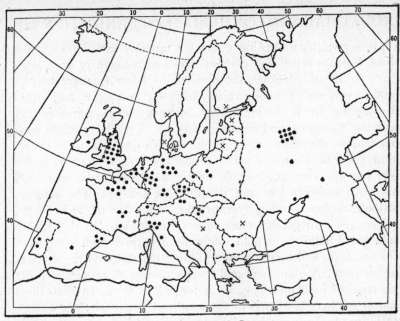

WORKERS IN THE TEXTILE INDUSTRIES

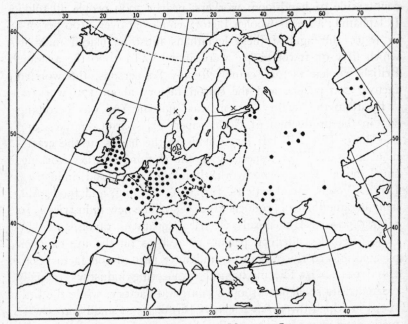

WORKERS IN THE METAL AND MACHINE INDUSTRIES

Each dot on these two maps represents 1 per cent of the European total engaged in each industry. (Reprinted by permission from *Economic and Social Geography,* by Huntington, Williams and Van Valkenburg, published by John Wiley & Sons. Inc.)

and machine tools, the rise of industries to make parts for cycles and cars, and the War's need for mass production.

The Spread of the Factory System on the Continent.—In spite of laws forbidding the emigration of artisans and the export of equipment, jennies, mules, and frames appeared in France soon after they were at work in England, and British workmen were procured to help in building and using them. In 1782 a Watt engine was bought by the Creusot iron works, and in 1788 a cotton factory at Sens, set up by a Manchester man, was using Arkwright's machines and employing 600 workers. The gathering of workers in central workshops was a fairly well-known French practice, and the government did its utmost to encourage the introduction of machinery. The Revolutionary and Napoleonic Wars deprived France of some export markets, but kept English goods out, stimulated cotton and woolen production, and caused little spinning mills to crop up in many places. When peace came, progress was slow for a time, but after 1830 became more rapid, especially in the iron, cotton, and coal industries. British methods were introduced to the Creusot works; mechanical engineering shops and coal mines were developed; Lille and Alsace-Lorraine extended spinning factories, installed power looms, and built their own machines, while mechanized paper mills grew rapidly in number. By 1850 there had "certainly been nothing which deserves to be called an industrial revolution" (Sée), but the movement was well started.

Belgium was quicker than France in adopting the new technique and organization. Its iron and coal deposits and its long industrial tradition fitted it for successful imitation of British models. During the Napoleonic War it was a French munitions center, and after 1815 mining, metallurgy, machine-building, and textile work were developed rapidly, in some places by Britons. The Dutch rulers improved its credit facilities, and when independence came (1830) the Belgian government actively furthered large-scale production and factory extension. By 1850 Belgium stood close to Great Britain in the development of the new industrialism and railroad transportation, and had supplied machines and capital for some German industries.

At that date little more than a beginning of industrial change was visible in Germany. Even before 1800 there had been some interest in British industrial developments, and Stein was suspected of having come to steal ideas when he visited Boulton's factory in 1786. The spinning jenny was soon in use in German homes and shops, and when Napoleon closed the continent to British goods some German industries expanded to fill the gap. After 1815 these war-time growths shriveled under British competition, and even the older staple export industries were battered. Silesia's great linen trade, fed by a vast *Verlagssystem*, lost much of its foreign and domestic market to British machine-made goods. German "shear steel" and Solingen cutlery had no superiors in Europe, but lost ground to Sheffield, while high tariffs reduced the Russian demand for linens and woolens. In the towns the small workshop prevailed, and Prussia in 1843 had fewer apprentices and journeymen than masters. In the country almost every peasant family made the goods it needed or worked for a *Verleger*, and commercial production was scarce outside the Rhineland, Westphalia, Saxony, and Silesia.

It was in these areas that the first steps toward new industrial methods were taken. The *Zollverein* (1834), the coming of the railroads, the weakening of guild control, state encouragement, the gradual accumulation of capital, and the example of western neighbors helped to quicken development after 1835. The textile, coal, and iron industries led, traveling slowly along familiar British lines. They were accompanied by machine-making, and by the rise of sugar factories, alcohol distilleries, and chemical plants. After 1870 the advance was much more rapid, especially in the newer fields of steel and the chemical and electrical industries. In the four decades of the Empire the lands east and west of the lower Rhine were crowded with industrial plants of all kinds, while the Berlin region, Saxony, Silesia, and minor areas became industrialized to a high degree. A combination of British factory technique, of rich mineral resources, of old-standing craftsman's skill, and of interest in science took Germany through a rapid and fundamental industrial transformation.

By 1850 a few textile mills had appeared in Austria, Italy, Spain, and Russia. To the enthusiasts for the Italian *Risorgimento* the machines, railroads, and steamships which had made England "so industrious, commercially so active, so enterprising, so powerful" offered hope. Factories would strengthen Italy for her struggle with Austria, railroads would link the parts of the country together—"stitch the boot"—while steamships and a

Suez Canal would put Italian ports back on world trade routes. In Lombardy, Tuscany, and Piedmont bourgeois and landlord put money into silk or cotton mills, and hired Englishmen to manage and instruct their workers. Till 1870 the stress was on textile mills, but when cheap "hydro" became available plants were erected to treat metals, chemicals, or rubber, and to make automobiles. Spain built cotton mills in Barcelona and at scattered water-power sites in the Pyrenees, and eventually harnessed some rivers so thoroughly that their beds are now quite dry. The factories of Austria grew after 1850 to supply a large imperial home market and some foreigners with glass, hardware, chemicals, textiles, implements, and beer.

In the days before emancipation the Russian landlords operated some workshops and mines with serf labor, and other capitalists ran them with hired workers. Government aid took the form of high tariffs after 1815, but until improved transportation opened the way to markets little industrial expansion was possible. During the eighteen-nineties Witte pursued an active policy of industrial stimulation, and much foreign capital and management went into textile plants, mines, metallurgical works, machine factories, and oil wells. War and revolution injured the semi-developed industrial equipment, and the Bolshevik efforts at restoration were soon expanded into an ambitious plan for making the country self-sufficing.

In the first Five-Year Plan (1928) the Bolsheviks glorified machinery, power, and large-scale operations as no capitalistic poet had ever done. In mass production they saw a way to a communistic society that would produce enough for all. But they stood the program of industrialization on its head, for whereas in other countries consumers' goods, such as cloth, clothes, boots, food, and furniture, were usually the first to be produced in factories, the Russians concentrated their attack on the heavy industries which provide "capital," "durable," or "producers' goods," such as iron and steel, machines, rolling stock, tractors, and electric power. They did so because they wished to be independent of foreign producers, and also because the heavy industries provided the materials needed for defense. By 1932, after just over four years' effort, some of the objectives of the Plan had been reached, but the output of coal, steel, iron, and some other essentials was below expectation. In the second Five-Year Plan the emphasis was still chiefly on the heavy and capital goods industries, and the advance has been greatest in the development of power stations, coal mines, oil wells, metal plants, and of factories which make machinery for industry, agriculture, and transportation. The consumer was, however, given more consideration, and provision was made for the erection of hundreds of factories in which the "light industries" would produce consumers' goods.

The Decline of the Handicrafts and Homework.—When the factory system invaded fields occupied by domestic or small workshop producers the latter retreated, but only after waging a long battle. State hostility to any technical change that might injure manual workers had vanished by 1800, for most governments were convinced that factories, machines, and engines spelled progress. Spasmodic attacks on mills or equipment achieved virtually nothing. In places a group of strongly organized workers might delay an innovation for a time, but resistance was eventually overcome. Hence the speed at which a transformation took place was determined by the size of the gap between costs under the new order and those under the old, and by the ability of factory goods to displace hand-made products. Factory spinning advanced rapidly because the machines did more, better, and cheaper work, yet made possible a higher wage than could be earned with a spinning wheel. Weaving passed into the factory more slowly because a superior power loom was only gradually evolved. The clothing trades lingered long in the home because the sewing machine could be used there, and because many women and girls, unable to leave home, were compelled to earn an income or to supplement the inadequate earnings of the breadwinner by doing outwork at wages which made the product as cheap as that of a clothing factory.

In some industries, such as cardboard box, chain, and nail-making, domestic or small workshop labor was cheap enough to prevent for a long time the search for machines. In other industries manual skill, whether well or ill paid, resisted displacement because the quality of work could not be mechanically reproduced or because the volume of demand did not justify machine production. Classic instances were: (1) the Sheffield and Solingen cutlery industries, in which master cutlers worked at home or in small shops, producing knives, razors, and tools such as machines could not fashion; (2) the Lyons cottage weavers of fine silks, who after 1894 were able to get electric power to drive looms in their homes; (3) the producers of those expensive and distinctive garments or personal and domestic accessories for which Paris and London were famous, or of the clocks and watches of Switzerland. In addition, there was a motley of peasant industries producing for use, for direct sale to the consumer, or for a *Verleger*. Belgian lace, Harris tweeds, German toys, Italian embroidery, Turkish carpets, and the spare-time products of Russian, Italian, and other workers do not have much difficulty overcoming the "sales resistance" of buyers satiated with factory products.

The extent of non-factory production is still considerable today. Germany's late industrialization kept many of the handicrafts strong until well after 1900, and the combination of electric power, voluntary associations, and government solicitude after that date helped many of them to hold their own. The associations helped the small or part-time producer in his buying and selling, and aided him to get cheap credit. In 1925 five per cent of the German population was employed in handwork (especially in cloth- or clothes-making, or in peasant industries), and in 1928-1929 the money turnover of these occupations was said to be about 15 per cent of that of the whole country. On the eve of the War nearly 30 per cent of Germany's industrial workers toiled in establishments employing not more than five persons.

In France about 2,300,000 small masters and homeworkers were found in 1921, mostly in the textile and needle industries, but also making shoes, lace, artificial flowers, jewelry, and religious ornaments, or working on feathers and furs. Swiss *Hausindustrie* in 1900 employed over 100,000 people, but in 1929 only 35,000, thanks largely to the growth of watch factories and to the imposition by various countries of heavy tariffs on Swiss timepieces. In Great Britain, according to one estimate, there are about half a million homeworkers. A sweated industries exhibition in 1906 revealed the variety of goods made partly or entirely at home or in small shops. Among them were the usual clothing products, cardboard and match boxes, chains, clay pipes, nails, tennis balls, brushes, bead decorations, jewel cases, military embroidery, and coffin tassels. Whether competing with a factory or monopolizing the field, the homeworker was spending long hours at tedious, monotonous jobs, in unhealthy conditions, for low wages. Since that exhibition was held the state has protected the homeworker's earnings, and machinery has annexed some of his (or rather her) field.

The Commercial Unit.—Although the large unit gradually dominated industry, the small one clung more tenaciously to distribution. As a greater percentage of the population became urban and specialized in its work, as living standards rose, and as new kinds of goods or services were introduced, the number of workers engaged in commerce increased both absolutely and relatively. In Germany wholesale and retail trade occupied 8.7 per cent of all gainfully employed workers in 1907, and 11.7 per cent in 1925. The percentage of British insured workers engaged in distributing trades rose from 11.8 in 1923 to 15 in 1929. In France the distributors more than doubled in number between 1866 and 1906, while the population grew only three per cent; and Professor Gide jestingly predicted that at this rate all the French people would become tradesmen in less than two centuries. In the wholesale field large warehouses and big capital or credit resources were needed, though a surprising number of men were able to find a little niche as brokers or agents; but in retail trade the small store was as firmly rooted as was the peasant in the countryside. It could be near the consumer, it needed little capital or credit, one or more members of the family supplied the labor, and part of the house could be used as shop. Some of the wares might be processed or made by the retailer, but the tendency toward the sale of nationally advertised packet goods or of factory products was evident long before 1900. Retail distribution attracted those who could do no other work and also those who had confidence in their ability to fight their own battles, to be free lances rather than privates. It was the hotbed of hope, and all too often the deathbed.

The advocate of rational economic organization finds in retail distribution one of his easiest targets, and points to the apparent oversupply of grocery stores, milk or bread distributors, filling stations, and tobacco shops. In Italy, England, and Germany there is one retail store for every 75 to 80 people. Britain is a nation of 500,000 shopkeepers with 1,500,000 assistants. During the War its people registered for food distribution at 150,000 stores, of which 137,000 were independently owned, 5500 were run by consumers' cooperative societies, and 7000 were chain stores.

The cooperative societies had been spreading over the country since 1844, attempting to benefit consumers by producing and distributing goods without profit. The chain stores and big department stores had become important only after about 1900, and were the first serious excursion of big business into the retail field. Yet half the customers patronized the "independents" during the War, leaving a quarter to the cooperatives and a quarter to the chains. The independent had only one-tenth as many customers to each shop as had the other stores, and since 1918 he has lost much ground to them. But he still shows remarkable tenacity. The growth of new suburbs, of new commodities, and of such new consumer habits as hiking, cycling, and motoring provides him with fresh opportunities to find a place in spite of, or away from, the giants. Some consumers prefer his individual personality and service; others like his willingness to sell on credit. He rarely makes a fortune, but he may scrape together a modest income, and if he fails some optimist is usually ready to take his place.

II.—THE ORGANIZATION OF ENTERPRISE.—THE INDUSTRIAL CAPITALIST

Of the men who developed or spread the new industrial order, some were merchants who turned manufacturer, and some were landowners who sold their land to obtain capital for an industrial venture or who plowed their rents into the exploitation of their mineral deposits or the processing of products taken from their soil. Landlords in Scotland helped to develop the iron industry, and those of Upper Silesia made fortunes from the iron, coal, and other minerals under their estates. In 1792, Benjamin Gott, a Leeds merchant who bought woolen cloth from domestic makers, erected a mill that eventually employed a thousand workers and housed every stage of production. When asked why he did this, he replied, "I was brought up as a merchant, and became a manufacturer rather from possessing capital than from understanding the manufacture. I paid for the talents of others in the different branches of manufacture." He was frequently unable to get all the cloths he wanted in the public market. Further, he was determined to break into the West of England's monopoly of superfine cloth production, and bid for the fine cloth trade, especially in the United States. In Scotland, David Dale, who began life as a hand-loom weaver and rose to be a great linen yarn importer, putter-out, and cloth merchant, sank his capital in a big cotton spinning mill at New Lanark in 1786. Many of his fellows who had made money sending goods to the American colonies and importing tobacco found their transatlantic trade ruined by the Revolution just at a time when the cotton machines offered a substitute field of action. They turned to the production of cotton, linen, glass, and later of iron and steel.

Such instances might be multiplied greatly; but in general the initiative and enterprise came from industry rather than commerce or land. Wedgwood, Boulton, Arkwright, Wilkinson, Krupp, Hadfield, and Vickers in Europe have their counterparts in Carnegie and Ford in America. This was natural, for the center of interest was now on problems of production rather than of sale. Industry was taking the risks, wrestling with technical difficulties, procuring capital, producing goods in a quantity or quality or at a price hitherto unknown, and eager to create new demands for its wares. The industrialist wanted more raw materials or new ones, and sought to get nearer the source of supply. He went to Germany to buy wool, bought cotton at the home port or from the American exporter, or obtained an interest in the mine or refinery that yielded the metal or coal he needed. He often found the existing commercial organization unsuited to his needs, and set out to find customers. Boulton toured Britain trying to make the country "steam-mill mad," Wedgwood used showrooms and circulars, the early ready-made clothes-makers found no stores except pawnshops available as retail outlets, and Krupp went over the heads of ministers to persuade the crown to buy his guns. The manufacturer sought to create and direct demand toward his products by advertising, sent partners or employees to live in important markets abroad, or appointed agents to whom he consigned goods at his own risk. In the intervals of such work he was actively supervising the operation of his plant, buying materials, improving equipment or methods, having occasional difficulties with his labor force, keeping one eye on his rivals and the other on his debtors, and hoping the bank would not reduce its loan to him.

The men who emerged as industrial capitalists had usually grown up in an industrial atmosphere, and often were self-made men. The ironmasters had iron in their blood. for many generations of ancestors had been nail- or lock-makers, smelters or founders, clockmakers, brass workers, or ironmongers. Krupp (1812-1887) inherited from his father a small iron works in Essen, with four workers, little capital and large liabilities. Wedgwood had behind him four generations of potters. The textile mill owners, with few exceptions, had learned the trade from childhood in cottage or farmhouse, had developed putting-out businesses, or were early machine-makers. Oldknow put out cotton to spinners and weavers, turned a discarded silk mill into a spinning factory, and then went on to build a bigger mill with sheds for weavers, dormitories for the pauper children brought from London, homes and shops for his other workers. Radcliffe saved money out of his wages as a weaver until he was able to start an enterprise. Eventually he fed yarn to a thousand looms, and could boast that his firm had all been raised "like a gathering snowball from a single spindle or single loom." Throughout the nineteenth century the textile industry continued to offer scope for the rise of ambitious men from the ranks. An investigation made about 1910 showed that forty-eight Lancashire manufacturers out of sixty-three chosen at random were "first generation" men who had come up from the wage-earning class. In a town of 100,000 inhabitants 139 employers were questioned; eighty-eight of them, owning half the looms in the town, were "self-made." In offering opportunity of this kind the textile trade was not alone.

The first problem these men faced was the raising of the necessary capital. The sum might be small. Robert Owen, a draper's clerk in Manchester, borrowed £100 in 1789, went into partnership with a mechanic who had skill but no funds, rented a workshop, bought wood, iron, and brass on credit, and soon had forty men at work making mules. Countless firms began with such small resources, but larger ventures needed much more. A big textile mill, fully equipped, might absorb £20,000, and the New Lanark mills changed hands for £60,000 in 1800. The capital in Boulton's hardware business was £20,000, and the capital of the Carron ironworks rose from £12,000 in 1760 to £150,000 in 1771. Once pioneers had shown what profits could be made, there might be little difficulty in finding a partner with spare capital; but even then funds often ran out, and the pioneers were hard pressed to obtain sufficient fixed and operating capital. Boulton supplemented his own inheritance and the dowry of his wife by taking a partner; but as he extended his plant he was forced to sell some of his property, raise a mortgage on his wife's, then sell some of it, and borrow from friends and bankers. He was often on the verge of insolvency, his hardware firm lost £11,000 in ten years on a capital of £20,000, and the steam engine enterprise was slow in changing from a liability to an asset. Wedgwood was no less harassed when he began to build his Etruria factory and homes for his workmen (1769). "I must either collect my debts, hire money, or take my place among the *Whereas's* [insolvents]," he wrote to his partner, a Liverpool merchant. "Collect— Collect, my friend—set all your hands and heads to work—send me the *L'argent* and you shall see wonders—£3,000! £3,000?—aye, £3,000, not a farthing less will satisfy my Architect for the next year's business; so you must collect, or take a place for me in the *Gazette*."

When the first financial hurdles had been surmounted the rest of the journey was rarely smooth. The industrial climber worked ceaselessly, and was often the first to enter the factory, but the last to leave. If he ground the face of his workers, as sometimes happened, he did not spare his own complexion. Customers complained that goods were defective. Krupp nearly lost his market when some of his guns split under fire. Wedgwood, "teased out of [his] life with dilatory and drunken idle worthless workmen," stumped on his wooden leg round the shops, breaking bad pieces of pottery and chalking on the bench, "This won't do for Josiah Wedgwood." War disturbed markets, buyers did not promptly pay what they owed even though long credit had been granted, bread cast on the water in consignments returned slowly, the banking and credit structure was defective, and the oscillation between boom and depression was violent. When booms burst the whole business fabric toppled over, smashing big firms as well as little, and ushering in three to six lean years. A town like Bradford had four panics between 1836 and 1844; of 318 firms in existence there in 1836, only 127 were alive in 1846. The bankruptcy list was no respecter of persons; the biggest merchants, manufacturers, and bankers were caught along with the minnows, and if an auctioneer was ever invited to dine at a rich man's house he must have spent much of his time wondering when the silver, glass, furniture, and wine cellar would come under his hammer.

When profits were made they had to be plowed back into the business until the firm seemed safely established. If profit was, as the economists said, the reward of risk, and interest the reward of abstinence, these men earned both. Sometimes they received neither, or lost both. If they were more fortunate, they eventually had money to spend according to their taste. Some of them found satisfaction in vulgar ostentation, as for instance the *nouveau riche* who went to church in a bright yellow chariot driven by a coachman decked in gold braid, and accompanied by three footmen in gaudy livery. Others became men of culture —if they had not been so originally; philanthropists, patrons of art, letters, music, science, and education; generous to their church and powerful in their party. They bought country estates, and had their pictures done in oils by the fashionable artist of the day. When they died the second generation carried on, but often lacked the ability or the concentration on one objective possessed by the founder. It developed an interest in railroads, banking, or politics, hunted, collected old furniture or books, obtained a title, and sent its children to famous schools or ancient universities. The firm might lose its drive, become set in habits, fail to keep its equipment and methods up-to-date, and ignore changes in market demands. If it carried on into the third generation its owners might sell out, break all connection with industry, and turn to the professions or to a life of leisure. There is no law of nature decreeing that the third generation should be the last, and a few firms had a longer life; but the story of many enterprises is summarized in the sad dictum, "Three generations from shirt sleeves to shirt sleeves," or in the happier one, "Three generations from shirt sleeves to bishop's gaiters, lawyer's wig, guardsman's uniform, or cabinet minister's knee-breeches."

III.—THE SPREAD OF JOINT-STOCK ORGANIZATION

Until at least 1850 most of the burden of financing industrial expansion was borne by the one-man firm, the partnership, and by loans from bankers or anyone else willing to make them. Some men, such as Krupp, struggled hard to avoid loans, but their capital was often inadequate in time of crisis, and Krupp was forced in 1873-1874 to the banker's door. He came away with a loan of 30,000,000 marks at 5 per cent, with an obligation to pay 37,000,000 marks in return, and with a strengthened belief in the greed of money merchants. The private firm, if such we may call the one-man firm or partnership, was also the unit that developed wholesale and retail trade, extended coal mining, built up fleets of sailing ships, and supplied the banking services of the eighteenth and early nineteenth centuries. It is still by far the most common type of enterprise in all countries. Even in England and Wales, the European stronghold of joint stock, 94 per cent of the industrial, commercial, and professional enterprises are private firms.

In England the partnership was restricted in its appeal for capital by the fact that all partners, whether active or sleeping, must share unlimited liability; but on the continent the *société en commandite* limited the liability of the passive partners to the loss of their investment, and thus permitted entrepreneurs to gather capital from outsiders. During the eighteenth century the funds supplied by the sleeping partners were cut up into shares of equal size, and during the early nineteenth century these shares became transferable. Thus there evolved a sleeping partnership with share capital—a *société en commandite sur actions*; the active partners were still liable without limit, but the ordinary shareholders had limited liability and an interest that could be sold. In countries adjacent to France the partnership developed in imitation of the French rule, especially when that rule was embodied in the *Code Napoléon* (1807). Germany had its *Kommanditgesellschaft*, or sleeping partnership, and also its *Kommanditgesellschaft auf Aktien*, which combined capital "raised through impersonal and freely saleable shares with the personal guidance and responsibility of a small body of fully liable" men who ran the business. In Germany as in France such partnerships were easily formed, were subject to little state inspection or regulation, and attracted investors who felt that unlimited liability would make the managers careful with other people's money. This feeling was not always a sound guide to investment, as there were ways of evading the full punishment for failure.

The full joint-stock company (*société anonyme, Aktiengesellschaft*) emerged from its limited field of foreign trade with the growing need for large permanent investments in canals, water or gas supplies, railroads, insurance companies, banks, and the new industries of the last fifty years. A large sum of fixed capital could best be raised in this way; but the joint-stock company could not advance far until the law cleared the path. The abuses of company promotion and stock speculation before 1720 had brought joint-stock into disfavor. In France a *société anonyme* could be formed only with official authorization by the state, and was subject to careful control; this provision of the *Code Napoléon* influenced adjacent countries. In England the Bubble Act of 1720 denied legal personality to companies that had not obtained a charter or a private act of parliament, and both documents were costly. The Act was not repealed till 1825, but had been a dead letter for many years. In 1825 many unincorporated companies, which were legally only big partnerships, were in existence with a nominal capital of at least £160,000,000, and many legal companies were operating canals, docks, waterworks, or insurance businesses. The former group included a swarm of mining companies recently formed to exploit Spanish American mines and British investors. Fraudulent promotion and wild speculation in this and other fields were rampant; companies with high-sounding titles appeared, using the names of famous persons on their lists of directors, issuing false prospectuses, publishing enthusiastic accounts of meetings that never took place, and in other ways separating the public from its savings. The bubble burst in 1825, four-fifths of the 600 new companies had vanished by 1827, and the dangers associated with joint stock were once more emphasized.

Yet the need for the joint-stock company could not be gainsaid, and eventually the essentials of the situation were recognized. A company needed large sums of money, a legal personality, and inexpensive easy formation. The investor needed limited liability, and wanted to know who controlled the use of his money, the purpose for which it was used, and the financial results of the enterprise. A company's creditors must know the character and condition of the debtor. The grant of privileges must be accompanied by publicity in the interests of investor and creditor. Between 1844 and 1862 incorporation was made cheap and easy in Great Britain and limited liability was granted. A company could gain official recognition by handing the state a memorandum of association, signed by seven persons, giving its name, purpose, directors, and nominal capital. When it had completed its preliminary work of raising the capital it must file articles of association; supply annual statements of its capital, shareholders, and directors; and publish a properly audited account of its financial position. In return for this publicity, its stockholders were exempted from liability for the company's debts beyond the amount of the nominal capital they held. The name of the firm must end with the word "Limited," thus indicating to creditors the nature of the assets of the debtor.

In France the need for individual authorization and the strict control had made the *société anonyme* far less popular than the *société en commandite sur actions*; but speculative abuses of the latter led to its closer regulation in 1856. In 1867 the formation of a *société anonyme* was made easier, publicity was demanded, and ordinary limited-liability joint-stock companies increased in importance. In most parts of Germany the formation of a joint-stock company was difficult until 1870, when it was made almost as easy as in England. The rush of promotion and speculation which followed the victory over France, the foundation of the empire, and the receipt of a big indemnity from Paris, caused a financial crash in 1873, and led to stricter control in later years. Publicity was imposed, the founders must shoulder heavy obligations, while managers, directors, and even shareholders must accept civil (or in certain cases criminal) liability.

Limited liability was a boon all entrepreneurs would like, but its price—publicity—was one they did not wish to pay. A company might therefore conceal its financial position by establishing "secret reserves," of which no one except the directors knew anything, by writing down heavily the value of its assets, or by other devices which made its condition look weaker or stronger than it really was. Governments fought these practices, stiffening company laws, forbidding secret reserves, placing stricter demands on auditors, and making directors personally liable for the accuracy of financial reports. But the increasing complexity of capital structures, and especially the growing interest which some concerns obtained in subsidiary companies, made control, prevention, and conviction more difficult. It is virtually impossible to enforce the demand for the truth, the whole truth, and nothing but the truth; and many published balance sheets are "collectors' specimens rather than business guides" (Smails).

The private firm longed for limited liability, but was even less willing than the companies to have its affairs made public. It eventually gained limited liability, yet retained its privacy, by foregoing the privilege of appealing to the public for capital. In 1892 Germany permitted the formation of private companies (*Gesellschaften mit beschränkter Haftung*). They could not have more than fifty stockholders, excluding employees; they could not invite the public to supply capital, or sell their stock on the exchanges, and they need not file annual financial statements. This combination of privacy and limited liability was very attractive to German firms, and was copied by other countries, e.g., by Great Britain in 1892 and 1907.

The limited-liability company was capable of great use and abuse. Alongside the companies which gathered capital together for production and profit were those formed to benefit promoters at the expense of investor and creditor. Private firms which had a good name were turned into public companies at an excessive capital value. Stock was sold in companies that were never intended to do much or that never could do much. "The committee member who thought a 'crop of fools' every ten years a natural phenomenon was too optimistic: the crop was more often annual" (Shannon); and a long series of investment manias stretches from the canals and railroads of the early days, through finance companies and hotels in the 'sixties, foreign mines, coal, iron, and skating rinks in the 'seventies, overseas land, gold, banks, and electricity in the 'eighties, bicycles in the 'nineties, to the rubber, gold, rayon, and gramophone booms of the present century. In each of them there were "bubble companies blown by men of strong lungs and brazen countenances," mines that were never dug outside a city office, speculators who were fortunate if they sold out in time, and investors who went empty away from the joint-stock race course.

Companies that were free from fraud might be sunk by the ordinary rocks in the channel. Inadequate capital or credit, unwise business policies, or depression wrecked many of them. Mr. Shannon has shown that one-third of the 20,500 British companies registered between 1856 and 1883 were small or abortive. Of the remainder, about one-sixth were sold, amalgamated, or reconstructed in later decades, 28 per cent were wound up compulsorily as insolvent, 32 per cent were wound up voluntarily, and

11 per cent sank unnoticed. One company out of three was dead before its fifth birthday, and one out of two before its tenth. Of the 20,500, only 1600 were alive in 1929, i.e., 8 per cent of the total projects, or 12 per cent of the companies that really began work. A smaller study by Professor MacGregor shows that of 1162 companies registered in 1880, 296 never began business, 654 failed, and 126 were alive in 1929. The course of joint-stock history was thus liberally strewn with failure, fraud, and false hopes. If the spare savings of the outsider were mobilized, so also were his credulity and cupidity. Men bought experience dearly, but did not make use of their purchase. The British government was slow to protect the investor by amending the law, and only in 1907 and 1929 were strong teeth put into it. Germany acted earlier, in 1884. But the lure and the risks are still great, for out of 277 new issues made in Great Britain during the boom year 1928, 101 were by companies which had disappeared by April, 1933. Of 109 new firms, 68 had vanished, and the stocks of 29 more had lost from four-fifths to all of their value.

The spread of joint stock depended on the existence of a class of people who possessed money and had developed the investing habit. To bring the money together, however, someone must wield the rake, and private bankers had developed some skill with that tool in raising loans for governments. They would "underwrite" a loan, i.e., be responsible for the raising of the money, take the bonds at a certain price and then try to sell them to the public at a higher figure. Some of them did the same for the early English railroads; but English private or joint-stock banks played a far smaller part in helping companies to get their capital than did continental banks. In France, Germany, Italy and elsewhere banks devoted part or the whole of their time, capital, and deposits to underwriting company stocks and bonds. They passed some of them on to the public, but they might (willingly or unwillingly) keep some. (See Chapter XXIV.) They made long-term loans to firms in which they were interested, had representatives on their boards, and brought pressure to bear on them whenever competition became destructive or fusion promised benefits.

The last fifty years have seen a great expansion in the number and capital sum of joint-stock companies. The number in Great Britain grew from less than 9000 in 1885 to 105,000 in

1930. Of the latter number, only about 10,000 were public companies whose shares were dealt with on the stock exchange; the remainder were private companies. The number of public companies in Switzerland rose fivefold between 1903 and 1928; that in Germany rose from 2100 in 1886 to 5400 in 1912, and then doubled between 1913 and 1926. Meanwhile the growth of individual businesses and the amalgamation of formerly independent units (see Chapter XXV) turned some companies into giants, especially in the railroad, banking, chemical, iron and steel, rayon, oil, shipping, and electrical fields. The area still held by small companies, by private companies, and by unincorporated enterprise is, however, relatively much larger in Europe than in the United States. In Great Britain there are at least 1,500,000 private industrial, commercial, and professional enterprises.

The joint-stock company dispersed ownership. The European is not so accustomed as is the North American to investment or speculation in stocks. Often he has less spare income, and puts what he has into savings banks, building societies, a hoard, or a house. But the War taught him to buy government bonds, and in every boom-time period of company promotion he has been urged to buy stocks of small denomination—five dollars or less— or been tempted by the announcement that he need pay down only a small fraction of the capital sum. Further, the capital structure of many firms was sufficiently varied to attract investors of all grades of timidity. The capital of a British railroad in 1923 consisted of bonds, guaranteed fixed interest stock, preferred stock, preferred redeemable stock, and ordinary shares. Every public company has therefore a long stockholders' list; that of one British bank contains 65,000 names, and a company may have more owners than employees. Joint stock also separated ownership from management. The rank and file of the stockholders exerted little influence, except when roused by adverse reports and unprofitable results. Control lay in the hands of a few large stockholders, of the board of directors, and of the managing officers. These officers were salaried experts, while the directors sold their business knowledge, experience, or name to a company (and possibly to several companies) for a fee. As firms became interlocked with one another or with the banks, a comparatively small group of men might direct the affairs of many companies. In Switzerland, for example, 3565 seats on the boards of less than a thousand companies were occupied by 1364 men in 1930; 533 held two or more seats, and 67 had ten or more.

The gulf between ownership and management was paralleled by the gulfs between labor and management and between owners and laborers. Personal contact—pleasant or otherwise—between wage earner and employer became increasingly difficult as firms grew in size, and reference to employees as "hands" became common. In a company the wage earner knew only a foreman, manager, or board of directors, who strove to earn dividends for owners scattered possibly over the face of the earth. These owners rarely knew much of the business, or even of the country or continent, in which their money was invested. Their only concern was with the check that came out of the machine into which they had put their money, or with market movements in the price of the stock they held. If one of them felt little responsibility for the Persian oil workers, Argentinian railroad men, Malay rubber cultivators, British seamen, Australian lead miners, and South African gold diggers who were producing profits for him, he could (or should) not be surprised if they in turn thought more of their own interests than his.

The joint-stock company mobilized capital in provisionally permanent heaps in its stocks, and borrowed for long terms by issuing bonds. Meanwhile governments gathered in great masses of money on long-term loans by selling bonds to construct railroads, harbors, or other public works, to improve fighting equipment, or to wage war. The growth of this vast capital market into which the buyer could go and purchase a title to interest or a hope of profit was possibly the outstanding financial development of the nineteenth century. If the world's railroads absorbed $100,000,000,000 of capital, the building of the great industrial units, the growing loan expenditure on defense, and the provision of the equipment needed in other countries or continents by governments, industries, mines, or land all offered inducements to the European investor (see Chapter XXVII). Growing familiarity with stock exchanges, the increasing facilities for underwriting issues and selling stocks or bonds, the expansion of financial columns in the press, and the accumulation of spare funds in the pockets of the middle class, of the rich, and of insurance companies—all helped to spread the investing and speculating habits, and to make income depend increasingly on interest or dividends. The day when real estate was the main form of property and source of unearned income had passed. In 1913-1914, 45 per cent of the gross capital that came to the notice of the British collectors of death duties consisted of stocks and bonds, and the huge issues of war loans during the next four years raised that percentage much higher. In the same year agricultural land, house property, and business premises accounted for only 19 per cent of the total capital sum, while probably one-ninth of the national income consisted of profits and interest on overseas investments.

BIBLIOGRAPHY

ASHLEY, W. J., *Economic Organization of England* (1914), chap. 8.

BERDROW, W., *Alfred Krupp* (Eng. trans., 1930).

BOWDEN, WITT, *Industrial Society . . . toward the End of the Eighteenth Century*, chap. 3, sections 1, 2.

CLAPHAM, J. H., *Economic Development of France and Germany, 1815-1914*, sections 11-15, 18-22, 23, 33, 60-66, 70-76, 97.

CLAPHAM, J. H., *Economic History of Modern Britain*, vol. i, chaps. 5, 6; vol. ii, chaps. 4, 8.

FONG, H. D., *The Triumph of the Factory System in England* (1930), chap. 1.

HIRST, F. W., *The Stock Exchange* (1911).

JONES, G. T. (ed. C. Clark), *Increasing Return: the Relation between the Size and the Efficiency of Industries* (1931).

MANTOUX, P., *The Industrial Revolution in the 18th Century*, part iii, chap. 2.

MARSHALL, A., *Industry and Trade* (1919), book ii, especially chaps. 3, 4, 8.

NUSSBAUM, F. L., *History of the Economic Institutions of Modern Europe*, part iv, chaps. 7, 9.

REDFORD, A., *Economic History of England, 1760-1860* (1931), chap. 6.

ROLL, E., *An Early Experiment in Industrial Organisation: A History of the Firm of Boulton and Watt (1775-1805)* (1930).

SOMBART, W., *Der Moderne Kapitalismus*, vol. iii, pp. 712-948.

UNWIN, G., *Samuel Oldknow and the Arkwrights* (1923).

ARTICLES

ALLEN, G. C., "Methods of Industrial Organisation in the West Midlands," in *Ec. Hist.*, January, 1929, pp. 535-553.

CHAPMAN, S. J., and ASHTON, T. S., "The Size of Businesses, Mainly in the Textile Industries," in *J. Royal Stat. Soc.*, April, 1914.

CHAPMAN, S. J., and MARQUIS, F. J., "The Recruiting of the Employing Classes from the Ranks of the Wage-earners," in *J. Royal Stat. Soc.*, January, 1912.

HARTSOUGH, M. L., "Business Leaders in Cologne in the 19th Century," in *J. E. B. H.*, February, 1930, pp. 332-352.

HEATON, H., "Benjamin Gott and the Industrial Revolution in Yorkshire," in *Ec. H. R.*, 1931, pp. 45-66.

HOWER, R. M., "The Wedgwoods: Ten Generations of Potters," in *J. E. B. H.*, February, 1932, pp. 281-313; and August, 1932, pp. 665-690.

HUNT, B. C., "The Joint-Stock Company in England" (1800-1844), in *J. P. E.*, February, 1935, pp. 1-33; and June, 1935, pp. 331-364.

HUTT, W. H., "The Factory System of the Early 19th Century," in *Economica*, March, 1926.

MACGREGOR, D. H., "Joint-Stock Companies and the Risk Factor," in *Ec. J.*, December, 1929, pp. 491-505.

POSTAN, M. M., "Recent Trends in the Accumulation of Capital," in *Ec. H. R.*, October, 1935, pp. 1-12.

SHANNON, H. A., "The Coming of General Limited Liability," in *Ec. Hist.*, January, 1931, pp. 267-291.

SHANNON, H. A., "The First Five Thousand Joint-Stock Companies," in *Ec. Hist.*, January, 1932, pp. 396-424.

SHANNON, H. A., "The Limited Companies, 1866-1883," in *Ec. H. R.*, October, 1933, pp. 290-316.

TODD, G., "Some Aspects of Joint-Stock Companies, 1844-1900," in *Ec. H. R.*, October, 1932, pp. 46-71.

Encyclopædia of the Social Sciences: See list of titles under "Business" and "Industry," vol. xv, pp. 548 and 551. See especially articles on Captain of Industry, Industrialism, Homework (Industrial), Joint-stock Company, Partnership, Retail Trade.

CHAPTER XXIV

CURRENCY AND BANKING SINCE 1800

THE complicated story of European banking since 1800 can perhaps be simplified by considering first the banking services that were needed. They were fourfold: *deposit, loan, transfer,* and *issue.*

The spread of the habit of depositing was facilitated by the growing use of the check and the establishment of branch banks and savings banks. By 1914 probably only 2 per cent of the deposits made in British banks were in coin. Silver and gold disks were used only in making small payments, such as wages, and for retail trade. Salaried persons and petty tradesmen had got into the check-writing habit, and one large employer was suggesting that the pay envelope be abolished. Further, when a bank made a loan to a client it no longer gave him cash or bank notes, but credited his account with the amount of the loan and allowed him to draw on it by check; or it allowed him to overdraw his account. On the continent deposits and checks were far less common, but were slowly coming into favor in the west after 1900.

Loans to agriculture have already been described. Those to the state might be short or long term. In general, banks were loath to tie up a large part of their funds in long-term bonds, but might underwrite the loan and sell it to the public at a higher price, or float it in return for a commission. Short-term loans were more attractive, since they would soon be repaid out of the proceeds of some tax, and banks might use part of their funds to buy "treasury bills." The most important class of bank loans consisted of those sought by industry and commerce. Here again the need might be long or short. Commerce turned its business over more rapidly than did industry, needed loans for shorter periods, and in the bill drawn by the seller produced a negotiable instrument that was acceptable enough to be discounted. A banker who had to be ready to meet the demands of his depositors dare not let his loans stretch too far into the future, and found in short-term loans to commerce a suitable field. He became a "commercial banker," and while he might make advances to some manufacturers for six or twelve months he preferred to let industry meet its long-term needs by floating stock or bonds.

Such an attitude was tenable where share capital was abundant, as in England, but failed to meet the requirements of a newer, poorer country like Germany in the early stages of its industrial expansion. Industry there needed both share and loan capital, but had a small investing public on which to draw. The German bank therefore helped by underwriting issues, by keeping part of them, and by making long-term loans. It was promoter, investor, and lender. "The distinctive feature of big German banking down to the crisis of 1931" was "the combination between the collection of capital from the public in the form of shares and deposits and its redistribution, in the form of speculative promotion of, and investment in, commercial and industrial enterprise" (Brinkmann). Thus we have a contrast between commercial banking and what may be called investment and industrial banking; but the same bank may do both.

Transfer services grew in importance with the growth of international trade and investment. The check simplified domestic payments, while machinery for the sale of foreign exchange and for the traffic in bills made it easy to remit any sum to any place in an envelope or cablegram. Finally, every nation needed a note issue, and learned by bitter experience that a good servant must be carefully regulated if it was not to become a costly master. The regulation of a bank which was given a monopoly of note issue was one of the most important legislative problems in modern banking history.

In 1800 these four services were being rendered by one or two big public banks, some large bankers or merchant bankers, and a host of small ones. Amsterdam had been injured by crises in 1763 and 1772, by the collapse of the Bank of Amsterdam, and by the decline of its commerce during the French occupation. Some of its great houses, such as the Hopes, carried on, but their business had declined. Meanwhile London went ahead, with its Bank of England and a swarm of private bankers and merchant bankers. The private bankers took deposits, honored checks, and made loans; the merchant bankers accepted, discounted, and dealt in home or foreign bills. Some firms, such as the Barings, had become well-known as loan underwriters. In 1773 a clearing house was established, in which the claims of each banker on his fellows could be set against their claims on him and easily adjusted. In the provinces the expansion of industry and trade produced an outcrop of country banks in the latter part of the century. On the continent Hamburg had a deposit and transfer bank; some banks of issue, modeled rather badly on the Bank of England, were at work; and many merchant banking firms in France, Switzerland, Frankfort, and Hamburg were well known outside their own countries. Only the last group possessed much vitality, and the stress of war or revolution after 1789 damaged or broke some of them.

England was more fortunate, for the war period (1793-1815) gave two great opportunities to bankers. The first was the raising of public loans and the transfer of the money to troops or allies. The second was the financing of the trade in war supplies and of the rapidly expanding cotton industry. The first opportunity did much to make Europe's greatest private banking firm, the Rothschilds. Nathan Mayer had gone from Frankfort into the Manchester cotton trade and then moved to London, where he gained profit and prestige by devising means for getting funds to Wellington in Spain. His brothers had been lending to Danish and other rulers, and by 1815 the five brothers, stationed in five centers—London, Vienna, Paris, Frankfort, and Naples—were on the way to eclipse the fame of the Fuggers. For seventy years the House of Rothschild had its finger in most financial pies. It made long- and short-term loans to governments, underwrote state and company issues, and financed railroad building in countries as far apart as Austria and Brazil. It bought cotton or tobacco in America, shipped it in its own vessels, gathered in much of the gold that came to London, and had its own refinery. It played a large part in financing the Crimean War, the struggle for Italian unity, and the transfer to Berlin of the billion-dollar indemnity imposed on France in 1871. Its power to provide or withhold credit might influence a decision between peace and war, and Disraeli did not exaggerate when he said the seven great powers of Europe were England, France, Russia, Prussia, Austria, the Barings, and the Rothschilds.

The trade in munitions and cotton stimulated a big crop of country banks. In 1797 there were 230 of them in England, but in 1814 there were 940. Since they were private partnerships they could issue notes, and as the country was off the gold standard from 1797 to 1821 the banker did not have to worry about redeeming his notes in gold or silver. He could issue as many as he wished, and since he knew his customers personally the extent of his lending and of his issue was determined by his confidence in his clients and his reading of trade prospects, rather than by the size of his gold or Bank of England note reserve. The end of the war showed his confidence had been excessive, for it pricked the price and credit bubble, and 240 banks stopped payment in 1814-1816. Ten years later the panic of 1825 dragged down another seventy banks and made their notes useless.

Joint-stock Banking.—These failures emphasized the need for a stronger banking system with adequate capital, and also for a more restrained issue of notes. The first need was met by permitting joint-stock banks to be set up outside a range of sixty-five miles from the Bank of England (1826), and inside that zone in 1833. The provincial banks could issue notes, but those nearer London must not break the Bank's monopoly. Armed with these powers, groups of manufacturers and merchants founded banks in the industrial towns, put much capital in them, and imported Scotch managers to run them. By 1836 over a hundred had been established, private banks were bought or squeezed out, branches and agencies were established, and the banks outside the London zone issued notes. Unfortunately, the boom of 1834-1836 led to excessive or speculative creation of joint-stock banks, to unhealthy extension of credit, to overissue of notes, and to disaster in 1836-1837. The formation of joint-stock banks was therefore made less easy, and the issue of notes was restricted in 1844. During the rest of the century most of the remaining private banks either became joint stock or disappeared before the superior ability and resources of their rivals. The latter scattered their branches, swallowed up private banks, and then began to amalgamate. Their number in Scotland fell from 36 in 1819 to 11 in 1873 and to 8 in 1928. England in 1844 had 400 banks, in 1891 she had 37 private and 106 joint-stock banks, but by the nineteen-twenties five joint-stock banks (out of sixteen), with 8000 branches, did five-sixths of the British banking business.

This movement toward a few large units with a legion of branches was found in most continental countries. Concentration was rapid in Germany after 1900, and by 1914 the thirty-six largest banks had 1500 branches, while five or six of them controlled nine-tenths of the joint-stock banking of the country. In 1929 the D banks—Deutsche, Discontogesellschaft, Dresdner, and Darmstädter—fell from four to three when the first two amalgamated. In France concentration came later and progressed more slowly; but against the 2700 private banks of 1907 must be placed the four leading commercial banks, with 2000 outposts at home or overseas. In Belgium concentration since 1918 has put most of the banking work into the hands of half a dozen firms. Bigness is no virtue in itself, but it tends to denote great aggregations of assets; to diversify interests, risks, and opportunities; to call for expert responsible direction; to limit cutthroat competition, and to make the state interested in saving a big bank from (possibly merited) disaster.

The Banks of Issue.—The crises of 1825 and 1836 provoked discussion concerning the principles that should govern the issue of notes. In the early 'forties about 280 banks were handing out paper promises to pay legal tender—gold or Bank of England notes—on demand, and the plethora of such promises had been partly responsible for both crises. For two decades controversy raged on the questions, "Who should issue notes?" and "What should control the size of the issue?" One school said banks should be free to expand or contract their issues in accordance with the state of trade, since the obligation to redeem notes on demand would be a sufficient brake. The opposing school doubted the prudence and restraint of bankers and urged that the volume of notes be related to the quantity of gold in hand. The second school won the day, and the Bank Charter Act of 1844 put the note issue on a rigidly regulated basis. Existing banks, with the sole exception of the Bank of England, must not increase the quantity of notes they had in use, and no bank formed after 1844 could issue any. If any bank failed, amalgamated, or changed its character, its right of issue lapsed into the hands of the Bank of England. By 1900 only forty banks retained the right of issue; by 1923 amalgamation had wiped out the last survivor of 1844, and the Bank of England's monopoly became complete.

That monopoly was strictly controlled. The Bank was allowed to issue notes to the amount of £14,000,000 on the security of its loans to the state. It could also put out notes equal to two-thirds the amount of the lapsed issues of the other banks, thus eventually bringing its total fiduciary issue to nearly £20,000,000. Beyond that point every note must be backed in full with gold. The notes were thus in effect gold certificates, as good as gold, and could be changed for gold at the Bank. The Bank's capacity to lend was now restricted by its holdings of a metal that was scarce till gold was found in California and Australia. The end of uncontrolled note issue did not end the susceptibility of the business world to attacks of boom, and when those fevers reached a critical height the Bank might be compelled by a drain on its gold to recall some loans or to refuse further aid, thus accentuating rather than allaying the crisis. In 1847, 1857, and 1866 this situation developed, and the Bank could do nothing legally to provide the credit that would relieve the tension. It therefore obtained authority to issue notes without a gold backing, and in 1857 actually did issue them. An Act that had to be suspended to save a situation seemed a poor statute, but it was not amended, and after 1866 did not need to be suspended until war came in 1914.

When Germany established its imperial note issue it improved on the British plan. The Reichsbank, founded in 1875, was given the monopoly of note issue, subject to the gradual expiry of issues made by about thirty existing banks. It could issue a certain amount of notes without a gold backing; it must cover fully all notes beyond that amount, but in order to meet emergency needs it could issue uncovered notes provided (1) that a tax of 5 per cent be paid on them, and (2) that the gold reserve did not sink below 30 per cent of the total issue. The tax would prevent these emergency powers from being abused.

In linking their notes to gold, Britain and Germany ignored entirely the practice of France. Bonaparte in 1800 encouraged the formation of the Bank of France to restore public credit and help business by issuing notes and discounting bills. Like the Bank of England, it was privately owned, given a monopoly of note issue in the capital (1803), confronted with an outcrop of provincial banks of issue, and given a national monopoly of issue (1848). Unlike the Bank of England, part of its governing body was chosen by the state, part of its profits went to the treasury, and its notes were not tied to gold. Instead a maximum issue was fixed, and the figure was increased at various times to 6,800,000,-000 francs ($1,300,000,000) in 1913. The Bank need not restrict its note issue if its reserve was shrinking, and need not raise its bank rate to attract gold imports as the Bank of England did. In 1908, a year of crisis, the French rate did not exceed 4 per cent, while the British rate rose to 8 per cent. Yet until 1914 the French note was always well backed with gold. During the War and the post-War inflation period the maximum limit was raised several times, notes were poured out to cover budget deficits, and in 1922 the Bank held one franc in gold for every seven francs of notes issued. In the currency reforms that followed devaluation of the franc the limit was abolished, but the Bank was ordered to keep a 35 per cent gold reserve. In 1933 the issue stood at 85,000,000,000 francs, or twelve times the pre-War limit; but the franc now had only one-fifth its former value, and as gold had flowed into France the issue had become more golden. In 1933 the gold reserve and the note issue were almost equal, and the note was more a gold certificate than in England.

Commercial Banking.—The banks of issue did more than handle notes. They were bankers for their governments, a tremendous job after 1914. They gradually overcame the hostility of the private and joint-stock banks and became central reserve custodians and bankers' banks. They rendered some service to commercial and financial houses, and in France and Germany went into what might be called the retail banking business. The Bank of France was nation-wide, with 600 branches, while the Reichsbank set up over a hundred branches and over four thousand sub-branches. It discounted bills for traders, accepted deposits, and transferred money from place to place or from customer to customer. Its notes, supplemented by silver, gold, and bills, were the chief medium of exchange, and checks were little used.

The Bank of England threatened for a time to enter the retail field, for after the crash of 1825 it began to establish branches in provincial towns and allowed merchants and manufacturers to open accounts. Gradually, however, it settled down to be a central institution for the private and joint-stock banks. They kept in their own vaults only as much gold as they needed for their day-to-day business, and put the rest in the Bank, thus creating a central reservoir. They could draw on their balances in the Bank as need arose, and if necessary borrow from the Bank as well. The amount they or anyone else could borrow depended on the willingness of the Bank to lend and on the gold reserve it held.

If the reserve was plentiful the Bank lent readily by rediscounting bills that the borrower had discounted, and at a low "bank rate." If the reserve was being drained, especially by export of gold, the Bank raised its rate. This step made loans dearer and was therefore supposed to check them; but since it raised the general rate at which all short-term loans were being made in the money market, foreigners might send funds to London to lend at this higher rate, and gold would flow back into the country and into the central reservoir. The bank rate therefore acted as a stimulant when borrowing was low, and a brake when it was high; it was a rather clumsy device for controlling the volume and price of credit, but so long as London was undisputed mistress of international finance a change in the rate was immediately reflected in every money market in the world.

The retail trade in credit and transfer was the work of the joint-stock banks, of merchant bankers, and of discount houses. British banks, working chiefly with money deposited by customers and repayable on demand, must keep their funds sufficiently liquid to meet such demands. The growing use of checks reduced the dependence on coins and notes, swelled the number of persons with bank accounts, increased the amount of funds in the banker's hands, and allowed him to make loans by depositing the sum in the borrower's account. Experience gradually taught him to keep about half of his assets in cash or at the Bank of England, in loans that could be called back at a moment's notice ("at call") or within a few days, or in gilt-edged securities that could quickly be turned into cash in the stock market. The idle cash earned nothing, the call or short-term loans earned a little, and the bonds gave a low yield; but liquidity was more important than income. The rest of the assets could be put a little further out of immediate reach; they might be used to discount bills that were still a few weeks from maturity, lent for a period of six to twelve months to merchant or manufacturer, or invested in still more bonds. There was, however, little contact with long-term advances or investments that were not easily convertible. Assets must not risk being "frozen" in industrial plant or equipment. Critics pointed to the services done to German industry by the banks, and demanded that British banks provide capital for industry as well as credit for commerce; but excursions into that field, especially since the War, have not been happy, for they have been in aid of sick industries. Healthy industries do not usually need such aid, and sick ones cannot pay the doctor's bill.

The commercial bank found plenty of work in financing domestic and international trade and in transferring payments inside the country or across boundaries. In the eighteenth century the bill on London was the medium of domestic trade, and in the nineteenth century the same bill became the paper money of world trade. The domestic bill passed out of use with the coming of the check, for sellers obtained loans or overdrafts instead of drawing and discounting bills. The foreign bill continued, however, to be widely used. When a Lancashire exporter sent cotton cloths to Boston it was natural that he should draw on London, but when a South American sold coffee to New York he did the same thing. All over the world foreign sellers obtained payment from foreign buyers through London. The reason for this was the widespread crisscross of British trading and shipping connections. The stability of sterling after 1819, the Rothschilds' ramifications, and the free gold market helped London, but skill and ingenuity in weaving a financial web helped more. The acceptance business (described in Chapter XV, Part III) expanded greatly when Amsterdam declined, a bill accepted by a London house was first-class paper in every part of the world, and in 1914 about £350,000,000 of such bills were at large. Alongside this accepting business was the work in bill discounting and bill-broking, and by 1830 there were firms which did little but discount or deal in bills. For their work they might borrow money at call or short notice from the banks, or rediscount at the Bank of England the bills they already had. In fact, the bank rate is the rate at which the Bank is ready to rediscount bills. At the same time banks with spare funds might buy bills from brokers, in addition to those discounted for their customers, and might accept bills drawn on them.

Pre-War London thus housed a financial system evolved to meet all kinds of requirements. Amalgamation and experience had produced a strong, flexible banking structure which regarded liquidity of assets and the safeguarding of the depositor as its two chief tasks, and which had escaped any serious blow since 1867. The facilities for obtaining call or short-term loans, for discounting and accepting, for buying foreign exchange, for buying or selling securities, for raising new capital, and for insurance against almost any kind of hazard were complete. Looking back on it, a Belgian banker sang its praises as follows: "Admirably organized, strong in knowledge and in traditions proved twenty times over, able to keep its head in times of difficulty and to help others, even by assuming for itself an excess of risk, organized to respond to the infinite diversity of the needs of international commerce—the market of the City was in truth the masterpiece of an incomparable and delicate mechanism for the distribution of products throughout the world" (Van Zeeland).

Continental Banking.—Much continental banking is concerned with the credit and transfer operations of home and external trade, and resembles in essentials the work of the British banks. The revolution of 1848 wrecked most of the French banks, and a new supply had to be built up. Some of them induced the public to deposit its money and used the funds chiefly to discount bills. The check was slow in finding favor, but bills were very popular, and were drawn for all kinds of transactions, even for amounts as low as five francs. They did not have to be "accepted"; they passed from hand to hand, and by the date of maturity might have two or three dozen signatures on the back or on the strip of paper that had been pasted on them. Banks discounted them, no matter how small the sum involved, and could rediscount them at the Bank of France.

During the 'fifties and 'sixties the investment bank came to the front. It had a forerunner in the Société Générale pour Favorizer l'Industrie Nationale, which was set up in Brussels in 1822, and which sold stock and bonds to secure money for commercial and industrial loans. In 1852 the Crédit Mobilier was established in Paris to oust the Rothschilds from the profitable field of underwriting and flotation. It sold its own stock to raise capital, used the money to buy bonds and stocks of new companies—some of which it promoted—and then sold some of these to investors. It overreached itself, and virtually collapsed in 1871, after having dabbled in railroads, harbors, gas, and ships. At the same time the Crédit Foncier (1852) sold bonds to provide mortgage credit, on the lines laid down by the Prussian Landschaften—except that it was not a cooperative bank. The Crédit Mobilier was copied in many other countries, especially in Germany. There the Darmstädter Bank (1853), the Discontogesellschaft (1856), and later creations supplied the capital and long-term needs of industry and railroads. Small and large banks alike became intimately tied up with industries, and used the money received by selling shares or by receiving deposits to serve either as capital-raising middlemen or as investors in industrial stock and bonds. The Reichsbank offered such a wide and varied service after 1875 that German banking opportunities for deposit and discount were rather limited at first, while the needs of industry were large. With industrial aid went control. The Deutsche Bank in 1920 had representatives on the governing bodies of over two hundred firms, the Dresdner Bank was closely bound up with Krupp, and the other banks shared in the direction of important industries.

When German manufacturers and merchants began to seek foreign markets the banks helped by establishing branches abroad or by setting up subsidiary banks to finance trade in overseas areas. Either alone or in conjunction with others, the Deutsche Bank placed branches or special banks in South America, the Levant, and the Far East. The overseas banks were run in Germany by boards containing representatives of manufacturing, shipping, machine-making, chemical, metal, insurance, and banking interests. They financed telegraph and cable ventures, handled South American loans, and generally tried to strengthen the German exporter's grip on distant markets. They proved that whether trade follows the flag or not, it certainly follows the banks.

Of banks in other countries little need be said. Holland got a bank in 1814 to take the place of the Bank of Amsterdam. The Bank of Belgium (1835) got into trouble in the crisis of 1847-1848, and in 1850 the National Bank of Belgium was founded and given a monopoly of the note issue. Private and joint-stock banks made Vienna the financial center of the Austro-Hungarian Empire. Italy had three banks of issue, three or four others which used their capital and much of their customers' deposits to finance industry on the German plan, and many small banks of deposit and discount. In Germany the banks controlled the industries they financed, but in Italy the industries controlled the banks and made them supply funds beyond the bounds of sound banking. Much foreign capital, especially German, fed Italian banks and industries. War cut off that supply, while post-War difficulties injured industries and made them bad debtors. The frozen assets held by the banks crippled the holder, and the post-War period was full of painful liquidation, amalgamation, and government action to aid or reform the banking system.

THE GOLD SUPPLY AND THE GOLD STANDARD

The growth of regulated bank note issues, the spread of bank deposits, and the improvements in the machinery for handling bills or buying drafts permitted the nineteenth century to do most of its business with pieces of paper. Yet behind the paper slips lay a supply of precious metal. Every transaction was in terms of some "unit of account" (pound, mark, franc, etc.) representing a fixed weight of gold or silver, and every piece of paper gave its possessor the right to obtain metal disks if he wished. The timid might prefer the chink of coins to the crackle of paper, and in times of crisis most people were timid. Banks of issue must be ready to pay coin or bullion to those who presented their notes, while a foreign debt might be paid by shipping bullion if bills of exchange could not be bought at a reasonable price. Precious metal was the normal foundation of the whole commercial and credit structure, even if people rarely went into the basement to look at it.

A broadening and strengthening of that foundation was essential to an increase in the weight of the superstructure, but Europe had to manage without any great increase in its precious-metal supply for the first half of the nineteenth century. Great Britain was best stocked with gold, but had far from enough, and the drain on her scanty supply did much to precipitate the crises of 1825, 1836, and 1847. On the continent gold was much scarcer, except in Holland and Portugal, and silver served as the chief coinage metal. In central Europe silver monometallism was the rule. In France bimetallism prevailed; gold and silver coins were legal tender and were freely coined at the mint, and one ounce of gold was declared to be worth 15.5 ounces of silver. But there were few French gold coins. In Belgium, Switzerland, Italy, and even Holland silver was the officially favored metal. When Holland in 1847 definitely abandoned bimetallism for a silver standard she virtually voiced the continent's belief that gold was inadequate in supply and useless as a currency basis.

Within five years the situation had been reversed and relieved by the gold discoveries in California and Australia. The world's output during the first half of the century averaged $6,000,000 a year; that of 1847 was $29,000,000, but that of 1853 was $150,000,000, and the annual average from 1851 to 1885 was about $120,000,000. When these two fields had nearly petered out in the early 'eighties, a new series of discoveries began. The first and richest was on the Rand, near Johannesburg in South Africa. Gold was found there in 1884, and by 1930 this field had yielded over $5,000,000,000 of gold. A quarter of all the gold mined since 1492 has come from South Africa. Close on the heels of the Rand discovery came smaller ones in western Australia and the Yukon. The total annual output mounted to a maximum of $470,000,000 in 1915, and to an average annual yield of nearly $400,000,000 for the years 1901 to 1930. Over half the gold mined since 1492 has been won since 1900.

Not all this treasure went to augment the monetary supply. India, China, and Egypt continued to be sinks, while jewelers, dentists, and others used it as raw material. Since 1900 about 45 per cent of the yield has gone in these channels, but sufficient was left to increase the stock of monetary gold as follows:

1835	2	billion dollars	
1889	3.5	"	"
1899	4.7	"	"
1909	6.8	"	"
1919	9.4	"	"
1929	11.1	"	"

This increase was far from regular. From 1850 to 1873 the supply increased at the rate of 4 per cent per annum; during the quieter years 1873 to 1895 it increased only 1.6 per cent each year; but between 1896 and 1914 it grew 3.7 per cent yearly, falling again to 1.8 per cent between 1918 and 1928.

The Spread of the Gold Standard.—The new gold made the wider adoption of the gold standard possible and the abandonment of bimetallism inevitable. There was now enough gold for currency and bank reserves, and gold coins were much more convenient than the heavy silver disks for many transactions. At the same time the golden flood made any attempt to maintain a fixed legal ratio between the two precious metals impossible. A government might declare that one ounce of gold was worth 15½ ounces of silver, and that the gold in one twenty-franc piece was equal in value to the silver in twenty one-franc coins. But in the bullion market gold sank in value as it became more plentiful; in 1848 an ounce of gold cost 15.85 ounces of silver, but in 1859 it cost only 15.19 ounces, and the gold in a twenty-franc piece would buy only 19.17 francs' worth of silver. If bimetallism was to be maintained the gold coins must be re-minted and be given a larger gold content to restore their value; otherwise Gresham's law would operate, the inferior gold coins would drive the superior silver ones out of circulation, and the latter would be melted down, hoarded, or exported to pay debts. Such re-minting was impracticable, and would have to be done frequently with every change in the relative value of the two metals. The alternative was to abandon any attempt to maintain the double currency standard. France, her franc-using allies (Belgium, Switzerland), and Italy tried to protect a modified bimetallism, and urged a world currency standard; but when the German Empire in 1871 swept aside its motley of state currencies in favor of a gold standard, the silver cause was lost. The Scandinavian countries followed Germany in 1872, Holland in 1873, Austria-Hungary and Russia a little later, while France and her allies in 1878 suspended the free coinage of silver. The United States and Japan joined the ranks of the gold-standard countries. Only China, Hong Kong, and Ethiopia were using silver as the standard of value in 1935.

This ostracism of a metal "which for thousands of years had enjoyed equal privileges with gold" (Helferrich) diminished greatly the demand for silver. Its price fell from $1.25 an ounce in 1866 to 43 cents in 1903. It became increasingly a by-product obtained in the extraction of other metals. Today 80 per cent of the output is obtained in this way, and would be produced regardless of its price. A period of industrial expansion and heavy demand for other metals, such as that of the nineteen-twenties, therefore sees a great outpouring of silver; yet its use is predominantly in industry rather than in mints. It might cease to be counted as a precious metal if the vested interests of silver-producing regions were not so politically powerful in some parts of the world.

The Gold Supply and the Price Level.—The supply of new precious metal had its influence on the general level of prices. The establishment of a satisfactory index number to record price movements is extremely difficult, but that task is simple when compared with any attempt to assess the influence of monetary and non-monetary influences. Price is influenced on the one hand by the total volume of purchasing power, and on the other by the volume of goods available seeking a buyer. In the great expansion of industrial and agricultural production during the nineteenth century, the combination of technological advance and of the raid on the fertile soils and subsoils of the New World might be expected to lower prices. At the same time the influx of gold increased the metallic and paper currency in circulation, expanded the basis on which credit could be granted, and thus tended to increase purchasing power and raise prices.

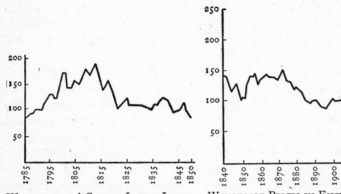

WAGE-EARNERS' COST OF LIVING INDEX IN ENGLAND, 1785-1850. (After Silberling.) 1790 = 100.

WHOLESALE PRICES IN ENGLAND, 1840-1930. (After Warren and Pearson.) 1880-1914 = 100.

The price level rose during the periods of great gold output but fell in periods of lower yield. Until 1849 the supply of new gold lagged far behind the volume of commodity production; in addition, the high levels of the Napoleonic war years vanished, and machinery reduced costs. Hence prices in England fell about 59 per cent between 1809 and 1849, or about 25 per cent between 1825 and 1849. During the years 1849 to 1873 gold poured in, gave the banks a bigger reserve, and increased the metallic currency of the leading countries by 30 per cent within a decade; but the volume of production of goods probably expanded more slowly. Prices rose in England 35 per cent between 1851 and 1854—one of the most rapid increases in peace-time history—and remained near the new level during most of the next twenty years. German prices rose 40 per cent, and the cost of living in Sweden 30 per cent. Between 1873 and 1896 the gold stream slackened, but the demand for gold grew as more countries adopted the gold standard, while the industrialization of Germany and the agricultural expansion of the New World increased the output of goods. Prices fell 40 per cent in England. Then came the inrush of African, Yukon, and west Australian gold, just as the fertile lands were reaching the end of their easy exploitation. Between 1895 and 1914 English prices rose 35 per cent, German 42, French 44, and Russian 52. The complaints of the farmer and the pleas of the bimetallist were silenced, but the voice of the wage earner rose loud, as his wages failed to keep pace with the rising cost of living. Thus the century of comparative peace between Waterloo and 1914 witnessed four general price movements —downward till 1850, upward till 1873, downward again till 1896, and upward till the eve of the War.

War and Post-War Developments.—In 1914 the gold standard prevailed throughout Europe. The unit of account was a coin containing a definite quantity of gold. Gold coins were in circulation, bullion was freely converted into coins by the mints, and coins could be melted down by any who wished to turn them back into bullion. Gold could be exported, and might be if a debtor found it was cheaper to ship gold to his creditor than to buy a bill or draft. In practice it rarely was cheaper, exchange rates did not move far from par, and little gold flowed across frontiers. The gold standard was not without its critics. These men condemned the waste of capital and labor involved in producing a metal for currency and reserves; they pointed to the fitful character of the flow; but their chief grievance was that the gold standard did not stand still. In terms of purchasing power the unit of account was uncertain; in 1896 it bought nearly twice as many goods as in 1873, and in 1913 only about 70 per cent as much as in 1896. When prices went down debtors had to give more goods to pay their debts, and creditors got more purchasing power than they had lent. When prices rose debtors escaped more easily, but creditors and fixed-income receivers suffered. The purchasing power of the unit of account must be "stabilized"; the purchasing power of money should remain unchanged from decade to decade.

Ten years of war and post-war currency history made those defects shine like virtues. In every belligerent country the paper currency expanded and the link with gold was snapped. In Great Britain the Treasury began to issue its own "currency notes" and

by 1919 had put out £350,000,000 worth, or six times as much
as the total Bank note issue on the eve of the War. In France the
limit on note issue was raised in order to allow the Bank of
France to print notes which it could lend the government. About
26,000,000,000 francs were lent, or five times as much as the
pre-War issue. In Germany the Reichsbank issued notes backed
with government bonds. In all countries paper paid the way, gold
was hoarded or raked into the reserve of the central bank, and
prices mounted. War finance methods could not easily be abandoned when peace came, and by 1920 wholesale price index numbers read as follows (1913 = 100):

Great Britain.... 307	Holland........ 292	Italy........... 624
France.......... 509	Sweden......... 359	Germany....... 1965

Some countries had still further to go along the road of inflation.
Germany's troubles called for ever more paper notes, her issue
reached fantastic heights in 1923, and her cost of living index
number rose to about 1,250,000,000,000 times its pre-War level.
In Austria and Poland inflation was only a little less extravagant;
in France, Italy, and Belgium the note issue rose rapidly to nearly
ten times its pre-War level as the printing press paid the government's bills. Only Great Britain, Scandinavia, Holland, and
Switzerland stood out from this general currency debauch.

By 1923 a return to gold seemed the only way of escape from
insanity. While some experts urged the cause of a "managed
currency," experience with mismanaged currencies had made the
gold standard look as solid as Gibraltar. Between 1923 and 1928
(inclusive) about thirty countries went back to the old standard
or to a modified version of it. In each case two questions had to
be answered: (1) What standard of value should be fixed? (2)
How should gold be used?

1. Where a currency had been smashed beyond repair, a new
currency was set up. Germany set up the Reichsmark, equal in
value to the pre-War mark (about 24 cents or one shilling) and
announced that 1,000,000,000,000 old paper marks equaled one
Reichsmark. Those who were creditors or had savings accounts
under the old currency saw the value of their claims wiped out,
and those who were debtors had their load removed. Where a
currency had been damaged but not ruined, it was devalued. Belgium put out a new coin, the belga, equal to five old francs;
France reduced the franc four-fifths, and Italy deprived the lira

of three-fourths of its value. Great Britain, Switzerland, Holland, and Scandinavia restored their units of account to the old gold value. Their policy benefited some people, but hurt others. The Englishman who bought American goods now got $4.86 worth of cotton and tobacco for every pound he spent, against about $3.50 just after the War; and the creditor who collected interest in pounds from foreign debtors got more pesos, milreis, or dollars. But the foreign buyer of British goods now had to give more francs, lire, or dollars to buy a pound's worth, and might get his needs met more cheaply elsewhere. The British seller who quoted the price of his goods in foreign currency obtained fewer pounds as the exchange value of sterling rose. If some men rejoiced that the pound could once more "look the dollar in the face," British export industries got little satisfaction therefrom. Their goods were too dear, and it is now generally agreed that the gold value of the pound should have been reduced. Great Britain was made a good country to sell in (because prices were high), and a bad country to buy from (for the same reason); but France, by reducing the gold value of its franc greatly, became a good country to buy from and a bad one to sell in. Foreigners got a lot of goods for their dollars, pounds, etc., but Frenchmen got few goods for their francs. The exporter benefited; the home manufacturer felt little competition from foreign rivals; but the investor who received interest in francs from abroad lost heavily.

2. Gold did not recover its old accessibility. During the War much of it had been gathered into the bank reserves, gold coins had disappeared from circulation, and people had become used to paper money. Gold was kept mobilized under the new plans. Free minting was not restored; coins could not be obtained for notes, but the central bank would hand over bullion bars. In England bars weighing 400 ounces could be obtained, but these were useless except to persons who wished to export gold. Thus gold was limited to reserve and exchange functions. France and Germany fixed a minimum gold reserve for their note issues. Britain added its "currency notes" to the fiduciary issue of the Bank of England (1928), and allowed a total issue of £260,000,000 to be made without gold backing. Beyond that point the old gold rule applied, but the Treasury could authorize a temporary increase in the fiduciary issue to meet emergencies.

Gold's ability adequately to serve reserve and exchange needs was partly a matter of supply and partly one of distribution. If the total world need for additional gold grew more rapidly than the total supply, scarcity would restrict credit expansion and purchasing power, thus reducing the price level. If any one country lost gold heavily, its bank credit facilities must be reduced, while if any other country received more gold than it could use or cared to use, the precious metal might be lost to one land and sterilized in the other.

These two possibilities worried the post-War world. That world must increase its monetary supply of gold about 3 per cent each year, said Professor Gustav Cassel, or its reserve would lag behind the needs of production and trade. But in the 'twenties the annual influx was only about 2 per cent, and the future offered no brighter prospect. While the supply grew too slowly, its distribution changed in ways disconcerting to many countries. The general change is shown in the following table:

STOCKS OF MONETARY GOLD

	1913		1930	
United States	1,924 million dollars		4,593 million dollars	
France	1,700	"	2,099	"
Germany	995	"	544	"
United Kingdom	770	"	730	"
World total	8,629	"	11,546	"

During and after the War gold flowed to America in payment for war and other supplies or because owners sought to get their funds away from the uncertain political and financial conditions of Europe. Until France stabilized the franc in late 1926, gold emigrated in search of safety. After she stabilized, the gold came back home, and more came to pay interest or reparations, to defray tourist expenses, and buy goods. Nervous men who sent their funds abroad for safety did not invest them in long-term loans, for they intended to recall them when the earth ceased to shake under their feet. Wide-awake men sent funds abroad to lend on short term if the interest rate was attractive, but brought them back when conditions changed. Further, the War created many new international obligations, especially reparations and interallied debts, which had to be discharged by buying large sums of foreign exchange or by sending bullion if supplies of exchange were inadequate. Finally, higher tariffs and the rise of new industries abroad made it more difficult for countries to export goods in order to pay their debts or pay for the goods they must import, and payment might therefore have to be made by shipping gold. These many influences made gold figure more largely as a means of international exchange, and made it far less secure as a credit basis. While France and the United States accumulated gold, London and other centers saw their supplies fluctuate or sink.

In attempting to cope with post-War financial strains and stresses, nearly every country relied increasingly on its central bank. The bank's note issue, its great loans to the state, and its mobilization of gold supplies had increased its power; and many observers felt that it could and should control the country's credit supply, protect the bullion reserve, and generally try to keep business on an even keel. In addition, the central banks might cooperate to strengthen some weak spot or help some necessary reconstruction. The Bank of England, the Federal Reserve Bank of New York, the Bank of France, and the Reichsbank joined hands to help stabilize the currencies of Belgium, Poland, and Roumania. New York agreed to help London to protect its gold reserve when England returned to the gold standard (1925). Under the Young Plan (1929) a Bank of International Settlements was set up at Basel, governed by representatives of the central banks of Belgium, England, France, Germany, Italy, and Japan, and of an American group. It was to receive reparations payments, disburse them, and do a limited amount of banking; but it was born in the year of the great crash, and could do little.

Since that crash, gold has not changed its post-War habits. By September, 1931, France and the United States held two-thirds of the world's monetary stock, but the central banks of other countries had seen their reserves shrink. In the summer of 1931 Austria, faced with a bank crisis, forbade gold exports. Then the Darmstädter Bank closed its doors and Germany imitated Austria. These events hurt England, and a drain of gold from London led to the suspension of the right to demand gold at the Bank (September, 1931). This action began a stampede: by the end of the year ten European countries were off the gold exchange standard, a dozen had severe restrictions on the traffic in currency, and only France, Holland, Belgium, and Switzerland—the gold *bloc*—remained faithful, but shaken. Outside Europe most other countries banned gold exports, and in the bank crisis of early 1933 the United States joined the great majority.

To the old complaint that the gold standard would not stand still must now be added the new one that it would not stand up. The props that had kept it standing before 1914 have been broken, the rules that made it possible to play the game no longer apply. One of those rules was that the creditor in the balance of payments should be (1) a free market in which debtors could pay their dues by sending goods, and (2) an investor ready to lend or invest part of the balance due to him in the debtor country. London, the great creditor of pre-War days, conformed to those rules; but New York and Paris were not open markets for the goods of their debtors, France was not a great external investor, and the United States ceased to be one after 1928. Another rule was that the payments due by debtors were largely for loans that had gone into productive investments; but many of the heavy burdens of the post-War days were the price of war and defeat. Some of these have been blotted out by the dropping of reparations and interallied debts; but the channels along which debtors can send their goods have become more choked than ever they were before 1929.

BIBLIOGRAPHY

BAGEHOT, W., *Lombard Street* (1873; new ed., 1917).

BIRNIE, A., *Economic History of Europe, 1760-1930*, chap. 6.

CLAPHAM, J. H., *Economic History of Modern Britain*, vol. i, chaps. 7, 13; vol. ii, chap. 9.

CLAPHAM, J. H., *Economic Development of France and Germany*, chaps. 6, 13.

CONANT, C., *History of Modern Banks of Issue* (6th ed., 1927).

CORTI, E., *The Rise of the House of Rothschild* (1928); *The Reign of the House of Rothschild* (1928).

ELLINGER, B., *Credit and International Trade* (1935).

FAY, C. R., *Great Britain from Adam Smith to the Present Day*, chap. 6.

FEAVEARYEAR, A. E., *The Pound Sterling* (1931).

GREGORY, T. E., Introduction to Tooke and Newmarch's *History of Prices* (1928).

GREGORY, T. E., *Select Statutes, Documents, and Reports Relating to British Banking* (1929), Introduction.

HAWTREY, R. G., *Currency and Credit* (3rd ed., 1928).

KEYNES, J. M., *Treatise on Money* (1930), chap. 30.

LAYTON, W. T., *Introduction to the Study of Prices* (new ed., 1934).

LE CHEMINANT, K., *Colonial and Foreign Banking Systems* (1924).

MARSHALL, A., *Industry and Trade*, book ii, chap. 9.

POWELL, E. T., *The Evolution of the Money Market* (1915).

REDFORD, A., *Economic History of England, 1760-1860*, chaps. 7, 12, 15.

RIESSER, J., *The German Great Banks and Their Concentration* (1911).

Van Dillen, J. G. (ed.), *A History of the Principal Public Banks* (1934).
Whale, P. B., *Joint Stock Banking in Germany* (1930).
Willis, H. Parker, and Beckhart, B. H., *Foreign Banking Systems* (1929).

ARTICLES

Gardner, W. R., "Central Gold Reserves, 1926-1931," in *Am. Ec. R.*, March, 1931, pp. 56-65.
Kitchin, J., "Gold Production: a Survey and a Forecast," in *Rev. Ec. Stat.* (Harvard), May, 1929, pp. 64-67.
Preston, H. H., "Europe's Return to Gold," in *Harv. Bus. Rev.*, April, 1931, pp. 319-329.
Sayers, R. S., "The Question of the Standard, 1815-1844," in *Ec. Hist.*, February, 1935, pp. 79-102.
Sayers, R. S., "The Question of the Standard in the Eighteen-Fifties," in *Ec. Hist.*, January, 1933, pp. 577-602.
Smith, L., "England's Return to the Gold Standard in 1925," in *J. E. B. H.*, February, 1932, pp. 228-258.
Encyclopædia of the Social Sciences: Articles on Banking (Commercial), Branch Banking, Central Banking, Credit Control, Investment Banking, Money Market; Bimetallism, Coinage, Gold, Monetary Unions, Money, Silver; Rothschild Family.
Social Science Abstracts: See Index for articles published 1928-1932. Supplement by examining files of *Economic Journal, American Economic Review, Quarterly Journal of Economics, Journal of Political Economy, Economica,* and *Foreign Affairs.*
League of Nations: *Memorandum on Commercial Banks, 1913-1929* (1931).
League of Nations: *Report of the Gold Delegation of the Financial Committee* (1932).
Macmillan Committee: Report on Finance and Industry (British Parliamentary Paper, Cmd. 3897:1931).
A New Estimate of American Investments Abroad (U. S. Dept. of Comm., Trade Information Bulletin No. 767 [1931]).

CHAPTER XXV

COMPETITION, COMBINATION, AND CONTROL

"COMPETITION," "progress," and "evolution" were the three popular words of the nineteenth century that future historians may adopt as summarizing its works and its philosophy. The first was regarded as an important factor in producing the second and controlling the third. "Competition is the law of progress"; "Competition is the life of trade"—these were unquestionable truisms in 1850. The economist and the political theorist alike regarded free competition as the road to maximum individual and social wealth and welfare, as the spur to efficiency, the enemy of incompetence, and the guardian of the consumer. When the scientists began to talk about evolution, their phrases seemed to support this view, for competition was apparently the law of progress in plants and animals as well. The survival of the fittest, the weakest to the wall, the extermination of those who could not adapt themselves to the world in which they lived—these were the laws of earth, air, and water. Competition was evidently "at once a process of selection, an economic organization, and an agency of social development" (Hamilton).

Free competition was more than a slogan: it was often a fact, a condition that became more common as monopolies or regulations imposed by governments disappeared and as new fields were opened to competitive enterprise. In the realm of external trade, the gateway to trade with Asia was thrown open with the passing of the East India Companies. The door to America was opened on equal terms to all comers with the end of colonial status north and south of the Gulf of Mexico. The abolition of guild privileges, the repeal of apprenticeship laws, the end of serfdom, the scaling down of tariffs in some countries, and the improvements in transportation gave a larger and longer range of free enterprise. (See Chapter XXVII.) The dislike of monopolies might lead the state deliberately to foster competition and to frown on any "restaint of trade."

Given this greater degree of freedom, competition could pervade almost every side of economic life. There were abundant opportunities for two or more persons or groups to strive against each other for economic advantage, whether as buyers or as sellers. There was competition between rival providers of the same goods or services; wherever capital or labor was receiving a high reward newcomers would invade the field, and few producers or traders could expect to remain long undisturbed in the enjoyment of a fertile preserve. There was competition between old industries, methods, or commodities and new ones: manual skills were challenged by new mechanical devices, native workers were jostled by immigrants, and townsmen by rural rivals. Yet when a new generation had vanquished the old, the victors might soon become so numerous that conflict between them became cutthroat. What did it profit enterprise if the spinning wheel, the charcoal burner, the sailing ship, the canal, and the cobbler were pushed aside only to make room for too many mules, mines, blast furnaces, steamers, and shoe factories? The increase in productive or transporting capacity that characterized each boom left many industries overloaded with equipment when depression came. There was competition between rival industries and products, between margarine and butter, between shoddy and other kinds of cloth, between iron and steel, between gas and electricity, and so forth. Finally, there was competition between buyers of raw materials, foodstuffs, and manufactured articles, and if it was intense at any point in the passage of goods from the point of primary production to that of final consumption, the price to be paid by the purchaser might rise high.

At its best, or worst, competition was often "imperfect," a mixture of monopolistic and competitive factors. Some firms had well-known and popular trade-marks, had customers who would never dream of going elsewhere for goods, or had a geographical location which virtually freed them from fear of rivals. Some businesses had a natural monopoly, as in the supply of gas, electricity, or street car services. Some firms began with a monopoly resting on some patent, and some were such successful competitors that they killed all their rivals and established a monopoly. To deal out such slaughter may have been the dream of every competitor, but the dream rarely came true. In many great industries, such as textiles, coal, iron, steel, and shipping, competition was severe, even though the number of rivals was small.

Consequently there gradually dawned a realization that perhaps cooperation, rather than competition, was the life of trade and even the law of self-preservation. Competition was a means, not an end; the end of business was profit, and if competition jeopardized that end some better means must be sought. Labor had pointed one way, and in its trade unions had tried to establish the principle that competition for jobs should not be allowed to push wages below a recognized standard. From this defensive attitude it had passed on to attempts to raise that standard. Capital took these two leaves out of labor's book, and added many more to them; it tried to assure profit and then to increase it by limiting or even eliminating competition.

When rival sellers of the same goods or services join hands we have a *horizontal* combination. Thousands of these combinations have appeared during the last sixty years. At the same time there has been some vertical combination, when a firm doing one kind of work has acquired control of the sources of its raw material or of the industries which use its finished product. Vertical combination has been most common in the iron and steel industries. A blast furnace owner who has to buy his ore, coal, and limestone may be at the mercy of the producers of those materials; if he has to sell his iron to the steel-maker he may have keen rivalry in that market and not be able to make a sale at a profitable price. If the steel-maker in turn sells raw steel to the makers of steel products he also may not find a market or be forced to sell at a loss. If, however, one firm can gather in all processes, from the mining of the coal and ore to the production and sale of the finished article, material is obtained at cost, middlemen's profits are eliminated, a market is assured for the iron and steel, and expansion can be combined with diversification. If, in addition, vertical rivals combine horizontally the industry gets the benefits of both possible arrangements.

Vertical Combinations.—Instances of vertical combination (or *integration*) can be found before 1800. Wedgwood acquired a three-fourths interest in one Cornish clay company, and joined with thirteen other potters to form another. His supply of raw material was thus assured, while his showrooms, salesmen, and partner guaranteed that energetic efforts would be made to sell his wares. As the iron industry grew after 1760 on coke fuel, British ironmasters acquired coal mines. After unhappy experiences in buying coal and ore, Alfred Krupp acquired coal mines in Germany, iron mines in Spain, and a fleet of ore boats. He developed the production of armor plate and of guns; his successor took over a big machine plant, and in 1896 bought the *Germania* shipyards, the birthplace of many submarines, at Kiel. In Britain, one big Sheffield firm built up, by amalgamation and absorption, a complete enterprise: ore mines in Spain, coal mines in Yorkshire, limestone quarries in Derbyshire, coke ovens, blast furnaces, converters, and rolling mills; factories making cannon, projectiles, small arms, and ammunition; engineering and shipbuilding works on the Clyde, and a strong interest in the largest shipyards in Belfast. A soap magnate (Lever) secured control of the source of his ingredients; a prosperous chain-store grocer (Lipton) began to process some of the goods sold in his shops, and then to acquire tea and cocoa plantations. The British consumers' cooperative movement began with retail stores, but from that went on to wholesale purchasing, to manufacturing goods needed by consumers, to farming, ownership of tea and palm oil plantations, to banking, insurance and operation of ships.

During the War and post-War years Germany witnessed the rocket-like rise and fall of a vast integration. Hugo Stinnes, who had begun selling coal in 1892 and then become head of a "mixed plant" which had mines, coke ovens, and blast furnaces, sprawled over the German economic countryside and reached across its borders. To naturally related interests in coal, steel, steel goods, and shipping, he added lumber, films, newspapers, banks, hotels, oil-fields, telegraph companies, insurance offices, and shoe factories. When he died in 1924, just as sanity was coming back to German currency and finance, there was no one capable of following him on his ramshackle throne. The vast aggregation fell to pieces, and the firm returned to its old interests—coal, iron, steel, and shipping.

Horizontal Combinations.—While integrations might seek economies in buying raw materials and sure markets for the product, horizontal combinations strove chiefly to limit competition. They were of three kinds: (1) Rivals might agree not to sell below a set price, not to exceed a certain output, or not to invade one another's market. (2) A central selling agency might be set up to enforce agreements by taking out of producers' hands the disposal of their wares. (3) Rivals might end competition by partial or complete amalgamation.

Agreements fixing prices, limiting output, or sharing out markets are probably as old as markets. From 1592 to 1844 the coal dealers of Newcastle had their Vend, which restricted output and regulated prices. In 1621 the Privy Council ordered them to disband, and in 1710 an act was passed "to dissolve the present and prevent the future combination of coal-owners, lightermen, masters of ships, and others to advance the price of coals, in prejudice of the Navigation, Trade, and Manufactures of this Kingdom." But the Vend continued until canals and railroads allowed other coal fields to break its monopoly of the coal trade. During the second half of the eighteenth century ironmasters, potters, cutlers, and others met to fix prices and conditions of sale, formed associations to protect their interests, and voiced their wishes to labor and the government. During the first two-thirds of the nineteenth century we hear less of such action, but after 1870 the restriction of competition became more general. In the United States the "trust" became an ogre, and "trust-busting" a popular political pastime. In Europe Germany led, and manufacturers or traders in other countries began to follow.

The German movement became pronounced during the depressed days that followed the promotion boom of 1871-1873. It gained further strength when the tariff of 1879 sheltered industries from some external competition, and it did not have a hostile law to check it. American railroads, oil refiners, and others were forbidden by common law and then by federal or state law to come together for mutual salvation. British, American, French, or Austrian courts would not enforce a trade agreement on anyone who wished to violate it; they might praise the rebel and punish the loyalists for conspiracy in restraint of trade. Germany recognized agreements as legal, forced one or two industries to make them, enacted laws regulating associations, and provided a special court to pass judgment on the rights and duties of their members. The Kartell (or cartel) could therefore grow in numbers and develop freely as a voluntary association of independent enterprises for the purpose of improving profits by exerting monopolistic influence on the market. By 1906 nearly 400 cartels existed in Germany; but in 1932, 2400 cartels controlled the sale of 56,000 commodities. Nearly all had been formed for a period

of years, and vanished unless renewed. Most of them simply
made agreements on price, output, or division of market; some
had rather elaborate machinery for enforcing the agreement, but
several of them took the work of selling out of the producers'
hands and marketed the goods of all firms through a central sales
bureau.

Of the many well-known cartels, only three need be described.
The Westphalian coal producers, faced with overcapacity and
falling prices, formed associations in 1877 and 1878 to control
exports and then prices. Their efforts failed, for new mines were
opened, agreements were broken, prices were cut, and owners
preferred to continue producing at a loss rather than close their
pits. At last in 1893 the Rhenish-Westphalian Coal Syndicate
was formed, to sell the coal of 170 mines which produced over
half Germany's output. It fixed the maximum output for each
mine, its central bureau at Essen took delivery of all coal at a
fixed price and sold it at the best price obtainable. Where rival
coal (especially British) could be brought in cheaply the bureau
sold at competitive prices, but where there was little effective
competition (i.e., in the Rhineland and Westphalia) it charged
high prices. After defraying operating expenses it shared its surplus among the members in proportion to their quotas, whether
they had produced up to the quota or had kept below it.

During the War the whole industry was regulated. When peace
came the government forced all mines into eleven district syndi-
cates, and placed over them (1) an Imperial Coal Union to fix
quotas, allocate markets, and fix maximum prices; and (2) an
Imperial Coal Council, consisting of representatives of producers,
consumers, labor, and the state, to plan and control the industry
in terms of the general welfare. The Council did little, the Union
did much; and when the troubles with the mark and with the
French in the Ruhr ended, the coal interests began to put their
house in order. Old mines or poor coal seams were abandoned,
machinery was installed, new methods of wage payment were introduced, and high-sounding phrases about rationalization and
research were voiced at frequent conferences. In the Ruhr coal
field seventy-seven firms closed their pits, leaving seventy companies with 175 mines to carry on more intensive work. Such
plans revealed a unity or community of interest far beyond the
aims or methods of 1893. But the savings in wages were counter-

balanced by the interest on the new equipment; the cost of production and the price were not appreciably reduced and over-capacity still dogged the heels of the industry.

The second famous German cartel attempted to bring order out of the chaotic exploitation of the world monopoly of potash. Potash mining was begun by the Prussian government in 1861 at Stassfurt, but refining was done by private enterprise, as was mining after 1865. Huge profits attracted too much capital; and competition, combined with improved methods, reduced prices nearly two-thirds in ten years. In 1877 four big mines were at work, though two of them could have met all the demand. Losses were heavy and in 1879 a cartel was formed. A sales syndicate was soon set up, and while the government kept prices low for German farmers, the syndicate tried to charge high prices for foreign sales. Its efforts were thwarted as firms outside the syndicate tapped deposits, and in 1910 the imperial government had to take control of the industry. Maximum domestic and minimum export prices were imposed on all producers, production was limited and apportioned, and all sales were to be made by the syndicate. In 1921 the sinking of new shafts was forbidden till 1928, the "monster of unrestricted competition" was thus slain, and inefficient mines were closed down. Germany's monopoly of potash was broken by the loss of Alsace, but an agreement was made (1925) with the Alsatian producers to share out the world market in the ratio of 70 for Germany to 30 for France.

The third important cartel was in the steel industry. In 1904 several cartels which controlled the sale of steel, rails, railroad ties, and girders united in the Steel Union (Stahlwerksverband), with headquarters at Düsseldorf. The Union sold certain raw steel products, such as ingots, rails, and shapes, known as "A products"; but it only regulated the output of "B products"— pipes, wire, plates, sheets, axles, wheels, rims, and other goods which required more manufacture and were less standardized. By 1914 it included thirty steel works; it sold goods at home at the best possible price, and let the surplus go abroad at whatever price it could get. That price was usually much below the home price, and the Union was accused of "dumping" goods overboard at a loss in order to maintain high prices at home. It knew, as nearly every producer in every country knew, that the cost of making one unit of goods was lower if production was large than if it was medium or small. If only part of the large production was sold at home in the protected market, and if the rest was sold abroad at bare cost or even at a loss, the total profit would be larger than on an output limited by domestic demands.

The War left the steel industry with a vast excess capacity. It also gave it vast profits; and during the days of inflation the industry put them into integrations, taking over all kinds of firms that used its products, and amalgamating horizontally to unite big rivals. Six giant firms produced 90 per cent of the country's steel, but consumption at home and abroad would not absorb more than half the metal the plants could produce. German steel magnates therefore sought agreement with their foreign rivals, and in 1926 the Continental Steel Cartel came into being. It included the raw steel-makers of Belgium, France, Germany, and Luxembourg; in 1927 those of Czechoslovakia, Austria, and Hungary joined, but Britain and Sweden were important European non-members. For five years it was to limit the total output and allot quotas to each country; but no agreement could be reached on prices.

Cartels of various kinds were to be found in most other countries and in some fields of international trade before the war, and after 1918 new ones came into being while old ones passed on from the regulation of competition to something stronger. In France the Comptoir Métallurgique de Longwy was formed in 1876 by four owners of blast furnaces, to push the sale of their pig iron; it gave each member his fraction of the market and fixed prices, but did not restrict output, and it dealt only with the domestic market. Comptoirs handled the sale of many steel products, and reduced the variety of sizes and patterns of such things as girders to a few standards; but French industry was far more individualistic than German, few products were suitable for control, and association or combination was therefore insignificant.

In Great Britain a few industries that were in the hands of a small number of firms reached agreement to restrict competition. The railroads charged uniform fares and freights; shipping firms made agreements with one another and with foreign rivals; banks adopted common lists of charges; and associations, sometimes with sales agencies, tried to benefit producers of thread, salt, steel rails, and bedsteads. But the big staple industries—coal and textiles—were in the hands of thousands of firms; there were 1700 coal-mining companies and about 3000 cotton businesses. The manufacturer was as stubbornly individualistic as his American counterpart, and in a free-trade country foreign competition was always at hand to check any attempt to push prices high at home or in the export trade. After the War the troubles of cotton, steel, and coal were often said to be due to the excessive number of units, the lack of cooperation between them, and the persistent survival of overcapacity, obsolete plants, and antiquated organization. Political pressure was exerted to induce mine owners to collaborate in reorganizing and cartelizing their industry. The iron and steel industry was given tariff protection in 1932 on condition that it overhaul its structure, and Lancashire was lectured by the rest of the country on the need for price regulation to stop price cutting, on the virtues of vertical and horizontal combination, on the folly of retaining redundant or old machinery, and on the value of cooperative marketing bureaus. The results have not been spectacular, and it has been impossible to get unanimous approval of even the most modest schemes for cooperation in the cotton industry.

International Cartels.—International cartels existed before the War in industries run by a few large units. On most of the world's ocean lanes shipping "rings" or "conferences" fixed freights and fares, and tried to prevent outsiders from stealing the traffic by offering shippers a rebate of 10 per cent, provided they did not patronize free-lance ships. The rebate was not paid until six months after the goods had been sent, and was canceled if in the meantime the shipper was found to have been disloyal. In the armaments industry a few giant producers supplied a limited number of customers, and could share out the markets with ease and skill. The European rail-makers formed a cartel in 1883, and strengthened it in 1904; while international agreements to control the sale of aluminum, electric bulbs, calcium carbide, plate glass, bottles, and enamelware were reached before 1914. At least a hundred cartels crossed national frontiers. The War broke some of them; but when peace came they were soon mended, and many new ones were added, affecting steel, potash, oil, rayon, nitrates, dyes, copper, zinc, tin, nickel, mercury, linoleum, paper, glue, and wood pulp. Many of these cartels were attempts to repair the damage done to pre-War trade conditions and markets by the redrawing of the European map. Whatever the treaty-makers did, industrialists must avoid internecine conflict and seek profit through harmony.

A Critique of Cartels.—The chief cartels were in industries with great capital structures and heavy overhead costs. They sought to secure profitable prices in the home market and avoid ruinous international competition. They rested on compacts that ran for ten years, five years, or less, that expired unless renewed, and could be modified in the light of experience. Renewal was usually a stormy procedure, as each firm strove to get a better quota. Cartels did not interfere with the actual methods of production, and each firm could be as efficient as it wished. They were most effective when the number of firms was small, when the product was capable of standardization and mass production, when raw materials were scarce and localized, when patents gave a monopoly that could not easily be invaded, when great sums of capital were needed to set up new firms, or when tariff and transport costs impeded external competition.

Where these conditions were present, prices were maintained at a stable level, and while they might not rise much in boom days, they did not fall much during depression. Since 1929 some German cartels have been disciplined by the government for holding prices up while the world price level was falling. The cartel may have charged a price that gave it the greatest net return, rather than an exorbitant figure, but there is little evidence that it experimented with various prices to discover which one yielded that return. It gave the higher rather than the lower figure the benefit of the doubt. Further, a cartel usually took control of an industry that had too many firms and excess producing capacity. By bringing higher prices and giving each member a share of the market, it might keep alive businesses that had obsolescent and inefficient plants, thus perpetuating overcapacity. In practice it rarely succeeded in establishing or maintaining complete control of its industry. New firms arose outside the ring, and the international cartels were seldom all-inclusive. Hence a cartel that maintained a high price level stimulated its members and out-siders to increase output; a cartel that restricted output as well encouraged independents to increase theirs. It seems probable that cartel efforts in maintaining prices before 1929 did much to encourage excessive production, and that similar efforts after

1929 did something to prolong the depression. In the international field, where cartels were weaker, even the most imposing of them were unable to prevent heavy falls in the price of their products, but in the domestic field price maintenance was more successful.

State Aid and Control.—The modern state may oppose restrictive policies which seem to be extorting excessively high prices from the consumer; but it is often willing to listen to the cry of producers who complain that excessively low prices are ruining them, and may impose control schemes on them or give its support to plans they formulate. State intervention in the case of coal and potash has already been mentioned. In the post-War period the state also sought to restore profit to some primary producers by adopting cartel practices. Two schemes, for the control of rubber and sugar, were especially ambitious. Faced with a severe fall in rubber prices, planters in Ceylon and Malaya induced the British government in 1922 to adopt the Stevenson Plan for regulating rubber exports. Each planter was to be permitted to export, virtually duty-free, only 60 per cent of his "standard production," i.e., the amount produced in 1920. If he wished to export more he must pay a prohibitive export duty. As the price of rubber fell, the exportable percentage was reduced; as the price rose, more could be sent abroad. The Plan raised the price of rubber somewhat; then America recovered from the depression of 1920-1922, began to buy more cars fitted with balloon tires, and the price of rubber soared, reaching $1.23 a pound in 1925, against a low point of 13 cents in 1922. From that pinnacle it descended equally rapidly, as tire-makers were stimulated to reclaim old rubber, as planters smuggled their product, and as the Dutch East Indian planters and natives (who had refused to cooperate with the British) increased their output greatly. By 1928 it was evident that a restriction plan which applied to only part of the producers was futile and even harmful, since those outside the scheme would reap the benefit while those inside it would gain temporary advantage but lose in the long run. When the Plan was abandoned (1928) the Dutch had improved their methods, lowered costs, and more than doubled their share of the world's market; the British share had dropped a third; the world output was more than twice that of 1922, and the indicator was set at full steam ahead. Within two years the market was glutted, rubber was selling at less than eight cents a pound, and the Dutch were eager for restriction. They got their way, and the planting of new areas was forbidden. As prices rise the natives will probably expand their output, and the tire will spin its vicious circle once more.

Sugar rivaled rubber in its post-War sufferings. Europe's output dropped during the War from 8,300,000 tons to 2,600,000, but Cuba's yield rose from 2,700,000 to 4,000,000 tons under the stimulus of a price that passed 22 cents a pound. That stimulus had shriveled to 5 cents by 1924, but even at that price Cuba kept production high. Meanwhile Europe revived its beet fields, Great Britain and the United States expanded theirs, while the propagation of a new kind of cane that gave a greater yield per acre and made cultivation profitable at 2 cents a pound caused a great extension of cane-growing in Java. The world yield rose from 17,000,000 tons in 1919-1920 to 29,000,000 in 1928-1929. In 1929 the price fell to 1¾ cents, and in 1930 to 1 cent. Even Java was now willing to consider restriction plans; and in 1931 Cuba, five European producers, and Java agreed, under the Chadbourne Plan, to restrict output, reduce area, ration exports, and gradually get rid of the huge surplus stocks. The governments were to help in carrying out the plan. Since Russia, the British Empire, and the United States are outside the scheme, the equilibrium, if established, may easily be disturbed again.

A list of the commodities that have been subjected to control by producers, by the state, or by both, is a long one. The list of staples "in which there has been no appreciable measure of general artificial control at any time" (Rowe) is short. It contains coal, wool, silk, rayon, hides, phosphates, meat, dairy products, flax and jute; but some of these have been under partial or national control by cartels or by producers' groups with state aid. Mr. Rowe's study of the various control efforts shows that the results were often identical with those already associated with the cartels. Schemes which sought to maintain price by holding back supplies encouraged producers to increase output, provoked overcapacity, and piled up stocks which broke the market. In many industries—sugar, rubber, copper—some goods were produced at high cost, but others at much lower costs; American copper from old mines and plants could not profitably be sold at less than 16 to 18 cents a pound, but South American, European, and African producers could sell for 11 or 12 cents. Plans that sought to protect the high-cost producer intensified the efforts of the low-cost areas, and led to a glut. Nearly all the controlled industries had expanded to overcapacity even before the crash came in 1929. Where consumption kept pace with capacity in good times, control erred in trying to maintain boom prices in depressed days, for the community with smaller spending power could not pay them, and either bought less or sought substitutes. Thus the activities of controllers were one cause of the glutted commodity markets of 1929, and prolonged the depression by trying to prevent prices from reaching a level "that would automatically eliminate submarginal producers and extend the margin of demand, thereby adjusting the supply to the effective demand" (Weidenhammer).

This cold-blooded verdict may be sound economics, but it ignores the age-long refusal of men to submit passively to automatic elimination, and the deep-rooted belief that control can produce desired results. Control has always been an attractive weapon to the strong and a life belt eagerly grabbed by the sinking. The elimination of submarginal *production* does not eliminate the submarginal *producer*. He still lives, with an appetite, unpaid debts, and a vote. Like his rulers, he learns little and forgets little from experience, is not eager to be the victim of long-run tendencies or economic laws, and may believe that the remedy for unsuccessful control is not *laissez faire*, but more control.

Amalgamations and Concerns.—The cartel left the individuality of its member firms untouched, and was content to control their sales. The cartel movement therefore was accompanied, supplemented, and partly supplanted by one which went much further, knit firms more tightly together, and in some instances merged many firms in one great company. Closer union was obtained in several ways:

1. Community of interest might be found in the "concern" (*Konzern*). A group of independent businesses retained their legal entities, but adhered to a common policy of production, sale, and finance under the direction of some central authority. Their directorates might be interlocked; a bank, a holding corporation, or a Stinnes might own sufficient stock in each of them to be able to make them work together; or they might exchange stock with

one another. They divided the field of production, shared patents or processes, and did not get in one another's way.

2. One company might purchase another or others, or a new company might be formed to take over a number of existing firms.

3. A "holding company" might secure sufficient shares in several operating companies to give it control over their policies. It might get these shares by giving their owners its own stocks or bonds, and possibly some cash as well. The owners might be persuaded to make the exchange by being offered two or three times as much new stock as they surrendered, thus imposing on the industry the task of producing profits and interest on a much larger face value of securities.

These developments were visible in Europe before 1914, but the War, the post-War boom, and the years of inflation and rationalization in Germany speeded the movement up greatly. In Great Britain the sewing-cotton firm of J. and P. Coats amalgamated with its four chief British rivals in 1895-1896, obtained a controlling interest in smaller firms, gradually spread to the continent and to America, and eventually held a virtual monopoly of the world's thread industry. In similar fashion, by buying and building, Lever became the colossus of the soap world, with factories in many lands, and tropical plantations or trading posts in Asia and Africa. In 1929 Lever Brothers joined hands with the Margarine Union, which had been formed by the amalgamation in 1927 of two Dutch companies, and which controlled most of the continental margarine and soap trade. The accompanying chart gives some idea of the vast ramifications of this Anglo-Dutch combination, known as Unilever. Few European or North American faces or clothes could now be washed without paying tribute to the "soap trust"; but the activities of the Unilever galaxy included the production of vegetable oils in the tropics, the catching of whales and seals in the antarctic, the production and sale of margarine, perfumes, soap, and cattle foods, and the operation of chains of grocery stores, fish shops, and restaurants. British shipping gradually became concentrated in the hands of a few great lines, the "big five" banks by 1919 held 85 per cent of the country's bank deposits, and in 1926 Imperial Chemical Industries, Ltd., was formed as a holding corporation to obtain stock in three large and about fifty small chemical

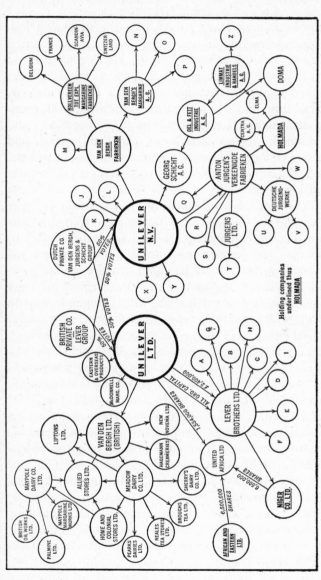

THE SOAP AND MARGARINE COMBINE

The dairy, tea, and other stores represented by the circles in the top left corner are large groups of chain stores selling dairy produce and groceries. The circles containing letters A–Z include a hundred and forty subsidiaries which are concerned with fishing, whaling, sealing; producing, transporting or selling soap, oil seeds, candles, jam, cocoa, margarine, vegetable oils, perfumes, cattle foods, and candies; or operating grocery stores, fish shops, and restaurants. They are located in Great Britain, Holland, Belgium, France, Germany, Scandinavia, Switzerland, Ireland, Nigeria, the Congo, the Dutch East Indies, North America, and Australia. (From the *Economist*, reprinted by permission of the Editor.)

firms. In 1929 four leading electrical equipment firms passed under the control of a holding company.

In Germany combination was strongest in the steel, electrical, and chemical industries. In 1926 the United Steel Company fused four large firms, with ore mines, coal pits, and big interests in machine works. In the preceding year thirteen chemical and dye firms had united in the *Interessengemeinschaft Farbenindustrie*, one big financial unit. The dye and chemical industry in all countries evolved such units. It needed well-staffed laboratories and long costly research; its products were many and varied, and production rested on large equipment, secret techniques, or patents. A large firm could enjoy the economies of *joint-cost* production: the cost of making commodity *A* would be reduced if the waste product could be made into commodity *B*, the waste from *B* turned into *C*, and so forth. Half a dozen large German firms and a few small ones had by 1904 sorted themselves into two groups, which in 1916 established community of interest, exchanged information, and joined hands to produce synthetic nitrogen, liquid fuel, rayon, explosives, and camera films. In 1925 the two groups merged in a single firm, which sought in vain to reach an *entente* with the British trust. With France, where three leading chemical firms were merged in 1927, and with Switzerland, Belgium, and Italy agreement was reached, and this continental group controlled 70 per cent of the world's dye production.

In the international field some important combinations emerged. In 1886 Nobel established the first international trust, the Nobel Dynamite Trust, Ltd. This holding company controlled the German, British, and some other dynamite companies, and reached agreement with producers in other countries. In 1907 the "Royal Dutch Company for the working of petroleum wells in the Netherlands Indies" united with the Shell Transport and Trading Company, a British concern. Each company was already an international holding company, and the Royal Dutch-Shell, controlling hundreds of subsidiaries in all parts of the world, eventually rivaled (and even surpassed in volume of business) any of the units of the Standard Oil group. It also made friends with its two smaller rivals in the eastern hemisphere—the Anglo-Persian and the Burmah Oil Companies.

In the post-War world some huge international combinations appeared. Severe dizziness is the only reward for any attempt to

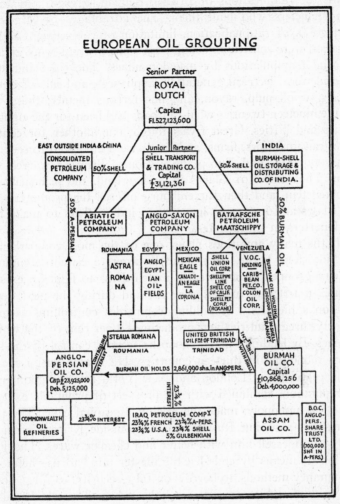

EUROPEAN OIL GROUPING

This diagram shows in general the cooperation between the three great combines—Royal Dutch Shell, Anglo-Persian, and Burmah Oil. It omits the wholly owned subsidiaries which market the oil in various countries, and also the producing or prospecting companies. Cooperation between the combines has ended the rivalry that once existed between them for markets. (From the *Economist*, reprinted by permission of the Editor.)

follow the ramifications of British, Belgian, French, and American financiers who built them. The advantages of large-scale production, of rationalization, limitation of competition, and integration were sometimes sought, but some projects were gigantic financial manipulations by megalomaniacs. The chief industries affected were electrical generation, appliances, and sale of power; forests, wood pulp, rayon, and non-ferrous metals; these were for the nineteen-twenties what railroads had been for the eighteen-forties and 'fifties. Great rivals fought one another for control; American financiers, firms, and funds were mobilized to seek foreign conquests; and Europeans welcomed them or warred with them. The canton of Glarus in Switzerland, the principality of Leichtenstein, and then Luxembourg offered the promoters "liberal" laws and low taxes in order to induce them to make their headquarters in those states.

Of the many ambitious plans, one of the most comprehensive and notorious began when Ivar Krueger, a Swedish engineer, in 1913 grouped some Swedish match firms to fight an existing group. In 1917 he fused the rivals, and during the next decade built up a hierarchy of holding companies controlling factories in forty-three countries and producing 80 per cent of the world's matches. By lending $350,000,000 he secured control of the state match monopoly in thirteen countries. He floated vast issues of stock, especially in London and New York, and the glamour of his reputation, combined with the prospect of profitable exploitation of a monopoly, made the raising of capital easy. The price of matches rose, but Russia remained outside Krueger's empire, ready to undersell him with better and cheaper wares. The justification of means by ends led the master mind to use heterodox accountancy methods, to borrow on false security, to forge bonds, and to deceive his associates and the public. The whirlwinds of 1929 shook the skyscraper of match boxes, a lot of short-term loans could not be met, and in 1932 a tawdry suicide in a Paris hotel bedroom ended the career of this northern Napoleon.

Many such figures strutted as supermen on the post-War stage. Some escaped by death, others by imprisonment, others by legal loopholes or skillful lawyers. To them, the production of commodities for sale seemed less important than the production of stocks and bonds for sale. They were playing a great game, with power and profit as the prize. They were also giving the public what it wanted, and supplying a demand just as real as, was that for rayon or radios. Their contribution to productive efficiency

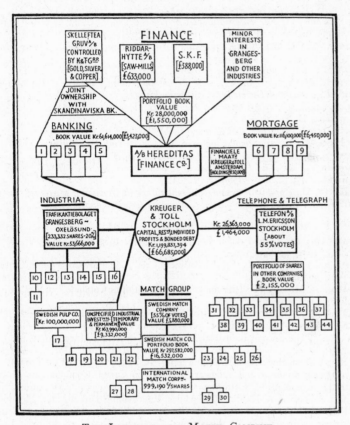

THE INTERNATIONAL MATCH COMBINE

Squares 10-13 and 15 handled iron ore; 14 was a railroad; 16 was a power and engineering firm; 17 controlled thirteen large producers of sulphur pulp; 18-30 were match companies in Scandinavia, Great Britain, Poland, Peru, San Domingo and other places; 31-44 manufactured or operated telephones. (From the *Economist,* reprinted by permission of the Editor.)

was often negligible, or was swallowed up by the heavier burden of capital charges imposed on the industry. Europe, like America, had little cause to be thankful to some of the financial wizards who waved their wands over it. The task of running businesses so large was beyond the capacity of men so little; the task of ruining them was not, and their eventual failure spread loss on wage earners, investors, and creditors alike.

BIBLIOGRAPHY

CARTER, G. R., *The Tendency toward Industrial Combination* (1913).

DOMERATZKY, L., *The International Cartel Movement* (U. S. Dept. of Comm., Trade Information Bulletin No. 556 [1928]).

ELLIOTT, W. Y., and others, *International Control in the Non-Ferrous Metals* (1935).

KNIGHT, BARNES, and FLÜGEL, *Economic History of Europe,* chap. 18.

LEVY, H., *Monopolies, Cartels, and Trusts in British Industry* (1927).

LEVY, H., *Industrial Germany* (Eng. trans., 1934).

LIEFMANN, R., *Cartels, Concerns, and Trusts* (Eng. trans., 1932).

MACGREGOR, D. H., *Industrial Combination* (1906), parts i, ii.

MARSHALL, A., *Industry and Trade* (1919), book iii, chaps. 1-6, 9-13.

PLUMMER, A., *International Combines in Modern Industry* (1934).

STOCKDER, A. N., *German Trade Associations* (1924).

STOCKING, G. W., *The Potash Industry: a Study in State Control* (1931).

TSCHIERSCHKY, S., *Kartellpolitik* (1930).

WARRINER, D., *Combination and Rationalization in Germany, 1924-1928* (1931).

WHITTLESEY, C. R., *Governmental Control of Crude Rubber* (1931).

ARTICLES

ABRAMS, M. A., "The French Copper Syndicate, 1887-1889," in *J. E. B. H.*, May, 1932, pp. 409-428.

DOMERATZKY, L., "Cartels and the Business Crisis," in *Foreign Affairs*, October, 1931, pp. 34-53.

HARTSOUGH, M. L., "The Rise and Fall of the Stinnes Combine," in *J. E. B. H.*, February, 1931, pp. 272-295.

JAMES, C. L., "International Control of Raw Sugar Supplies," in *Am. Ec. R.*, September, 1931, pp. 481-497.

JEVONS, S., "The Second Industrial Revolution," in *Ec. J.*, March, 1931, pp. 1-18.

ROWE, J. W. F., *Studies in the Artificial Control of Raw Material Supplies*, Royal Econ. Soc., Special Memoranda, Nos. 23 (1930), and 29 (1931).

Encyclopædia of the Social Sciences: Articles on Cartel, Combinations (Industrial), Competition, Cutthroat Competition, Employers' Associations, Export Associations, Holding Companies, Interlocking Directorates, Monopoly, Price Stabilization, Restraint of Trade, Stabilization (Economic), Trusts, Unfair Competition, Valorization; Hudson, G.; Leverhulme, Lord; Melchett, Lord; Ballin, A.; Stinnes, H.; Kreuger, I.; Nobel, A. B.; Loewenstein, A.

Social Science Abstracts: See Index.

CHAPTER XXVI

BUSINESS FLUCTUATIONS

THE economic course of the nineteenth century, like that of all earlier centuries since at least the sixteenth, was marked by alternations of comparative prosperity and depression. A period of prosperity would be characterized by plentiful employment, growing demands for goods and services, increased investment, rising wages and prices, expanding domestic and external trade, and a general confidence that all was well with the world. Then, suddenly or gradually, these conditions were reversed; demand, prices, wages, employment, and profits declined; investment dried up; relief problems became acute; and the optimists of yesteryear declared that the world was going to the dogs. Then gradually the clouds would lift, signs of recovery would reveal themselves, men would be called back to work, and the apparently stalled car would move forward once more. The experience of at least three centuries suggests that the normal course of economic life is for conditions to be getting better, to be getting ready to get worse, to get worse, and to be getting ready to get better.

These ebbs and flows affected social and political life as well as economic conditions. The marriage rate, the consumption of alcohol, tobacco, and other non-essentials, and the number of convictions for drunkenness or disorderly conduct rose with the curves of employment and production. On the other hand, larceny and petty theft became less common, and the calls on public and private charity declined. Industrial unrest became more marked as prosperity grew more pronounced, for wage earners sought to get a higher price for their labor. The stream of emigration widened, especially when good conditions in Europe synchronized with similar conditions in the New World. A period of depression reversed all these trends, and if it lasted long enough it might cause an outcrop of radical ideas, of schemes for social, political, or economic reform, and even of violence. Governments might be overthrown at the barricades or at the ballot box, and employers who had introduced new machines might be attacked. Most of the anti-machine riots between 1750 and 1850 came in days of depression, when starving men saw in the new equipment the thief that had stolen bread from their hands. A curve showing the fluctuations in business conditions would be a fitting and illuminating frontispiece to any book on modern political, diplomatic, or social history.

Early students of business fluctuations were impressed by the fact that the intervals separating the tips of booms or the troughs of depressions were roughly of equal length. In the seventeenth century the interval was often eight to ten years; after 1760 big crises descended on British trade every nine to eleven years—in 1763, 1773, 1783, 1793, 1815, 1825, 1836, 1847, 1857, 1866, 1873, 1882, 1893. But some of these crises were caused by the beginning or ending of a war, which cannot be predestined to happen according to schedule. Further, the turns of the tide since 1880 have been less regular and more frequent, and if we examine the periods between the dates given above we find many minor undulations which upset the simple notion of a nine-to-eleven-year cycle. The most that can be said is that alterations of good and bad trade are recurrent but not periodic. The business cycle, unlike leap year, is not bound by arithmetic; depression comes when conditions are ripe for it, not by decree of the calendar.

The length and severity of a depression depended partly on the intensity of the boom that preceded it, and also on the general trend of prices during the period. In times of rising price levels (1849-1873 and 1896-1920) recovery usually came fairly quickly, and Professor Thorp has shown that in England and the United States there were about three years of good trade to every one of bad during these periods. During the years 1815-1849 and 1873-1896, when price levels were generally sinking, recovery was much slower and more fickle; in the second period England had only about five months of prosperity for every year of depression.

Booms and depressions varied in their range. The capital goods industries were especially active in boom days, but were prostrate during depression. Farmers and industries producing consumers' goods (e.g., shoes, clothes, food) poured out large streams of wares even in dark days; they made little profit, and when prosperity returned they enjoyed a great increase of net earnings rather than a great increase in the volume of business. In prosperous years some industries, such as agriculture, dying ventures like canals, or industries exposed to competition from new rivals at home or abroad (e.g., coal or railroads), might be sick. Finally, whole countries might stand apart from the general world trend, flourishing while others were ailing, or vice versa. Since 1790, according to Professor Thorp, the years of international diversity in business conditions have outnumbered the years of similarity. Nevertheless, the growing commercial and financial interdependence of the world in the last hundred years has tended to make disaster or good fortune in one country react on the others.

The booms of the first half of the nineteenth century usually ended with a bang as the bubble burst. A period of intense energy terminated suddenly in a crisis that often degenerated into a panic; the financial heart seemed to have stopped beating, bankruptcy stared men in the face, and in a few days or weeks business was headed for the abyss. After the panic of 1866 Great Britain gradually learned how to avert these crises, and henceforth business slid down a hill instead of falling over the edge of a precipice. France also succeeded in avoiding sudden disasters, and the United States sought escape by erecting its Federal Reserve System after the crisis of 1907. In 1914 most observers were disposed to say that crises were things of the past, but the events of 1920 and 1929 showed they were overconfident.

Causes of Fluctuations.—In 1895, 230 explanations of business fluctuations were listed. Since that time production has continued unflaggingly, and no cartel has been formed to limit output. The theories sometimes contradict each other, but usually differ in the emphasis they give to different factors. Their number reflects the great variety of points at which something can go wrong with the economic machine, with the judgment of those who steer it, or with the power supply that moves it. No two recessions have been quite alike in their causes and consequences, or in the extent to which they were influenced by some special or extraneous event. Nevertheless, certain general factors usually played a part in taking business up into a boom, dragging it down, and pulling it out of the slough of despond.

The first general feature was personal—the optimism and forgetfulness of the average farmer, manufacturer, banker, trader, and investor. Individuals acting under the stimulus of profit behaved in much the same manner time after time. Like the Bourbons, they learned nothing and forgot nothing. If they did, a younger generation, proud of its superior wisdom, insisted on buying its own experience. Good trade begat optimism, optimism begat overoptimism, which in turn begat depression, whose child was pessimism and whose grandchild was overpessimism. But business sentiment was as subject to climate and environment as to heredity, and responded rapidly to the first sign of spring and sunshine.

The second general feature was the behavior of production. When the producer considers what he will produce and how much, his decision tends to be governed by the current levels of demand, prices, and profits, and by the expectation that these levels will be maintained at least until his goods are ready for market. If many producers independently decide that conditions justify an extension of output, the supply eventually placed on the market may exceed the demand. If the commodity is a comparatively new one (e.g., bicycles, radio sets, automobiles, tires, or a new kind of cloth), production flourishes until the new demand has been met; but when fashions change or every potential purchaser has been supplied, demand falls off as rapidly as it grew. The expansion of production sharpens the demand for raw materials, credit, and labor, and may raise the price of these things so much that the margin left for profit is pared down unless the price of the finished product can be raised or some saving in cost can be effected; but at the height of a boom neither may be possible.

In the field of agriculture, climatic conditions might play havoc with production and shake trade. While Europe depended chiefly on its own farm supplies, a bad season raised food prices to such an extent that consumers had less income available for buying manufactured goods, and farmers lost some of their purchasing power if the higher prices failed to counteract the effect of the short crop. In England the abnormal need for food imports in lean years was not necessarily accompanied by any abnormal expansion of exports, and the task of paying for the emergency food imports might cause a drain of gold abroad. This reduced the banks' ability to make new loans or continue old ones, and as credit became tight business in general was checked. When New World supplies of farm produce were available, scarcity in

Europe was not counterbalanced by high prices, and the shrinkage in farmers' income hurt those who supplied them with goods and credit.

Every period of prosperity was marked by a great expansion in the production of capital goods—machines, buildings, roads, canals, railroads, ships, power generators, metals, etc. While a railroad was being laid and equipped, material and labor were wanted; when it was finished they were not. A demand for factories or houses stirred the building industry, but when the buildings had been erected the industry lacked work. The same experience was undergone by industries that made the more durable consumers' goods. Bicycles, cars, sewing machines, or cameras last for years, and the European is far less eager (or able) than the American to scrap his two-year-old model for a new one. Hence the capital goods industries and those producing durable consumption goods have proceeded by "bumps and jerks"; and Mr. Dennis Robertson suggests that "most of the great upward and downward swings of trade in the nineteenth century, from the great English railway boom of the 'forties to the great German electrical boom of the late 'nineties, can be explained in terms of . . . the essential bumpiness and jerkiness of the process of investment in capital equipment." He also points out that the troubles of 1929 sprang partly from the fact that during the preceding years three leading lines of production—primary foodstuffs and raw materials, capital goods for production and transport, and durable consumers' goods—had developed rapidly and simultaneously to the point of "glut and indigestion."

The third general feature was the behavior of investment and speculation. Investment was stimulated by the belief that interest or profit would be forthcoming, and speculation lived on the faith that goods, stocks, or bonds could be sold at a higher price than had been paid for them. This faith shone most brightly on the new field of production, transportation, and investment that characterized every period of revival. Each boom had at least one attractive novelty to add to the established list of profit-producers. When something happened to check the upward price movement, when interest or profit was not forthcoming, and when buyers failed to appear or refused to pay what had been expected, the mirage melted away.

The fourth feature was the behavior of credit. In the later

stages of a depression the lack of borrowers lowered interest rates, and led bankers to welcome a resumption of requests for loans. Those who could present a good case secured credit cheaply, and with returning confidence the banker grew more loath to say, "No." As the requests became more numerous, banks might raise their rates somewhat, but allow their total loans to expand, safe in the knowledge that their reserves were a healthily large fraction of their liabilities. When, however, the ratio of reserves to liabilities became endangered either by overliberal lending or by a drain on reserves, the banks would change their tune, raise their rates, refuse to grant new loans or extend old ones, and call in money that was out on call or short notice. The collapse of some great firm, a sudden turn in commodity prices, fear of war, or some such untoward event at home or abroad might frighten them; but whatever the cause, a reversal of policy shook the credit fabric, and drove borrowers to sell goods, bills, or stocks at whatever price they could obtain in order to repay their debts. If the scramble for money became widespread the whole house of cards might be blown over. The counsel of perfection which urges that banks should be cautious when business men are enthusiastic, and courageous when the rest of the business world is gloomy, has rarely been followed, and the banking brake has seldom been applied sufficiently early. Rather has it been applied belatedly but fiercely, throwing the passengers against a windscreen that was not shatter-proof.

Business did not operate *in vacuo* or in a world of its own making. Physical factors such as drought, flood, or famine played their part; accidental discoveries of gold or scientific discoveries of new processes or commodities exerted their influence; and political events such as revolution, war, or peace might shake the business world to its very foundation. War imposed on the productive system vast demands for special kinds of products, and left behind a distorted equipment, a fantastic price level, and a great body of creditors' claims to wealth not yet produced. At least three periods—those following 1815, 1871, and 1918—were marked by business fluctuations with post-war complications.

The Chief Fluctuations, 1750-1914.—During the sixteenth to eighteenth centuries crises were caused by commercial excesses or miscalculations, the closing of markets by war or tariff, the collapse of prices on the coming of peace, speculation in commodities, bonds, or stocks, political upheavals, famine, the repudiation of a royal debt, or the failure of a big venture. The end of the Seven Years' War in 1763 smashed war prices and played havoc with Amsterdam and Hamburg. The overstocking of the American market with cloth and hardware, followed by the non-importation resolutions of the colonists, ruined many British producers and merchants in 1773-1775. In 1793 the outbreak of war between England and France and the excesses of the canal boom wrecked many businesses, while in 1810-1811 overfond hopes led English exporters to glut the newly opened South American markets with goods that could not be sold or paid for.

The end of the Napoleonic War brought, not "Peace and Plenty," but "Peace and Beggary." Agriculture lost its high prices without shedding its high costs, and nearly twenty years elapsed before readjustment was completed. Industry lost its army orders. The continental markets were now open, and exporters poured goods into them, only to find that Europe was too poor to buy. Bad harvests, a potato famine in Ireland, the failure of banks, and the demobilization of armies all added to the chaos. Every European town had its bread lines and soup kitchens, a third of the population of munitions or textile centers was idle, and governments sought salvation behind higher tariffs, complete prohibition of imports, and ruthless suppression of expressions of discontent.

Out of this misery Europe crept after 1820, and in the west went on to the boom and crash of 1825. That collapse was due to overinvestment in home industries, speculation in commodities, and the lure of overseas trade, loans, and investments. Liberated Latin America wanted loans, its potentialities as a market were exaggerated, and vast quantities of goods were consigned there. Every mining company assured investors it had found a new Potosi; loans were raised for one non-existent republic; and diversification of investment was offered when a company was promoted to drain the Red Sea and salvage Pharaoh's chariots. In late 1825 the companies became suspect; the republics did not pay their interest, a few big bankruptcies started a panic, the notes of the private banks could not be redeemed in gold, and depression came to a country "one portion of which [had] exhibited a degree of knavery and another a degree of gullibility altogether unparalleled even in the disastrous period of the South Sea mania."

After 1830 recovery gained pace throughout western Europe. The new governments in Belgium and France, the formation of the *Zollverein*, the rise of the German wool industry, the extension of textile factories, the coming of the early railroads, the westward movement in the United States, and the expansion of the Asiatic market stimulated all kinds of enterprise. Prices of raw materials mounted, joint-stock banks multiplied, and bank notes supplied borrowers' needs. The crash came in September, 1836, when the Bank of England, faced with a drain of gold abroad, raised its rate, and when the collapse of the American boom prostrated all who had cast their bread across the Atlantic. The growing interdependence of countries and continents made the depression severe and long, for a promise of revival was wrecked by the closing of the Bank of Belgium in 1838, by the American suspension of specie payments in 1839, and by widespread bad harvests in 1839 and 1840.

After six dreary years recovery came in 1843, and a world which refused to learn anything rushed ahead again to the crash of 1847. The British railroad boom floated £250,000,000 of shares in those four years; conversion of the British national debt to a lower interest rate in 1844 stirred investors to seek higher yields elsewhere; and in Germany industry, railroads, and peasants were competing for credit. Hence a period of bad harvests in the British Isles and many parts of the continent shook rural credit, raised food prices, and rocked the whole commercial structure. The Irish potato blight of 1845 and 1846 was paralleled by the failure of rye, wheat, fruit, and potato crops in Germany. This rural tragedy and the pricking of the railroad bubble brought double disaster, and when the Bank of England tried to use a higher bank rate to draw gold back to its coffers, the effect on the cost of credit in general was unhappy.

The depression of 1847 was short-lived. Quick on its heels came the California gold discoveries, which broadened the gold base of banking and started the price level moving upward. America's railroad system grew from 9000 to 31,000 miles during the 'fifties, and much of the capital and iron was imported; Canada had only sixty-six miles of railroad in 1850 and 2000 in 1860, while Australia needed great quantities of capital and goods when gold lifted her to adolescence and colonial autonomy. In continental Europe railroad gangs were hard at work, and in Germany industrial expansion became marked. The Crédit Mobilier type of financing became popular, and in England the first installment of limited liability was granted in 1855. The Crimean War created a great demand for war supplies, and iron steamships were being built in increasing numbers. In 1857 the collapse in the value of American railroad securities shook the United States, and the crisis spread to Liverpool, to north Germany and to north Europe generally. The investment banks and their creations were affected both by the American debacle and by their own mistakes or excesses, and the crisis of 1857 was far more international in scope than most of its predecessors.

Yet the next one was almost purely national, domestic, and confined to Great Britain. It sprang from the abuses of the new financial toy, the limited liability company. Companies were floated for diverse purposes, and investment companies cropped up to find them funds. Some were overconfident, others were underethical, and most were short-lived. In them one of the oldest and most reputable firms of bill brokers and discounters, Overend and Gurney, became heavily involved; and when, on "Black Friday," May 11, 1866, it closed its doors, dismay descended on Lombard Street. "Strong men were paralysed, and rich men fancied they were poor in an hour." The Bank Charter Act was suspended and the bank rate rose to 10 per cent. Railroad troubles added to those caused by this spectacular collapse, and in 1867 it was said that the British constitution consisted of four parts—Queen, Lords, Commons, and liquidators of public companies.

Recovery was rapid, for a railroad boom in the United States and central Europe expanded the iron and steel industry. The completion of the Suez Canal led to the building of vessels for that route, the Franco-German War needed supplies, and the indemnity of $1,000,000,000 led to vast credit inflation and the promotion of countless tame or wildcat ventures in Germany. Agricultural produce was selling at profitable prices, seasons were good, and all seemed well. In 1873, however, the boom burst in Vienna, New York, and Berlin; in September of that year New York had its "Black Friday," and for two decades enterprise was beset with difficulty. The slump of 1873 lasted till 1879, improvement marked the years 1879-1882, but a new spasm of sickness filled the years 1882-1886. Four years of recovery followed, but from 1890 to 1896 lean years prevailed. When clouds cleared in one quarter a storm brewed in another; when Philadelphia got on to its feet Vienna slipped and fell; if trouble subsided in the Argentine it cropped up in Australia.

Europe's difficulties were partly those of production and price and partly those of finance. While farmers were facing new supplies of produce from Russia and the New World, manufacturers found their plants swollen to overcapacity and faced the competition of new rivals. When the railroad boom vanished, iron and steel masters could produce 2,500,000 tons of steel rails (1876), but consumption declined to about 500,000 tons, and the price of rails fell 60 per cent between 1872 and 1881. The check to demand hurt the coal industry. The expiration of Bessemer's patent and the discovery of the Gilchrist-Thomas process made steel cheap and rendered many iron plants obsolete. The industrial advance of Germany, France, the United States, and Japan ended the days of Britain's easy supremacy, and increased the area over which excessive or misdirected production could bring stagnation and destroy profitable enterprise.

The financial troubles of the 'seventies to 'nineties began with the French indemnity payment. The transfer drew much gold from Paris and London, helped Germany on to the gold standard and blew an overlarge credit bubble in Berlin, but unsettled the French and British money markets. The slump in iron and steel injured the banks interested in metallurgical industries. The demand for gold by countries that went on the gold standard revived in part the old scarcity of that metal, while the abandonment of silver and the consequent slump in the price of silver reduced the ability of India, China, and South America to pay interest or buy goods. This reduction led the South American republics to default, and brought the Barings to the edge of bankruptcy in 1890. Trouble in the Near East caused Turkey and Egypt to repudiate bonds, held chiefly by British creditors. The discovery of gold in South Africa and the French plans for a Panama Canal provoked an investment boom in 1887-1889; but the gold was slow in appearing and the canal project failed. A period of heavy capital exports to Australia and New Zealand ended disastrously in 1892-1893. A crisis in America in 1893 piled trouble higher still. Gross darkness seemed to cover the earth.

These two decades were full of gloom but devoid of any panic in London, Paris, Berlin or Vienna. When Barings tottered, the Bank of England and the other banks came to the aid of the stricken veteran, guaranteed all its liabilities, and staved off a crisis. Joint action averted minor crises on at least two other occasions, and where necessary the Bank of France came to the aid of the Bank of England. Hence trade fluctuated, but panics were averted, and after 1896 difficulties due to falling prices ended as the price curve began to climb. Fluctuations came as frequently as before, but did not last as long. The collapse of the overexpanded German electrical industry in 1901, the end of the South African War in 1902, and a bad storm in Wall Street in 1907 spread gray skies over several countries; but there was no tornado.

Post-War Fluctuations.—The end of hostilities in November, 1918, was followed by eighteen months of hectic economic energy. To the normal demand for goods was added an abnormal replacement demand, since many wares needed by civilians had been worn out and could not be replaced during the War. Devastated areas must be rebuilt, soldiers needed civilian clothes, houses were wanted, and warehouse shelves were empty. Purchasing power was great: war-time savings, soldiers' bonuses, and war profits were spent as people "had their fling" in sheer reaction and search for forgetfulness. Government spending diminished slowly, peace loans followed on the heels of war loans, and paper money rolled off the printing presses. Companies extended their plants and increased their capital, financiers bought up businesses, recapitalized them at inflated figures, and sold the shares to a public of pigeons. Banks were swept along by the jubilant stream and their loans rose high. Unemployment vanished from the victorious countries, and British wholesale prices advanced from 217 in April, 1919, to 313 a year later. In the new world born of the War, all could fiddle merrily, unless they lived on fixed incomes or in defeated countries; and the new popular music was, appropriately, jazz.

This "victory ball" ended in 1920. The speculative bubble burst in Japan, famine and rebellion descended on China, and the monsoon rains, which decided the success or failure of India's crops, were scanty. The price of silver collapsed, consumers had spent their savings, some urgent demands had been satisfied, governments began to retrench, while the Bank of England and the Federal Reserve Board decided that the credit supply had become excessive. They raised the bank rate and thus pricked the balloon. In a year British prices fell from 313 to 199, and American from 247 to 145. Profits vanished, unemployment rose to 18 per cent in Britain, capital issues ended, bankruptcy courts worked overtime, and Europe settled down to look at its post-War features. The collapse was as spectacular as the boom had been, but those continental countries which had failed to enjoy the latter did not escape the former.

Between 1920 and 1930 Europe and the world at large passed through a complete business cycle with post-war complications. The liquidation of war and the readjustment to peace was a huge task, even for countries that had been spared revolution or loss of territory. Trade channels had been blocked; some markets had become impoverished; some industries had swollen equipment and labor force; currencies were in chaos; rates of wages, interest, and taxes had found new levels; and many countries had expanded production greatly to supply their own needs or to feed markets formerly served by the belligerents.

By 1925 Europe had made a remarkable recovery in many directions. Its output of wheat, corn, rye, beet, wool, potatoes, coal, iron, and steel was near or above pre-War levels, and its production of the new goods—oil, electricity, electrical appliances, automobiles, and rayon—was mounting. Coal, shipbuilding, shipping, steel, cottons and woolens were sick from lack of buyers or from excess capacity, fierce competition, and fallen prices. Not one of Britain's staple export industries had regained its pre-War position in 1929, and two-fifths of the unemployed army of a million workers belonged to these industries. Germany's experience was similar: export markets were more easily lost than regained. Meanwhile, farmers everywhere complained that the price of their produce had fallen too near the cost of production, but that the price of the industrial goods they had to buy remained too high. But while some industries lost customers, others found new ones. In the first place, the devastated areas must be rebuilt; the supply of houses, offices, shops and public buildings must catch up with the demand; suburban "dormitories" were required for those who commuted between a city job and a semi-rural home, while roads must be made or improved to bear the growing load of motor traction. The construction industry was busy, and according to one estimate employed about 14 per cent of the industrial workers of western Europe in 1925. This construction, supplemented by the equipping of new industries and the remodeling of old ones, gave much work to the capital goods industries. In the second place, the demand for new comforts and luxuries, though less strong in Europe than in North America, was broad enough to bring new industries and service occupations into being. Hence the decline in the number of weavers, miners, and shipbuilders was more than counterbalanced by the growth of employment in virtually new occupations, ranging from the making of cars and cycles to the preservation of feminine beauty and the sale of prepared foods.

The expansion of production was encouraged by these capital and consumption needs, by the protection governments were willing to give, by the behavior of prices, and by the comparative ease with which capital could be obtained at home, in London or in New York. The stream of American capital, like the English one a century earlier, ran high to other continents till 1928, and British investors resumed their export of loans and investments, though on a smaller scale than before 1914. After falling rapidly in 1920, prices recovered somewhat and remained fairly steady (in countries with stable currencies) at 40 to 60 per cent above pre-War levels. The trend was slowly downward, but the movement was not marked enough to check production, and schemes for price maintenance helped to keep some prices at a level that encouraged producers to expand output.

The rest of the story is world history rather than European. Till 1928 production and purchase advanced at about the same pace; but hints of saturation then began to be evident, prices of foodstuffs and raw materials began to fall a little more quickly, and surplus stocks grew large enough to overshadow the market. By mid-1929 the prices of minerals were breaking, wool brought much lower prices in the auction rooms, while bumper wheat crops in 1928 and the reentry of Russia wrecked grain prices. This fall came just at a time when the flow of capital to primary producing countries was checked. London, Paris, and New York ceased to export loans, for the money could earn more in the boiling stock markets of New York and London. Hence the debtor primary producers had to pay for their imports and pay their interest bills by sending out produce that was shrinking rapidly in value and by supplementing it with gold from their bank reserves. The silver countries were also hit by a rapid fall in the price of silver.

The depression of 1929 thus began largely as a result of increasing stringency in the agricultural borrowing countries; but other factors played their part. The most urgent replacement and reequipment demands of Europe were eventually met. The flow of American capital, which had financed much reconstruction and had allowed some Europeans to pay their debts and buy goods with borrowed money, came to an end. Instead, there must now be a greater flow of payments to America, and this stream was swollen by funds going to be lent or used for speculation in stocks. Since America was not a great market for European goods, the transfer was made partly in gold. The concentration of gold in New York and Paris weakened the credit basis of many European banking systems, and forced central banks to raise their rates in order to protect reserves from depletion.

Meanwhile Europeans had been sucked into a stock and promotion boom of their own, in which borrowers as well as banks—especially the "industrial banks"—were deeply involved. In January, 1929, an Italian bank came to grief after "bulling the Bourse." A Belgian bank nearly foundered after financing an unhappy cork trust. A big Viennese bank nearly sank under the load of embarrassed firms it was carrying, and a Rothschild had to withdraw funds from New York to save it. Just at that moment (September) the arrest of a flashy British promoter for forging stock certificates upset London, sent stock prices diving down, forced the Bank to raise its rate, compelled investors to sell American stocks to get funds, drove British lenders to pull their loans out of the New York call market, and thus added one more cloud to the Manhattan horizon. Within a month the sky showed nothing but clouds; the major boom in America and the minor boom in Europe had ended. To the fall in prices of primary products was added that in the price of all salable things, but especially of those pieces of paper that had poured out of the financial mills of the electrical, oil, public utilities, and non-ferrous metal magnates.

For three years, till the summer of 1932, gloom grew relentlessly deeper in every part of the world. Wholesale price index numbers fell 30 per cent in Great Britain, 35 per cent in Germany, 40 per cent in France and Italy, and nearly 50 per cent in Holland. Primary products suffered much more severely than did manufactured articles, and a League of Nations composite index number for eight of the former fell nearly 70 per cent between 1929 and 1932. The general decline in two or three years was as great as that in any preceding two or three decades, and the shrinking pains were consequently most acute. One-fifth or a quarter of the wage earners might be out of work, but in the capital goods industries every second worker was a victim of the collapse of the great construction and equipment boom. The index number used by the League of Nations to record European industrial activity (excluding Russia) sank from 111 in 1929 to 77 in 1932, that of raw material production from 116 to 81, but that of foodstuffs production scarcely declined at all. The volume of world trade declined about a quarter, and its value about two-thirds. In every country the all-absorbing political problem was to find ways that would bring relief and lead to recovery. Ancient landmarks were swept away, the reestablished gold standards were abandoned, imports were almost throttled. The reparations problem was solved by abandoning payment, and the interallied debts were settled in the same way. Despair and distress led many to decide that this was the end of democracy and to welcome dictatorship; they led some to believe that this was the twilight of capitalism.

The boom of the nineteen-twenties was the thirteenth—and the greatest—since Waterloo. The depression that followed was the fourteenth—and the deepest. In the second half of 1932 signs appeared to prompt the hope that the worst was over. Prices, production, volume of trade and employment began to rise, were checked by the American crisis in early 1933, and then resumed their ascent. The long depression, like a severe long war, left deep scars on the body politic and economic; but only an incorrigible optimist would assert that the sight of these scars will keep the business world from eagerly embracing its fourteenth boom or precipitating its fifteenth depression. In other chapters some effects of the depression of 1929 on public policy are described.

Looking back on them, it seems apparent that many efforts of groups or of the state to maintain wages, prices, profits, and employment and to protect producers from disaster were short-sighted, futile, or even harmful. Some of them kept costs high while prices were falling, and thus made enterprise unprofitable. Some of them kept prices high while the incomes of those who would normally buy the goods fell, and thus reduced consumption. Some preserved firms which through over-capitalization, over-capacity, or inefficiency should be allowed to pass away. Some benefited one group or section (e.g., the farmer or the producer for the home market), at the expense of another (e.g., the wage earner or the exporter). It is at least arguable that partial control of economic effort is doomed to fail simply because it is partial and is exposed to the influence of the uncontrolled sections; either everything must be controlled or nothing. To control everything is a vast task, possible only in a self-sufficing autocratic collectivist (or communistic) state. To control what chiefly affects one's interests is the desire of every cartel, trade union, or other type of sectional organization; to seek state aid in furthering those interests is almost an automatic reflex action. Hence it is probably humanly impossible to leave a depression to work itself out, and the best that can be hoped for is that control of currency and credit may be in a measure successful in preventing prosperity from degenerating into a boom or in mitigating the severity of the recession.

BIBLIOGRAPHY

The literature on business fluctuations is enormous; most of it is concerned with theoretical explanations, with a little historical material. The following books are useful:

ALLEN, G. C., *The Industrial Development of Birmingham and the Black Country, 1860-1927* (1929).

BEALES, H. L., " 'The Great Depression' in Industry and Trade," in *Ec. H. R.,* October, 1934, pp. 65-75.

BEVERIDGE, W. H., *Unemployment* (1909 and 1930), chaps. 3, 4.

CLAPHAM, J. H., *Economic Development of Modern Britain,* vol. ii, chap. 9.

CLAPHAM, J. H., *Economic Development of France and Germany,* section 35.

HANSEN, A. H., *Cycles of Prosperity and Depression in the United States, Great Britain, and Germany* (1921).

HANSEN, A. H., *Business Cycle Theory: Its Development and Present Status* (1927).

HAWTREY, R. G., *Good and Bad Trade* (1913).

HEATON, H., "An Early Victorian Business Forecaster," in *Ec. Hist.,* January, 1933, pp. 553-576.

HENDERSON, W. O., "Trade Cycles in the 19th Century," in *History*, July, 1933, pp. 147-153.

HYNDMAN, H. M., *Commercial Crises of the Nineteenth Century* (1908).

LEVI, L., *History of British Commerce* (1872).

MITCHELL, W., *Business Cycles: the Problem and Its Setting* (1927).

NEWBOULD, J. T. W., "The Beginnings of the World Crisis, 1873-1896," in *Ec. Hist.*, January, 1932, pp. 425-441.

OGBURN, W. F., and JAFFÉ, W., *The Economic Development of Post-War France* (1929).

OHLIN, B., *The Course and Phases of the World Economic Depression* (1931), especially chap. 7.

PERRIS, G. H., *Industrial History of England* (1914).

ROBBINS, L., *The Great Depression* (1934).

ROSENBERG, H., *Die Weltwirtschaftskrisis von 1857-1859* (1934).

SILBERLING, N. J., "British Prices and Business Cycles, 1779-1850," in *Rev. of Econ. Statistics* (Harvard), 1923.

SOMBART, W., *Der moderne Kapitalismus*, vol. iii, chap. 35.

THORP, W. L., *Business Annals* (1926).

WELLS, D. A., *Recent Economic Changes* (1890).

Encyclopædia of the Social Sciences: Boom, Business Cycles, Conjuncture, Crises, Inflation and Deflation, Promotion, Stabilization (Economic), Unemployment.

The *Macmillan Report* (1931) and the League of Nations *World Economic Survey, 1931-1932*, describe the events leading up to 1929. The League's annual survey of *World Production and Prices* goes back to 1925, and its *Monthly Bulletin of Statistics* is valuable.

CHAPTER XXVII

INTERNATIONAL TRADE AND COMMERCIAL POLICY SINCE 1800

During the century between Waterloo and the outbreak of the War in 1914 the world's population probably doubled, but the value of its international trade grew twentyfold, from two billion to forty billion dollars. By 1929 it had climbed to sixty-nine billions, largely because of higher prices, but by 1932-1933 shrinking volume and falling prices had dragged its value down to less than twenty-five billions.[1] For the expansion of foreign trade Europe was chiefly responsible, and the exchange of goods between European countries or between them and other continents accounted for two-thirds of the trade of 1913, and 56 per cent of that of 1930. Great Britain was the largest trader; in 1913 her exports and imports comprised a sixth of the world's trade, and in 1929 a seventh. France was England's nearest rival in the early nineteenth century, but Germany advanced rapidly in every way after its union and industrialization, and in 1913 one-eighth of the world's trade touched her ports. From at least 1840 the United States increased its share, and in 1929 the total value of its foreign trade equaled that of Great Britain.

The growth of trade across frontiers increased greatly the dependence of Europeans on foreign buyers and sellers. In 1800 Great Britain could just about feed herself; but in 1914 she imported all her oil, four-fifths of her wheat, half her meat, and large fractions of her dairy produce and industrial raw materials. In return she exported at least a quarter of the goods she produced. Probably one-fifth of German production was exported, but France remained comparatively self-sufficing. Some of the smaller countries concentrated on the production of export staples,

[1] These figures obviously count every commodity twice, once as an export from one country, and once as an import into another. The total value of imports in 1929 was $35,600,000,000; the total value of exports was $33,000,000,000. The difference represents the cost of insurance and freight.

bought much abroad, and stood at the top of a list giving the value
per capita of foreign trade.

FOREIGN TRADE PER HEAD OF POPULATION, 1929

New Zealand	$334	Sweden	$158
Denmark	252	France	102
Holland	243	Germany	97
Canada	241	U.S.A.	77
Belgium	227	Italy	46
Switzerland	213	Poland	21
United Kingdom	196	U.S.S.R.	6

In the nineteenth century, as in all earlier ones, domestic trade
was by far the most important branch of commerce. It expanded
with the growth of production and population, the increasing specialization of labor, the improvement of transport facilities, and
the removal of political barriers. The domestic area was increased by such events as the union of England with Scotland
(1707) and with Ireland (1801), the establishment of the *Zollverein* (1834) and then of the German Empire (1871), the
liberation and unification of Italy, and the creation of the Austro-
Hungarian Empire.

Next in importance came trade between European countries,
and trade beyond Europe came third. Great Britain was the only
country that bought or sold more goods outside Europe than
within. In 1913 her exports were divided roughly equally among
Europe (33.5 per cent), the British Empire (37.2 per cent), and
foreign countries outside Europe (29.3 per cent). Her five best
customers were India, Germany, Australia, the United States, and
France; the five chief markets in which she bought goods were
the United States, Germany, India, France, and the Argentine.
Each list contains two European countries and three distant ones;
but if we group together the seven small countries on the continent's western fringe (Norway, Sweden, Denmark, Holland, Belgium, Spain, and Portugal) their total trade with Great Britain
would put them second on each list. Germany came second in
dependence on other continents; yet in 1913 three-fourths of her
exports went to nearby European countries and over half her
imports came from them. The rest of Europe had far less contact
with other continents. Denmark sent nine-tenths of its exports to
Great Britain, Germany, Norway and Sweden. Belgium in 1926
sold nearly 60 per cent of her exports to four neighbors, and
Holland sold 65 per cent to four. Half Finland's trade was with

Germany and Britain, while Czechoslovakia, an inland industrial country, bought or sold only 15 per cent of its goods outside Europe.

Europe's international trade can be divided into three classes: (1) exchange of tropical and semi-tropical products for those of temperate or cold zones; (2) exchange between agricultural and industrial regions; (3) exchange between industrial areas. The first class is partly intracontinental, but chiefly intercontinental. Europe could draw on its Mediterranean fringe for some semi-tropical products; but when areas with the same kind of soil and climate were settled in America and the antipodes, and when refrigeration became possible, Greece, Italy, and Spain were supplemented by California, Florida, South Africa, and Australia. There was no suitable European area big enough for growing much cotton, the Ottoman Empire was slow to seize its opportunity, and favorable conditions in the United States tied Europe to the cotton states of the south. As early as 1828 some Lancashire men saw the danger of relying mainly on one source of supply, and urged manufacturers and the British government to encourage the growth of good cheap cotton elsewhere. The American Civil War reinforced such pleas, and led to expanded cultivation in India, the West Indies, Guiana, Natal, Australia, the Ottoman Empire (especially Egypt), Brazil, and the French, Dutch, and Portuguese possessions. The yield was inferior, costly, and unsuitable for some purposes; manufacturers were glad to get back to the American supply as soon as possible; and when peace reduced prices some of the mushroom growth ended. After 1900 the American preeminence became less secure; the yield per acre decreased, and the boll weevil forced cultivators to grow plants which matured early enough to escape the pest but which produced a poorer fiber. Meanwhile cotton growing spread over other areas and cotton manufacturing developed in the Orient. In 1929 Lancashire and the southern states could bewail in unison the departure of their old supremacy, for while Asiatic mills had annexed Lancashire's low-grade trade, the world's spindles were using more cotton grown outside the United States than inside.

No other commodity from warm latitudes approached cotton in importance; but the combined demand for rice, cocoa, coffee, tea, silk, copra, cane sugar, spices, bananas, jute, palm oil, and rubber created a large volume of trade. The demand for many of these commodities was elastic, for the quantity sold depended largely on the price. Hence cheaper production and reduced ocean freights brought them within the reach of the middle classes and then of wage earners. Further, the nineteenth century developed an ever-growing need for oils and fats for dressing leather and making soap, paint, linoleum, margarine, lubricants, salad oil, cooking oil, and candles. Since the supply of animal fats was inadequate, the oilseeds of the tropics were raided. Coconuts, cotton seeds, palm kernels, and various nuts were crushed to yield oils, the refuse was made into cakes for fattening cattle, and the husks could be made into paper. Finally, the tropics yielded rubber; until 1900 the supply came solely from Brazil and the Congo, but after that date the "wild" rubber from those areas was rapidly supplanted by the "tame" product of plantations in Ceylon and the East Indies. Most of these new or expanding demands for tropical produce became acute after about 1860, and led European entrepreneurs and governments to develop a keen interest in "darkest Africa," India, the East Indies, and Oceania.

The second kind of international trade was between agricultural, forest, or mineral areas and industrial regions. The highly industrialized west drew food and raw materials from the primary producing lands of the north, east, and south, and supplemented them by drawing on the rest of the world. Apart from the tropical goods, most of the primary products that entered Europe augmented the continent's own yield, and the farm imports were largely the offspring of European plants or animals that had been exported. The Greater Europe to which white men had been migrating since 1500 had areas and climates in which European grains, fruits, and livestock could flourish. The kangaroo and the bison were of little use for export purposes, but the transplanted animals, grains, and fruits found a good home. American foodstuffs were not unknown in Europe in the eighteenth century, but their influence was seriously felt only after 1850. South American hides were being shipped to Europe by 1800, and by 1914 the Argentine had become Europe's chief beef provider. By 1818 Australian wool had appeared in London auction rooms, and in 1850 Australia, South Africa, and South America supplied two-thirds (50,000,000 lb.) of Britain's wool imports. In 1913 over half the world's wool was produced in the antipodes, and the position has not changed since. Little of the fiber was retained for domestic use; Australia, the chief producer, sent at least four-fifths of her wool clip across the equator. Great Britain took a third of her post-War exports, and continental European countries bought half of them.

In the non-ferrous metal market Europe also had to lean on the Americas, Africa, and Australia for part of its supply. Of oil Europe had enough so long as oil was needed chiefly for lamps and lubricants. When in 1873 the Nobel brothers began to exploit systematically the Baku oil field, they started a development which by 1900 was producing half the world's oil and a quarter more than the United States yield. After 1900 Baku declined, just when the car was changing the character and size of the demand. War and revolution threw the Russian industry into chaos, but the Bolsheviks restored order, and in 1932 production was nearly double that of 1900. Russia is today second, but a poor second, among world producers. Her output, supplemented by that of Roumania, Galicia, and Albania, can meet only half Europe's needs, and the continent must therefore draw on North and South America, the Dutch East Indies, Persia, and Iraq.

The third kind of international trade was that between industrial countries. The continental industrial countries were not simple facsimiles of Great Britain. They were able to make for themselves some goods that they had formerly imported, and Britain lost some markets for textiles, iron, and metal products. But among industrial nations there was a sufficient degree of specialization to make each a good customer of the others. Differences in natural resources, in labor costs, in technical knowledge, tradition, and equipment, and priority in developing a new industry or process gave the manufacturers in one country an advantage or even a virtual monopoly. Each country had its strong points: it might excel in the fabrication of high-grade consumers' goods, of articles that lasted a long time, or of wares that were "cheap and nasty," and it might be better than its rivals at making some producers' goods or semi-manufactured commodities. The French were best in silk work, in making certain woolen fabrics, and in producing perfumes and other luxury goods, but relied on other countries for steel, machinery, electrical appliances, and cheap products made on a large scale. England was best in making fine yarns or fabrics, leather, and certain machines; for a time she was ahead of others in producing cheap cottons, and she could place coal in some continental markets at a lower price than was asked for domestic coal. But Englishmen who wanted chemicals, dyes, musical instruments, and many kinds of special machines were best served by German, French, or American manufacturers. German potash, dyes, lenses, Essen steel and Solingen tools were well known outside the country, while certain German toys, crockery, trinkets, knitwear, and metal goods stood alongside Yorkshire shoddy, Birmingham hardware, American tools, and (later) Japanese cottons, cups and matches as wares of low quality and price bought by the poorer sections of the European population. Hence the exchange of industrial products among the manufacturing countries of Europe was larger than that with the agricultural countries. Germany sent three-quarters of her industrial exports to the other industrial countries; Great Britain was in 1913 her best customer, and she bought more from Great Britain than did any other country except India. Discussion of international trade in terms of rivalry, conflict, and war usually ignores such fairly important facts.

Influences on the Development of International Trade.— The volume and character of international exchange were influenced by the growth in the number of buyers, by the expansion in the quantity of goods seeking a purchaser, and by the removal (or erection) of barriers across the path between seller and buyer. Improved transportation, communication, and marketing methods reduced the physical obstacles and economic impediments, especially those of high freights and middleman's costs. The discovery of mineral deposits (such as gold), of new uses for raw materials (such as nitrates, oilseeds, and lumber), or of methods by which regions could be made more productive (e.g., through irrigation or the propagation of suitable kinds of grains) knit new areas into the commercial fabric as producers and buyers. The economies of large-scale production led to the pouring out of goods in excess of local needs, and made many European industries depend on exports for the sale of part of their wares. Long before the "law of diminishing cost of production" or of "increasing return" ceased to operate, the pile of Wedgwood ware, Lancashire cottons, or German steel was more than could be sold to domestic consumers, and the manufacturer must seek foreign buyers.

In his search he was helped by the growing accessibility of areas that had been politically barred. The American Revolution opened the front door to all countries, and made the use of the back one no longer necessary. When Napoleon drove the Portuguese royal family from Lisbon to Rio de Janeiro in 1807, direct trade with Brazil became legal; and as the Spanish American colonies established their independence during the next two decades Mexico and South America could be approached openly by foreign traders. Cuba remained Spanish, but her trade was freed from colonial restrictions in 1809, and she became a profitable market as well as producer of nearly a fifth of Europe's sugar (1830). The East India Company's monopoly ended in India in 1813 and in China in 1834. China gave the white man scant respect or privilege until her defeat in the first opium war led to the opening of five ports, the cession of Hong Kong to Britain (1842), and the fixing of the Chinese tariff at a mere 5 per cent. France and the United States quickly followed Britain's lead in claiming concessions, and the second opium war (1856) opened more ports. Two years earlier (1854) the United States had pushed open the long-closed door of Japan, and Europeans quickly slipped in. The oriental market gradually grew in importance; in 1913 India bought 13 per cent of all British exports, China and Japan bought 6 per cent, and four cotton cloths out of every ten made in Lancashire were sold in the Orient. No other European country made much impression, and China, India, and Japan took only 4 per cent of German exports; but Holland found an increasingly valuable market in her East Indian empire.

The emigration of Europeans and the export of capital promoted the outflow of goods. Between Waterloo and the end of mass emigration in the nineteen-twenties, about 55,000,000 people left Europe to make their homes in other continents; 19,000,000 of them went from the British Isles, 9,000,000 from Italy, 6,000,000 from Germany, 5,000,000 from Austria-Hungary, 4,000,000 from Spain, and about 2,000,000 from Scandinavia. The United States took 36,000,000 of them, South America nearly 10,000,000, Canada over 4,000,000, and Australasia a smaller number. These people played a large part in the rural expansion of the countries to which they went, and in increasing the demand for European goods. Eventually they helped to develop industries in their adopted lands, and thus dispensed with some imports; but Europe's sales to the United States, Canada, and Australia are larger today than they would have been if the stream of emigration had not run in such force for over a century.

With this flow of labor went a stream of capital; but in addition the white man's capital sometimes went where the white man could not, i.e., to the tropics, and some of it took a much shorter journey, from one European country to another. After 1815 London became a reservoir from which loans and investments flowed to all parts near and far. Lenders' fingers were burned in Greece, Spain, Portugal, Spanish America, and North America, but they got better, and by 1850 the amount of new investment made abroad each year was probably equal to the amount that was being made at home. The colonies, South America, and the United States attracted great sums for railroads, banking, mining, oil plantations, and public utilities. By 1930 about 3000 companies were registered in the United Kingdom but operated abroad; other companies were registered and operated abroad, and these two groups had a total capital of at least $10,000,-000,000. In addition, nearly as much had been lent to foreign and colonial governments, and the total investment overseas was about $20,000,000,000, or about a quarter of the country's national wealth. Of that sum, only about a twelfth was in Europe; the rest had gone into the political and economic development of other continents.

No other country had such a large stake abroad. France began to export capital after 1850, and by 1914 her investments were worth nearly $9,000,000,000. Little of this sum (about 10 per cent) had gone into her colonies, although she kept that field closed to foreigners; some had gone to Latin America or the United States, and the Santa Fé Railroad was virtually French property in 1914; but most of it had gone into businesses or government loans in eastern Europe. Paris was the largest market in the world for government securities; and while the French investor was given lessons in caution by the failures of the Crédit Mobilier and the Panama project, his government steered him toward public borrowers that proved almost as insecure. A quarter of his total investments in 1914 were in Russia, and much was in Turkey and Austria-Hungary. German foreign investment began after 1880, and by 1914 had reached $6,000,000,000. Holland invested much in her East Indian colonies, as did Belgium in the Congo.

The influence of these capital movements on international trade was twofold. In the first place, the outward flow was largely in the form of goods or services. Heavy investments by Europeans filled ships with cargoes of consumers' or capital goods. The investor would export goods in payment for goods imported, and ship more goods as capital exports. His annual trade statistics would show a "favorable commodity (or visible) balance of trade," and the borrowing country would have an "unfavorable" commodity balance of trade. In the second place, the payment of interest or dividends was made by the shipment of goods from the debtor country. In 1914 Germany was entitled to receive $400,000,000 from her external investments; but during and after the War she changed from a creditor to a debtor, with an obligation to pay at least as much as she formerly received. Great Britain had to sell a quarter of her foreign investments during the War to pay for supplies, but by 1929 she had recovered the lost ground, and in that year was entitled to about £230,000,000 in interest and dividends from overseas. This sum might be left abroad and invested or lent, in which case no goods would need to be sent to pay the creditor. If part of it was sent to its owner, goods would flow to the creditor country in payment of interest or profit as well as in payment for goods exported. The creditor country would thus have an "unfavorable commodity balance," not because foreigners were subtly extracting its gold or, like simpletons, were giving more than they received, but because they were paying their debts as well as paying for their purchases.

Imports of goods may represent more than payment for commodity exports, import of capital, repayment of a loan, or annual remittance of interest or profit. They may be payment for shipping or banking services, insurance premiums, remittances by emigrants to their relatives in the Old World, or tourist expenditures. In 1913 British shipping earned about £100,000,000 by carrying foreign persons or goods. Payment was made for these "invisible exports" by sending goods. When American tourists were transported, entertained, fed (and fleeced) in Europe, the host received payment in imports of goods. When a London accepting house, marine insurance broker, or bank rendered a service to persons in other continents, reward came in the form of additional imports.

When we gather together all this medley of visible and invisible items in the relations between people living in different countries, the result is a balance sheet strangely different from one that merely records the value of commodity movements. In 1913 the commodity balance of a number of countries was as follows:

	Imports of Commodities (in million $)	Exports of Commodities (in million $)	Surplus of Exports (+) or Deficit (−) (in million $)
Canada	634	432	−202
Russia	708	783	+ 75
U. S. A.	1894	2330	+436
France	1642	1327	−315
Germany	2563	2403	−160
Netherlands	1575	1239	−336
Italy	702	483	−219
U. K.	3208	2556	−652

Canada was still importing capital heavily, and had a huge surplus of imports. Russia had reached the stage where she was supplying about five rubles from her own savings for every one borrowed abroad, and her exports of interest exceeded her imports of capital. The United States had virtually ceased to import capital, and was now investing abroad; but her obligations as debtor, as patron of foreign ships, and as tourist obliged her to export a large surplus of goods each year. Italy was not an important creditor country, but her export of human beings was followed by large remittances from Italians overseas; her ships drew much revenue from foreign patrons, and her large tourist traffic supplied her with much credit abroad. France, Germany, and the Netherlands were creditors and shippers, while France, Germany and Switzerland drew much from tourists. The outstanding figure in the table is that of the United Kingdom. Since 1854 the British commodity balance has been weighted with increasing heaviness on the import side, in spite of heavy capital exports. In 1928-1929 the excess of imports was about $1,900,000,000. Against this sum the country could place the following invisible exports:

	1928–1929	1930–1931
Shipping, net income	$ 650,000,000	$ 400,000,000
Investments, net income	1,250,000,000	825,000,000
Financial and other fees, commissions, etc.	520,000,000	280,000,000
Total invisible exports	$2,420,000,000	$1,505,000,000
Less excess of imports	1,900,000,000	2,055,000,000
Balance	+$520,000,000	−$550,000,000

When all the imports had been paid for, half a billion dollars were still in hand in 1929. This was a healthy condition; but if the sale of goods abroad declined, if shipping or other earnings fell away, if debtors defaulted or dividends were not forthcoming, the plus sign might turn into a minus. The second column shows that it did so in 1931, for two years of depression reduced visible and invisible exports so much that the country was half a billion dollars short of the credits needed to pay for its imports. The deficit could be met by borrowing, by selling securities, or by exporting gold. The last method was not feasible, the others meant living on one's capital. The realization of the state into which the country's foreign trade had sunk was in part responsible for the abandonment of free trade. In France similar losses of invisible exports were felt, Germany's decline of exports rendered her unable to pay external debts or to buy much foreign supplies, while in debtor countries like Australia a fall in the value of exports made the payment of interest abroad difficult and the purchase of foreign goods almost impossible.

In trade across national boundaries, the goods that went from country A to country B were rarely identical in value with the goods B was sending to A, even when allowance had been made for invisible items. B might buy a large surplus from A, and in turn sell a large surplus to C; C might in turn have a large favorable balance with D, and so on. But somewhere along this alphabetical road would be a country or countries that sold a large surplus to the original seller, A, thus paying that country for the surplus it had sold to B. Trade did not balance "bilaterally," i.e., between two countries; it balanced multilaterally, through the sum total of all transactions and the final cancellation of visible and invisible debts and credits. When describing the services rendered by tramp ships (Chapter XXII) we followed a steamer which moved seven cargoes between thirty-one ports in six con-

tinents. It would not be fanciful to say that the West Australians
who bought the first cargo of British goods paid for it by selling
goods to eastern Australians; that they in turn paid by selling to
South Americans, who sold to Indians, who sold to Americans,
who sold to Australians, who rounded out the transactions by
sending goods to England to pay the original exporter.

Dr. Hilgerdt has recently shown how this multilateral trade
operated before 1929 to make possible the payment of the sum—

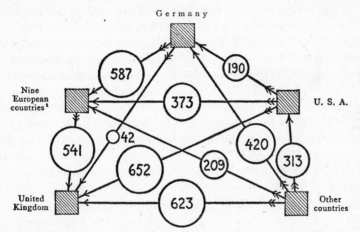

WAYS OF TRANSFER TO THE UNITED KINGDOM, AS REVEALED BY BILATERAL
TRADE BALANCES IN 1929

Excess of imports, in millions of gold dollars, of the country (or group)
shown to the left of each amount. (From F. Hilgerdt, "The Approach to Bi-
lateralism," in *Index*, August, 1935.)

nearly $1,900,000,000—due to the United Kingdom for invisible
exports. Of that amount, at least two-thirds was owed by non-
European countries, excluding the United States. Yet these countries sent to the United Kingdom only just over $600,000,000 of
goods more than they imported from her. They did, however, send
surplus exports, chiefly food and raw materials, worth nearly
$1,000,000,000 to other industrial countries, and "employed their
export surplus with the United States and the industrial countries of Continental Europe for payments to England. England
in her turn employed the currencies she thus obtained for purchases of various products, particularly industrial goods, in the
last-mentioned countries. These latter were to a considerable
extent dependent upon their export surplus with England for

their supply of foreign raw materials and foodstuffs. This system of triangular or rather multilateral trade, extending over the whole world, was one of the most important expressions of international economic interdependence" (Hilgerdt).

Commercial Policy.—International trade, like domestic, is a matter of personal or corporate buying and selling. With the exception of Russia since 1917, nations do not trade with one another as political units. Germany does not sell to England; individuals in Germany sell goods to individuals in England. The latter buy from Germans, rather than from Englishmen or Americans, because Germans are the only producers or because they produce a better or cheaper article. The Englishman gets what he wants, or he gets more value for his money, and the German sells to him rather than to his fellow countrymen because he gets more money for his value than he would by putting his wares on the German market or by not producing them at all. If producers in all countries made the same goods and offered them at the same price, there would be no international trade. They do not, because of differences in natural resources, in the supply and cost of land, labor, and capital, in the organization and equipment of production, and in the stage of economic development that has been reached.

The state may take one of two attitudes toward these differences. It may welcome them, on the ground that the greatest economic good is gained when each area specializes on that line of production for which physical and human resources fit it, and when the specialists freely exchange their cheap goods regardless of national boundaries. If in this world of free exchange one region pulls ahead of another by superior equipment, resources, or methods, the world at large benefits by the lower cost of production, and the laggard high-cost producer should either find ways to meet his rival or pass out of the picture as obsolete, just as the ox cart, canal, stagecoach, and spinning wheel did.

Against this free-trade view is opposed the protectionist policy. It has two central tenets. The first is that differences in the content of production are not permanent or preordained. No country has a monopoly of natural resources; iron ore and coal are widespread, cotton can be imported into Barcelona or Bremen as well as into Liverpool, there is no industrial skill or aptitude in working machines that cannot be acquired, and smoke will find its way out of factory chimneys just as easily on the banks of the Rhine, Dnieper, or Seine as around the Mersey. Lancashire, Lille, and Liège won a comparative economic advantage simply because they were first in the field; but any other country can do what they are doing if it has the necessary fuel and raw material and cares to make the effort. Moreover, it *should* make that effort, for a fully developed industrial equipment is necessary to national dignity, to national defense, and to national wealth. It is humiliating to depend on the foreigner for goods that could be made in the homeland; it is dangerous to depend on him for things that will be needed during a war in which he may be the enemy; and it is foolish to be satisfied with the ill-paid tasks of hewing wood and drawing water while he rakes in the vast profits of industry, commerce, and transportation. Hence new industries should be encouraged to come into being and nursed through childhood and adolescence by tariffs, bounties, or other political aids.

The second protectionist tenet is that differences in price, even in fully developed industries, should be wiped out rather than welcomed. The state cannot regard competition between one of its industries and a foreign rival as a gladiatorial contest, in which the spectators—the consumers—may callously vote "thumbs down" on the defeated native. The foot race or horse race provides a better analogy, for those whose record shows them to be especially swift are handicapped or given additional weight to carry. A native industry on which an army of farmers, capitalists, or wage earners depends must not be sunk merely because consumers can get goods cheaper elsewhere. If international trade, resting on differences in price, is harmful to vested home interests, the difference must be minimized by a tariff.

The controversies that have raged round these issues have filled European political history, as they have North American, during the last hundred and twenty years. In them economic theory has been used as a weapon by each side, but has rarely been a deciding factor. Vested interests have clamored for free trade or protection according to their circumstances and needs; and infant industries, having got their own way by crying in the nursery, have pursued the same tactics through to postgraduate days and even in the old folks' home. Consumers have rarely raised their voices, and policy has been shaped chiefly to meet the wishes of producers. Meanwhile the state, needing revenue, has found in the tariff a device that would provide a measure of protection and yet produce a substantial income if it was not raised too high.

Trends in Commercial Policy.—The French Revolution descended on a continent that was moving fitfully but surely toward greater freedom in colonial and international trade. The biggest step was the Anglo-French treaty of 1786, which admitted French wine and spirits (but not silk) more easily into British ports, and in return allowed English cottons, iron, and pottery to enter France. The British makers of these wares, eager to find markets for their expanding output, urged their government to make similar treaties with other countries; but the French manufacturers cried out that they were ruined by the cheap imports, and sent delegates to England to discover the secrets of British production. Revolution and war prevented the treaty from having a fair test, and Napoleon tried to exclude British goods from the continent with his Continental System after 1806. He did not succeed, but the war did check the movement toward easier exchange. It also gave protection to some industries, raised customs dues in order to find additional revenue, and imposed a high price level on all countries.

When peace shattered the war economy and price level, producers in every land cried for protection. English landlords and farmers clamored for the Corn Laws; a ban was placed on wheat imports so long as the price of English grain did not exceed 10/– a bushel, and a tax of 6d. per pound was levied on foreign wool. Some goods (especially silk) were still prohibited entry, some goods (especially wool and machines) could not be exported, and 1500 items on the customs list sought to provide a combination of protection and revenue. In France manufacturers and farmers secured high or higher duties in 1816, 1822, and 1826; the Napoleonic policy of keeping out enemy goods was crystallized into one of keeping out all goods by a virtually prohibitive tariff. In Russia the czar dreamed of rapid industrialization behind a high tariff wall, while Prussia tried to protect both her old industries and her war-time offspring (1818).

After 1820 the tide turned, and the next half-century saw a broadening movement toward freer trade. Great Britain led, egged on by her merchants, bankers, and manufacturers. Their arguments had already been voiced by the new industrialists before 1789. In the first place, they hoped for the opening of more

the emperor's policy, tried to cope with the crushing deficit and burden of war debt by raising the tariff. The trade treaties stood in the way, for the last of the important ones did not expire till 1877. Meanwhile industrial depression, agricultural competition, and financial need grew great, and in 1881 rates were raised somewhat. As in Germany, the agriculturists demanded more and more protection as prices continued to sink, and got it. In 1892 the whole tariff was put on a higher basis and also on a new one. Two schedules of rates were prepared—a maximum and a minimum; Germany had virtually the same plan in her "general" and "conventional" lists. By making treaty concessions to France, a country could get the benefit of the minimum rate; by fixing the maximum high enough, foreigners could be scared into granting substantial concessions; while by fixing the minimum rates high enough, a substantial protection could be granted even against favored rivals. Thus the tariff became a bargaining weapon; its use led to endless bickering, and to tariff wars when one side retaliated against the other for some real or imaginary act of discrimination. France had tariff wars with Italy and Spain, and Germany had a fierce one with Russia (1893-1894). Rates were frequently altered: France had thirty changes between 1892 and 1913.

The tariff history of Austria, Russia, and Italy ran along similar lines. Great Britain, Holland, Belgium, and Scandinavia moved slowly or stood still. In Great Britain the landed interests were politically too weak, the industrialists and wage earners too strong to permit the taxing of food and raw materials. Every depression produced some demand for "retaliation," "fair trade," or some kindred plan for hitting the countries that taxed British goods; but when a depression ended the agitation went into recess. In 1903 Joseph Chamberlain began a campaign for "tariff reform" and imperial preference. The first meant a tariff on imported manufactures, in order to protect British industry against dumping and the products of ill-paid foreign producers. The second meant a duty on imported food, with a lower rate on imperial produce than on goods from foreign countries. In return the dominions and colonies would admit British goods at preferred rates, though some enthusiasts talked of Empire Free Trade, of an Imperial *Zollverein*, with goods passing duty-free between one member of the family and the others.

This scheme was in such flat contradiction to the policy of the preceding sixty years that it threw the country into acute intellectual and emotional turmoil. Certain criticisms were made. (1) Dumping might hurt some producers but it gave other industries cheap raw material. (2) A tariff would not help British export industries. (3) A tariff on food would raise the cost of living, while a tariff on manufactures would raise the price of some goods which were the raw materials of many industries. (4) The overseas empire supplied only a third of the food and raw materials Britain imported, and bought only about a third of the exports. Preference would benefit the less at the expense of the greater. (5) The dominions, wedded to protection of their own infant industries, would give only such preference as was innocuous to their own people. These arguments were repeated and refuted during the pre-War decade; the Conservative party eventually adopted protection and preference, but the free traders (Liberals) were in power, and Labor was strongly opposed to tariffs.

Pre-War protection and encouragement were not content with tariffs, and some of the machinery of mercantilism was rebuilt. Bounties were given on some products. The building of merchant marines was fostered by exempting from duty any materials imported by shipyards, by granting lower railroad rates on goods that were to be carried on native vessels, by lending funds at low rates or free of interest for the construction of steamers, by paying Suez Canal dues, and by giving subsidies. In 1881 France began to give subsidies, and one of them in 1893 was so generous that a ship could sail around the world, carrying only ballast most of the way, and yet make a profit. Finally, obstacles could be placed in the path of rural imports by veterinary or pest control rules, and foreigners could be forced to make goods inside a country instead of outside by restricting the validity of patents.

Commercial Policy during and after the War.—In 1914 an optimistic free trader could find evidence that the protectionist tide was turning. German industrialists were wanting free trade in foodstuffs, and German farmers were demanding freer trade in manufactured wares. Farm prices were mounting and the agricultural depression had ended. In America Woodrow Wilson's election had been followed by some tariff reduction in 1913, and in Britain elections fought on the tariff issue revealed a solid mass

of free-trade orthodoxy. In comparison with the commercial policies of the post-War years, those of 1914 now look like free trade,
or at least like very moderate protection. As Professor Heckscher remarks, trade followed largely the same channels as it
would have done under free trade. The net effect of protection
on industry was probably slight. The priority of Britain and
Belgium might have checked or retarded the development of the
textile and metal industries in France, Germany, and Austria;
but in the newer industries there was no such priority, and German expansion after 1879 rested on other assets far more than
on its tariff. To agriculture the tariff may have rendered a greater
service, for it is possible that French and German farmers could
not have turned their land to meat and dairy production as easily
as did the British and Danish.

The War was partly the result of economic rivalry; its conduct
was largely dependent on the mobilization of economic resources;
and its end had far-reaching economic consequences. While it was
being waged, each side gave thought to plans that would strengthen
itself and injure the other when peace came. Germans talked of
"Middle Europe," an economic union binding the lands from
Hamburg to Constantinople. The Allies held an economic conference in Paris (1916) to consider how they could help each other
and ostracize the enemy later on. They held other less public meetings to consider how they could help themselves to the eagles'
flesh and feathers when the birds had been shot, and victory allowed them to put some of these plans into the peace treaty. The
transfer of territory at home and in the colonies, of coal, iron ore,
potash, ocean-going ships, and of personal or corporate property
was a comprehensive feat; but the imposition of heavy reparation
obligations was an impracticable demand for a sum beyond Germany's capacity to pay and the creditors' willingness to receive in
the only way possible, i.e., by a vast annual German surplus export
of goods and services.

The post-War years were so abnormal that vigorous control of
international trade was inevitable. Goods from countries with
sinking exchange rates were so cheap in lands with steady currencies that the bargains must be kept out and the home industries
"safeguarded." "Key industries" that had grown up during the
War must not be exposed to the competition of more mature foreign rivals. Industries that had been swollen by War demands

must not be allowed to shrink excessively if protection could prevent it. Unemployment, the need for revenue, and the ideal of self-sufficiency all made the building of high tariff walls popular politics. Further, there were more walls. Europe went into the war with twenty-two states, but emerged with twenty-nine, and 7000 miles of new customs walls. New-found national pride and hatred of old rulers stimulated efforts to foster industries which could never serve more than a small domestic market, or to such unnecessary tasks as the building of a Polish port, Gdynia, when Danzig was already there, available and competent.

In the general movement toward protection even the free-trade stalwarts, Holland and Great Britain, were involved. In 1915 Great Britain put duties on automobiles and other luxuries to save shipping space and husband her available dollars for buying war supplies. In 1919, partly as a token of gratitude for the part played by the dominions and colonies in the War, she granted a preference on all dutiable goods from imperial sources, e.g., on automobiles from Canada. Certain key industries (such as dye-making) and others were protected later from imports that were cheap because of depreciated currencies; but when in 1923 the government appealed to the public on a program of mild protection and preference it was heavily defeated.

By 1927 currency stability had returned, tempers had cooled, and a world economic conference in Geneva (1927) said the time had come to begin reducing or removing trade barriers. Export and import prohibitions, and the arbitrary or discriminatory practices which they allowed, had produced "deplorable results." Fifty nations agreed to do something, some trade treaties were negotiated, some prohibitions disappeared, and proposals for a "United States of Europe," for a European Economic Union, or at least for a tariff truce were discussed. The League of Nations Assembly discussed the truce in September, 1929, but the ground was shaking under its very feet, and during the next five years restraint ran riot. In every land imports were anathema, and must be reduced; but exports must be encouraged. Yet the exports one country encouraged were the imports other lands impeded, and the net result was a heavy decline in both. Action by one country provoked retaliation by others, and trade wars injured both sides. Emergency measures tended to become permanent policies, and the benefits that might be conferred on industries producing for a

domestic market were counteracted by the injury done to exporting industries.

Four main weapons were used. (1) Tariffs were raised. Some
French duties increased fourfold, and Germany's tariff rose to the
sky. Great Britain, faced with much "distress dumping" into the
one surviving free-trade market, confronted with an adverse balance of trade, and shaken by the financial crisis of 1931, deserted
free trade, and joined what has been called the International Trade
Suicide Club. In February, 1932, she imposed a tariff, ranging
from 10 per cent upward, on most imports from *foreign* countries,
but let *imperial* products enter free or at a lower rate.

(2) The actual quantity of goods to be admitted was limited
by fixing a quota. Goods that had to be sold somehow somewhere
might jump a tariff, and trade treaties might prevent rates from
being put too high. France discovered this, and in 1930-1931 her
exports fell away while importers poured goods in. She therefore
began to limit the admission of lumber and wine (August, 1931)
and within a year had over 1100 commodities on the quota list.
She might fix the total amount to be admitted, or the amount to
be sent from each country; and the quota might arbitrarily be
altered at a moment's notice. Many other countries adopted this
plan.

(3) Imports were checked by controlling the sale of foreign
exchange. If an importer could not get dollars he could not buy
American goods; if he could get no foreign bills or drafts he
could import nothing. In some countries preference was given to
the government's need for foreign exchange to pay interest
abroad; in others it was given to those who wished to import
certain goods or buy from certain countries, but other buyers
could get none. Hence it might be impossible for a German agent
to send a British or American author the royalties collected on the
sale of his works. British firms which had sent cloth or clothes to
Vienna or the Balkans could not get payment except by taking
produce and selling it in England. Some governments took this
barter to great lengths: Poland agreed to exchange coal for Bul-
garian tobacco and for liners built in Italian shipyards; Brazilian
coffee was exchanged for Roumanian oil or Ruhr coal, and in
many trade treaties each country pledged itself to buy a certain
quantity (or proportion) of its imports from the other. In an
Anglo-Russian agreement (1934) Russia promised to buy more

goods until her purchases from Great Britain nearly equaled her sales to that country.

(4) Countries which left the gold standard allowed the exchange value of their currencies to fall or deliberately pushed it down. This action was expected to stimulate exports, since it made goods cheaper to foreign buyers. If the pound sterling fell from $4.86 to $3.50, an American could buy a pair of English shoes costing £2 for $7, instead of having to pay $9.72. At the same time imports would be checked, since the English buyer who once obtained $4.86 worth of goods for twenty shillings would now have to pay nearly twenty-eight. In practice, these results were obtained in only a limited degree. Other countries made the cheap exports dearer by raising the duties on them, or kept them out by quotas. Further, if one country reduced the value of its currency, rival exporting nations did the same and perhaps did it more drastically. The dollar was devalued and brought back to about its old parity with sterling, but Japan depreciated her currency about twice as much as did America or England. Competitive currency depreciation of this type was therefore of temporary and doubtful advantage to exporters, and made the cost of necessary imports or of external debt payments much higher.

Thus the impact of depression has driven the commercial policies of most countries on to a new stage, or pushed them back to an old one, that of the seventeenth century. "From a mere tariff subsidy to aid and protect certain domestic industries, the goals aimed at have shifted to the protection of the balance of payments, the stability of the currency, and even to the more ambitious program of autarchy or self-sufficiency" (Hansen). Trade has become regimented and controlled almost as much as in war-time, and self-sufficiency has been embraced as a desirable ideal by those who cannot buy abroad what they need because they cannot sell abroad the things they have to offer. Economic disarmament has proved to be as difficult as any other kind of disarmament; in 1933 a World Economic Conference met to take steps which nearly every student of economic problems said were essential to recovery and sanity. It failed to reach agreement on a single vital point, and its agenda looked like "a mausoleum of blighted hopes." By that time the value of world trade had fallen by 65 per cent since 1929, and the volume by about 27 per cent. From these figures the pessimist could draw the conclusion that international trade was doomed to be of declining importance in world economy. He could strengthen his belief by pointing to the growing ability of the industrial scientist to make commodities formerly imported, to the erection of industrial plants in countries that were once large importers of manufactured goods, and to the decline in the migration of capital and people across frontiers. It was admittedly easier in 1933 to discern the forces working to diminish international trade than to see those which might expand it. Yet the optimist could retort that even in the greatest depression in modern history, and in spite of the multiplication of barriers, world trade showed "astounding vitality" and "marvelous tenacity." The catastrophic fall in its value was chiefly the result of the decline in prices; the actual volume, or quantum, dropped only just over a quarter. Reviving prices would blot out some of the slump in value; general recovery would make men desire, and be able to pay for, more of the foreign goods they needed. "The restless energy and initiative of private enterprise finds unsuspected outlets for foreign trade even when confronted with an intricate tangle of restrictions and barriers" (Hansen). Only the future can decide which view is right.

BIBLIOGRAPHY

ALLEN, G. C., *British Industries and Their Organisation* (1933).

ASHLEY, P., *Modern Tariff History* (1910).

ASHLEY, W. J., *The Tariff Problem* (1911).

BARNES, D. G., *History of the English Corn Laws, 1660-1846* (1930).

BENAERTS, P., *Les origines de la grande industrie allemande* (1933), chaps. 1, 2.

BIRNIE, A., *Economic History of Europe, 1760-1930* (1930), chap. 5.

BLAND, TAWNEY, and BROWN, *English Economic History: Select Documents,* section iii, pp. 689-711.

BOGARDUS, J. F., *Europe: A Geographical Survey,* chap. 9.

BOWDEN, WITT, *Industrial Society in England toward the End of the Eighteenth Century,* pp. 164-193.

BOWLEY, A. L., *England's Foreign Trade in the Nineteenth Century* (1905).

CLAPHAM, J. H., *Economic History of Modern Britain,* vol. i, chap. 12; vol. ii, chap. 6.

CLAPHAM, J. H., *Economic Development of France and Germany, 1815-1914,* sections 16, 23, 28, 29, 47, 55, 67, 78, 88.

DAWSON, W. H., *Evolution of Modern Germany,* chap. 4.

DAWSON, W. H., *Protection in Germany* (1908).

DAY, C., *History of Commerce,* chaps. 34-42.

DUNHAM, A. L., *The Anglo-French Treaty of Commerce of 1860* (1930).

FAY, C. R., *Great Britain from Adam Smith to the Present Day,* Introduction and chaps. 2-5, 7.

FAY, C. R., *Imperial Economy . . . 1600-1932* (1934).

FEIS, H., *Europe the World's Banker, 1870-1914* (1930).

HEATON, H., *The British Way to Recovery* (1934), chaps. 4-6.
HOFFMAN, R. J. S., *Great Britain and the German Trade Rivalry, 1875-1914* (1933).
HORROCKS, J. W., *A Short History of Mercantilism* (1925), chaps. 11 to end.
JENKS, L. H., *Migration of British Capital to 1875* (1927).
KEYNES, J. M., *Economic Consequences of the Peace* (1919), chaps. 1-3.
KNOWLES, L. C. A., *Industrial and Commercial Revolutions in the 19th Century in Great Britain*, part vi.
KNOWLES, L. C. A., *Economic Development in the 19th Century*, part v.
LEVASSEUR, E., *Histoire du commerce de la France de 1789 à nos jours* (1912).
LEVI, LEONE, *History of British Commerce* (1872).
LIETH, C. K., *World Minerals and World Politics* (1931).
LIST, F., *The National System of Political Economy* (Eng. trans., 1904).
MCCLURE, W., *World Prosperity as Sought through the Economic Work of the League of Nations* (1933). See table of contents.
MEREDITH, H. O., *Protection in France* (1904).
OGG, F. A., and SHARP, W. R., *Economic Development of Modern Europe*, chaps. 12-14, 16, 28.
OHLIN, B., *Interregional and International Trade* (1933).
PORTER, G. R. (ed., F. W. HIRST), *Progress of the Nation* (1912).
REES, J. F., *Short Fiscal and Financial History of England, 1815-1918* (1921).
VAUCHER, P., *Post-War France* (1934), chaps. 3, 7.
VINER, J., *Dumping* (1923).
WAGNER, A., *Agrar- und Industriestaat* (1902).

ARTICLES

DIETRICH, E. B., "French Import Quotas," in *Am. Ec. R.*, December, 1933, pp. 661-674.
DUNHAM, A. L., "The Development of the Cotton Industry in France and the Anglo-French Treaty of Commerce," in *Ec. H. R.*, January, 1928, pp. 281-307.
DUNHAM, A. L., "Government Aid to Industry in the French Economic Reforms of 1860," in *Ec. Hist.*, May, 1927, pp. 291-306.
DUNHAM, A. L., "The Attempt of President Thiers to Restore High Protection," in *J. E. B. H.*, February, 1929, pp. 302-324.
HENDERSON, W. O., "The Rise of German Industry" (review article), in *Ec. H. R.*, April, 1935, pp. 120-124.
KINDERSLEY, R., "British Overseas Investments," an annual article in *Ec. J.*, e.g., in June, 1930, 1932, and 1933.
SÉE, H., "The Normandy Chamber of Commerce and the Commercial Treaty of 1786," in *Ec. H. R.*, 1930, pp. 308-313.
SNOW, E. C., "The Relative Importance of Export Trade," in *J. Royal Stat. Soc.*, 1931, pp. 373-431.
WHITTLESEY, C. R., "Exchange Control," in *Am. Ec. R.*, December, 1932, pp. 585-604.
League of Nations: *Memorandum on International Trade and Balances of Payments, 1912-1926* (1927). Brought up to date in later years. *Review of World Trade* (Annual).
Encyclopædia of the Social Sciences: See list of titles under Commerce, Economic Policy, and Tariff, in vol. xv, pp. 549, 550, and 556.
Index (Stockholm): Consult files since 1931 for series of studies on "The World's Staples" and on recent commercial policies.
Report of the Commission of Inquiry into National Policy in International Economic Relations (University of Minnesota Press, 1934), especially Part III, by A. H. Hansen.

CHAPTER XXVIII

LABOR CONDITIONS AND REGULATION

THE three outstanding facts in the history of European labor during the last two centuries are (1) the increase in the proportion of the population engaged in industry, transportation, mining, and commerce; (2) the increase in the percentage that worked under factory conditions and depended entirely for its income on the sale of its labor, and (3) the relative and absolute growth in the number of town-dwellers.

The Distribution of Population and Occupations.—The relation between industrialization and urbanization is fairly close. In predominantly agricultural countries at least 80 per cent of the population live on the land or in villages; the remaining 20 per cent reside in the towns that run the necessary industries, transportation, commerce, government, and professional services. This distribution between town and country prevails in Russia, Roumania, Bulgaria, and other parts of "agricultural Europe." It was found in England, France, and Germany until these countries began their modern industrial expansion. Its disturbance was possible when high farming allowed a smaller proportion of cultivators to carry a bigger non-agricultural population, or when imports achieved the same purpose. In the case of Great Britain, high farming and high imports caused the most far-reaching redistribution of occupations. In 1760 agriculture employed possibly two-thirds of the population, but in 1931 only 7 per cent of the "gainfully employed" persons in England and Wales were working on the land, while 47 per cent were engaged in mining and manufacturing. Scotland came next, with 10 farmers to 47 miners or makers; but no continental country had become so neglectful of the land—even Belgium had 19 land workers to set against 46 miners or manufacturers. The trend away from agriculture was, however, general throughout northern and western Europe. In Sweden 80 per cent of the labor force worked on the land in 1800, 72 per cent in 1870, and 41 per cent in 1930. In Germany the percentage of land workers fell from 42 in 1880 to 30 in 1925. By the nineteen-twenties Scotland, Belgium, Switzerland, Holland, Austria, Germany, and England and Wales had more people mining or manufacturing than farming.

The same story is told by the change in the relative size of the rural and urban populations. Between about 1870 and 1920 the percentage of the population classified as rural fell as follows:

> In England and Wales from 38 to 21
> In Germany · " 61 to 38
> In France " 68 to 54
> In Denmark " 71 to 57

In France there was a considerable *absolute* decline, and in Germany and England a slight one in the size of the rural population during that half century. In the two latter countries urbanization was especially marked. In 1831 a quarter of the population of England and Wales lived in towns of 20,000 people or more; in 1931 two-thirds of them lived in such places. In the latter year three out of every ten Germans and four out of every ten Englishmen lived in towns of 100,000 people. In 1800 Germany had only two towns of that size—Berlin and Hamburg. In 1914 she had forty-six, of which sixteen were in the lower Rhineland. No Strauss has composed a waltz about the Lower Rhine and its grimy landscape, nor have bagpipes found a theme to do justice to the industrialization that gathered a quarter of the Scottish population into Glasgow.

The rise of the provincial industrial and commercial towns was eventually eclipsed by the expansion of the capital cities. The latter combined politics and pleasure with commerce, finance, and industry. Their very size attracted light industries that needed to be near the consumer rather than near supplies of fuel or raw material, and their position at the heart of the financial and transportation systems made them economic as well as political capitals. Since the War the influx of industry and population into them has been the outstanding feature of internal migration. By 1930 Greater London housed more than 8,000,000 people, or over a fifth of the total population of England and Wales. Greater Paris held an eighth (4,800,000) of the French people, while the Berlin area contained 4,300,000 people, of whom three-quarters had been born elsewhere.

The expansion of industry, transportation, and commerce could possibly in some cases be met by the natural increase of the local population; but where economic growth was rapid, migration or even immigration supplemented the available labor supply. Mr.

Redford has shown that in England between 1800 and 1850 there was comparatively little long-distance movement from the south and east to the north or west, but rather a series of short journeys. The growing industries and the higher wages they offered drew in people from the hinterland, the void thus created was filled by people from the ring farther out, and so forth. There was a little long-distance transfer of pauper children or their elders, but the strange brogue most commonly heard in the industrial hives of northern England and Scotland was Irish. By 1850 one-tenth of the population of some northern industrial centers and nearly one-thirtieth of the population of England and Wales was Irish-born —a fact that influenced wages, housing conditions, and public health.

In Germany the same long and short migrations were experienced, with the lands east of the Elbe playing the part of Ireland. Rural regions fed adjacent towns, but those who left the east had to travel farther afield, leaving their places to be filled by Poles. The sons of peasant families were almost as easily lured from the soil as were the children of farm laborers. France, Belgium, and Austria shared with Germany a sense of alarm at the rural exodus. In France even the countryside could not provide all the industrial labor needed, and employers had bureaus to obtain foreign workers before 1914. In that year 1,500,000 foreigners were employed, and after the War another million were added. A sixth of them were engaged in agriculture, nearly half the miners in 1927 were foreign, and in heavy metal plants twenty nationalities might be represented. French industry ranked second to American as "an epitome of world labor."

The Chief Occupational Groups.—The following table gives the percentage of the total "gainfully employed" workers in each main occupational group in the nineteen-twenties:

Country	Agri-culture	Manu-facturing	Mining	Trade	Communi-cation and Transport	Profes-sions	Personal Service
England and Wales.....	7	40	7	14	7	4.5	12
Germany....	30	38	3	12	5	4	—
France......	38	31	2	11	6	3.5	4.5
Belgium.....	19	40	7	11	8	3.5	5
Holland.....	24	36	2	12	10	6.5	—
Switzerland..	26	44	—	12	5	5.3	6
Roumania...	80	8	—	3	2	1.3	—
Russia......	87	6	6	1	2	2.3	—

The first six countries in this table are well developed industrially and commercially, while the last two join with Poland, Bulgaria, and Lithuania in having over three-fourths of their workers engaged on the land. If we add the first three columns together, we find that in England and Wales only 54 per cent of the workers were engaged in primary and secondary production, and that in the continental industrial countries 62 to 71 per cent were thus

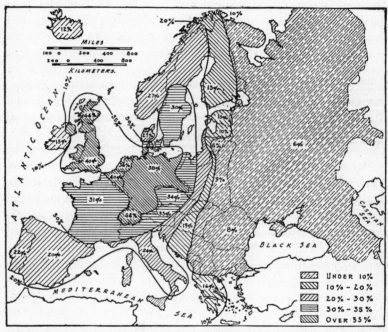

PERCENTAGE OF THE WORKING POPULATION ENGAGED IN MANUFACTURING

employed. Trade, including finance, absorbed between 10 and 14 per cent of the labor force in ten out of the twenty-four European countries, but was an insignificant form of occupation in the rural lands. Communication and transportation gave employment to between 5 and 10 per cent of the working population in the economically advanced countries, but to only 1, 2, or 3 per cent in agricultural Europe. Hence, if we add the fourth and fifth columns together, we see that in the west one worker out of every five or six was engaged in moving or marketing.

The last two columns indicate the important part played by professional and personal service. Professor Clapham has pointed out that the number of female domestic servants in England in 1830 was probably more than 50 per cent greater than that of the workers in the cotton industry. He has also reminded us that only six English cities in 1851 had populations greater than the army of "general domestic servants" employed in London homes. In 1931, 2,400,000 persons in England and Wales were engaged in "personal service"; 1,330,000 were female domestic servants. There were 750,000 professional workers who were rendering those skilled services that modern society and economic life increasingly require. The lawyer and doctor play a larger part than ever before in safeguarding life and property; but to these expanded ancient professions have been added those of the accountant, engineer, teacher, architect, and scientist, each resting on a body of skill and knowledge acquired by long training and tested by some examining board. In western Europe one worker out of about every twenty is rendering professional service of some kind.

Women's Work.—Of the "gainfully employed" in the nineteen-twenties, about three-tenths were female in England and Wales and in Germany. The transfer of some industries to the factory and the rise of new occupations affected the economic position of women in several ways. While production was domestic, mothers and daughters supplemented the agricultural or industrial labors of the men. Their sex did not exempt them from heavy and disagreeable occupations, and their earnings, where they received wages, were a scanty reward for long hours of drudgery. When the factory came it upset domestic arrangements. In the first place, it took woman's staple industrial occupation out of the home, and for a time made spinning a job done by men and children or young persons. In the second place, it eventually made weaving a woman's occupation. Women had to choose between going to the mill and neglecting their homes or staying at home and becoming economically dependent on other members of the family. For a time some refused to go or let their children go; but this hostility to the factory gradually broke down, and the mother and children might go out to work, leaving the father at home at his hand loom. Eventually men found jobs in the mill, women and young persons filled the spinning and weaving sheds, and young women often continued to work as long as they could after marriage. About 65 per cent of the labor in the British textile industry is female; in some Lancashire towns 40 per cent of the married women and 50 to 60 per cent of all the women work if they can get a job.

The rise of the ready-to-wear clothing industry offered another field to women workers, and they comprised two-thirds of the English labor force in 1931. In the preparation of tobacco they held three-fourths of the jobs, and in the pottery industry half of them. In other occupations where great physical strength was not required, where a task could be learned quickly, where semi-automatic machinery had to be fed, where standard parts were assembled by hand, where products had to be packed, or where nimble fingers were needed, women did the work as well as men did and were willing to accept lower wages. These light occupations have increased greatly in number and size during the last twenty years, and the scope for female labor has extended. In non-factory occupations—commerce, hotels, retailing, clerical work, laundries, and the like—women supplied nearly half the labor force in the post-War decade. In personal service there were four women to each man in 1931, and thrice as many stenographers as soldiers and sailors. The teaching profession was not so predominantly feminine in Great Britain as in North America, but the law, medicine, and nursing had a steadily increasing number of women practitioners. In the professions as a whole there were more women than men.

The heavy industries remained in men's hands. During the War women entered many of them, but when peace came the old conditions were quickly restored. The social structure of English agriculture keeps the farmer's wife largely to domestic duties, and in 1931 only 5 per cent of the gainfully occupied land workers were female, against over 40 per cent in France and over 50 per cent in Germany. In many other walks of life, both among wage earners and among the middle class, convention decrees that a woman shall quit her job when she marries; she works only if she must supplement her husband's income, and in 1931 only 9.7 per cent of British married women were working. Consequently the war-time belief that women would displace men has been upset by the character of the work and by the limited supply of women available. In Fascist countries women have been told their work is that of wife and mother, and have been excluded from fields that men want. In Russia, on the other hand, they have been gathered into the new industries in vast numbers, and by 1932 comprised about 30 per cent of the gainfully employed, which is about the same as in England and Wales.

Labor Conditions.—Of the 19,000,000 gainfully employed persons in England and Wales in 1931, at least 16,000,000 were dependent on the sale of their labor to some employer. Their material welfare was determined by their ability to make a sale, the price they obtained, the conditions under which they had to work to deliver their commodity, and the price they had to pay for the goods they needed as consumers. The spread of factory production introduced few new elements into labor conditions. The wage relation was already well and widely established. Long hours —twelve a day, and more in busy seasons—were general, and the chief new feature was the extension of the field over which the discipline of regular working hours prevailed. The employment of children was regarded as normal, natural, and even beneficial; and the frequent instances of maltreatment of apprentices suggest that cruelty was not absent from the craftsman's shop. The new features of child labor were the gathering of children together, the discipline of hours and of the machine, and the higher earnings. Modern industry has introduced new dangers to health, life, and limb, but has put many ancient ones to flight. It has destroyed the value of certain old types of skill, but created many more new ones. Boredom, monotonous repetition, physical strain, wet feet, poisonous fumes, low wages paid in truck, and bad housing were not invented about the same time as the mule or the puddling process. The really important innovation was the consciousness that such conditions were inhuman, and then that they were bad economics as well as bad humanics.

THE STATE REGULATION OF WORKING CONDITIONS

A basic principle of industrial capitalism is that he who takes the initiative and risks the loss of his funds shall have the control. A second principle is that labor is a commodity, to be bought by time or by the piece. From these two principles it would follow that the employer is an autocrat, whose power is limited only by the terms of the contract made with those whose labor he buys. In theory that contract is one mutually satisfactory to both sides, for while the employer need not buy, the employee need not sell unless he is satisfied with the price and conditions of sale. If labor is scarce the laborer may have ground for such satisfaction, but if it is relatively abundant the terms may be offered by the employer with a "Take it or leave it" gesture. Further, the terms may be limited by what the firm can afford to offer in the light of competitive conditions inside the industry or of trade conditions in general. The individual male adult laborer is rarely in a position to argue over the terms of the contract; the woman worker may have little bargaining power, and any suggestion that the young person or child is a free agent is grotesque. Hence in practice the employer would largely determine the conditions of purchase; but his power has been limited from two quarters—by the interference of the state and by the strength of organized labor.

The development of labor legislation began in 1802, and progressed slowly at first; but after 1850 the area of control expanded more easily, and by 1914 the leading industrial countries had comprehensive codes regulating most aspects of the labor contract. The movement did not originate in any broad economic or political philosophy; it spent its childhood in an atmosphere hostile to state control, and some of its earlier triumphs were tolerated only on the ground that they dealt with children, whose economic well-being could not be left to *laissez faire* and the play of free enterprise. The motive behind most early extensions of regulation was humanitarian.

The awakening of western Europe to a consciousness that certain things were cruel, intolerant, and inhuman was one of the most remarkable events of the late eighteenth and early nineteenth centuries. Political theory may have been partly responsible, by its stress on the rights of the individual or by Bentham's plea for the maximization of pleasure, the minimization of pain, and the greatest good for the greatest number. The work of Howard and Beccaria led to prison reform, a gradual softening of the penal code, and a more sparing use of the death sentence. In the religious field Wesleyans, Quakers, evangelical Episcopalians and, later, High Churchmen worked among the poor and gave new meaning to the brotherhood of man. In literature Mrs. Gaskell, Kingsley, Disraeli, and Dickens made people uncomfortable about economic and social conditions merely by describing them; and the agitations of Wilberforce for slave emancipation, of Owen, Oastler, and Shaftesbury for factory reform, and of others for education or public health were all indications of a new kind of social conscience.

The task of awakening this conscience was hard and results came slowly. Wilberforce was "overwhelmed for a time by the avalanche of the French Revolution and Napoleonic War, baffled by the intractable inertia of public apathy, and bewildered by the cynical hypocrisy which enables uninspired religion always to resist the Holy Ghost with a serenely good conscience" (Archbishop Temple). The reformer often overdid his denunciation, saw evils only when they were far enough away from his own personal interests, was motivated by political partisanship or personal spleen, or was consumed by an intolerance that defeated or delayed his purpose. But in the long run the community and the state came to look on labor conditions through new spectacles, and decided that some of them, no matter how venerable or profitable, should not be tolerated any longer.

Labor legislation developed by answering a series of questions. (1) Which workers were to be protected? The early answer was, "Only those who are unable to fight their own battles." This at first meant children, then young persons, and then women. Men were supposed to be strong enough to look after their own interests, as individuals, as trade unionists, and as citizens. Indirectly, however, the regulation of hours of labor for women and young persons influenced the hours of men who worked in the same industries; while laws dealing with shipping conditions, wages, the eight-hour day, workmen's compensation, social insurance, and health or safety requirements affected male labor directly. Further, the scope of protection gradually spread from factories to mines, workshops, retail stores, home workers, and even to agriculture.

(2) At what age should persons be allowed to begin work? Should females be forbidden entirely to enter certain occupations, such as mining? Once an age limit was fixed, the tendency was to raise it by stages from nine years to thirteen or fourteen, and the movement has probably not stopped yet.

(3) For what hours should work be permitted? Should night work or overtime be allowed? What statutory holidays should be provided? The answer to these questions was a gradual reduction in the length of the working day from twelve toward eight, the

prohibition of night work for women, and the provision of legal holidays or weekly days of rest.

(4) What should be done to protect the health, strength, and safety of workers? Gradually rules were framed dealing with sanitation, ventilation, the fencing of machinery, the control of dangerous or poisonous trades, and all other aspects of the working environment. As occupational diseases became better understood, protective measures became more effective.

(5) Could or should the state regulate wages? Employers and economists thundered a unanimous "No"; but since 1900 the discovery of sweating, the power of some labor groups, and the problems created by the War have led to the erection of machinery for the regulation of some wages.

(6) All the above questions referred to the person actually at work. But what happened to the worker who could not earn an income, the victim of sickness, accident, old age, or unemployment? Could he be cast aside, to depend on his savings, family, friends, or union, or to fall back on poor relief? The number of such persons was too great and the resources at their disposal were too scanty to make this method adequate. Workmen's compensation might take care of the victim of accident, but the needs of the others must be met by schemes of insurance in which employer, employee and the state participated.

In answering these questions different countries pioneered. Great Britain led in dealing with minimum age, maximum hours, and working conditions. Germany was the first to deal with insurance, and Australia led in wages regulation. International imitation was widespread. England dealt with sweating by copying wages boards from Australia, with health insurance by imitating Germany, but pioneered in unemployment insurance, and Germany copied that scheme from her. Many laws made national and compulsory the working conditions voluntarily established by the best employers. Most of the things for which factory reformers asked were already to be found in the better factories, or were urged by many employers who wished to adopt them but were prevented by the competition of their rivals. This policy of bringing backward employers up to the standards prevailing elsewhere was applied to the international field when the International Labor Organization was set up in 1919 to secure standardization of labor regulation throughout the world.

The First Stages.—The first factory act (1802) was passed to protect British pauper children who had been handed over by local poor relief authorities as apprentices to some cotton factory owners. The treatment of these paupers had often been bad when they were forced on to tradesmen or craftsmen; it was no better if they remained in the relief authority's hands, and in the early factories apprentices were at the mercy of their master or of his manager or foreman. That children of six should work twelve hours, or more in busy seasons; that a rush of orders should be met by working two shifts of twelve hours; that discipline should be enforced with fist or lash; that food and bedding should be frugal, and that fevers should sweep over mills and towns crowded with paupers and Irish—all these things were natural, but protest against them was inevitable. Hence the "Health and Morals of Apprentices Act" was passed with little opposition. Its interest lies in the things it dealt with: (1) *Sanitation*. Mill walls and ceilings must be whitewashed twice a year; ventilation and lighting must be adequate. (2) *Hours*. The working day must not exceed twelve hours, and night work must be abolished. (3) *Education*. Instruction in the three R's must be provided. (4) *Inspection*. Two visitors—one a local justice and the other a clergyman—were to inspect factories, and offending employers were to be fined.

This act achieved virtually nothing. It applied only to apprentices in cotton factories; but "free" children were now available in increasing numbers, the visitors did not do their job, and the country was too busy beating Napoleon to bother about labor problems. But here and there employers were improving working conditions of their own accord, and when peace came one of them —Robert Owen—went out to preach the cause of factory reform. Owen (1771-1858) was a Welshman who made a fortune in Scotland and lost most of it trying to plant an ideal community in America. He was the father or sponsor of nearly every modern labor movement. Cooperation, trade unionism, friendly societies, the eight-hour day, factory laws, and socialism owed much to this man who "started out to help the masses and ended by wanting to change the whole system" (Cole).

Owen's first chance came when, as son-in-law and junior partner of David Dale, he became manager of the New Lanark cotton mills in 1800. Of the 2000 workers, 500 were pauper apprentices, and many of the remainder were "addicted to theft, drunkenness, and falsehood" (Owen). For twenty-three years Owen experimented in making a model mill and a model village. He ceased taking pauper apprentices, forbade children under ten to work, and sent them to school instead. He limited hours to twelve a day, less 1¾ hours for meals. He established a store to sell food at cost, improved houses, provided medical care, and set up a sick fund and a savings bank. His plans frightened his partners, but he made profits, and New Lanark became one of the seven wonders of Britain. Visitors went to see it and sometimes to study it. Owen's influence was great even in high quarters, and his recommendations on factory reform and on other matters were given respectful attention. Then in 1817 he shattered that influence by making an attack on religion. The prestige of a great reforming business man was changed into the menace of an atheistic radical visionary. His political power faded, and the factory act for which he had fought was a pale reflection of his proposals.

That act (1819) forbade children under nine to work in cotton factories, thus introducing an age limit. "Young persons," i.e., those from nine to sixteen years, must not work more than twelve hours, i.e., a 72-hour week. In 1825 Saturday work was limited to nine hours, and in 1831 the upper age was raised to eighteen years. Thus by 1831 persons nine to eighteen years old could not legally work more than sixty-nine hours a week in cotton factories. There was no inspection worth the name, no provision dealing with women, and no regulation of any industry except cotton. But by 1831 a storm had blown up which blew *laissez faire* out of a much wider area of industry, and led to the first really effective piece of labor legislation.

The storm king was Richard Oastler. Factories had been multiplying in the Yorkshire woolen and worsted industries, and during the 'twenties many of the larger employers had not merely provided decent working conditions and limited hours but had decided that legislation was as necessary for woolen factories as for cotton. One of them interested Oastler in factory conditions. Oastler had failed in business as dealer in dyestuffs, and was now estate agent for a big landlord. He had spent much time in the anti-slavery and other agitations, and now (1830) transferred his hot temper and lurid vocabulary from owners of Negro slaves to factory slave-owners. His blistering letters to the press and his speeches demanding a ten-hour working day aroused great enthusiasm and equal resentment. Committees were formed, supported by employers, clergymen, doctors, and wage earners; and Michael Sadler persuaded parliament to appoint a committee to investigate factory conditions. It was far from being a judicial investigation, there was no cross-examination of witnesses, and much of the evidence was either suspect or at least partisan; but its general conclusion that the labor of children and young persons needed to be regulated could not be gainsaid and was supported by a royal commission which studied the matter further in 1833.

The result was the factory act of 1833. (1) It applied to cotton, wool, and linen mills, but exempted lace factories and had saving clauses for silk mills. (2) No child under nine could be employed. (3) Children between nine and thirteen years must not work more than nine hours a day or forty-eight hours a week, and must spend three hours a day in school. The beginning of compulsory education was thus embodied in a factory act. (4) Young persons (thirteen to eighteen years) must not work more than twelve hours a day or sixty-nine a week, and no one under eighteen years could work at night (after 8.30 P.M. or before 5.30 A.M.). (5) Inspection was at last effectively provided. Four factory inspectors were appointed, whose business was to enforce the act and bring offenders to court.

To pass an act was one thing, to enforce it was another. The inspectors faced a herculean task, confronted with the apathy of some parents and the hostility of some employers. Children seldom had birth certificates, and forged or bogus certificates were often presented. Factory clocks were not always reliable, schools were not everywhere available, and teachers were frequently illiterate. Fines were sometimes so light that employers escaped any real punishment. Yet the inspectors stuck to their task; the best employers supported them, fines gradually were increased, school facilities improved, the inspectors stressed the importance of safety and sanitary precautions, while the long depression from 1836 to 1842 and some improvements in machinery eased the demand for young workers and long hours. The agitation for a ten-hour day continued, and Lord Shaftesbury, who had become champion of factory reform in 1832, hammered away at the government. In 1844 children (under thirteen) were ordered to spend not more than 6½ hours in the factory and the other half day in school. Women were put under the same time limit as young persons, i.e., a maximum sixty-nine-hour week. In 1847, 1850, 1853, and 1874 the ten-hour day became the rule for young persons and women in textile mills, and since few men could work without female or juvenile aid men's work was automatically restricted.

Every step in this story had been bitterly fought by some employers. The plea of *laissez faire* soon was abandoned, for it could not be applied to children. Opponents therefore denied that factory labor was bad in itself; the work was light, the factory was healthier than other places in which children worked; the labor was productive of thrift and preferable to loafing or getting into mischief in the streets; and factory conditions were not in general as black as in those particular extreme cases over which so much fuss was made. Further, industry could not bear the cost of reduced hours; overhead costs had to be met, reserves must be built up to provide new machinery and buildings, competition was fierce, and when the employer had plowed into his business all that it needed he had not a very great margin left over. To reduce working hours by a twelfth or to impose a ten-hour day would more than wipe out that margin. The danger of competition from lands which had no labor laws was also stressed, and textile manufacturers asked why their industry should be singled out for interference while workers in other occupations remained untouched.

The employers' case cannot be dismissed as the lies of a lobby. Their enterprises were all too often skating on very thin ice; their need for fixed and operating capital was intense and incessant; the protest of the reformers was an attack of a new conscience or a new discontent on old labor conditions which many employers had endured themselves; and the motives of the reformers were not always disinterested or free from party politics. If the landlords who denounced the dirty north would look at the wages or the houses of laborers on their estates, or at the London slums and tenements from which much of their own income was drawn, they might remember a proverb about glass houses. As for Oastler and his loose tongue, he would have been invited to consult a psychiatrist if there had been any in the 'thirties.

The textile industry managed, however, to survive its tribulations. Regulation equalized competitive conditions at one important point, mechanical improvement reduced the dependence on young fingers, and after 1850 brighter days came for both capital and labor. Meanwhile other industries were subjected to similar regulation. In 1842 the foul conditions under which pauper apprentices, free children, and women were working in mines were exposed. Boys under ten, and women and girls were forbidden to work underground, and mine inspectors were appointed. In the 'sixties and 'seventies the range of regulation was extended to all kinds of factories and workshops; the employment of women and children in agricultural gangs was restricted, and the long fight to prevent the sweeping of chimneys by sending children up them ended successfully (1875). The safety of ships, passengers, and crew was guarded by providing for inspection of vessels, preventing unseaworthy ones from sailing, investigating wrecks, issuing certificates to officers, and marking a line on the side of the ship (the Plimsoll line) to limit the amount of cargo that could be loaded (1876). The minimum age for beginning work was supplemented by a minimum age for leaving school, and the joint result was that work could not begin till the twelfth to fourteenth birthday. Health and safety precautions were imposed by legislation or by local sanitary rules. Industries which were exposed to special danger from fumes or the handling of poisons (e.g., potteries, lead works, paint factories, and match factories) were subjected to laws or to orders prepared by government experts after 1900. By that year the country's biggest occupation, retail trading, had become subject to regulation, by limiting the hours that employees could work, and by demanding a weekly half-holiday. Outworkers, the survivors of the putting-out system, received attention in 1891. Their homes were to be inspected by the local health officer, and they were to be given detailed "particulars" of the work to be done and the rate of pay.

In most of this legislative advance the interests of women, young persons, and children were paramount, but after 1900 the state began to respond to pleas for aid to male adults. In 1908 the eight-hour day was imposed on coal mining. In 1912 the miners gained another point by securing the imposition of a legal minimum wage on the industry. While the state thus granted the wishes of the strongest group of wage earners in the kingdom, it protected the weakest by establishing "trade boards" to fix minimum wages for sweated industries (1909). It also took up the task of insurance against sickness and unemployment (1911-1912).

Continental Factory Legislation.—France and Germany followed Britain's example in framing factory laws. France in 1841 limited children's hours to eight, and young persons' to twelve; in 1848 she passed a general twelve-hour act for all workers, but as she provided no inspectors till 1874 the early laws had little effect. In 1906 a Ministry of Labor was established, and a labor code began to be framed; but a weekly day of rest was still far from universal and a half-holiday on Saturday was rare. After the War the eight-hour day became widespread, compensation for accident or industrial disease was improved, and minimum wage provisions appeared. Prussia studied child labor conditions in 1818 and 1832, passed a law to protect children and young persons in 1839, and provided inspectors in 1853; but there, as in other German states, the laws were ineffective. When the empire came, Bismarck was indifferent or hostile to labor legislation; he disliked compulsion and prohibition, hated the Social Democrats who were advocating effective control, and believed that other things were more important. Hence little was done till 1891, when an industrial code was framed. It ran along familiar British lines, and was frequently amended or supplemented by law or by administrative decree. After the revolution of 1918 an eight-hour law was passed. In other countries the rise of factories led to similar legislative or administrative action.

Industrial Insurance.—The chief continental contribution to the worker's welfare was the development of compulsory insurance. Imperial Germany had its Marxian socialists, whose growing strength and talk of an impending social revolution worried Bismarck. It also had its "state socialists," many of them university professors, who urged the extension of state activity for the amelioration of the wage-earner's lot. This policy was far closer to the German concept of statesmanship than was *laissez faire,* and Bismarck accepted it, refusing to be scared by the charge that it was socialistic. He was also wise enough to see that tangible tokens of state solicitude might wean the laboring class from the Social Democrats. That solicitude should deal less with the conditions under which men worked, and more with the dread insecurity of work and income that hung like Damocles' sword over the wage earner. The wise and valuable policy was to provide insurance.

Insurance against loss of income was part of the policy of some friendly societies and trade unions. Bismarck extended such voluntary efforts into a nation-wide scheme, based on two principles: (1) All workmen in certain trades must be compelled to insure themselves. (2) All parties must contribute to the premiums; the funds must be built up by payments from the employer, the employee, and in some cases from the state. These principles were first translated into a sickness insurance plan, which began in 1883 with 10 per cent of the total population, but was extended till in 1926 it covered a third (21,000,000 workers). In 1925 it was expanded to cover the worker's family dependents and the middle class as well, thus embracing 60 per cent of the population. Contributions amounted to about 2 per cent of wages, of which the employer paid two-thirds. When a worker fell sick, he received free medical attention and medicine, and half to three-fourths of his wages for six months. Gradually other benefits were added, such as X-ray or dental work, hospital care, maternity benefits for workers' wives, and treatment for rickets, tuberculosis, etc. The extension to the whole family was accompanied by increasing attention to preventive work, and to raising the general level of working-class health. In 1929 the total cost of the scheme was about $415,000,000.

Accident insurance was established in 1884 as a better method than workmen's compensation. All premiums were paid by the employer; but for the first thirteen weeks a victim of accident was technically a "sick person," drawing on the sickness fund. After that period he drew on the accident fund as long as he was disabled; if he was permanently totally helpless he obtained full wages, and if he was killed his dependents received a pension up to three-fifths of his wages. These liabilities induced employers to take great care to prevent accidents. Old age and invalidity insurance came in 1888. Employer and employee paid equal premiums, and the state added something. If a person became unable, through illness, to earn more than a third of the usual wage he was classified as an invalid; otherwise he began to draw old age benefits at seventy. Actually most people became eligible before they reached three score and ten.

Germany never regretted these schemes, and frequently extended or improved them. They put a bottom to poverty—except that which came from unemployment. The sickness scheme was widely copied abroad, and by 1930 twenty-five countries had compulsory systems, while fifteen had voluntary ones. In Austria 75 per cent of the employees and 34 per cent of the whole population were compulsorily covered, and in Denmark 45 per cent of the population were participants in a voluntary scheme. Great Britain in 1911 embraced the plan, and, by 1928, 15,000,000 workers (nearly nine-tenths of the employed class and a third of the total population) were assured of medical attention and some income while absent from work because of sickness.

Unemployment was a hazard to be met in two ways: by helping the workless man to find a job and giving him support till he did. In 1883 an employment exchange was set up privately in Berlin, to which masters and men could resort, and the depression of 1893 led to the establishment of many public and private exchanges. A nation-wide scheme was gradually evolved, which filled over 6,000,000 vacancies in 1929. Great Britain established labor exchanges in 1909, which in 1929 filled 5000 jobs a day. Meanwhile the second method of meeting unemployment was tried in a small way by trade unions. In Ghent, Cologne, Berlin, Switzerland, and elsewhere municipalities or other local bodies supplemented the payments made by the unions or other voluntary bodies. The really important step, however, was taken when in 1911 Great Britain began a compulsory insurance scheme for seven occupations and 2,250,000 workers. In 1916, 1,250,000 women munition workers were added, and in 1920 the range was extended to include all employees except those in agriculture, domestic work, the civil service, and the higher clerical ranks. By 1930 nearly 12,000,000 workers were insured.

The original plan was a modest and cautious insurance contract which applied to some capital goods industries whose employment cycle was fairly well known. The employee paid five cents a week, the employer paid the same, and the state added three cents. When a man had paid dues for a certain time, he became eligible to draw 7/- ($1.75) a week for fifteen weeks in one year. He obtained the money at the labor exchange, and the exchange could test the genuineness of his condition by offering him any suitable job it had on its books. This plan would have proved actuarially sound and capable of extension if pre-War conditions had persisted; but post-War circumstances led to extension into dangerous fields, and some of the original industries, especially shipbuilding, became unusually subject to depression. The benefits were made more generous, the act was amended fourteen times between 1920 and 1927, and the scheme was converted into a plan to relieve heavy unemployment out of levies imposed on employers and those who were at work. In the post-War decade $2,500,000,000 was paid to some 20,000,000 beneficiaries; the contributions were insufficient to meet even pre-depression needs, and in 1928 the fund was $125,000,000 in debt. By 1931 the debt had risen to nearly $600,000,000.

Critics pointed out the danger of shifting from benefits based on a contract to relief based on status, and felt that the effect would be to prevent governments, employers, and unions from attacking the causes of unemployment. Mr. Clay suggests that the system was partly responsible for maintaining wages at too high a level, since trade unions no longer had to support their unemployed and hence resisted any reduction of wages to rates at which employment could be given. The abuses and shortcomings of the scheme did not, however, destroy its central merit. Some sort of provision had to be made to cope with post-War unemployment, and insurance was more efficacious than any scheme improvised in an emergency or based on charity.

Other countries—Italy, Austria, Poland, and Germany—adopted insurance plans based on the British pattern. The German scheme of 1927 tried to avoid some of England's mistakes, emphasized the search for work, and recognized that insurance could not take care of all. By February, 1929, 17,000,000 workers were covered, but there was no time to build up much reserve before hard times came. During four years a deficit of $365,000,000 accumulated, and the rate of contributions was increased from 3 to 3½ per cent of wages. In 1931 the government refused to carry any heavier load, and virtually abandoned the insurance aspect of the scheme. British and German experience suggest that in a deep depression no insurance plan can cope with the whole problem without substantial aid from the public purse.

Industrial Fatigue.—The motive behind early factory reform was humanitarian or political. Factory laws placed human welfare above profits. By 1900, however, there was some recognition that output was not strictly proportionate to the length of the working day, and some study of industrial fatigue had been made. American efficiency experts experimented, and in Germany Ernst

Abbe noticed that his reduction of working hours from nine to eight in the Zeiss optical works at Jena was followed by an increase in output. During the early stages of the War production had to be expanded, and the factory laws of every country were suspended. The results on the work and the worker were disastrous, and in Great Britain especially the factors that influence output began to be studied seriously.

The conclusions reached by such studies have shown that shorter hours, sanitary and safe conditions, and most other items of factory legislation were not merely good for the worker but good for the employer. Industrial fatigue reduces the quantity and quality of the product, causes spoiled work and damage to tools or machines, is responsible for many accidents and much sickness, rouses a feeling of staleness and resentfulness, and thus provokes industrial unrest. Once this many-sided relationship was recognized, many questions cropped up. What was the optimum working day? The evidence, though far from exhaustive, certainly showed that a 48-hour week was more productive than one of 55 or 60 hours, and that in heavy manual tasks hourly output increased with a still shorter week. Long working periods, say of four or five hours, were found to be too long, and needed to be broken by a rest pause. Light, ventilation, dust, fumes, the provision of seats and of facilities for obtaining proper meals—all influenced the operation and output of the plant. Such discoveries provided a basis for further legislation, and gave employers certain guiding principles on which they could formulate labor policies far in advance of the minimum conditions required by law.

International Aspects of Labor Legislation.—Almost every proposal for industrial legislation encountered the objection that it would harass native industries in competition with lands that had backward labor laws or none at all. As early as 1850 Daniel Le Grand, a Swiss factory reformer, was urging governments to take common action, but without avail. In 1890 an international convention at Berlin approved a few simple proposals, such as the non-employment of children in mines. A similar convention at Berne in 1905-1906 recommended that the use of phosphorus for making matches be restricted, since it attacked the bones and produced a disease known as "phossy jaw." Beyond this, little was accomplished. The War gave an opportunity for more ambitious effort. It is hard today to recapture the enthusiastic belief that from the conflict would emerge not merely a better international order but also a better social order. The war to end war was also to end social injustice. While the peasants were stirred by being promised land, wage earners were urged to intensify their efforts by promises of better working conditions and rewards.

The fulfillment of these promises (and the fear of the specter in Russia) led to the inclusion in the Covenant of the League of Nations of a pledge that all members would "endeavour to secure and maintain fair and humane conditions of labour for men, women and children . . . and for that purpose will establish and maintain the necessary international organizations." Part XIII of the Treaty of Versailles created the organization and stated the two principles that were to guide its work. (1) "Universal peace . . . can be established only if it is based upon social justice"; but conditions exist involving "such injustice, hardship, and privation to large numbers of people as to produce unrest so great that the peace and harmony of the world are imperiled." (2) "The failure of any nation to adopt humane conditions of labour is an obstacle in the way of other countries which desire to improve the conditions in their own countries." The desirable objectives and essentials of social justice included the living wage, the eight-hour day, the abolition of child labor, the restriction of work by young persons and women, the payment to men and women of "equal remuneration for work of equal value," and the right of workers to form associations. "Labour should not be regarded merely as an article of commerce."

To obtain these objectives was the task of the International Labor Organization. All members of the League were automatically members of the Organization, and other countries could join if they wished. The Organization consisted of an International Labor Office and an annual conference. To the conference each country sent a delegation representing the government, employers, and wage earners. Various aspects of labor regulation were discussed, and any draft convention or recommendation that was approved by two-thirds of the conference was forwarded to the member governments. They in turn were pledged to submit the proposal to the "competent legislative authority," i.e., usually to parliament. The "authority" could accept or reject as it thought best; it was under no compulsion except that of considering the recommendations made by the majority at the conference.

The first conference was held at Washington in 1919, the second at Genoa in 1920, and the later ones met at Geneva, where the Office has become an efficient bureau of research and information on every aspect of labor problems. The Washington conference did more in a month than had been achieved in thirty years, for the delegates agreed on proposals bearing on hours of labor, unemployment, night work, child labor, and many other topics. Genoa examined problems of employment on ships, and the Geneva meetings have dealt with a wide range of subjects. By 1935 seventy draft conventions or recommendations had been made, and about 650 ratifications had been made by different countries. The net effect has not been great on the countries with advanced labor laws, but backward lands have been brought far forward. The new states have been provided with laws ready made, and the leveling up of industrial legislation has been substantial. Freedom to associate in trade unions has spread in some regions, but has been impaired in lands that have succumbed to dictatorship. Hours of labor have tended toward the eight-hour day in Europe, and have been subjected to control and reduction in Asia. Provisions for health, accident prevention, unemployment, and factory inspection have become much more thorough, while the continuous work of the Office provides a clearing house, a searchlight, and a stimulant. The living wage, "equal pay for equal work," and many other objectives that seemed just around the corner in 1919 are still there; but if international action has failed to do some things its friends hoped for, it has done more than its enemies wished, and has given large sections of Europe's working population a protection undreamed of two decades ago.

BIBLIOGRAPHY

Birnie, A., *Economic History of Europe, 1760-1930*, chaps. 12, 14.

Beveridge, W. H., *The Past and Present of Unemployment Insurance* (1930).

Bland, Tawney, and Brown, *English Economic History: Select Documents*, pp. 502-524, 571-618.

Carr-Saunders, A. M., and Wilson, P. A., *The Professions* (1933).

Carroll, M. R., *Unemployment Insurance in Germany* (1929).

Clapham, J. H., *Economic History of Modern Britain*, vol. i, chaps. 8, 14; vol. ii, chaps. 10, 11.

Clapham, J. H., *Economic Development of France and Germany, 1815-1914*, sections 17, 49, 68, 69, 79, 80, 81.

Cole, G. D. H., *Robert Owen* (1925).

Day, C., *The Distribution of Industrial Occupations in England, 1841-1861* (1927).

FAY, C. R., *Great Britain from Adam Smith to the Present Day,* chaps. 16, 17.

FLORENCE, P. S., *Economics of Fatigue and Unrest* (1924).

GOLDMANN, F., and GROTJOHN, A., *Benefits of the German Sickness Insurance System* (1928).

HAMMOND, J. L. and B., *The Town Labourer* (1917); *The Skilled Labourer* (1920); *The Age of the Chartists* (1930); *Lord Shaftesbury* (1923).

HILL, A. C. C., and LUBIN, I., *The British Attack on Unemployment* (1934), parts iii, iv.

HUTCHINS, B. L., and HARRISON, A., *History of Factory Legislation* (1911).

JOHNSTON, G. A., *International Social Progress* (1924).

OGG, F. A., and SHARP, W. R., *Economic Development of Modern Europe,* chaps. 17, 18, 24, 25, 29.

PINCHBECK, I., *Women Workers and the Industrial Revolution* (1930).

REDFORD, A., *Labour Migration in England, 1800-1850* (1926).

SPATES, T. G., and RABINOVITCH, A. S., *Unemployment Insurance in Switzerland* (1933).

VERNON, H. M., *Industrial Fatigue and Efficiency* (1921).

WEBER, A. F., *The Growth of Cities in the 19th Century* (1899).

WILLIAMS, H. (ed.), *Man and the Machine* (1934).

The Treaty of Versailles, part xiii.

ARTICLES

DERRY, T. K., "Repeal of the Apprenticeship Clauses of the Statute of Apprentices," in *Ec. H. R.,* January, 1931, pp. 67-87.

FLORENCE, P. S., "The Theory of Women's Wages," in *Ec. J.,* March, 1931, pp. 19-37.

GREGORY, T. E., "Rationalization and Technological Unemployment," in *Ec. J.,* December, 1930, pp. 551-567.

OUALID, W., "Foreign Workers in France," in *Int. Lab. Rev.,* August, 1929, pp. 161-184.

RENOLD, C. G., "The Present Position of Skill in Industry," in *Ec. J.,* December, 1928, pp. 593-604.

SHANNON, H. A., "Migration and the Growth of London, 1841-1891," in *Ec. H. R.,* April, 1935, pp. 79-86.

WARD, G., "The Education of Factory Child Workers," in *Ec. Hist.,* February, 1935, pp. 110-124.

Unsigned, "The Number of Women in Agriculture in Germany, France, and Czechoslovakia," in *Int. Lab. Rev.,* July, 1929, pp. 84-95.

Encyclopædia of the Social Sciences: See list of articles on Labor and Industry in vol. xv, pp. 551 and 552.

Students who have access to the publications of the International Labor Office will find there a mine of information. See especially the *International Labor Review* (monthly), *Industrial and Labor Information* (weekly), and the numerous special reports and studies. The *Labour Gazette* (British), *Monthly Labor Review* (U. S. Bureau of Labor Statistics), and Canadian *Labor Gazette* contain much European news on labor affairs.

CHAPTER XXIX

THE LABOR MOVEMENT

WHILE the state built some defenses around labor, wage earners built some for themselves, and in the trade union and cooperative movements revealed a capacity for voluntary association which rivaled that of the medieval guildsmen. The trade union sought to protect the worker in his capacity as earner; co-operation served him as spender, and when unionism joined forces with socialist groups, or built up a party of its own, the labor movement ran on three wheels—unionism, cooperation, and politics.

The associations formed to guard and improve working conditions or wages during the later Middle Ages and in subsequent centuries had two features in common with the modern movement. In the first place, they usually consisted of skilled workers—printers, tailors, cloth-dressers, wool-combers, cutlers, or ship-wrights. All through the nineteenth century unionism was strongest among the skilled crafts. The organization of semi-skilled, unskilled, casual, or women workers was difficult, came late, and has been least successful. The newer industries which use much automatic machinery and can quickly train workers are almost as weakly organized in Europe as in Detroit. In the second place, labor organizations had to face the hostility of employers and of the law. Common or statute law banned their existence or their activities in England till 1824, and when they ceased to be illegal they did not become legal persons, while their actions might still be illegal. Fifty years more elapsed before they became legal entities, and even in 1909 the courts were denying their right to do certain things. In other countries legal impediments lasted longer still, and the close connection between unionists and socialists tended to bring to the former some of the hatred bestowed on the latter. Freedom of association was still far from complete in some countries in 1914.

Apart from its legal aspect, the story of trade unionism is that of seeking the best type of organization, of winning and keeping members, of formulating aims, of confronting employers, of securing recognition by them, and of developing strategy and tactics. The central aim was to replace individual bargaining between workman and employer by collective bargaining, and to obtain standard wage rates, standard hours, and standard conditions which would prevent one worker from undercutting his fellow by offering to sell his labor more cheaply. In the last resort this aim might have to be sought by refusing to sell any labor—a strike; or the employer might refuse to buy any—a lockout. Gradually, however, recognition paved the way to peaceful negotiation, to conciliation and arbitration; the last resort became more remote, and was reached only after protracted efforts failed to reach agreement. The cost of industrial warfare and the injury done to the country at large induced governments to foster conciliation and arbitration or, by passing a law, to settle the dispute. When unions became politically minded and powerful, legislation might be influenced by their programs or by the need for their votes. In England the program combined various economic, social, or political reform proposals with hopes of a gradual approach to a socialist state. On the continent the language was more revolutionary, but the accomplishment was only reformist until Russia put talk to the test.

Trade Unionism in Great Britain.—By 1800 many skilled workers were accustomed to joint action and even to membership in a formal organization. Sometimes workers came together to resist an attack on their wages or hours, or to demand an improvement, and dispersed when the dispute was over; but some trades had elaborate organizations, which started as friendly societies to help the sick or unemployed, but soon began to look after the employed. The wool-combers enforced a claim for a minimum wage and refused to work with non-unionists. The cloth-finishers forbade the employment of "snakes" (non-members), fixed a maximum age at which apprentices could be indentured, and were strong enough to command the respect of their employers. The member of a union in one part of the country was welcomed and looked after by the kindred group in other areas if he went seeking work, and a national sense of craft solidarity was thus fostered.

The last decade of the eighteenth century saw a great increase in organized activity. The men employed in the rapidly growing cotton industry formed societies, the miners were grouping, cloth-finishers were protesting against machines, and various workers were seeking the enforcement of the apprenticeship law to check the spread of the factory system. High prices, war strain, and revolutionary ideas ruffled the waters, and manufacturers or politicians suspected a Jacobin was behind every bush. Hence the Combination Laws of 1799 and 1800 made general the special laws passed in earlier decades; they forbade combinations to raise wages, reduce hours, organize a strike, or restrain employer or employee from doing as he wished. They were followed by the suspension and then the repeal of the laws regarding apprenticeship and wage regulation, and the wage earner was thus left defenseless by the state, yet forbidden to defend himself.

The Combination Laws achieved little. There were some prosecutions under them or under the common law, but unions continued to grow, even if they had to grow underground. Masters either did not dare or did not wish to attack them, and collective bargaining continued more or less openly. In 1824 a parliamentary inquiry reported that the Laws had not merely been ineffective in preventing unions of employers or of employees, but had tended to produce mutual irritation and distrust, to give a violent character to unions and thus to render them highly dangerous to the peace of the community. Persecution could not kill a necessity. This report, coming at a time when war hysteria had subsided and when coercion and restraint were being discarded in other directions, led to the repeal of the Laws (1824). The result was an outburst of organizing activity and a series of strikes, for trade was booming and wage earners wished to make up for lost time. Frightened by this new birth of freedom, Parliament in 1825 said that combinations were not illegal, but that any act of violence, threat, intimidation, or force was a penal offense. Unions could live, but must walk circumspectly.

During the next decade labor used its modified freedom vigorously. The period was full of agitation over Catholic emancipation, parliamentary reform, factory acts, the Corn Laws, the Poor Law, and other issues; Owen was describing his utopian socialist dreams, and workers wished to regain the wages lost during the depression that came in 1825. Local unions of mechanics, builders, miners, spinners, or other skilled workers sprang up; some of them joined hands on a national basis, and in 1833-1834 Owen built up his Grand National Consolidated Trades

Union. In it he sought to gather all kinds of workers and groups. Male and female, skilled and unskilled, rural and urban workers would form a mighty army that would demand an eight-hour day and then proceed to transform capitalism into some sort of cooperative commonwealth. The movement was aggressive, for the ten-hour agitation had sharpened the wage-earner's temper and tongue; but a series of strikes and lockouts broke it, and employers retaliated by refusing to employ any unionists. A group of farm laborers at Tolpuddle (Dorsetshire) was arrested in 1834 and sent to Australia for having taken secret union oaths (in violation of an old law passed at the time of a naval mutiny in 1797); and the beginning of the long depression in 1836 completed the wreckage of the grandiose schemes of the early 'thirties. Some of the local unions survived as small groups of craftsmen, and in 1851 some of these provided what became known as the New Model for labor organization.

That New Model was the Amalgamated Society of Engineers (A.S.E.), a fusion of local and sectional societies of engineers, machinists, blacksmiths, and kindred metal workers. It limited its membership to certain skilled and properly trained craftsmen. Its constitution concentrated control in the hands of the central body in London and imposed strict discipline on the branches, especially in such matters as starting a strike. Its permanent officials were skilled administrators rather than fiery enthusiasts, whose business was to develop collective bargaining and settle disputes peacefully wherever possible. It welcomed publicity, avoided the fantastic secret society ritual of some of its predecessors, and set out to destroy the bourgeois distrust of unionism by letting all see that it had no wild revolutionary or subversive aims. Finally, it was a friendly society as well as a trade union. Its members paid large dues, and in return received aid in time of sickness, unemployment, or old age as well as when they were on strike. This aid kept members loyal and solid.

The New Model worked well, and other skilled trades copied it. Between 1851 and 1890 the fourteen largest unions disbursed nearly £8,000,000 in benefits. About half this money went to help unemployed members, and nearly a quarter went to the sick; 8 per cent was spent on giving members a decent funeral, and only 6 per cent (£460,000) was strike pay. Unionism had evidently found the right track, with cautious leaders, a conciliatory policy, and loyal disciplined members. In the 'sixties the legal position became obscured by the courts, but seemed to be cleared up by acts of 1867 to 1876. Under these laws unions could register, and thus buy, hold, and protect property. The right to strike was assured, strikers could peacefully persuade others to leave their work, and no action taken by a union was to be illegal unless it would be illegal if committed by an individual. Further, the union was a registered body, but not a corporation. Its funds could not be called on to pay for any damage or loss of trade caused by a strike. This immunity was shattered in 1901 when the Taff Vale Railway Company sued the union to which its striking employees belonged, and was granted £23,000 for damage done when 208 men left their jobs without giving notice. In 1906, however, the Trade Disputes Act repaired the rent in union immunity, and said that unions could not be sued for breaches of contract or "tortious acts" committed in the course of a labor dispute.

Collective Bargaining.—The first task of a union was to gain recognition and to get an employer (or group of employers) to deal with the union through its representative rather than with his men as a separate group or as individuals. Recognition came slowly; in the 'thirties, the 'fifties, and even later some employers demanded that their men sign a document swearing they were not and would not become unionists. When recognition came, the way was open for peaceful discussion of disputes, and in 1860 the Nottingham hosiery trade established a conciliation board. On it sat an equal number of representatives of each side, and if it failed to reach agreement an arbitrator was called in. Below it were district and factory subcommittees, who settled most matters without bothering the central body. During the discussions work continued undisturbed; but if in the last resort the arbitrator's award was unsatisfactory to either side, a strike or lockout was permissible.

The Nottingham plan or something akin to it was widely copied, and most large industries established permanent machinery and methods of procedure for dealing with disputes or with matters that might lead to disputes. Acts of 1896 and 1908 gave the Board of Trade power to arbitrate or appoint a conciliation board if asked to do so by conflicting parties, or to mediate between disputants if it saw a chance of bringing a quarrel to an end. Between 1900 and 1909, 7500 disputes—750 a year—came before

the 300 boards or standing joint committees. Only 104—ten a
year—went away unsettled, to cause a stoppage of work. These
figures suggested that the day of industrial warfare was passing;
but the years 1911-1913 belied the hope, for war in the mining,
transport, and other industries shook the economic life of the
country, and a scheme was hatched for a "Triple Alliance" of
miners, railroadmen, and water transport workers, binding 1,350,-
000 workers together (1914). Peace was evidently leaving the
industrial front before it left the international. Yet, in 1911, 4500
disputes went to conciliation or arbitration, and only thirteen of
them led eventually to a stoppage of work.

The Spread of Unionism.—After 1890 unionism spread from
the skilled crafts both upward and downward. In 1888 the ill-paid
girls in a London match factory struck successfully. In 1889 ten
thousand dock workers paralyzed the port of London for five
weeks, attracted world-wide support in their claim for sixpence
an hour, and won a great victory. These successes contradicted
the belief that unskilled or casual workers were incapable of
organization. At the same time the "black-coat brigade"—teachers, clerks, shop-workers, civil servants, musicians, and actors—
began to realize that preservation and improvement of their standard of living could be guaranteed only by united action. Between
1892 and 1913 the membership of British unions rose from
1,576,000 to 4,135,000.

This broadening of membership was accompanied by a widen-
ing of policy and methods. The new unions could not collect high
dues from ill-paid workers, could not undertake friendly society
work, but must concentrate on improving labor conditions. Some
of their leaders were soaked in the ideas of Henry George, William Morris, John Ruskin, or even of Karl Marx, for the British
social conscience was being stirred again as it had been in the
'twenties and 'thirties. This time the range of its disquietude was
wider than Negro, factory, chimney, or mine slaves; it took in
the whole economic and social system, and especially that part of
it which condemned possibly a third of the population to live
below a meager poverty line. Young intellectuals had formed the
Fabian Society (1884) and were seeking ways to reach socialism
by political action. Workmen were buying red ties and reading
William Morris' utopian *News from Nowhere* or Robert Blatch-

ford's pink peppery socialist newspaper, *The Clarion*. Some were trying to understand the translated first volume of Marx's *Capital*.

Even the old unions began to feel the need for adding the political weapon to their armory. In 1874 the miners of Northumberland had won a seat in the House of Commons for their leader, Thomas Burt, and in 1885 ten unionists were in the House; but they had no distinct Labor creed and ranked as good loyal Liberals. In the 'nineties, however, the socialists, the new unionists, and the old ones were brought together in what became the Labor party in 1906. The unions supplied the funds, many of the candidates, and most of the votes. In 1909 a court ruling (the Osborne judgment) forbade them to make political levies, but an act of 1913 permitted them to do so, provided that members who did not wish to contribute to a party which was not theirs could claim exemption.

Organized labor now had a chance to pursue its aims along two roads. On the political road it was soon able to accomplish much. In 1906 it won 29 seats in the House of Commons, and in 1910 won 42. It supported social legislation introduced by the Liberal government, and as that government was dependent on the Labor vote for a majority after 1910 the new party's influence was greater than its size. The reversal of the Taff Vale and Osborne judgments, the payment of members of parliament, and the introduction of national insurance and old age pensions helped the unionist and the union. Laws improving workmen's compensation, giving the miner an eight-hour day and a minimum wage, banning the use of white phosphorus in making matches, establishing trade boards to eliminate sweating, stamping out the last traces of night work for women in industry, and improving working conditions in retail stores—all owed much to the presence of a small but strategically strong Labor party in parliament. But the moderately socialistic part of the party's program was less easy of accomplishment and when in post-War days Labor was in power socialism drew little nearer. Further, the childhood of the party was spent in a period of rising prices, but wages stood still or mounted very slowly. At the same time ideas were slipping in from France which suggested that the state was useless to wage earners, political action futile, and conciliation a device for delay. This combination of increased prices and imported ideas was partly responsible for the outburst of strikes between

1910 and 1913. The strikes did some good, forced up some wages, and drove parliament to provide a minimum wage for coal miners. But they were costly, drained union funds, and brought to light the strength of the employers' organization. Hence the War found both sides strengthening the weak spots in their armor, making alliances, and filling war chests. If the advocates of votes for women and the opponents of home rule for Ireland were preaching force to the utmost, unionists might easily accept the same creed.

Labor and the War.—By 1915 it was evident that the production front had to be given as much attention as the destruction front. The War was seen to be an engineer's war, and the Munitions Act of 1915 organized capital and labor for such a fight. Labor accepted compulsory arbitration, virtually abandoned the right to strike, and agreed to the suspension of all trade union rules which "might restrict production or employment." Unionism had kept the boundary lines between crafts almost as clear as did the medieval guildsman. One job was a bricklayer's task, another a mason's; the shipwright and the boilermaker, the plumber and the coppersmith, all had their preserves marked out by rule or tradition, and the line between the skilled man and the laborer was equally sharply drawn. Now all such restrictions were to be cast aside for the duration of the War, and skilled labor could be "diluted." In return for these sacrifices by labor, employers were to have their profits limited, and excess profits were to be handed over to the state.

This Act achieved its main purpose, and eventually the whole field of mining, manufacture, and transport was controlled by the state. The wage-regulating activities of the trade boards were extended, and farm laborers' wages were fixed in the same way. There was much inevitable friction, delay in adjusting wages, suspicion of victimization, and hatred of profiteering. In addition, nerves were wracked by overtime, deficient food or housing, grim casualty lists, and growing doubt concerning the real aims of the War. Peace brought a great release of discontent, a welter of ideas, and a vast expansion in union membership. The enrollment in 1920 (8,350,000) was double that of 1913. In three years (1919-1921) 3700 disputes affected 6,000,000 workers and involved a loss of 150,000,000 working days. Demands for higher wages to meet high prices, or for reduced hours were the chief causes. There was a clamor for nationalization of mines and railroads, and Labor's failure to win many seats at the election held just after the armistice (1918) left it with only the industrial weapon.

The post-War story is shadowed by the depression in the staple industries that were the old stronghold of labor organization. Membership fell rapidly after 1920, and by 1932 was down to 4,400,000, or a little higher than the pre-War level; but much remained of the pre-War and War-time gains. Recognition is general, with few exceptions. Reduced hours have not been lengthened. Joint industrial councils set up as part of the Whitley plan for improving industrial relations have extended the range of conciliation and collective bargaining, even into the civil service. In 1931, eight million workers had their wages regulated by collective agreements or by the state. But the largest group of unionists was in a sick industry—coal mining—and the relations between the miners and their employers were bitter. Twice, in 1921 and 1926, did the miners go to battle, and twice they were defeated. The first strike did untold harm to those who used coal, as well as to the export trade. The second was for a few days supported by a general strike of all unionists. The general strike failed, and the miners' strike dragged on for months. It damaged the coal industry and many others as well. It also led parliament to pass a law banning general strikes and forbidding unions to collect political levies except from those members who definitely said they wished to pay them.

Continental Unionism.—Labor organization on the continent lagged almost half a century behind that in Great Britain. There was virtually no movement till the 'sixties or 'seventies, and only after 1890 was much progress made. By 1912, however, there were about 7,000,000 unionists, of whom half were in Germany. The War and its aftermath caused a great expansion in membership and influence, but depression and dictatorship led to a heavy decline in numerical strength or economic power.

The late start was partly the result of late industrialization. It was partly due to the fact that many skilled workers were employed in small shops, were employers, or were independent workers. In France this was especially true, for in 1911 there were about as many employers and self-employed persons as there were non-agricultural wage and salary earners; only in mining, railroad transportation, iron, and textiles were large groups of workers gathered together. Further, the opposition of employers and of the state was more bitter and protracted. An employer like Krupp was ready to be benevolent, but insisted on being a despot; from the beginning he adopted a policy of high wages, developed welfare work of various kinds, and was ready to "do the right thing." But he must define "right," and tolerated no interference. "We want only loyal workers, who are grateful in soul and body that we offer them bread." There were many like him, paternal and philanthropic; but many despots were not benevolent, and all regarded the union official as an impertinent intruder. They refused to recognize or negotiate, formed employers' unions, and resorted frequently to the lockout. In the first ten years of the present century nearly 3000 lockouts were declared in Germany, and some of them were frankly intended to smash a union or exhaust its funds.

The hostility of the state died slowly, and some outburst of revolutionary labor sentiment or of socialistic propaganda often put new life into it when it seemed at death's door. The restrictions imposed on labor organization by France in 1791 were not fully withdrawn till 1884. Belgium allowed organization in 1866, but had a clause against strikes in its penal code till 1921. In Germany trade unionism really started in 1868 under the auspices of two socialist bodies which in 1875 fused into the Social Democratic party. Hence Bismarck in 1878 made little distinction between the political and industrial wings when he set out to kill the socialist movement, and put them both under a ban. In ten years 108 unions were dissolved by the authorities. Only in 1890 was the ban removed, and in later years German unionists received many unwelcome decisions from the courts. In other countries the right of association came slowly, in full or partial form—in Austria in 1867, in Holland in 1872, in Finland and Poland in 1905, and in Russia in 1906. The hostile laws did not achieve their full purpose. Where organization was needed men found ways around them or under them. The laws annoyed and impeded the unions, but did not kill them.

The close association between socialism and unionism led to the establishment of non-socialist unions. In 1868, while the socialists were busy enlisting recruits, another movement was gathering together workers who were not socialists. These Radical unions, led by Max Hirsch, repudiated political action, sought amicable relations with employers, and developed friendly society work. After 1890 the Catholic Church began to form unions, for it was afraid that its laity might be drawn into the socialist fold and imbibe the anti-religious doctrines preached by some socialists. German unionism thus marched under three banners—"free" (Social Democratic), Radical, and Christian. But the armies were very unequal in size, for while the free unions in 1913 had over 2,500,000 members, the Christian unions had only 340,000, and the Radical only 100,000. This division of forces was found in other European countries where Catholicism was strong, e.g., in Austria, Holland, and Belgium. In some countries differences of nationality divided workers. Czechs and German-Austrians had separate camps in Bohemia; Belgium had its socialist unions, its Catholic unions and also its Walloon and Flemish groups. In all countries, however, the non-socialist or anti-socialist organizations were comparatively small.

Continental unionism was seen at its best in the German free unions. They were few in number but large in size; in 1914 there were only forty-seven of them, and in 1931 only thirty; Great Britain had over 1100. In 1912 thirty-five metal trades formed the German Metal Workers' Federation, the largest union in the world, with 900,000 members in 1928. The Building Workers' Federation had nearly 500,000 members. The giants were allied in the General Commission of Trade Unions, which was founded in 1890 and in 1919 became the German General Federation of Labor, representing 4,600,000 workers in 1928. The free unions worked in close contact with the Social Democrats, but their business was economic, not political. They concentrated on securing better wages, hours, and working conditions, and provided friendly society benefits. Recognition and agreements came gradually; the large-scale and heavy industries were the most difficult to influence, but even there some concessions were won before 1914. In 1910, 9700 "movements" reduced hours for 1,300,000 workers and increased wages for 800,000. Of these movements, two-thirds were settled peacefully, and only one-third caused a strike or lockout. Some unions ran labor exchanges, and used them to ask higher wages from employers who sought workers. Much money was spent on education and propaganda, with libraries, lectures, classes, and daily or weekly papers. Elaborate

"Charter of Labor" (1927) enunciated the rights and obligations of capital and labor alike, and asserted the state's right to control all forces of production in the interests of the "moral, political, and economic unity" of the nation. "Private initiative in the field of production is the most efficacious and most useful instrument in the interests of the nation"; but the objects of production are "the well-being of the producers and the development of the national strength," and the labor of the entrepreneur, of the intellectual, of the technician, or of the manual worker is "a social duty." Organization of employers and of workers is free, "but only the syndicate legally recognized and under the control of the State" has any power.

Translated into legislation, these declarations provided for one union in each industry or profession. This union would bargain collectively with the employers' organization and make agreements binding on the whole industry. Strikes or lockouts were made penal offenses, and any dispute that was not settled by conciliation must go to a labor court. The union officials were appointed by the state, not by the members, and the old non-Fascist unions melted away. Between 1926 and the end of 1933, 650 national and nearly 12,000 local collective agreements were filed, and thirty-four disputes were settled by courts; two lockouts, about 150 strikes, and 660 violations of agreements were punished. In 1934 a corporation was established for each of twenty-two branches of production. Each corporation contains representatives of capital and labor, and of the Fascist party, and is presided over by a minister of state. The corporation drafts general rules concerning labor, production, and prices, advises the government on economic matters, acts as a conciliation board, regulates apprenticeship and vocational training, and establishes labor exchanges. At the top of the tree is a National Council of Corporations, similarly constituted and presided over by the head of the government. It acts as a coordinating body, advises the political heads on economic matters, regulates the relations between different industries, and fixes wages or salary rates.

On paper the plan seems a comprehensive and logical attempt at state supervision and a "planned economy," replacing *laissez-faire* individualism and the clash of classes. But the gap between plan and practice has been wide as yet. The corporations have still to prove their worth. The National Council of Corporations has never yet been listened to or even consulted when really important economic problems called for solution, and has done little more than indorse decisions already made by the government. The large business and landed interests have been able to get much of their own way and to exert great influences on Fascist policy; but the chief work of the heads of the trade unions since 1926 has been to persuade the members to accept serious wage reductions. Labor has gained little to compensate it for the loss of freedom, and it has scanty opportunity for escape or for effective protest.

Italy and Germany defeated the advocate of the class struggle and put him under authoritarian control in the interests of capitalism and nationalism. Russia put the proletarian victor in the class struggle under similar control in the interests of communism. In that country there was little unionism in 1914 or even at the time of the first revolution in 1917. After the second revolution workers' councils were going to run industry; the old technicians and managers were evicted or deposed, new ones were elected, committees were everywhere, and workshops became talkshops. The destruction of capitalism soon looked like the destruction of production as well, and during the years 1918-1921 the workers' committees gave place to less direct and more disciplined control by a big union in each industry. This plan was in turn abandoned after 1921. State trusts were set up to manage nationalized undertakings, and were freed from labor control. Hence the unions had real work to do in protecting their members. The state fixed a minimum wage, and then left matters to collective bargaining. Lenin himself had emphasized the need for adopting the methods of large-scale machine industry and for studying the technique of management as developed in America. By 1920 rigid discipline had been imposed, overtime was common, piece-work wages and bonuses for rapid work were paid, and wages were developing the differences in size that existed elsewhere.

In carrying out the Five-Year plans, the unions could play a part as agents of the state, urging or cajoling workers to strenuous endeavor, pointing out defects in productive methods, and generally helping to "put the plan over." Their defensive work was chiefly the drafting of wage agreements, but these agreements were limited by the amount of money allotted for wages in the plans, and were based on reward according to output or position rather than on the early doctrine of reward according to need. Hence the wage policy was little different from that of capitalist industry, and the gaps between skilled and unskilled earnings, or between those of artisan, foreman, and technician, are large. The unions also have much to do with education, propaganda, and recreational facilities. They are under party control, and their offices, as well as the factory and other councils, are usually filled with party men. This insures harmony between union and party, allows unionist critics to be removed easily, gives the plans the fullest possible opportunity of being carried out, and makes workers pay the price that the leaders think must be paid for rapid industrialization. What may happen if the workers decide the price is too high, only the future can tell.

Consumers' Cooperation.—Consumers' cooperation originally was intended to be producers' cooperation as well. Owen and other utopian socialists believed that society could be regenerated by the establishment of communities based on the principles of mutual cooperation, community of property, and equal means of enjoyment, but devoid of the harmful influence of private property, competition, and profit-seeking. These communities would produce all that their members needed; employment and enjoyment would go hand in hand. All such communities failed, but the belief that they could be successfully built and run died hard. When a group of Rochdale (Lancashire) weavers considered what could be done to improve their miserable condition and established the Rochdale Pioneers' Society (1844), their plan embraced not merely the opening of a retail store. In addition they hoped to secure houses, manufacture goods, buy or lease land, and "as soon as practicable . . . proceed to arrange the powers of production, distribution, education, and government, or, in other words, to establish a self-supporting home colony of united interests."

This was almost pure Owenism; but the starting point was not a model village. It was a small store in a mean street, selling flour, butter, sugar, oatmeal and candles. Wholesale trading, a flour mill, a cotton mill, a Turkish bath, a sick and burial society, and a building society were in later years added to the list of the Rochdale Pioneers' activities, and the cooperative movement which sprang from their success grew to great dimensions as producer. But it never reached a point where it could employ more than a small fraction of its members, and its policy centered on serving them as consumers, not on finding them jobs.

Even a little retail store required capital, and the society that founded it needed rules and working principles. There had been cooperative societies and stores before 1844, but most of them had failed. The Pioneers combined the desirable features of experiments that had gone before, made them work, and then made them known over a wide field. Those features were as follows:

1. Capital was provided by the members, in units of £1, payable in installments as low as a shilling, and withdrawable if the member desired to get his money back. In addition, members could use the society as a savings bank, but on capital and deposits alike only a fixed rate of interest was paid.

2. The best obtainable goods were to be supplied, and full weight and measure were to be given. This rule was almost a revolution in retailing. Flour was often adulterated, tea was colored with Prussian blue, sand was mixed with sugar, the price of milk rose as the quantity of chalk and water fell, while weights and measures were uncertain quantities. "Traders treated the workingman's stomach as a sort of wastepaper basket" (Fay); and although muckrakers published exposures of these practices under such titles as *Death in the Pot*, there was little effective state action to get pure food until about 1875 in England, 1876 in Germany, and much later in other countries. *Caveat emptor*—let the buyer beware—was good *laissez faire* in the food market as in the stock market, and the Pioneers' rule was far ahead of commercial practice or public policy.

3. Market prices were charged, and credit was neither given nor asked. No attempt was made to sell "at cost," for costs were not known at the time of sale, and a policy of undercutting rivals might lead to reprisals. Credit was avoided, bad debts were thus evaded, and the society could get cash discounts by paying for its goods when it obtained them.

4. By selling at market price a society had a surplus left over when all costs, including interest on capital, had been met. In a private store this surplus would be the tradesman's profit; in a joint-stock company it would be distributed among the stockholders in proportion to their capital. In a cooperative society it was returned quarterly or semi-annually to the consumer from whom it had been taken, in the form of a "dividend on purchases"

and in proportion to the amount of his purchases. It was a refund of an overcharge. In some societies the pre-War "divvy" was 15 per cent, and the wage-earning family that spent most of its income at the "co-op" received a substantial sum on "divvy day."

5. The Pioneers were democrats, imbued with Chartist ideas of manhood suffrage, vote by ballot, and annual parliaments. They decreed that "the principle of one member one vote should obtain in government, with equality of the sexes in membership." Management was to be in the hands of periodically elected officers and committees, and frequent financial statements were to be issued. The principle of "one member one vote," as distinct from "one share one vote," was natural in a cooperation of consumers rather than of capitalists. The demand for financial publicity was made as early as was the state demand for publicity in joint-stock company affairs, and the grant of votes to women came seventy-three years before it came in national politics.

6. The Pioneers knew the shortcomings in their own education and saw the value of cooperative propaganda. They resolved "that a definite percentage of profits should be allotted to education." In 1844 factory children were getting a meager education, but an effective system of state elementary education was at least a quarter of a century away, while secondary schools, libraries, or adult education were still further in the future. In 1852 the rule was made that 2½ per cent of the surplus should be spent in educational work.

The Pioneers succeeded where hundreds of societies had failed. The dividend bound wage earners to the store just as friendly society benefits bound them to the new model unions. The Rochdale group grew from twenty-eight members in 1844 to over 20,000 by 1913, the funds from £28 to £400,000, and the employees from one part-time salesman to over 400 workers. Other towns and villages established societies, especially throughout the midlands and north, and later in the south.

> By 1900, 1440 retail societies had 1,700,000 members.
> By 1914, 1385 " " " 3,050,000 "
> By 1932, 1200 " " " 6,760,000 "

This last figure is about one-seventh of the total population of the British Isles, and since a member is usually the head of a family it can safely be interpreted as indicating that at least half the population was obtaining some of its supplies from retail

societies. In 1930 the share capital of these societies was over
£110,000,000, and the sales nearly £220,000,000.

From retail distribution the next step was to production or to
purchase on a large scale. Some societies began to produce part
of the goods they sold, and by 1923 the retail societies produced
or prepared one-sixth of the things they needed. But this was not
enough. Large-scale importation or production was best done by
some central organization, and in 1863 the English Cooperative
Wholesale Society (C.W.S.) was established with headquarters
in Manchester. Five years later came a Scottish C.W.S. The
capital was supplied by the retail societies, and on it a fixed rate of
interest was paid. The C.W.S. procured, made, and sold goods to
the member societies, and at the end of the year distributed any
net surplus among them in proportion to their purchases. The
dividend-on-purchases principle was thus applied to wholesale
as well as to retail trade.

The C.W.S. took cooperation out into world trade, for the
necessaries of life of the British artisan had to be drawn from
every corner of the globe. Soon the C.W.S. name plate appeared
on doors in Ireland, New York, Rouen, Copenhagen, Hamburg,
Montreal, Sydney, Colombo, and elsewhere. From purchase overseas to production overseas sometimes seemed a desirable step.
Tea plantations were bought in Ceylon, a concession was obtained
in Sierra Leone, and for a time 10,000 acres of wheat land were
held on the Saskatchewan prairie. Some goods from Europe
were carried to England in C.W.S. ships, but the economies in
that enterprise were small. The really great successes came in the
preparation and manufacture of materials in factories scattered
over the country. Foodstuffs, cloth, clothes, shoes, tobacco, soap,
furniture, fruit, coal, and other commodities can be obtained
from C.W.S. sources of supply. In 1930, 46,000 persons produced or processed goods worth £36,000,000. In 1872 the C.W.S.
began banking, and by 1923 kept current accounts for 1000 societies and 12,500 unions, friendly societies, or kindred bodies.
The net surplus was distributed in proportion to the amount of
custom. Insurance began in 1867 and was gradually extended to
cover most risks. In 1904 a collective life insurance plan was
formulated under which all the members of a retail society were
automatically insured without exception or medical examination.
The administration of this huge many-sided business was con-

ducted on democratic lines. Control rested in the hands of meetings of delegates from the member societies, and management was directed by elected committees consisting of men who belonged by birth, training and sympathy to the wage-earning class. The failures have been few, the successes substantial. The critic may with truth point out that management in the retail and wholesale societies has been conservative, and that there has been a reluctance to step into new fields. This has not been entirely the leaders' fault, for often the brake has been applied fiercely by the individual members and progressive officers have been dethroned. The critic also points out, with some degree of truth, that this great organization of consumers may give scant thought to the welfare of its 260,000 employees. Working men, probably stalwart unionists, may, when clothed in authority as committeemen or directors, subordinate the interests of the employees to the desire of a big dividend. This criticism has far less force than it once had; the growth of unionism among cooperative employees and the frank facing of the labor problem by managements have placed the cooperative societies in the front rank as employers in the distributive trades.

On the continent, consumers' cooperation spread among townsmen almost as easily as did agricultural cooperation among farmers, and in rural regions the same organization might serve the peasants both as consumers and as producers. In 1929 it was estimated that there were 40,000,000 members in 60,000 consumers' societies in over thirty countries. The strongholds outside Great Britain were Germany and Russia, but all northern Europe had its stores and wholesale societies. Germany had 4,000,000 members; France had 3,500,000 members and 7500 stores. In Hungary, Switzerland, Czechoslovakia, Denmark, and Finland one-tenth or more of the population was enrolled. Russia began late, but after 1905 the growth of consumers' societies was rapid. By 1914, 10,000 societies were at work, and by January, 1918, 35,000 societies with 11,000,000 members were handling nearly half the country's retail trade. The Bolsheviks made the cooperatives an instrument of the state for handling retail distribution, but with NEP the societies became voluntary and self-governing again. Between 1921 and 1930 their membership rose to 43,000,000, and their central wholesale organization, *Centrosoyus,* ran elevators, mills, cold-storage plants, canning factories, soap works, etc., and did much educational and welfare work. Hence the machinery built up by the consumers' cooperatives is the chief means for the distribution of necessaries in Russia today.

The dream of the Rochdale Pioneers that cooperation could create a new social order has faded. In the big staple occupations that produce and distribute consumers' goods cooperation has a field that is far from fully exploited today; but other industries, such as lighting, transport, machine-making, metal production, luxury and export trades are beyond its reach, if only because it would be difficult to keep track of the consumer and pay him his dividend. In the field most suited to its work it has now to face not merely the corner "neighborhood store" run on a non-wage-paying basis by its proprietor, but also the chain stores with their great capital resources, elaborate displays, and low cash prices. In its struggle with these it has a tradition of working-class loyalty and middle-class good will, and the rapid growth of membership since the War shows that it is not losing its appeal. In so far as it can retain loyalty and offer tangible benefits, the self-interest of consumers will bring them to its door and allow a large area of economic endeavor to use capital without being capitalist.

BIBLIOGRAPHY

BIRNIE, A., *Economic History of Europe, 1760-1930,* chaps. 7-10.
BLAND, TAWNEY, and BROWN, *English Economic History: Select Documents,* pp. 619-646.
CLAPHAM, J. H., *Economic History of Modern Britain,* vol. ii, chaps. 4, 11.
COLE, G. D. H., *The World of Labour* (1912) ; *Organized Labour* (1924).
FAY, C. R., *Great Britain from Adam Smith to the Present Day,* chaps. 19, 20.
FAY, C. R., *Cooperation at Home and Abroad* (1920).
FINER, H., *Mussolini's Italy* (1935).
FORD, G. S., (editor), *Dictatorship in the Modern World* (1935).
FREEMAN, J., *The Soviet Worker* (1932).
GIDE, C., *Consumers' Cooperative Societies* (1921).
HAIDER, C., *Capital and Labor under Fascism* (1930).
HALL, F., and WATKINS, W. P., *Cooperation* (1934), chaps. 5, 6, 8, 10, 13, 15, 19, 31.
LAIDLER, H. W., *A History of Socialist Thought* (1927).
LAWTON, L., *Economic History of Soviet Russia* (1932).
LEVINE, L., *Syndicalism in France* (1914).
MONTGOMERY, B. G., *British and Continental Labor Policy* (1922).
MÜLLER, H., *Geschichte der deutschen Gewerkschaften* (1918).
OGG, F. A., and SHARP, W. R., *Economic Development of Modern Europe,* chaps. 19, 20-23, 30.
PITIGLIANA, F., *The Italian Corporative State* (1933).
RICHARDSON, J. H., *Industrial Relations in Great Britain* (1933).
RÜHLE, D., *Karl Marx* (1929).

SANDERS, W. S., *Trade Unionism in Germany* (1916).
SAPOSS, D., *The Labor Movement in Post-War France* (1931).
SOMBART, W., *Socialism and the Social Movement* (Eng. trans., 1909).
WEBB, S. and B., *History of Trade Unionism, 1666-1920* (1920).
WEBB, S. and B., *The Consumers' Cooperative Movement* (1921).

ARTICLES

ANSELMI, A., "Trade Associations and Corporations in Italy," in *Int. Lab. Rev.*, January, 1935, pp. 6-27.
CHILDS, S. L., and CROTTET, A. A., "Wages Policy in Russia," in *Ec. Hist.*, January, 1932, pp. 442-460.
CHILDS, S. L., and CROTTET, A. A., "Trade Unions in the Soviet State," in *Ec. Hist.*, January, 1933, pp. 617-628.
HAMMOND, J. L., "The Industrial Revolution and Discontent," in *Ec. H. R.*, January, 1930, pp. 215-228.
HEWES, A., "The Transformation of Soviet Trade Unions," in *Am. Ec. R.*, December, 1933, pp. 605-619.
PLUMMER, A., "The General Strike During One Hundred Years," in *Ec. Hist.*, May, 1927, pp. 184-204.
Encyclopædia of the Social Sciences: See list of titles on Labor, Socialism, and Cooperation in vol. xv, pp. 552, 556, 550. See especially the articles on Trade Unions, Socialism, Syndicalism, the Labor Movement, Bolshevism, Russian Revolution, Gosplan, Fascism, National Socialism, Consumers' Cooperation, Producers' Cooperation, Collectivism.

CHAPTER XXX

PUBLIC ENTERPRISE, POPULATION, AND MATERIAL WELFARE

IN THIS concluding chapter, three topics hitherto neglected or lightly touched will be briefly examined.

PUBLIC ECONOMIC ENTERPRISE

While cooperation invaded the field of enterprise from one side, the state or its political subdivisions occupied some of it from the other. It sank capital, employed various kinds of workers, produced goods or rendered services. The motives that led it to do so were seldom formally socialistic, for socialist thought or propaganda achieved little of its real purpose outside Russia. The pioneers in state or municipal enterprise were good capitalists, autocrats, Liberals, or Conservatives, eloquent denouncers or ruthless suppressors of the red menace. They acted because certain pieces of equipment that were economically, socially, or politically necessary could not be provided by private enterprise or could be better provided by the state or municipality.

These needs were connected especially with communication, transportation, or the rise of large towns. The factors that led to public ownership of railroads have already been noted (Chapter XXII). The addition of telegraphs and telephones to the state postal system was a natural step to Europeans. A very brief experience sufficed to show that radio broadcasting must be regulated to prevent chaos on the air, that monopoly was essential in countries with a small area, and that the educational and propagandist value of the new voice could best be realized under public or quasi-public ownership. Roads could not be provided on a profit-making basis by making the traffic pay tolls, and waterways could not be self-supporting. A canal like the Kiel or the Panama had naval as well as commercial value, and its construction by the state was a piece of defensive work as well as commercial aid. A harbor that needed costly improvements must be cared for by city or state, and if a port like London was to render efficient service its miles of quays and acres of docks must be coordinated under one public authority.

The growth of large towns gave a great stimulus to public enterprise. The nineteenth-century town needed houses, light, water and sewage systems, fire protection, paved streets, sidewalks, and street traction. Private enterprise provided the houses. The return on capital was sufficiently attractive to induce investors and speculative builders to erect them. Absence of building regulations allowed, and the high cost of urban land forced, builders to crowd as many houses as possible on each acre in England or to erect tenements with many stories on the continent; but that crowding would in any case have been unavoidable until, late in the century, better street transportation allowed population to be dispersed in suburbs. The small rent that wage-earning tenants could pay (say $1 to $1.50 a week) limited the amount that could be spent on each house if the rent was to yield enough to cover interest, taxes, and depreciation. All recent schemes for better housing have come back to the unpleasant fact that there must be some relationship between the amount a tenant can pay and the cost of erecting his habitation. As the standard of living rose, tenants could afford better homes and pay street-car or train fares to get to them. Hence, to take one instance, the percentage of the Scottish population living under "one family one room" conditions fell from 26 in 1861 to 14 in 1891 and to 8 in 1921.

Up to 1914 the private builder put a roof over Europe's head, but was finding the task less and less profitable in face of higher costs and taxes. The War stopped building, led to restrictions on increases in rents, piled heavier taxation on real estate, and increased the interest rate on mortgage loans. By 1919 there was an acute shortage of dwellings, and little inclination on the part of private capital to fill the gap. Housing therefore became a public concern. Municipalities and other local authorities built great blocks of tenements (e.g., in Vienna) to provide additional homes and replace slum dwellings, or laid out and constructed new suburbs. In England subsidies were given by the state to private builders or to local governments; between 1919 and 1929, 600,000 houses were erected by local authorities, 400,000 by private subsidized enterprise, and 600,000 by private builders on their own initiative without aid. The reduction of interest rates during the depression made loans cheap once more; but taxation, land costs, and wages are still high, and it is virtually impossible to build houses that can be profitably let at rents many wage earners can afford.

On the continent the same condition has prevailed. Germany by 1930 had erected 1,500,000 houses, but the rents absorbed a third of the wage-earner's income, against a sixth in older dwellings; cheaper flats were planned, but even these deplete low incomes severely. France had to rebuild its devastated areas and add to its housing accommodation elsewhere. Russia built vast blocks of flats, which were largely dormitories with central restaurants and kitchens. Hence one of the great private enterprises of the nineteenth century has become in large part a public one; a necessary of life cannot be produced at a price that many consumers can afford to pay.

Some of the other components of a modern town were first provided by private enterprise but later passed into public hands. Probably no European sewage system is a private service, but many water supplies were inaugurated by a company of "undertakers" and later passed under municipal control. State pressure and civic action sprang from the "awakening of the sanitary conscience" after about 1840, an awakening for which social reformers, such as Edwin Chadwick (1800-1890), rather than medical men were responsible. A widespread epidemic of cholera in and after 1830 gave urgency to the study of urban health, and led to a recognition of the importance of an adequate water supply, a sewage system, and paved streets. Cleanliness was found to be next to healthiness as well as to godliness. The cost was great, and the opposition from vested interests was not all the avarice of property-owners. When Glasgow closed polluted wells and supplied water from a mountain lake, one aged woman demanded access to her old well on the ground that the new water had "got neither taste nor smell." Eventually civic action and machine-made cheap pipes rid western Europe of its dirt diseases—typhoid, cholera, and dysentery. Glasgow, for instance, had epidemics in 1818, 1830, 1837, 1847, 1851, and 1853. It then began to clean up, and the epidemic of 1869-1870 was the last of the long line. The bacteriological work begun by Pasteur, Lister, and Koch added a new weapon to the armory of preventive medicine, and by 1900 public health was a service with a great capital outlay and a skilled labor force. Yet even in the post-War world the water that emerges from some continental faucets is drunk at one's peril.

Private enterprise carried gas, electrical, and street-car services through their formative experimental stages. It might continue to operate these local monopolies under some civic control, but they were a fit field for municipal effort, either because private capital was slow in providing them or because private owners seemed to be charging high monopoly prices. The German towns had traditions which made operation of public utilities a natural activity; Dresden and Leipzig acquired gas plants in the eighteen thirties, and by 1910 four-fifths of the German gas production was in municipal hands. Electrical generation and street-car services passed into or were built by the same hands, while a compromise between public and private interests was found in the "mixed" enterprise. A "mixed" venture was financed jointly by public funds and private investment, and the former might contribute more than the latter. It was run as a commercial business by officers elected by the two owners, subject to government regulation or to a limit on the amount of profit that could be made. It was thus a combination of private enterprise and socialism; it gained the advantages of efficient management associated with the former, yet protected the consumer and gave the public purse part of the profit.

This mixture began to be made in Germany about 1900, when the electrical age dawned. The western German cities saw their little power plants endangered by large private producers and distributors. They set out to build great rival units, but the threatened power war was stopped by the imperial government and the towns began to buy stock in the companies. By 1913 they owned a third of the shares in the largest company and chose over half the directors. Mixing became popular after the War, and in Prussia alone the cities had nearly 500 mixed enterprises. Of 150 city transit systems, sixty were fully public property and fifty were mixed. Almost a third of the electricity came from mixed plants, and most of the rest from public generators. Many housing schemes, warehouses, docks, airports, and theatres were mixed undertakings.

In other countries similar combinations of state or municipal capital and private investment were also found. England produced some rather different ones. She began the practice by buying shares in the Suez Canal and carried it a stage further by acquiring an interest in the Anglo-Persian Oil Company (1912). When a company constructing the Manchester Ship Canal reached the verge of bankruptcy in 1890 the city of Manchester advanced £5,000,000 and took a share in the control of the waterway. Apart from this instance the English municipal field remained unmixed, and the utilities were either entirely private or fully public. The latter supplied two-thirds of the electricity, two-fifths of the gas, and four-fifths of the urban transportation in the nineteen-twenties. By that decade it had become evident that the generation of electricity by hundreds of public and private plants was unsatisfactory. If each town had its own plant much production would be small scale and uneconomical; yet municipal law might forbid towns to join hands in producing power or to sell it outside their own boundaries. In 1926 the state stepped in to coordinate and expand production and distribution. It established a public trust, the Central Electricity Board, which would borrow money in order to cover the whole country with a network of high-tension wires along which power would be distributed from a small number of large generating stations. Retail distribution remained in the hands of the existing municipal or joint-stock units; they would close down their small inefficient stations, buy power at cost, and sell it. The result is thus a composite of state, municipal, and private enterprise, with the state acting to achieve a rational reorganization that could not have been accomplished in any other way.

Even a brief description of other state or municipal enterprises would occupy many paragraphs. It would start with maternity hospitals and end with cemeteries or crematoria. Doctors, chemists, nurses, and undertakers are civil servants in some places. Educational institutions, libraries, orchestras, and theatres comprise one of the largest public enterprises, and the building up of this service is largely an achievement of the last seventy years. Public landownership and utilization are found in both town and village, for many German communities own the land on which they stand, and a seventh of the area of pre-War Germany was public forest. The state ownership and exploitation of mineral deposits was best seen in the Prussian coal and potash mines; the state coal mines in 1914 supplied the railroads and sold 12,000,000 tons of coal. The king of Prussia was probably the largest coal merchant in the world. In Holland four out of ten mines that have greatly expanded coal production in that country since 1913 belong to the state, and one of them is the largest and most modern pit in Europe.

All governments have some factories, workshops, shipyards, arsenals, etc., to produce the goods they need for their social, defense, or administrative needs. They are the biggest printers in many countries, and their uniform or boot-making factories, shipyards, and munitions plants are large employers. Beyond this self-service lies a wide range of enterprises to serve the public, sometimes in competition with private enterprise. The post office operates a large savings bank in Great Britain and many other countries, and in some central European countries allowed people to have current checking accounts in pre-War days. Municipalities in Germany run savings banks, and some German states have ordinary banks. The Bank of Sweden is the oldest state bank in the world, for the Banks of England and France are joint-stock organizations. In the financial crisis of 1931 the German government took over many shares of the Darmstädter and Dresdner banks, and when it merged the two into the Dresdner Bank it held two-thirds of the share capital, thus making a "mixed" enterprise. Switzerland began insurance work before 1900, and other governments have since entered into insurance of ships or of credit on goods exported to countries whose ability to pay was uncertain.

The provision of market facilities is an old public service, and was followed by retail trading in some places. Italian cities ran bread shops and drug stores; Budapest in 1914 was selling meat, poultry, and dairy produce; and Swiss authorities in 1910-1911 tried to reduce the cost of living by selling fish, vegetables, groceries, and coal. In these cases the motive was usually a reduction in living costs by creating competition; but in another field the motive was monopoly, for either moral or monetary reasons. Government monopolies control the production or sale (or both) of tobacco, alcohol, matches, and salt in ten to sixteen countries, while similar restraint is imposed by some governments on quinine, gasoline, lotteries, sugar, flax, pistols, and printed posters. Alcohol is monopolized either to prevent its abuse or to draw large revenue from the consumer, but the monopoly on most of the other commodities is frankly for revenue purposes by imposing indirect taxation through high prices. The trade may be handled by the state, farmed out, or run by a mixed company; Sweden, for instance, owns the greater part of the stock of the firms which handle tobacco and alcohol, and appoints some members of the managing board.

It is evident from the above catalogue that public enterprises cover most human needs from the cradle to the grave, and that a person with seven-league boots—or their modern equivalent, the airplane—could flit round Europe, even keeping out of Russia, and yet satisfy most of his needs under state or municipal auspices. The total number of public employees (excluding the defense forces) in England and Wales in 1921 was about 1,600,000, or nearly 10 per cent of the gainfully employed population. Of this number, well over half were engaged in enterprises rather than in regulation or purely administrative work. In 1911 the civic enterprises of the United Kingdom had a capital value of over £500,000,000, or one-eighth the amount invested overseas. In the same year the German state railways employed nearly 700,000 workers, and in 1929 one out of every fifteen civilian workers in France and Germany was on the public payroll, though only a part (possibly a half) was engaged in supplying goods or services.

To the question, "How did public enterprise fare?" no simple general answer can be given. Success and failure jostled each other just as they did in private enterprise. There was no evil genius presiding over state or municipal effort, nor was there any fairy godmother hovering over partnerships and companies. Some public enterprises gave the laborer good treatment and the consumer a good article or service at a low price; others did not. Some were efficiently managed, made ends meet, and produced a surplus; others were badly run, squandered their capital and revenue, and met perennial deficits by drawing on the pocket of the taxpayer or money-lender. Some regarded themselves as existing for the benefit of the community, others reversed the view. Some were public benefits, others were public nuisances. Success, whether measured in terms of the quality and price of the service rendered, or in terms of the balance sheet, or both, depended on many factors, some of them common to all forms of enterprise but some peculiar to public effort.

Of the latter factors, one or two may be noted. In the first place, a political unit—state, county, or city—was not necessarily a suitable economic unit. It might be too large or too small, and for municipal enterprise was often the latter. A street-car, gas, or electric service might stop at the city authority's boundary; the German railways were planned to meet state needs, and a canal or railroad built to give an outlet inside national territory might defy (at heavy cost) the fact that the nearest or cheapest outlet was through another country's territory. Only gradually has localism given place to regionalism; the American student who knows the tenacity of states' rights will understand the difficulties attending schemes for merging local units into a Greater Berlin or a Greater London, or for fusing a larger territory into an economic region.

In the second place, political units tended to run economic enterprises with political machinery driven by political power. The organization, procedures, and type of person necessary for diplomacy, defense, or justice were not always suitable for running railroads, ships, or a post office. Excessive centralization in the hands of a political chief, routine methods, red tape, protracted discussion, and the pressure of lobbies were out of place in a business venture. Political pressure was often the most harmful influence. Some railroad lines were constructed for military reasons and could not be expected to pay; others were built in response to pressure from voters whose support must be retained, but whose patronage of the line would do little more than "pay for the axle grease." The coal barons and the Junkers were powerful in determining Germany's water and rail policies. The French tobacco monopoly was exposed to the pressure of planters, retailers, and factory operatives; each was a big electoral influence, and controlled several seats in the legislature. Hence the state bought local leaf at a higher price than foreign, let the retailers dictate prices, and dared not enforce discipline in factories which in 1929 were said to have 4000 workers more than were needed. When in 1924 the German railroads were handed over to be operated by a company, over a million workers were on the government's payroll. During the next five years this number was gradually reduced by 30 per cent; in face of the railroad workers' vote no government would have dared to take such a step.

In the nineteenth century the public employee tended to be

treated worse than his fellow in private industry. His wages were low, and his civil rights were impaired. He must not join a union, or a cooperative society (in Belgium), or go to mass or be a socialist (in France). A strike was treated as rebellion. These conditions, relics of the time when the state employee was a public *servant*, have faded away before the growing political and economic strength of public service organizations, and the employee at times threatens to become a public *master*. Between the upper millstone of the consumer demanding cheaper service and the nether one of the employee sticking to (or adding to) his rights, the lot of the administrator of a public enterprise may be unenviable.

In the third place, a public enterprise is exposed to public criticism in legislature and press as no private venture is. The "whole temper and character of public and parliamentary criticism" is "to concentrate on mistakes and to ignore successes, to attach more discredit to the loss of £100 than credit to the gain of £100,000" (Salter). Such criticism is often carping, or is inspired by those who have private interests to promote. It tends to encourage the public employee to take the safe course and avoid the risks inseparable from technical experiment and advance. No legislature would have provided the $5,000,000 spent on eighteen years' work to discover the structure of the indigo molecule and devise methods for producing the dye on a large scale. Public enterprises have, in consequence, often lacked enterprise, and the work of experiment and innovation has had to come from elsewhere.

The disabilities of public enterprise, like those of private, are not all incurable. The mixed organization on the continent allies the material welfare of the public with the stimulus of private profit. In Great Britain the Port of London Authority (1909), the British Broadcasting Corporation (1927), the Central Electricity Board (1926), and the London Transport Board (1933) were set up by parliament as special bodies to take charge of a particular task. Their powers were outlined in the statute that brought them into being; their sources of capital or income were provided for, and the government chose their governing bodies or prescribed the manner of their choice. They were then left free to get on with their job and to make ends meet, without bothering about snipers in the legislature. In German towns the traditional autocracy of the burgomaster and of the civic heads gave a measure of immunity from democratic or sectional clamor, and the German civil service did its work with a high degree of efficiency. How far the demand for political orthodoxy—to Fascist, Nazi, or communist party—may interfere with the quality of administration east of the Rhine only the future can tell. If faith is more important than works the work may suffer. To run a public enterprise successfully, it is more important to have a good accountant or engineer than a sound Fascist or pure Aryan.

The further extension of public enterprise in a capitalistic world is not so much a matter of converting voters as of facing problems as they arise. The pressure of facts has been responsible for most of the extensions of recent years, and the plea for nationalization has had far less effect than the need for it. If further steps are taken, they will probably be due to the financial breakdown of private ventures, such as the British railways or the coal industry, or to an outburst of hostility to banking policy. Yet the control of banking policy by the state today is about as effective as it would be if the banks were owned by the state. Mining, the heavy industries, foreign trade, luxury production, and agriculture have little to gain from state operation; and any guess at future developments would probably see the state, the towns, the cooperative societies, and free enterprise sharing out the continent's work much as they do today.

Russia is the great exception. The collectivization of agriculture is really a revised reversion to the Mir, and the industrialization of the country up to 1928 was little more than a restoration, under state auspices, of the damaged equipment of czarist days. The two Five-Year Plans stepped out into new territory, though it has been suggested that they really tackled a problem that Peter the Great faced over two centuries earlier—that of establishing equilibrium between town and county by fostering the town. If there had been no revolution it seems safe to suppose that American and other capital would have flowed into Russia in a broad stream in the post-War decade and that industrial development would have been substantial. On the other hand, part of the income that the Bolsheviks earmarked for capital investment would have gone to pay interest on external debts. The communists tried to carry through in five or ten years an industrial development greater than that of the period since Waterloo. They had to modernize and mechanize industries that were manual or ill-equipped, and in addition they had to expand greatly the capital goods industries. They were helped by foreign experts and by such foreign machines as they could afford to buy. But they lacked great capital imports, important materials, and good transportation, and were handicapped by the unsuitability of the Russian temperament for the routine, discipline, and carefulness needed for factory work with complicated equipment. The repair shops (and the first-aid rooms) were the busiest places in the country. A capital outlay of 80,000,000,000 rubles ($40,000,000,000) was planned in the first five years, a sum twice as large as the total American export of capital during and after the War; but to squeeze the greater part of this out of the country's current income involved an abstinence sterner than that of the early industrial capitalists of the west.

These obstacles could be overcome only by ruthless discipline, reinforced by enthusiasm for the cause and by promises of better days later on. In broad outline the first plan succeeded: most of the objectives were reached, and in four years. The output of coal, chemicals, iron, lumber, and electric power doubled or trebled, and that of tractors rose far more. A nation had learned something of a new language, the language of mass machine production. But its fingers were not yet as efficient as its tongue. They were still often "all thumbs," and even such automatic machines as could be mastered by an immigrant in Detroit in two or three days were beyond the comprehension of many a Russian factory worker. It may be that the treatment of the stomach had something to do with the shortcomings of the hands, for consumers' goods were still scarce and the standard of living was lower than in pre-War days. Production of all kinds has not yet reached the point where the problem of disposing of the product has become important. If Russia gets to the stage where the twin needs for capital goods and consumers' goods are adequately met, and where a high standard of living can be guaranteed to all, many of the achievements described in the preceding ten chapters of this book will, in comparison, seem insignificant.

POPULATION TRENDS

Europe doubled its population during the nineteenth century, an achievement unknown in any earlier similar period of time. The following rough table tells the tale:

In 1800 Europe may have had 190,000,000 people.
In 1900 Europe had, according to census returns, 400,000,000 people.
In 1930   "   "   "   "   "   "   505,000,000   "

Between Waterloo and 1914 the population of the British Isles
rose from 19,000,000 to 46,000,000, in spite of the heavy fall in
Ireland. That of England and Wales nearly quadrupled, rising
from 10,000,000 to 37,000,000. That of the German Empire rose
from 40,000,000 in 1871 to nearly 70,000,000 in 1914. Italy at
unification (1871) had 27,000,000 people, and 41,000,000 in
1930. European Russia probably trebled its population between
the emancipation of the serfs and 1914, while among the smaller
countries Holland grew from 2,600,000 in 1829 to 7,600,000 a
century later. The French population nearly doubled between
Waterloo and Sedan, and then became almost stationary.

Behind these figures lay movements in the birth rate, the death
rate, and the stream of emigration. Defective statistics prevent us
from seeing clearly what was happening until at least 1850. The
reduction in the death rate which began in the eighteenth century
was checked and partly undone by the concentration of population
in towns during the nineteenth. Scurvy had gone, smallpox was
reduced to "a minor peril" (Marshall), and infant mortality had
been lessened. But the new industrial towns were death traps; bad
sewers, which leaked into the water supply, were worse than no
drains at all, and crowded dwelling areas made the spread of
infectious or contagious diseases easy. Only after 1870 did the
fight for public health begin to show statistical results, and its
effects were first enjoyed by the young and strong, rather than by
the infants or the old. The death rate among children under one
year old was as high in England and Wales at the end of the
century as in the middle (153 per thousand births), but after 1900
it dropped rapidly to 68 in 1926-1930. Throughout Europe at
large the general death rate has fallen greatly only within the last
seventy years, but in that period it has been at least halved in most
countries. Public and private health improvements can claim most
of the credit, but part of the progress "was due to the increased
wealth per head and better nourishment of the poor" and part "to
the gradual acclimatisation of the people to town life" (Marshall).

Alongside this decline in death rates was a contemporaneous or
slightly later fall in birth rates. If the typical mid-nineteenth-
century mother boasted that she knew how to rear children
because she had given birth to eight and buried five, her grand-

daughter could retort that she had brought her two or three off-spring safely through the years to maturity. Mr. Kuczynski has shown that in western and northern Europe (the British Isles, France, Belgium, Holland, Switzerland, Germany, the Scandinavian countries and Finland), the birth rate fell from 31 in 1850 to about 18 in 1930. In southern Europe the decline is far less marked, and in Russia has been scarcely perceptible. Later marriages and the spread of birth control are chiefly responsible, and while the decline began to be visible by 1880 its pace has been rapid since 1900 and even more so since 1920. In northern and western Europe the gap between birth and death rates is diminishing. In 1931 the births in an area holding two-fifths the total population of Europe exceeded the deaths by only 800,000, and there were 2,000,000 more females between fifteen and thirty years of age than under fifteen years. The difference between the size of rich or middle class and poor families had vanished or was doing so rapidly in Germany and Sweden, as was also that between rural and urban families in France. In Germany, once a land with one of the highest birth rates in Europe (40.9 per thousand in 1876), a birth rate of 20.5 is needed to maintain the population unchanged in size; but since the War the rate has fallen to 17.5 (in 1930). In England and Wales the rate was 36.3 in 1876; in 1934 it was 14.8.

This development must produce stationary and then declining populations in those countries which for four centuries have been the energetic and dominant economic and political regions of Europe. By 1950 the human tide will be receding in those areas. According to one estimate, 1935 would mark the turning point in France, and population will have fallen a million below its 1921 level by 1956. According to another estimate, 1944 will be the great divide in Great Britain, with a loss of over 3,000,000 by 1956 and of 12,000,000 by 1976 if present trends continue. Further reduction of death rates is difficult, since most of the factors that cause premature death have been exploited almost to the limit, except perhaps in France. Such a development, visible already over other parts of the world where the white race has gone, would indeed be "a turning point in human history" (Beveridge). Its economic effects are already apparent in certain directions. (1) Agriculture has felt the slower growth in the demand for foodstuffs and basic raw materials. (2) Less of the family income is needed to clothe and feed the smaller number of mouths and bodies. When doctors saved more infant lives and factory laws forbade the child to work, they placed an additional burden on the breadwinner, and the task of supporting several children grew increasingly heavy until the eldest were old enough to go to work. In a smaller family the burden was much lighter, savings might be accumulated, children could be given a better education, and the new commodities or services—the bicycle, cinema, radio, etc.—could be afforded by many whose parents had fought a grim fight to make ends meet. The "retreat from parenthood" thus meant a more comfortable life for the childless and for the smaller family. (3) The change in the age distribution of the population has not yet made its influence seriously felt. Only the statistician has grasped the significance of a declining percentage of children or young persons and an increasing percentage of middle-aged and old. As this trend becomes more evident, the expenditure on training the young may fall, or at least cease to grow as it did after 1870. On the other hand, the ailments and care of the elderly and old will grow in importance; childless couples who have not provided for their own old age may be a heavy burden on the state, and schemes for old age pensions and annuities will be more necessary. Stability and security will seem more important economically and politically than will opportunities for enterprise and advancement. But those countries which still possess youth and energy, and which want outlets for their teeming populations, may not be willing to let the older ones enjoy either stability or security undisturbed.

The Trend of Economic Welfare

At the end of a long trail it may be worth while to attempt an estimate of the contribution made by the last two centuries to the material welfare of Europe's people. The main fact is that a combination of improving technique and organization made possible the maintenance of a vastly greater population, much of it at a higher standard of living, and without needing the labor of many women and children. Man's command over nature was increased; material wealth was produced in far greater abundance and variety; and actual physical want, which was once so common that it was regarded as natural, became comparatively rare. Natural resources were not so rich as in the New World, yet had to support a far larger population; hence it is doubtful whether the organization and equipment of North America, if applied to European resources, could have given each person an income as large as was dug out of the prairies, the cotton belt, the forests, the coal seams, the iron ore ranges, and the oil fields. Poverty still persisted, for there was not enough wealth produced to let every family live in comfort—even if all large incomes had been shared out among the poor. But the progressive farmer and the factory worker were far better off in 1914 than their counterparts were in 1815 or 1715. One English statistical study concluded that the ordinary person in 1913 was four times as well off in real commodities as was the person in the corresponding place in the social scale in 1801.   .   *

For the mass of wage earners, material welfare depended on the size and regularity of their earnings and on the behavior of the price level. Wage statistics are few and unsatisfactory until well after 1850, but some trends can be traced. In England wages fell slowly between 1815 and 1850, but retail prices dropped much more. There were, however, periods of depression and of famine, which made wages scarce on many occasions. During the next quarter-century wages rose much more than prices, and after 1875 the heavy fall in prices did not check the rise in wages. After 1900 wages virtually stood still while prices rose, provoking widespread labor unrest. The rapid increase of wage rates during the War period was not all canceled in the depressed aftermath. Unskilled workers and those employed in industries "sheltered" from foreign competition kept most, but the producers of export goods lost much. The wage-fixing activities of trade boards and agricultural wages boards shielded the workers in those occupations, while the steady fall in prices up to 1929 increased "real" wages. Between 1880 and 1930 real wages increased by a half, and those of the lower-paid workers by more. In Germany both money and real wages rose after 1850, and especially after 1875, but rising prices ate up gains made after 1900. War increases in earnings were inadequate, and the wage earner suffered severely during inflation; but by 1929 real wages had passed the pre-War level, only to be plunged down by depression. The French story is roughly similar, save that wages did not rise between 1880 and 1900. Thus increased productivity, trade union organization, and periods of prosperity have been reflected in higher money wages; but depression or rising prices have injured purchasing power.

The actual money wage has ceased to be the sole source of labor's income. To it has to be added the contribution of employers and the state to insurance, and the value of the other social services (education, hospitals, pensions, housing subsidies, and poor relief). Mr. Clay estimates that these contributions and outlays in Great Britain amounted in 1911 to 9 per cent of the country's wage bill: but in 1929-1930 they were one-fifth (£300,000,000) of that bill, or more than the interest on the national debt. Apart from the employers' contributions to insurance premiums, this great sum came from taxation, and hence in large measure from the middle class and rich in the form of heavy income tax, death duties, or property taxes. British wealth distribution, like that of most other countries, is such that a large fraction of the income from property goes to a small fraction of the population; but the tax machine redistributes part of it among those who receive wages or who, through lack of work, lack wages. Of Germany the same is partly true.

The result of the decrease in the size of the family, of the increase in the lowest wages, and of the spread of social services has been a reduction in the amount of acute poverty. Professor Bowley found that the percentage of people living below a "poverty line" in five English industrial areas fell by half between 1913 and 1924. In 1890 over 30 per cent of the people of London were living below a poverty line of 21/- per family per week. Forty years later real wages had increased on an average by one-fifth, and the number below the line had fallen to 25 per cent. Among other results were the improved level of health, the wider educational opportunities, the better care of the sick and unemployed, and the assistance given to nearly 1,600,000 widows, children, and orphans of insured persons or to old people under pension schemes in 1929.

Against these gains must be placed the loss of income of workers in depressed industries of the post-War period and of the more heavily taxed middle class. Against them can also be placed the charge that the price of subsidy and security added to the cost of production for export, and thus handicapped the staple industries in their struggle with foreign rivals. A more serious charge is that the guarantee of income tended to reduce the "sense of economic responsibility, the sense of the connection between economic causes and effects, in the mass of the population" (Clay). A social service may come to be regarded as a vested right, as something that society must provide whether it can afford the cost or not. A fixed wage rate, a fixed insurance or relief payment is expected, regardless of whether industry or the state can pay the money and remain solvent.

This irresponsibility runs through the whole of an economic society based on a money economy and on specialization. A man who has to get water from a stream soon becomes aware that the supply is running low; but a man who turns a faucet which is connected with a reservoir a hundred miles away knows little and bothers little about the volume of supply available. Growing specialization has made one man an exporter and another an importer, one a provider of capital and another a seller of labor, one a debtor and another a creditor, one a servant of his street and another the servant of the world. In such circumstances it is hard to see the "altogetherness of everything," or to feel a responsibility for the effect of one's actions or demands on people who live around the corner or over the horizon. The wage earner knows by experience how insecure is his position and income; so also does the farmer, the manufacturer, and every other section of a society that has little sense of economic unity. Each seeks to stabilize its position, and insulate itself against insecurity. The collective bargain makes labor costs rigid, the cartel tries to make prices rigid, the tariff seeks to protect the home-producer's income from the competition of cheaper foreign wares, the wages board imposes a minimum wage that is not easily altered, the lender seeks an investment that will bring him a fixed rate of interest for many years ahead, and the farmer wants a guaranteed price. But economic change is unavoidable, and insecurity is its price. "A system that tries to insulate everybody from the shocks caused by economic change may succeed in directing attention altogether from the need of anticipating and adjusting ourselves to economic change" (Clay).

Europe's capacity for anticipating and adjusting itself to economic change is impaired by the political strength of economic vested interests. A heavier disability is the legacy of national antipathies, the memory of conflicts, and the absorption of a large part of income in paying the cost of past wars or of paving the way for future struggles. Whenever men of good will from different countries gather together, their plans for a wealthier and happier Europe call for economic and military disarmament and for cooperation in exploiting the still rich resources of the continent. Their recommendations fail to win acceptance because they are forward-looking while international relations are all too often backward-looking. The post-War years gave some hope that governments, banks, and business men might find ways of working together, but this thin veneer of cooperation was torn off when depression came. The chief ill effect of that depression may prove to be the sharpening of political and economic nationalism, the checking of a promising start in international cooperation, and the festering of war sores that seemed to be healing. The War made Europe poor; the depression made her poorer, and made her embark on policies that may make her poorer still.

BIBLIOGRAPHY

ASHLEY, W. J., *The Progress of the German Working Classes* (1904).

BOWLEY, A. L., *Some Economic Consequences of the Great War* (1930), chaps. 2, 6, 7, 8.

BOWLEY, A. L., and HOGG, M. H., *Has Poverty Diminished?* (1925).

BUER, M. C., *Health, Wealth, and Population in the Early Days of the Industrial Revolution* (1926).

CARR-SAUNDERS, A. M., and JONES, D. C., *The Structure of English Society as Illustrated by Statistics* (1927).

CLAPHAM, J. H., *Economic Development of France and Germany*, sections 36, 99.

DAVIES, E., *The Collectivist State in the Making* (1914).

DAWSON, W. H., *Municipal Life and Government in Germany* (1914).

HAMMOND, J. L. and B., *The Bleak Age* (1934).

HOOVER, C. B., *The Economic Life of Soviet Russia* (1931).

HOWE, F. C., *Socialized Germany* (1915).

KUCZYNSKI, R. R., *The Balance of Births and Deaths*, vol. i: *West and Northern Europe* (1928); vol. ii: *Eastern and Southern Europe* (1931).

THOMPSON, C. D., *Public Ownership* (1925).

ARTICLES

BOWLEY, A. L., "Wages in the United Kingdom during the Last Hundred Years," in *J. Royal Stat. Soc.*, 1906, pp. 148-192.

CANNAN, E., "The Changed Outlook in Regard to Population," in *Ec. J.*, December, 1931, pp. 519-533.

HAMMOND, B., "Urban Death Rates in the Early 19th Century," in *Ec. Hist.*, January, 1928, pp. 419-428.

HOOVER, C. B., "Economic and Social Consequences of Russian Communism," in *Ec. J.*, September, 1930, pp. 422-441.

HOPPER, B., "The Soviet Touchstone—Industrialization," in *Foreign Affairs*, April, 1930, pp. 379-398.

HOPPER, B., "Soviet Economy in a New Phase," in *Foreign Affairs*, April, 1932, pp. 453-464.

KUCZYNSKI, R. R., "The World's Population," in *Foreign Affairs*, October, 1928, pp. 30-40.

MARSHALL, T. H., "The Population of England and Wales from the Industrial Revolution to the World War," in *Ec. H. R.*, April, 1935, pp. 65-78.

WINTERTON, P., "Soviet Economic Development since 1928," in *Ec. J.*, September, 1933, pp. 442-452.

Unsigned, "The German Family Budget Inquiry of 1927-1928," in *Int. Lab. Rev.*, October, 1930, pp. 524-532.

Encyclopædia of the Social Sciences: See list of titles on Public Health, Public Welfare, Housing, Consumption, and Economic Policy in vol. xv, pp. 554, 555, 553, 550.

INDEX

Abbe, Ernst, 704
Abbeville, 162, 346
Abyssinia, 235, 239
Acre, 157, 158
Africa, and Europe, 9; exploration of, 231, 233, 661; gold, 155, 231, 239, 247, 437, 611, 614; produce, 24, 32, 155, 239-241, 661; trade with, 44, 57, 88, 155, 158, 281, 239-241
Agents, 179, 326, 355, 373, 584
"Agricultural Europe," 408, 471, 493, 685
Agriculture, and New World competition, 420, 437, 438-439, 454-455, 465-466, 472, 473, 650, 676-678; commercial, 36-37, 51, 57, 92, 112-117, 121, 303, 408, 420, 437, 447, 465, 471-473, 478, 479, 493, 494, 498; depressions, 433, 437-440, 454-455, 460, 466, 470, 493-494, 644, 647, 652, 655; Dutch intensive, 117, 280, 445; early modern, 262-263, 280, 287-289, 303-308; effect of World War on, 429-433, 441-444, 457-458, 460, 462, 468-470, 487-498, 744; Egyptian, 20-21; expansion of settlement, 123-129, 433, 445, 466; Greek, 35-37; income from, 108-110, 252, 280, 303-304, 306-307, 478, 494, 498; laborers in, 95, 97, 115, 118, 119, 350, 431-432, 433, 435, 440, 447, 451, 457, 459-460, 472-473, 479, 492, 685-687, 721; landlords' enterprise, 117, 121, 280, 303, 424-427, 430, 449, 473, 484; large-scale, 36-37, 44, 47, 51-52, 63-64, 114, 127, 447, 460-461, 462, 472, 479, 484, 487, 489; medieval, 68-70, 91-131; Mediterranean, 34-35; modern, chaps. xviii-xx; modern improvements in technique, 306, 308, chaps. xviii-xx; Moslem, 68-70, 262-263; origins of, 15-16; Roman, 47-48, 50-52, 63-65; science and, 436-437, 441, 449-450, 467-468; stimuli to improvement, 112, 114, 115, 280, 303, 423-430, 437, 448-450, 454, 462; subsist-

ence, 92-93, 112-113, 408, 493; yield of wheat, 106, 422, 424-425, 454-455, 466
See also Denmark, England, France, Germany, Holland, Ireland, Italy, Low Countries, Russia; Capital, Cooperation, Credit, Food supply, Grain trade, Land tenure, Latifundia, Leasehold tenures, Machinery, Peasant proprietorship, Prices, Protection, State, Village.
Airplane, 553, 555, 557; limits to commercial use, 558
Aktiengesellschaft, 590
Albuquerque, 257, 259
Alcabala, 265
Aleppo, 143, 258, 556, 557
Alexander the Great, 43, 51
Alexandria, trade of, 44-45
Alsace-Lorraine, 468, 469, 521, 579, 627
Alum, 155, 191, 310
Aluminum, 524
Amalfi, 85, 86-87, 156, 157
Amalgamations, 633-640; railroad, 545, 548-549, 552; banks, 602-603, 607, 628, 634
Amber, 29, 30, 55, 78, 153, 155
Amboyna, 259, 274
America, American capital in Europe, 653-654; colonial market, 303, 322, 331, 348, 365, 400, 504, 647, 663; colonial policy, 244-245, 266-270, 274-275, 294-296, 328-332, 398, 400, 673, 677; colonial trade, 325-328, 329, 330; Dutch in, 242, 275-276, 328; economic effects of colonization, 324-328; in, 244, 322-333, 359, 360, 362, 364; European capital in, 322-324, 568, 601, 609, 647, 648, 649, 650, 665; exploration, 225, 235, 241; French in, 235, 294-296, 363-364; immigration, 264, 294, 324-325, 664; modern exports, 420, 438-439, 512, 514, 523-524, 561, 568-